Navigating Social Security Disability Programs

Navigating Social Security Disability Programs

A Handbook for Clinicians and Advocates

James Randall Noblitt and
Pamela Perskin Noblitt

BLOOMSBURY ACADEMIC
NEW YORK • LONDON • OXFORD • NEW DELHI • SYDNEY

BLOOMSBURY ACADEMIC
Bloomsbury Publishing Inc
1385 Broadway, New York, NY 10018, USA
50 Bedford Square, London, WC1B 3DP, UK
29 Earlsfort Terrace, Dublin 2, Ireland

BLOOMSBURY, BLOOMSBURY ACADEMIC and the Diana logo
are trademarks of Bloomsbury Publishing Plc

First published in the United States of America by ABC-CLIO 2020
Paperback edition published by Bloomsbury Academic 2025

Cover photo: (smartboy10/iStockphoto)

Library of Congress Cataloging-in-Publication Data
Names: Noblitt, James Randall, author. | Noblitt, Pamela Perskin, author.
Title: Navigating social security disability programs : a handbook for
clinicians and advocates / James Randall Noblitt, Pamela Perskin Noblitt.
Description: Santa Barbara, California : Praeger, An Imprint of ABC-CLIO, 2020. |
Includes bibliographical references and index.
Identifiers: LCCN 2019048430 (print) | LCCN 2019048431 (ebook) |
ISBN 9781440870019 (print) | ISBN 9781440870026 (ebook)
Subjects: LCSH: Disability insurance—Law and legislation—United States. |
Social security—Law and legislation—United States.
Classification: LCC KF3650 .N63 2020 (print) | LCC KF3650 (ebook) |
DDC 368.4/300973—dc23
LC record available at https://lccn.loc.gov/2019048430
LC ebook record available at https://lccn.loc.gov/2019048431

ISBN: HB: 978-1-4408-7001-9
PB: 979-8-7651-3664-5
ePDF: 978-1-4408-7002-6
eBook: 979-8-2161-2201-2

To find out more about our authors and books visit www.bloomsbury.com
and sign up for our newsletters.

This book is dedicated to those who created the Social Security Administration and those who aspired to ensure that the aged and the disabled of all ages would not suffer from lack of financial support and health care in their hour of need. It is also dedicated to those who persevere to achieve justice within the system, and those who tirelessly work to reform it and expand its reach. We also dedicate this book to those who benefit from Social Security's programs and those who are struggling through the process of obtaining benefits. We hope this book helps you achieve your goals and find respite.

Finally, as always, we dedicate this book to our children and grandchildren, who always lift us up with their love and support.

Contents

Preface

Social justice is for everyone, including people with disabilities.
—Marlee Matlin

Unless an impairment is so clearly articulated, so evident that it cannot be interpreted as some mundane, benign condition, almost no claim for disability can be approved without the full cooperation of the applicant's treating clinicians. In 2016, of 2,582,092 initial applications for Social Security Disability Insurance (SSDI) benefits, slightly more than one-third were approved and, on reconsideration only 12% more were approved. Of the claimants who were denied benefits at the initial application and reconsideration levels, 698,579 appealed and requested a hearing before an administrative law judge (ALJ). At the hearing level, benefits were approved for 46% of claimants, while 35% of the claims were denied and 20% dismissed.[1] Why is there such a wide disparity between approvals at the initial application (IA) level and the hearing level? The reasons are time, preparation, and the opportunity to present a more complete picture of the claimant's level of disability before an ALJ.

At the IA level, claimants complete an application online, over the phone, or in person at a Social Security Administration field office in their community. In response to the Administration's request for medical records, claimants often bring, if anything, the summary patient notes provided by their treating doctor, not official treatment notes. They have no clinician opinions except, occasionally, a brief note written on letterhead or a prescription form, sometimes dated, with a few scribbled words or computer-generated sentences that state something along the lines of, "My patient is completely disabled and deserves disability" and is signed by Somebody MD or PhD. That doesn't float. According to the Social Security Administration (SSA), it is only by meeting Social Security's specific definition of disability and stringent requirements that people qualify for receipt of either SSDI or Supplemental Security Income (SSI) benefits.

The process for obtaining benefits begins with an application that is first evaluated by the SSA to ascertain whether the applicant meets the required work history and Social Security contributions for SSDI or the income and assets test for SSI. If those standards are met, the claim is forwarded to the state Disability Determination Services (DDS), where its claims examiners request that the claimant provide treatment records from the clinicians and facilities from whom care was received from as early as a year prior to the onset of the disabling condition, if relevant, through the present. The clinicians are also requested to complete a brief form estimating their patient's residual functional capacity (RFC). The claims examiners, along with physicians and psychologists employed or contracted by Social Security, evaluate the records and make a decision as to whether the applicant meets Social Security's definition of disability.

The problem with this scenario is that not all clinicians respond to requests for records and opinions regarding their patient's application for benefits. Or they do not respond in a timely way. Or their records are inadequate to the task of identifying the severity of an impairment or how the impairment impacts on the ability to perform typical work tasks. Or irrelevant records are submitted that obscure or deemphasize salient information documenting a potentially disabling condition. For example, dermatological treatment records may document the patient's long history of acne that conceals episodes of suspected melanoma. If there is not enough information for a determination of disability in the treatment records, the claimant can be sent to a clinician contracted by the DDS for a physical or psychological evaluation. The examiner will opine as to whether the claimant has severe exertional or nonexertional impairments that prevent the performance of the claimant's past work or any other work in the national economy. The SSA will factor in the claimant's age, education, the exertional level of past work, and English fluency to determine whether the claimant meets the criteria for SSDI or SSI. In other words, applicants for benefits are reliant on the assessment of strangers who do not know them personally and who are relying on whatever treatment records have been obtained and an analysis based on a brief, perfunctory examination.

By the time claimants reach the hearing stage, the passage of time, while representing a significant hardship to most applicants for benefits, provides the opportunity for the claim to be developed, for clinicians to respond for requests of treatment records and professional opinions, and for the claimant's representative to develop and articulate a theory of the case. However, while this delay provides for better preparation of the claimant's case, it also represents a burden to the claimant, who is already struggling with the problems associated with illness or injury, treatment, unemployment, financial distress, and basic survival.

We will make the point, repeatedly, throughout this book: the full understanding and cooperation of the treating clinician is essential to a favorable disposition of an SSDI or SSI claim. And, the earlier the records and opinions are submitted, the likelier the claimant will enjoy an earlier favorable decision. We will also make the argument that clinicians have a duty to their patients to become acquainted with the relevant Social Security disability programs, regulations, definitions, and language to identify patients who may meet SSDI and SSI criteria. This book is intended to be a guide for clinicians on behalf of patients who may become disabled at some point and who may need SSDI or SSI benefits to provide health insurance and a monthly income. It is also a reference and resource to which clinicians can refer when considering whether a patient's impairment meets the criteria for disability and how that finding can be expressed in a way that is compatible with Social Security's regulations and language. To this end, we have incorporated into the appendixes Social Security's Listings of Impairments for Adults and Children (Appendixes A and B) to provide clinicians with ready access to pertinent information as they develop the treatment record, or offer professional opinions that conform to Social Security's complicated definition of disability. The appendixes also offer sample impairment questionnaires (Appendixes C, D, E, F), sample progress note template for psychological services (Appendix G), and a list of compassionate allowances as of 2019 (Appendix H). The appendixes also offer a list of compassionate allowances as of 2019 (Appendix H), sample impairment questionnaires (Appendixes C, D, E, F), and sample progress note template for psychological services (Appendix G).

Although the Listings of Impairments can be found online, it is our belief that consolidating the relevant definitions, rationale, language, regulations, descriptions, and case studies into one volume will arm clinicians with the information they need to respond to queries by Social Security and claimants' representatives as well as to recognize when their own patients may need to be evaluated for disability benefits.

Our professional training seldom focuses on practical matters such as office management, accommodations to health insurance companies, and coding and billing, and it certainly does not focus on interactions with Social Security. But these issues are consequential both to our patients and our professional practice. Our role as health-care professionals is to give succor to our patients, to cure their ills if we can, and to give comfort where we cannot. Assisting our patients who meet the criteria for disability benefits is our responsibility—one that we cannot meet if we are uninformed.

In the course of my (Randy Noblitt's) private practice of clinical psychology, I had a large caseload of trauma survivors who presented with often debilitating symptoms associated with post-traumatic stress disorder (PTSD), borderline personality disorder, and dissociative disorders and who frequently displayed symptoms that were incompatible with sustained, competitive work tasks. These patients showed signs of disorientation, disconnection from reality, paranoid ideation, self-destructive impulses, emotional lability, impaired concentration, poor self-regulation, social anxiety, diminished judgment, obsessive compulsivity, and other emotional and behavioral characteristics unsuited for competitive work settings.

In the late 1990s, one of my patients, a survivor of childhood incest, was an entomologist who worked for an international chemical company. As a woman in a highly stressful job within a department primarily populated by males, she experienced significant harassment, pay inequity, and gender-based internal politics that obstructed her ability to rise within the company, which triggered the feelings of helplessness and vulnerability she felt when she was being abused by her father. She struggled through her workdays to maintain her equilibrium but fell apart at home at night. She began to decompensate, and it was clear that she would not be able to continue to work at that level. She was in such a specialized field that few jobs were available that were not equally stressful. She frequently expressed her frustrations about knowing she had to take time to deal with her worsening symptoms of PTSD but that a sustained absence would cause her to lose her job and with it the salary and health insurance on which she relied. I knew little about SSDI other than its availability as a resource for disabled people and assumed it was a straightforward process that would readily grant her claim, so I advised her to investigate it as a way of subsidizing her survival while she worked toward developing better coping skills and managing her symptoms more effectively. She did look into the program but found the application process overwhelming, dehumanizing, and stigmatizing, and she knew the outcome after months of waiting would be uncertain. Caught between her recognition that she would not be able to maintain her ability to adequately perform her job and that she could not count on obtaining SSDI, she withdrew from therapy, quit her job, and ended her life.

Her story is not unique, but to me it was personal. I subsequently made my practice more sensitive to my patients' inability to continue to perform full-time jobs and determined to find out how to best advocate for them in the disability determination process. My office manager, who coincidentally is my wife and coauthor, began to speak directly to the local Social Security field office personnel to find out how disability was determined, how SSDI and SSI benefits were awarded, and what other programs might be available to my incapacitated patients. The more she delved into the workings of Social Security, the more she came to understand the importance of framing treatment notes and opinions around symptoms and resultant limitations. She was able to use her newfound knowledge to obtain SSDI and SSI benefits for others among my patients who were unable to work because of the severity of their psychological impairments. We developed a template for progress notes that focused more on how symptoms interfered with a patient's ability to consistently perform basic job tasks (see Appendix G). We studied the *Blue Book*, a publication by the Social Security Administration that included the Listings of Impairments, to better understand the elements of disability as defined by Social Security. Finally, we learned to write narrative reports for our patients who applied for SSDI and SSI that incorporated the Administration's language, definitions, and regulations and were instrumental in supporting our patients' applications for benefits.

Not only were we successful in supporting our patients' being approved for disability benefits but, with few exceptions, most of them recovered sufficiently to rejoin the workforce and often to excel both professionally and personally, beyond their expectations.

One such patient, Claire, had been so debilitated, incapable of even self-care, that she was psychiatrically hospitalized for months at a time. When she was not hospitalized, her living circumstances were unstable as she couch-surfed from one place to another, sometimes in unsuitable and unsafe environments. Once she obtained her SSDI and SSI benefits, she was able to obtain a safe, stable living situation, qualify for food stamps to ensure adequate nutrition, and receive more and better treatment, both medical and psychological. Over time she learned to dominate her fears, reclaim mastery of her own life, and return to the workforce. She began working at a local store, part of a national retail chain. Progressing through the ranks, she ultimately achieved a management position at the company's national headquarters. Is she completely cured? Of course not. But she is functional, productive, self-sufficient, and a contributing member of society. This is the gift of Social Security—giving her the tools to recover and live her life as fully as possible. This was a situation where I was able to assist my patient beyond serving as her psychotherapist, by helping her navigate the Social Security application system and by properly documenting the relevant information that was needed to support her claim.

People do not want to apply for or receive Social Security disability benefits. Not only is their condition stigmatizing but so is their identification as SSDI recipients. There is a common term used by the political right regarding Social Security, Social Security Disability Insurance, and Medicare—*entitlements*. Those who receive these benefits are labeled as deadbeats by a significant segment of society, and that is further stigmatizing and isolating. Let us be clear: Social Security, Social Security Disability, and Medicare are not entitlements—they are earned benefits supported by those workers' tax dollars. And Supplemental Security Income and Medicaid should not be pejoratively labeled entitlements. They are an essential part of the social safety net that a civil society creates to sustain its most vulnerable members.

We believe that clinicians want to contribute constructively to their patients' lives. Our hope is that this book will be a tool to help them achieve that aspiration.

Note

1. https://cpollardlaw.com/2016-social-security-disability-decision-statistics.

Acknowledgments

We would like to express our gratitude to the many applicants for Social Security Disability Insurance and Supplemental Security Income benefits who shared their struggles with us to help us understand the system from their perspective. And our thanks go as well to the clinicians who expressed to us their confusion and frustration in their efforts to support their patients' applications for benefits. We are grateful to the researchers, many of whom we have cited, who have shared their expertise and findings that exposed us to other ideas, perceptions, and interpretations of disability and Social Security regulations. Special thanks to Michael Stephen Stretton III, direct payment non-attorney, a veritable guru of all things Title II and Title XVI. Thank you, Praeger and especially Debbie Carvalko, for your confidence in and support of our work. And thank you to those who represent the interests of SSDI and SSI claimants who are deeply motivated to find justice for their clients.

Introduction

> Those who are weak have great difficulty finding their place in our society. The image of the ideal human as powerful and capable disenfranchises the old, the sick, the less-abled. For me, society must, by definition, be inclusive of the needs and gifts of all its members. How can we lay claim to making an open and friendly society where human rights are respected and fostered when, by the values we teach and foster, we systematically exclude segments of our population? I believe that those we most often exclude from the normal life of society, people with disabilities, have profound lessons to teach us. When we do include them, they add richly to our lives and add immensely to our world.
>
> —Jean Vanier, *Becoming Human*

According to the World Health Organization, "disability is part of the human condition. Almost everyone will be temporarily or permanently impaired at some point in life, and those who survive to old age will experience increasing difficulties in functioning" (WHO, 2011, p. 3). The widespread presence of disability is awakening the growing recognition of this traditionally hidden human experience. Some disabling conditions are readily observable, but others such as cardiovascular conditions, pain, and psychological disorders can be invisible (Norstedt, 2019). People with disabilities have been historically stigmatized, marginalized, and excluded from full participation in their communities, neighborhoods, and from competitive employment. Their disabilities and perceived vulnerability have sometimes made them the targets of bullying and crime. During the 1960s, along with the emerging civil rights movement, people with disabilities engaged in increased political action against oppressive and discriminatory practices. Along the lines of the Lesbian, gay, bisexual and transgender movement, some people with disabilities began "coming out" and asserting their legal and social rights (Corrigan, Kosyluk, & Rüsch, 2013; Evans, 2019). The Americans with Disabilities Act (ADA) of 1990 was one such watershed moment in this advocacy movement. This federal law prohibits discrimination against people with disabilities as one component of people's collective civil rights. Internationally, the United Nations adopted a Convention on the Rights of Persons with Disabilities (UN General Assembly, 2007) to articulate its support for disability rights. Disability studies (DS) is now an academic discipline, with the first program having been established at Syracuse University in 1994 (Simon, 2013). Interest in DS has fostered programs at a number of universities nationally and internationally as well as an interdisciplinary organization, the Society for the Study of Disabilities, which publishes *Disabilities Studies Quarterly*.

For the most part, disability is a social construct; distinguishable from impairment, a more objectively definable attribute. Both are potentially stigmatizing. People with disabilities are often more impeded by common social preconceptions than from their own objective limitations. *Ableism* is one such prejudice, as it is the idea that the value of an individual is a reflection of what that person can do.

Those of us in health-care professions are commonly immersed in ableist thinking, and we may show this bias in unintended microaggressions that can be hurtful to the people we are serving. Many people with disabilities also belong to other marginalized groups and may be cumulatively affected by multiple microaggression themes (Lui & Quezada, 2019). K. J. Conover (2015) developed, in an area of ongoing research, a 20-item Ableist Microaggressions Scale that yielded four factors experienced by her research participants with disabilities: helplessness, minimization, denial of personhood, and otherness. We should note that hostility and aggression are not the only discriminatory attitudes and behaviors that may harm people with disabilities. The tendency to exclude, ignore, patronize, and pity may also detrimentally affect their quality of life (Dunn, 2019; Nario-Redmond, Kemerling, & Silverman, 2019).

Conflict is often embedded in the relationships between people with disabilities and their treating clinicians, whose job is to clearly see the illness processes that are present and use medical diagnoses and other scientific language where warranted. Attributions of disability by health care providers are often stigmatizing. Thomas Dirth and Nyla Branscombe (2018) described a *social identity approach* (SIA) to disability that considers the identifications that people with disabilities make with groups of other disabled people, as well as with people without disabilities. Perceiving similarities with others may help define one's own identity and it may provide effective sources of social support. Such identifications may be comforting, uplifting, and empowering; and in other instances, they may not be. The authors contrast the SIA that has been advocated by the DS movement and the more traditional biomedical approach that is common in health care and law. Doron Dorfman described a woman who was empowered by her disability identity and assisted by Social Security Administration (SSA) benefits:

> At twenty-eight years old, Lisa moved to Berkeley. It was the late 1970s and the height of the disability rights movement. Since a car accident injured her spinal cord at the age of sixteen, Lisa has been paraplegic and a wheelchair user. Growing up in the Midwest, where there were only a few people with significant visible disabilities, Lisa remembers clearly the message she received from everyone except her parents—that her life was pretty much over: "That I probably wouldn't be able to live independently. Going to college would be very limited, if at all . . . That I was unattractive, you know, probably would not have a mate. All the stereotypes were just full-blown. And I sensed it immediately from the way [other people], even the medical world, were relating to me."
>
> In Berkeley, Lisa felt that everything was accessible and everyone was friendly. She began learning about the concepts underlying the new social movement, her community, and her claimed, empowered disability identity.
>
> Lisa, like more than 18 million other Americans with disabilities, has an ongoing, long-term relationship with the Social Security Administration SSA; Disability Statistics and Demographics Rehabilitation and Research Training Center (2014, p. 76). She has been receiving disability benefits since the age of eighteen.
>
> Lisa says obtaining her benefits was a "horrible experience." She felt at the time that the SSA representatives constantly suspected her of "gaming the system," treated her with disrespect, and brought her to tears more than once. She felt unable to voice her opinion or tell her story to the representatives, who, she believed, cared nothing about her needs. All in all, Lisa felt that she had no control over the process. She believes the procedure of obtaining benefits was unfair because it made her present an image of herself as someone different from who she really was, as someone completely dependent, helpless, and even "pathetic"—an image she believes with the common social perception of a person with disabilities. (Dorfman, 2017, pp. 195–196)

Dorfman's portrayal of Lisa is consistent with the reports we have heard from other SSDI and Supplemental Security Income (SSI) claimants and recipients. The process of applying for SSA benefits is potentially overwhelming, and it often feels disrespectful and dehumanizing. However, without these benefits, many people with disabilities may be left homeless, food-insecure, and unable to obtain adequate medical care.

We encourage people with disabilities to continue working in their jobs or careers for as long as they can. The ADA helps by prohibiting disability-related discrimination, and requires reasonable accommodations and accessibility in the workplace and other public facilities. In some instances, continued employment is not possible, and obtaining Social Security benefits may become critical to one's survival. This book is an introduction for clinicians and advocates to the Social Security programs. The reader will notice a shift in our language as we move from discussing the disability rights movement to explaining Social Security programs in the United States. The biomedical model with its *patients*, *doctors*, and *illnesses* terminology will appear more frequently as we progress through this book because this kind of language and thinking is essential to the SSA. As we make this transition in thinking and language, we hopefully continue to be mindful of disability as a kind of diversity while maintaining our awareness of the pervasive ableism and other biases that undermine the well-being of people with disabilities. Ideally, we will retain our humility and respect for the humanity of all who seek health care.

The SSA defines disability as a physical or mental impairment that is so severe that it has lasted or is expected to last at least 12 months or result in death; and it prevents the individual from earning at the level of substantial gainful activity (SGA) while performing any full-time work within a competitive work setting.[1] The Social Security Act provides two programs to address the survival needs of people who are so incapacitated that they can no longer engage in sustained or consistent full-time work. Social Security Disability Insurance (SSDI) benefits are available to individuals who meet the criteria for disability and have a sufficient history of paying into the Social Security system through payroll deductions or self-employment contributions.[2]

SSDI benefits are based on a complicated formula called *covered earnings* that factors in the claimant's earnings on which Social Security taxes were paid. The SSA calculates the beneficiary's monthly payment based, in 2019, on 90% of the first $926 of the individual's average indexed monthly earnings (AIME), which is added to the claimant's primary insurance amount (PIA), the benefit to which the individual would be entitled if taking early retirement at age 62. An additional 32% of the AIME on earnings from $926 to $5,583 is added to the PIA. Another 15% of AIME over $5,583 is added to the mix and the total equals the PIA the worker will receive in SSDI money benefits monthly up to a maximum amount of $2,861 for a nonblind disabled person in 2019. The average monthly benefit in 2019 is $1,234.

SSI is the second program, and is based on economic need in addition to meeting the same physical or mental evidentiary requirements for SSDI benefits. Recipients are paid a small monthly income set by the federal government and in some cases supplemented by state governments. SSDI beneficiaries receive Medicare, and SSI beneficiaries receive Medicaid (or their state's equivalent). Disability determination for federal benefits is based on the severity of the impairment(s), the limitations imposed by the disability, and other factors that prevent the claimant from engaging in typical work activities without any accommodations that are not available to all employees. An accommodation could be telecommuting, modified schedules, more frequent breaks during the day, longer breaks during the day, enhanced supervision, greater tolerance for absence and tardiness, or reduced quotas, among other things.

The SSA tasks the Disability Determinations Services (DDS), a federally funded state agency with offices in every state, with evaluating claimants' impairments and resultant limitations to assess whether they meet the criteria for SSDI or SSI. To make this assessment, the DDS requests treatment records from all clinicians and facilities consulted by the applicant for up to one year prior to the alleged onset date (AOD) to the present. Although most treating clinicians provide requested medical records, the great majority refuse to respond to requests for their opinions about their patients' work limitations. When treating clinicians fail to provide their assessments of their patients' limitations, disability determination is left to the opinions of nontreating, often nonexamining, clinicians contracted by the DDS and based solely on a review of the available medical records and, sometimes, a perfunctory, one-time examination. As expected, these clinicians' assessments often fail to identify nuanced or subtle symptomatology or complications, particularly those that may affect employment. This is not necessarily due to lack of clinical expertise but because many of the effects of illness, injury, or psychological disorders are not apparent to the casual, albeit professional, observer, and may not be noted in the patient's records. Thus significant factors that contribute to the claimant's inability to engage in sustained employment may go unidentified, and benefits may be denied because of inadequate medical documentation.

Until January 18, 2017, Social Security recognized the *treating physician rule*[3] that gave the treating physician "great if not controlling weight" in the disability determination process. That rule was modified and, as of March

27, 2017, the treating physician's opinion is only found credible if the treatment records support the doctor's opinions. In other words, there is no special consideration given to the views of treating clinicians whose treatment records do not fully substantiate their opinions. This is a problem because clinicians do not typically include opinions regarding the patient's capacity to perform exertional and nonexertional work activities in the treating records. For example, doctors don't usually include such things as for how long their patients can sit, stand, or walk at one time, or the total number of hours they can engage in each of these activities in the course of an eight-hour workday. Sometimes a doctor may advise patients about the maximum weight they can lift or whether they should elevate their legs when sitting. But even when these limitations are part of the treatment plan, they are not always recorded. Instead, the doctor may say something like, "If it hurts, stop doing it," rather than recommending specific postural restrictions. On the other hand, without the perspective of treating providers, the Administration only has the opinions of clinicians employed or contracted by the SSA as nonexamining or examining acceptable medical sources (AMSs). This represents a distinct disadvantage to claimants who have no treating doctors' opinions to balance those of Social Security's agents.

Furthermore, there is often bias against individuals who apply for disability benefits. There is a misperception among many, clinicians included, that people seeking disability benefits are slackers who prefer to live off monthly "entitlements" rather than going to work. This is a harsh and largely untrue presumption. In the United States, people are largely defined by the work they do. When we meet someone new, what is one of the first things we say? "What do you do?" Our work provides us with financial rewards, identity, stability, structure, and social status. It may be that the foundation of our social life is our work, which introduces us to coworkers, suppliers, customers, and others, who may create their own community. Work also often makes health insurance and other benefits available. My coauthor, Pam Noblitt, has represented more than 1,000 claimants for SSDI or SSI benefits and, with very few exceptions, knew her clients to be incapable of full-time work under Social Security regulations. And in every case, her clients mourned the loss of their ability to work. Work brought them money, independence, status, structure, a social outlet, job satisfaction, and, most importantly, self-esteem. Even minimum-wage earners generally receive higher compensation for their work than their disability benefits provide. A poignant example of this is reflected in the story of one woman, 52 years old, who had only a ninth-grade education but had been employed for more than 30 years as a restroom attendant at a five-star hotel in downtown Los Angeles. Marion was forced to stop working after being felled by a devastating stroke that paralyzed her dominant right upper and lower extremities and adversely affected her vision, speech, and memory. The claimant spoke in glowing terms about her job: how she helped women by maintaining a spotless restroom, how she brought sewing supplies to assist women in need of a quick mending job, and how she advised the hotel to make available a secluded lounge area to accommodate nursing mothers or women just needing a private place to rest. She spoke of her friends at work and how much she missed their social interactions during and after work hours. Her story was repeated with little variation by virtually all the clients my coauthor represented, no matter how exalted or menial their past work. Inability to perform one's past work or any work is as stigmatizing to most claimants as the disability itself.

Furthermore, the average SSDI benefit of $1,234 a month equals an annual income of $14,808, just $2,318 above the federal poverty line of $12,490 for an individual and below the poverty line of $16,910 for a family of two. People with a history of work even at the minimum wage of $7.25 an hour could earn more than they receive in disability benefits. SSDI and SSI are often the last refuge of the desperately ill, hopelessly injured, and those without other resources. We know of no claimant who doesn't appreciate this option but who would not rather be working.

Our position is that clinicians have an ethical duty to their patients to respond to reasonable requests for information that may result in benefits to which they are lawfully entitled in the spirit of the Hippocratic oath's admonition to first do no harm. When clinicians fail to respond to requests for health records or professional opinions, this nonresponse can result in arbitrary denial of benefits that may jeopardize their patient's survival. However, to be able to respond to such requests, it is incumbent that the clinicians understand the nature of work, what constitutes work, and how physical and psychological symptoms interfere with one's ability to perform work. It is this purpose for which this book is written: to provide clinicians with a basic understanding of Social Security programs for the disabled, the definitions and language employed by the SSA, clinicians' role in the disability determination process, their professional ethical responsibility to participate in disability determination, and use of best practices to incorporate and record disabling features in patients' health records.

The SSA recognizes only certain clinicians as acceptable medical sources for the purpose of providing professional opinions regarding the claimant's medically determinable impairments, symptoms, and limitations. Acceptable medical sources include licensed physicians (MDs and DOs), and licensed or board-certified psychologists at the independent practice level. Licensed or certified school psychologists or similarly qualified mental-health-care professionals in school settings are acceptable medical sources for impairments of intellectual ability, learning disabilities, or borderline intellectual functioning only; licensed optometrists are acceptable medical sources for visual disorders, visual acuity, and visual fields, depending on state licensing limitations; licensed podiatrists for foot and ankle impairments only; and licensed speech and language pathologists for speech impairment only. For claims filed on or after March 27, 2017, additional AMSs include licensed physician assistants, licensed audiologists, and advanced practice nurses (APNs), including certified nurse midwives (CNWs), nurse practitioners (NPs), certified registered nurse anesthetists (CRNAs), and clinical nurse specialists (CNSs). However, even a clinician who is not yet a recognized acceptable medical source should maintain and submit treatment records and can still render opinions. If the records and opinions are consistent with those of the acceptable medical sources, they can still add weight to the claimant's case. The Administration has expanded its recognition of clinicians and will likely do so again in the future to encompass the expanding field of health-care providers.

This book is also written to provide useful information to advocates for people with disabilities who may qualify for one of the Social Security programs, including family members, friends, clergy, social workers, and others. Many people know about SSDI and SSI, but few understand the regulations, language, and definitions employed; the complexities of the disability determination process; or the difficulties involved in obtaining benefits. We explain the available programs, time frames, importance of treatment, health records, professional opinions, deadlines, and other aspects of the obstacle-strewn path to obtaining benefits that many assume to be automatically conferred as needed.

In this book, my coauthor and I discuss many of the limitations and biases associated with Social Security disability programs. For example, there are systemic biases in the disability determination process, including prejudices against younger individuals—that is, between the ages of 18 and 45—women, people of color, claimants whose disabilities are psychological, and lower wage earners (Johnson, 2017). But in the interests of full disclosure, we admit to our own biases. We generally advocate for disability applicants. We believe that in the United States, no one should be denied safe shelter, adequate and nutritious food, access to health care, and dignity because they are ill or injured and unable to work. Ideally, this is what Social Security is intended to remedy. In our experience, most people would prefer to work and very few favor the acceptance of disability benefits over the fulfillment derived from work. We acknowledge our own biases but nevertheless strive to present factual information. In legal venues it is always critically important to render factually accurate information. This is true whether one is an applicant or health-care provider.

We also believe that clinicians with greater knowledge of the Social Security system will serve their patients more effectively. As the U.S. population grows older, along with the availability of increasingly sophisticated methods for identifying illnesses, we anticipate increases in the diagnosis of disabling conditions generally. Some health-care professionals may choose to develop specialties in Social Security disability-related assessments, but all clinicians need a working knowledge of Social Security Disability. Clinicians who are well versed in the Social Security system will be better equipped to understand how the system operates, the criteria by which claimants are assessed, and the benefits and limitations of SSDI and SSI programs. These health-care providers will have improved skills in determining whether patients meet SSDI or SSI standards, in responding to requests from Social Security, in referring eligible patients to apply for benefits, and in providing appropriate support and documentation for claimants.

Finally, this book is not intended to be a comprehensive guide to the Social Security disability process or to fully equip advocates with the necessary tools to represent claimants for Social Security disability programs. Rather, it is designed to offer a description of available programs, the general process of applying for benefits, the definition of disability, examples of impairments considered by the SSA to be disabling, how disability is measured, descriptions of the clinician's role in the disability determination process, and some guidance in navigating the disability benefits maze. We hope this book will be a bridge to greater understanding between clinicians and patients, and clinicians and the SSA, so that they can develop mutually cooperative relationships that result in the application of justice for people with disabilities.

Notes

1. Basic Definition of Disability, 20 C.F.R. §404.1505.
2. "Social Insurance Programs," published by the Social Security Administration, https://www.ssa.gov/policy/docs/progdesc/sspus/oasdi.pdf.
3. Evaluating Opinion Evidence for Claims Filed before March 27, 2017. 20 C.F.R §404.1527(d)(2).

CHAPTER ONE

An Overview of Social Security Disability Programs

> We do not believe that in this country freedom is reserved for the lucky, or happiness for the few. We recognize that no matter how responsibly we live our lives, any one of us at any time may face a job loss, or a sudden illness, or a home swept away in a terrible storm. The commitments we make to each other through Medicare and Medicaid and Social Security, these things do not sap our initiative, they strengthen us. They do not make us a nation of takers; they free us to take the risks that make this country great.
> —President Barack Obama, "Inaugural Address," January 21, 2013

Social Security Disability Insurance

In 1956, SSDI benefits became available to eligible workers from the ages of 50 to 64 and adult children of qualified workers whose disabling conditions predated their 18th birthday under Title II of the Social Security Administration Act. The Social Security Amendments Act of 1972 resulted in an expansion of SSDI to include younger workers, reduced the mandatory waiting period from six months to five, increased the availability of benefits to adult children whose disabling conditions occurred prior to their 22nd birthday, and created the SSI program Title XVI of the Social Security Administration Act that provided for disabled people who were low wage earners or who never worked or who hadn't worked within five years of becoming too disabled to work. SSDI and SSI continue to serve disabled workers and others who meet program criteria today, with annual alterations, amendments, clarifications, and additions to the Social Security regulations (SSRs).

Workers who are either employed or self-employed contribute to Social Security through taxes on their earnings. These payroll taxes are collected through the Federal Insurance Contributions Act (FICA) and are subsequently deposited into the four Social Security trust funds managed by the secretary of the Treasury. One of the trust funds covers Old Age Survivors Insurance (OASI), while a second oversees Disability Insurance (DI). The other two trust funds manage Medicare Part B (provider benefits) and Medicare Part D (prescription drug benefits). In addition to payroll taxes, Social Security is funded by taxation of benefits, net interest income, and General Fund reimbursements.

SSDI is available to eligible individuals who paid into the Social Security fund. Retirement benefits are calculated based on lifetime earnings and the average earnings during the 35 years prior to achieving retirement age, as those are most likely to reflect the worker's highest prior income level. Workers tend to reach their highest earnings level as they mature and gain experience and expertise. SSDI benefits are based on the claimant's last 15 years of earnings prior to becoming too incapacitated to perform full-time work or earn at least substantial gainful activity. The SSA also factors in the *average indexed monthly earnings* (AIME), the median income for the job(s) the worker previously performed. Thus disability benefits may be paid at a slightly higher rate than early retirement benefits available to eligible individuals 62 years of age but younger than their designated Social Security retirement age, but the benefits are often less than the amount they would have received based on their actual retirement age according to their birth year.

SSDI is designed to provide income and health insurance benefits for two populations: workers whose medical conditions are terminal or whose conditions are unlikely to improve, and workers who, with financial support and access to adequate medical and psychological support, can recover enough to rejoin the workforce. Toward that end, Social Security provides beneficiaries with opportunities to return to work without losing benefits until they have had the opportunity to demonstrate that they can perform full-time jobs in a competitive work setting on a sustained basis. Beneficiaries who return to work can continue to receive SSDI benefits for up to nine months (consecutively or cumulatively), and this is considered a *trial work period*. The trial work period is triggered by gross income equaling or exceeding *substantial gainful activity* (SGA).[1] At the end of the trial work period, the beneficiary enters a 36-month *extended period of eligibility* (EPE) during which monthly earnings are monitored, and SSDI provides a benefit payment for months where earnings may fall below SGA and no money benefit when they meet or exceed SGA. For the next five years following the extended period of eligibility, workers can apply for *expedited reinstatement* if income falls below SGA or stops completely. The SSA will pay benefits for six months while the claim is processed. In order to deny reinstatement, the Department of Disability Determination must prove that the worker's medical condition substantially improved since last receiving benefits. If a former beneficiary were to file a new application for SSDI, the burden of proof would fall on the claimant. If a beneficiary returns to the workforce but is unable to persist as either an employed or self-employed worker for longer than six months, that is considered an *unsuccessful work attempt* (UWA). During this period, the beneficiary's earnings are monitored, and if earnings meet or exceed substantial gainful activity, the SSDI benefit is reduced. Medicare benefits continue uninterrupted. An UWA is included in the nine months of the trial work period. An SSDI beneficiary is entitled to one nine-month trial work period every five years.

To be sure, it is worth noting that there is no such thing as permanent disability so far as Social Security is concerned. Disability continues only until the claimant recovers enough to return to the workforce or dies. In either scenario, there is a limit to the term of disability, although it can last months, years, or even decades. A younger individual who is approved for benefits is usually scheduled for periodic assessments of ongoing disability by Disability Determination Services (DDS) at the direction of the judge who approved benefits. This means that the individual's medical records are updated, and treating clinician opinions are solicited to determine whether the beneficiary still meets the criteria for disability benefits. Reevaluations are typically scheduled at two- to three-year intervals, however, due to a reduced workforce, such reassessments may be deferred or ignored.

Disabled Widow Benefits

Disabled widow benefits (DWB) are available to disabled spouses or former spouses of individuals who were beneficiaries of SSDI benefits prior to and at the time of their deaths. This program is available to widowed or divorced spouses of individuals if they had been married for at least 10 years and if the deceased individuals had been awarded SSDI prior to their deaths or had been awarded benefits posthumously. This benefit is available to a spouse who was either a full-time homemaker without independent earnings or one whose earnings were substantially less than the deceased partner's. To be eligible, a claimant must be 50 years of age or older and meet Social Security's disability criteria. If approved, the individual receives SSDI based on the spouse's earnings record.

Disabled Child Benefits

Disabled child benefits are provided to adult children who met the criteria for disability under Social Security before the age of 22 and continue to meet that criteria. These adult children can receive benefits based on the earnings record of whichever parent contributed the most into Social Security upon that parent's death or attainment of retirement age, and providing the child has remained unmarried and has not earned greater than substantial gainful activity. Assuming the medical evidence supports disability commencing before age 22, the adult child would receive approximately half the value of the parent's Social Security retirement benefit and, upon the parent's death, may be entitled to receive the parent's full retirement benefit for the remainder of his or her own life. The child's benefit is not deducted from and has no impact on the parent's disability or retirement benefit.

An exception can be made regarding from which parent the disabled child can benefit. In one situation, a claimant was a 35-year-old woman who was on the autism spectrum but had been undiagnosed until well into adulthood. Her older sister was diagnosed with severe autism as a young child, and the claimant's parents thought their younger daughter had no such disability compared with her sister's extreme behavioral issues. The older sister received SSI as a child and as an adult, and when her father attained the age of 66, she was granted disabled child benefits based on his income record. The claimant never lived independently away from her family and her only jobs were for extended-family-owned enterprises; she never worked more than part time or earned greater than substantial gainful activity. As the claimant grew older, her symptoms became increasingly severe and she exhibited extreme anxiety, panic, fears, mood swings, and obsessive compulsivity. She was awarded benefits based on her mother's earnings record. If her earnings had been taken from her father's benefits, it would have reduced the amount received by her older sister and herself. Although her mother's earnings were less than her father's, the claimant received more from her mother's earnings record than she would have from her father's. Just as when an SSDI claimant has minor children and the claimant receives an additional money benefit to help support the minor children, the amount is the same, approximately half of the claimant's benefit, whether there is one child or four. When the youngest child reaches 18, the additional benefit ends. This provision is similar to disabled child benefits. Whether there is one disabled child or more, the amount allocated for minor dependent children and disabled adult children is the same, regardless of the number of children.

Posthumous Benefits

Sadly, claimants for SSDI benefits may pass away before benefits have been awarded. A claimant's parent, spouse, or child may pursue the claim and receive the claimant's back due benefits as the *substitution of party* (SOP) for the claimant. Under these circumstances, Medicare health insurance and monthly cash benefits are not awarded. If the deceased individual never applied for disability benefits, the spouse, child, or parent has until three months after the death of the disabled individual to file an application on behalf of the deceased. The same regulations apply to the deceased claimant regarding disability determination, including the severity of the condition, limitations caused by the impairment, earnings record or meeting other financial considerations. The claimant's demise is not evidence of a severe disability unless the death is directly attributable to the impairment or complications of the impairment noted on the application. For instance, an individual who cited cardiac disease as the debilitating condition but who passed away after being hit by a car would not qualify for posthumous disability benefits. However, if such an individual was driving a car, suffered a severe heart attack, and subsequently crashed the car and expired, it could be deduced that the person's passing was a direct consequence of the stated severe impairment.

Supplemental Security Income

For those who did not contribute to the Social Security fund at all, did not contribute enough, or did not contribute within the five years prior to meeting the criteria for disability, or who are disabled children under the age of 18 or disabled adults over the age of 65, SSI may be available. SSI is not based on earnings, is funded by federal income tax and other general revenue but is administered by the SSA.

Some individuals who worked and contributed to Social Security but had very low paying jobs or whose working life was cut short due to illness or injury will receive far less than the average monthly benefit of \$1,234.[2] If their monthly benefit is less than the *federal benefit rate* (FBR) which is the SSI monthly benefit payment of $771 in 2019, and if they meet the financial requirements for SSI, those SSDI beneficiaries can receive concurrent benefits up to $771 per month for an individual living independently (paying for food and housing). However, if the beneficiary is receiving other income, the SSI benefit is reduced by that amount. Additionally, those receiving both SSDI and SSI will also receive both Medicare and Medicaid (or their state's equivalent). An individual who receives as little as one dollar in SSI in addition to SSDI benefits is entitled to both Medicare and Medicaid. Some individuals who receive SSDI and SSI may also be eligible for the *Qualified Medicare Beneficiary* (QMB) program. This program provides for Medicaid to pay the Medicare Part B premium, giving the insured a boost in the monthly SSDI money benefit and 100% health insurance coverage.

SSDI applicants whose anticipated benefits exceed $771 a month may still be entitled to SSI benefits if they meet the financial qualifications temporarily. For example, an individual who is hospitalized or recovering from surgery and cannot perform at a part-time job, and thus has no income for an extended period between the date of disability and the decision date for disability determination, may be eligible to receive back due SSI benefits. But once the SSDI benefits are approved, SSI will be discontinued, and the person will not receive future monthly benefits from SSI. Or it is possible for an individual to be approved for SSI on initial application and be denied SSDI benefits. In that case, the claimant may receive SSI while the SSDI claim is pending. If the claimant's SSDI monthly benefit is greater than $771, SSI will be suspended, and the claimant will receive only SSDI benefits. In only one other circumstance can an SSDI beneficiary receive disability benefits from another federally sponsored disability program: Veteran's Administration disability benefits.

Disabled U.S. Veterans of the Uniformed Services

In only one other circumstance can an SSDI beneficiary receive concurrent benefits: when the claimant is a disabled veteran of the Uniformed Armed Services,[3] defined as:

- serving in the uniformed services on active duty or
- in active duty for training or
- in inactive duty training and
- discharged under other than dishonorable conditions and

- at least 10% disabled by an injury or disease that was incurred in or aggravated during active duty or active duty for training, or inactive duty training.

The disability may be evident and acknowledged during active duty or may not become evident until after discharge. For example, post-traumatic stress disorder (PTSD) symptoms may not appear or become problematic for some time after discharge, although they can be attributed to the veteran's military service. Or, as in the case of Agent Orange[4] exposure, it was not considered harmful to humans at the time of its dispersal during the Vietnam War but was later found to be carcinogenic and has since been implicated in other physical and mental symptoms and disorders and birth defects in the children of those exposed to the chemicals.

Determination by the Veterans Administration that one is disabled does not necessarily translate to legally recognized disability by the SSA and vice versa. Each agency has its own process and criteria for disability determination. The Veterans Administration ascribes disability on a percentage basis, with 10% being the minimal allowable for benefits up to 100% disability. Veterans with a single disability rated at 60% or more than one disability with a total rating of 70% may be deemed unemployable. Their ratings may be reassessed to 100% to account for their unemployability. Disability payments are based on the percentage of impairment, not on the veteran's earnings. Veterans who are determined to be at least 30% disabled are eligible to receive additional allowances for their dependents. Disabled veterans' status can change, and any improvement or deterioration can result in decreased or increased proportional level of disability. Veterans who are found to qualify for SSDI are also eligible to receive Medicare in addition to their veterans' health-care benefit. SSDI benefits are based on the claimant's ability to perform any full-time job within a competitive work setting and having a qualifying disabling condition that has lasted or is expected to last for 12 months or result in death (see Appendixes A and B). Thus consideration of a veteran's disabled status might not result in a finding of disability by Social Security without additional evidence supporting Social Security's eligibility requirements. Finally, veterans disability benefits are nontaxable, and additional allowances may be made available to beneficiaries who require additional assistance in terms of caregiving, durable equipment, modification to housing, modified vehicles, and other disability-related expenses. The Code of Federal Regulations, volume 38 (38 C.F.R.) addresses all matters related to the Department of Veterans Affairs.

Notes

1. SGA in 2019 is $1,200 per month for nonblind individuals and $2,040 for statutorily blind individuals.

2. Average SSDI benefit in 2019 per https://www.ssa.gov.

3. U.S. Department of Veterans Affairs, https://www.benefits.va.gov/compensation/types-disability.asp.

4. Agent Orange is an herbicide and defoliant best known for its use during the Vietnam War to expose enemy combatants and deprive them of cover and food.

CHAPTER TWO

Clinical Assessment of the Ability to Work

Your work is going to fill a large part of your life, and the only way to be truly satisfied is to do what you believe is great work. And the only way to do great work is to love what you do.

—Steve Jobs

What Is Disability?

The SSA defines disability as a medically determinable physical or mental impairment that is so severe it prevents an individual from engaging in full-time work in a competitive work setting at any job within the national economy. This definition is foundational in Social Security disability determination. Impairments that significantly limit an individual's strength, endurance, mobility, intelligence, cognition, concentration, attention, persistence, and pace of performance would affect that person's ability to perform any work. Furthermore, Social Security's definition of disability requires that the impairment must have lasted or be expected to last at least 12 months or result in death (see Appendixes A and B). Finally, the individual must be able to perform work without special accommodations not available to coworkers (see Appendix A, §12.00 C4). These accommodations may range from modified quotas or schedules to increased breaks or rest periods, liberal absenteeism policies, or assistive devices necessary to accomplish work-related tasks.

Since most children do not work, the impact of their severe medical or mental impairments is considered relative to school performance at grade or age level, behavioral and social adaptation, and meeting developmental milestones appropriately and timely. However, children who have impaired functioning secondary to their physical or mental impairments may be provided accommodations through their school or outside agencies to enable them to attend and tolerate school and other programs (see Appendix B, §112.00D). In these circumstances, special accommodations may actually strengthen their claim of disability. Children with special needs are evaluated more liberally than working-age adults because children are still developing, and there is potential for enough improvement for them to leave the disability roles as adults. Some children's disabilities are so severe that they might not survive to adulthood, thus emphasis is placed on making their life as comfortable as possible and guaranteeing their access to appropriate health care. School and social interactions with peers may be such children's greatest source of succor.

Under Social Security's guidelines for SSI benefits for children, disability assessment incorporates the child's school experience to further demonstrate the child's level of impairment and limitations that obstruct the child's ability to navigate school, which emulates competitive work in its structure, schedule, social interaction, submission to authority, and ability to exercise individual concentration, attention, persistence, and pace. To evaluate the child's residual functional capacity, school provides a laboratory of intellectual, behavioral, physical, and emotional activities that children are expected to meet based on age and grade level. To this end, Social Security seeks the cooperation of the child's school as part of the disability determination process and reviews school-provided information that includes:[1]

- copies of the child's school records, including those of academic performance, psychological evaluation, attendance, and behavior;
- standardized and other specialized testing;
- school-based therapeutic interventions (e.g., speech and language therapy, the use of other special services including placement in special education classes or other specially adapted settings);
- individualized education programs (IEPs);
- other periodic assessments of the child (e.g., comprehensive triennial assessments); and
- assessments by teachers and other qualified personnel about the child's activities and functioning, such as what the child can and cannot do or is limited in doing. Social Security uses a federally approved form, the Teacher's Questionnaire (SSA-5665) to request information from teachers.

The SSA has developed an inventory of specific medical and mental impairments called a Listing of Impairments. There is a Listing of Impairments for adults and one for children. The Administration has divided the adult listing of impairments[2] into 14 categories that include:

1.00 Musculoskeletal System (see Appendix A, §1.00),
2.00 Special Senses and Speech (see Appendix A, §2.00),
3.00 Respiratory Disorders (see Appendix A, §3.00),
4.00 Cardiovascular System (see Appendix A, §4.00),
5.00 Digestive System (see Appendix A, §5.00),
6.00 Genitourinary Disorders (see Appendix A, §6.00),
7.00 Hematological Disorders (see Appendix A, §7.00),
8.00 Skin Disorders (see Appendix A, §8.00),
9.00 Endocrine Disorders (see Appendix A, §9.00),
10.00 Congenital Disorders That Affect Multiple Body Systems (see Appendix A, §10.00),
11.00 Neurological Disorders (see Appendix A, §11.00),
12.00 Mental Disorders (see Appendix A, §12.00),
13.00 Cancer (Malignant Neoplastic Diseases, see Appendix A, §13.00), and
14.00 Immune System Disorders (see Appendix A, §14.00).

There are 15 categories of impairments for children under the age of 18. The child listing of impairments[3] includes:

100.00 Low Birth Weight and Failure to Thrive (see Appendix B, §100.00),
101.00 Musculoskeletal System (see Appendix B, §101.00),
102.00 Special Senses and Speech (see Appendix B, §102.00),
103.00 Respiratory Disorders (see Appendix B, §103.00),
104.00 Cardiovascular System (see Appendix B, §104.00),
105.00 Digestive System (see Appendix B, §105.00),
106.00 Genitourinary Disorders (see Appendix B, §106.00),
107.00 Hematological Disorders (see Appendix B, §107.00),
108.00 Skin Disorders (see Appendix B, §108.00),
109.00 Endocrine Disorders (see Appendix B, §109.00),
110.00 Congenital Disorders That Affect Multiple Body Systems (see Appendix B, §110.00),
111.00 Neurological Disorders (see Appendix B, §111.00),

112.00 Mental Disorders (see Appendix B, §112.00),
113.00 Cancer (Malignant Neoplastic Diseases, see Appendix B, §113.00), and
114.00 Immune System Disorders (see Appendix B, §114.00).

The criteria for the subcategories of impairments are so specific and difficult to satisfy that meeting a listing is rare. However, with adequate documentation, a medical expert may opine that the claimant's limitations "equal" a listing. The opinion that a claimant's disability equals a listing is demonstrated by showing that the claimant's limitations are similar or identical to the limitations of a listing that refers to a different condition. An example might be an individual who experiences chronic migraine headaches for which there is no listing, but an argument can be made that the individual in the throes of a migraine has functional limitations equal to the listing for epilepsy. Epileptic seizures occur unpredictably and often with little warning. Prophylactic medications may not be effective in preventing all seizures and carry their own adverse effects, including grogginess and drowsiness. The individual is incapacitated by the seizure for seconds or minutes followed by a postictal phase that can last for some hours, during which the individual is unable to function due to disorientation, confusion, and fatigue. So, too, migraine headaches occur at unpredictable intervals and give little or no warning to individuals experiencing them. The course of the headache can last for several hours, during which the individual is incapable of full functioning due to pain, nausea, vomiting, phonophobia, photophobia, and sometimes other visual disturbances. Claimants who meet or equal a listing may be awarded benefits, assuming they meet the other required criteria for disability.

The SSA has developed a list of particularly devastating conditions that, if treatment records establish a diagnosis of one of them for a claimant, they should trigger an expedited favorable disposition. This list of Compassionate Allowances conditions continues to grow. Many of the conditions are quite rare but always catastrophic and are brought to the attention of the SSA by the public, physicians, agencies, and organizations. The 233 conditions comprising the current list of Compassionate Allowances[4] can be found in Appendix H.

What Is Work?

Work consists of combined mental effort and physical exertion resulting in an intellectual or tangible product. A geologist finds likely gas-producing fields. An oil field worker excavates, develops, and maintains wells that produce the gas. A truck driver delivers gas. A meter reader measures the amount of consumed gas. An accounting clerk calculates the cost of the gas. A billing clerk sends consumers billing statements. A receivables clerk receives and records payment. An accountant records profits and losses; calculates withholding, payroll, and taxes; and prepares financial documents. The payroll clerk pays the geologist, oil field worker, truck driver, meter reader, accounting clerk, billing clerk, receivables clerk, accountant, and payroll clerk. But what constitutes the work each of these individuals performs consists of a variety of skills, both physical and mental.

All work requires attention, concentration, persistence, and pace.[5] The worker must be able to focus attention on the task at hand. The worker must be able to concentrate on the task to complete it in an accurate and timely way. The worker must persist to meet deadlines or quotas. And the worker must perform at a pace consistent with coworkers and management expectations. Thus, to adequately assess a patient's ability to work, a clinician must be aware of signs and symptoms that interfere with these essential elements of work: attention, concentration, persistence, and pace.

Symptoms that interfere with attention, concentration, persistence, and pace include: (1) pain; (2) fatigue; (3) altered mental status secondary to mental impairment, injury, medical condition, or adverse effects of prescribed medication; (4) gastrointestinal distress (i.e., urinary or bowel frequency or urgency, nausea, vomiting); (5) malaise (a general feeling of weakness, illness, or discomfort); (6) restricted movement or use of extremities; (7) sensory reduction or loss; (8) shortness of breath, weakness, syncope or near syncope, and dizziness secondary to respiratory or cardiovascular distress or neurological impairment; (9) cognitive impairment; and (10) intellectual deficits. Some of these symptoms are objective and can be observed or proven by diagnostic testing and imaging. Other symptoms are subjective and experienced in ways unique to every person. The treating clinician is in the best position to assess the presence of symptoms and their effect on the patient.

Pain particularly affects mobility, mood, and emotions. It is observable on some level objectively, but often it is experienced more subjectively. Each person experiences pain differently. Each person has a different threshold for pain. And each person has a different tolerance for pain alleviation. The effect of pain on these four characteristics of work, whether constant or intermittent, may impede the worker's ability to function within a competitive work setting. Pain is distracting and may inhibit work activity on a variety of levels. Pain may affect the worker's ability to perform physical tasks and limit the amount of time spent sitting, standing, or walking or the amount of weight that can be lifted or carried, pushed or pulled. Coping with pain often requires medication, and pain-reducing medication frequently causes drowsiness, grogginess, and gastrointestinal distress. These adverse effects may impact on the worker's ability to operate machinery, concentrate, and pay attention and may require more frequent and lengthy bathroom breaks. Sometimes pain cannot be managed by medication alone, and activity, temperature, infection, or emotions can exacerbate pain, resulting in needed bed rest or therapeutic interventions such as physical therapy that affect the worker's ability to be present for work 40 hours every week. Finally, pain can impact the individual's mood and emotional equilibrium. It can cause or exacerbate existing depression and anxiety.

Similarly, fatigue interferes with attention, concentration, persistence, and pace. It is especially detrimental to thinking, judgment, and memory; and fatigue is dangerous for individuals operating or directing the operation of machinery. Fatigue accompanies many illnesses and their treatment and is also symptomatic of depression. The effect of fatigue on the ability to sustain full-time employment must be a consideration in any clinical assessment of disability.

Altered mental status, evident in people who are disoriented to person, place, or time, is symptomatic of a variety of psychiatric disorders, and can be a side effect of various medications. Disorientation is also characteristic of the postictal phase following a seizure. Individuals who experience altered mental status are unable to reliably engage in the competitive workforce. People so disoriented may be unable to consistently maintain a schedule, understand or carry out instructions, remember orally delivered directions or instructions, be able to appropriately operate machinery, or otherwise engage in common exertional or nonexertional, work-related tasks.

Gastrointestinal distress, nausea, vomiting, and bladder or bowel incontinence or urgency may require immediate access to a bathroom, frequent bathroom breaks, and bathroom breaks of significant duration. These symptoms frequently accompany various medical conditions and can be side effects of several prescribed medications or treatments. They are distractions to both the worker experiencing the symptoms and to coworkers and others with whom such an individual interacts within the workplace. This condition affects work schedules within the department, completion of assignments, meeting quotas, and appropriately interacting with coworkers and the public. Such issues are often accompanied by significant distress and anxiety, and the patient is constantly on guard for emergency situations that are distracting and embarrassing.

Individuals who experience chronic or intermittent malaise, who feel sickly, weak, fatigued, and uncomfortable, may have trouble at all levels of work. Much like people who are in pain, people who feel ill may be unable to focus on anything other than their own symptoms. People who are sick may feel increased anxiety that further impairs their functioning. Furthermore, individuals with infectious diseases may pose a threat to coworkers and the public, whereas individuals with autoimmune diseases may be endangered by exposure to opportunistic infection for which they have little or no resistance.

Individuals who have musculoskeletal conditions, burns, amputations, medical conditions such as multiple sclerosis, peripheral neuropathy, Tardive dyskinesia, Parkinson's disease, or who may have suffered a stroke (cardiovascular or cerebrovascular accident) may experience reduced ability to manipulate their own bodies. They may have lost the use or control of one or more extremities inhibiting their ability to stand, walk, balance, kneel, stoop, or bend, or to lift, carry, push, pull, or reach, or the ability to engage in fine or gross manipulations in either or both hands or the fingers of either or both hands. Clearly, these limitations impose obvious restrictions on one's ability to work. Even if one's work is primarily cerebral, physical limitations still impact on the ability to perform within a competitive work environment.

Sensory reduction or loss applies to vision, hearing, and speech as well as touch. Speech is not entirely a sensory function, but the ability to hear is critical in both receptive and expressive language, and the SSA combines speech with the sensory deficits in both the adult and child listings of impairments. People with sensory loss or reduction may be able to perform some work, but they may be unable to participate in the competitive workforce. Such individuals might require special accommodations by their employers. An impaired sense of touch may also create significant obstacles in the workplace. People who suffer from diabetic peripheral neuropathy, for example, maybe unable to feel the ground beneath their feet, leading to disbalance and an increased risk of falling. Similarly, neuropathy or tremulousness of the hands interferes with fine and gross manipulations. These problems can severely limit the ability to reliably perform jobs requiring simple mobility and dexterity.

Cognitive impairment can result from illness, stroke, or injury adversely affecting the individual's capacity for thinking, processing information, understanding, remembering, and judging. Even mild cognitive impairment may be a barrier to competitive work if it interferes with a person's ability to learn or retain information, remember simple instructions, work without close supervision, and make simple work-related decisions.

Intellectual deficits, depending on severity, limit work options and may prevent full participation in a competitive work setting. Depending on the nature of the deficits and the limitations they impose, the claimant may be able to perform simple repetitive tasks within a competitive work environment. Or, if the deficits are profound, close supervision in a sheltered environment may be the best option such an individual can manage.

For Social Security's purposes, work is the concentrated, organized physical and mental effort to produce something for which one is paid. To qualify as work, it must be performed on a full-time basis, 8 hours a day, 40 hours a week. It must be performed within a competitive work setting as opposed to a sheltered or protected work environment. Sheltered work may include a family-owned or operated business where the individual can come and go at will and who is given only simple tasks performed voluntarily or with constant supervision. To be considered work, it must produce earnings that meet the standard of substantial gainful activity. SGA for 2019 is a monthly income of $1,220 for nonblind individuals and $2,040 for the statutorily blind. Persons still working and earning at least SGA typically will not qualify for disability benefits through Social Security unless it can be demonstrated that the work setting is not competitive or the work is not consistent or the work can only be performed if the worker is provided accommodations unavailable to the other employees. Accommodations can consist of assistive devices such as voice-controlled computer access or production accommodations such as modified work schedules or reduced production quotas.

Assessment for SSDI and SSI benefits requires a reasonable understanding of jobs, the training, skills and strength required, as well as the intellectual capacity to perform the work. All jobs have certain levels of nonexertional prerequisites to execute the requirements of work, including attention, concentration, persistence, and pace. Workers must be physically and mentally present and available to work. They must be able to concentrate on the task at hand. They must be able to persist until the job is completed. They must be able to work at a pace consistent with deadlines, quotas, and coordinated activities with coworkers. Additionally, all jobs require some level of training. Even a simple, repetitive job requires some instruction and supervision before the job can be performed independently. The more complex the job, the greater the specific vocational preparation (SVP) necessary to perform it.

The level of exertion typically needed to perform jobs is described as sedentary, light, medium, heavy, or very heavy. Sedentary jobs require the worker to lift no more than 10 pounds occasionally and are performed primarily from the seated position, with standing and walking performed only occasionally. Light work involves standing and walking throughout the workday, with frequent lifting and carrying up to 10 pounds and occasional lifting and carrying up to 20 pounds. Medium work requires lifting and carrying up to 25 pounds frequently and up to 50 pounds occasionally. Heavy work means frequently lifting and carrying up to 50 pounds and occasionally lifting and carrying up to 100 pounds, while very heavy work requires frequently lifting and carrying 50 pounds or more and occasionally lifting or carrying 100 pounds or more.[6]

Specific vocational preparation is a term coined by the *Dictionary of Occupational Titles*, a publication by the U. S. Department of Labor that is used by Social Security to describe the level of training or education necessary to perform various jobs. The less skilled a job, the less time is necessary to learn to perform it independently. A job that can be mastered with only a short demonstration has a specific vocational preparation (SVP) of 1. A job that requires more than a short demonstration and training of up to one month has an SVP of 2. A job that requires more than one month to three months of training has an SVP of 3. A job that requires training between three and six months has an SVP of 4. A job identified as an SVP 5 position requires training of between six months and one year. An SVP of 6 requires training of between one and two years, while an SVP of 7 requires two to four years of training or education. An SVP of 8 denotes a job necessitating four to 10 years of training or education and an SVP of 9, the highest skill set cited by the *Dictionary of Occupational Titles*, requires more than 10 years of training and education. An SVP of 1 or 2 is considered unskilled, 3 or 4 is semiskilled, and 5 and above denote levels of skilled work.

The following scenario may prove illustrative in developing an understanding of exertional and preparatory requirements for various jobs. A trucking company was founded and operated by Mr. Smith. Mr. Smith employs an administrative staff to purchase and maintain a fleet of trucks, recruit and manage drivers and maintenance staff, provide employee benefits, make payroll, and secure and maintain the premises. Employees include a chief operating officer (COO), chief financial officer (CFO), accountant, bookkeeper, accounts receivable clerk, accounts payable clerk, secretarial and clerical support staff, human resources director and staff, marketing director, sales staff, dispatchers, drivers, mechanics, mechanics helpers, security guards, janitors, and supervisors for each department. Each job has different strength requirements, different sets of skills, and different training. All employees perform their duties autonomously and in concert or coordination with one another. The jobs of COO, CFO, and human resources manager of the company are highly skilled. They are considered sedentary positions with an SVP level of 8. Industrial truck mechanics perform at the medium level of exertion and are highly skilled with an SVP of 7. However, the position of truck driver is semiskilled and performed at the medium exertional level with an SVP of 4. The dispatcher job is skilled and sedentary with an SVP of 5. Both the jobs of security guard and janitor are semiskilled with an SVP of 3, but the security guard job is performed at the light exertional level while the job of janitor requires medium exertional activity. The jobs of accountant and bookkeeper are both sedentary, but the accountant has an SVP of 8 while the bookkeeper has an SVP of 6. Accounts receivable and payable clerks have an SVP of 5 and are sedentary, while general office clerks perform at the light exertional level with an SVP of 3. Although there is a correlation between education and specific vocational preparation, sometimes the SVP is more closely related to acquired skills and experience.

Measuring Disability

The determination of disability can only be conferred by the commissioner of the SSA or the commissioner's designees, including Social Security field offices, state Disability Determination Services, administrative law judges, the Appeals Council, or federal courts. Clinicians' opinions that a patient is disabled are not accorded any weight by Social Security in the disability determination process because clinicians' definitions of disability are generally incompatible with that of the SSA. However, treating clinicians' opinions can influence the disability determination process if their treatment records support their assessment of exertional or nonexertional limitations resulting from their patient's condition and treatment. The opinion of the treating physician is not accorded any greater weight than the opinion of nontreating or examining-only clinicians unless treatment records are supportive of the doctor's opinion. However, if the treating clinicians' treatment records support their professional opinions and the Administration's contracted examining or nonexamining clinical opinions result in substantially different conclusions, the Administration or administrative law judge is more likely to find the examining or nonexamining professionals' opinions less credible and give the treating source greater influence in disability determination.

Clinicians typically do not consider disability as a designation for their patients. In a general sense, clinicians measure their patient's condition along a continuum of severity of symptoms where they, at their most severe, are addressed by either more aggressive curative interventions or palliative care. The progress notes of medical professionals generally reflect repetition of the patient's history, diagnoses, and treatment and add current vital signs (i.e., blood pressure, pulse, weight, height), complaints, symptoms, recent laboratory findings, treatments, medications, and referrals. A common method for health-care professionals' note taking is known as SOAP notes, and these notes include the patient's subjective report, objective findings, assessment, and plan.

For mental-health-care professionals, notes are frequently reflective of the patient's mental status, presentation, stressors, behavioral or emotional responses, symptoms, observations, and response to treatment. Often the notes are sparse and oblique. Psychologists and other mental-health-care professionals may feel a special obligation to protect their patients' confidentiality and are aware that their notes can have unintended consequences in a variety of legal contexts, including employment, divorce, child custody, and criminal and civil actions. However, for the purpose of disability determination, thorough, accurate and well-maintained treatment records are most helpful.

Furthermore, in disability determination there must be a clear link between the identified symptoms and functional limitations. Disability is based on severity of symptoms that interfere with exertional and nonexertional activities resulting in the claimant's inability to engage in either past work or any other full-time work in the national economy. Thus, if clinicians render an opinion about the patient's functional limitations, there must be corresponding evidence in the records.

Toward that end, clinicians should consider recording progress notes that identify the patient's job and describing any physical and mental limitations experienced as a result of injury, illness, or mental impairment. This note-keeping process would not only provide valuable information for insurers, agencies, and adjunctive health-care services that may be prescribed but would also benefit claimants by providing concrete examples of the effect of signs and symptoms of possible *medically determinable impairments* (MDIs). For each visit, physicians could easily incorporate a few lines in their records that chart their patients' limitations. For example, consultative examiners regularly opine as to the weight the claimants can frequently and occasionally lift and carry; for how long they can sit, stand and walk; and whether they have the capacity to use their hands to grip, grasp or engage in fine and gross manipulations. The examiners base their opinions not on empirical evidence but on their impressions, which are founded on a single, sometimes perfunctory, examination. My coauthor regularly queries her clients following their consultative examinations and asks, for example, whether the examiner actually had them lift or carry something of a specific weight. The response has been uniformly and categorically, "No."

Most clinicians use a formula for progress notes that addresses history, diagnoses, procedures, hospitalizations, symptoms, and vital and other signs. However, these data do not particularly advance an understanding of how or why their patients may meet disability criteria. Treatment records that reflect patients' actual measured functioning are often more helpful. For those professionals qualified to evaluate functions such as lifting, carrying, sitting, standing, and walking, this can be accomplished by adding a few props to the routine examination. For example, a gallon jug of water is a common reference used by administrative law judges (ALJs) to determine the weight a claimant could comfortably lift or carry on a constant, frequent, or occasional basis, thus forming the foundation of engaging in sedentary, light, or medium work. Clinicians can request the patient lift a gallon jug of water weighing slightly more than eight pounds, from the ground level, table height, and shoulder height with both right and left hands, and record success or failure, the ease in doing so or the effort that had to be expended, as well as other practical exercises such as grip strength, all of which provide relevant information. These can be introduced at random examinations or at specific intervals. The information extrapolated from such exercises informs the examiner of the patient's capacity to engage in activities essential to most work. However, clinicians would have to bear in mind that these exercises are performed outside the stress of the competitive work setting, without time limits or other restrictions. Or clinicians can include a questionnaire in the new patient information packet where patients can describe their work activities. Such a form could be revisited annually to account for changes in job or job activities and their ability to perform them. Marfeo et al. (2013) suggest "developing new measurement instruments of behavioral health and physical functioning relevant for Social Security work disability evaluation purposes."

Health-care professionals should also consider their patients' levels of adaptive psychological functioning, or what the SSA refers to as mental residual functional capacity (MRFC). The SSA's four general categories of MRFC include the ability to (1) "understand, remember, or apply information; (2) interact with others; (3) concentrate, persist, or maintain pace; and (4) adapt or manage oneself."[7] Within the four general categories, there are 20 subcategories, as follows:

A. Understanding and Memory

1. The ability to remember locations and work-like procedures
2. The ability to understand and remember very short and simple instructions
3. The ability to understand and remember detailed instructions

B. Sustained Concentration and Persistence

4. The ability to carry out very short and simple instructions
5. The ability to carry out detailed instructions
6. The ability to maintain attention and concentration for extended periods
7. The ability to perform activities within a schedule, maintain regular attendance, and be punctual within customary tolerances
8. The ability to sustain an ordinary routine without special supervision
9. The ability to work in coordination with or proximity to others without being distracted by them
10. The ability to make simple work-related decisions
11. The ability to complete a normal workday and workweek without interruptions from psychologically based symptoms and to perform at a consistent pace without an unreasonable number and length of rest periods

C. Social Interaction

12. The ability to interact appropriately with the general public
13. The ability to ask simple questions or request assistance
14. The ability to accept instructions and respond appropriately to criticism from supervisors
15. The ability to get along with coworkers or peers without distracting them or exhibiting behavioral extremes
16. The ability to maintain socially appropriate behavior and to adhere to basic standards of neatness and cleanliness

D. Adaptation

17. The ability to respond appropriately to changes in the work setting
18. The ability to be aware of normal hazards and take appropriate precautions
19. The ability to travel in unfamiliar places or use public transportation
20. The ability to set realistic goals or make plans independently of others[8]

Each of these component features of nonexertional activity is essential to competitive work. Together they define one's capacity to work independently and in concert with others, to perform tasks accurately and efficiently, to be socially appropriate, and to be present and available for work. Even a moderate level of impairment in any of these attributes reduces functionality, and the more impaired the individual's ability to perform any of these activities, the less likely that person is capable of participating in the full-time competitive workforce. Multiple moderate impairments may be more incapacitating than one or two severe impairments.

Perhaps the most common rationale for a finding of disability is based on the claimant's incapacity to work a full-time work schedule, 8 hours a day, 40 hours a week, due to impairments or treatment. Social Security rulings 96-8p and 96-9p provide that either a claimant must be able to perform at the assessed residual functional capacity on a sustained basis (i.e., an eight-hours-a-day, five-days-a-week schedule or the equivalent) or a finding of disability is warranted. Claimants who are off task even 10% of the workday in addition to legally mandated rest and meal breaks are not completing a full-time workday. Of course, no one can be on task 100% of the time, but 10% of an 8-hour workday equals 48 minutes. Forty-eight minutes in addition to two mandated 15-minute rest breaks and one 30-minute meal break would mean the individual is available to engage in work activities 6.2 hours a day, which would not constitute a full-day's work per Social Security's definition. Workers may experience occasional episodes of malaise or fatigue that interferes with attention, concentration, persistence, and pace. But if such occurrences happen on a regular basis for a sustained period, that worker is not performing a full-time job. People who are distracted by chronic conditions such as pain, gastrointestinal or urinary symptoms, fatigue, or low energy, or who experience constant psychological symptoms including obsessive compulsivity, anxiety, or depression, are unlikely to be on task and available for work more than 90% of the workday.

Another justification for a finding of disability is based on the consideration of age, past relevant work, education, and work experience. Pursuant to SSR 85-15, Titles II and XVI:[9] Capability to Do Other Work—The Medical-Vocational Rules as a Framework for Evaluating Solely Nonexertional Impairments: "If a person has a severe medically determinable impairment which, though not meeting or equaling the criteria in the Listing of Impairments, prevents the person from doing past relevant work, it must be determined whether the person can do other work. This involves consideration of the person's RFC and the vocational factors of age, education, and work experience."

The SSA recognizes that nonexertional impairments, whether acknowledged as the claimant's primary impairment or the consequence of underlying secondary symptoms, treatment, unemployment, stress, or other factors, may prevent an individual from reliably performing the basic functions of work. This ruling takes the role of stress and other nonexertional impairments into consideration when assessing disability. The claimant's tolerance for typical work-related stressors such as quotas, schedules, time limits, and interacting with supervisors, coworkers, and the public may increase stress. Greater stress may be associated with more complex or demanding work. Thus, if claimants cannot tolerate higher levels of stress, the judge will ask the vocational expert whether, given the claimant's limitations, that individual could perform unskilled jobs requiring only simple, repetitive tasks. A claimant who is incapable of performing even unskilled simple and repetitive tasks is effectively disabled.

Notes

1. https://www.ssa.gov/disability/professionals/childhoodssi-pub049.htm.
2. See Appendix A.
3. See Appendix B.
4. https://www.ssa.gov/compassionateallowances/conditions.htm.
5. https://secure.ssa.gov/poms.nsf/lnx/0425020010
6. SSR 83-10: Titles II and XVI: Determining Capability to Do Other Work—The Medical Vocational Rules of Appendix 2.
7. https://www.ssa.gov/disability/professionals/bluebook/12.00-MentalDisorders-Adult.htm#12_00F.
8. As listed on Social Security Administration Form SSA-4734-F4-SUP.
9. SSR 85-15, https://www.ssa.gov/OP_Home/rulings/di/02/SSR85-15-di-02.html.

CHAPTER THREE

Disability Determination

> Disability and health are difficult concepts to define and measure. In fact, the appropriate definition of disability depends on the reason behind its measurement.
>
> —Daniel Mont

There are essentially four paths to a determination of disability: a diagnosis of one of the conditions on the growing list of Compassionate Allowances; meeting or equaling one or more of the conditions on the adult or child listing of impairments; showing evidence of inability to perform past work or any other work based on functional limitations reflected in treatment records and opined by a treating clinician, consultative examiner, or medical expert; or being found to meet the Medical-Vocational Guidelines based on age, education, English fluency, and exertional limitations.

Disability determination relies on multiple factors that address physical and mental limitations that are incompatible with full-time competitive employment. The basic assumptions and language used by the SSA are somewhat at odds with those of medicine and psychology. For Social Security's purposes, disability for adults is tied to the capacity to sustain full-time employment, or for children, age appropriate behaviors, school functioning, and meeting developmental milestones. Clinicians often see severe conditions as challenges, not as disabilities, because they do not understand work, the exertional and nonexertional requirements of work, Social Security regulations, and the role of Social Security as a mechanism for survival. There is also some confusion between the guidelines for SSDI and SSI and the ADA.

The ADA was first established in 1990 and followed by the ADA Amendments Act (ADAAA) passed by Congress in 2008 and enacted in 2009. The ADA defines disability as "an impairment that substantially limits one or more major life activities; a record of such an impairment; or being regarded as having such an impairment." It further identifies by example what is considered substantial limitations to include: "caring for oneself, performing manual tasks, seeing, hearing, eating, sleeping, walking, standing, lifting, bending, speaking, breathing, learning, reading, concentrating, thinking, communicating and working."[1] The ADAAA also lists *major bodily functions* including, but not limited to, functions of the immune system; normal cell growth; and digestive, bowel, bladder, neurological, brain, respiratory, circulatory, endocrine, and reproductive functions."[2] The ADA is a protection for disabled individuals to participate in usual and customary activities associated with daily life and in the workforce by requiring accessible access and egress including hallways and doorways wide enough to accommodate wheelchairs and walkers, accessible bathrooms, ramps, handicapped parking, and other amenities to afford equal entrée to places of business and public buildings and venues. Individuals with disabilities who can work and want to work are protected under the ADAAA from discrimination on the basis of their disabilities and are provided with the tools and accessibility to allow them to perform their work. However, this act does not define work as full time, whereas inability to engage in full-time work is fundamental to the definition of disability for the Social Security disability programs.

Diagnoses, Symptoms, and Limitations in the Assessment of Disability

Social Security's definition of disability is generally inconsistent with the way that clinicians consider the term. Most clinicians view disability as a challenge to be overcome by advances in medicine, science, and technology. Clinicians typically think in terms of treatable versus terminal. And even terminal illness may be treatable such that treatment can extend life quality and duration. The usual medical conception of disability exists as a level of extreme severity but not necessarily in a way that is compatible with Social Security's definition.

Diagnoses of severe medical or psychological conditions with their attendant symptoms and adverse effects of treatment may be considered disabling by clinicians, but treatment records often do not reflect the seriousness of the claimants' disabilities because, as a general rule, clinicians do not equate symptoms and the effects of treatment with functional limitations. While the records may mention pain, malaise, or fatigue, these symptoms are not always qualified or associated with functional limitations such as poor memory, diminished concentration, impaired judgment, drowsiness, increased distractibility, impaired cognitions, reduced persistence, and weakened resilience. Unless these symptoms are documented as obstacles to performance within a competitive work environment, they exist only as abstract concepts in the disability determination process.

Contributing Factors in Disability Determination

The Administration considers other factors in addition to the severity of the claimant's impairments and functionality. These factors include age, obesity, education level, transferability of skills, and English fluency. These issues reflect the patient's capacity to perform jobs as well as the kinds and numbers of jobs for which the claimant is suited. If a claimant can no longer perform past work as a result of impairment, the question arises as to whether that individual can perform other work. If the work is significantly different from past work, it is a legitimate concern as to whether age, educational level, obesity, transferability of skills, or English fluency may be a barrier to learning new skills, adapting to a new work setting, integrating with a different population of coworkers, applying previously learned skills, performing new skills, or acclimating to a new industry.

Clinicians should bear in mind the definition of sedentary work as described in Social Security Regulation (SSR) 96-9p,[3] and be prepared to consider their patients' ability to perform any work based on their symptoms and resultant limitations:

> The ability to perform the full range of sedentary work requires the ability to lift no more than 10 pounds at a time and occasionally to lift or carry articles like docket files, ledgers, and small tools. Although a sedentary job is defined as one that involves sitting, a certain amount of walking and standing is often necessary in carrying out job duties. Jobs are sedentary if walking and standing are required occasionally and other sedentary criteria are met. "Occasionally" means occurring from very little up to one-third of the time, and would generally total no more than about 2 hours of an 8-hour workday. Sitting would generally total about 6 hours of an 8-hour workday. Unskilled sedentary work also involves other activities, classified as "nonexertional," such as capacities for seeing, manipulation, and understanding, remembering, and carrying out simple instructions.[4]

Additional nonexertional abilities necessary to all work are thinking; paying attention; concentrating; making simple work-related decisions; working independently without constant supervision; being aware of hazards and taking appropriate precautions; behaving appropriately with coworkers, peers, and the public; working in coordination with or proximity to others; and, above all, maintaining the daily work schedule and being present for work with absences limited to fewer than once per month. An individual incapable of performing at this level may be too impaired to work at any full-time competitive job.

Age

The SSA classifies adults by age.[5] Between ages 18 and 50, individuals are "younger aged." Ages 50 to 55 are identified as "approaching advanced age." Between ages 55 and 60, individuals are considered of "advanced age." Over age 60, individuals are identified as "closely approaching retirement age." The matter of age reflects an element of a claimant's ability to adjust to "other work." Depending on the claimant's past work, it may be considered too great a hardship for that individual to learn a new job or job skill due to the adversity of age, which carries with it age-related memory or concentration deficiencies or strength or mobility deficits that may exist because of other, age-related physical limitations. Social Security uses the Medical-Vocational Guidelines, also known as the grid rules,[6] to assign disability status to workers who may not meet or equal one or more conditions in the Listing of Impairments but who may demonstrate incapacity for full-time work due to severe limitations associated with their medical or mental impairments and exacerbated by age-related limitations.

The grid rules consist of factors including the claimant's age, level of education, exertional level required by past work, and the maximum skill level of past relevant work, along with the exertional level at which the claimant is currently capable of performing. If a claimant is younger (18–49 years of age), age is not considered to be a significant obstacle to working at any skill or exertional level, although, depending on other factors, workers aged 45–49 may be considered to be at somewhat of a disadvantage relative to those age 44 and under. Workers aged 50–54 are considered approaching advanced age, and their age along with work history and education may impose significant limitations on their ability to perform available jobs. Claimants 55 years old and above are considered of advanced age.

The exertional level of jobs is also considered. Jobs are classified as sedentary, light, medium, heavy, or very heavy. Skill levels range from unskilled to highly skilled. Due to the combined effect of a severe impairment that results in significant limitations in the worker's ability to perform past work, lack of transferable skills based on the person's specific vocational preparation (SVP) level, and, finally, limitations by age, education, or both, a worker may be found disabled based on the grid rules, even if the impairment does not meet or equal a listing. If the available jobs that meet the claimant's exertional and educational limitations require learning a new job in a new field in a new setting and would represent a more-than-moderate adjustment to the new work, a finding of disability may be based on the grid rules.

Obesity

Although it is not a listed impairment, obesity is recognized as a complicating factor that can compromise various body systems and exacerbate or worsen existing impairments and precipitate others. Obesity adds stress to the cardiovascular, musculoskeletal, endocrine, and respiratory systems, to name the most obvious (see Appendix A, §§3.00O, 100Q, 4.00I; Appendix B, §104.00G). It can also affect mood, emotions, and behavior and contribute to mental impairments, including depression and anxiety. Obesity may increase the risk for development or exacerbation of osteoarthritis, sleep apnea, type 2 diabetes mellitus, hypertension, and various cancers. Social Security considers the ways that obesity may adversely affect pain, fatigue, and physical activity. Obesity can interfere with such activities as bending, stooping, kneeling, crawling, balancing, sitting, standing, and walking, and even fingering and handling. As such, "if the person's obesity, alone or in combination with another impairment(s), significantly limits his or her physical or mental ability to do basic work activities, we find that the impairment(s) is severe. We find, however, that the impairment(s) is "not severe" if it does not significantly limit [a person's] physical or mental ability to do basic work activities."[7]

The SSA does not rely on weight or the body mass index (BMI) and does not employ clinical descriptions of obesity such as "extreme" or "morbid" to assess severity. It relies on the effect of obesity on the individual's residual functional capacity (RFC).

Education

Like age, education level is a determinant of what work an individual can do. Individuals who did not graduate high school, who did not receive a general equivalency diploma (GED), who were special education students, or who are not fluent in English are disadvantaged in the competitive job market and have only unskilled work available to them as a rule. Some individuals with little formal education may have held skilled jobs as mechanics, electricians, plumbers, or other trades. However, these are all physically laborious jobs, and an individual who can no longer meet physical demands may be incapable of performing any other work.

Of course, it should also be noted that the older the claimants, the more remote their education is likely to have been. Thus the value of a high school diploma granted in 1978 may be somewhat less relevant in 2019 than a diploma earned in 1988. Likewise, a GED may also be problematic because of the obvious holes in the GED holder's education, which may also be true of some individuals who were homeschooled. School requires students to be present, participate in classroom discussion, engage in socially appropriate behaviors, meet schedules and deadlines, comply with teachers' authority, interact effectively and appropriately with fellow students on group assignments, and demonstrate the requisite level of grade-appropriate expertise. Formal education provides students with tools beyond academics, including cooperation, negotiation, compromise, persistence, familiarity with hierarchy of authority, and leadership. In short, school is preparation for work, and those who have not experienced a complete school experience may be disadvantaged in the competitive job market, having potentially not developed the social skills or emotional intelligence of their formally school-educated peers. Although contemporary homeschooling has become increasingly sophisticated and encourages peer interactions and activities, previously it was less formal, did not include socialization exercises, was often conducted in isolation, and was not necessarily guided by trained teachers.

English Fluency

Individuals who cannot communicate in English, who cannot read, write, and speak English with a full appreciation for the nuances of the language, are at a decided disadvantage in the competitive job market. Lack of English fluency diminishes the number of jobs that they would be able to perform. Some industries such as agriculture, domestic service, and manufacturing employ large numbers of non-English-speaking workers such that a lack of English fluency may not represent a hardship to employee or employer. However, jobs in such industries may not have unskilled sedentary jobs available, thus leaving the worker with fewer job possibilities.

Transferability of Skills

Skilled and semiskilled jobs typically require the acquisition of levels of expertise based on education, training, and experience that are applied foundationally where one skill builds on another. As an example, an office manager is a skilled job with an SVP of 7. To have attained the level of expertise and be able to manage an office, the manager must have first mastered the lesser skilled jobs that encompass office work. If a skilled or semiskilled worker becomes too medically or mentally impaired to perform that skilled job but retains the ability to perform a simpler, less complex skilled or semiskilled job for which the worker already has the skills, and such jobs exist in sufficient numbers within the national economy, that individual may not be considered disabled. Workers with transferable skills cannot have those skills transferred to a higher skilled job but only to jobs less skilled than the past relevant work, which would include any job performed for more than three months within the 15 years prior to the alleged onset date. Furthermore, the skills may be transferable to jobs in industries other than the claimant's past relevant work. Thus an individual who had spent the past fifteen years in the banking industry may have skills that are transferable to retail sales, general clerical work, or other work.

Clinicians whose patients may be considering or applying for disability benefits should think about how their patients' conditions and symptoms may be exacerbated by age and obesity. And while they may not be in a position to assess how their patients' education or English fluency affect job performance, they may be able to record observations in their notes that reflect how these qualities may create barriers to their patients' learning. For example, a 50-year-old, obese agricultural worker with a minimal education achieved in his native Central American country suffered a severe injury to his back. While being evaluated for the back injury, he was found to have an A1c of 8, placing him in the severe diabetic range. The clinical staff of the hospital attempted to counsel the patient, in Spanish, on the essential medication and nutrition regimen he needed to follow to avoid further damage to his health. At subsequent follow-up appointments, the patient's A1c continued to soar, and it was clear he was not following medical advice. The clinical staff requested the patient be accompanied by a close family member to his next appointment. At that appointment, the patient was accompanied by his wife and 20-year-old son. As the doctor explained the gravity of the patient's health problems, his wife and son were surprised, since the patient had not reported his diabetes to them. The son took charge of administering his father's insulin and assisted his mother in modifying the family diet to accommodate his father's diabetes. Fortunately, the clinical staff made note of the necessity of family intervention to address the patient's serious medical condition, explaining that on his own, the patient did not understand the seriousness of his illness and lacked the capacity to absorb the requisite information to mitigate his disease process. This illustrates the importance of the medical staff's attention to their patients' non-medical needs including English fluency, education, and judgment as well as the value of patient advocacy by family, friends, or other resources such as religious or non-profit organizations.

Notes

1. 42 U.S. Code §12101—Findings and purpose.
2. 42 U.S. Code §12101—Note.
3. Policy Interpretation Ruling Titles II and XVI: Determining Capability to Do Other Work—Implications of a Residual Functional Capacity for Less Than a Full Range of Sedentary Work.
4. SSR 96-9p.
5. Your Age as a Vocational Factor, 20 C.F.R. §404.1563.
6. Medical-Vocational Guidelines, 20 C.F.R., Appendix 2 to Subpart P of Part 404.
7. SSR 19-2p, applicable May 20, 2019.

CHAPTER FOUR

Complicating Factors in Disability Determination

> Because deep down we know that what matters in this life is more than winning for ourselves. What really matters is helping others win, too, even if it means slowing down and changing our course now and then.
>
> —Fred Rogers

Disability determination is never straightforward, and a variety of factors can cause an otherwise clearly benefits-worthy claim to be denied. These complicating factors include lack of treatment, drug and alcohol abuse, noncompliance with treatment, lack of clinical support, and evidence of malingering.

Lack of Treatment

In the United States, employers commonly provide options for health insurance, including the opportunity to purchase health insurance for employees and their dependents through a group plan. Some employers may cover the premium in whole or in part, at least for employees, and any remaining portion of their own and their dependents' premiums are deducted from their paychecks. However, if the claimant is uninsured or loses insurance benefits due to loss of employment, treatment may be inconsistent, limited to emergency rooms or urgent care, and without continuity. Although the claimant can legitimately assert that treatment was too expensive and thus impossible to obtain, the SSA would argue that if the individual is too sick to work, then seeking adequate treatment should be the individual's priority and that there are free and low-cost treatment options. Evidence of a severe impairment that has existed since the claimant's alleged onset date can only be found in the treatment records. It is possible that a claimant can be found disabled without treatment records if, for example, a consultative examiner finds support of a condition that meets a listing or observes and records the presence of exertional or nonexertional limitations that place the claimant at less than sedentary functional capacity. However, this scenario is atypical.

Another circumstance where it may be possible to obtain a favorable decision without consistent records might occur if an individual who had been without treatment experienced a significant worsening of a physical or mental condition and was found to meet a listing or at least found too impaired to perform work activities on a full-time basis. There might be a determination that the individual is disabled, but the alleged onset date could be amended to the date that the claimant became completely incapacitated per Social Security regulations.

For instance, consider Robert, a 49-year-old claimant with hypertension, and whose insulin-dependent type 1 diabetes was poorly controlled, resulting in diabetic proliferative retinopathy that affected his vision and eventually led to his failure to pass the vision test for his commercial driver's license, thereby ending his employment as a truck driver. The loss of his job meant the loss of his health insurance. After unsuccessfully seeking other employment, Robert applied for SSDI benefits and continued to seek treatment from free and low-cost clinics, but as his finances dwindled, he became homeless and no longer had the money to purchase insulin or the ability to refrigerate it when he could buy it. He was denied benefits at the initial application and requested reconsideration. Robert's condition deteriorated to the point that he developed chronic renal disease and worsened again as he went into kidney failure. He was denied again at reconsideration and requested a hearing. He was emergently hospitalized and diagnosed with end-stage renal disease (ESRD), for which hemodialysis was prescribed five times weekly. Social Security granted Robert benefits as of his application date despite the lack of consistent treatment records because ESRD meets a listing and clearly had to have been developing over time to have reached this level of severity. Robert was also immediately entitled to Medicare, even though he had not met the 29-month eligibility period, because individuals with chronic renal disease or ESRD who require hemodialysis or kidney transplantation receive immediate access to Medicare due to the urgency of otherwise prohibitively expensive medical intervention.

On the other hand, Karen, also 49 years old, lost her job and health insurance when she could no longer perform her job as a waitress. She had bilateral carpal tunnel syndrome, but even after having carpal tunnel release surgery on both wrists, she showed continuing symptoms of numbness and loss of grip strength in her bilateral hands. Karen applied for and received workers' compensation benefits when it was determined her carpal tunnel syndrome resulted from repetitive work-related injury, but workers' compensation provided medical treatment for her carpal tunnel syndrome only, not for the depression she suffered due to her ongoing pain, unemployment, loss of income, and struggle for survival. When Karen appeared before ALJ at her hearing, she alleged severe major depression in addition to her bilateral carpal tunnel syndrome. However, since she was not receiving any treatment for her depression because she could not afford it, the depression was found not to be contributory to her claim of disability, and her carpal tunnel syndrome did not, in the opinion of the vocational expert, prevent her from performing her past work or any other work that was a light, semiskilled job per the *Dictionary of Occupational Titles* (*DOT*). Her claim was denied. The judge's rationale was that the consultative examiner found that Karen could still perform a full range of light work, including waiting tables, despite her carpal tunnel syndrome.

Drug Abuse and Alcoholism

The relationship between substance abuse and disability is one of the many perplexing and misunderstood questions that arise in the disability determination process. Drug abuse and alcoholism (DAA)[1] was previously recognized as a disabling condition and incorporated into the SSA catalogue of disabilities during the period from the inception of the SSDI program in 1972 until 1994. There was unanimity of agreement among many mental health providers at around the same time who regarded drug and alcohol abuse as a disease process (Kahle & White, 1991). The ending of this category of impairment in 1994 coincided with the Republican control of Congress and its revised interpretation of what qualifies as a disability. The result was a repudiation of drug abuse and alcoholism as disabling conditions because they were construed to be a consequence of poor self-control, self-indulgence, and deficient character rather than medical or psychological disorders (Greenberg & Baumohl, 1996). Drug abuse and alcoholism are now used as a rationale for denying benefits.

Specifically, Social Security deems that if drug or alcohol use is a material cause of a claimant's disabling condition or if drug or alcohol abuse exacerbates the claimant's impairments, the claim may be denied. However, if sobriety or abstinence would not affect the condition, and if the impairments, limitations, and other requirements for benefits are present, the claim may be awarded (Noblitt & Noblitt, 2012).

Although DAA frequently occurs with other psychological disorders, it can also be associated with physical impairments. It is becoming increasingly difficult for people to obtain adequate pain relief due to contemporary fear of addictions among prescribing health-care professionals. People have been known to self-injure in order to obtain prescriptions for opioids. Street drugs and alcohol are often employed as self-medication against pain, anxiety, and depression. The use of illicit drugs and alcohol is sometimes cultural, sometimes self-perceived as a necessity. Stigma continues to be associated with seeking mental health care, and, rather than doing so, some are inclined to self-medicate with drugs or alcohol to mitigate their symptoms (Khantzian & Albanese, 2008). For others, there may be more practical concerns. If they cannot afford health insurance or health care, they may turn to drugs or alcohol because these are accessible and more affordable for managing physical pain and psychological distress.

As noted previously, the use of drugs or alcohol is a disqualifier from receiving SSDI or SSI benefits if the use of drugs or alcohol is a material cause of signs or symptoms. However, if discontinuation of substances would not improve the claimant's impairments, the issue of DAA may not prevent an award of benefits. For example, assume an individual with a significant back injury was experiencing severe pain, self-treated with alcohol, and subsequently developed gastritis, pancreatitis, and cirrhosis of the liver. The individual stopped drinking but still had cirrhosis, pancreatitis, and gastritis. The claimant can still be awarded benefits, but the judge may amend the alleged onset date to the date of sobriety. This may reduce the back due benefits and delay eligibility for Medicare, but the claimant would receive monthly money benefits. It is also possible that although the judge finds the claimant qualifies for disability, if the date of sobriety falls after the date last insured,[2] the claimant will not be eligible for SSDI but may meet the eligibility requirements for SSI if the financial criteria are met.

There are some psychological impairments with symptoms or characteristics that commonly include drug or alcohol use or abuse, such as post-traumatic stress disorder, anxiety disorders, dissociative disorders, bipolar disorder, some personality disorders, and schizophrenia and schizotypal disorder. In fact, the use of drugs and alcohol can sometimes be diagnostic for such conditions. It is helpful if the clinician's treatment notes incorporate this information, but the claimant's representative also can include diagnostic material from the *Diagnostic and Statistical Manual of Mental Disorders* (*DSM-5*) in a prehearing brief or during cross-examination of a medical expert, or in opening or closing arguments at the hearing.

No matter how impressive or well-articulated the arguments for awarding benefits to a claimant with a history of drug or alcohol use or abuse may be, the ultimate decision rests with the ALJ, and the judge's decision may be influenced by personal, political, or cultural beliefs. Judges are human, and, like the rest of us, they have personal biases that unconsciously guide their decisions, so they sometimes disregard or reinterpret the regulations in support of their own personal beliefs (Vendel, 2005). This may result in a successful appeal of an unfavorable or partially favorable decision, but it imposes a considerable delay for desperate claimants. Likewise, favorable decisions not founded on the regulations or supported by the evidence may also be reviewed by the Appeals Council and reversed or remanded for a new hearing. The best option for claimants is for the treating clinicians to explain any DAA issues in the treatment records, with clear explanations as to the materiality of the DAA to the claimants' disabling symptoms.

There is another DAA problem that may arise: the use of medical marijuana. An increasing number of states have legalized medical marijuana, and others have decriminalized possession along with medical and recreational use. However, Social Security is regulated by the federal government, and, as of the writing of this book, the federal government does not recognize medical or recreational marijuana as a legitimate substance for use by claimants. Different jurisdictions and different judges may assess the use of marijuana more leniently than others and grant benefits regardless of marijuana use. Others, however, may deny a claim on the basis of the use of federally illegal substances or consider that its use does not constitute treatment even in cases where research suggests the efficacy of medical marijuana or some of its component features for the treatment of some cancers, immune disorders (e.g., multiple sclerosis, HIV/AIDS), reduction of pain and inflammation, reduction of side effects from chemotherapy, management of glaucoma, seizure activity, substance use disorders, and mental disorders.[3]

Noncompliance with Treatment

The notion of noncompliance with treatment suggests that compliance is always a choice, and, when claimants are uninterested or unmotivated to participate in effective treatment of their impairments, the Administration interprets the attitude as an indication that disability claims are exaggerated or unfounded. However, clinicians may indicate noncompliance in the treatment records to reflect the patient's failure to fill prescriptions, attend appointments, consult with specialists, agree to various treatment modalities or therapies, or comply with nutritionist's advice, among other issues, without explanation. Often, these examples of noncompliance are due to patients' financial constraints, transportation problems, symptom exacerbations, misunderstanding of the severity of their impairments, and other legitimate reasons. For example, patients may be offered a surgical remedy that they refuse due to the associated risks, unsure outcome, cost, recovery period, and so forth. Nevertheless, when noncompliance is recorded by clinicians or facilities, the Administration is likely to interpret such observations as representing willful noncooperation. Perhaps if clinicians could either use different language or provide an explanation when they report on noncompliance, it would clarify for the record that the patients' actions were not in defiance of medical advice. Such an approach to documentation is intended to add clarity and reduce the risk of prejudicial interpretation.

In some circumstances, noncompliance is a feature of the alleged disability. As an example, people diagnosed with schizophrenia are often resistant to treatment. They may refuse to take prescribed antipsychotics or to reside in structured and monitored housing. My coauthor represented a 40-year-old gentleman, George, who was diagnosed with schizophrenia as an 18-year-old college freshman. After his initial hospitalization, he refused further medication. His parents agreed not to recommit him to a hospital or restricted housing if he would agree to work in his father's small business, an assaying operation. His parents were concerned that he was vulnerable to victimization and could be lost to homelessness without their protection. George was given a redundant position under close supervision in his father's business. He made his own schedule and came and left at will. He was paid a salary and his father deducted his Social Security and Medicare taxes to ensure his son was protected with retirement and disability benefits. His father's long-time employees were very familiar with George's psychological problems and behavioral eccentricities and were protective of him. For 22 years, George worked in his father's business and maintained his own apartment with the help and support of his mother and sister, who visited his apartment several times a week to do his housekeeping, go shopping, put away groceries, prepare meals, help with laundry, and pay his bills. Sadly, George's father passed away suddenly. The business was sold to an associate who was familiar with George's special circumstances and agreed to retain him. However, George was unsettled by his father's death and changes to the business implemented by the new owner and, after a few weeks, he did not return to the office. During the intervening 22 years, George had received no treatment for schizophrenia. However, he was obsessed with his heart and was convinced he had cardiac disease. He regularly visited his internist and a cardiologist, who performed an array of diagnostic tests that revealed mild, intermittent arrhythmia in an otherwise healthy heart. When George was unable to find other work due to his behavioral eccentricities, his mother encouraged him to apply for disability insurance benefits. His actual impairment was psychiatric, as he had been diagnosed with schizophrenia, but his only treatment for schizophrenia was a brief involuntary hospitalization 22 years prior, and his most consistent treatment records reflected a history of nonsevere cardiac issues. Pam reached out to the cardiologist to query whether George's complaints about his heart could represent somatoform disorder or conversion disorder. The doctor agreed that it was a likely rationale to explain George's perceived symptoms for which there was no medical evidence. The cardiologist wrote a lengthy narrative describing George's nonexistent cardiac problems, his irrationality regarding the reality of a heart condition, and his eccentric behaviors (e.g., responding aloud to auditory hallucinations). The doctor had taken copious notes during George's visits and requested a psychiatrist to review them and offer an opinion. The psychiatrist agreed that George's cardiac symptoms appeared to be delusional and reflective of somatoform disorder. At the hearing, a medical expert (ME) testified that the conclusions of the nonexamining psychiatrist along with the treating cardiologist were consistent with the claimant's history. He agreed that George's past work was unskilled and sedentary and was performed in a sheltered work environment with special accommodations. He testified that George's diagnosis of somatoform disorder, based on his history, the observations of his treating cardiologist, and the review of the doctor's notes by the psychiatrist, met a listing (adult listing §12.07) and entitled the claimant to a fully favorable decision.

This case illustrates a common thread among applicants for disability benefits. They and their providers and advocates assume that the claimant's impairments obviously rise to the level of disability—even without evidence. But the procedure for obtaining federal disability benefits is a legal process whereby the burden of proof of disability falls to the claimant. The existence of even a listed disorder is not a guarantee of benefits without evidence of treatment.

Lack of Treating Clinician Support

The language of medicine is sometimes mismatched to the language of Social Security. In medical terminology, positive equals negative, and negative equals positive. There has been some confusion with the use of the term *rule out* for the purposes of differential diagnosis, and administrative law judges have been known to gauge the severity of the claimant's condition based on the number of medications prescribed or hospital admissions. Although most employees of the SSA and Disability Determination Services (DDS) understand the basic terminology of health-care professions, there are nevertheless common misunderstandings regarding the relevance of various treatment strategies and their effects. It is not unusual for a judge to make an unfavorable decision on a claim for benefits if, in the judge's opinion, the claimant is undermedicated or has not been referred for hospitalization or surgery. For example, a claimant who was diagnosed with severe spinal stenosis with impingement on the S1 nerve root was denied benefits on the basis of not having been referred for surgical intervention. Due to the claimant's prior adverse reaction to regional anesthesia, an epidural was not an option for surgery. The claimant's cardiologist determined that the claimant's underlying cardiac impairments were incompatible with general anesthesia, making surgery inadvisable. The judge wrongly concluded that the lack of surgery was an indication of nonseverity. Although the claimant eventually won the claim on appeal, another 18 months elapsed before a favorable decision was handed down, resulting in significant hardship before a just resolution was achieved. It would have been helpful to the claimant if the treating clinician had provided a brief narrative at the time of the hearing to explain the decision to forgo surgery, although such a report was furnished when the case was appealed.

Surgery and other interventions carry their own risks and cannot guarantee positive outcomes. Almost all medications can cause a variety of adverse side effects, some of which are quite severe. Patients have a right to be fully informed about the potential risks and benefits of treatment in order to make decisions that are in their own best interest. Patients should not be coerced into agreeing to treatment modalities by their doctors, insurers, or the SSA. Likewise, they should not be punished for their personal choices regarding their health care.

Left to their own devices, DDS personnel will make assumptions when weighing the evidence for disability. When records alone are submitted in support of a claim, the Administration or a judge may or may not be able to assess the severity of the impairment and the limitations imposed on the claimant's functioning. A judge who feels unable to render a decision can direct the claimant to be examined by a clinician: a *consultative examiner* (CE), who is presumably a specialist in the area of medicine associated with the claimant's impairments. We say "presumably" because we have seen cases where the assigned CE for a 55-year-old gentleman with severe cardiac issues was an obstetrician-gynecologist, and another man with myositis ossificans progressiva, known as "stone man disease," was referred to an internist who had no real knowledge about the disease and postulated that the claimant's condition might improve with physical therapy. For the record, increased activity is known to exacerbate the symptoms and accelerate this condition's disease process.

In many cases, clinicians, hospitals, and agencies ignore requests for treatment records made by Social Security and often charge exorbitant fees for records requested by claimants and their representatives that are beyond their capacity to pay. Even smaller fees for copies in the neighborhood of 15 to 25 dollars may be excessive when the claimant has no income and must obtain records from many different clinicians and facilities. Several states have legislated to protect the right of claimants for Social Security and other disability programs to obtain a complete record of treatment at no cost. For example, California has memorialized this protection in the state's Health and Safety Statutes §123110.[4] However, the statute has no real enforcement policy, and the penalty, if pursued, is only 100 dollars to noncooperating treatment sources. Furthermore, as of January 1, 2018, California's statute only applies to the claimant and to representatives not requesting a fee for representation. This places a burden on claimants who are unemployed, often uninsured, and struggling to survive. And representatives are generally unable to cover the expense of records. They may be willing to pay for records in special circumstances, but paying for records from multiple sources multiplied by several of their cases is more than most representatives in private practice can afford, and representatives employed by larger firms are often barred from undertaking such an expense. Representatives are only paid if their representation results in a favorable decision. Even if a representative has the greatest confidence in the claimant's case, there is no guarantee of a win. Hence many of the representatives we know of are salaried employees of companies dedicated to SSDI/SSI representation or rely on other jobs to support their work as claimant advocates and lack the financial resources to pay for client treatment records.

Pam's experience in more than 1,000 claimant representations provides context for the real cost of the lack of treating clinician support. She typically accepts clients who received denials at the initial and reconsideration application levels, which means that they have likely been unable to work for at least 12 to 18 months and often longer. Depending on the region where the claimants reside, requests for hearings may, on average, take between 11 and 22 months to be accepted and an additional number of days, at least 75 days, before the hearing dates are set. This means that claimants may have been out of work and without health insurance for three or more years. If they are their own sole support, such claimants may be destitute or even homeless and without health care other than what is afforded by emergency room visits. If a claimant is living with a spouse or others and was the primary breadwinner, the family unit may be suffering from loss of income and the added burden of caring for the sick or injured claimant's needs. Even if the claimant lives with family and is not the primary breadwinner, the loss of income and added costs of care can cause irreparable damage to all concerned.

One might think that homeless SSA claimants would be readily approved, but this is not the case (Kauff, Clary, Lupfer, & Fischer, 2016). These applications are confounded by the claimants' overwhelming obstacles, their lack of family support, and their lack of reliable means of communication, such as telephones, mailing addresses, or other contact information. According to Jacqueline F. Kauff and her colleagues (2016), an estimated 46% or more "of the homeless or those at risk of homelessness have one or more chronic general medical conditions, and as many as 67% have received a psychiatric diagnosis during their lifetimes" (p. 1098). Mark Amdur (2018) observed that some people may be denied Social Security benefits because they are too disabled to complete the process. This is especially true of homeless people.

Are there circumstances where clinicians should advocate for their patients? We know there are some individuals who are so overwhelmed by their impairments and other adverse circumstances that they cannot negotiate the complex machinery of the Social Security system on their own. One federal agency, the Substance Abuse and Mental Health Services Administration (SAMHSA) has a specific program, SOAR (SSI/SSDI Outreach, Access, and Recovery; see SAMHSA, 2019), that advocates for homeless people who are eligible for SSA benefits. SOAR provides training and support to local communities and agencies that implement SOAR initiatives. Research has shown that SOAR-assisted Social Security claims were approved at higher rates than a comparison group that did not use the SOAR approach among homeless individuals (Kauff et al., 2016). A study by Lowder, Desmarais, Neupert, and Truelove (2017) also showed that homeless, SOAR-supported disability claimants were more successful than their comparison group of non-SOAR claimants, but the authors also found varied outcomes among subgroups of homeless SSA applicants. Lowder et al. (2017) found that older applicants and those living in institutions had higher rates of disability approval; but among women and adults who received public assistance, the rates of approval were lower.

Being sick in America is expensive. Even those with health insurance must pay premiums, deductibles, and copayments; medication and medical supply costs; the cost of durable appliances such as crutches, walkers, wheelchairs, and oxygen; the cost of transportation to appointments; and the cost of special dietary needs. It is also extremely stressful to worry not only about one's health but also about matters of survival of self and loved ones. Without the cooperation of treating sources, applicants for SSDI or SSI benefits have little or no chance of obtaining the support needed for recovery or survival.

As claimants' financial resources dwindle, they frequently become more dependent on emergency department care, which is often administered by busy interns and residents and can result in abrupt changes to previously effective treatment regimens. The lack of continuity of care and personal relationships with health-care providers increases the chance of errors in treatment and documentation and reduces the likelihood of provider compliance with requests for records and professional opinions. The overall effect is to increase the potential for worsening of the claimant's condition while decreasing the potential for adequate longitudinal documentation for disability benefits. The importance of compliance with requests for medical records and treating doctors' opinions cannot be overstated.

Malingering

When a patient seeks evaluation for treatment, most clinicians assume that person is in genuine distress. Malingering, representing oneself with medical, physical, or psychological symptoms to achieve some secondary gain, is not representative of most clinicians' experience. But it is always a question for those evaluating disability claimants, and clinicians are expected to respond to queries by the agency and the ALJs.

Malingering is often difficult to prove or disprove (Institute of Medicine, 2015; Merckelbach, Dandachi-FitzGerald, van Helvoort, Jelicic, & Otgaar, 2019). People's perceptions of pain, malaise, and other symptoms are highly subjective and as unique as the individuals experiencing them. Individuals seeking drugs may be legitimately in pain. Persons presenting with vague, migrating, or transitory symptoms may be in real distress.

Many medical conditions are rare enough that significant numbers of clinicians have no experience with them. Other conditions can only be diagnosed by process of elimination. Individuals without access to consistent health care are more likely to be identified as malingerers because they lack a history and relationship with a health-care provider who is familiar with their ability to articulate how they feel and how they are affected. They may be falsely identified as drug seekers and their complaints discounted. Because medical records are accessible among clinicians' offices, hospitals, insurers, and other agencies, inaccurate allegations of malingering or drug seeking may create bias and may sabotage the claimant's future efforts to obtain accurate assessment and effective treatment, a circumstance that I witnessed with regard to how one of my own patients was treated several years ago.

My patient was diagnosed with dissociative identity disorder and was sometimes psychiatrically hospitalized due to her intense and overwhelming dissociative episodes. While being treated as an outpatient, this 38-year-old woman began complaining of heart palpitations and near syncope. We had a sphygmomanometer in the office and checked the patient's blood pressure, which appeared to be dangerously high. One of my staff walked the patient to the hospital emergency room across the parking lot from our office building and remained with her while she was seen in the emergency department and asked to describe her symptoms. Her blood pressure was still high, but the ER staff discounted her recitation of symptoms upon checking her treatment records because they believed her to be having a dissociative experience that would self-correct. My staff member asked for a cardiologist to examine the patient but was informed no one was available and that she should make an appointment with her own doctor. The client died in her sleep that night, secondary to advanced heart disease according to the autopsy report. The patient's credibility was undermined by her psychiatric diagnosis in the eyes of the emergency room physician, who discharged her without administering a more thorough examination.

Credibility

The credibility of a claimant's allegations are questioned repeatedly at every level of the application process. Are the claimant's complaints, symptoms, and limitations consistent with the diagnosis? Are the symptoms and limitations reflected in the clinical treatment notes or justified by the level of care? Is the claimant exaggerating or minimizing? My coauthor offers an example of how credibility can affect a judge's decision-making, in the case of a young adult who had lived independently and worked as a heavy equipment operator. "John" suffered a severe, traumatic brain injury in a motorcycle mishap. He was in a coma for four weeks and hospitalized for two additional months before he returned home to his parents. He required a feeding tube and physical and occupational therapy to relearn how to walk, write, swallow, manipulate eating utensils, and engage in self-care. At the age of 30, John remains in his parents' home, unable to live independently since the accident. He addresses his parents as "Mommy" and "Daddy." He has regressed to his adolescent self. He has very poor short-term memory and ability to concentrate. He cannot perform simple household chores unsupervised and is prohibited from using the stove after several incidents of burning food and inadvertently causing kitchen fires. However, when the judge insisted on hearing the claimant's testimony outside the presence of his mother, the claimant's legal guardian, John could not distinguish between his past and current life. He spoke of drinking alcohol, operating heavy equipment (his former occupation), and carousing with his buddies. When the judge took the mother's testimony, she refuted everything her son testified to, explaining that John could not drink alcohol because his injury resulted in seizures and he was now taking neuroleptic medication daily. He had no money or access to alcohol. He had no friends and was always with one or both of his parents. He did not drive and could not operate heavy equipment due to his seizure history and medication, and his driver's license was revoked. Furthermore, John was no longer leaving home alone because he got lost in the same neighborhood where he lived from childhood. However, at the hearing, the ALJ asked John questions about what he liked to do for fun, and John described his passion for fishing and how he fished whenever possible. The judge's inquiries were couched in friendly terms as he encouraged John to elaborate on when, where, and how he fished. John's medical records did describe the extent of his injuries and physical rehabilitation as well as his prescribed medications, all of which were supportive of his mother's testimony. However, John's evaluation by a consultative examiner reflected John's testimony in that he made the same assertions to the psychologist as he had to the judge. The judge ruled unfavorably in John's case, citing his testimony as not credible and equating John's ability to fish and derive pleasure from it as an admission that his condition was not severe and his limitations not so profound as to prevent full-time competitive work. John's decision has been appealed and, as of this writing, is awaiting a decision by the Appeals Council.

In yet another example of how credibility can be challenged, my coauthor represented a client whose reported diagnosis was dysautonomia, a collection of several medical conditions affecting the autonomic nervous system. Of those conditions, the client experienced postural orthostatic tachycardia syndrome (POTS) and neurocardiogenic syncope. She was also diagnosed with Addison's disease, rheumatoid arthritis, and Sjögren's syndrome. The client's symptoms were extreme and included severe intractable headaches, syncopal and near syncopal episodes, atypical seizure-like activity described by the claimant as electric shocks, temperature dysregulation, vertigo, dizziness, fatigue, malaise, intermittent fevers, muscle and joint pain, chest pain, chronic abdominal pain, nausea, diarrhea, vomiting, memory and concentration deficits (brain fog), anxiety, and depression. The claimant professed sensitivity and adverse reactions to medications from available traditional health-care providers and sought treatment from naturopathic and unconventional treating sources. The ALJ was clearly skeptical of the claimant's condition and could not make a decision based on one hearing. Thus a supplementary hearing was scheduled approximately six months after the first. The judge engaged an ME to opine on the claimant's impaired status based on her treatment records. The ME offered his opinion that the claimant's impairments would be responsive to traditional medical interventions and that the reported severity of her symptoms was exaggerated. He found that the claimant's impairments were not severe and that she did not meet or equal any of the Listings of Impairments. Given the ME's testimony, the judge's questions to the vocational expert did not reflect the significant limitations noted in her records and expressed in her testimony, and the vocational expert opined that the claimant could perform her past work and other work available in the national economy. Unsurprisingly, the judge issued an unfavorable decision based on the assumption that the claimant obtained significant positive reinforcement for her symptoms through her family's attention, sympathy, and advocacy. The judge also found the claimant's testimony and the treatment records and opinions offered by her nontraditional treating sources to be less than credible because they were inconsistent with traditional medical views and her naturopath was not an acceptable medical source.

In one last example, credibility was also a determinant in tipping the scales toward an unfavorable decision. My coauthor recounted a case where her client, a native Spanish-speaker, requested an interpreter because she felt insecure with her English language skills. During the hearing, it was evident that the claimant understood a great deal despite her lack of fluency. Her concern had primarily been that she would not understand the nuances of legal language and wanted the support of someone who could accurately translate English to the claimant's native language, as is any claimant's right. However, the judge viewed this maneuver as a manipulation to add the limitation of non-English fluency and found the claimant to be not credible and thus denied her claim.

Credibility is generally a subjective interpretation that may be more reflective of a judge's perceptions and biases than is any inaccuracy or deception on the claimant's part. Claimants are often punished for the poverty of their vocabularies or poor communication skills. They are frequently penalized for knowing too much about the clinical aspects of their disease or injury, as if the judge suspects them of gaming the system. Claimants who describe every pain as excruciating may not be exaggerating—they may truly experience their pain as reported. There are also claimants who minimize their problems. This is particularly true of male claimants who may be embarrassed by some of their symptoms and their effects. The stigma of disability often affects how claimants perceive and present themselves. These claimants will be adversely judged if their testimony is inconsistent with medical records or provider opinions, even if the inconsistencies are minor figures of speech.

Claimants are typically prepared for their testimony by their advocates: an attorney or nonattorney representative. They are advised to tell the truth and to clearly articulate their answers—to use their words instead of nodding or shaking or pointing. They are advised to keep their answers short, not to answer questions not asked, and not to go off on tangents. Claimants should always take prescribed medication as scheduled on the day of their hearing. Some claimants have resisted this, but it's important that the judge see claimants as they are: how medication affects them; if they are groggy or dizzy; and whether they have problems articulating, following the discussion, or remembering relevant dates and events; or require a recess to go to the restroom. Claimants are advised not to exaggerate, elaborate, or embellish their symptoms or limitations. My coauthor recalled clients who reported under oath that they could not lift or carry more than five pounds, but they carried briefcases, backpacks, medical records, and even handbags that weighed more. Or they told the judge they could not sit for more than 15 minutes at a time after sitting in the hearing office for more than an hour. Or they reported that they could not walk for more than a few feet unassisted after having to walk many times that distance just to walk from the parking lot to the hearing office. Claimants are not being deceitful or attempting to game the system. They are usually trying to be truthful and transparent. But for many such people, symptoms and limitations are fluid. They have good days and bad days. Circumstances vary, and it is not always possible to respond to a simple question simply.

At the hearing level, claimants are encouraged to be consistent and realistic if they want the judge to take their testimony seriously. If a claimant makes a statement about not being able to walk unassisted for more than a few steps, yet clearly had to walk a greater distance to the hearing office and the judge does not ask for clarification, the representative will elicit further information from the claimant. For example, the representative will ask how long it took to walk from the parking lot to the hearing office. How often did the claimant have to stop to rest and for how long? Likewise with regard to the matter of weight that can be lifted or carried or for how long the claimant can sit. The representative should be familiar with how the claimant responds to pain and medication, how the claimant's impairments limit functioning and how the claimant compensates for those limitations, so that any damaging testimony can be remediated through additional clarification.

Notes

1. This is the term used by SSA. The *DSM-5* uses the expression *substance use disorders* instead.

2. See chapter 7 for a complete explanation of the *date last insured*.

3. https://www.drugabuse.gov/publications/drugfacts/marijuana-medicine.

4. *(Amended by Stats. 2017, Ch. 513, Sec. 1. (SB 241) Effective January 1, 2018.)* (d) (1) Notwithstanding any provision of this section, and except as provided in Sections 123115 and 123120, a patient, former patient, or the personal representative of a patient or former patient, is entitled to a copy, at no charge, of the relevant portion of the patient's records, upon presenting to the provider a written request, and proof that the records or supporting forms are needed to support a claim or appeal regarding eligibility for a public benefit program. These programs shall be the Medi-Cal program, the In-Home Supportive Services Program, the California Work Opportunity and Responsibility to Kids (CalWORKs) program, social security disability insurance benefits [*sic*], Supplemental Security Income/State Supplementary Program for the Aged, Blind and Disabled (SSI/SSP) benefits, federal veterans service-connected compensation and nonservice connected pension disability benefits, and CalFresh.

(2) Although a patient shall not be limited to a single request, the patient or patient's personal representative shall be entitled to no more than one copy of any relevant portion of his or her record free of charge.

(3) This subdivision shall not apply to any patient who is represented by a private attorney who is paying for the costs related to the patient's claim or appeal, pending the outcome of that claim or appeal. For purposes of this subdivision, "private attorney" means any attorney not employed by a nonprofit legal services entity.

CHAPTER FIVE

The Role of Clinicians in Disability Determination

> Our prime purpose in life is to help others. And if you can't help them, at least don't hurt them.
>
> —Dalai Lama

Clinicians train for many years to competently diagnose and treat the various diseases and injuries that people sustain. Their adversaries are illness, pain, and the many conditions that interfere with a long and full life. Their weapons are medications and other therapies, technology, surgical interventions, calm reassurance, and sincere empathy. Restoration and recovery are their goals; disability and death are their natural enemies. This is perhaps the irony of their role in the disability determination process: when health-care professionals accept that their patients are disabled, they are admitting that to some degree their treatments have failed.

Duty of Clinicians to Patients

Clinicians owe their patients their professional expertise, their best health-care advice, their honest opinions, and compassion. They owe it to their patients to treat them with respect and not to patronize them. Clinicians should be transparent and explain the limitations of medicine and science. Not all medical or psychological impairments can be successfully treated, and patients should not be subjected to painful or expensive procedures where there is little or no expectation of improved quality of life. When requested, clinicians also have a duty to their patients to provide accurate treatment records and professional opinions. Health-care providers should be willing to share their observations and opinions regarding their patients' diagnoses and symptoms that may limit, or not limit, their ability to perform functional and nonfunctional tasks common to full-time competitive work. If clinicians are unable or unwilling to support patients' applications for benefits by providing records in a timely way and offering their professional opinions as to the effect of patients' symptoms on their ability to perform full-time work, they should communicate this directly to patients in the event that disability is a possible outcome of their illness or injury. My coauthor has sometimes had clinicians respond to requests for an opinion regarding their patients' limitations as being "beyond their scope." It is our hope that this book helps arm clinicians with a better understanding of disability determinations so that they are better prepared to respond to these requests when called upon.

Duty to Respond to Requests for Treatment Records

In the spirit of "first do no harm," clinicians should consider the impact of noncompliance with requests for treatment records. Claimants for Social Security disability benefits are frequently in desperate circumstances. They are unemployed, sick or injured, and often uninsured. They have frequently exhausted all financial resources, including savings, retirement funds, and loans from family and friends. The acquisition of benefits to which they are entitled is their only hope for survival. Even claimants who live with family members or friends or partners are often in a tenuous state economically. Deprived of the financial resources to sustain the household, a claimant's psychological and emotional equilibrium is rocked. The claimant may forgo necessary treatment, including prescribed medication and procedures, because of an unwillingness to accrue further indebtedness or put additional financial strain on loved ones. Individuals, particularly women, may feel compelled to remain in an abusive relationship because they are dependent on the abusive partner for housing, food, health care, and transportation. The resulting instability affects the claimant's capacity for coping with impairments, so making appropriate judgments, complying with treatment, and making progress toward recovery or at least greater functionality becomes more difficult. Claimants' treatment records are their only objective evidence of disability, and, without the full cooperation of their treatment providers, claimants are even more vulnerable in the disability determination process. Whether requested by the SSA, the claimant, or the claimant's representative, the clinician has a duty to comply with requests for records.

Disabled People as an Underserved Community

We recommend that health-care professionals be mindful that some of their patients may have medically determinable impairments that meet Social Security's definition of disability and that any of their patients may become too disabled to continue to perform full-time jobs. Disability as defined by the SSA is not rare, although it is difficult to prove without adequate documentation. According to Erickson Cornish et al., "persons with disabilities are a large and growing minority group in the United States, second only to combined ethnic groups at 34%" (2008, p. 489). Clinicians may see patients with severe physical and mental disorders, so they should be equipped with an understanding of the available programs that may benefit these patients. We recommend that individual clinicians in all disciplines become familiar with the ADA and the relevant SSA regulations so that they will be better able to evaluate their patients and appropriately and accurately document their findings in their professional records, as well as make suitable referrals and recommendations for supportive services and local, state, and federal disability programs. To this end, we have included the Listings of Impairments for Adults and Children in this volume (see Appendixes A and B).

Clinicians' Ethical Considerations and Disability Determination

The various health-care professions include physicians and surgeons, physician's assistants, nurses, dentists, optometrists, chiropractors, podiatrists, physical therapists, occupational therapists, pharmacists, psychologists, social workers, marriage and family therapists, and counselors, among others. Some, but not all, are licensed to practice independently. Licensed clinicians are required to follow the ethics codes of their respective professional licensing boards. These rules of practice are not all identical, but they typically include the injunction to do no harm, to work within a circumscribed scope of practice, to maintain confidentiality, to obtain informed consent, to keep accurate records, and to maintain one's professional competence through continuing education. In addition to these enforceable rules, there are often a list of aspirational ethical principles. For example, the American Psychological Association (2002) lists the following "General Principles":

Principle A: Beneficence and Nonmaleficence

Principle B: Fidelity and Responsibility

Principle C: Integrity
Principle D: Justice
Principle E: Respect for People's Rights and Dignity (p. 1060)

The last principle. "Respect for People's Rights and Dignity," specifically includes disability as a factor that must be considered in addressing human rights and dignity. The APA Ethics Code further expressly prohibits unfair discrimination or harassment on the basis of disability. Other health-care professions have similar expectations and requirements.

Thus clinicians should be mindful of their specific professions' ethical rules and principles to include their applicability to patients with disabilities. Ethical practice demands that clinicians do no harm, be trustworthy, honest, and treat people justly with respect for their humanity. Health-care providers should be competent to work with people who have disabilities, because all providers are likely to have at least some professional interactions with them. One effort to establish core competencies for health-care providers who work with people with disabilities was recently developed by The Alliance for Disability in Health Care Education and Ohio Disability and Health Program and was summarized by Catherine Graham (2019). This list of competencies includes

- contextual and conceptual frameworks on disability,
- professionalism and patient-centered care,
- legal obligations and responsibilities for caring for patients with disabilities,
- teams and systems-based practice,
- clinical assessment, and
- clinical care over the lifespan and during transitions.

"Legal obligations and responsibilities for caring for patients with disabilities," refers to practices that are consistent with the ADA and the Social Security Act (Alliance for Disability in Health Care Education, 2018). We concur: clinicians should be aware of the applicable ADA and SSA laws and ethical requirements, and their professional work should appropriately meet those requirements.

Another important consideration is to do thorough and comprehensive clinical evaluations. For those patients who have multiple identified problems, each problem should be documented along with its respective diagnoses. Often claimants have a primary diagnosis with other co-occurring symptoms and diagnoses. Research has found that when careful assessments are conducted, it is common for SSA applicants to have multiple diagnoses and that incomplete evaluations are a common source of denials (Amdur, 2018). Claimants with financial resources may be willing to pay for comprehensive clinical evaluations performed by either their treating clinician(s) or an independent medical examiner (IME). Unless there is a medical necessity to justify an extensive examination and the resultant comprehensive report, medical insurance may not pay for such a service, which can cost hundreds to thousands of dollars. Without the ability to obtain a thorough medical or psychological evaluation, the SSA or ALJ will rely on the only purported comprehensive evaluation in the record—a report by a consultative examiner (CE). Unfortunately, SSA does not typically pay CEs for their time but rather pays for each evaluation. Consultative examiners are typically paid at a rate of under $150 for each evaluation, depending on the region of the country where they practice. Evaluations by psychologists that include psychological testing may be paid at a slightly higher rate. No matter what CEs are paid, it is significantly less than what is typically paid for the same service in private practice by patients or insurers. Consultative examiners are frequently clinicians who are supplementing their incomes at the beginning or end of their careers. Pam's clients have reported, almost without exception, that they appeared for their examination at offices that were usually in "low rent" districts. The waiting room was crowded and examinations brief and perfunctory. As a claimant's representative, Pam always advises her clients to be accompanied to a CE appointment and for their companion to document the time spent with the examiner. In almost every case, claimants are with the examiner for under 15 minutes for a medical evaluation and 30 minutes for a psychiatric evaluation, as confirmed by companions who accompanied them to appointments. Claimants are referred to psychologists when psychological testing is required. Pam has reviewed CE reports that reflected administration of psychological tests such as the Wechsler Adult Intelligence Scale (WAIS), which typically takes 45 to 75 minutes to administer but the claimant reported having been at the appointment for under an hour. Upon querying the claimants, she has found that only selected elements of the WAIS were administered, although such modification was not delineated in the CE reports. "The consultant's incentive is to maximize profit by conducting as quick an interview as acceptable" (Amdur, 2018, p. 30). One of our concerns is that the SSA's policies favor people who are economically privileged over those who are impoverished. When patients have abundant economic resources, they can afford extensive medical evaluations that are more comprehensive and better documented. Those living in poverty may not have their own personal physicians and their medical care often consists of sporadic emergency room visits when they are in crisis.

Sadly, clinicians are sometimes unresponsive to requests for records by the SSA, patients, or claimants' representatives. Additionally, many hospitals and medical practices engage outside medical record storage facilities such as BACTES and ShareCare, which charge a fee for copying and sending records. These companies have no relationship with the patient, and provision of records is contingent on payment. Unfortunately, claimants who are unemployed and have extremely limited financial resources may lack the ability to pay for these necessary records, and their problems are multiplied by being confronted with expenses for every hospital, physician, or other medical professional consulted since their alleged onset date. Several states have enacted statutes to make medical records available to claimants for disability benefits at no charge, however these file storage companies do not honor these statutes because penalties for noncompliance are directed toward clinicians and facilities and not to third-party file storage agencies. The companies may be further emboldened because they may be headquartered in states where there are no statutes in support of free and complete records for disability claimants.

Clinicians sometimes monetize their records and may place unreasonable value on the cost of copying and transmitting treatment records. The rationale for this may be part of their overall profitability plan. We know of cases in the past where the fees for copying records from multiple medical offices has totaled in the thousands of dollars for a single claimant. On the other hand, some offices simply may be unwilling to devote time and energy to responding to such requests. Records requested by Social Security are paid at a rate of around 15 dollars per request regardless of the number of pages in the records. Some records requests are accompanied by a request for completion of a brief questionnaire documenting the clinician's opinion regarding the limitations the claimants may experience that affect their ability to perform certain work-related activities. Years ago, after I established a private clinical psychology practice in Dallas, I began to receive requests for records from the SSA. Pam, who managed my office at the time, consulted an older, established practice administrator to ask for more advice about how to respond to Social Security requests. She was told, "Oh, you can throw those away." This is not an unusual reaction to receipt of SSA requests, Pam learned. Based on her experience as a claimant's representative, she has found that the number of clinicians willing to submit records only slightly exceeds those who are willing to complete an impairment questionnaire, which is, in effect, their opinion regarding their patients' functionality. However, in some instances, we believe it to be a strategy to avoid having to submit their records for scrutiny by Social Security. Clinicians who accept Medicare and Medicaid (or their states' version of Medicaid) may be concerned that communications with Social Security may impact their reimbursements from Medicare and Medicaid. We know of no direct evidence that this is a legitimate concern, but perhaps others may be more knowledgeable regarding any such connection. However, we think it is unlikely that the SSA maintains a master list of clinicians who support their patients' claims of disability.

It is the responsibility of the ALJ to fully develop the claimant's *exhibit file* prior to and sometimes following the hearing. If advised of outstanding evidence by the claimant or claimant's representative from sources unresponsive to requests for same, the judge can request those records, and if the sources are still unresponsive, the judge may subpoena them. Unfortunately, while the ALJ has subpoena power, there is no associated enforcement authority as ALJs have no sanction power. On the other hand, most recipients of subpoenas recognize their duty to respond appropriately. The request for treatment records does not represent a challenge or threat to the clinician. The clinician's treatment is not the subject of investigation. It is the fact that symptoms were evaluated, diagnoses were made, and treatment rendered that gives the records value, and that value is only to the claimant.

Documentation of Services

Treatment records are maintained to document patients' medical history, current condition and treatment including diagnoses, diagnostic testing, laboratory results, prescribed medications, and other treatments for the purpose of continuity of care as well as to document billable services. Records typically include vital signs, past medical history, new complaints, prescribed treatment, adverse effects of treatment, allergies, hospitalizations, and referrals for imaging, testing and specialists.

Psychotherapy notes generally provide insight into the patient's orientation to person, place and time, past history, any psychological testing results, current medications, suicidality, diagnoses with respective signs and symptoms, current functioning, recommendations, and referrals. Out of respect for patient confidentiality and sensitivity regarding psychological, emotional, and behavioral disorders, treatment records may not include information that details severity or documents functionality. Treatment records seldom include criteria by which Social Security can establish physical or mental limitations secondary to a medical or mental condition, although they may refer to the patients' experience of pain including severity, frequency, and location.

Health Insurance Portability and Accountability Act (HIPAA)

The Health Insurance Portability and Accountability Act of 1996 (HIPAA) was primarily designed for those insured under group policies through employers to protect their coverage if their employment is terminated or they change employers. In addition, it prevents discrimination against group policy members with certain medical or preexisting conditions and prevents the establishment of lifetime limits for coverage. HIPAA standards have subsequently been applied to all health insurers. Under HIPAA, patients and their agents have access to their treatment records which must be provided within 30 days of requests to inspect, review or receive copies of the records. HIPAA also provides for medical record security and imposes specific requirements for maintaining and disseminating medical information. Thus, health-care providers and facilities must be HIPAA compliant in record storage and release.

CHAPTER SIX

Psychological Disabilities

> Although stigmatizing attitudes are not limited to mental illness, the public seems to disapprove persons with psychiatric disabilities significantly more than persons with related conditions such as physical illness. Severe mental illness has been likened to drug addiction, prostitution, and criminality. Unlike physical disabilities, persons with mental illness are perceived by the public to be in control of their disabilities and responsible for causing them. Furthermore, research respondents are less likely to pity persons with mental illness, instead reacting to psychiatric disability with anger and believing that help is not deserved.
>
> —Patrick W. Corrigan and Amy C. Watson (2002, p. 16)

Thus far we focused primarily on physical impairments, but psychological disabilities are another broad group of SSA's *medically determinable impairments*. According to Goldman, Frey, and Riley, "Individuals with mental disorders and intellectual limitations represent the largest single category of individuals on the disability rolls" (2018, p. 458). In chapter 2 we described the Listings of Impairments for adults and children. Included among the listings are 12.00 Mental Disorders for Adults (see Appendix A, §12.00) and 112.00 Mental Disorders for Children (see Appendix B, §112.00). In chapter 2 we also introduced the SSA's four categories of mental residual functional capacity—understanding and memory, sustained concentration and persistence, social interaction, and adaptation—which are considered necessary for work. In this chapter we discuss psychological disabilities in greater detail.

In 2016 the SSA revised their Listings of Mental Impairments partly to better correspond with the most recent edition of the American Psychiatric

Association's *Diagnostic and Statistical Manual of Mental Disorders* (*DSM-5*; APA, 2013). These changes became effective January 17, 2017. SSA's listings of adult mental disorders now consist of 11 categories:

12.02 Neurocognitive disorders (see Appendix A, §12.02);
12.03 Schizophrenia spectrum and other psychotic disorders (see Appendix A, §12.03);
12.04 Depressive, bipolar, and related disorders (see Appendix A, §12.04);
12.05 Intellectual disorder (see Appendix A, §12.05);
12.06 Anxiety and obsessive-compulsive disorders (see Appendix A, §12.06);
12.07 Somatic symptom and related disorders (see Appendix A, §12.07);
12.08 Personality and impulse-control disorders (see Appendix A, §12.08);
12.10 Autism spectrum disorder (see Appendix A, §12.10);
12.11 Neurodevelopmental disorders (see Appendix A, §12.11);
12.13 Eating disorders (see Appendix A, §12.13); and
12.15 Trauma- and stressor-related disorders (see Appendix A, §12.15).[1]

The SSA's listings for mental disorders for children are organized in 12 categories:

112.02 Neurocognitive disorders (see Appendix A, §112.02);
112.03 Schizophrenia spectrum and other psychotic disorders (see Appendix A, §112.03);
112.04 Depressive, bipolar, and related disorders (see Appendix A, §112.04);
112.05 Intellectual disorder (see Appendix A, §112.05);
112.06 Anxiety and obsessive-compulsive disorders (see Appendix A, §112.06);
112.07 Somatic symptom and related disorders (see Appendix A, §112.07);
112.08 Personality and impulse-control disorders (see Appendix A, §112.08);
112.10 Autism spectrum disorder (see Appendix A, §112.10);
112.11 Neurodevelopmental disorders (see Appendix A, §112.11);
112.13 Eating disorders (see Appendix A, §112.13);
112.14 Developmental disorders in infants and toddlers (see Appendix A, §112.14); and
112.15 Trauma- and stressor-related disorders (see Appendix A, §112.15).

All of these listings, with the exception of 112.14, apply to children from the age of 3 to 18. Listing 112.14 is for children from birth to age 3.[2]

Although the SSA's revised child and adult Listings of Mental Impairments are closer in similarity to the *DSM*-5 categories than previously, they are still not identical. The *DSM*-5 includes 20 major diagnostic groupings for both adults and children that consist of neurodevelopmental disorders; schizophrenia spectrum and other psychotic disorders; bipolar and related disorders; depressive disorders, anxiety disorders; obsessive-compulsive and related disorders; trauma- and stressor-related disorders; dissociative disorders; somatic symptom and related disorders; feeding and eating disorders; elimination disorders; sleep-wake disorders; sexual dysfunctions; gender dysphoria; disruptive, impulse-control, and conduct disorders; substance-related and addictive disorders; neurocognitive disorders; personality disorders; paraphilic disorders; other mental disorders and additional codes (APA, 2013). The *DSM*-5 also lists an additional category, *medication-induced movement disorders and other adverse effects of medication*, that is not considered a mental disorder but is nonetheless important to assess and track (APA, 2013). In the assessment of disability, the effects of medication can be debilitating and must also be considered.

Disability is one of the general defining characteristics of *DSM* diagnoses, whereby a "criterion requiring distress or disability has been used to establish disorder thresholds" (APA, 2013, p. 21). In reviewing the *DSM*'s definitions for clinical diagnoses, it is clear that "significant distress or disability in social, occupational, or other important activities" (APA, 2013, p. 20) is an essential criterion in making *DSM* diagnoses.

In this chapter we discuss the SSA's Listings of Mental Impairments for adults and children. The more general Listings of Impairments for adults can be found in Appendix A, and for children in Appendix B of this book. In order to minimize redundancy in our discussion of these listings, we have combined the adult and child listings as follows: neurocognitive disorders; schizophrenia spectrum and other psychotic disorders; depressive, bipolar, and related disorders; intellectual disorder; anxiety and obsessive-compulsive disorders; somatic symptom and related disorders; personality and impulse-control disorders; autism spectrum disorder; neurodevelopmental disorders; eating disorders; developmental disorders in infants and toddlers (it is only a child listing by definition); and trauma- and stressor-related disorders.

Neurocognitive Disorders

This is the first category of the Mental Impairments listings (§12.02 for adults and §112.02 for children) and corresponds to the *DSM*-5 category of the same name. This SSA listing was labeled organic mental disorders prior to January 17, 2017, and the name change reflected alterations in the evolving *DSM* terminology. As we have stated throughout this book it is challenging to meet a listing because of the listings' exacting criteria. The neurocognitive disorders listing includes major neurocognitive disorder; dementia of the Alzheimer type; vascular dementia; dementia due to a medical condition such as a metabolic disease (e.g., late-onset Tay-Sachs disease); human immunodeficiency virus infection; vascular malformation; progressive brain tumor; neurological disease (e.g., multiple sclerosis, Parkinsonian syndrome, Huntington disease) or traumatic brain injury; or substance-induced cognitive disorder associated with drugs of abuse, medications, or toxins.[3] (Also see Appendixes A, §12.02, and B, §112.02.)

As one can see, the SSA listing of neurocognitive disorders is a varied category of impaired brain functioning ranging from Alzheimer's disease to neurotoxic poisoning. Thus the claimant might be listed under the neurologic disorders (§11.00) unless the neurological disorder *only* results in mental impairment or if there is a co-occurring mental condition that is not caused by the neurological disorder (see Appendix A, §11.00G).

In the *DSM*-5 the diagnosis major neurocognitive disorder is characterized by cognitive impairments that "interfere with independence in everyday activities (i.e., at a minimum, requiring assistance with complex instrumental activities such as paying bills or managing medications" (APA, 2013, p. 602). In order to be considered a listing, the diagnosis of neurocognitive disorders must also meet the following criteria A and B, or A and C:

A. Medical documentation of a significant cognitive decline from previous functioning in one or more of the cognitive areas:

   1. complex attention,
   2. executive function,
   3. learning and memory,
   4. language,
   5. perceptual-motor, or
   6. social cognition;

AND

B. Extreme limitation of one, or marked limitation of two, of the following areas of mental abilities:

   1. understand, remember, or apply information;
   2. interact with others;

3. concentrate, persist, or maintain pace;
4. adapt or manage oneself;

OR

C. The disorder in this listing category is "serious and persistent," with a medically documented history of the disorder over a period of at least two years and evidence of both

 1. medical treatment, mental health therapy, psychosocial support(s), or a highly structured setting(s) that is ongoing and that diminishes the symptoms and signs of the mental disorder; and
 2. marginal adjustment, with minimal capacity to adapt to environmental changes or to new demands in one's life.[4]

Schizophrenia Spectrum and Other Psychotic Disorders

As the next category of SSA Mental Impairments (see Appendix A §12.03 for adults and Appendix B §112.03 for children), this listing is a diagnostic category with the same name in the *DSM-5* and is associated with "delusions, hallucinations, disorganized speech, or grossly disorganized or catatonic behavior, causing a clinically significant decline in functioning."[5] In addition to impaired thought processes and diminished emotional expression, schizophrenia is associated with limited adaptive social functioning. Many of the commonly prescribed medications also have side effects that may further diminish the patient's physical health (e.g., significant weight gain) and sedative affects that can reduce the alertness needed for many jobs. To meet the criteria for schizophrenia spectrum and other psychotic disorders as an SSA listing, it is also necessary to meet criteria A and B, or A and C, as follows:

A. medical documentation of one or more of these three:

 1. delusions or hallucinations,
 2. disorganized thinking (speech), or
 3. grossly disorganized behavior or catatonia;

AND

B. extreme limitation of one, or marked limitation of two, of the following areas of mental functioning:

 1. understand, remember, or apply information;
 2. interact with others;

3. concentrate, persist, or maintain pace;
4. adapt or manage oneself;

OR

C. The mental disorder in this listing category is "serious and persistent"; that is, with a medically documented history of the disorder over a period of at least two years, and there is evidence of both

   1. medical treatment, mental health therapy, psychosocial support(s), or a highly structured setting(s) that is ongoing and that diminishes the symptoms and signs of the mental disorder; and
   2. minimal capacity to adapt to environmental changes or to demands of daily life.

Depressive, Bipolar, and Related Disorders

This listing (§12.04 for adults and §112.04 for children) is divided into two *DSM-5* categories: depressive disorders, and bipolar and related disorders. It includes "an irritable, depressed, elevated, or expansive mood, or . . . a loss of interest or pleasure in all or almost all activities, causing a clinically significant decline in functioning."[6] To meet this listing there must be medical documentation of meeting criteria A and B, or A and C.

Criterion A consists of 1 or 2:

1. Depressive disorder, characterized by five or more of the following:
   a. depressed mood,
   b. diminished interest in almost all activities,
   c. appetite disturbance with change in weight,
   d. sleep disturbance,
   e. observable psychomotor agitation or retardation,
   f. decreased energy,
   g. feelings of guilt or worthlessness,
   h. difficulty concentrating or thinking, or
   i. thoughts of death or suicide;
2. bipolar disorder, characterized by three or more of the following:
   a. pressured speech,
   b. flight of ideas,
   c. inflated self-esteem,
   d. decreased need for sleep,

e. distractibility,
f. involvement in activities that have a high probability of painful consequences that are not recognized, or
g. increase in goal-directed activity or psychomotor agitation;

AND

B. Extreme limitation of one, or marked limitation of two, of the following areas of mental functioning:
   1. understand, remember, or apply information;
   2. interact with others;
   3. concentrate, persist, or maintain pace;
   4. adapt or manage oneself;

OR

C. The mental disorder in this listing category is "serious and persistent;" with a medically documented history of the existence of the disorder over a period of at least two years, and there is evidence of both:
   1. medical treatment, mental health therapy, psychosocial support(s), or a highly structured setting(s) that is ongoing and that diminishes the symptoms and signs of the mental disorder; and
   2. marginal adjustment, that is, minimal capacity to adapt to environmental changes or to new demands of life.[7]

Intellectual Disorder

This SSA listing (see Appendix A §12.05 for adults, Appendix B §112.05 for children) is found under the *DSM-5* category of neurodevelopmental disorders, in its subcategory intellectual disability. It refers to "significantly subaverage general intellectual functioning, significant deficits in current adaptive functioning, and manifestation of the disorder before age 22."[8] The *DSM-5* definition of the diagnosis requires that onset must be "during the developmental period" (APA, 2013, p. 33) but does not specify a precise age or age range. The previous diagnostic manual, the *DSM-IV-TR* used the term *mental retardation* for this diagnosis, with the onset stipulated as "before age 18 years" (APA, 2000, p. 49). The commonly used term *mental retardation* was changed to *intellectual disability* by a 2010 federal statute known as Rosa's Law.[9] The SSA instead decided to use "intellectual disorder" for this listing in order to not presuppose disability.[10] For SSA purposes the onset must begin before age 22. In order to be considered a listing, it needs to meet criterion A or B.

Criterion A requires all three of the following:

1. significantly subaverage general intellectual functioning required to participate in standardized testing of intellectual functioning; and
2. significant deficits in adaptive functioning currently manifested by dependence upon others for personal needs (e.g., toileting, eating, dressing, or bathing); and
3. evidence of current intellectual and adaptive functioning and of the history of the disorder demonstrates or supports the conclusion that the disorder began prior to attainment of age 22.

OR
criterion B requires all three of the following:

1. significantly subaverage general intellectual functioning, evidenced by a or b:
    a. a full-scale (or comparable) IQ score of 70 or below on an individually administered standardized test of general intelligence, or
    b. a full-scale (or comparable) IQ score of 71–75, accompanied by a verbal or performance IQ score (or comparable part score) of 70 or below on an individually administered standardized test of general intelligence; and
2. significant deficits in adaptive functioning currently manifested by extreme limitation of one, or marked limitation of two, of the following areas of mental functioning:
    a. understand, remember, or apply information; and/or
    b. interact with others; and/or
    c. concentrate, persist, or maintain pace; and/or
    d. Adapt or manage oneself; and
3 The evidence about the current intellectual and adaptive functioning and about the history of the disorder demonstrates that the disorder began prior to attainment of age 22.[11]

Anxiety and Obsessive-Compulsive Disorders

This listing (see Appendix A §12.06 for adults and Appendix B §112.06 for children) is in the *DSM-5* under anxiety disorders and includes "social anxiety disorder, panic disorder, generalized anxiety disorder, agoraphobia, and obsessive-compulsive disorder."[12] The diagnosis needs to meet criteria A and B, or A and C to be considered a listing:

A. Medical documentation of the requirements of paragraph 1, 2, or 3:
   1. anxiety disorder, characterized by three or more of the following:
      a. restlessness,
      b. easily fatigued,
      c. difficulty concentrating,
      d. irritability,
      e. muscle tension, and/or
      f. sleep disturbance.
   2. panic disorder or agoraphobia, characterized by one or both of the following:
      a. panic attacks followed by a persistent concern or worry about additional panic attacks or their consequences, and/or
      b. disproportionate fear or anxiety about at least two different situations (e.g., using public transportation, being in a crowd, being in a line, being outside of your home, being in open spaces);
   3. obsessive-compulsive disorder, characterized by one or both of the following:
      a. involuntary, time-consuming preoccupation with intrusive, unwanted thoughts, and/or
      b. repetitive behaviors aimed at reducing anxiety;

AND

B. Extreme limitation of one, or marked limitation of two, of the following areas of mental functioning:
   1. understand, remember, or apply information;
   2. interact with others;
   3. concentrate, persist, or maintain pace;
   4. adapt or manage oneself;

OR

C. the mental disorder in this listing category is "serious and persistent;" with a medically documented history of the disorder over a period of at least two years, and there is evidence of both:
   1. medical treatment, mental health therapy, psychosocial support(s), or a highly structured setting(s) that is ongoing and that diminishes the symptoms and signs of the mental disorder; and
   2. marginal adjustment, that is, with minimal capacity to adapt to environment changes or to new demands of life.[13]

Somatic Symptom and Related Disorders

The SSA listing (§12.07 for adults and §112.07 for children) considers these to be physical symptoms "that cannot be fully explained by a general medical condition, another mental disorder, the direct effects of a substance, or a culturally sanctioned behavior or experience."[14] They are in the *DSM*-5 with the same name. This listing also needs to meet criteria of one or more of the following:

A. Medical documentation of *one* or more of the following:

1. symptoms of altered voluntary motor or sensory function that are not better explained by another medical or mental disorder;
2. one or more somatic symptoms that are distressing, with excessive thoughts, feelings, or behaviors related to the symptoms; or
3. preoccupation with having or acquiring a serious illness without significant symptoms present;

AND

B. Extreme limitation of one, or marked limitation of two, of the following areas of mental functioning:

1. understand, remember, or apply information;
2. interact with others;
3. concentrate, persist, or maintain pace; and/or
4. adapt or manage oneself.[15]

Personality and Impulse-Control Disorders

The listing (see Appendix A §12.08 for adults and Appendix B §112.08 for children) can be found in two separate *DSM*-5 chapters: first, under personality disorders, and second, under disruptive, impulse-control, and conduct disorders.

> These disorders are characterized by enduring, inflexible, maladaptive, and pervasive patterns of behavior. Onset typically occurs in adolescence or young adulthood. Symptoms and signs may include, but are not limited to, patterns of distrust, suspiciousness, and odd beliefs; social detachment, discomfort, or avoidance; hypersensitivity to negative evaluation; an excessive need to be taken care of; difficulty making independent decisions; a preoccupation with orderliness, perfectionism, and control; and inappropriate, intense, impulsive anger and behavioral expression grossly out of proportion to any external provocation or psychosocial stressors.[16]

> Examples of disorders in this category include paranoid, schizoid, schizotypal, borderline, avoidant, dependent, obsessive-compulsive personality disorders, and intermittent explosive disorder.[17]

This diagnosis must also meet the criteria below to qualify as a listing:

A. Medical documentation of a pervasive pattern of one or more of the following:

1. distrust and suspiciousness of others,
2. detachment from social relationships,
3. disregard for and violation of the rights of others,
4. instability of interpersonal relationships,
5. excessive emotionality and attention seeking,
6. feelings of inadequacy,
7. excessive need to be taken care of,
8. preoccupation with perfectionism and orderliness, or
9. recurrent, impulsive, aggressive behavioral outbursts;

AND

B. Extreme limitation of one, or marked limitation of two, of the following areas of mental functioning:

1. understand, remember, or apply information;
2. interact with others;
3. concentrate, persist, or maintain pace; and/or
4. adapt or manage oneself.[18]

Autism Spectrum Disorder

The listing (see Appendix A §12.10 for adults and Appendix B §112.10 for children) is found in the *DSM*-5 with the same terminology as within the chapter dedicated to neurodevelopmental disorders.

> These disorders are characterized by qualitative deficits in the development of reciprocal social interaction, verbal and nonverbal communication skills, and symbolic or imaginative activity; restricted repetitive and stereotyped patterns of behavior, interests, and activities; and stagnation of development or loss of acquired skills early in life. Symptoms and signs may include, but are not limited to, abnormalities and unevenness in the development of cognitive skills; unusual responses to sensory stimuli; and behavioral difficulties, including hyperactivity, short attention span, impulsivity, aggressiveness, or self-injurious actions.

Examples of disorders that we evaluate in this category include autism spectrum disorder with or without accompanying intellectual impairment, and autism spectrum disorder with or without accompanying language impairment.[19]

For this diagnosis to be considered a listing, it must also include

A. Medical documentation of *both* of the following:

  1. qualitative deficits in verbal communication, nonverbal communication, and social interaction; and
  2. significantly restricted, repetitive patterns of behavior, interests, or activities;

AND

B. Extreme limitation of one, or marked limitation of two, of the following areas of mental functioning:

  1. understand, remember, or apply information;
  2. interact with others;
  3. concentrate, persist, or maintain pace; and/or
  4. adapt or manage oneself.[20]

Neurodevelopmental Disorders

The SSA listing for neurodevelopmental disorders may be confusing to clinicians who are already familiar with the *DSM*-5 diagnoses. As we have already pointed out, the *DSM*-5 has an entire chapter devoted to neurodevelopmental disorders, and the *DSM* considers neurodevelopmental disorders to include intellectual disability, language disorder, autism spectrum disorder, attention-deficit/hyperactivity disorder, specific learning disorder, and motor disorders. The SSA, however, includes intellectual disorder (§12.05 for adults and §112.05 for children) and autism spectrum disorder (12.10 for adults and 112.10 for children) as separate listings, and we have discussed them previously in this chapter. The SSA listing for neurodevelopmental disorders refers to disorders

> characterized by onset during the developmental period, that is, during childhood or adolescence, although sometimes they are not diagnosed until adulthood. Symptoms and signs may include, but are not limited to, underlying abnormalities in cognitive processing (e.g., deficits in learning and applying verbal or nonverbal information, visual perception, memory, or a

> combination of these); deficits in attention or impulse control; low frustration tolerance; excessive or poorly planned motor activity; difficulty with organizing (time, space, materials, or tasks); repeated accidental injury; and deficits in social skills. Symptoms and signs specific to tic disorders include sudden, rapid, recurrent, nonrhythmic, motor movement or vocalization.[21]

Examples of this listing include specific learning disorder, borderline intellectual functioning, and tic disorders such as Tourette syndrome. The listing neurodevelopmental disorders requires

A. Medical documentation of the requirements of paragraphs 1, 2, or 3:
   1. *One* or both of the following:
      a. frequent distractibility, difficulty sustaining attention, and difficulty organizing tasks; and/or
      b. hyperactive and impulsive behavior (e.g., difficulty remaining seated, talking excessively, difficulty waiting, appearing restless, or behaving as if being "driven by a motor");
   2. significant difficulties learning and using academic skills; or
   3. recurrent motor movement or vocalization

AND

B. Extreme limitation of one, or marked limitation of two, of the following areas of mental functioning:
   1. understand, remember, or apply information;
   2. interact with others;
   3. concentrate, persist, or maintain pace;
   4. adapt or manage oneself.[22]

Eating Disorders

This SSA listing (see Appendix A §12.13 in adults or Appendix B §112.13 in children) is discussed in the *DSM-5* chapter on feeding and eating disorders.

> These disorders are characterized by disturbances in eating behavior and preoccupation with, and excessive self-evaluation of, body weight and shape. Symptoms and signs may include, but are not limited to, restriction of energy consumption when compared with individual requirements; recurrent episodes of binge eating or behavior intended to prevent weight

gain, such as self-induced vomiting, excessive exercise, or misuse of laxatives; mood disturbances, social withdrawal, or irritability; amenorrhea; dental problems; abnormal laboratory findings; and cardiac abnormalities.

Examples of disorders in this category include anorexia nervosa, bulimia nervosa, binge eating disorder, and avoidant/restrictive food disorder.[23]

The diagnosis of eating disorders must also meet criteria A and B to be considered a listing:

A. Medical documentation of a persistent alteration in eating or eating-related behavior that results in a change in consumption or absorption of food and that significantly impairs physical or psychological health,

AND

B. Extreme limitation of one, or marked limitation of two, of the following areas of mental functioning:
   1. understand, remember, or apply information;
   2. interact with others;
   3. concentrate, persist, or maintain pace;
   4. adapt or manage oneself.[24]

Developmental Disorders in Infants and Toddlers

Developmental disorders in infants and toddlers (§112.14) is a listing that is unique to children under three years of age and is

a. characterized by a delay or deficit in the development of age-appropriate skills, or a loss of previously acquired skills, involving motor planning and control, learning, relating and communicating, and self-regulating;
b. inclusive of developmental coordination disorder, separation anxiety disorder, autism spectrum disorder, and regulation disorders of sensory processing (difficulties in regulating emotions, behaviors, and motor abilities in response to sensory stimulation). Some infants and toddlers may have only a general diagnosis of "developmental delay."[25]

This listing requires medical documentation of impairment in the following developmental abilities:

1. Ability to plan and control motor movement. This criterion refers to the developmental ability to plan, remember, and execute controlled motor

movements by integrating and coordinating perceptual and sensory input with motor output. Using this ability develops gross and fine motor skills, making it possible to engage in age-appropriate symmetrical or alternating motor activities to include grasping and holding objects with one or both hands, pulling oneself up to stand, walk without holding on, and go up and down stairs with alternating feet. These examples illustrate the nature of the developmental ability. Documentation of all the examples is not required, according to SSA.

2. Age-appropriate ability to learn and remember. This criterion refers to the developmental ability to learn by exploring the environment, engaging in trial-and-error experimentation, putting things in groups, understanding that words represent things, and participating in pretend play. Using this ability develops the skills that help one understand what things mean, how things work, and how one can make things happen.
3. The ability to interact with others. This criterion refers to the developmental ability to participate in reciprocal social interactions and relationships by communicating feelings and intents through vocal and visual signals and exchanges, physical gestures and contact, shared attention and affection, verbal turn taking, and understanding and sending increasingly complex messages.
4. The ability to regulate physiological functions, attention, emotion, and behavior. This criterion refers to the developmental ability to stabilize biological rhythms (e.g., by developing an age-appropriate sleep/wake cycle); control physiological functions (e.g., by achieving regular patterns of feeding); and attend, react, and adapt to environmental stimuli, persons, objects, and events.[26]

Trauma- and Stressor-Related Disorders

These disorders (see Appendix A §12.15 for adults and Appendix B §112.15 for children) are found in the *DSM-5* chapter of the same name.

a. These disorders are characterized by experiencing or witnessing a traumatic or stressful event, or learning of a traumatic event occurring to a close family member or close friend, and the psychological aftermath of clinically significant effects on functioning. Symptoms and signs may include, but are not limited to, distressing memories, dreams, and flashbacks related to the trauma or stressor; avoidant behavior; diminished interest or participation in significant activities; persistent negative emotional states (e.g., fear, anger) or persistent inability to experience positive emotions (e.g., satisfaction, affection); anxiety; irritability; aggression; exaggerated startle response; difficulty concentrating; and sleep disturbance.

b. Examples of disorders in this category include PTSD and other specified trauma- and stressor-related disorders (such as adjustment-like disorders with prolonged duration but without prolonged duration of stressor).[27]

To be considered a listing, trauma- and stressor-related disorders must meet criteria A and B, or A and C:

A. Medical documentation of all of the following:

1. exposure to actual or threatened death, serious injury, or violence;
2. subsequent involuntary re-experiencing of the traumatic event (e.g., intrusive memories, dreams, or flashbacks);
3. avoidance of external reminders of the event;
4. disturbance in mood and behavior; and
5. increases in arousal and reactivity (e.g., exaggerated startle response, sleep disturbance);

AND

B. Extreme limitation of one, or marked limitation of two, of the following areas of mental functioning:

1. Understand, remember, or apply information (see Appendix A §12.00E1);
2. interact with others;
3. concentrate, persist, or maintain pace;
4. adapt or manage oneself;

OR

C. The disorder in this listing category is "serious and persistent," with a medically documented history of the disorder over a period of at least two years, and there is evidence of both:

1. medical treatment, mental health therapy, psychosocial support(s), or a highly structured setting(s) that is ongoing and that diminishes the symptoms and signs of the mental disorder (see Appendix A §12.00G2b); and
2. marginal adjustment, that is, minimal capacity to adapt to changes in one's environment or to demands that are not already part of daily life (see Appendix A §12.00G2c).[28]

There is a psychological component to almost every disability claim, even when mental health issues are not the primary complaint and mental health care providers can play an active role in the assessment of disability (Noblitt & Noblitt, 2010; Noblitt & Noblitt, 2017). Physical impairments secondary to illness or injury provoke feelings of stress, worry, fear, depression, hopelessness, helplessness, guilt, shame, and anxiety that may exacerbate physical symptoms such as pain, gastrointestinal distress, blood pressure, disturbed sleep, and disturbed appetite. People who are sick or injured, who cannot work, and who are torn by anxiety over how they will survive their medical or psychological disorder experience a range of emotions from mood swings to irritability, from depression to suicidal ideation. Medications designed to address physical and psychological symptoms often carry adverse effects, including those that may affect cognitions, concentration, orientation, and emotions. The psychological impact of physical illness or injury should always be considered when evaluating the whole person for Social Security disability benefits. If the claimant exhibits symptoms of a psychological disorder secondary to the impairment on which the claim of disability is made, it should be documented in the treating clinician's progress notes, and appropriate referrals for specialist care should be made.

Notes

1. https://www.ssa.gov/disability/professionals/bluebook/12.00-MentalDisorders-Adult.htm.
2. https://www.ssa.gov/disability/professionals/bluebook/112.00-MentalDisorders-Childhood.htm.
3. https://www.ssa.gov/disability/professionals/bluebook/12.00-MentalDisorders-Adult.htm.
4. Summarized from https://www.federalregister.gov/documents/2016/09/26/2016-22908/revised-medical-criteria-for-evaluating-mental-disorders.
5. https://www.federalregister.gov/documents/2016/09/26/2016-22908/revised-medical-criteria-for-evaluating-mental-disorders.
6. https://www.federalregister.gov/documents/2016/09/26/2016-22908/revised-medical-criteria-for-evaluating-mental-disorders.
7. Adapted from https://www.federalregister.gov/documents/2016/09/26/2016-22908/revised-medical-criteria-for-evaluating-mental-disorders.
8. https://www.federalregister.gov/documents/2016/09/26/2016-22908/revised-medical-criteria-for-evaluating-mental-disorders.
9. https://www.congress.gov/111/plaws/publ256/PLAW-111publ256.pdf.
10. https://www.federalregister.gov/documents/2016/09/26/2016-22908/revised-medical-criteria-for-evaluating-mental-disorders.
11. Adapted from https://www.federalregister.gov/documents/2016/09/26/2016-22908/revised-medical-criteria-for-evaluating-mental-disorders.
12. https://www.federalregister.gov/documents/2016/09/26/2016-22908/revised-medical-criteria-for-evaluating-mental-disorders.

13. Adapted from https://www.federalregister.gov/documents/2016/09/26/2016-22908/revised-medical-criteria-for-evaluating-mental-disorders.

14. https://www.federalregister.gov/documents/2016/09/26/2016-22908/revised-medical-criteria-for-evaluating-mental-disorders.

15. Adapted from: https://www.federalregister.gov/documents/2016/09/26/2016-22908/revised-medical-criteria-for-evaluating-mental-disorders.

16. https://www.federalregister.gov/documents/2016/09/26/2016-22908/revised-medical-criteria-for-evaluating-mental-disorders.

17. Adapted from https://www.federalregister.gov/documents/2016/09/26/2016-22908/revised-medical-criteria-for-evaluating-mental-disorders. The CFR appendixes for the Adult and Child listings are directed toward the consumer of Social Security Services. We adjusted the language to make this section consistent with the rest of the book and improve readability and thus refer to these excerpts as adaptations. The exact language for the Listings appears in Appendixes A and B.

18. Adapted from https://www.federalregister.gov/documents/2016/09/26/2016-22908/revised-medical-criteria-for-evaluating-mental-disorders.

19. https://www.federalregister.gov/documents/2016/09/26/2016-22908/revised-medical-criteria-for-evaluating-mental-disorders.

20. Adapted from https://www.federalregister.gov/documents/2016/09/26/2016-22908/revised-medical-criteria-for-evaluating-mental-disorders.

21. https://www.federalregister.gov/documents/2016/09/26/2016-22908/revised-medical-criteria-for-evaluating-mental-disorders.

22. Adapted from https://www.federalregister.gov/documents/2016/09/26/2016-22908/revised-medical-criteria-for-evaluating-mental-disorders.

23. Adapted from https://www.federalregister.gov/documents/2016/09/26/2016-22908/revised-medical-criteria-for-evaluating-mental-disorders.

24. Adapted from https://www.federalregister.gov/documents/2016/09/26/2016-22908/revised-medical-criteria-for-evaluating-mental-disorders.

25. Adapted from https://www.federalregister.gov/documents/2016/09/26/2016-22908/revised-medical-criteria-for-evaluating-mental-disorders.

26. Adapted from https://www.federalregister.gov/documents/2016/09/26/2016-22908/revised-medical-criteria-for-evaluating-mental-disorders.

27. Adapted from https://www.federalregister.gov/documents/2016/09/26/2016-22908/revised-medical-criteria-for-evaluating-mental-disorders.

28. Adapted from https://www.federalregister.gov/documents/2016/09/26/2016-22908/revised-medical-criteria-for-evaluating-mental-disorders.

CHAPTER SEVEN

Application Process for Social Security Disability Programs

> When Franklin D. Roosevelt launched Social Security in 1935, he did not present it as expressing the mutual obligation of citizens to one another. . . . Rather than offer a communal rationale, FDR argued that such rights were essential to "true individual freedom," adding, "necessitous men are not free men."
>
> —Michael J. Sandel, Justice: What's the Right Thing to Do?

Who Is Eligible for Social Security Disability Programs?

Social Security Disability Insurance (SSDI) is available to any disabled worker aged 18 and over (see Appendix A) who becomes too impaired to work and who has worked for at least 10 years, with five of those years immediately preceding the date when severe physical or mental impairments left the claimant without the capacity to sustain full-time work. For every year of employment, the worker accrues up to four credits—that is, a maximum of four credits per year and based on one credit for every $1,360 of earnings. Workers aged 62 or older must accumulate 40 credits (10 work years). For SSDI eligibility, workers aged 31 to 42 must have at least 20 earned credits (5 years), 6 to 18 credits (14 months to 6 years) from ages 24 to 30, and from ages 18 to 24, only 6 credits (14 months).

Workers of advanced age or even nearing retirement age are eligible to apply for SSDI as long as they were working at a full-time job prior to their date last insured. Workers who already receive Social Security retirement benefits can still apply for SSDI if they are injured or develop a disabling condition and must stop working. If their disability benefit is greater than their retirement benefit, their monthly payments will be adjusted accordingly. For example, Ann, age 66, received Social Security retirement benefits while she worked full-time as a community college lecturer, and she had no plans to retire. She took a fall at the bus stop and fractured her hip, requiring hip replacement surgery. While hospitalized, she contracted pneumonia and a secondary opportunistic infection. The injury and complicating health problems stretched her strength to the extent that she felt too weak and fragile to return to the pressure of full-time work. Her physicians suggested that the injury and subsequent illnesses had taxed her system such that she would require a lengthy rehabilitation and advised against her return to full-time employment. She applied for SSDI and received a small increase in her monthly benefits as well as back due benefits by the time her claim was appropriately adjudicated. Because she was over her Social Security retirement age, she was able to work part-time substitute teaching and tutoring without a restriction on the income she could earn.

Individuals who have been convicted of a crime and are incarcerated may apply for SSDI benefits if they are eligible and their impairment is severe and imposes substantial limitations on exertional or nonexertional work-related activities, but inmates cannot receive payments until they are released from prison. Benefits for people who already receive SSDI at the time they are incarcerated are suspended until a month after they are released. Medicare Part A remains in force during incarceration, but claimants are responsible for paying the premium for Medicare Parts B and D (premiums are usually deducted from monthly SSDI payments). Supplemental Security Income recipients also have their SSI benefits suspended for the duration of their incarceration, but they can be restored the month the beneficiaries are released from custody.

People who believe they have medical or psychological impairments so severe that they are incapable of working at a full-time job in a competitive work setting may apply for SSDI benefits. Many people make the mistake of waiting too long before applying, and this can compound their problems. The process of applying for SSDI benefits is typically quite lengthy and arduous. Applicants should anticipate that their initial application (IA) for benefits is unlikely to be approved. Thus they should explore alternative means of financial support and ongoing medical care during the interim period between applying for benefits and obtaining them. Currently, it can take three to four months or longer from the IA to receipt of an approval or denial. If the response is a denial, the claimant can appeal for reconsideration and expect another three to four months' wait for a decision. The claimant can then appeal to have the case heard by an ALJ. At the hearing level, it can take from about 7 months in less populated regions and up to 22 months in more densely populated areas from the time the claimant requests a hearing until the ALJ schedules a hearing. Once the hearing is held, the judge renders a decision, and again, depending on the judge's workload, this may take between 30 and 90 days and sometimes longer. In other words, the entire process can take between 13 and 30 months for resolution. And if the claimant receives an unfavorable decision and can demonstrate the judge committed errors in interpreting the regulations or failed to fully develop the claimant's file or made some other error that affected the hearing outcome, or if the claimant has new evidence in support of a disability determination, the claimant can request a review by the Appeals Council. The Appeals Council can uphold the ALJ's decision, reverse the decision, or remand the case for a new hearing before the same ALJ. Administrative law judges can and do reverse their original decisions on remand when new evidence is presented or there is a reinterpretation of the regulations. Sometimes they are unmoved, and claims remain denied. However, claimants have additional recourse. The claimant can appeal again to the Appeals Council. If the Appeals Council agrees that the judge's decision is in error, they can again reverse the decision or remand the case to a new judge. If the new judge upholds the prior decision, the claimant can file a new application or appeal to federal court. If the Appeals Council upholds a judge's unfavorable decision, either after the initial hearing, at the remand stage, or upon a hearing before a new ALJ, the claimant can file a civil action in U.S. District Court within 60 days of receipt of the Appeals Council denial. However, federal civil actions can take years to resolve.

While many disabilities are the consequence of unexpected injuries or illness, many others result from degenerative disease processes, complications from preexisting medical conditions, consequences of long-term treatment, and worsening of symptoms due to natural aging. For example, many people have well-controlled type 2 diabetes that has little impact on their lives. However, they may subsequently develop known complications of diabetes, including peripheral neuropathy, proliferative retinopathy, circulatory problems, and kidney failure. Individuals with known health problems may have the luxury of planning for the eventuality of disability and thus be better prepared to survive the SSDI waiting process. But for most people, disability catches them unawares, and they are unprepared for the bureaucracy and obstruction inherent in the disability determination process.

Workers who become sick or injured may try to remain employed in the hope that they will recover and be able to return to their jobs. They may be able to use their paid sick days and vacation days and take advantage of the Family Medical Leave Act (FMLA). The act, signed into law in 1993, provides workers who have been employed for at least one year by a company of at least 50 employees, and who have worked at least 1,250 hours in the prior 12 months, with the ability to take up to 12 weeks of unpaid leave to care for an ailing family member; to care for a new child through childbirth, adoption, or foster parenting; to recover from injury or illness; or for other similar medically related reasons. Although unpaid, employees continue to be covered by any health insurance benefits of employment as well as other benefits such as 401K investiture, employer-provided short- or long-term disability insurance, among others. As of the writing of this book (2019), seven states—California, Washington, New York, New Jersey, Connecticut, Rhode Island, Massachusetts—and the District of Columbia offer additional paid FMLA benefits and protections.

Some employers offer short-term (STD) or long-term disability (LTD) insurance benefits. These may be paid by the employer or by employee contribution or a combination of these. The duration of benefits may vary, so it is important to understand from the outset for how long they will be available. Additionally, most such insurance policies require the beneficiary to apply for SSDI benefits. It should be understood that receipt of SSDI will not increase the monthly financial benefit provided by the private LTD policy. If the beneficiary is approved for SSDI, the benefit amount will be deducted from the LTD monthly benefit, and some or all of past due benefits payable by SSDI will be recouped by the LTD carrier.

Most states offer disability insurance programs (DI or SDI). Typically, these programs provide around 60% of the claimant's monthly salary for about one year from approval. Generally, there are no health insurance benefits associated with these state programs. However, some states may offer Medicaid-equivalent health insurance. Individuals contemplating the need to apply for SSDI should certainly investigate what programs their state offers. Again, if the claimant is awarded SSDI benefits, some of the claimant's back due benefits will repay state disability benefits.

Individuals whose injuries or illnesses occurred in the workplace or in performance of their work and that result in a disabling condition may make a claim under their state's workers' compensation program. Workers' compensation programs provide both cash benefits and medical treatment, but treatment is confined to only the condition associated with the work-related illness or injury. Many individuals who have received workers' compensation complain about substandard care from medical personnel contracted by workers' compensation, and about the control workers' compensation has over the claimant's treatment. The advice of the claimant's treating physicians is often ignored, and authorization for medical tests and treatment are frequently delayed or denied. Again, if the claimant's SSDI application is approved, back due benefits will be used to repay workers' compensation.

Workers who are union or professional association members may also be entitled to DI or other benefits. Some unions or associations may offer such programs as a member benefit, while some may make group rates for private disability or health insurance available to members.

Those applicants who are near retirement age can apply for Social Security retirement benefits as early as age 62. This will not disqualify them from applying for SSDI. However, early retirement beneficiaries may receive a lower monthly financial benefit than if they had waited for full retirement age. If they are later found disabled, their benefits will be adjusted to the amount to which they would be entitled in disability benefits, and they would receive back due benefits. Early Social Security retirement benefits do not include Medicare eligibility until the age of 65.

Adding to the financial concerns for individuals awaiting a decision by Social Security as to their application for benefits is the necessity to obtain ongoing medical or psychological treatment. Consistent treatment is not only necessary to the claimant's well-being and potential for recovery but it is evidentiary. If claimants are not receiving treatment, or if there is no evidence that their disabling condition persists, they are conceding that they are not still disabled. Even if they are terminally ill, there must be evidence of ongoing care, even if it is only palliative, in order to demonstrate proof of their disabling condition. A diagnosis of stage IV cancer is not in and of itself evidence of disability.

If an individual is hospitalized due to serious illness or injury, or if the individual is a patient of a large clinical practice or managed health-care organization, there may be an opportunity to meet with a social worker to discuss options that may be available in the community, such as eligibility for housing support, food support, home health care, subsidized prescription medication, free or low-cost clinics, and other services. Agencies such as Catholic Charities and Jewish Family Services may also have social workers available to make such referrals. One does not need to be Catholic or Jewish to take advantage of the services these agencies offer. It is always good to know what assistance may be available during the prolonged application process and beyond. However, if the individual receives any city, county, state, or federal benefits, including welfare or general relief, food stamps, or certain other services, repayment may be elicited from back due benefits if the SSDI or SSI claim is approved.

Initial Application

The initial application for SSDI (Title II of the Social Security Act) benefits or SSI (Title XVI of the Social Security Act) benefits can be filed online, by phone, or in person at any SSA field office. The applicant must produce full name and all other names by which they have been known, Social Security number, date of birth, address, citizenship or permanent resident status, and contact information. Applicants must also identify current and former spouse information, including Social Security numbers and birthdates, date of marriage and, where applicable, date of divorce or death of spouse. The names of any dependent children aged 18 and under along with their Social Security numbers will also be required. Applicants must provide information about the disabling condition, doctors and hospitals where treatment has been received, and corresponding dates of diagnosis and treatment. Finally, a complete work history for the 15 years preceding disability, including employers, jobs, and description of duties, must be developed.

The majority of IAs are denied whether initiated by the claimant or a representative, but they are even more likely to be denied when pursued by the claimant alone. We don't have to wonder why the majority of claims for benefits are denied at the initial and reconsideration appeal levels. Most claimants naively assume that their diagnosis and severe symptoms should automatically identify them as disabled. They are unaware that the burden of proof is theirs. They do not understand what constitutes proof and assume that providing their diagnoses and the members of their treatment team is sufficient.

Unfortunately, what is presented above as a list of documents requested by Social Security at the IA level does not describe the full extent of what is necessary for the SSA to make a completely informed decision. Furthermore, there is no appreciation for the effort required for the claimant to accumulate the information. Therefore, most initial applications are woefully incomplete and do not provide the level of support necessary. Claimants are advised to bring their supportive documentation to their nearest Social Security field office, but that seemingly simple task may be beyond their capacity to perform.

People who are sick, injured, in pain, medicated, confused, disoriented, exhausted, emotionally drained, and without financial resources and reliable support may be incapable of completing this task. Disability is demonstrated by the claimant's incapacity to perform simple tasks unsupervised, the same requirement needed for negotiating the disability application process. Perhaps the best evidence for disability is the claimant's inability to accumulate the requisite materials, organize their delivery, communicate with health-care providers and obtain records, and meet all of the SSA demands that are associated with the IA process.

Additional information will be requested, including the applicant's description of how the disabling condition limits capacity to function, as well as any third-party observations about the claimant, usually completed by a spouse, parent, or child with intimate knowledge of the claimant's situation. Without a good understanding of Social Security's language and regulations, the applicant may be unable to discern what information is relevant and what is extraneous. Although a qualified representative's assistance at the IA stage is unlikely to guarantee an award of benefits, the representative will be in a better position to lay a stronger foundation for a favorable decision at the hearing level.

The SSA will request records from all treating clinicians identified by the claimant. If health-care providers do not respond to the SSA's request for records, or if the records do not adequately address the limitations experienced by the claimant as a result of the impairment, the Administration will often require the claimant to attend a consultative examination. In the absence of any supportive documentation, the claim will likely be denied unless the claimant's age and work history dictate a finding of "disabled" according to the Medical-Vocational Guidelines, or grid rules.[1] Younger claimants who do not meet a listing or who do not meet the criteria for compassionate allowance[2] will most likely have their claims denied.

The claimant's application is reviewed by various staff at the SSA, both clerical and medical professionals, to determine if the claimant meets the eligibility requirements based on a five-step sequential evaluation process:

1. At the first step, Social Security considers the claimant's work history, if any. If the claimant is performing substantial gainful activity, Social Security will find the claimant is not disabled.
2. The medical severity of the impairment(s) is then considered. If the impairments do not constitute a severe, medically determinable physical or mental impairment that meets the duration requirement, or a combination of impairments that is severe and meets the duration requirement, a finding of not disabled will be made.

3. At the third step, consideration is made regarding the medical severity of the impairment(s) and whether the impairment meets or equals one of the listings of this subpart and meets the duration requirement. If the impairment meets or equals a listing and the duration requirement, a finding of disability will be rendered.
4. Now the claimant's residual functional capacity and past relevant work are evaluated. If the claimant can still perform past relevant work, Social Security will find the claimant not disabled.
5. At the last step, Social Security considers its assessment of the claimant's residual functional capacity, age, education, and work experience to see if the claimant can reasonably make an adjustment to other work. If the claimant can make an adjustment to other work, Social Security will find the claimant not disabled. If an adjustment to other work cannot be made, Social Security will find the claimant disabled.[3]

While the field office of the SSA evaluates the applicant's nonmedical information to assess eligibility, including work history, marital status, age, and Social Security Old-Age, Survivors, and Disability Insurance (OASDI) coverage, at step 2 of the sequential evaluation, it defers to the Disability Determination Services (DDS), a state agency that develops the claimant's medical records to evaluate whether the claimant meets the medical eligibility standard of disability based on the existing treatment records. The DDS reviews medical records of claimants at the IA and reconsideration stages to assess whether they meet the level of severity necessary for a finding of disability. The agency is also responsible for making similar assessments for Medicaid applicants. If there is insufficient supportive documentation from treating clinicians and facilities, the DDS will refer the applicant for a consultative evaluation by a local medical professional contracted by the DDS on behalf of the SSA.

Contributions to Social Security are deducted from payroll via FICA, the Federal Insurance Contributions Act. These monies essentially act as insurance premiums that apply to old-age retirement benefits and SSDI benefits. Depending on their earnings history, claimants' premiums may be paid as far as five years into the future after they stop working. These contributions are calculated to determine the claimant's *date last insured* (DLI). It must be demonstrated that the claimant's impairments became severe enough to qualify for benefits prior to the DLI.

Applicants for SSI benefits must meet a financial test in addition to the medical or mental impairment criteria that limit applicants to having no more than $2,000 ($3,000 for a couple) in financial resources (cash or money in a checking or savings account or property or other items that can be sold for cash). This total is independent of

- ownership of the house the claimant lives in,
- ownership of one car used for transportation of the claimant or household member,
- burial fund of no greater than $1,500 each for the claimant and spouse,
- life insurance policies owned by the claimant with a face value of $1,500 or less each,
- household goods,
- personal effects, and
- burial plots for immediate family.

Sadly, even if the applicant has what may appear to be solid evidence in support of a finding of disability, only 33% of initial applications in 2016 were approved.[4]

Reconsideration

If the initial application for benefits is denied, the claimant can appeal for reconsideration of the initial decision within 60 days of receipt of the decision. Unfortunately, the percentage of applications approved at the reconsideration level is only around 12%. Upon receipt of denial, the claimant has 60 days to request a hearing before an ALJ. Social Security's own statistics show that claimants have the greatest chance for approval at the hearing level.

Exhibit File

Beginning with the initial application for benefits for either SSDI, SSI or both, an exhibit file containing both medical and nonmedical documentation relevant to the disability determination process is collected and organized into sections. The basic organization of the file is usually completed by the time the hearing is scheduled, but new evidence can be submitted up to five business days in advance of the scheduled hearing. The exhibit file is divided into the following sections:

A. Payment Documents/Decisions, composed of the Disability Determination Explanation and Transmittal, and prior decisions;
B. Jurisdictional Documents/Notices, generally containing Acknowledgment of Hearing Requests, Notice of Hearing, Appointment of Representative, and other hearing-related notices;
D. Nondisability Development, information relevant to SSDI and SSI eligibility such as Workers' Compensation and Public Disability queries, SSDI and SSI

applications, Summary Earnings Query, Detailed Earnings Query, Certified Earnings Record, New Hire/Quarter Wage/Unemployment Query;

E. Disability-Related Development, referring to Disability Reports, Work History, Function Reports, Disability Determination Services, Disability Worksheet, Exhibit List, Representative's Brief, and the Resume of the Vocational Expert (VE) and Medical Expert (ME); and

F. Medical Records.

At the hearing, the ALJ will refer to the exhibit list and ask for clarifying information from the claimant or representative, and will use the relevant exhibits in Section E to ask the VE to identify the claimant's past work, and medical records in Section F to pose hypotheticals to the VE regarding future work. The VE will only have access to the E exhibit file but will be able to hear the claimant's elocution as to impairments and resultant limitations. The claimant's representative will use the exhibit list to bring relevant evidence to the ALJ's attention and to support a theory of the case that may result in a finding of disabled. The medical expert (ME) will have access only to the F exhibits as well as the claimant's testimony.

Hearing Level

Claimants who request a hearing enjoy the greatest chance for a favorable outcome. Approximately 43% of individuals who applied for Social Security disability benefits were approved at the hearing level in 2016. It is at the hearing level where the claimant comes face to face with a real person, a judge, and can present the case for disability, providing evidence in the form of treatment records, clinician opinions, and the testimony of the claimant and any relevant witnesses who may appear.

Of course, not all judges are created equal, and each has a unique approach to the interpretation of regulations and value placed on different aspects of the claimant's situation. Judges often recognize certain elements of the claimant's record to be more or less supportive than others. Whereas some judges place greatest emphasis on the claimant's past work and earnings record, others are more concerned with age. Assuming a medically determinable impairment is present, the judge may rely on the claimant's consistent work record, high earnings, or age as the determining factor in making a favorable or unfavorable decision.

My coauthor recounted a recent experience where she represented three claimants on the same day before the same judge. She believed all the cases to be equally strong but knew from experience that the judge was unlikely to grant all three. Pam rated her clients according to the strength of the severe medical impairments and found them to be equal. All of the claimants were in their mid-40s and thus would not benefit from the grid rules. All were well-educated professionals. However, whereas two of the claimants had long and lucrative careers, the third had been working as a contract worker overseas, had worked in the United States for only eight years, and had the lowest earnings of the three claimants. Indeed, the judge made fully favorable decisions on the other two claimants and denied the claim of the client with the lowest earnings. That decision is in the process of an appeal before the Appeals Council, and, based on the existing evidence as well as two RFCs submitted by the claimant's clinicians after the hearing, there is hope for a better outcome at the appeals level.

Claimants or their representatives have no control over assignment of judges, and, once assigned, the judge is unlikely to be changed unless special circumstances arise, such as the claimant relocating from one jurisdiction to another or the judge's extended incapacity, death, or retirement. However, just because a judge may have particular biases or a reputation for having a lower grant rate does not mean the claimant has no chance to win. This is perhaps where the value of representation is most evident in that the representative's experience with individual judges helps to develop the presentation of the case and emphasize those elements to which the judge is most likely sensitive. The representative can craft a prehearing brief that lays out the facts of the case, articulating the applicable regulations, suggesting possible listings of impairments that may be met or equaled, and, in the case of those claimants to whom the grid rules apply, citing those as well.

Office of Hearings Operations

The Office of Hearings Operations (OHO) schedules and conducts disability determinations for both SSDI and SSI claimants. There are 10 regional OHOs, located in Boston (R1), New York (R2), Philadelphia (R3), Atlanta (R4), Chicago (R5), Dallas (R6), Kansas City (R7), Denver (R8), San Francisco (R9), and Seattle (R10). The regional hearing centers oversee 164 hearing offices and two satellite offices. There are also five National Hearing Centers with three satellite offices. However, even with a staff of approximately 1,600 ALJs and 9,100 support staff, the system is badly overtaxed; depending on the residence of the claimant and the region it falls under, it can take between one and two years from the request for hearing to the hearing date. In 2017 there were 2,179,728 applicants for SSDI benefits, of which 762,141 or 34.96% were ultimately granted.

Administrative Law Judge

The ALJ is an appointed position and requires that the applicant be an attorney in good standing and licensed in any state or the District of Columbia, who has practiced for at least seven years and passed a qualifying examination. The ALJ's duty is to adjudicate findings of fact in various civil venues, with the majority of ALJs being assigned to the SSA. Administrative law judges are federal employees and are paid an average of around $160,000 annually. They can only be removed from office for cause.

The hearing process varies from ALJ to ALJ, but there are some consistent features. The hearings are small and include only the judge, the claimant, the hearing assistant, and the claimant's representative when retained. Almost always a vocational expert is either physically present or available by telephone. Depending on the judge and the complexities of the case, an ME may also testify. The claimant is entitled to produce witnesses and the claimant or representative may question witnesses, including the VE and ME. Hearings vary in length from 15 minutes to more than an hour. Some judges wear a robe; others do not. Judges may appear in person or via video teleconferencing. Claimants may object to video hearings and are generally afforded a live hearing when possible. Claimants and witnesses, including vocational and medical experts, are sworn to tell the truth under penalty of perjury. The hearings are recorded via audio for review during any appeals process. Claimants and representatives who must travel 75 miles or more from their home to the nearest hearing office may be able to receive reasonable reimbursement for travel expenses to and from the hearing office.

At each of the OHOs, one of the judges serves as chief ALJ and is tasked with supervising the staff to ensure regulations are met, assigning cases to the ALJs, and keeping up with new policies and regulations.

The ALJ may dismiss the claimant's application if it is determined that the claimant does not meet the eligibility requirements. The application can also be dismissed if the claimant fails to meet deadlines, fails to appear at consultative examinations, or fails to appear at the hearing without good cause, which could be acute exacerbation of illness or injury, hospitalization, transportation issues, weather emergencies, or similar situations that occur unpredictably. The ALJ can make a "fully favorable" decision that reflects the judge's agreement with the facts of the case, that the severity of the claimant's condition and subsequent limitations are as presented in the evidence from the date(s) designated. The ALJ may also render a "partially favorable" decision. Such a decision reflects the judge's agreement that the claimant is disabled but disagrees with the date of disability or other factors. The judge's partially favorable decision may also be made in cases where the judge determines that the claimant was disabled for at least 12 months but is no longer found to be disabled. In situations where claimants request the judge only consider their previous disabled status, acknowledging that they have now recovered sufficiently to return to work, this would provide for a *closed period of disability* that entitles the claimants to back due benefits for the period of disability but no future monthly financial benefit or Medicare or Medicaid health insurance. An "unfavorable decision" is rendered if the judge believes that the claimant's physical or mental impairments are not severe, that the claimant's severe impairments did not occur within the prescribed time period, that the claimant's earnings were insufficient for Title II eligibility, that the claimant's earnings post the alleged onset date indicate insufficient level of severity, or that the claimant is still capable of full-time work within a competitive work environment.

In a decision, an ALJ can direct that a *representative payee* be assigned to manage the beneficiary's money benefits. A representative payee is required when the beneficiary is a minor. Generally, the representative payee is a parent, although some other responsible adult may be elected. Representative payees are also required for beneficiaries who are incompetent due to psychological impairments, a history of drug and alcohol abuse, or other circumstances. The representative payee is responsible for managing the claimant's SSA income, assuring that essential bills are paid and that the money is used only for the recipient's benefit. Representative payees are required to present to the SSA, on demand, an accounting of how they allocate the beneficiaries' benefits.

Judges' findings are based on the legal standard of *preponderance of evidence*. That is to say that as all the evidence is weighed, the judge must consider whether the evidence is more likely to favor the claimant's allegation of disability or not. A helpful summary of the kinds of evidence that are considered by the SSA can be found in Michael Stretton's chapter, "Understanding the Three Types of Evidence Used by the Social Security Administration in Resolving Disability Claims" (2017). Stretton explains that the three general categories are objective, subjective, and opinion evidence. "Objective medical evidence is medical evidence that can be verified by other healthcare professionals using medically acceptable clinical or laboratory techniques" (2017, p. 7). Medical laboratory findings (including objective psychological testing) and clinical signs are considered examples of objective evidence, although the interpretations of medical objective findings can be considered opinion evidence.

Patients' descriptions of their health problems and limitations are considered subjective evidence. The SSA looks for consistency in the documentation and testimony regarding these different kinds of evidence. Ultimately, the body of evidence to be considered is composed of medical records, opinions from treating clinicians, nonexamining clinicians including employees of the Administration as well as MEs, and examining clinicians such as consultative examiners or independent medical examiners, along with the claimant's testimony. While the hearings process for Social Security disability claims is supposed to be nonadversarial pursuant to Social Security regulations,[5] there are both good and bad judges, and the bad judges can demonstrate incompetence and political, racial, economic, gender, sexual orientation, or social bias; or they can assume the role of a prosecuting attorney, intimidating the claimant and encouraging an adversarial environment (Vendel, 2005). If these tactics result in an unfavorable decision, the decision may be appealable but will also delay the process even further, as the appeals process is lengthy and unpredictable. Conversely, there are judges who may be inclined to grant cases where evidence is not complete or completely supportive and the judge may rely on instinct and experience rather than the letter of the law. The Appeals Council may also review favorable decisions and reverse or amend the judge's finding or remand for a new hearing if the decision is unsupported by the evidence.

The best judges are those who weigh their decisions based on the evidence, regulations, and humanity. They understand the nature of work, the effect of symptoms and medications on the ability to perform work activities, the difference between work activities and activities of daily living, and they are realistic in their appraisal of the claimants who appear before them. My coauthor represented a young woman who applied for benefits as an adult child whose impairments developed early in life and now, at age 20, left her without the capacity to engage in full-time work. She has a combination of severe orthopedic, cardiac, gastrointestinal, and psychiatric conditions that have dogged her since adolescence. She has undergone multiple surgeries and psychiatric hospitalizations and was prescribed a plethora of medications. Despite being armed with very supportive treatment records and multiple medical opinions from treating clinicians that reflected her severely reduced physical and mental functional capacity, the judge found the claimant not disabled because she was capable of self-care in the completion of her activities of daily living (dressing, bathing, toileting, food preparation, eating, and light housekeeping) and testified that she had a boyfriend. Of course, this decision warrants appeal. However, given the current state of affairs where only around 13% of unfavorable decisions are granted a new hearing or reversed by the Appeals Council, even such an egregious decision may not warrant the Appeals Council's attention.

Medical Expert

The *medical expert* (ME) is a licensed physician or psychologist with a specialty consistent with the claimant's medically determinable severe impairment who reviews the treatment records and testifies under oath regarding the claimant's diagnosis, prognosis, and whether the claimant meets or equals one of the Listing of Impairments compiled by the SSA. The ME does not examine the claimant and, indeed, has never seen the claimant prior to the hearing. The ME may ask clarifying questions of the claimant with the judge's permission. The ME can be cross-examined by the claimant or representative. Occasionally, there is new evidence revealed at the hearing or post hearing that may require input from an ME. The ALJ can query the ME via written interrogatories that are proffered to the claimant or claimant's representative, along with the ME's response. The claimant or the claimant's representative can also pose interrogatories to the ME that the ME is compelled to answer.

MEs can be helpful or harmful to the claimant's case. Their knowledge of the applicant is limited to what is in the record, although they may ask clarifying questions of the individual as well as rely on their observations of the claimant at the hearing, when testifying in person. Although they are required to be specialists in the general area of medicine most aligned to the claimant's most severe condition, they may not have experience or specific knowledge of the claimant's diagnosed condition. For example, one of Pam's clients suffered from polymyositis, an inflammatory disease of the voluntary and involuntary muscles that causes pain and weakness as the inflamed muscles deteriorate. The condition is incurable and progressive, and the currently available treatment is only palliative. A diagnosis of polymyositis is one of the featured conditions in the Listing of Impairments under the category of immune system disorders for both adults (§14.05) and children (§114.05), if qualifying criteria are met. The ME, whose curriculum vitae represented him as an expert on polymyositis, testified by phone from out of state. He testified that the client bore some responsibility for her condition due to her overweight state, which he opined contributed to her shortness of breath. And since the client's treating rheumatologist reported that she scheduled the claimant for in-person visits every four months, the ME suggested the claimant's condition was not severe. The treating rheumatologist did not restrict the claimant to office visits every four months. The four-month scheduling represented the minimum in-person appointments the physician required of her patient. The claimant was free to come in more frequently in response to the waxing and waning nature of the disease process, and her medical records revealed periods of weekly visits and hospitalizations. The ME focused on the inflammatory disease process without due consideration of the fact that polymyositis is also an autoimmune disorder, leaving the claimant vulnerable to opportunistic infection, which is particularly concerning because the claimant's breathing was impaired secondary to accelerated weakening of her diaphragmatic muscles that inhibited her ability to engage in physical activities and even extended talking. Furthermore, the medical treatment of choice, high-dose steroids, carry significant adverse effects including severe malaise, fatigue, and involuntary weight gain, yet because of her inflamed voluntary and involuntary muscles, she was unable to exercise. As a result of her long-term, high-dose steroid use and enforced inactivity, the claimant gained significant weight and developed type 2 diabetes mellitus. Finally, the ME testified that stress was not a factor in the course of polymyositis. Immediately following the hearing, Pam wrote a comprehensive post-hearing brief in response to the ME's testimony, citing the claimant's treatment records, her treating physicians' professional opinions, and current research, and was able to refute the ME's testimony. In her fully favorable decision posted a month later, the ALJ gave the ME little weight and determined the claimant was indeed completely disabled under Social Security's regulations. However, ALJs often defer to the opinions expressed by the MEs, giving them the benefit of the doubt when it comes to disability determination.

Vocational Expert

The role of the VE is defined by Social Security's Program Operations Manual System (POMS). The function of the VE is to identify the claimant's past work for the ALJ using the definitions derived from the *Dictionary of Occupational Titles* (*DOT*), a publication of the Department of Labor, last revised in 1992. The volume identifies occupations, provides the code numbers by which they are sorted in the *DOT* and provides the required exertional and nonexertional aspects of these jobs along with the necessary training based on specific vocational preparation (SVP) levels. The VE may query the claimant for additional information about how jobs were performed or whether jobs were combined with other jobs, or other details that affected work activities and performance. For example, the claimant's job may be described in the *DOT* as a medium job but was performed by the claimant at the heavy exertional level. Or the claimant may have been a working supervisor who both performed a job with the added responsibilities of hiring, firing, scheduling, and customer service. After the judge has heard testimony, the VE is posed a number of hypothetical questions during which the judge and the claimant's representative offer scenarios where the claimant's functional capacity is limited by physical or mental impairments, and the VE offers opinions as to whether past jobs or any other jobs can be performed under those restrictions. The VE is charged with opining whether the claimant can perform past work or any other work in the national economy despite any physical, psychological, behavioral, or cognitive limitations without consideration of special accommodations not available to other workers in the same work setting. The VE testifies about specific jobs, their requirements, and whether they exist in sufficient numbers nationally to make them viable options for the claimant. What constitutes sufficient numbers of jobs has not been defined by the SSA and is at the discretion of the judge. The VE may also testify about jobs and how they are performed based on professional experience. For example, the claimant may not be able to sit or stand for prolonged periods and requires the ability to sit and stand at will. This level of activity is not discussed in the *DOT*, but the VE may be aware of jobs that can be performed with a sit/stand option based on experience that may include research and observations in the field. Without regard to the claimant's past level of renumeration or whether the claimant can actually be hired, the VE's testimony strongly influences the judge's disability determination. Theoretically, if the claimant was a surgeon who, due to cerebral hemorrhage, has lost the skills and dexterity to continue performing as a surgeon and the vocational expert opines that the claimant is able to perform the work of a ticket taker at a movie theater, a job that exists in significant numbers nationally, the claimant will be found not disabled, even though the work of a ticket taker would be paid at a significantly lower wage than the surgeon's previous income. As long as the work is full time, can be performed without accommodations, takes place in a competitive work setting, and the wages are equal to or greater than SGA,[6] the claimant is not disabled. The jobs cited by the VE are frequently obscure and, due to current technology, may not be as available as the VE represents them to be. For example, the job of "addresser" is often provided as a sedentary unskilled job. The *DOT* describes this job as follows:

> *DOT* CODE: 209.587-010, TITLE(s): ADDRESSER (clerical) alternate titles: addressing clerk; envelope addresser. Addresses by hand or typewriter, envelopes, cards, advertising literature, packages, and similar items for mailing. May sort mail.

In our computerized era, the job of addressing envelopes, cards, advertising literature, packages, and similar items by hand or typewriter is rare, if it exists at all. As of this writing, the job of addresser is not listed on the website for the Bureau of Vital Statistics. And because the *DOT* has not been updated since 1992, there are a plethora of jobs that have been created over the last quarter century and are not referenced in the *DOT*. Thus the VE must sometimes improvise to find a correlation between jobs defined in the *DOT* and the claimant's recently developed position.

The VE does not review the medical evidence in the claimant's Social Security file. The VE may hear testimony regarding the claimant's impairments but is not qualified to make determinations as to how the claimant's physical or mental limitations affect work, other than in the context of the hypothetical questions introduced by the judge or the claimant's representative.

Appeals Council

All decisions by the ALJs are subject to review by the Appeals Council. Claimants may also appeal partially favorable and unfavorable decisions to the Appeals Council. The Appeals Council (AC) is composed of approximately 60 administrative appeals judges who are charged with reviewing appeals requests and the cases to which they apply and to determine whether the appeal is substantiated by the record. The Appeals Council can deny the appeal, reverse the ALJ's decision, or remand the case back for another hearing. At the first appeal, the case is remanded to the same judge who initially heard the case unless the claimant has moved to a different jurisdiction or the judge is no longer available due to retirement, relocation, illness, or death. If the judge again denies the claim on remand, the decision can be appealed again. If the appeal is granted and remanded, a new judge in the same OHO is assigned to hear the case, unless the claimant is under the jurisdiction of a different OHO due to relocation.

A request for a review of the ALJ's decision must be based on judicial error or new evidence not available at the hearing. A common error judges make is failing to assign the evidence-supported opinions of treating clinicians enough influence over disability determination. Over the years, the importance of treating physicians' opinions has been degraded. The treating physician rule has been amended such that opinions must be in sync with the treatment records. Unfortunately, treatment records are frequently lacking in professional observations and, more often than not, are repetitive and confusing. In the interest of efficient time and risk management, treatment records are relatively bare-bones documents composed of the SOAP formula: subjective, objective, assessment, and plan. The records reflect the patient's vital signs, prior diagnoses and treatments, prescribed medications and procedures, and new complaints, without editorial comment. This antiseptic approach rarely sheds light on the claimant's experience of limited function and leaves much of the information open to interpretation by the beholder. The claimant or the claimant's representative must often read between the lines to extrapolate supportive evidence from the records. For example, doctors typically work during regular business hours during the week and rarely on weekends or holidays, just like most other workers. Thus they schedule office visits and procedures during the hours most people work, and their patients must conform to their schedule. And we all know from experience that doctors' schedules are flexible to account for emergent situations. A 10-minute appointment can easily result in a much greater expenditure of time between the time required to be transported to and from the clinician's office or hospital; the check-in process, waiting for the clinician's availability, the examination, discussions with the clinician, laboratory work-ups, imaging studies, and check-out can easily evolve into several hours. Thus a review of time spent at clinician appointments, in- or outpatient procedures, physical or occupational therapy, psychotherapy, and hospitalization may be reflective of the severity of the claimant's condition and is evidence of the claimant's unavailability to work.

Another error commonly resulting in an unfavorable decision is the false equation between activities of daily living and other activities performed by the claimant in a nonwork setting and actual competitive work. There is a significant distinction between performing light housekeeping at home and performing work activities in a competitive work setting. At home, even among those of us not experiencing physical or psychological limitations, tasks can be performed at leisure, without the pressure of time, quotas, supervisory demands, interaction with others, the distraction of additional assignments, deadlines, and structured schedules. We are free to complete tasks at our convenience and in the order and manner of our choosing. We can empty the clothes dryer and fold laundry in front of the television. We can take a break and lie down for 30 minutes or an hour in the midst of completing chores. We can take medication that may leave us a bit foggy without concerning ourselves about its impact on our work product. We can take as many bathroom breaks of any duration necessary without answering to supervisors or compromising schedules. Nevertheless, a judge may base a decision on a claimant's occasional gardening activity despite severe back problems, even though another part of the claimant's testimony indicates that it takes several days to recover from the effort. The judge may mischaracterize occasional gardening at home as the equivalent of performing a full-time job at the light exertional level. These are clearly not the same and would offer a reasonable argument for appeal.

One more error still is the misinterpretation of severe impairments as nonsevere and the judge's neglect to consider the combined effect of severe and nonsevere impairments. Let's consider the case of an obese (BMI = 39.0) 45-year-old woman with severe rheumatoid arthritis who formerly worked for many years as an office manager, a light exertional activity job performed at the skilled level. She also has type 2 diabetes mellitus, which is generally considered nonsevere. Conditions that frequently accompany diagnoses of diabetes include hypertension and hyperlipidemia (high blood pressure and high cholesterol). These conditions often require prescription medication to contain and control symptoms. However, the claimant is prescribed steroids for her rheumatoid arthritis, which causes involuntary weight gain that exerts additional stress on her back, hips, knees, and ankles. Furthermore, her diabetes exacerbates her hypertension, requiring additional medications to reduce her blood pressure. One of these medications is a diuretic that causes her to need frequent bathroom breaks. The claimant's pain, unemployability, and financial distress cause her to experience depression and anxiety. The medications prescribed to address these conditions aggravate her diabetes, hypertension, hyperlipidemia, and obesity, which further accelerate her joint pain. The claimant is treated monthly by a rheumatologist, internist, psychiatrist, and psychotherapist. She is prescribed a total of three oral medications for hypertension, two for diabetes, one for hyperlipidemia, one for anxiety, and one for depression. She is also prescribed a weekly drug delivered via injection, methotrexate, which carries severe side effects such as liver damage, skin reactions, lymphoma, rapid tumor growth, and immune deficiency. Consideration of the effects of all the claimant's conditions, their effects on her functionality, along with the effects of her medications would most certainly qualify her for SSDI benefits if the facts of the case are properly adjudicated. Unhappily, such is often not the case and is thus grounds for appeal.

An additional judicial error is the failure to fully develop the claimant's file. It is the responsibility of both the claimant and the judge to request treatment records for all relevant impairments from all treating clinicians from approximately one year prior to the alleged onset date to the most recent treatment prior to the hearing. Judges frequently fail to pursue records, and claimants' Social Security files may be woefully inadequate to the task of determining disability. Claimants are at a disadvantage in the accumulation of treatment records. Clinicians and medical facilities often resist release of records, delay delivery, or simply ignore requests. Some offices and hospitals store their records with a third party and direct patients to request records from the third-party facilities, which adds a new dimension of complexity to be dealt with. Additionally, doctors' offices, hospitals, and other medical facilities typically demand payment for copying the records before agreeing to release them. Although some states require that a free and complete copy of relevant medical records be released to patients who have a claim for SSDI benefits, not all offices comply with these requests in a timely way. At facilities in states where such records are not made freely available, the costs for records may be prohibitive. Most importantly, the majority of applicants for Social Security disability programs are sick, medicated, weak, emotionally fragile, and financially disadvantaged. They lack the physical, emotional, and sometimes intellectual ability to track down records and convey them to Social Security. ALJs may request records, and Social Security will pay a "reasonable fee" of around 15 dollars for them, but medical offices and hospitals often ignore these requests. ALJs have subpoena power but no enforcement power, so it's not uncommon for records requests to fall through the cracks and be insufficiently pursued, judge's duty notwithstanding, due to the overwhelming population of disability applicants.

Even the most reasonable rationale to appeal an unfavorable decision is no guarantee that the decision will indeed be successfully appealed. In recent years, it has become increasingly unlikely that an appeal will result in a more favorable outcome. Presently, there is only a 13% likelihood that an unfavorable decision will be reversed on appeal or at remand.

Representation for Disability Insurance Benefits

The judge, although trained as an attorney and not a clinician, is making a determination as to the legitimacy of the applicant's claim based on medical evidence. The system is fraught with inequity, bias, ineffectiveness, and expediency, almost none of which operates in the claimant's favor. It is in applicants' best interest to engage a professional qualified to represent claimant at the hearing level. The Federal Code of Regulations specifies the qualifications for acceptable representation for disability claimants:[7]

> (a) You may appoint as your representative in dealings with us, any attorney in good standing who—
>
> (1) Has the right to practice law before a court of a State, Territory, District, or island possession of the United States, or before the Supreme Court or a lower Federal court of the United States;

(2) Is not disqualified or suspended from acting as a representative in dealings with us; and
(3) Is not prohibited by any law from acting as a representative.

(b) You may appoint any person who is not an attorney to be your representative in dealings with us if the person—

(1) Is generally known to have a good character and reputation;
(2) Is capable of giving valuable help to you in connection with your claim;
(3) Is not disqualified or suspended from acting as a representative in dealings with us; and
(4) Is not prohibited by any law from acting as a representative.

(c) We may refuse to recognize the person you choose to represent you if the person does not meet the requirements in this section. We will notify you and the person you attempted to appoint as your representative if we do not recognize the person as a representative.

Qualified individuals, attorneys, and nonattorneys may receive compensation for representation via direct payment from the claimant's back due benefits if a favorable or partially favorable decision is awarded. Representatives, whether attorneys or non-attorneys, are entitled to a fee of 25% of back due benefits up to a maximum of $6,000. Nonattorneys who provide Social Security disability representation may be called nonattorney representatives (NARs), accredited disability representatives (ADRs), or eligible for direct payment nonattorneys (EDPNAs). These professionals must pass an examination, earn annual continuing education credits in Social Security disability regulations, pass a background check, and carry professional liability insurance to maintain certification. The nonattorney program is administered for the SSA by CPS HR Consulting. Claimants' representatives may be self-employed, employed by a firm or company, contracted by firms or companies, or may operate as part of a nonprofit agency. There are benefits and disadvantages to these various avenues for representation, and claimants should feel free to explore their options. The most important criteria for representation include accessibility to the client, experience, knowledge of the hearing office and—hopefully—an understanding of the assigned judge's hearing style, understanding of the regulations, and willingness to be available to the client. The hearing process is confusing and arduous, and the representative should serve as a guide as well as an advocate. Furthermore, most ALJs require claimants to obtain representation at the hearing level. In my coauthor's experience, claimants who appear for a scheduled hearing without representation often have their cases continued by the judge until a representative is retained. Hearing offices generally maintain a list of representatives, most of whom are in local firms or affiliated with nonprofits. The list is not comprehensive or all-inclusive, and claimants are not restricted to selecting a representative from a hearing office list.

Notes

1. https://www.ssa.gov/OP_Home/cfr20/404/404-app-p02.htm. Appendix 2 to Subpart P of Part 404—Medical-Vocational Guidelines.
2. See chapter 2.
3. Evaluation of Disability in General, 20 C.F.R. §404.1520.
4. https://cpollardlaw.com/2016-social-security-disability-decision-statistics.
5. Federal Court SSR 13-1p; Titles II and XVI: Agency Processes for Addressing Allegations of Unfairness, Prejudice, Partiality, Bias, Misconduct, or Discrimination by Administrative Law Judges (ALJs).
6. "Substantial gainful activity" in 2018 is $1,180 per month for nonblind people and $1,970 for blind people.
7. Who May Be Your Representative, 20 C.F.R. §404.1705.

CHAPTER EIGHT

Claimants and Advocates: Navigating the Disability Determination Process

> The Torah does not just command us to give to the poor but to advocate on their behalf. We are told in Proverbs 31:9 to "speak up, judge righteously, champion the poor and the needy." We learn that *tzedakah*, helping fellow human beings in need, is not simply a matter of charity but of responsibility, righteousness, and justice. As Jews, we see a moral obligation to advocate for children, the elderly, the poor, the disenfranchised, the sick, the disabled, and the "stranger among us."
>
> —Religious Action Center of Reform Judaism

> Truly, I say to you, as you did it to one of the least of these my brothers, you did it to me.
>
> Matthew 25:31–46

Who applies for Social Security Disability? Workers who cannot work are the natural applicants for SSDI benefits. But there are different levels of workers. There are professionals whose special skills, talents, and training place them among the most highly compensated members of the workforce. Then there are those who have no special skills and who labor at menial, unskilled jobs and who are paid substantially less. Subsequently, those with the highest level of earnings may receive as much as

$2,861 per month from SSDI, while those whose earnings were low may have benefits so low that they can be augmented by SSI benefits to the maximum monthly benefit of $771. Currently, the average monthly benefit for disabled workers is $1,234.[1] Often, higher earners have private short- and long-term disability insurance, and others may have savings, investments, property, or other assets that may provide additional financial support. But a recent review of the average American family's financial condition found that 40% of Americans would be overwhelmed by a $400 emergency.[2] Many Americans live paycheck to paycheck due to rising costs and stagnant wages. A sudden injury or a chronic illness can make short shrift of whatever savings have been accrued by the worker, leaving the worker and any dependents without minimal resources for survival over the course of the disability determination process.

The disability determination process is a team enterprise. People who are ill or injured may lack the energy, persistence, or capacity to file applications and documents, meet deadlines, keep up with appointments, diagnoses, treatments, and procedures that are intrinsic to the Social Security disability programs. They may be so immersed in survival efforts—housing, food, medical treatment—that the process of obtaining disability benefits becomes a bridge too far. They will often require assistance at every level if they are able to realize success, receive benefits, and hopefully achieve some level of recovery.

The representative must rely on the claimant and the claimant's relationship with treating clinicians to obtain records and opinions. Representatives, like those they represent, may not have the financial resources to afford multiple treatment records from multiple sources. Some states mandate the release of treatment records at no cost to the patient who is applying for Social Security benefits or to the individual or company representing the patient. Some states, like our home state of California, recently amended its health and safety statutes to provide records at no cost to claimants only, not to their representatives, unless the representative is employed by a nonprofit not accepting a fee for representation. Thus, if the claimant engages a representative not affiliated with a nonprofit, the claimant may need to make the request for records.

There are no requirements to compel treating clinicians to offer professional opinions regarding their patients' functional limitations other than their consciences and the Hippocratic oath advising them to "first do no harm." Some clinicians are willing to complete *residual functional capacity* (RFC) questionnaires or provide narrative reports in support of their patients' claims as their duty and as part of the cost of doing business. Others may charge for their time. Still others will refuse to offer opinions.

The representative may recommend that the client consult with another clinician who may be more willing to render an opinion. Some representatives may recommend an independent medical evaluation (IME). This would be a one-time appointment with a specialist in the discipline most compatible with the claimant's primary complaint. The clinician would examine the claimant, review all treatment records, write a comprehensive narrative report, and, if requested, complete an RFC questionnaire. This procedure is more extensive than the consultative examination offered by Social Security. It can also be quite expensive, costing from $500 to $2,500, depending on the claimant's impairments, the specialty of the clinician, the number of pages of medical records to review, the type of examination required, and the length and detail of the narrative report. Such evaluations have not demonstrated themselves to be influential in the decision-making process, and many ALJs deem them to be little more than bought-and-paid-for support. In my coauthor's experience, such an evaluation and subsequent report by a treating clinician are much more valuable. If the clinician is unwilling to provide this service at no additional cost and if the claimant has the capacity to pay for such a comprehensive report, it could make the difference between winning or losing the disability claim. On the other hand, there are no guarantees that such an investment will reap positive results. The clinician's report must be objective and supported by the treatment records, and it might not be completely supportive of the claimant's allegations of disability. Careful consideration of the value of such an action must be made in consultation with the representative based on the representative's knowledge of the assigned judge, the political makeup of the claimant's place of residence, the strength of the claimant's case, and the claimant's ability to pay for it.

Planning for Disaster

In today's world, everyone appears to be preparing for retirement with the abundant opportunities for saving and investing advertised on television, radio, and the internet. We all optimistically assume we will retire from our jobs at the appropriate age and enjoy a comfortable retirement living off our 401(k)s, pensions, and Social Security. However, an August 27, 2018, survey by CNBC reported that 21% of Americans have no retirement savings and an additional 10% have less than $5,000 in savings. Twenty-five percent of respondents reported having savings in excess of $200,000 and 16% between $75,000 and $199,999. The average retirement savings was $84,821, far less than the recommended minimum retirement savings of $1,000,000. The main obstacles to savings were identified as stagnant earnings, increased cost of living, other financial priorities, and unexpected financial emergencies.[3] Even fewer people are prepared for illness or injury that may cut their working life short.

The reality is that our workforce is aging, and, as we age, we are more prone to illness and injury. We need a plan so that if disaster strikes, we have a strategy for survival. As we have discussed in previous chapters, obtaining SSDI benefits is uncertain and dependent on many variables beyond our control. The process is complicated, confusing, and most importantly, time-consuming. When claimants become too incapacitated to sustain full-time employment, they lose not only income but usually their health insurance coverage as well. Thus, during this extended period between job loss, applying for benefits, and a hearing that may or may not resolve some of their most pressing issues, the claimant's health is strained further with less access to appropriate and continuous treatment. It is not uncommon for claimants to have drained their savings, borrowed from friends and family, and still been unable to support themselves and receive adequate ongoing medical treatment while they await a decision on their application for benefits.

Furthermore, some individuals, particularly those who are self-employed, tend to underreport personal income, paying themselves at a lower salary than justified but paying for personal expenses through their business or simply not reporting income earned "under the table" in order to reduce their tax burden. While this may make good financial sense in the short term, it is important to remember that Social Security benefits, whether for disability or retirement, are based on earnings as reported to the Internal Revenue Service. The lower the reported income, the lower the benefit the worker will receive at a time when it is most needed. A lower reported income may reduce one's tax burden, but it can spell disaster when the worker is no longer capable of work.

This situation is exemplified by Dan P., who was a self-employed sales representative for a women's ready-to-wear company. He traveled throughout his territory three weeks out of the month for 40 years. Although he made an excellent living and provided very well for his family, according to the earnings reported to the IRS, his income appeared to be in the middle-class category. Dan had very high expenses related to work that, on the advice of his accountant, he was able to offset as deductions on his personal income taxes to further reduce his annual tax burden, and he made tax-exempt contributions to his union pension fund with the expectation that he and his wife would be well cared for in their "golden years." Sadly, the union pension on which he relied did not materialize: the union went bankrupt in the 1980s, just before Dan reached the age of

65, hence he continued working for as long as he was able. When Dan was forced to retire due to deteriorating health at the age of 75 in 1995, his OASDI benefit was $900 a month. His wife had not worked outside the home during their 53-year marriage but received $450 a month from Social Security based on Dan's earnings record. Both Dan and his wife had significant age-related health issues that, despite having Medicare, cost them more than $900 a month for prescriptions alone. Ultimately, Dan and his wife exhausted their savings and were forced to move in with their daughter and her family in their final years. These were not exactly the golden years they anticipated. Finally, after Dan passed away in 2005 just short of their 63rd wedding anniversary, his wife was left with only the $900 a month in Social Security to which Dan had been entitled, for the last five years of her life. When the Social Security beneficiary dies, the surviving spouse receives only the benefit of the higher earner, even though the survivor's cost of living is likely to increase due to worsening health conditions and age-related incapacity. She remained with her daughter's family for those last five years.

Workers would be wise to carefully interview accountants, financial advisors, and other professionals with whom they consult for financial planning and be sure the professional is well-versed in Social Security benefits and their role in developing a protective financial strategy. Women historically have lower Social Security benefits because they often earn less than their male counterparts, they are more likely to take extended time away from work to bear and raise their children and to take care of disabled or elderly parents, they are more likely to work part-time or modified schedules, and they are more likely to hold less well-paying jobs. Women should also understand that under Social Security regulations, they (or men who earn less than their spouse) are entitled to approximately one-half of their spouses' retirement benefit as long as they were married for at least 10 years. This is true even for divorced couples or widows and widowers.

Survival Strategies

The most likely scenario after applying for SSDI is that the claimant will be denied at the initial and reconsideration levels and will need to get to the hearing level for the best chance of obtaining benefits. Thus the applicant will need to be financially and medically sustained for at least two years. Paradoxically, people who are sick or injured will frequently experience increased expenses at the same they are experiencing diminished income. Those who live independently and are their own sole support may be in the most tenuous position unless they have abundant savings adequate to sustain them for at least two years. But even for claimants who were not the primary breadwinners in their family, the loss of a second income may be disastrous to the family. The family mortgage or tuition for children may be reliant on the claimant's income.

Most people receive health insurance as a benefit of employment that is fully paid or partially paid by the employer. When employees cease working, their insurance is generally terminated. The employee may be offered health insurance coverage through the Consolidated Omnibus Budget Reconciliation Act (COBRA) of 1985. This program provides for up to 18 months of insurance coverage; however, the premiums for this coverage are not underwritten by the employer and the cost may be prohibitive. Health insurance through private policies as well as plans available through the Affordable Care Act (ACA) (also known as Obamacare) are being eroded by the current administration and may, by the time this book is published, exclude preexisting conditions entirely or cover them only at extra cost. The ACA has been found unconstitutional by a Texas Supreme Court justice, and, as of this writing, its future is as yet unclear. This case will likely be referred to the Supreme Court, but the administration has advised that the ACA will remain in place until that time.

Individuals should familiarize themselves with any programs available through their city, county, or state that provide disability benefits. Most states offer some short-term disability relief. State sponsored DI benefits are typically limited to approximately two-thirds of the claimant's monthly earnings for a maximum of one year. Usually, applicants must apply for state disability within a year of their last employment. Generally, no health insurance benefit is included. Some individuals resort to applying for unemployment benefits. People do what they must to survive, but applying for and receiving unemployment insurance benefits require applicants to attest to being able to work and willing to actively pursue jobs for as long as they receive benefits or until the benefits are exhausted. This may create problems at the hearing level, where the judge may challenge the claimants' credibility based on a history of lying to obtain unemployment benefits. Of course, claimants could reasonably report that they were willing to work if a job could be found that accommodated their capacity for exertional or nonexertional activities. But the matter would still be resolved at the discretion of the judge.

If the claimant is a member of a union or works for a company, short- or long-term DI may be available as a benefit of union membership or employment. If not, and if financially feasible, it may be worth the investment to obtain a private DI policy. These policies typically provide income replacement or a portion thereof for a period of time. The period of coverage is often less for psychological disability than physical disability. These short- and long-term policies define disability more liberally than Social Security does, and most such policies require beneficiaries to apply for Social Security disability benefits to subrogate the private policy's losses.

For injuries or medical or psychological conditions that are sustained in the course of one's work or on the work premises, workers' compensation may be available to the worker. Generally, workers' compensation provides money and health care for the specific injury or illness directly attributable to the work or workplace. Thus the worker may still require health insurance for other medical or mental disorders unrelated to the on-the-job injury or illness. As an example, Sylvia J. experienced a slip-and-fall injury while performing her job as a retail store clerk. She suffered an injury to her back and hip and was transported to the hospital by ambulance, where emergency room doctors assessed her injuries and determined she had fractured her hip and two vertebrae in her lumbar spine. While she was hospitalized, she suffered a stroke due to an occluded carotid artery. Although workers' compensation benefits covered her care for her fractured hip and back, it denied coverage for expenses related to her stroke or its treatment since the injury was considered noncontributory to the stroke.

Veterans of the uniformed services who have a medical or psychological disorder, whether service-connected or not, or an injury or illness that occurred or was exacerbated while on active duty or training for duty, can receive care at any Veterans Administration Medical Center. Veterans may apply for VA disability benefits for any service-connected injury or condition. However, disability benefits may only be allotted based on severe conditions that meet the VA criteria for disability and are based on the percentage of the whole body that is affected. Veterans may have one or several impairments. Each impairment is ascribed a number value, and the combined value of all impairments determine the veteran's disability rating. The lowest rating is 10% and the highest 100%. Veterans receiving VA disability benefits may also apply for and receive SSDI benefits. However, the disability determination for these programs are very different, and qualification for one does not guarantee qualification for the other, although some circuits, including the 9th Circuit, may consider receipt of VA disability benefits as part of the disability determination process.

All claimants feel that time is of the essence, and the seemingly interminable wait for the disability determination process to play out can be extremely stressful for people in desperate circumstances. In some instances, it may be possible to either accelerate the hearing schedule or bypass the hearing by requesting the ALJ to render a favorable decision based on the existing record.

A claimant or the claimant's representative can write a *dire need* letter to the Office of Hearings Operations (OHO) or directly to the ALJ if assigned. Through this correspondence, the claimant may request an accelerated hearing date if significant financial need can be demonstrated. An example of circumstances that justify dire need include house foreclosure; eviction from a rented home or apartment; inability to pay for utilities, with the expectation that they will be cut off; or inability to pay for necessary medical treatment, including essential medication. The dire need letter should include the specific financial hardship(s) with evidence of same including notices of foreclosure or eviction, past due utility bills, and bank statements.

Another strategy for facilitating faster response times for Social Security and OHOs is for the claimant or the claimant's representative to contact the claimant's congressional representative and request a congressional inquiry of the claim for disability benefits. When a congressperson indicates interest in a constituent's claim, the OHO, ALJ, and staff are obligated to assign high priority to such inquiries, investigate the rationale for the inquiry, and respond to the congressperson and staff promptly, accurately, and courteously.[4]

Finally, if the claimant's case is strong, the individual's medical or psychological condition is worsening, and the existing evidence may support a fully favorable finding without the claimant's appearance, the claimant's representative may submit an *on the record* (OTR) request addressed to the Chief ALJ at the appropriate Office of Hearings Operations if a hearing judge has not been assigned, or to the assigned ALJ. An OTR is not appropriate in all cases, and a claimant's representative will use this tool only when it is in the claimant's best interest. In general, the claimant's appearance at a hearing can demonstrate the severity of the incapacity and put a human face on the case for disability. Even if the ALJ denies a finding based on the OTR, it does not interfere with the claimant's appearance at a scheduled hearing, and the OTR may trigger an acceleration of the scheduling process.

Common Mistakes Claimants Make

Delaying Application for SSDI Benefits

People who are sick or injured generally believe they will recover their health and be able to return to the workforce, so considering applying for

Social Security disability benefits is not their first impulse. Some people will apply for workers' compensation when applicable, short-term DI benefits when available, or state disability benefits with the expectation that they will be able to return to work by the time such benefits are exhausted. Thus the number one mistake claimants make is delaying their application for Title II benefits. Several concerns are at issue. First, because the process of obtaining Social Security is so lengthy and obstructive, the sooner application is made, the better. If the claimant recovers before receiving a hearing date, the application can be withdrawn. But if there is no improvement, or at least enough improvement to trigger a return to work, the claimant's place in line is secured. This is not just a survival issue. The sooner the claimant applies for benefits, the sooner medical records can be accessed, and the more likely the claimant will be able to enlist the support of treating clinicians. The longer the claimant is unemployed, the more likely it is that fewer treatment options will be available. If insurance is lost, access to the claimant's doctors may be lost as well. Clinicians may be more cooperative with the disability determination process while the claimant is an active patient and still paying for services.

Also, Social Security looks at three relevant dates as they relate to disability benefits: alleged onset date (AOD), application date, and date last insured (DLI). The AOD is used to determine eligibility for Medicare. It is typically the date that either the claimant stopped work altogether or the date that the claimant stopped receiving earnings. Claimants for SSDI must be disabled for at least five months before they can receive cash benefits from SSDI. Some workers may be on sick leave or take a leave of absence under the Family and Medical Leave Act (FMLA) or receive short-term disability payments but not actually terminate employment until a later date, so their AOD may not actually coincide with their last official day of work. Disability beneficiaries are eligible for Medicare 29 months from the onset of disability. The regulation actually states 24 months, but there is an additional 5-month waiting period calculated from the AOD. The DLI represents the last date the claimant is covered for SSDI benefits. SSDI is like any other insurance, meaning the policyholder must be insured upon becoming too disabled to work. Typically, the DLI extends beyond the date last worked, or the date last paid, and, depending on the claimant's earnings record, can be as much as five years into the future after the claimant stops working. When claimants delay application for benefits, they may find themselves with their DLI in the past. Thus they have the more difficult task of demonstrating they met Social Security's definition of disability before their DLI. Furthermore, new symptoms, diagnoses, and limitations may not be considered, and the judge may find that the claimant did not meet the disability criteria before the DLI and is thus not entitled to SSDI benefits, although the judge may make the determination that the claimant is now disabled and is eligible for SSI if the financial criteria are met. On the other hand, if the claimant applies as soon as work becomes impossible, ongoing symptoms, diagnoses, complications, and limitations may be considered as continuing or complicating factors of the original complaint. Also, claimants who make application sooner rather than later may have some income replacement through workers' compensation or state disability while their SSDI applications are processed, and may be able to extend their access to continuity of care, support their household, and forestall making drastic changes such as selling their home, moving in with relatives, applying for general relief, requesting food assistance, and taking other steps that add stress and discomfort to an already overwhelming situation.

SSI beneficiaries do not need to deal with the AOD or DLI. Their application date is also the date used to determine the date they are considered to have become too disabled to work. If the claimant began the application process prior to completing the application, the date the process was begun is called the protective filing date, which can add to the claimant's eligibility for receiving current benefits and becomes the earliest date for calculating back due benefits. SSI benefits are paid the first month after the application or protective filing date.[5]

Not Appealing Denial at Initial or Reconsideration Stage

Yet another common mistake made by claimants is giving up after receiving denials at the initial or reconsideration stages. Some claimants feel ashamed that they have been denied benefits, taking that denial as a sign that they are not truly disabled or believed. Others attempt a return to work because they do not believe they can wait for a hearing for the possibility of a favorable decision. But even for claimants who feel able to return to work, it is worthwhile to appeal to the hearing level if their medical or psychological condition has lasted for more than 12 months. Even when claimants find they can sustain employment for nine months or longer, consecutively or cumulatively, because their condition has improved, they may still be eligible for a closed period of disability. The claimant who is unable to sustain employment for at least nine months cumulatively within a 60-month time frame, which would represent a trial work period, may be eligible for continuing disability benefits. It is always wise to appeal to the next level of consideration unless there is certainty of medical improvement significant enough to support a long-term return to work and if the five-month waiting period has been exhausted.

Missing Deadlines

Missing important deadlines is yet another error common to claimants. Claimants are afforded 60 days to request an appeal of a denied application, request a denial for reconsideration, request for a hearing before an ALJ, or appeal a judge's decision. Missing deadlines may result in a dismissal of the claim unless there is good cause for the deadline to have been missed. When claimants miss a deadline, they sometimes walk away from their claim and stop pursuing it. They may attempt a return to work or try to survive without the assistance Social Security can provide. If their efforts fail, they may start the application process all over again, but, as previously noted, this may result in a diminution of benefits due to the passage of time that may exceed the date last insured, leave the claimant with "stale" medical records, and make it more difficult to obtain new evidence. It may be possible to reinstate an earlier onset date if the claimant reapplies, but that is at the discretion of the Administration.

Assessing Clinicians

When potential clients request representation, my coauthor always asks, "Do the doctors who treat you support your application for disability?" to which they almost always respond, "Of course!" Unfortunately, we have learned this optimistic assessment of the treating clinicians is sadly off base. Many clinicians are wary of providing any service for which they are uncompensated, particularly when it comes to offering professional opinions to Social Security. Other clinicians may work as part of a medical practice whose policy is to deny the provision of professional opinions for the purpose of facilitating the disability determination process. Thus, early in the professional relationship with providers, it may be wise to ask the clinician's opinion on SSDI or SSI, whether they understand Social Security disability programs, and if they have or would support patients who are eligible for those programs. It is important for claimants to understand their clinician's perspective and to consider changing clinicians to someone more receptive before it may become necessary to make application.

Clinicians may be reluctant to offer professional opinions regarding their patient's limitations resulting from the effects of illness, injury, or treatment. They may be concerned that offering opinions that suggest the patient meets disability criteria may interfere with reimbursements for services rendered to their patients who are Medicare or Medicaid beneficiaries. There is a relationship between these agencies and the SSA, but, to our knowledge, clinicians who treat Medicare and Medicaid patients have not been penalized for offering supportive opinions on behalf of their patients applying for Social Security disability programs. Some clinicians who are asked to provide professional opinions may fear the impact such opinions can have on their professional liability. Others may be politically antagonistic toward "entitlements" and be unwilling to cooperate with a system to which they are philosophically opposed. And some clinicians are unwilling to provide a service that is not reimbursable. While it may be possible for some claimants to pay for the clinician's time to complete a RFC questionnaire that translates symptoms and their treatment into the language of Social Security Disability, most do not have the financial resources to do so. Whatever the clinician's position with regard to Social Security, it is better for the patient to know sooner rather than later so as to be able to plan for future concerns. For example, an individual may be diagnosed with type 2 diabetes, which is a controllable and relatively benign condition as long as it is monitored and treated. But despite compliance with medical advice, diabetes can worsen and thus create potentially debilitating conditions such as cardiovascular disease, blindness, and kidney failure, leading to limitations so severe that full-time competitive work becomes moot. A patient would do well to carefully interview prospective physicians while the patient is in relatively good health rather than wait and discover, while in crisis, that the physician's position on Social Security disability benefits is unsupportive. Also, while clinicians may be willing to provide professional opinions on behalf of their patients, they may be employed by a practice that does not permit them to do so. Thus the policy of the clinician's practice should be examined with a mind toward preparing for a potential health crisis.

Treatment and Opinions

Applicants for Social Security disability programs are often in a veritable catch-22 situation. On the one hand, they may have lost their medical insurance and must allocate all available resources to survival expenses such as food and shelter. On the other hand, without treatment, their health suffers more, and they do not have evidence of their ongoing disability. It is of paramount importance for claimants to pursue treatment, not only to obtain support for their claim but for their own well-being, to prevent further deterioration, realize some quality of life, and obtain the most achievable level of recovery. To that end, it is necessary to explore all publicly available treatment resources, including mental health clinics, medical clinics, and dental clinics. Most metropolitan areas offer one or more health centers that offer free or sliding-scale services to financially distressed and uninsured people. A claimant who is a veteran of the U.S. uniformed services and has better than a less-than-honorable discharge can obtain treatment through the Veterans Administration. These resources can often be quite good, and opportunities for developing professional relationships with clinicians and staff are more likely than in hospital emergency departments.

Although hospital emergency departments are excellent for emergent care, they cannot be relied upon for preventive treatment or continuity of care. Emergency departments are frequently staffed by a rotating group of medical students, interns, and residents. Some may simply authorize continuation of prior treatment based on existing diagnoses, while others may make entirely new diagnoses and prescribe different treatment. Not only can this have disastrous results but there is no opportunity to develop a personal relationship with clinicians and staff who, upon learning more about the patient, may gain greater insight into the patient's lifestyle, stressors, nutrition, social support system, capacity for self-care, intelligence, judgment, and other factors that can affect health and health care. Emergency departments are also very expensive and discourage reliance on their services for other than emergency situations.

Many communities offer free or low-cost mental health services, including psychiatric and psychotherapy services. The clinical staff is generally well-equipped to treat severe mental illnesses, and those so afflicted will often find knowledgeable and compassionate care and support for applicants for disability benefits. They may also have resources for additional services such as housing and food support.

Universities with medical schools, dental schools, chiropractic schools, and postgraduate psychology programs may offer free or low-cost services provided by students and supervised by faculty who are licensed to practice medicine, dentistry, chiropractic services, and psychological services. Medical and dental schools often offer free or low-cost clinics to give students practical experience. Postgraduate psychology students may provide testing and therapy services under supervision. Sometimes service is limited to students, faculty, and staff. However, other programs may be open to the public. Furthermore, some medical schools and pharmaceutical companies engage in research of certain medical and psychological conditions. An individual who has a condition being researched, and meets the criteria for participation in the research, may have the opportunity to receive free treatment, interact with specialists who may be able to refer them to clinicians willing to treat them longer-term, and, in some cases, be compensated for their time and travel expenses. Research opportunities may be announced through media outlets or can be located on the websites of medical schools and pharmaceutical companies.

Most pharmaceutical companies offer patient-assistance programs to make prescription drugs accessible to financially disadvantaged patients. They generally require completion of a comprehensive application that provides details of the patient's health and financial status to determine if the criteria established for assistance is met. Some medications may require supervision by the prescribing physician, who may be needed to take on a gatekeeper role to dispense and monitor the medicine. Patients may participate in more than one patient-assistance program if they are prescribed multiple medications manufactured by different pharmaceutical companies. This is certainly an option worth exploring, since medication represents a major portion of health-care expense.

Clinicians do not typically think of their patient's conditions in terms of how the patient's symptoms limit ability to perform basic work activities, so their opinions are generally restricted to diagnoses, prognoses, treatment planning, prescribed medications, and medical interventions. However for Social Security's purposes, professional opinions refer to a clinician's assessment of the patient's ability to perform the basic functions of work, which include their patient's minimal physical capacity to sit, stand, walk, lift, carry, bend, stoop, kneel, push, pull, reach (including overhead reaching), and use one's hands for fine and gross manipulations. Opinions regarding their patient's ability to perform the nonexertional components of all work must also be addressed, such as the ability to concentrate for extended periods, pay attention, understand, remember and carry out simple instructions, perform within a schedule, make simple work-related decisions, adapt to changes in the workplace, work in cooperation and coordination with coworkers, tolerate typical work stressors, and interact appropriately not only with coworkers but also with supervisors and the public. Claimants whose clinicians indicate severe impairments that limit their ability to engage in necessary exertional and nonexertional work activities are at a more advantageous position than claimants without such support.

Social Security will typically send clinicians a brief questionnaire with requests for records. The purpose of the questionnaire is for the clinician to express an opinion regarding how the claimant's condition, symptoms, and treatment affects that patient's RFC. Unfortunately, few clinicians respond to this request. Likewise, claimants' representatives may also request their clinician to complete a similar but usually more extensive questionnaire to translate clinical findings into the language of Social Security. Patients have a different relationship with their treatment providers than a representative could, thus clinicians are more likely to respond to a patient's request than a representative's. Still, few providers respond to these requests. My coauthor usually suggests that the client bring the questionnaire to an appointment and ask the provider to complete it during the visit. The questionnaire can be instructive for the clinician providing relevant information not typically considered during the course of scheduled appointments, and the benefit to the patient may be priceless.

Notes

1. https://www.investopedia.com/ask/answers/082015/what-are-maximum-social-security-disability-benefits.asp.
2. *Report on the Economic Well-being of U.S. Households for 2018*, https://www.cnbc.com/2019/05/23/millions-of-americans-are-only-400-away-from-financial-hardship.html.
3. https://www.cnbc.com/2018/08/27/1-in-3-americans-have-less-than-5000-dollars-saved-for-retirement.html.
4. HALLEX, chapter I-1-6.
5. SI 00601.009 Application Effective Date.

CHAPTER NINE

The Past, Present, and Future: Public Policy and Social Security

> If a free society cannot help the many who are poor, it cannot save the few who are rich.
>
> —John F. Kennedy, Inaugural Address, January 20, 1961

With an already overburdened Social Security system, we are anticipating an increasing number of claimants as the baby boomer generation reaches retirement age and beyond. As concerns increase regarding the ongoing solvency of the SSA trust funds and the Medicare program in the face of rising numbers of participants and increasing costs, there has been much speculation that without significant adjustments, these social programs will fail. Presently, one political party favors raising the tax base of the wealthiest citizens while the opposing party advocates for privatization. There are, however, alternatives to these considerations that could sustain these essential social programs into the foreseeable future. In order to consider these options, we must first explore the programs themselves and what each entails.

The SSA was established under President Franklin Delano Roosevelt in direct response to the hardships resulting from the Great Depression in the United States. A program to provide income to retirees was signed into law on August 14, 1935. The plan was to provide economic security to American workers that would supplement savings or pensions when the worker was no longer able to perform a job. At the time of enactment, retirement age was 65 years. However, for individuals born in 1930, the median life expectancy was 58 years for men and 62 years for women. Thus many people never lived long enough to collect their Social Security benefit, and, if they did receive it, it was not for long. However, the life expectancy for individuals in the United States has risen almost every year since 1930 so that children born in 2007 can expect to live to a median age of 77.9 years. These people can expect to receive Social Security benefits for at least 10 years. The Medicare bill, which added medical insurance to the retirement benefit, was signed into law by President Lyndon Baines Johnson in 1965. Over time, Social Security income has become the primary support for American retirees, many of whom have outlived their savings and private retirement benefits. And today, many private health insurance benefits automatically terminate or transition to secondary insurance when the policyholder reaches age 65, even if that individual is still employed. Also, Medicare premiums are significantly lower than private or employer-supported group health insurance premiums, encouraging voluntary transfer to Medicare and increasing the burden on Medicare.

In addition to providing income and health insurance to our senior citizens, the SSA offers disability benefits for individuals who meet the criteria established by the Administration. The program for providing disability benefits under Social Security was enacted in July 1956. From that time forward, the process of applying for and obtaining disability benefits has been fraught with problems that have permitted nondisabled individuals to receive benefits while simultaneously denying benefits to individuals who are truly and profoundly disabled under the definition of disability adopted by the SSA. At the root of these serious problems is the fundamental injustice upon which the system is based: delay. Many individuals applying for benefits, no matter how severe their medical or psychological condition, feel their claims are arbitrarily denied, forcing them to either continue through a convoluted appeals process or to abandon their quest for relief. This belief stems from the lack of clarity provided to the public regarding how the SSA processes claim, how disability is defined, and the time it takes for records to be received and organized, reviewed, and responded to, usually with a denial and the need to appeal that decision. The process is so complicated and obstructive that the vast majority of claimants must retain the services of advocates to represent their interests, thus depriving them of a percentage of their desperately needed financial resources.

At issue is the entitlement of individuals to seek benefits under SSDI or SSI benefits, the definition of disability under Social Security, the bureaucracy of the disability determination process, the accessibility and compliance of the health-care professions, and the confusing disability determination process. Because of these deficiencies, some people die before they obtain any relief. In an article that originally appeared in the *Milwaukee Journal Sentinel* on December 27, 2018, and subsequently in *USA Today*, reporter Mark Johnson recounted the story of Christine Morgan, a then 60-year-old woman diagnosed with fibromyalgia, spinal stenosis, diabetes, kidney disease, hypertension, and depression. Ms. Morgan filed for SSDI in October 2016, after her symptoms became so severe she could not sustain employment at any of her former jobs, including 10 years at the U.S. Department of Housing and Urban Development, five years working at an assessor's office in California, and jobs at McDonald's. Her claim for SSDI was denied at the application and reconsideration levels, and she appealed her denial on August 7, 2017. She was granted a hearing that took place more than a year later, November 7, 2018. At the time the article was published, she had not received a ruling on her claim. Johnson used Ms. Morgan's story to illustrate the delays at every level of the disability determination process that some claimants do not live to see resolved. As he wrote, "In fiscal year 2016, 8,699 Americans died on the disability insurance waiting list. That number rose to 10,002 in 2017." Johnson further cited the SSA's own revealing figures: "According to the Social Security Administration, the average wait for an appeal to be heard and decided is 540 days across the country."[1]

Other claimants may become hopelessly and permanently disabled without hope of meaningful recovery due to delays. Conditions that could have been successfully treated and from which afflicted individuals might have been able to undergo significant enough rehabilitation to rejoin the workforce are irrevocably worsened through the progressive nature of the disease process and lack of continuity of care with appropriate medical interventions. My coauthor is currently representing a client who has been experiencing extreme orthopedic impairment since adolescence. He experiences chronic back pain secondary to congenital spinal stenosis impinging on the nerve root and interfering with his ability to stand and walk, and recurrent herniated nucleus pulposus. He has undergone multiple surgical interventions, including several hemilaminectomies, laminectomies, microdiscectomies, and medial facetectomy and foraminotomy, all at L4, L5, and S1 (Lumbar spine, fourth and fifth vertebrae, and sacrum. Together, L5 and S1 are the lumbosacral joint.). Despite these interventions, the client at the age of 28 experiences chronic back pain, weakness and numbness in his bilateral lower extremities, and urinary incontinence. Due to his impairments, he has been unable to engage in sustained full-time employment, and, since his last nine-hour surgery, his surgeon has advised that he cannot endure the physical exertion or stress of a competitive work setting. Although he is in desperate financial straits, having exhausted his savings, and has been forced to move back into his mother's house, where he is unable to contribute to the household, he is even more anxious to obtain Medicare health insurance in the hope that it will avail him of more and better health care that can eventually improve his health and return him to the workforce. He has been forced to rely on MediCal (California's version of Medicaid), which is accepted by very few physicians and facilities due to its low rate of reimbursement.

The SSA defines disability as the inability to work at either the full-time job(s) one was able to perform for the 15 years prior to the alleged onset of disability or any other job as a consequence of a medical condition that has lasted or is expected to last for at least 12 months or result in death (see Appendixes A and B). And while this may appear to be a rather straightforward and uncomplicated definition, it is extremely difficult to provide the level of evidence required to support allegations of disability under this premise. These obstacles to obtaining the benefits to which claimants are entitled exhaust their financial, physical, and emotional endurance over the course of a process that can take many months and even years to conclude. Many of the problems are logistic, and others are the logical outcome of an overburdened, understaffed, and poorly defined process.

The application procedure for Social Security disability benefits is not user-friendly for the general public. The information for claimants is confusing such that if and when the need should arise, potential claimants are unprepared to make a timely application and thus may lose their window of opportunity to prove their disability status. An application for Social Security Disability or SSI benefits may be filed at any time. However, the greater duration of time between the onset of the disabling impairments and the application date, the more difficult it is to provide evidence for the disabling conditions. Some individuals delay application because they expect they will recover from their medical or mental impairments and be able to return to the workforce. Others are simply unaware of the program, its requirements, or their eligibility for benefits. Still others are ashamed or embarrassed by their incapacity and stigmatized by their diagnoses, and they only apply for benefits when all other options have been exhausted. During that period between injury or onset of illness and application for benefits, these people may lose their health insurance, reducing their access to needed and appropriate health care. Only when recovery is not forthcoming or patients become aware of their rights are they likely to apply for disability assistance. Since monetary benefits are calculated from the application date, individuals who delay application may lose months or years of eligibility and seriously erode their access to medical evidence that would support their claims. Depending on licensure and the state in which they practice, medical and mental health professionals are not required to indefinitely maintain treatment records of inactive patients. Thus a delay in requesting medical records may result in their unavailability and—thus—the loss of substantive medical support for their alleged impairments.

Another concern is the date last insured (DLI) with regard to the timetable for qualifying for disability benefits. Workers pay into the Social Security system through payroll deduction. In essence, they are paying a premium for government-sponsored and administered disability and retirement insurance. The premiums are paid approximately five years into the future, depending on the consistency of the claimant's work and earnings history. Thus, a person who stops working in 2005 will likely have a DLI at the end of one of the quarters of 2010: March 31, June 30, September 30, or December 31. In order to qualify for SSDI benefits, individuals must demonstrate that their impairments met the established level of severity prior to that DLI. Since the DLI qualification is generally unknown to the public, claimants are frequently unprepared to address this issue. As a result, they may sometimes not meet the criteria under SSDI but may still qualify for SSI, depending on whether the economic criteria are met.

Individuals who lose health-care benefits due to loss of employment or other financial resources also typically lose their relationship with their long-term treating clinician and indeed with any continuity of care. Therefore, it may be impossible to obtain needed medical opinions in support of their disability claims. Without medical support in the form of consistent treating records and opinions, individuals have little or no chance to prove entitlement to disability benefits. Individuals without access to health insurance must generally rely on public health clinics, free clinics, and hospital emergency departments. Although medical records are maintained and can be obtained from such sources, the records typically reflect conflicting diagnoses, prescriptions, and treatment plans based on the provider of services. And such facilities are rarely willing to provide medical opinions for the disability determination process.

In fact, it is paradoxical that even when clinicians in private or public health venues agree or even suggest that their patient is appropriate for disability benefits, they are frequently unwilling to provide the necessary professional opinion in support of such claims. The SSA relies on both nonexamining and examining practitioners to grant or deny disability claims. Nonexamining clinicians review available medical records and make a determination without any personal contact with the claimant. Consultative examiners (CEs) are clinicians in the appropriate medical specialty who are charged with the task of reviewing available medical records and performing a physical examination or, if a psychologist, administering and interpreting psychological testing. Unfortunately, consultative examinations are generally perfunctory, records are often scanty or absent, and the end result is frequently a far less accurate assessment of the claimant's health status than would be made by the treating clinician.

Likewise, the testimony of a medical expert (ME) is sometimes required at the hearing level to interpret the medical records for the ALJ conducting the hearing and making a determination as to whether the claimant's impairment or impairments meets the criteria for a disabling medical or mental condition under the SSA guidelines. The ME's testimony is limited by the content of the medical records, including the assessment of the consultative examiner, and is thus not as likely to be consistent with the claimant's experience or the treating clinician's perspective of the issues. There may also be bias on the part of the medical expert. Physicians and psychologists may specialize in the same areas of expertise but hold differing views regarding severity, symptom management, and resultant limitations. For example, there have been controversies around whether conditions such as Lyme disease, fibromyalgia, and autism spectrum disorder can be considered disabling impairments that focus on generalizations rather than individual cases.

While the SSA is interested in both the claimant's diagnosis and the features and symptoms of the diagnosis and treatment, its particular focus is on the exertional (physical) limitations and nonexertional (psychological, cognitive, behavioral, emotional, and intellectual) limitations affecting the claimant's ability to perform work activities. Exertional limitations are measured by considering such questions as to how long an individual can sit, stand, or walk, how much the individual can lift or carry, the capacity to perform fine and gross manipulations with hands and fingers, and the ability to push, pull, bend, stoop, and kneel. Nonexertional limitations involve one's ability to concentrate, remember, perform tasks within a schedule, tolerate the stress inherent in the workplace, and other such activities associated with any full-time work performed within the competitive workforce. Thus it is specifically these kinds of limitations that the treating clinicians are requested to address. Individuals whose medical or psychological condition severely limits their ability to perform a full-time job within a competitive work setting are considered to be disabled under the SSA's guidelines.

What constitutes evidence in the medical records that supports disability determination? Let us first consider why treatment records are maintained. For practical purposes, medical records exist for only three reasons: to document the objective findings of treatment providers; to ensure continuity of care; and to justify medical decisions and actions for the purpose of insurance reimbursement, medical review board requirements, and liability questions for malpractice and other civil or criminal actions. Treatment records often include repetitive, arcane, and irrelevant minutia that may obfuscate or exaggerate the level of care rendered. Sometimes the documentation includes unnecessary detail as a means of protecting the provider or facility with overinclusion of data; at other times, it presents only the bare minimum of detail both in response to time pressures and to obscure the precise nature of the treatment provided. Records are maintained to reduce liability of the treating sources. Both over and underinforming can shield the provider by passing responsibility for interpretation of the records to the next treating source.

Treatment records document the findings of the providers based on laboratory tests, imaging, physical examination, mental status examination, observation, and patient complaints and feedback and the perspective they bring to the process. Different medical specialists may reach conflicting conclusions, often fueled by their relationship with the patient, their professional biases, and their stake in the outcome. For example, a surgeon may suggest that a patient's postsurgical prognosis is good, but that may be generated from the standpoint of the patient having survived the operation and not from any long-term recovery prospects. Responsibility for recovery may be foisted onto the postsurgical treatment and to the patient himself.

However, records may often be deliberately misleading, particularly when recorded for the purpose of insurance reimbursement rationalization or defending specific medical choices. For example, until the publication of the fifth edition of the *Diagnostic and Statistical Manual of the American Psychiatric Association* (*DSM*–5), the global assessment of functioning (GAF) was regularly used as a kind of subjective shorthand to describe the patient's level of social adaptation and psychological efficiency. Very low GAF scores—under 50—were used to signify incompetence or justify voluntary or involuntary hospitalization. Likewise, higher GAF scores were used to defend hospital discharge or deny disability. In reality, the GAF score is an estimation by the assessor. It is not based on any actual testing or true science. It is an opinion based on the patient's presentation and often on the provider's understanding, knowledge, and experience. And since the GAF can be incentivized as a justification for treatment or discharge when there is an advantage to the provider for either choice, the reliability of this device is questionable. Many times, during the 1980s and 1990s, my staff and I despaired of the "magic GAF" that was low enough to justify long-term psychiatric hospitalization until the patient's insurance ran out, at which point the GAF would magically rise just enough to justify discharge but leave the patient without the insurance resources to pursue outpatient treatment. As of the publication of the *DSM–5*, the GAF is no longer used and has been replaced by the World Health Organization Disability Assessment Schedule 2.0 (WHO-DAS 2.0). The WHODAS 2.0[2] is:

- a generic assessment instrument for health and disability;
- used across all diseases, including mental, neurological, and addictive disorders;
- short, simple, and easy to administer (5 to 20 minutes);
- applicable in both clinical and general population settings;
- a tool to produce standardized disability levels and profiles;
- applicable across cultures, in all adult populations; and
- directly linked at the level of the concepts to the International Classification of Functioning, Disability and Health (ICF).

WHODAS 2.0 covers six domains of functioning, including:

- cognition—understanding and communicating;
- mobility—moving and getting around;
- self-care—hygiene, dressing, eating, and staying alone;
- getting along—interacting with other people;
- life activities—domestic responsibilities, leisure, work, and school;
- participation—joining in community activities.

The WHODAS can be completed by a physician, psychologist, family member, or caregiver. Its acceptance as a diagnostic or predictive tool by the SSA is as yet unknown. Like the GAF, the WHODAS is subjective and reliant on the respondent's perspective.

There has been a long-standing debate between the political right and left about the notion of a government-facilitated social safety net. The left has sought to expand benefits to ensure the health, safety, and security of the population, whereas the right has repeatedly fostered campaigns designed to delegitimize Social Security programs and recategorize them as "entitlements." However, this was not always the case. During the 1984 presidential debates, Republican candidate Ronald Reagan defended Social Security when he proclaimed,

> Social Security, let's lay it to rest once in for all. . . . Social Security has nothing to do with the deficit. Social Security is totally funded by the payroll tax levied on employer and employee. If you reduce the outgo of Social Security, that money would not go into the general fund to reduce the deficit. It would go into the Social Security trust fund. So Social Security has nothing to do with balancing the budget or erasing or lowering the deficit.

Upon achieving office, Reagan promoted Social Security reform by tasking the Congress to eliminate fraud and abuse. Unfortunately, President Reagan also fulfilled his campaign promise of substantial tax breaks that especially impacted the wealthy as a means of implementing his "trickle-down" philosophy of the economy. However, when the tax breaks resulted in a significant addition to the federal deficit, the Congress used the Social Security Trust Fund surplus to pay for the deficits caused by his tax breaks for the rich. This act of raiding Social Security became traditional for Republican administrations and supported by Republican majority Congresses, and Reagan's example was emulated by President George Herbert Walker Bush, to fund the tax breaks under his administration, and President George Walker Bush, to fund both the Iraq war and his own tax breaks. Although there is an understanding that these funds will be repaid, the repayment will be from the general fund that is already overburdened with debt and underfunded by taxation. Under the current Trump administration, Social Security, Medicare, and the ACA are all under threat of diminished funding, reduced benefits, and restricted access (Rosenbaum, 2018).

Political perspectives further influence how social welfare programs flourish and are valued. The Republican political party platform reflects the conservative values of less government, lower taxes, and fewer regulations. Traditionally, Republicans have been socially and fiscally conservative, and they typically support governmental policies that promote personal responsibility, limited government, national defense, individual liberty, free markets, lower taxes, and traditional American values. The Democratic party, on the other hand, sees government as the primary mechanism for alleviating social injustice; supporting initiatives such as public education and social welfare programs to protect the poor, disabled, and disadvantaged through progressive taxation; and protecting individual and human rights and civil liberties of all people regardless of differences in race, ethnicity, culture, gender, or sexual orientation. The Republican party favors privatization, thus monetization of public programs ranging from prisons to education to Social Security, whereas the Democratic party is invested in maintaining the integrity of programs that serve the greater good by funding such initiatives through public monies supported by taxes.

Over time, we have seen the Social Security system become increasingly burdened as applicants for benefits increase and SSA personnel experience reductions in force. As a consequence, the wait times for decisions have increased and the rate of favorable decisions has decreased. Social Security provides statistical information regarding the annual applications for benefits and their determinations.[3] In 2015, there were 2,505,290 claimants who applied for disability benefits under Title II and Title XVI. Of that number of combined SSDI and SSI claims, 901,422 applicants were denied based on technical issues, 573,186 were denied on medical grounds, and 28,138 were denied for nonmedical reasons. A total of 607,175 claims were initially approved, but 2,077 claims were subsequently denied after a favorable decision was made, leaving a total of 605,098 approved claims. As of the date this information was published in July 2016, 393,292 claims were still pending a final decision, which likely means that they were appealed to the Appeals Council or federal district court. Claims awarded in 2015 amounted 28.7%. In 1999, the total number of applications was 1,265,037 of which 708,797 or 56.0% were awarded benefits. In 16 years, the numbers of SSDI and SSI applicants almost doubled, but the percentage of awards was almost half of what it was previously.

Denials subsequent to a favorable decision occur when the decision is reviewed by the Appeals Council where a problem may be found with the medical evidence, the claimant's earnings history, or some other factor not available to the ALJ at the time of the hearing. The ALJ may have based a decision on a clinician's opinion without substantiation in the medical records. Or the AC may find that the ALJ's decision was too generous based on the available facts. The AC may determine that the claimant was not disabled at the time of the DLI and only met the definition of disability after that date. Or there may be technical issues including citizen or permanent resident status, or even a fraudulent Social Security number. If there is an issue with medical evidence, it might have been avoided by better compliance on the part of the treating physicians, better record-keeping, and a better understanding of Social Security regulations, definitions, and the listings.

Pam notes that she has observed a reduction in efficiency at the SSA at the local level, reflected in less well-prepared exhibit files, communications problems with hearing offices, longer wait times for decisions following hearings, and longer wait times between receipt of fully favorable decisions and award of benefits. This has been attributed to a reduction in force among general staff at the SSA office and the Offices of Hearings Operations, too few administrative law judges, and a series of government shutdowns, most recently from December 22, 2018 through January 25, 2019, that interfered with processing new applications, obtaining treatment records, scheduling consultative examinations, scheduling hearings, and writing and delivering decisions.

However, the greatest challenge facing Social Security's programs for old age and disability benefits is its projected insolvency. For the SSA, solvency means the ability of its trust funds to pay all scheduled benefits on timely basis.[4] At present and based on current revenues, the SSA anticipates it will remain solvent until between 2033 and 2035, after which it will be able to meet only 76% of its scheduled benefits.[5] However, a subsequent report indicated the SSA will remain solvent through 2052.[6] The rapid depletion of the four trust funds is blamed on several converging issues: the baby boomer population's achieving retirement age, the lower U.S. birthrate, SSA tax rates at only 12.4%, stagnant wages, reduced workforce, and the cap on Social Security tax limited to only $132,900 of income as of January 1, 2019.[7]

The Administration has called for legislative action to rescue this essential social safety net, and several bipartisan proposals have been submitted by the House and Senate from 1993 to as recently as July 24, 2019.[8] Social Security's chief actuary (and former supervisory actuary) since 1993, Stephen C. Goss, ASA, MAA, has reviewed each of these proposals and responded via written memoranda regarding their efficacy. In general, most of these offerings have resulted in limited benefit to the system, and some have actually reduced the programs' long-term viability. However, elements of some of the proposals and the overall positive effects of two of them, which encompass these elements, show promise, if the Senate is receptive.

The Social Security 2100 Act (January 30, 2019), chaired by Representative John Larson and cosponsored by Senators Richard Blumenthal and Chris Van Hollen proposed the following:

- Section 101. Increase the first PIA[9] formula factor from 90 percent to 93 percent for all benefits payable for months of entitlement January 2020 and later, including benefits for those becoming newly eligible both before and after January 2020.

- Section 102. Use the Consumer Price Index for the Elderly (CPI-E) increase rather than the Consumer Price Index for Urban Wage Earners and Clerical Workers (CPI-W) increase to calculate the cost-of-living adjustment (COLA), effective for December 2019 and later COLAs. We assume this change would increase the COLA by an average of 0.2 percentage point per year.
- Section 103. Increase the special minimum PIA, beginning for workers who become newly eligible for retirement or disability benefits or die in 2020 or later. For workers becoming newly eligible or dying in 2020, the minimum PIA for 2020 for workers with 30 or more years of coverage (YOCs) is 125 percent of the annual poverty guideline for a single individual published by the Department of Health and Human Services for 2019, divided by 12. For workers becoming newly eligible or dying after 2020, the minimum PIA for their initial year of eligibility is increased by the growth in the national average wage index (AWI). For all affected workers, the minimum PIA is increased after their year of initial eligibility by the COLA.
- Section 104. Replace the current-law thresholds for federal income taxation of OASDI [Old-Age, Survivors, and Disability Insurance] benefits with a single set of thresholds at $50,000 for single filers and $100,000 for joint filers for taxation of up to 85 percent of OASDI benefits, effective for tax year 2020. These thresholds would be fixed and not indexed to price inflation or average wage increase. The amount of revenue from taxation of OASDI benefits that would be allocated to the HI Trust Fund will be at the same level as if the current-law computation (in the absence of this provision) were applied. The net amount of revenue from taxing OASDI benefits, after the allocation to HI, would be allocated to the combined Social Security Trust Fund.
- Section 201 and Section 202. Apply the combined OASDI payroll tax rate on covered earnings above $400,000 paid in 2020 and later. Tax all covered earnings once the current-law taxable maximum exceeds $400,000. Credit the additional earnings that are taxed for benefit purposes by: (a) calculating a second average indexed monthly earnings (AIME) reflecting only additional earnings taxed above the current-law taxable maximum, (b) applying a 2-percent factor on this newly computed AIME to develop a second component of the PIA, and (c) adding this second component to the current-law PIA.
- Section 203. Increase the combined OASDI payroll tax rate to 14.8 percent, fully effective for 2043 and later. The combined rate is increased by 0.1 percentage point each year starting in 2020, reaching the ultimate 14.8 percent rate for 2043 and later.
- Section 204. Beginning in 2020, establish a new Social Security Trust Fund by combining the reserves of the separate OASI and DI Trust Funds and managing all future financial operations of the program on a combined basis.

Chief Actuary Goss concluded that the effect of this Act would be as follows:

> For the 75-year (long-range) period as a whole, the current-law unfunded obligation of $13.2 trillion is replaced by a positive trust fund reserve of $2.1 trillion in present value assuming enactment of the proposal. This change of $15.3 trillion results from
>
> - a $18.9 trillion net increase in revenue (column 2), primarily from additional payroll tax, minus
> - a $3.7 trillion net increase in cost (column 3), primarily from the special minimum PIA provision, the change in computing the COLA, increases in current and future benefits from replacing the 90 percent factor in the PIA formula with 93 percent, and additional benefits from earnings taxed above the current-law taxable maximum.[10]

Chief Actuary Goss responded to a second proposal by Senator Van Hollen in reference to S. 1950, the "Strengthen Social Security by Taxing Dynastic Wealth Act of 2019" on June 25, 2019. This Act has only two propositions:

- Section 1. For the estate tax, gift tax, and generation skipping transfer (GST) tax, return the respective exemption thresholds and tax rates to 2009 levels for deaths after 2019 and gifts made after 2019, with those levels not indexed in future years. All proceeds from the estate tax, gift tax, and GST tax would go to the combined OASDI Trust Fund.
- Section 2. Combine the separate Old-Age and Survivors Insurance (OASI) and Disability Insurance (DI) Trust Funds into one Social Security Trust Fund effective January 1, 2020.

Chief Actuary Goss determined that enactment of the provision in section 1 alone "would improve the long-range OASDI actuarial balance by an estimated 0.58 percent of taxable payroll, and would improve the OASDI annual balance by 0.78 percent of payroll for the 75th projection year (2093)," whereas enactment of section 2 alone "would have a negligible effect (between −0.005 and 0.005 percent of taxable payroll) on the long-range OASDI actuarial balance and on the annual deficit for the 75th projection year (2093)."[11]

In summary, significant changes to the funding for the Social Security trust funds will likely protect its mission well into the future by raising the cap on earnings that are taxable for OASDI and Medicare. Furthermore, replacing the tax liability for Social Security recipients—from the current rate of 50% for incomes between $25,000 and $34,000 and up to 85% for more than $34,000 income for individuals filing separately and 50% tax for combined incomes of between $32,000 and $44,000 up to 85% for combined incomes over $44,000, with an increased income of $50,000 for single filers and $100,000 for joint filers for taxation of up to 85% of OASDI benefits, effective for tax year 2020—would effectively increase the value of OASDI benefits and raise many recipients up from poverty. Also, beneficiaries receiving retirement benefits are often still in the workforce, accounting for their higher earnings beyond what OASDI pays. These older workers continue to contribute to OASDI and Medicare through their payroll taxes and should not be penalized for continued productivity.

Not addressed in these proposals to increase the financial viability of Social Security is the effect of the reduced U.S. birthrate. With fewer workers to replace those who are retired or disabled, less in tax revenues is being collected to support the current system. A friendlier immigration system that includes permanent resident and guest worker programs would help to alleviate the strain on the Social Security trust funds by encouraging undocumented immigrants out of the shadows to undertake legitimate jobs that subscribe to federally mandated minimum wage and health and safety standards, and thereby to make contributions to the Social Security and Medicare trust funds.

Unfortunately, the legislative potential for saving Social Security is countered by the conservative majority in the Senate who are opposed to increased taxation and a fairer, more liberal immigration policy. They favor, in fact, privatizing Social Security and Medicare and, to that end, are reluctant to act in defense of the existing programs. Thus any protective actions or expansion of OASDI and Medicare hinge on the election of a Democratic majority in the Senate and retaining the current House majority.

Notes

1. "Turned Down for Federal Disability Payments, Thousands Die Waiting for Appeals to Be Heard," https://www.usatoday.com/story/news/nation/2018/12/27/thousands-die-waiting-social-security-disability-insurance-appeals/2420836002/.
2. https://www.who.int/classifications/icf/whodasii/en/.
3. https://www.ssa.gov/policy/docs/statcomps/di_asr/2016/sect04.html#chart11.
4. https://www.ssa.gov/policy/docs/ssb/v70n3/v70n3p111.html.
5. https://www.ssa.gov/OACT/solvency/index.html.

6. https://www.nytimes.com/2019/04/22/us/politics/social-security-medicare-insolvency.html.

7. https://www.ssa.gov/OACT/COLA/cbb.html.

8. https://www.ssa.gov/OACT/solvency/index.html.

9. "Primary insurance amount," the benefit due the retiring worker or SSDI beneficiary.

10. https://www.ssa.gov/OACT/solvency/LarsonBlumenthalVanHollen_20190130.pdf.

11. https://www.ssa.gov/OACT/solvency/CVanHollen_20190625.pdf.

Epilogue

> Let us realize the arc of the moral universe is long but it bends toward justice.
>
> —Martin Luther King Jr.

This book has presented an overview of the SSA's disability programs for clinicians and advocates. As the reader can see, the SSA incorporates both conventional health-care knowledge and thinking but also relies on a system of complex decision logic with its own distinct administrative rules and guidelines. Personally, I was not prepared for the requests for information that I began to receive from the SSA in the early 1980s after becoming a licensed psychologist in Texas. The patients who apply for SSA disability benefits are also often ill equipped for the ordeal of the application process. Both my coauthor and I hope that this book helps prepare other clinicians for their eventual interactions with the SSA. Ideally this book will also contribute to further discussion as to what professional competencies are needed among the various health-care disciplines that treat people with disabilities. In chapter 5 we summarized the "Core Competencies on Disability for Health Care Education" published by the Alliance for Disability in Health Care Education (2018). As we stated in chapter 5, these core competencies refer to practices that are consistent with the ADA and the Social Security Act (Alliance for Disability in Health Care Education, 2018). Familiarity with SSA policies prepares clinicians for developing treatment records that are meaningful and relevant if the patient becomes an SSDI claimant.

We encourage clinicians to consider these competencies and begin discussions of the fundamental and general competencies that should be encouraged or required within their respective professions. In addition to developing disability-related core competencies, health-care professionals might consider formulating practice guidelines and other policies that serve to better protect their patients with disabilities. For example, a disability-informed approach to clinical care might specifically address the initial phases of patient contact to include the patient's current capacity to perform activities of daily living, employment status, work activities description, education history, English fluency, and other information relative to subsequent questions of disability eligibility.

All health-care professionals have a legal and ethical obligation to respect their patients' privacy and confidentiality. Such policies are often initially discussed as part of the informed consent process where clinicians explain how they maintain privacy as well as the clarifying legitimate reasons that patients' information might be shared. When patients apply for SSA benefits, they also authorize the release of their health-care information and records, but it would often be helpful if clinicians and their patients had already begun a conversation about such a possibility early in their treatment relationship. Record-keeping policies and the availability of health records are often also discussed during the patient's giving informed consent. Patients need to know their clinicians' policies for allowing them to review their own records as well as the procedures for sending copies of records to their other health-care providers or to resources such as the SSA.

Throughout this book we have made the case that appropriate documentation is critical in disability determination. The best documentation usually comes from the patient's own treating professionals because those clinicians have the most thorough knowledge of the claimant and more opportunities to conduct longitudinal assessments over the course of the treating relationship. It is the history of the patient's treatment that informs the clinician of symptoms and their frequency and intensity, response to treatment, adverse effects of medication, and other information that could not be assessed with only a cursory examination. How and when do the diagnoses first appear? What particular signs and symptoms have been noted? Are there laboratory or other objective findings that confirm or disconfirm the patients reported symptoms? What is the expected prognosis and actual course of the illness over time? These questions require that clinicians carefully track and document work-related abilities and disabilities within their respective scope of practice.

In some cases, patients may need support and encouragement in seeking disability benefits if they have medically determinable impairments that are severe and cause limitations that prevent full-time work. Along the lines of the SAMHSA's SOAR program described in chapter 4, there are patients who may need support and possibly referrals to someone who can assist them in the application process. Additionally, patients will need to understand the process they are confronting, the likely length of time it will take for their claim to be processed, the likelihood of at least initial disapproval, the stigma of disability, and the loss of autonomy engendered by reduced income, debilitating symptoms, and impaired functioning (Whittle et al., 2017). Patients may need referrals to federal, state, and local programs that offer food and housing assistance, free and low-cost treatment, durable medical equipment, and patient-assistance programs for free and low-cost prescription drugs.

Chapter 5 explains the essential role of the treating clinician in the disability determination process and how the claimant's case can rise or fall on clinicians' cooperation through provision of detailed records that support their patient's allegations of disabling symptoms, and professional opinions that conform to the Administration's definition of disability. Chapter 6 focuses on psychological disability and how psychological factors can play a role in other disabling conditions, while chapter 7 describes the SSDI application process, hearings, and appeals. Chapter 8 provides advice to clinicians and advocates on how to negotiate the complexities of SSDI and SSI claims. Finally, in chapter 9, we address Social Security as public policy and how it is threatened by an aging workforce, financial and political constraints that interfere with customer service and expediency, and steps that may save OASDI into the future.

Our overriding message is that there should be a collaborative relationship between clinicians, the SSA, and the claimants' representatives in service to patients' legitimate applications for SSDI and SSI benefits. Furthermore, each life has value, and all individuals are entitled to live their best possible life. As a civil society, we are obliged to protect our most vulnerable members, to raise them up and give them the tools to survive with dignity. We may not be able to right all the world's wrongs, but we can lift up our neighbors and ease their suffering.

In summary, we are recommending a high standard of professional care for all people, including those with disabilities. Providers should be fully competent to produce thorough documentation that is consistent with SSA requirements, and opinions consistent with Social Security's definition of severity, duration, and residual functional capacity. Some clinicians may strive for more than clinical competence and engage in political advocacy for the well-being and sustainability of all people, including those with disabilities. Perhaps the principled choice is to set aside political and personal biases in deference to the rights of claimants for SSDI and SSI, lending our support to this underserved community.

APPENDIX A

Listing of Impairments (Adult)

Disability Evaluation Under Social Security

Listing of Impairments—Adult Listings (Part A)

The following sections contain medical criteria that apply to the evaluation of impairments in adults age 18 and over and that may apply to the evaluation of impairments in children under age 18 if the disease processes have a similar effect on adults and younger children.

1.00 Musculoskeletal System

A. Disorders of the musculoskeletal system may result from hereditary, congenital, or acquired pathologic processes. Impairments may result from infectious, inflammatory, or degenerative processes, traumatic or developmental events, or neoplastic, vascular, or toxic/metabolic diseases.

B. Loss of function.

1. General. Under this section, loss of function may be due to bone or joint deformity or destruction from any cause; miscellaneous disorders of the spine with or without radiculopathy or other neurological deficits; amputation; or fractures or soft tissue injuries, including burns, requiring prolonged periods of immobility or convalescence. The provisions of 1.02 and 1.03 notwithstanding, inflammatory arthritis is evaluated under 14.09 (see 14.00D6). Impairments with neurological causes are to be evaluated under 11.00FF.

Source: Code of Federal Regulations, Title 20, Chapter III, Part 404, Subpart P, Appendix 1. Available online at https://www.govinfo.gov/app/details/CFR-2012-title20-vol2/CFR-2012-title20-vol2-part404-subpartP-app1.

2. How we define loss of function in these listings.

a. General. Regardless of the cause(s) of a musculoskeletal impairment, functional loss for purposes of these listings is defined as the inability to ambulate effectively on a sustained basis for any reason, including pain associated with the underlying musculoskeletal impairment, or the inability to perform fine and gross movements effectively on a sustained basis for any reason, including pain associated with the underlying musculoskeletal impairment. The inability to ambulate effectively or the inability to perform fine and gross movements effectively must have lasted, or be expected to last, for at least 12 months. For the purposes of these criteria, consideration of the ability to perform these activities must be from a physical standpoint alone. When there is an inability to perform these activities due to a mental impairment, the criteria in 12.00ff are to be used. We will determine whether an individual can ambulate effectively or can perform fine and gross movements effectively based on the medical and other evidence in the case record, generally without developing additional evidence about the individual's ability to perform the specific activities listed as examples in 1.00B2b(2) and 1.00B2c.

b. What we mean by inability to ambulate effectively.

(1) Definition. Inability to ambulate effectively means an extreme limitation of the ability to walk; i.e., an impairment(s) that interferes very seriously with the individual's ability to independently initiate, sustain, or complete activities. Ineffective ambulation is defined generally as having insufficient lower extremity functioning (see 1.00J) to permit independent ambulation without the use of a hand-held assistive device(s) that limits the functioning of both upper extremities. (Listing 1.05C is an exception to this general definition because the individual has the use of only one upper extremity due to amputation of a hand.)

(2) To ambulate effectively, individuals must be capable of sustaining a reasonable walking pace over a sufficient distance to be able to carry out activities of daily living. They must have the ability to travel without companion assistance to and from a place of employment or school. Therefore, examples of ineffective ambulation include, but are not limited to, the inability to walk without the use of a walker, two crutches or two canes, the inability to walk a block at a reasonable pace on rough or uneven surfaces, the inability to use standard public transportation, the inability to carry out routine ambulatory activities, such as shopping and banking, and the inability to climb a few steps at a reasonable pace with the use of a single hand rail. The ability to walk independently about one's home without the use of assistive devices does not, in and of itself, constitute effective ambulation.

c. What we mean by inability to perform fine and gross movements effectively. Inability to perform fine and gross movements effectively means an extreme loss of function of both upper extremities; i.e., an impairment(s) that interferes very seriously with the individual's ability to independently initiate, sustain, or complete activities. To use their upper extremities effectively, individuals must be capable of sustaining such functions as reaching, pushing, pulling, grasping, and fingering to be able to carry out activities of daily living. Therefore, examples of inability to perform fine and gross movements effectively include, but are not limited to, the inability to prepare a simple meal and feed oneself, the inability to take care of personal hygiene, the inability to sort and handle papers or files, and the inability to place files in a file cabinet at or above waist level.

d. Pain or other symptoms. Pain or other symptoms may be an important factor contributing to functional loss. In order for pain or other symptoms to be found to affect an individual's ability to perform basic work activities, medical signs or laboratory findings must show the existence of a medically determinable impairment(s) that could reasonably be expected to produce the pain or other symptoms. The musculoskeletal listings that include pain or other symptoms among their criteria also include criteria for limitations in functioning as a result of the listed impairment, including limitations caused by pain. It is, therefore, important to evaluate the intensity and persistence of such pain or other symptoms carefully in order to determine their impact on the individual's functioning under these listings. See also §§ 404.1525(f) and 404.1529 of this part, and §§ 416.925(f) and 416.929 of part 416 of this chapter.

C. Diagnosis and evaluation.

1. General. Diagnosis and evaluation of musculoskeletal impairments should be supported, as applicable, by detailed descriptions of the joints, including ranges of motion, condition of the musculature (e.g., weakness, atrophy), sensory or reflex changes, circulatory deficits, and laboratory findings, including findings on x-ray or other appropriate medically acceptable imaging. Medically acceptable imaging includes, but is not limited to, x-ray imaging, computerized axial tomography (CAT scan) or magnetic resonance imaging (MRI), with or without contrast material, myelography, and radionuclear bone scans. "Appropriate" means that the technique used is the proper one to support the evaluation and diagnosis of the impairment.

2. Purchase of certain medically acceptable imaging. While any appropriate medically acceptable imaging is useful in establishing the diagnosis of musculoskeletal impairments, some tests, such as CAT scans and MRIs, are quite expensive, and we will not routinely purchase them. Some, such as myelograms, are invasive and may involve significant risk. We will not order such tests. However, when the results of any of these tests are part of the existing evidence in the case record we will consider them together with the other relevant evidence.

3. Consideration of electrodiagnostic procedures. Electrodiagnostic procedures may be useful in establishing the clinical diagnosis, but do not constitute alternative criteria to the requirements of 1.04.

D. The physical examination must include a detailed description of the rheumatological, orthopedic, neurological, and other findings appropriate to the specific impairment being evaluated. These physical findings must be determined on the basis of objective observation during the examination and not simply a report of the individual's allegation; e.g., "He says his leg is weak, numb." Alternative testing methods should be used to verify the abnormal findings; e.g., a seated straight-leg raising test in addition to a supine straight-leg raising test. Because abnormal physical findings may be intermittent, their presence over a period of time must be established by a record of ongoing management and evaluation. Care must be taken to ascertain that the reported examination findings are consistent with the individual's daily activities.

E. Examination of the spine.

1. General. Examination of the spine should include a detailed description of gait, range of motion of the spine given quantitatively in degrees from the vertical position (zero degrees) or, for straight-leg raising from the sitting and supine position (zero degrees), any other appropriate tension signs, motor and sensory abnormalities, muscle spasm, when present, and deep tendon reflexes. Observations of the individual during the examination should be reported; e.g., how he or she gets on and off the examination table. Inability to walk on the heels or toes, to squat, or to arise from a squatting position, when appropriate, may be considered evidence of significant motor loss. However, a report of atrophy is not acceptable as evidence of significant motor loss without circumferential measurements of both thighs and lower legs, or both upper and lower arms, as appropriate, at a stated point above and below the knee or elbow given in inches or centimeters. Additionally, a report of atrophy should be accompanied by measurement of the strength of the muscle(s) in question generally based on a grading system of 0 to 5, with 0 being complete loss of strength and 5 being maximum strength. A specific description of atrophy of hand muscles is acceptable without measurements of atrophy but should include measurements of grip and pinch strength.

2. When neurological abnormalities persist. Neurological abnormalities may not completely subside after treatment or with the passage of time. Therefore, residual neurological abnormalities that persist after it has been determined clinically or by direct surgical or other observation that the ongoing or progressive condition is no longer present will not satisfy the required findings in 1.04. More serious neurological deficits (paraparesis, paraplegia) are to be evaluated under the criteria in 11.00ff.

F. Major joints refers to the major peripheral joints, which are the hip, knee, shoulder, elbow, wrist-hand, and ankle-foot, as opposed to other peripheral joints (e.g., the joints of the hand or forefoot) or axial joints (i.e., the joints of the spine.) The wrist and hand are considered together as one major joint, as are the ankle and foot. Since only the ankle joint, which consists of the juncture of the bones of the lower leg (tibia and fibula) with the hindfoot (tarsal bones), but not the forefoot, is crucial to weight bearing, the ankle and foot are considered separately in evaluating weight bearing.

G. Measurements of joint motion are based on the techniques described in the chapter on the extremities, spine, and pelvis in the current edition of the "Guides to the Evaluation of Permanent Impairment" published by the American Medical Association.

H. Documentation.

1. General. Musculoskeletal impairments frequently improve with time or respond to treatment. Therefore, a longitudinal clinical record is generally important for the assessment of severity and expected duration of an impairment unless the claim can be decided favorably on the basis of the current evidence.

2. Documentation of medically prescribed treatment and response. Many individuals, especially those who have listing-level impairments, will have received the benefit of medically prescribed treatment. Whenever evidence of such treatment is available it must be considered.

3. When there is no record of ongoing treatment. Some individuals will not have received ongoing treatment or have an ongoing relationship with the medical community despite the existence of a severe impairment(s). In such cases, evaluation will be made on the basis of the current objective medical evidence and other available evidence, taking into consideration the individual's medical history, symptoms, and medical source opinions. Even though an individual who does not receive treatment may not be able to show an impairment that meets the criteria of one of the musculoskeletal listings, the individual may have an impairment(s) equivalent in severity to one of the listed impairments or be disabled based on consideration of his or her residual functional capacity (RFC) and age, education and work experience.

4. Evaluation when the criteria of a musculoskeletal listing are not met. These listings are only examples of common musculoskeletal disorders that are severe enough to prevent a person from engaging in gainful activity. Therefore, in any case in which an individual has a medically determinable impairment that is not listed, an impairment that does not meet the requirements of a listing, or a combination of impairments no one of which meets the requirements of a listing, we will consider medical equivalence. (See §§ 404.1526 and 416.926 .) Individuals who have an impairment(s) with a level of severity that does not meet or equal the criteria of the musculoskeletal listings may or may not have the RFC that would enable them to engage in substantial gainful activity. Evaluation of the impairment(s) of these individuals should proceed through the final steps of the sequential evaluation process in §§ 404.1520 and 416.920 (or, as appropriate, the steps in the medical improvement review standard in §§ 404.1594 and 416.994).

I. Effects of treatment.

1. General. Treatments for musculoskeletal disorders may have beneficial effects or adverse side effects. Therefore, medical treatment (including surgical treatment) must be considered in terms of its effectiveness in ameliorating the signs, symptoms, and laboratory abnormalities of the disorder, and in terms of any side effects that may further limit the individual.

2. Response to treatment. Response to treatment and adverse consequences of treatment may vary widely. For example, a pain medication may relieve an individual's pain completely, partially, or not at all. It may also result in adverse effects, e.g., drowsiness, dizziness, or disorientation, that compromise the individual's ability to function. Therefore, each case must be considered on an individual basis, and include consideration of the effects of treatment on the individual's ability to function.

3. Documentation. A specific description of the drugs or treatment given (including surgery), dosage, frequency of administration, and a description of the complications or response to treatment should be obtained. The effects of treatment may be temporary or long-term. As such, the finding regarding the impact of treatment must be based on a sufficient period of treatment to permit proper consideration or judgment about future functioning.

J. Orthotic, prosthetic, or assistive devices.

1. General. Consistent with clinical practice, individuals with musculoskeletal impairments may be examined with and without the use of any orthotic, prosthetic, or assistive devices as explained in this section.

2. Orthotic devices. Examination should be with the orthotic device in place and should include an evaluation of the individual's maximum ability to function effectively with the orthosis. It is unnecessary to routinely evaluate the individual's ability to function without the orthosis in place. If the individual has difficulty with, or is unable to use, the orthotic device, the medical basis for the difficulty should be documented. In such cases, if the impairment involves a lower extremity or extremities, the examination should include information on the individual's ability to ambulate effectively without the device in place unless contraindicated by the medical judgment of a physician who has treated or examined the individual.

3. Prosthetic devices. Examination should be with the prosthetic device in place. In amputations involving a lower extremity or extremities, it is unnecessary to evaluate the individual's ability to walk without the prosthesis in place. However, the individual's medical ability to use a prosthesis to ambulate effectively, as defined in 1.00B2b, should be evaluated. The condition of the stump should be evaluated without the prosthesis in place.

4. Hand-held assistive devices. When an individual with an impairment involving a lower extremity or extremities uses a hand-held assistive device, such as a

cane, crutch or walker, examination should be with and without the use of the assistive device unless contraindicated by the medical judgment of a physician who has treated or examined the individual. The individual's ability to ambulate with and without the device provides information as to whether, or the extent to which, the individual is able to ambulate without assistance. The medical basis for the use of any assistive device (e.g., instability, weakness) should be documented. The requirement to use a hand-held assistive device may also impact on the individual's functional capacity by virtue of the fact that one or both upper extremities are not available for such activities as lifting, carrying, pushing, and pulling.

K. *Disorders of the spine*, listed in 1.04, result in limitations because of distortion of the bony and ligamentous architecture of the spine and associated impingement on nerve roots (including the cauda equina) or spinal cord. Such impingement on nerve tissue may result from a herniated nucleus pulposus, spinal stenosis, arachnoiditis, or other miscellaneous conditions.

1. Herniated nucleus pulposus is a disorder frequently associated with the impingement of a nerve root. Nerve root compression results in a specific neuroanatomic distribution of symptoms and signs depending upon the nerve root(s) compromised.

2. Spinal *arachnoiditis*.

a. General. Spinal arachnoiditis is a condition characterized by adhesive thickening of the arachnoid which may cause intermittent ill-defined burning pain and sensory dysesthesia, and may cause neurogenic bladder or bowel incontinence when the cauda equina is involved.

b. Documentation. Although the cause of spinal arachnoiditis is not always clear, it may be associated with chronic compression or irritation of nerve roots (including the cauda equina) or the spinal cord. For example, there may be evidence of spinal stenosis, or a history of spinal trauma or meningitis. Diagnosis must be confirmed at the time of surgery by gross description, microscopic examination of biopsied tissue, or by findings on appropriate medically acceptable imaging. Arachnoiditis is sometimes used as a diagnosis when such a diagnosis is unsupported by clinical or laboratory findings. Therefore, care must be taken to ensure that the diagnosis is documented as described in 1.04B. Individuals with arachnoiditis, particularly when it involves the lumbosacral spine, are generally unable to sustain any given position or posture for more than a short period of time due to pain.

3. Lumbar spinal stenosis is a condition that may occur in association with degenerative processes, or as a result of a congenital anomaly or trauma, or in association with Paget's disease of the bone. *Pseudoclaudication*, which may result from lumbar spinal stenosis, is manifested as pain and weakness, and may impair ambulation. Symptoms are usually bilateral, in the low back, buttocks, or thighs, although some individuals may experience only leg pain and, in a few cases, the leg pain may be unilateral. The pain generally does not follow a

particular neuro-anatomical distribution, i.e., it is distinctly different from the radicular type of pain seen with a herniated intervertebral disc, is often of a dull, aching quality, which may be described as "discomfort" or an "unpleasant sensation," or may be of even greater severity, usually in the low back and radiating into the buttocks region bilaterally. The pain is provoked by extension of the spine, as in walking or merely standing, but is reduced by leaning forward. The distance the individual has to walk before the pain comes on may vary. Pseudoclaudication differs from peripheral vascular claudication in several ways. Pedal pulses and Doppler examinations are unaffected by pseudoclaudication. Leg pain resulting from peripheral vascular claudication involves the calves, and the leg pain in vascular claudication is ordinarily more severe than any back pain that may also be present. An individual with vascular claudication will experience pain after walking the same distance time after time, and the pain will be relieved quickly when walking stops.

4. Other miscellaneous conditions that may cause weakness of the lower extremities, sensory changes, areflexia, trophic ulceration, bladder or bowel incontinence, and that should be evaluated under 1.04 include, but are not limited to, osteoarthritis, degenerative disc disease, facet arthritis, and vertebral fracture. Disorders such as spinal dysrhaphism (e.g., spina bifida), diastematomyelia, and tethered cord syndrome may also cause such abnormalities. In these cases, there may be gait difficulty and deformity of the lower extremities based on neurological abnormalities, and the neurological effects are to be evaluated under the criteria in 11.00ff.

L. Abnormal curvatures of the spine. Abnormal curvatures of the spine (specifically, scoliosis, kyphosis and kyphoscoliosis) can result in impaired ambulation, but may also adversely affect functioning in body systems other than the musculoskeletal system. For example, an individual's ability to breathe may be affected; there may be cardiac difficulties (e.g., impaired myocardial function); or there may be disfigurement resulting in withdrawal or isolation. When there is impaired ambulation, evaluation of equivalence may be made by reference to 14.09A. When the abnormal curvature of the spine results in symptoms related to fixation of the dorsolumbar or cervical spine, evaluation of equivalence may be made by reference to 14.09C. When there is respiratory or cardiac involvement or an associated mental disorder, evaluation may be made under 3.00ff, 4.00ff, or 12.00ff, as appropriate. Other consequences should be evaluated according to the listing for the affected body system.

M. Under continuing surgical management, as used in 1.07 and 1.08, refers to surgical procedures and any other associated treatments related to the efforts directed toward the salvage or restoration of functional use of the affected part. It may include such factors as post-surgical procedures, surgical complications, infections, or other medical complications, related illnesses, or related treatments that delay the individual's attainment of maximum benefit from therapy. When burns are not under continuing surgical management, see 8.00F.

N. After maximum benefit from therapy has been achieved in situations involving fractures of an upper extremity (1.07), or soft tissue injuries (1.08), i.e., there have been no significant changes in physical findings or on appropriate medically acceptable imaging for any 6-month period after the last definitive surgical procedure or other medical intervention, evaluation must be made on the basis of the demonstrable residuals, if any. A finding that 1.07 or 1.08 is met must be based on a consideration of the symptoms, signs, and laboratory findings associated with recent or anticipated surgical procedures and the resulting recuperative periods, including any related medical complications, such as infections, illnesses, and therapies which impede or delay the efforts toward restoration of function. Generally, when there has been no surgical or medical intervention for 6 months after the last definitive surgical procedure, it can be concluded that maximum therapeutic benefit has been reached. Evaluation at this point must be made on the basis of the demonstrable residual limitations, if any, considering the individual's impairment-related symptoms, signs, and laboratory findings, any residual symptoms, signs, and laboratory findings associated with such surgeries, complications, and recuperative periods, and other relevant evidence.

O. Major function of the face and head, for purposes of listing 1.08, relates to impact on any or all of the activities involving vision, hearing, speech, mastication, and the initiation of the digestive process.

P. When surgical procedures have been performed, documentation should include a copy of the operative notes and available pathology reports.

Q. Effects of obesity. Obesity is a medically determinable impairment that is often associated with disturbance of the musculoskeletal system, and disturbance of this system can be a major cause of disability in individuals with obesity. The combined effects of obesity with musculoskeletal impairments can be greater than the effects of each of the impairments considered separately. Therefore, when determining whether an individual with obesity has a listing-level impairment or combination of impairments, and when assessing a claim at other steps of the sequential evaluation process, including when assessing an individual's residual functional capacity, adjudicators must consider any additional and cumulative effects of obesity.

1.01 Category of Impairments, Musculoskeletal

1.02 ***Major dysfunction of a joint(s) (due to any cause)***: Characterized by gross anatomical deformity (e.g., subluxation, contracture, bony or fibrous ankylosis, instability) and chronic joint pain and stiffness with signs of limitation of motion or other abnormal motion of the affected joint(s), and findings on appropriate medically acceptable imaging of joint space narrowing, bony destruction, or ankylosis of the affected joint(s). With:

A. Involvement of one major peripheral weight-bearing joint (i.e., hip, knee, or ankle), resulting in inability to ambulate effectively, as defined in 1.00B2b;

OR

B. Involvement of one major peripheral joint in each upper extremity (i.e., shoulder, elbow, or wrist-hand), resulting in inability to perform fine and gross movements effectively, as defined in 1.00B2c.

1.03 ***Reconstructive surgery or surgical arthrodesis of a major weight-bearing joint***, with inability to ambulate effectively, as defined in 1.00B2b, and return to effective ambulation did not occur, or is not expected to occur, within 12 months of onset.

1.04 ***Disorders of the spine*** (e.g., herniated nucleus pulposus, spinal arachnoiditis, spinal stenosis, osteoarthritis, degenerative disc disease, facet arthritis, vertebral fracture), resulting in compromise of a nerve root (including the cauda equina) or the spinal cord. With:

A. Evidence of nerve root compression characterized by neuro-anatomic distribution of pain, limitation of motion of the spine, motor loss (atrophy with associated muscle weakness or muscle weakness) accompanied by sensory or reflex loss and, if there is involvement of the lower back, positive straight-leg raising test (sitting and supine);

OR

B. Spinal arachnoiditis, confirmed by an operative note or pathology report of tissue biopsy, or by appropriate medically acceptable imaging, manifested by severe burning or painful dysesthesia, resulting in the need for changes in position or posture more than once every 2 hours;

or

C. Lumbar spinal stenosis resulting in pseudoclaudication, established by findings on appropriate medically acceptable imaging, manifested by chronic nonradicular pain and weakness, and resulting in inability to ambulate effectively, as defined in 1.00B2b.

1.05 ***Amputation (due to any cause)***

A. Both hands;

or

B. One or both lower extremities at or above the tarsal region, with stump complications resulting in medical inability to use a prosthetic device to ambulate effectively, as defined in 1.00B2b, which have lasted or are expected to last for at least 12 months;

or

C. One hand and one lower extremity at or above the tarsal region, with inability to ambulate effectively, as defined in 1.00B2b;

or

D. Hemipelvectomy or hip disarticulation.

1.06 *Fracture of the femur, tibia, pelvis, or one or more of the tarsal bones.* With:

A. Solid union not evident on appropriate medically acceptable imaging and not clinically solid;

and

B. Inability to ambulate effectively, as defined in 1.00B2b, and return to effective ambulation did not occur or is not expected to occur within 12 months of onset.

1.07 *Fracture of an upper extremity* with nonunion of a fracture of the shaft of the humerus, radius, or ulna, under continuing surgical management, as defined in 1.00M, directed toward restoration of functional use of the extremity, and such function was not restored or expected to be restored within 12 months of onset.

1.08 *Soft tissue injury (e.g., burns)* of an upper or lower extremity, trunk, or face and head, under continuing surgical management, as defined in 1.00M, directed toward the salvage or restoration of major function, and such major function was not restored or expected to be restored within 12 months of onset. Major function of the face and head is described in 1.00.

2.00 Special Senses and Speech

A. *How do we evaluate visual disorders?*

1. *What are visual disorders?* Visual disorders are abnormalities of the eye, the optic nerve, the optic tracts, or the brain that may cause a loss of visual acuity or visual fields. A loss of visual acuity limits your ability to distinguish detail, read, or do fine work. A loss of visual fields limits your ability to perceive visual stimuli in the peripheral extent of vision.

2. *How do we define statutory blindness?* Statutory blindness is blindness as defined in sections 216(i)(1) and 1614(a)(2) of the Social Security Act (Act).

a. The Act defines blindness as central visual acuity of 20/200 or less in the better eye with the use of a correcting lens. We use your best-corrected central visual acuity for distance in the better eye when we determine if this definition is met. (For visual acuity testing requirements, see 2.00A5.)

b. The Act also provides that an eye that has a visual field limitation such that the widest diameter of the visual field subtends an angle no greater than 20 degrees is considered as having a central visual acuity of 20/200 or less. (For visual field testing requirements, see 2.00A6.)

c. You have statutory blindness only if your visual disorder meets the criteria of 2.02 or 2.03A. You do not have statutory blindness if your visual disorder medically equals the criteria of 2.02 or 2.03A or meets or medically equals the criteria of 2.03B, 2.03C, 2.04A, or 2.04B because your disability is based on criteria other than those in the statutory definition of blindness.

3. *What evidence do we need to establish statutory blindness under title XVI?* To establish that you have statutory blindness under title XVI, we need evidence showing only that your central visual acuity in your better eye or your visual field in your better eye meets the criteria in 2.00A2, provided that those measurements are consistent with the other evidence in your case record. We do not need documentation of the cause of your blindness. Also, there is no duration requirement for statutory blindness under title XVI (see §§ 416.981 and 416.983 of this chapter).

4. *What evidence do we need to evaluate visual disorders, including those that result in statutory blindness under title II?* To evaluate your visual disorder, we usually need a report of an eye examination that includes measurements of your best-corrected central visual acuity (see 2.00A5) or the extent of your visual fields (see 2.00A6), as appropriate. If you have visual acuity or visual field loss, we need documentation of the cause of the loss. A standard eye examination will usually indicate the cause of any visual acuity loss. A standard eye examination can also indicate the cause of some types of visual field deficits. Some disorders, such as cortical visual disorders, may result in abnormalities that do not appear on a standard eye examination. If the standard eye examination does not indicate the cause of your vision loss, we will request the information used to establish the presence of your visual disorder. If your visual disorder does not satisfy the criteria in 2.02, 2.03, or 2.04, we will request a description of how your visual disorder affects your ability to function.

5. *How do we measure best-corrected visual acuity?*

a. *Visual acuity testing.* When we need to measure your best-corrected central visual acuity (your optimal visual acuity attainable with the use of a corrective lens), we use visual acuity testing for distance that was carried out using Snellen methodology or any other testing methodology that is comparable to Snellen methodology.

(i) Your best-corrected central visual acuity for distance is usually measured by determining what you can see from 20 feet. If your visual acuity is measured for a distance other than 20 feet, we will convert it to a 20-foot measurement. For example, if your visual acuity is measured at 10 feet and is reported as 10/40, we will convert this measurement to 20/80.

(ii) A visual acuity recorded as CF (counts fingers), HM (hand motion only), LP or LPO (light perception or light perception only), or NLP (no light perception) indicates that no optical correction will improve your visual acuity. If your central visual acuity in an eye is recorded as CF, HM, LP or LPO, or NLP, we will determine that your best-corrected central visual acuity is 20/200 or less in that eye.

(iii) We will not use the results of pinhole testing or automated refraction acuity to determine your best-corrected central visual acuity. These tests provide an estimate of potential visual acuity but not an actual measurement of your best-corrected central visual acuity.

b. *Other test charts.* Most test charts that use Snellen methodology do not have lines that measure visual acuity between 20/100 and 20/200. Some test charts, such as the Bailey-Lovie or the Early Treatment Diabetic Retinopathy Study (ETDRS), used mostly in research settings, have such lines. If your visual acuity is measured with one of these charts, and you cannot read any of the letters on the 20/100 line, we will determine that you have statutory blindness based on a visual acuity of 20/200 or less. For example, if your best-corrected central visual acuity for distance in the better eye is 20/160 using an ETDRS chart, we will find that you have statutory blindness. Regardless of the type of test chart used, you do not have statutory blindness if you can read at least one letter on the 20/100 line. For example, if your best-corrected central visual acuity for distance in the better eye is 20/125+1 using an ETDRS chart, we will find that you do not have statutory blindness because you are able to read one letter on the 20/100 line.

c. *Testing using a specialized lens.* In some instances, you may perform visual acuity testing using a specialized lens, such as a contact lens. We will use the visual acuity measurements obtained with a specialized lens only if you have demonstrated the ability to use the specialized lens on a sustained basis. We will not use visual acuity measurements obtained with telescopic lenses.

d. *Cycloplegic refraction* is an examination of the eye performed after administering cycloplegic eye drops capable of relaxing the ability of the pupil to become smaller and temporarily paralyzing the focusing muscles. If your case record contains the results of cycloplegic refraction, we may use the results to determine your best-corrected central visual acuity. We will not purchase cycloplegic refraction.

e. *Visual evoked response (VER) testing* measures your response to visual events and can often detect dysfunction that is undetectable through other types of examinations. If you have an absent response to VER testing in your better eye, we will determine that your best-corrected central visual acuity is 20/200 or less in that eye and that your visual acuity loss satisfies the criterion in 2.02 when these test results are consistent with the other evidence in your case record. If you have a positive response to VER testing in an eye, we will not use that result to determine your best-corrected central visual acuity in that eye.

6. How do we measure visual fields?

a. *General.* We generally need visual field testing when you have a visual disorder that could result in visual field loss, such as glaucoma, retinitis pigmentosa, or optic neuropathy, or when you display behaviors that suggest a visual field loss. When we need to measure the extent of your visual field loss, we use visual field testing (also referred to as perimetry) carried out using automated static threshold perimetry performed on an acceptable perimeter. (For perimeter requirements, see 2.00A9.)

b. *Automated static threshold perimetry requirements.*

(i) The test must use a white size III Goldmann stimulus and a 31.5 apostilb (asb) white background (or a 10 candela per square meter (cd/m^2) white background). The stimuli test locations must be no more than 6 degrees apart horizontally or vertically. Measurements must be reported on standard charts and include a description of the size and intensity of the test stimulus.

(ii) We measure the extent of your visual field loss by determining the portion of the visual field in which you can see a white III4e stimulus. The "III" refers to the standard Goldmann test stimulus size III (4 mm^2), and the "4e" refers to the standard Goldmann intensity filter (0 decibel (dB) attenuation, which allows presentation of the maximum luminance) used to determine the intensity of the stimulus.

(iii) In automated static threshold perimetry, the intensity of the stimulus varies. The intensity of the stimulus is expressed in decibels (dB). A perimeter's maximum stimulus luminance is usually assigned the value 0 dB. We need to determine the dB level that corresponds to a 4e intensity for the particular perimeter being used. We will then use the dB printout to determine which points you see at a 4e intensity level (a "seeing point"). For example:

A. When the maximum stimulus luminance (0 dB stimulus) on an acceptable perimeter is 10,000 asb, a 10 dB stimulus is equivalent to a 4e stimulus. Any point you see at 10 dB or greater is a seeing point.

B. When the maximum stimulus luminance (0 dB stimulus) on an acceptable perimeter is 4,000 asb, a 6 dB stimulus is equivalent to a 4e stimulus. Any point you see at 6 dB or greater is a seeing point.

C. When the maximum stimulus luminance (0 dB stimulus) on an acceptable perimeter is 1,000 asb, a 0 dB stimulus is equivalent to a 4e stimulus. Any point you see at 0 dB or greater is a seeing point.

c. *Evaluation under 2.03A*. To determine statutory blindness based on visual field loss in your better eye (2.03A), we need the results of a visual field test that measures the central 24 to 30 degrees of your visual field; that is, the area measuring 24 to 30 degrees from the point of fixation. Acceptable tests include the Humphrey Field Analyzer (HFA) 30-2, HFA 24-2, and Octopus 32.

d. *Evaluation under 2.03B*. To determine whether your visual field loss meets listing 2.03B, we use the mean deviation or defect (MD) from acceptable automated static threshold perimetry that measures the central 30 degrees of the visual field. MD is the average sensitivity deviation from normal values for all measured visual field locations. When using results from HFA tests, which report the MD as a negative number, we use the absolute value of the MD to determine whether your visual field loss meets listing 2.03B. We cannot use tests that do not measure the central 30 degrees of the visual field, such as the HFA 24-2, to determine if your impairment meets or medically equals 2.03B.

e. *Other types of perimetry.* If the evidence in your case contains visual field measurements obtained using manual or automated kinetic perimetry, such as Goldmann perimetry or the HFA "SSA Test Kinetic," we can generally use these results if the kinetic test was performed using a white III4e stimulus projected on a white 31.5 asb (10 cd/m^2) background. Automated kinetic perimetry, such as the HFA "SSA Test Kinetic," does not detect limitations in the central visual field because testing along a meridian stops when you see the stimulus. If your visual disorder has progressed to the point at which it is likely to result in a significant limitation in the central visual field, such as a scotoma (see 2.00A6h), we will not use *automated* kinetic perimetry to determine the extent of your visual field loss. Instead, we will determine the extent of your visual field loss using automated static threshold perimetry or manual kinetic perimetry.

f. *Screening tests.* We will not use the results of visual field screening tests, such as confrontation tests, tangent screen tests, or automated static screening tests, to determine that your impairment meets or medically equals a listing or to evaluate your residual functional capacity. We can consider normal results from visual field screening tests to determine whether your visual disorder is severe when these test results are consistent with the other evidence in your case record. (See §§ 404.1520(c), 404.1521, 416.920(c), and 416.921 of this chapter.) We will not consider normal test results to be consistent with the other evidence if the clinical findings indicate that your visual disorder has progressed to the point that it is likely to cause visual field loss, or you have a history of an operative procedure for retinal detachment.

g. *Use of corrective lenses.* You must not wear eyeglasses during visual field testing because they limit your field of vision. You may wear contact lenses to correct your visual acuity during the visual field test to obtain the most accurate visual field measurements. For this single purpose, you do not need to demonstrate that you have the ability to use the contact lenses on a sustained basis.

h. *Scotoma.* A scotoma is a field defect or non-seeing area (also referred to as a "blind spot") in the visual field surrounded by a normal field or seeing area. When we measure your visual field, we subtract the length of any scotoma, other than the normal blind spot, from the overall length of any diameter on which it falls.

7. *How do we determine your visual acuity efficiency, visual field efficiency, and visual efficiency?*

a. *General. Visual efficiency,* a calculated value of your remaining visual function, is the combination of your *visual acuity efficiency* and your *visual field efficiency* expressed as a percentage.

b. *Visual acuity efficiency.* Visual acuity efficiency is a percentage that corresponds to the best-corrected central visual acuity for distance in your better eye. See Table 1.

Table 1—Visual Acuity Efficiency

Snellen best-corrected central visual acuity for distance		Visual acuity efficiency (%) (2.04A)
English	Metric	
20/16	6/5	100
20/20	6/6	100
20/25	6/7.5	95
20/30	6/9	90
20/40	6/12	85
20/50	6/15	75
20/60	6/18	70
20/70	6/21	65
20/80	6/24	60
20/100	6/30	50

c. *Visual field efficiency.* Visual field efficiency is a percentage that corresponds to the visual field in your better eye. Under 2.03C, we require kinetic perimetry to determine your visual field efficiency percentage. We calculate the visual field efficiency percentage by adding the number of degrees you see along the eight principal meridians found on a visual field chart (0, 45, 90, 135, 180, 225, 270, and 315) in your better eye and dividing by 5. For example, in Figure 1:

A. The diagram of the left eye illustrates a visual field, as measured with a III4e stimulus, contracted to 30 degrees in two meridians (180 and 225) and to 20 degrees in the remaining six meridians. The visual efficiency percentage of this field is: ((2 × 30) + (6 × 20)) / 5 = 36 percent.

B. The diagram of the right eye illustrates the extent of a normal visual field as measured with a III4e stimulus. The sum of the eight principal meridians of this field is 500 degrees. The visual efficiency percentage of this field is 500 / 5 = 100 percent.

d. *Visual efficiency.* Under 2.04A, we calculate the visual efficiency percentage by multiplying your visual acuity efficiency percentage (see 2.00A7b) by your visual field efficiency percentage (see 2.00A7c) and dividing by 100. For example, if your visual acuity efficiency percentage is 75 and your visual field efficiency percentage is 36, your visual efficiency percentage is: (75 × 36) / 100 = 27 percent.

8. *How do we determine your visual acuity impairment value, visual field impairment value, and visual impairment value?*

a. *General. Visual impairment value*, a calculated value of your loss of visual function, is the combination of your *visual acuity impairment value* and your *visual field impairment value.*

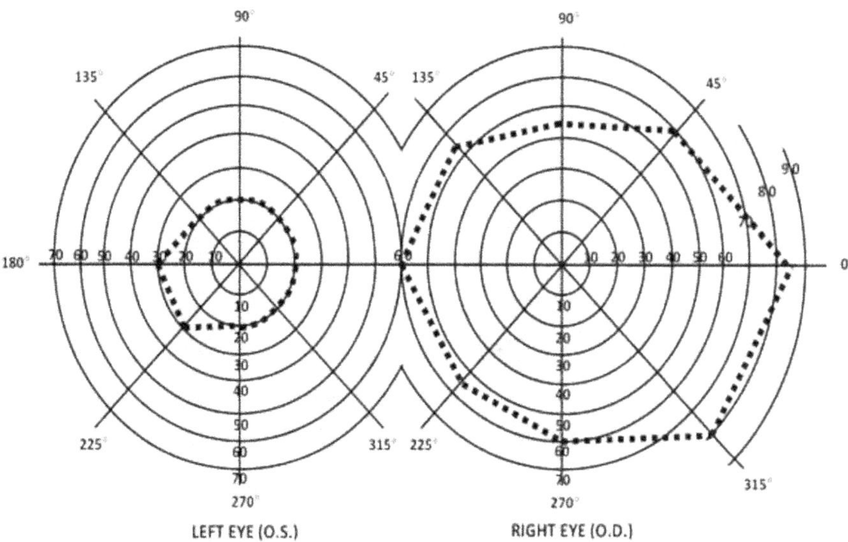

Figure 1

b. *Visual acuity impairment value.* Your visual acuity impairment value corresponds to the best-corrected central visual acuity for distance in your better eye. See Table 2.

c. *Visual field impairment value.* Your visual field impairment value corresponds to the visual field in your better eye. Using the MD from acceptable automated static threshold perimetry, we calculate the visual field impairment value by dividing the absolute value of the MD by 22. For example, if your MD on an HFA 30-2 is −16, your visual field impairment value is: |−16| / 22 = 0.73.

d. *Visual impairment value.* Under 2.04B, we calculate the visual impairment value by adding your visual acuity impairment value (see 2.00A8b) and your visual field impairment value (see 2.00A8c). For example, if your visual acuity impairment value is 0.48 and your visual field impairment value is 0.73, your visual impairment value is: 0.48 + 0.73 = 1.21.

9. *What are our requirements for an acceptable perimeter?* We will use results from automated static threshold perimetry performed on a perimeter that:

a. Uses optical projection to generate the test stimuli.

b. Has an internal normative database for automatically comparing your performance with that of the general population.

c. Has a statistical analysis package that is able to calculate visual field indices, particularly MD.

d. Demonstrates the ability to correctly detect visual field loss and correctly identify normal visual fields.

Table 2—Visual Acuity Impairment Value

Snellen best-corrected central visual acuity for distance		Visual acuity impairment value (2.04B)
English	Metric	
20/16	6/5	0.00
20/20	6/6	0.00
20/25	6/7.5	0.10
20/30	6/9	0.18
20/40	6/12	0.30
20/50	6/15	0.40
20/60	6/18	0.48
20/70	6/21	0.54
20/80	6/24	0.60
20/100	6/30	0.70

e. Demonstrates good test-retest reliability.

f. Has undergone clinical validation studies by three or more independent laboratories with results published in peer-reviewed ophthalmic journals.

B. How do we evaluate hearing loss?

1. *What evidence do we need?*

a. We need evidence showing that you have a medically determinable impairment that causes your hearing loss and audiometric measurements of the severity of your hearing loss. We generally require both an otologic examination and audiometric testing to establish that you have a medically determinable impairment that causes your hearing loss. You should have this audiometric testing within 2 months of the otologic examination. Once we have evidence that you have a medically determinable impairment, we can use the results of later audiometric testing to assess the severity of your hearing loss without another otologic examination. We will consider your test scores together with any other relevant information we have about your hearing, including information from outside of the test setting.

b. The otologic examination must be performed by a licensed physician (medical or osteopathic doctor) or audiologist. It must include your medical history, your description of how your hearing loss affects you, and the physician's or audiologist's description of the appearance of the external ears (pinnae and external ear canals), evaluation of the tympanic membranes, and assessment of any middle ear abnormalities.

c. Audiometric testing must be performed by, or under the direct supervision of, a licensed audiologist or an otolaryngologist.

2. *What audiometric testing do we need when you do not have a cochlear implant?*

a. We generally need pure tone air conduction and bone conduction testing, speech reception threshold (SRT) testing (also referred to as "spondee threshold" or "ST" testing), and word recognition testing (also referred to as "word discrimination" or "speech discrimination" testing). This testing must be conducted in a sound-treated booth or room and must be in accordance with the most recently published standards of the American National Standards Institute (ANSI). Each ear must be tested separately.

b. You must not wear hearing aids during the testing. Additionally, a person described in 2.00B1c must perform an otoscopic examination immediately before the audiometric testing. (An **otoscopic examination** provides a description of the appearance of your external ear canals and an evaluation of the tympanic membranes. In these rules, we use the term to include otoscopic examinations performed by physicians and otoscopic inspections performed by audiologists and others.) The otoscopic examination must show that there are no conditions that would prevent valid audiometric testing, such as fluid in the ear, ear infection, or obstruction in an ear canal. The person performing the test should also report on any other factors, such as your cooperation with the test, that can affect the interpretation of the test results.

c. To determine whether your hearing loss meets the air and bone conduction criteria in 2.10A, we will average your air and bone conduction hearing thresholds at 500, 1000, and 2000 Hertz (Hz). If you do not have a response at a particular frequency, we will use a threshold of 5 decibels (dB) over the limit of the audiometer.

d. The SRT is the minimum dB level required for you to recognize 50 percent of the words on a standard list of spondee words. (Spondee words are two-syllable words that have equal stress on each syllable.) The SRT is usually within 10 dB of the average pure tone air conduction hearing thresholds at 500, 1000, and 2000 Hz. If the SRT is not within 10 dB of the average pure tone air conduction threshold, the reason for the discrepancy must be documented. If we cannot determine that there is a medical basis for the discrepancy, we will not use the results of the testing to determine whether your hearing loss meets a listing.

e. Word recognition testing determines your ability to recognize a standardized list of phonetically balanced monosyllabic words in the absence of any visual cues. This testing must be performed in quiet. The list may be recorded or presented live, but in either case the words should be presented at a level of amplification that will measure your maximum ability to discriminate words, usually

35 to 40 dB above your SRT. However, the amplification level used in the testing must be medically appropriate, and you must be able to tolerate it. If you cannot be tested at 35 to 40 dB above your SRT, the person who performs the test should report your word recognition testing score at your highest comfortable level of amplification.

3. *What audiometric testing do we need when you have a cochlear implant?*

a. If you have a cochlear implant, we will consider you to be disabled until 1 year after initial implantation.

b. After that period, we need word recognition testing performed with any version of the Hearing in Noise Test (HINT) to determine whether your impairment meets 2.11B. This testing must be conducted in quiet in a sound field. Your implant must be functioning properly and adjusted to your normal settings. The sentences should be presented at 60 dB HL (Hearing Level) and without any visual cues.

4. *How do we evaluate your word recognition ability if you are not fluent in English?*

If you are not fluent in English, you should have word recognition testing using an appropriate word list for the language in which you are most fluent. The person conducting the test should be fluent in the language used for the test. If there is no appropriate word list or no person who is fluent in the language and qualified to perform the test, it may not be possible to measure your word recognition ability. If your word recognition ability cannot be measured, your hearing loss cannot meet 2.10B or 2.11B. Instead, we will consider the facts of your case to determine whether you have difficulty understanding words in the language in which you are most fluent, and if so, whether that degree of difficulty medically equals 2.10B or 2.11B. For example, we will consider how you interact with family members, interpreters, and other persons who speak the language in which you are most fluent.

C. How do we evaluate vertigo associated with disturbances of labyrinthine-vestibular function, including Ménière's disease?

1. These disturbances of balance are characterized by a hallucination of motion or a loss of position sense and a sensation of dizziness which may be constant or may occur in paroxysmal attacks. Nausea, vomiting, ataxia, and incapacitation are frequently observed, particularly during the acute attack. It is important to differentiate the report of rotary vertigo from that of "dizziness" which is described as light-headedness, unsteadiness, confusion, or syncope.

2. Ménière's disease is characterized by paroxysmal attacks of vertigo, tinnitus, and fluctuating hearing loss. Remissions are unpredictable and irregular, but may be long-lasting; hence, the severity of impairment is best determined after prolonged observation and serial reexaminations.

3. The diagnosis of a vestibular disorder requires a comprehensive neuro-otolaryngologic examination with a detailed description of the vertiginous episodes, including notation of frequency, severity, and duration of the attacks. Pure tone and speech audiometry with the appropriate special examinations, such as Bekesy audiometry, are necessary. Vestibular function is accessed by positional and caloric testing, preferably by electronystagmography. When polytomograms, contrast radiography, or other special tests have been performed, copies of the reports of these tests should be obtained in addition to appropriate medically acceptable imaging reports of the skull and temporal bone. Medically acceptable imaging includes, but is not limited to, x-ray imaging, computerized axial tomography (CAT scan) or magnetic resonance imaging (MRI), with or without contrast material, myelography, and radiocnuclear bone scans. "Appropriate" means that the technique used is the proper one to support the evaluation and diagnosis of the impairment.

D. Loss of speech.

In evaluating the loss of speech, the ability to produce speech by any means includes the use of mechanical or electronic devices that improve voice or articulation. Impairments of speech may also be evaluated under the body system for the underlying disorder, such as neurological disorders, 11.00ff.

E. How do we evaluate impairments that do not meet one of the special senses and speech listings?

1. These listings are only examples of common special senses and speech disorders that we consider severe enough to prevent an individual from doing any gainful activity. If your impairment(s) does not meet the criteria of any of these listings, we must also consider whether you have an impairment(s) that satisfies the criteria of a listing in another body system.

2. If you have a medically determinable impairment(s) that does not meet a listing, we will determine whether the impairment(s) medically equals a listing. (See §§ 404.1526 and 416.926.) If you have an impairment(s) that does not meet or medically equal a listing, you may or may not have the residual functional capacity to engage in substantial gainful activity. Therefore, we proceed to the fourth, and if necessary, the fifth steps of the sequential evaluation process in §§ 404.1520 and 416.920. When we decide whether you continue to be disabled, we use the rules in §§ 404.1594, 416.994, or 416.994a, as appropriate.

2.01 Category of Impairments, Special Senses and Speech

2.02 Loss of Central Visual Acuity. Remaining vision in the better eye after best correction is 20/200 or less.

***2.03 Contraction of the visual field in the better eye,* with:**

A. The widest diameter subtending an angle around the point of fixation no greater than 20 degrees;

OR

B. An MD of 22 decibels or greater, determined by automated static threshold perimetry that measures the central 30 degrees of the visual field (see 2.00A6d).

OR

C. A visual field efficiency of 20 percent or less, determined by kinetic perimetry (see 2.00A7c).

2.04 *Loss of visual efficiency, or visual impairment, in the better eye:*

A. A visual efficiency percentage of 20 or less after best correction (see 2.00A7d).

OR

B. A visual impairment value of 1.00 or greater after best correction (see 2.00A8d).

2.07 Disturbance of labyrinthine-vestibular function (Including Ménière's disease), characterized by a history of frequent attacks of balance disturbance, tinnitus, and progressive loss of hearing. With both A and B:

A. Disturbed function of vestibular labyrinth demonstrated by caloric or other vestibular tests; and

B. Hearing loss established by audiometry.

2.09 Loss of speech due to any cause, with inability to produce by any means speech that can be heard, understood, or sustained.

2.10 Hearing loss not treated with cochlear implantation.

A. An average air conduction hearing threshold of 90 decibels or greater in the better ear and an average bone conduction hearing threshold of 60 decibels or greater in the better ear (see 2.00B2c).

OR

B. A word recognition score of 40 percent or less in the better ear determined using a standardized list of phonetically balanced monosyllabic words (see 2.00B2e).

2.11 Hearing loss treated with cochlear implantation.

A. Consider under a disability for 1 year after initial implantation.

OR

B. If more than 1 year after initial implantation, a word recognition score of 60 percent or less determined using the HINT (see 2.00B3b).

3.00 Respiratory Disorders

A. *Which disorders do we evaluate in this body system?*

1. We evaluate respiratory disorders that result in obstruction (difficulty moving air out of the lungs) or restriction (difficulty moving air into the lungs), or that interfere with diffusion (gas exchange) across cell membranes in the lungs. Examples of such disorders and the listings we use to evaluate them include chronic obstructive pulmonary disease (chronic bronchitis and emphysema, 3.02), pulmonary fibrosis and pneumoconiosis (3.02), asthma (3.02 or 3.03), cystic fibrosis (3.04), and bronchiectasis (3.02 or 3.07). We also use listings in this body system to evaluate respiratory failure (3.04D or 3.14), chronic pulmonary hypertension (3.09), and lung transplantation (3.11).
2. We evaluate cancers affecting the respiratory system under the listings in 13.00. We evaluate the pulmonary effects of neuromuscular and autoimmune disorders under these listings or under the listings in 11.00 or 14.00, respectively.

B. *What are the symptoms and signs of respiratory disorders?* Symptoms and signs of respiratory disorders include dyspnea (shortness of breath), chest pain, coughing, wheezing, sputum production, hemoptysis (coughing up blood from the respiratory tract), use of accessory muscles of respiration, and tachypnea (rapid rate of breathing).

C. *What abbreviations do we use in this body system?*

1. *ABG* means arterial blood gas.
2. *BiPAP* means bi-level positive airway pressure ventilation.
3. *BTPS* means body temperature and ambient pressure, saturated with water vapor.
4. *CF* means cystic fibrosis.
5. *CFRD* means CF-related diabetes.
6. *CFTR* means CF transmembrane conductance regulator.
7. *CO* means carbon monoxide.
8. *COPD* means chronic obstructive pulmonary disease.
9. *DLCO* means diffusing capacity of the lungs for carbon monoxide.
10. FEV_1 means forced expiratory volume in the first second of a forced expiratory maneuver.
11. *FVC* means forced vital capacity.
12. *L* means liter.

13. *mL CO (STPD)/min/mmHg* means milliliters of carbon monoxide at standard temperature and pressure, dry, per minute, per millimeter of mercury.
14. *PaO_2* means arterial blood partial pressure of oxygen.
15. *$PaCO_2$* means arterial blood partial pressure of carbon dioxide.
16. *SpO_2* means percentage of oxygen saturation of blood hemoglobin measured by pulse oximetry.
17. *6MWT* means 6-minute walk test.
18. *VI* means volume of inhaled gas during a DLCO test.

D. *What documentation do we need to evaluate your respiratory disorder?*

1. We need *medical evidence* to document and assess the severity of your respiratory disorder. Medical evidence should include your medical history, physical examination findings, the results of imaging (see 3.00D3), pulmonary function tests (see 3.00D4), other relevant laboratory tests, and descriptions of any prescribed treatment and your response to it. We may not need all of this evidence depending on your particular respiratory disorder and its effects on you.
2. If you use *supplemental oxygen*, we still need medical evidence to establish the severity of your respiratory disorder.
3. *Imaging* refers to medical imaging techniques, such as x-ray and computerized tomography. The imaging must be consistent with the prevailing state of medical knowledge and clinical practice as the proper technique to support the evaluation of the disorder.
4. *Pulmonary function tests* include *spirometry* (which measures ventilation of the lungs), *DLCO* tests (which measure gas diffusion in the lungs), *ABG* tests (which measure the partial pressure of oxygen, PaO_2, and carbon dioxide, $PaCO_2$, in the arterial blood), and *pulse oximetry* (which measures oxygen saturation, SpO_2, of peripheral blood hemoglobin).

E. *What is spirometry and what are our requirements for an acceptable test and report?*

1. Spirometry, which measures how well you move air into and out of your lungs, involves at least three forced expiratory maneuvers during the same test session. A forced expiratory maneuver is a maximum inhalation followed by a forced maximum exhalation, and measures exhaled volumes of air over time. The volume of air you exhale in the first second of the forced expiratory maneuver is the FEV_1. The total volume of air that you exhale during the entire forced expiratory maneuver is the FVC. We use your highest FEV_1 value to evaluate your respiratory disorder under 3.02A, 3.03A, and 3.04A, and your highest FVC value to evaluate your respiratory disorder under 3.02B, regardless of whether the values are

from the same forced expiratory maneuver or different forced expiratory maneuvers.

2. We have the following requirements for spirometry under these listings:
   a. You must be medically stable at the time of the test. Examples of when we would not consider you to be medically stable include when you are:
      i. Within 2 weeks of a change in your prescribed respiratory medication.
      ii. Experiencing, or within 30 days of completion of treatment for, a lower respiratory tract infection.
      iii. Experiencing, or within 30 days of completion of treatment for, an acute exacerbation (temporary worsening) of a chronic respiratory disorder. Wheezing by itself does not indicate that you are not medically stable.
      iv. Hospitalized, or within 30 days of a hospital discharge, for an acute myocardial infarction (heart attack).
   b. During testing, if your FEV_1 is less than 70 percent of your predicted normal value, we require repeat spirometry after inhalation of a bronchodilator to evaluate your respiratory disorder under these listings, unless it is medically contraindicated. If you used a bronchodilator before the test and your FEV_1 is less than 70 percent of your predicted normal value, we still require repeat spirometry after inhalation of a bronchodilator unless the supervising physician determines that it is not safe for you to take a bronchodilator again (in which case we may need to reschedule the test). If you do not have post-bronchodilator spirometry, the test report must explain why. We can use the results of spirometry administered without bronchodilators when the use of bronchodilators is medically contraindicated.
   c. Your forced expiratory maneuvers must be satisfactory. We consider a forced expiratory maneuver to be satisfactory when you exhale with maximum effort following a full inspiration, and when the test tracing has a sharp takeoff and rapid rise to peak flow, has a smooth contour, and either lasts for at least 6 seconds or maintains a plateau for at least 1 second.
3. The spirometry report must include the following information:
   a. The date of the test and your name, age or date of birth, gender, and height without shoes. (We will assume that your recorded height on the date of the test is without shoes, unless we have evidence to the contrary.) If your spine is abnormally curved (for example, you have kyphoscoliosis), we will substitute the longest distance between your outstretched fingertips with your arms abducted 90 degrees in place of your height when this measurement is greater than your standing height without shoes.

b. Any factors, if applicable, that can affect the interpretation of the test results (for example, your cooperation or effort in doing the test).

c. Legible tracings of your forced expiratory maneuvers in a volume-time format showing your name and the date of the test for each maneuver.

4. If we purchase spirometry, the medical source we designate to administer the test is solely responsible for deciding whether it is safe for you to do the test and for how to administer it.

F. *What is a DLCO test, and what are our requirements for an acceptable test and report?*

1. A DLCO test measures the gas exchange across cell membranes in your lungs. It measures how well CO diffuses from the alveoli (air sacs) of your lungs into your blood. DLCO may be severely reduced in some disorders, such as interstitial lung disease (for example, idiopathic pulmonary fibrosis, asbestosis, and sarcoidosis) and COPD (particularly emphysema), even when the results of spirometry are not significantly reduced. We use the average of two of your unadjusted (that is, uncorrected for hemoglobin concentration) DLCO measurements reported in mL CO (STPD)/min/mmHg to evaluate your respiratory disorder under 3.02C1.

2. We have the following requirements for DLCO tests under these listings:

   a. You must be medically stable at the time of the test. See 3.00E2a.

   b. The test must use the single-breath technique.

      i. The VI during the DLCO maneuver must be at least 85 percent of your current FVC, and your time of inhalation must be less than 4 seconds. (See 3.00E for our rules for programmatically acceptable spirometry.) If you do not have an FVC measurement on the same day as the DLCO test, we may use your FVC from programmatically acceptable spirometry administered within 90 days of the DLCO test.

      ii. Your breath-hold time must be between 8 and 12 seconds.

      iii. Your total exhalation time must be less than or equal to 4 seconds, with a sample collection time of less than 3 seconds. If your FVC is at least 2.0 L, the washout volume must be between 0.75 L and 1.0 L. If your FVC is less than 2.0 L, the washout volume must be at least 0.5 L.

3. The DLCO test report must include the following information:

   a. The date of the test and your name, age or date of birth, gender, and height without shoes. (We will assume that your recorded height on the date of the test is without shoes, unless we have evidence to the contrary.) If your spine is abnormally curved (for example, you have kyphoscoliosis), we will substitute the longest distance between your outstretched fingertips with your arms abducted 90 degrees in place of your height when this measurement is greater than your standing height without shoes.

b. Any factors, if applicable, that can affect the interpretation of the test results (for example, your cooperation or effort in doing the test).

c. Legible tracings of your VI, breath-hold maneuver, and volume of exhaled gas showing your name and the date of the test for each DLCO maneuver.

d. At least two acceptable (see 3.00F2) DLCO measurements within 3 mL CO (STPD)/min/mmHg of each other *or* within 10 percent of the highest value.

4. We may need to purchase a DLCO test to determine whether your disorder meets 3.02C1 when we have evidence showing that you have a chronic respiratory disorder that could result in impaired gas exchange, unless we can make a fully favorable determination or decision on another basis. Since the DLCO calculation requires a current FVC measurement, we may also purchase spirometry at the same time as the DLCO test, even if we already have programmatically acceptable spirometry.

5. Before we purchase a DLCO test, a medical consultant (see §§ 404.1616 and 416.1016 of this chapter), preferably one with experience in the care of people with respiratory disorders, must review your case record to determine if we need the test. The medical source we designate to administer the test is solely responsible for deciding whether it is safe for you to do the test and for how to administer it.

G. What is an ABG test, and what are our requirements for an acceptable test and report?

1. *General.* An ABG test measures PaO_2, $PaCO_2$, and the concentration of hydrogen ions in your arterial blood. We use a resting or an exercise ABG measurement to evaluate your respiratory disorder under 3.02C2.

2. *Resting ABG tests.*

   a. We have the following requirements for resting ABG tests under these listings:

      i. You must be medically stable at the time of the test. See 3.00E2a.

      ii. The test must be administered while you are breathing room air; that is, without oxygen supplementation.

   b. The resting ABG test report must include the following information:

      i. You name, the date of the test, and either the altitude or both the city and State of the test site.

      ii. The PaO_2 and $PaCO_2$ values.

c. We may need to purchase a resting ABG test to determine whether your disorder meets 3.02C2 when we have evidence showing that you have a chronic respiratory disorder that could result in impaired gas exchange, unless we can make a fully favorable determination or decision on another basis.

d. Before we purchase a resting ABG test, a medical consultant (see §§ 404.1616 and 416.1016 of this chapter), preferably one with experience in the care of people with respiratory disorders, must review your case record to determine if we need the test. The medical source we designate to administer the test is solely responsible for deciding whether it is safe for you to do the test and for how to administer it.

3. *Exercise ABG tests.*

   a. We will not purchase an exercise ABG test.

   b. We have the following requirements for exercise ABG tests under these listings:

      i. You must have done the exercise under steady state conditions while breathing room air. If you were tested on a treadmill, you generally must have exercised for at least 4 minutes at a grade and speed providing oxygen (O_2) consumption of approximately 17.5 milliliters per kilogram per minute (mL/kg/min) or 5.0 metabolic equivalents (METs). If you were tested on a cycle ergometer, you generally must have exercised for at least 4 minutes at an exercise equivalent of 5.0 METs.

      ii. We may use a test in which you have not exercised for at least 4 minutes. If you were unable to complete at least 4 minutes of steady state exercise, we need a statement by the person administering the test about whether the results are a valid indication of your respiratory status. For example, this statement may include information about your cooperation or effort in doing the test and whether you were limited in completing the test because of your respiratory disorder or another impairment.

   c. The exercise ABG test report must include the following information:

      i. Your name, the date of the test, and either the altitude or both the city and state of the test site.

      ii. The PaO_2 and $PaCO_2$ values.

H. *What is pulse oximetry, and what are our requirements for an acceptable test and report?*

1. Pulse oximetry measures SpO_2, the percentage of oxygen saturation of blood hemoglobin. We use a pulse oximetry measurement (either at rest, during a 6MWT, or after a 6MWT) to evaluate your respiratory disorder under 3.02C3 or, if you have CF, to evaluate it under 3.04F.

2. We have the following requirements for pulse oximetry under 3.02C3:
   a. You must be medically stable at the time of the test. See 3.00E2a.
   b. Your pulse oximetry measurement must be recorded while you are breathing room air; that is, without oxygen supplementation.
   c. Your pulse oximetry measurement must be stable. By "stable," we mean that the range of SpO_2 values (that is, lowest to highest) during any 15-second interval cannot exceed 2 percentage points. For example: (1) the measurement is stable if the lowest SpO_2 value during a 15-second interval is 87 percent and the highest value is 89 percent—a range of 2 percentage points. (2) The measurement is not stable if the lowest value is 86 percent and the highest value is 89 percent—a range of 3 percentage points.
   d. If you have had more than one measurement (for example, at rest and after a 6MWT), we will use the measurement with the lowest SpO_2 value.
   e. The pulse oximetry report must include the following information:
      i. Your name, the date of the test, and either the altitude or both the city and State of the test site.
      ii. A graphical printout showing your SpO_2 value and a concurrent, acceptable pulse wave. An acceptable pulse wave is one that shows the characteristic pulse wave; that is, sawtooth-shaped with a rapid systolic upstroke (nearly vertical) followed by a slower diastolic downstroke (angled downward).
   f. We may need to purchase pulse oximetry at rest to determine whether your disorder meets 3.02C3 when we have evidence showing that you have a chronic respiratory disorder that could result in impaired gas exchange, unless we can make a fully favorable determination or decision on another basis. We may purchase pulse oximetry during and after a 6MWT if your SpO_2 value at rest is greater than the value in Table V.
   g. Before we purchase pulse oximetry, a medical consultant (see §§ 404.1616 and 416.1016 of this chapter), preferably one with experience in the care of people with respiratory disorders, must review your case record to determine if we need the test. The medical source we designate to administer the test is solely responsible for deciding whether it is safe for you to do the test and for how to administer it.
3. We have the following requirements for pulse oximetry under 3.04F:
   a. You must be medically stable at the time of the test. See 3.00E2a.
   b. Your pulse oximetry measurement must be recorded while you are breathing room air; that is, without oxygen supplementation.
   c. If you have had more than one measurement (for example, at rest and after a 6MWT), we will use the measurement with the lowest SpO_2 value.

d. The pulse oximetry report must include your name, the date of the test, and either the altitude or both the city and State of the test site. If you have CF, we do not require a graphical printout showing your SpO_2 value and a concurrent, acceptable pulse wave.

I. *What is asthma and how do we evaluate it?*

1. *Asthma* is a chronic inflammatory disorder of the lung airways that we evaluate under 3.02 or 3.03. If you have respiratory failure resulting from chronic asthma (see 3.00N), we will evaluate it under 3.14.
2. For the purposes of 3.03:
   a. We need evidence showing that you have listing-level (see Table VI in 3.03A) airflow obstruction at baseline while you are medically stable.
   b. The phrase "consider under a disability for 1 year" in 3.03B does not refer to the date on which your disability began, only to the date on which we must reevaluate whether your asthma continues to meet a listing or is otherwise disabling.
   c. We determine the onset of your disability based on the facts of your case, but it will be no later than the admission date of your first of three hospitalizations that satisfy the criteria of 3.03B.

J. *What is CF and how do we evaluate it?*

1. *General*. We evaluate CF, a genetic disorder that results in abnormal salt and water transport across cell membranes in the lungs, pancreas, and other body organs, under 3.04. We need the evidence described in 3.00J2 to establish that you have CF.
2. *Documentation of CF*. We need a report signed by a physician (see §§ 404.1513(a) and 416.913(a) of this chapter) showing both a and b:
   a. One of the following:
      i. A positive newborn screen for CF; or
      ii. A history of CF in a sibling; or
      iii. Documentation of at least one specific CF phenotype or clinical criterion (for example, chronic sino-pulmonary disease with persistent colonization or infections with typical CF pathogens, pancreatic insufficiency, or salt-loss syndromes); *and*
   b. One of the following definitive laboratory tests:
      i. An elevated sweat chloride concentration equal to or greater than 60 millimoles per L; or
      ii. The identification of two CF gene mutations affecting the CFTR; or
      iii. Characteristic abnormalities in ion transport across the nasal epithelium.

c. When we have the report showing a and b, but it is not signed by a physician, we also need a report from a physician stating that you have CF.

d. When we do not have the report showing a and b, we need a report from a physician that is persuasive that a positive diagnosis of CF was confirmed by an appropriate definitive laboratory test. To be persuasive, this report must include a statement by the physician that you had the appropriate definitive laboratory test for diagnosing CF. The report must provide the test results or explain how your diagnosis was established that is consistent with the prevailing state of medical knowledge and clinical practice.

3. *CF pulmonary exacerbations.* Examples of CF pulmonary exacerbations include increased cough and sputum production, hemoptysis, increased shortness of breath, increased fatigue, and reduction in pulmonary function. Treatment usually includes intravenous antibiotics and intensified airway clearance therapy (for example, increased frequencies of chest percussion or increased use of inhaled nebulized therapies, such as bronchodilators or mucolytics).

4. For 3.04G, we require any two exacerbations or complications from the list in 3.04G1 through 3.04G4 within a 12-month period. You may have two of the same exacerbation or complication or two different ones.

   a. If you have two of the acute exacerbations or complications we describe in 3.04G1 and 3.04G2, there must be at least 30 days between the two.

   b. If you have one of the acute exacerbations or complications we describe in 3.04G1 and 3.04G2 and one of the chronic complications we describe in 3.04G3 and 3.04G4, the two can occur during the same time. For example, your CF meets 3.04G if you have the pulmonary hemorrhage we describe in 3.04G2 and the weight loss we describe in 3.04G3 even if the pulmonary hemorrhage occurs during the 90-day period in 3.04G3.

   c. Your CF also meets 3.04G if you have both of the chronic complications in 3.04G3 and 3.04G4.

5. CF may also affect other body systems such as digestive or endocrine. If your CF, including pulmonary exacerbations and nonpulmonary complications, does not meet or medically equal a respiratory disorders listing, we may evaluate your CF-related impairments under the listings in the affected body system.

K. *What is bronchiectasis and how do we evaluate it?* Bronchiectasis is a chronic respiratory disorder that is characterized by abnormal and irreversible dilatation (enlargement) of the airways below the trachea, which may be associated with the accumulation of mucus, bacterial infections, and eventual airway scarring. We require imaging (see 3.00D3) to document this disorder. We evaluate your bronchiectasis under 3.02, or under 3.07 if you are having exacerbations or complications (for example, acute bacterial infections, increased shortness of breath, or coughing up blood) that require hospitalization.

L. *What is chronic pulmonary hypertension and how do we evaluate it?*

1. Chronic pulmonary hypertension is an increase in the blood pressure of the blood vessels of the lungs. If pulmonary hypertension is not adequately treated, it can eventually result in right heart failure. We evaluate chronic pulmonary hypertension due to any cause under 3.09.
2. Chronic pulmonary hypertension is usually diagnosed by catheterization of the pulmonary artery. We will not purchase cardiac catheterization.

M. *How do we evaluate lung transplantation?* If you receive a lung transplant (or a lung transplant simultaneously with other organs, such as the heart), we will consider you to be disabled under 3.11 for 3 years from the date of the transplant. After that, we evaluate your residual impairment(s) by considering the adequacy of your post-transplant function, the frequency and severity of any rejection episodes you have, complications in other body systems, and adverse treatment effects. People who receive organ transplants generally have impairments that meet our definition of disability before they undergo transplantation. The phrase "consider under a disability for 3 years" in 3.11 does not refer to the date on which your disability began, only to the date on which we must reevaluate whether your impairment(s) continues to meet a listing or is otherwise disabling. We determine the onset of your disability based on the facts of your case.

N. *What is respiratory failure and how do we evaluate it?* Respiratory failure is the inability of the lungs to perform their basic function of gas exchange. We evaluate respiratory failure under 3.04D if you have CF-related respiratory failure, or under 3.14 if you have respiratory failure due to any other chronic respiratory disorder. Continuous positive airway pressure does not satisfy the criterion in 3.04D or 3.14, and cannot be substituted as an equivalent finding, for invasive mechanical ventilation or noninvasive ventilation with BiPAP.

O. *How do we consider the effects of obesity when we evaluate your respiratory disorder?* Obesity is a medically determinable impairment that is often associated with respiratory disorders. Obesity makes it harder for the chest and lungs to expand, which can compromise the ability of the respiratory system to supply adequate oxygen to the body. The combined effects of obesity with a respiratory disorder can be greater than the effects of each of the impairments considered separately. We consider any additional and cumulative effects of your obesity when we determine whether you have a severe respiratory disorder, a listing-level respiratory disorder, a combination of impairments that medically equals the severity of a listed impairment, and when we assess your residual functional capacity.

P. *What are sleep-related breathing disorders and how do we evaluate them?*

1. *Sleep-related breathing disorders* (for example, sleep apnea) are characterized by transient episodes of interrupted breathing during sleep, which disrupt

normal sleep patterns. Prolonged episodes can result in disorders such as hypoxemia (low blood oxygen) and pulmonary vasoconstriction (restricted blood flow in pulmonary blood vessels). Over time, these disorders may lead to chronic pulmonary hypertension or other complications.

2. We evaluate the complications of sleep-related breathing disorders under the listings in the affected body system(s). For example, we evaluate chronic pulmonary hypertension due to any cause under 3.09; chronic heart failure under 4.02; and disturbances in mood, cognition, and behavior under 12.02 or another appropriate mental disorders listing. We will not purchase polysomnography (sleep study).

Q. *How do we evaluate mycobacterial, mycotic, and other chronic infections of the lungs?* We evaluate chronic infections of the lungs that result in limitations in your respiratory function under 3.02.

R. *How do we evaluate respiratory disorders that do not meet one of these listings?*

1. These listings are only examples of common respiratory disorders that we consider severe enough to prevent you from doing any gainful activity. If your impairment(s) does not meet the criteria of any of these listings, we must also consider whether you have an impairment(s) that meets the criteria of a listing in another body system. For example, if your CF has resulted in chronic pancreatic or hepatobiliary disease, we evaluate your impairment under the listings in 5.00.
2. If you have a severe medically determinable impairment(s) that does not meet a listing, we will determine whether your impairment(s) medically equals a listing. See §§ 404.1526 and 416.926 of this chapter. Respiratory disorders may be associated with disorders in other body systems, and we consider the combined effects of multiple impairments when we determine whether they medically equal a listing. If your impairment(s) does not meet or medically equal a listing, you may or may not have the residual functional capacity to engage in substantial gainful activity. We proceed to the fourth step and, if necessary, the fifth step of the sequential evaluation process in §§ 404.1520 and 416.920 of this chapter. We use the rules in §§ 404.1594 and 416.994 of this chapter, as appropriate, when we decide whether you continue to be disabled.

3.01 Category of Impairments, Respiratory System

3.02 *Chronic respiratory disorders* due to any cause except CF (for CF, see 3.04) with A, B, C, or D:

A. FEV_1 (see 3.00E) less than or equal to the value in Table I-A or I-B for your age, gender, and height without shoes (see 3.00E3a).

OR

B. FVC (see 3.00E) less than or equal to the value in Table II-A or II-B for your age, gender, and height without shoes (see 3.00E3a).

Table I: FEV_1 Criteria for 3.02A

		Table I-A		*Table I-B*	
		Age 18 to attainment of age 20		Age 20 or older	
Height without shoes (*centimeters*) < means *less than*	Height without shoes (*inches*) < means *less than*	*Females* FEV_1 less than or equal to (L, BTPS)	*Males* FEV_1 less than or equal to (L, BTPS)	*Females* FEV_1 less than or equal to (L, BTPS)	*Males* FEV_1 less than or equal to (L, BTPS)
<153.0	<60.25	1.20	1.45	1.05	1.20
153.0 to <159.0	60.25 to <62.50	1.30	1.55	1.15	1.35
159.0 to <164.0	62.50 to <64.50	1.40	1.65	1.25	1.40
164.0 to <169.0	64.50 to <66.50	1.45	1.75	1.35	1.50
169.0 to <174.0	66.50 to <68.50	1.55	1.85	1.45	1.60
174.0 to <180.0	68.50 to <70.75	1.65	2.00	1.55	1.75
180.0 to <185.0	70.75 to <72.75	1.75	2.10	1.65	1.85
185.0 or more	72.75 or more	1.80	2.15	1.70	1.90

Table II: FVC Criteria for 3.02B

		Table II-A		*Table II-B*	
		Age 18 to attainment of age 20		Age 20 or older	
Height without shoes (*centimeters*) < means *less than*	Height without shoes (*inches*) < means less than	*Females* FVC less than or equal to (L, BTPS)	*Males* FVC less than or equal to (L, BTPS)	*Females* FVC less than or equal to (L, BTPS)	*Males* FVC less than or equal to (L, BTPS)
<153.0	<60.25	1.35	1.65	1.30	1.50
153.0 to <159.0	60.25 to <62.50	1.50	1.80	1.40	1.65
159.0 to <164.0	62.50 to <64.50	1.60	1.90	1.50	1.75
164.0 to <169.0	64.50 to <66.50	1.70	2.05	1.60	1.90
169.0 to <174.0	66.50 to <68.50	1.80	2.20	1.70	2.00
174.0 to <180.0	68.50 to <70.75	1.90	2.35	1.85	2.20
180.0 to <185.0	70.75 to <72.75	2.05	2.50	1.95	2.30
185.0 or more	72.75 or more	2.10	2.60	2.00	2.40

Table III: DLCO Criteria for 3.02C1

Height without shoes (*centimeters*) < means *less than*	Height without shoes (*inches*) < means *less than*	*Females* DLCO Less than or equal to (mL CO (STPD)/ min/mmHg)	*Males* DLCO Less than or equal to (mL CO (STPD)/ min/mmHg)
<153.0	<60.25	8.0	9.0
153.0 to <159.0	60.25 to <62.50	8.5	9.5
159.0 to <164.0	62.50 to <64.50	9.0	10.0
164.0 to <169.0	64.50 to <66.50	9.5	10.5
169.0 to <174.0	66.50 to <68.50	10.0	11.0
174.0 to <180.0	68.50 to <70.75	10.5	11.5
180.0 to <185.0	70.75 to <72.75	11.0	12.0
185.0 or more	72.75 or more	11.5	12.5

OR

C. Chronic impairment of gas exchange demonstrated by 1, 2, or 3:

1. Average of two unadjusted, single-breath DLCO measurements (see 3.00F) less than or equal to the value in Table III for your gender and height without shoes (see 3.00F3a); or
2. Arterial PaO_2 and $PaCO_2$ measured concurrently by an ABG test, while at rest or during steady state exercise, breathing room air (see 3.00G3b), less than or equal to the applicable values in Table IV-A, IV-B, or IV-C; or
3. SpO_2 measured by pulse oximetry (see 3.00H2) either at rest, during a 6MWT, or after a 6MWT, less than or equal to the value in Table V.

OR

D. Exacerbations or complications requiring three hospitalizations within a 12-month period and at least 30 days apart (the 12-month period must occur within the period we are considering in connection with your application or continuing disability review). Each hospitalization must last at least 48 hours, including hours in a hospital emergency department immediately before the hospitalization.

3.03 *Asthma*. (see 3.00I), with both A and B:

A. FEV_1 (see 3.00E1) less than or equal to the value in Table VI-A or VI-B for your age, gender, and height without shoes (see 3.00E3a) measured within the same 12-month period as the hospitalizations in 3.03B.

Tables IV-A, IV-B, and IV-C: ABG Criteria for 3.02C2

Table IV-A

(Applicable at test sites less than 3,000 feet above sea level)	
Arterial $PaCO_2$ (mm Hg) *and*	Arterial PaO_2 less than or equal to (mm Hg)
30 or below	65
31	64
32	63
33	62
34	61
35	60
36	59
37	58
38	57
39	56
40 or above	55

Table IV-B

(Applicable at test sites from 3,000 through 6,000 feet above sea level)	
Arterial $PaCO_2$ (mm Hg) *and*	Arterial PaO_2 less than or equal to (mm Hg)
30 or below	60
31	59
32	58
33	57
34	56
35	55
36	54
37	53
38	52
39	51
40 or above	50

Table IV-C

(Applicable at test sites over 6,000 feet above sea level)	
Arterial $PaCO_2$ (mm Hg) *and*	**Arterial PaO_2 less than or equal to (mm Hg)**
30 or below	55
31	54
32	53
33	52
34	51
35	50
36	49
37	48
38	47
39	46
40 or above	45

Table V: SpO_2 Criteria for 3.02C3

Test site altitude (feet above sea level)	**SpO_2 less than or equal to**
Less than 3,000	87 percent
3,000 through 6,000	85 percent
Over 6,000	83 percent

AND

B. Exacerbations or complications requiring three hospitalizations within a 12-month period and at least 30 days apart (the 12-month period must occur within the period we are considering in connection with your application or continuing disability review). Each hospitalization must last at least 48 hours, including hours in a hospital emergency department immediately before the hospitalization. Consider under a disability for 1 year from the discharge date of the last hospitalization; after that, evaluate the residual impairment(s) under 3.03 or another appropriate listing.

3.04 ***Cystic fibrosis***. (documented as described in 3.00J2) with A, B, C, D, E, F, or G:

A. FEV_1 (see 3.00E) less than or equal to the value in Table VII-A or VII-B for your age, gender, and height without shoes (see 3.00E3a).

Table VI: FEV_1 Criteria for 3.03A

		Table VI-A		*Table VI-B*	
		Age 18 to attainment of age 20		Age 20 or older	
Height without shoes (*centimeters*) < means *less than*	Height without shoes (*inches*) < means *less than*	*Females* FEV_1 less than or equal to (L, BTPS)	*Males* FEV_1 less than or equal to (L, BTPS)	*Females* FEV_1 less than or equal to (L, BTPS)	*Males* FEV_1 less than or equal to (L, BTPS)
<153.0	<60.25	1.65	1.90	1.45	1.60
153.0 to <159.0	60.25 to <62.50	1.75	2.05	1.55	1.75
159.0 to <164.0	62.50 to <64.50	1.85	2.15	1.65	1.90
164.0 to <169.0	64.50 to <66.50	1.95	2.30	1.75	2.00
169.0 to <174.0	66.50 to <68.50	2.05	2.45	1.85	2.15
174.0 to <180.0	68.50 to <70.75	2.20	2.60	2.00	2.30
180.0 to <185.0	70.75 to <72.75	2.35	2.75	2.10	2.45
185.0 or more	72.75 or more	2.40	2.85	2.20	2.55

Table VII: FEV_1 Criteria for 3.04A

		Table VII-A		*Table VII-B*	
		Age 18 to attainment of age 20		Age 20 or older	
Height without shoes (*centimeters*) < means *less than*	Height without shoes (*inches*) < means *less than*	*Females* FEV_1 less than or equal to (L, BTPS)	*Males* FEV_1 less than or equal to (L, BTPS)	*Females* FEV_1 less than or equal to (L, BTPS)	*Males* FEV_1 less than or equal to (L, BTPS)
<153.0	<60.25	1.65	1.90	1.45	1.60
153.0 to <159.0	60.25 to <62.50	1.75	2.05	1.55	1.75
159.0 to <164.0	62.50 to <64.50	1.85	2.15	1.65	1.90
164.0 to <169.0	64.50 to <66.50	1.95	2.30	1.75	2.00
169.0 to <174.0	66.50 to <68.50	2.05	2.45	1.85	2.15
174.0 to <180.0	68.50 to <70.75	2.20	2.60	2.00	2.30
180.0 to <185.0	70.75 to <72.75	2.35	2.75	2.10	2.45
185.0 or more	72.75 or more	2.40	2.85	2.20	2.55

OR

B. Exacerbations or complications (see 3.00J3) requiring three hospitalizations of any length within a 12-month period and at least 30 days apart (the 12-month period must occur within the period we are considering in connection with your application or continuing disability review).

OR

C. Spontaneous pneumothorax, secondary to CF, requiring chest tube placement.

OR

D. Respiratory failure (see 3.00N) requiring invasive mechanical ventilation, noninvasive ventilation with BiPAP, or a combination of both treatments, for a continuous period of at least 48 hours, or for a continuous period of at least 2 hours if postoperatively.

E. Pulmonary hemorrhage requiring vascular embolization to control bleeding.

OR

F. SpO_2 measured by pulse oximetry (see 3.00H3) either at rest, during a 6MWT, or after a 6MWT, less than or equal to the value in Table VIII, *twice* within a 12-month period and at least 30 days apart (the 12-month period must occur within the period we are considering in connection with your application or continuing disability review).

OR

G. Two of the following exacerbations or complications (either two of the same or two different, see 3.00J3 and 3.00J4) within a 12-month period (the 12-month period must occur within the period we are considering in connection with your application or continuing disability review):

1. Pulmonary exacerbation requiring 10 consecutive days of intravenous antibiotic treatment.
2. Pulmonary hemorrhage (hemoptysis with more than blood-streaked sputum but not requiring vascular embolization) requiring hospitalization of any length.

Tables VIII: SpO_2 Criteria for 3.04F

Test site altitude (feet above sea level)	SpO_2 less than or equal to
Less than 3,000	89 percent
3,000 through 6,000	87 percent
Over 6,000	85 percent

3. Weight loss requiring daily supplemental enteral nutrition via a gastrostomy for at least 90 consecutive days *or* parenteral nutrition via a central venous catheter for at least 90 consecutive days.
4. CFRD requiring daily insulin therapy for at least 90 consecutive days.

3.05 *[Reserved]*

3.06 *[Reserved]*

3.07 ***Bronchiectasis*** (see 3.00K), documented by imaging (see 3.00D3), with exacerbations or complications requiring three hospitalizations within a 12-month period and at least 30 days apart (the 12-month period must occur within the period we are considering in connection with your application or continuing disability review). Each hospitalization must last at least 48 hours, including hours in a hospital emergency department immediately before the hospitalization.

3.08 *[Reserved]*

3.09 ***Chronic pulmonary hypertension due to any cause*** (see 3.00L) documented by mean pulmonary artery pressure equal to or greater than 40 mm Hg as determined by cardiac catheterization while medically stable (see 3.00E2a).

3.10 *[Reserved]*

3.11 ***Lung transplantation*** (see 3.00M). Consider under a disability for 3 years from the date of the transplant; after that, evaluate the residual impairment(s).

3.12 *[Reserved]*

3.13 *[Reserved]*

3.14 ***Respiratory failure*** (see 3.00N) resulting from any underlying chronic respiratory disorder except CF (for CF, see 3.04D), requiring invasive mechanical ventilation, noninvasive ventilation with BiPAP, or a combination of both treatments, for a continuous period of at least 48 hours, or for a continuous period of at least 72 hours if postoperatively, *twice* within a 12-month period and at least 30 days apart (the 12-month period must occur within the period we are considering in connection with your application or continuing disability review).

4.00 Cardiovascular System

A. General

1. *What do we mean by a cardiovascular impairment?*

a. We mean any disorder that affects the proper functioning of the heart or the circulatory system (that is, arteries, veins, capillaries, and the lymphatic drainage). The disorder can be congenital or acquired.

b. Cardiovascular impairment results from one or more of four consequences of heart disease:

(i) Chronic heart failure or ventricular dysfunction.

(ii) Discomfort or pain due to myocardial ischemia, with or without necrosis of heart muscle.

(iii) Syncope, or near syncope, due to inadequate cerebral perfusion from any cardiac cause, such as obstruction of flow or disturbance in rhythm or conduction resulting in inadequate cardiac output.

(iv) Central cyanosis due to right-to-left shunt, reduced oxygen concentration in the arterial blood, or pulmonary vascular disease.

c. Disorders of the veins or arteries (for example, obstruction, rupture, or aneurysm) may cause impairments of the lower extremities (peripheral vascular disease), the central nervous system, the eyes, the kidneys, and other organs. We will evaluate peripheral vascular disease under 4.11 or 4.12 and impairments of another body system(s) under the listings for that body system(s).

2. *What do we consider in evaluating cardiovascular impairments?* The listings in this section describe cardiovascular impairments based on symptoms, signs, laboratory findings, response to a regimen of prescribed treatment, and functional limitations.

3. *What do the following terms or phrases mean in these listings?*

a. *Medical consultant* is an individual defined in §§ 404.1616(a) and 416.1016(a). This term does not include medical sources who provide consultative examinations for us. We use the abbreviation "MC" throughout this section to designate a medical consultant.

b. *Persistent* means that the longitudinal clinical record shows that, with few exceptions, the required finding(s) has been present, or is expected to be present, for a continuous period of at least 12 months, such that a pattern of continuing severity is established.

c. *Recurrent* means that the longitudinal clinical record shows that, within a consecutive 12-month period, the finding(s) occurs at least three times, with intervening periods of improvement of sufficient duration that it is clear that separate events are involved.

d. *Appropriate medically acceptable imaging* means that the technique used is the proper one to evaluate and diagnose the impairment and is commonly recognized as accurate for assessing the cited finding.

e. *A consecutive 12-month period* means a period of 12 consecutive months, all or part of which must occur within the period we are considering in connection with an application or continuing disability review.

f. *Uncontrolled* means the impairment does not adequately respond to standard prescribed medical treatment.

B. *Documenting Cardiovascular Impairment*

1. *What basic documentation do we need?* We need sufficiently detailed reports of history, physical examinations, laboratory studies, and any prescribed treatment and response to allow us to assess the severity and duration of your cardiovascular impairment. A longitudinal clinical record covering a period of not less than 3 months of observations and treatment is usually necessary, unless we can make a determination or decision based on the current evidence.

2. *Why is a longitudinal clinical record important?* We will usually need a longitudinal clinical record to assess the severity and expected duration of your impairment(s). If you have a listing-level impairment, you probably will have received medically prescribed treatment. Whenever there is evidence of such treatment, your longitudinal clinical record should include a description of the ongoing management and evaluation provided by your treating or other medical source. It should also include your response to this medical management, as well as information about the nature and severity of your impairment. The record will provide us with information on your functional status over an extended period of time and show whether your ability to function is improving, worsening, or unchanging.

3. *What if you have not received ongoing medical treatment?*

a. You may not have received ongoing treatment or have an ongoing relationship with the medical community despite the existence of a severe impairment(s). In this situation, we will base our evaluation on the current objective medical evidence and the other evidence we have. If you do not receive treatment, you cannot show an impairment that meets the criteria of most of these listings. However, we may find you disabled because you have another impairment(s) that in combination with your cardiovascular impairment medically equals the severity of a listed impairment or based on consideration of your residual functional capacity and age, education, and work experience.

b. Unless we can decide your claim favorably on the basis of the current evidence, a longitudinal record is still important. In rare instances where there is no or insufficient longitudinal evidence, we may purchase a consultative examination(s) to help us establish the severity and duration of your impairment.

4. *When will we wait before we ask for more evidence?*

a. We will wait when we have information showing that your impairment is not yet stable and the expected change in your impairment might affect our determination or decision. In these situations, we need to wait to properly evaluate the severity and duration of your impairment during a stable period. Examples of when we might wait are:

(i) If you have had a recent acute event; for example, a myocardial infarction (heart attack).

(ii) If you have recently had a corrective cardiac procedure; for example, coronary artery bypass grafting.

(iii) If you have started new drug therapy and your response to this treatment has not yet been established; for example, beta-blocker therapy for dilated congestive cardiomyopathy.

b. In these situations, we will obtain more evidence 3 months following the event before we evaluate your impairment. However, we will not wait if we have enough information to make a determination or decision based on all of the relevant evidence in your case.

5. *Will we purchase any studies?* In appropriate situations, we will purchase studies necessary to substantiate the diagnosis or to document the severity of your impairment, generally after we have evaluated the medical and other evidence we already have. We will not purchase studies involving exercise testing if there is significant risk involved or if there is another medical reason not to perform the test. We will follow sections 4.00C6, 4.00C7, and 4.00C8 when we decide whether to purchase exercise testing.

6. *What studies will we not purchase?* We will not purchase any studies involving cardiac catheterization, such as coronary angiography, arteriograms, or electrophysiological studies. However, if the results of catheterization are part of the existing evidence we have, we will consider them together with the other relevant evidence. See 4.00C15a.

C. *Using Cardiovascular Test Results*

1. *What is an ECG?*

a. *ECG* stands for *electrocardiograph* or *electrocardiogram.* An electrocardiograph is a machine that records electrical impulses of your heart on a strip of paper called an electrocardiogram or a *tracing.* To record the ECG, a technician positions a number of small contacts (or *leads*) on your arms, legs, and across your chest to connect them to the ECG machine. An ECG may be done while you are resting or exercising.

b. The ECG tracing may indicate that you have a heart abnormality. It may indicate that your heart muscle is not getting as much oxygen as it needs (ischemia), that your heart rhythm is abnormal (arrhythmia), or that there are other abnormalities of your heart, such as left ventricular enlargement.

2. *How do we evaluate ECG evidence?* We consider a number of factors when we evaluate ECG evidence:

a. An original or legible copy of the 12-lead ECG obtained at rest must be appropriately dated and labeled, with the standardization inscribed on the tracing.

Alteration in standardization of specific leads (such as to accommodate large QRS amplitudes) must be identified on those leads.

(i) Detailed descriptions or computer-averaged signals without original or legible copies of the ECG as described in listing 4.00C2a are not acceptable.

(ii) The effects of drugs or electrolyte abnormalities must be considered as possible noncardiac causes of ECG abnormalities of ventricular repolarization; that is, those involving the ST segment and T wave. If available, the predrug (especially digitalis glycosides) ECG should be submitted.

b. ECGs obtained in conjunction with treadmill, bicycle, or arm exercise tests should meet the following specifications:

(i) ECG reports must include the original calibrated ECG tracings or a legible copy.

(ii) A 12-lead baseline ECG must be recorded in the upright position before exercise.

(iii) A 12-lead ECG should be recorded at the end of each minute of exercise.

(iv) If ECG documentation of the effects of hyperventilation is obtained, the exercise test should be deferred for at least 10 minutes because metabolic changes of hyperventilation may alter the physiologic and ECG-recorded response to exercise.

(v) Post-exercise ECGs should be recorded using a generally accepted protocol consistent with the prevailing state of medical knowledge and clinical practice.

(vi) All resting, exercise, and recovery ECG strips must have the standardization inscribed on the tracing. The ECG strips should be labeled to indicate the date, the times recorded and the relationship to the stage of the exercise protocol. The speed and grade (treadmill test) or work rate (bicycle or arm ergometric test) should be recorded. The highest level of exercise achieved, heart rate and blood pressure levels during testing, and the reason(s) for terminating the test (including limiting signs or symptoms) must be recorded.

3. *What are exercise tests and what are they used for?*

a. Exercise tests have you perform physical activity and record how your cardiovascular system responds. Exercise tests usually involve walking on a treadmill, but other forms of exercise, such as an exercise bicycle or an arm exercise machine, may be used. Exercise testing may be done for various reasons; such as to evaluate the severity of your coronary artery disease or peripheral vascular disease or to evaluate your progress after a cardiac procedure or an acute event, like a myocardial infarction (heart attack). Exercise testing is the most widely used testing for identifying the presence of myocardial ischemia and for estimating maximal aerobic capacity (usually expressed in METs—metabolic equivalents) if you have heart disease.

b. We include exercise tolerance test (ETT) criteria in (chronic heart failure) and 4.04A (ischemic heart disease). To meet the ETT criteria in these listings, the ETT must be a sign-or symptom-limited test in which you exercise while connected to an ECG until you develop a sign or symptom that indicates that you have exercised as much as is considered safe for you.

c. In 4.12B, we also refer to exercise testing for peripheral vascular disease. In this test, you walk on a treadmill, usually for a specified period of time, and the individual who administers the test measures the effect of exercise on the flow of blood in your legs, usually by using ultrasound. The test is also called an exercise Doppler test. Even though this test is intended to evaluate peripheral vascular disease, it will be stopped for your safety if you develop abnormal signs or symptoms because of heart disease.

d. Each type of test is done in a certain way following specific criteria, called a *protocol*. For our program, we also specify certain aspects of how any exercise test we purchase is to be done. See 4.00C10 and 4.00C17.

4. *Do ETTs have limitations?* An ETT provides an estimate of aerobic capacity for walking on a grade, bicycling, or moving one's arms in an environmentally controlled setting. Therefore, ETT results do not correlate with the ability to perform other types of exertional activities, such as lifting and carrying heavy loads, and do not provide an estimate of the ability to perform activities required for work in all possible work environments or throughout a workday. Also, certain medications (such as beta blockers) and conduction disorders (such as left or right bundle branch blocks) can cause false-negative or false-positive results. Therefore, we must consider the results of an ETT together with all the other relevant evidence in your case record.

5. *How does an ETT with measurement of maximal or peak oxygen uptake (VO2) differ from other ETTs?* Occasionally, medical evidence will include the results of an ETT with VO2. While ETTs without measurement of VO2 provide only an estimate of aerobic capacity, measured maximal or peak oxygen uptake provides an accurate measurement of aerobic capacity, which is often expressed in METs (metabolic equivalents). The MET level may not be indicated in the report of attained maximal or peak VO2 testing, but can be calculated as follows: 1 MET = 3.5 milliliters (ml) of oxygen uptake per kilogram (kg) of body weight per minute. For example, a 70 kg (154 lb.) individual who achieves a maximal or peak VO2 of 1225 ml in 1 minute has attained 5 METs (1225 ml/70 kg/1 min = 17.5 ml/kg/min. 17.5/3.5 = 5 METs).

6. *When will we consider whether to purchase an exercise test?*

a. We will consider whether to purchase an exercise test when:

(i) There is a question whether your cardiovascular impairment meets or medically equals the severity of one of the listings, or there is no timely test in the evidence we have (see 4.00C9), and we cannot find you disabled on some other basis; or

(ii) We need to assess your residual functional capacity and there is insufficient evidence in the record to make a determination or decision.

b. We will not purchase an exercise test when we can make our determination or decision based on the evidence we already have.

7. *What must we do before purchasing an exercise test?*

a. Before we purchase an exercise test, an MC, preferably one with experience in the care of patients with cardiovascular disease, must review the pertinent history, physical examinations, and laboratory tests that we have to determine whether the test would present a significant risk to you or if there is some other medical reason not to purchase the test (see 4.00C8).

b. If you are under the care of a treating source (see §§ 404.1502 and 416.902) for a cardiovascular impairment, this source has not performed an exercise test, and there are no reported significant risks to testing, we will request a statement from that source explaining why it was not done or should not be done before we decide whether we will purchase the test.

c. The MC, in accordance with the regulations and other instructions on consultative examinations, will generally give great weight to the treating source's opinion about the risk of exercise testing to you and will generally not override it. In the rare situation in which the MC does override the treating source's opinion, the MC must prepare a written rationale documenting the reasons for overriding the opinion.

d. If you do not have a treating source or we cannot obtain a statement from your treating source, the MC is responsible for assessing the risk to exercise testing based on a review of the records we have before purchasing an exercise test for you.

e. We must also provide your records to the medical source who performs the exercise test for review prior to conducting the test if the source does not already have them. The medical source who performs the exercise test has the ultimate responsibility for deciding whether you would be at risk.

8. *When will we not purchase an exercise test or wait before we purchase an exercise test?*

a. We will not purchase an exercise test when an MC finds that you have one of the following significant risk factors:

(i) Unstable angina not previously stabilized by medical treatment.

(ii) Uncontrolled cardiac arrhythmias causing symptoms or hemodynamic compromise.

(iii) An implanted cardiac defibrillator.

(iv) Symptomatic severe aortic stenosis.

(v) Uncontrolled symptomatic heart failure.

(vi) Aortic dissection.

(vii) Severe pulmonary hypertension (pulmonary artery systolic pressure greater than 60 mm Hg).

(viii) Left main coronary stenosis of 50 percent or greater that has not been bypassed.

(ix) Moderate stenotic valvular disease with a systolic gradient across the aortic valve of 50 mm Hg or greater.

(x) Severe arterial hypertension (systolic greater than 200 mm Hg or diastolic greater than 110 mm Hg).

(xi) Hypertrophic cardiomyopathy with a systolic gradient of 50 mm Hg or greater.

b. We also will not purchase an exercise test when you are prevented from performing exercise testing due to another impairment affecting your ability to use your arms and legs.

c. We will not purchase an ETT to document the presence of a cardiac arrhythmia.

d. We will wait to purchase an exercise test until 3 months after you have had one of the following events. This will allow for maximal, attainable restoration of functional capacity.

(i) Acute myocardial infarction.

(ii) Surgical myocardial revascularization (bypass surgery).

(iii) Other open-heart surgical procedures.

(iv) Percutaneous transluminal coronary angioplasty with or without stenting.

e. If you are deconditioned after an extended period of bedrest or inactivity and could improve with activity, or if you are in acute heart failure and are expected to improve with treatment, we will wait an appropriate period of time for you to recuperate before we purchase an exercise test.

9. *What do we mean by a "timely" test?*

a. We consider exercise test results to be timely for 12 months after the date they are performed, provided there has been no change in your clinical status that may alter the severity of your cardiovascular impairment.

b. However, an exercise test that is older than 12 months, especially an abnormal one, can still provide information important to our adjudication. For example, a test that is more than 12 months old can provide evidence of ischemic heart disease or peripheral vascular disease, information on decreased aerobic capacity, or information about the duration or onset of your impairment. Such tests can be an important component of the longitudinal record.

c. When we evaluate a test that is more than 12 months old, we must consider the results in the context of all the relevant evidence, including why the test was performed and whether there has been an intervening event or improvement or worsening of your impairment.

d. We will purchase a new exercise test only if we cannot make a determination or decision based on the evidence we have.

10. *How must ETTs we purchase be performed?*

a. The ETT must be a sign- or symptom-limited test characterized by a progressive multistage regimen. It must be performed using a generally accepted protocol consistent with the prevailing state of medical knowledge and clinical practice. A description of the protocol that was followed must be provided, and the test must meet the requirements of 4.00C2b and this section. A radionuclide perfusion scan may be useful for detecting or confirming ischemia when resting ECG abnormalities, medications, or other factors may decrease the accuracy of ECG interpretation of ischemia. (The perfusion imaging is done at the termination of exercise, which may be at a higher MET level than that at which ischemia first occurs. If the imaging confirms the presence of reversible ischemia, the exercise ECG may be useful for detecting the MET level at which ischemia initially appeared.) Exercise tests may also be performed using echocardiography to detect stress-induced ischemia and left ventricular dysfunction (see 4.00C12 and 4.00C13).

b. The exercise test must be paced to your capabilities and be performed following the generally accepted standards for adult exercise test laboratories. With a treadmill test, the speed, grade (incline), and duration of exercise must be recorded for each exercise test stage performed. Other exercise test protocols or techniques should use similar workloads. The exercise protocol may need to be modified in individual cases to allow for a lower initial workload with more slowly graded increments than the standard Bruce protocol.

c. Levels of exercise must be described in terms of workload and duration of each stage; for example, treadmill speed and grade, or bicycle ergometer work rate in kpm/min or watts.

d. The exercise laboratory's physical environment, staffing, and equipment must meet the generally accepted standards for adult exercise test laboratories.

11. *How do we evaluate ETT results?* We evaluate ETT results on the basis of the work level at which the test becomes abnormal, as documented by onset of signs or symptoms and any ECG or imaging abnormalities. The absence of an

ischemic response on an ETT alone does not exclude the diagnosis of ischemic heart disease. We must consider the results of an ETT in the context of all of the other evidence in your case record.

12. *When are ETTs done with imaging?* When resting ECG abnormalities preclude interpretation of ETT tracings relative to ischemia, a radionuclide (for example, thallium-201 or technetium-99m) perfusion scan or echocardiography in conjunction with an ETT provides better results. You may have resting ECG abnormalities when you have a conduction defect—for example, Wolff-Parkinson-White syndrome, left bundle branch block, left ventricular hypertrophy—or when you are taking digitalis or other antiarrhythmic drugs, or when resting ST changes are present. Also, these techniques can provide a reliable estimate of ejection fraction.

13. *Will we purchase ETTs with imaging?* We may purchase an ETT with imaging in your case after an MC, preferably one with experience in the care of patients with cardiovascular disease, has reviewed your medical history and physical examination, any report(s) of appropriate medically acceptable imaging, ECGs, and other appropriate tests. We will consider purchasing an ETT with imaging when other information we have is not adequate for us to assess whether you have severe ventricular dysfunction or myocardial ischemia, there is no significant risk involved (see 4.00C8a), and we cannot make our determination or decision based on the evidence we already have.

14. *What are drug-induced stress tests?* These tests are designed primarily to provide evidence about myocardial ischemia or prior myocardial infarction, but do not require you to exercise. These tests are used when you cannot exercise or cannot exercise enough to achieve the desired cardiac stress. Drug-induced stress tests can also provide evidence about heart chamber dimensions and function; however, these tests do not provide information about your aerobic capacity and cannot be used to help us assess your ability to function. Some of these tests use agents, such as Persantine or adenosine, that dilate the coronary arteries and are used in combination with nuclear agents, such as thallium or technetium (for example, Cardiolyte or Myoview), and a myocardial scan. Other tests use agents, such as dobutamine, that stimulate the heart to contract more forcefully and faster to simulate exercise and are used in combination with a 2-dimensional echocardiogram. We may, when appropriate, purchase a drug-induced stress test to confirm the presence of myocardial ischemia after a review of the evidence in your file by an MC, preferably one with experience in the care of patients with cardiovascular disease.

15. *How do we evaluate cardiac catheterization evidence?*

a. We will not purchase cardiac catheterization; however, if you have had catheterization, we will make every reasonable effort to obtain the report and any ancillary studies. We will consider the quality and type of data provided and its relevance to the evaluation of your impairment. For adults, we generally see two types of catheterization reports: Coronary arteriography and left ventriculography.

b. For coronary arteriography, the report should provide information citing the method of assessing coronary arterial lumen diameter and the nature and location of obstructive lesions. Drug treatment at baseline and during the procedure should be reported. Some individuals with significant coronary atherosclerotic obstruction have collateral vessels that supply the myocardium distal to the arterial obstruction so that there is no evidence of myocardial damage or ischemia, even with exercise. When the results of quantitative computer measurements and analyses are included in your case record, we will consider them in interpreting the severity of stenotic lesions.

c. For left ventriculography, the report should describe the wall motion of the myocardium with regard to any areas of hypokinesis (abnormally decreased motion), akinesis (lack of motion), or dyskinesis (distortion of motion), and the overall contraction of the ventricle as measured by the ejection fraction. Measurement of chamber volumes and pressures may be useful. Quantitative computer analysis provides precise measurement of segmental left ventricular wall thickness and motion. There is often a poor correlation between left ventricular function at rest and functional capacity for physical activity.

16. *What details should exercise Doppler test reports contain?* The reports of exercise Doppler tests must describe the level of exercise; for example, the speed and grade of the treadmill settings, the duration of exercise, symptoms during exercise, and the reasons for stopping exercise if the expected level of exercise was not attained. They must also include the blood pressures at the ankle and other pertinent sites measured after exercise and the time required for the systolic blood pressure to return toward or to the pre-exercise level. The graphic tracings, if available, should also be included with the report. All tracings must be annotated with the standardization used by the testing facility.

17. *How must exercise Doppler tests we purchase be performed?* When we purchase an exercise Doppler test, you must exercise on a treadmill at 2 mph on a 12 percent grade for up to 5 minutes. The reports must include the information specified in 4.00C16. Because this is an exercise test, we must evaluate whether such testing would put you at significant risk, in accordance with the guidance found in 4.00C6, 4.00C7, and 4.00C8.

D. *Evaluating Chronic Heart Failure*

1. *What is chronic heart failure (CHF)?*

a. *CHF* is the inability of the heart to pump enough oxygenated blood to body tissues. This syndrome is characterized by symptoms and signs of pulmonary or systemic congestion (fluid retention) or limited cardiac output. Certain laboratory findings of cardiac functional and structural abnormality support the diagnosis of CHF. There are two main types of CHF:

(i) *Predominant systolic dysfunction* (the inability of the heart to contract normally and expel sufficient blood), which is characterized by a dilated, poorly contracting left ventricle and reduced ejection fraction (abbreviated EF, it represents the percentage of the blood in the ventricle actually pumped out with each contraction), and

(ii) *Predominant diastolic dysfunction* (the inability of the heart to relax and fill normally), which is characterized by a thickened ventricular muscle, poor ability of the left ventricle to distend, increased ventricular filling pressure, and a normal or increased EF.

b. CHF is considered in these listings as a single category whether due to atherosclerosis (narrowing of the arteries), cardiomyopathy, hypertension, or rheumatic, congenital, or other heart disease. However, if the CHF is the result of primary pulmonary hypertension secondary to disease of the lung (cor pulmonale), we will evaluate your impairment using 3.09, in the respiratory system listings.

2. *What evidence of CHF do we need?*

a. Cardiomegaly or ventricular dysfunction must be present and demonstrated by appropriate medically acceptable imaging, such as chest x-ray, echocardiography (M-Mode, 2-dimensional, and Doppler), radionuclide studies, or cardiac catheterization.

(i) Abnormal cardiac imaging showing increased left ventricular end diastolic diameter (LVEDD), decreased EF, increased left atrial chamber size, increased ventricular filling pressures measured at cardiac catheterization, or increased left ventricular wall or septum thickness, provides objective measures of both left ventricular function and structural abnormality in heart failure.

(ii) An LVEDD greater than 6.0 cm or an EF of 30 percent or less measured during a period of stability (that is, not during an episode of acute heart failure) may be associated clinically with systolic failure.

(iii) Left ventricular posterior wall thickness added to septal thickness totaling 2.5 cm or greater with left atrium enlarged to 4.5 cm or greater may be associated clinically with diastolic failure.

(iv) However, these measurements alone do not reflect your functional capacity, which we evaluate by considering all of the relevant evidence. In some situations, we may need to purchase an ETT to help us assess your functional capacity.

(v) Other findings on appropriate medically acceptable imaging may include increased pulmonary vascular markings, pleural effusion, and pulmonary edema. These findings need not be present on each report, since CHF may be controlled by prescribed treatment.

b. To establish that you have *chronic* heart failure, your medical history and physical examination should describe characteristic symptoms and signs of pulmonary or systemic congestion or of limited cardiac output associated with the abnormal findings on appropriate medically acceptable imaging. When an acute episode of heart failure is triggered by a remediable factor, such as an arrhythmia, dietary sodium overload, or high altitude, cardiac function may be restored and a chronic impairment may not be present.

(i) Symptoms of congestion or of limited cardiac output include easy fatigue, weakness, shortness of breath (dyspnea), cough, or chest discomfort at rest or with activity. Individuals with CHF may also experience shortness of breath on lying flat (orthopnea) or episodes of shortness of breath that wake them from sleep (paroxysmal nocturnal dyspnea). They may also experience cardiac arrhythmias resulting in palpitations, lightheadedness, or fainting.

(ii) Signs of congestion may include hepatomegaly, ascites, increased jugular venous distention or pressure, rales, peripheral edema, or rapid weight gain. However, these signs need not be found on all examinations because fluid retention may be controlled by prescribed treatment.

3. *Is it safe for you to have an ETT, if you have CHF?* The presence of CHF is not necessarily a contraindication to an ETT, unless you are having an acute episode of heart failure. Measures of cardiac performance are valuable in helping us evaluate your ability to do work-related activities. Exercise testing has been safely used in individuals with CHF; therefore, we may purchase an ETT for evaluation under 4.02B3 if an MC, preferably one experienced in the care of patients with cardiovascular disease, determines that there is no significant risk to you. (See 4.00C6 for when we will consider the purchase of an ETT. See 4.00C7–4.00C8 for what we must do before we purchase an ETT and when we will not purchase one.) ST segment changes from digitalis use in the treatment of CHF do not preclude the purchase of an ETT.

4. *How do we evaluate CHF using 4.02?*

a. We must have objective evidence, as described in 4.00D2, that you have chronic heart failure.

b. To meet the required level of severity for this listing, your impairment must satisfy the requirements of one of the criteria in A and one of the criteria in B.

c. In 4.02B2, the phrase *periods of stabilization* means that, for at least 2 weeks between episodes of acute heart failure, there must be objective evidence of clearing of the pulmonary edema or pleural effusions and evidence that you returned to, or you were medically considered able to return to, your prior level of activity.

d. Listing 4.02B3c requires a decrease in systolic blood pressure below the baseline level (taken in the standing position immediately prior to exercise) or below any systolic pressure reading recorded during exercise. This is because, normally, systolic blood pressure and heart rate increase gradually with exercise. Decreases in systolic blood pressure below the baseline level that occur during exercise are often associated with ischemia-induced left ventricular dysfunction resulting in decreased cardiac output. However, a blunted response (that is, failure of the systolic blood pressure to rise 10 mm Hg or more), particularly in the first 3 minutes of exercise, may be drug-related and is not necessarily associated with left ventricular dysfunction. Also, some individuals with increased sympathetic responses because of deconditioning or apprehension may increase their systolic blood pressure and heart rate above their baseline level just before and early into exercise. This can be associated with a drop in systolic pressure in early exercise that is not due to left ventricular dysfunction. Therefore, an early decrease in systolic blood pressure must be interpreted within the total context of the test; that is, the presence or absence of symptoms such as lightheadedness, ischemic changes, or arrhythmias on the ECG.

E. *Evaluating Ischemic Heart Disease*

1. *What is ischemic heart disease (IHD)? IHD* results when one or more of your coronary arteries is narrowed or obstructed or, in rare situations, constricted due to vasospasm, interfering with the normal flow of blood to your heart muscle (ischemia). The obstruction may be the result of an embolus, a thrombus, or plaque. When heart muscle tissue dies as a result of the reduced blood supply, it is called a myocardial infarction (heart attack).

2. *What causes chest discomfort of myocardial origin?*

a. Chest discomfort of myocardial ischemic origin, commonly known as angina pectoris, is usually caused by coronary artery disease (often abbreviated CAD). However, ischemic discomfort may be caused by a noncoronary artery impairment, such as aortic stenosis, hypertrophic cardiomyopathy, pulmonary hypertension, or anemia.

b. Instead of typical angina pectoris, some individuals with IHD experience atypical angina, anginal equivalent, variant angina, or silent ischemia, all of which we may evaluate using 4.04. We discuss the various manifestations of ischemia in 4.00E3–4.00E7.

3. *What are the characteristics of typical angina pectoris?* Discomfort of myocardial ischemic origin (angina pectoris) is discomfort that is precipitated by effort or emotion and promptly relieved by rest, sublingual nitroglycerin (that is, nitroglycerin tablets that are placed under the tongue), or other rapidly acting nitrates. Typically, the discomfort is located in the chest (usually substernal) and described as pressing, crushing, squeezing, burning, aching, or oppressive. Sharp, sticking, or cramping discomfort is less common. Discomfort occurring with activity or emotion should be described specifically as to timing and usual inciting factors (type and intensity), character, location, radiation, duration, and response to nitrate treatment or rest.

4. *What is atypical angina? Atypical angina* describes discomfort or pain from myocardial ischemia that is felt in places other than the chest. The common sites of cardiac pain are the inner aspect of the left arm, neck, jaw(s), upper abdomen, and back, but the discomfort or pain can be elsewhere. When pain of cardiac ischemic origin presents in an atypical site in the absence of chest discomfort, the source of the pain may be difficult to diagnose. To represent atypical angina, your discomfort or pain should have precipitating and relieving factors similar to those of typical chest discomfort, and we must have objective medical evidence of myocardial ischemia; for example, ECG or ETT evidence or appropriate medically acceptable imaging.

5. *What is anginal equivalent?* Often, individuals with IHD will complain of shortness of breath (dyspnea) on exertion without chest pain or discomfort. In a minority of such situations, the shortness of breath is due to myocardial ischemia; this is called *anginal equivalent*. To represent anginal equivalent, your shortness of breath should have precipitating and relieving factors similar to those of typical chest discomfort, and we must have objective medical evidence of myocardial ischemia; for example, ECG or ETT evidence or appropriate medically acceptable imaging. In these situations, it is essential to establish objective evidence of myocardial ischemia to ensure that you do not have effort dyspnea due to non-ischemic or non-cardiac causes.

6. *What is variant angina?*

a. *Variant angina* (Prinzmetal's angina, vasospastic angina) refers to the occurrence of anginal episodes at rest, especially at night, accompanied by transitory ST segment elevation (or, at times, ST depression) on an ECG. It is due to severe spasm of a coronary artery, causing ischemia of the heart wall, and is often accompanied by major ventricular arrhythmias, such as ventricular tachycardia. We will consider variant angina under 4.04 only if you have spasm of a coronary artery in relation to an obstructive lesion of the vessel. If you have an arrhythmia as a result of variant angina, we may consider your impairment under 4.05.

b. Variant angina may also occur in the absence of obstructive coronary disease. In this situation, an ETT will not demonstrate ischemia. The diagnosis will be established by showing the typical transitory ST segment changes during attacks of pain, and the absence of obstructive lesions shown by catheterization. Treatment in cases where there is no obstructive coronary disease is limited to medications that reduce coronary vasospasm, such as calcium channel blockers and nitrates. In such situations, we will consider the frequency of anginal episodes despite prescribed treatment when evaluating your residual functional capacity.

c. Vasospasm that is catheter-induced during coronary angiography is not variant angina.

7. *What is silent ischemia?*

a. Myocardial ischemia, and even myocardial infarction, can occur without perception of pain or any other symptoms; when this happens, we call it *silent ischemia*. Pain sensitivity may be altered by a variety of diseases, most notably diabetes mellitus and other neuropathic disorders. Individuals also vary in their threshold for pain.

b. Silent ischemia occurs most often in:

(i) Individuals with documented past myocardial infarction or established angina without prior infarction who do not have chest pain on ETT, but have a positive test with ischemic abnormality on ECG, perfusion scan, or other appropriate medically acceptable imaging.

(ii) Individuals with documented past myocardial infarction or angina who have ST segment changes on ambulatory monitoring (Holter monitoring) that are similar to those that occur during episodes of angina. ST depression shown on the ambulatory recording should not be interpreted as positive for ischemia unless similar depression is also seen during chest pain episodes annotated in the diary that the individual keeps while wearing the Holter monitor.

c. ST depression can result from a variety of factors, such as postural changes and variations in cardiac sympathetic tone. In addition, there are differences in how different Holter monitors record the electrical responses. Therefore, we do not consider the Holter monitor reliable for the diagnosis of silent ischemia except in the situation described in4.00E7b(ii).

8. *What other sources of chest discomfort are there?* Chest discomfort of nonischemic origin may result from other cardiac impairments, such as pericarditis. Noncardiac impairments may also produce symptoms mimicking that of myocardial ischemia. These impairments include acute anxiety or panic attacks, gastrointestinal tract disorders, such as esophageal spasm, esophagitis, hiatal hernia, biliary tract disease, gastritis, peptic ulcer, and pancreatitis, and musculoskeletal syndromes, such as chest wall muscle spasm, chest wall syndrome (especially after coronary bypass surgery), costochondritis, and cervical or dorsal spine arthritis. Hyperventilation may also mimic ischemic discomfort. Thus, in the absence of documented myocardial ischemia, such disorders should be considered as possible causes of chest discomfort.

9. *How do we evaluate IHD using 4.04?*

a. We must have objective evidence, as described under 4.00C, that your symptoms are due to myocardial ischemia.

b. Listing-level changes on the ECG in 4.04A1 are the classically accepted changes of horizontal or downsloping ST depression occurring both during exercise and recovery. Although we recognize that ischemic changes may at times occur only during exercise or recovery, and may at times be upsloping with only junctional ST depression, such changes can be false positive; that is, occur in the absence of ischemia. Diagnosis of ischemia in this situation requires radionuclide or echocardiogram confirmation. See 4.00C12 and 4.00C13.

c. Also in 4.04A1, we require that the depression of the ST segment last for at least 1 minute of recovery because ST depression that occurs during exercise but that rapidly normalizes in recovery is a common false-positive response.

d. In 4.04A2, we specify that the ST elevation must be in non-infarct leads during both exercise and recovery. This is because, in the absence of ECG signs of prior infarction, ST elevation during exercise denotes ischemia, usually severe, requiring immediate termination of exercise. However, if there is baseline ST elevation in association with a prior infarction or ventricular aneurysm, further ST elevation during exercise does not necessarily denote ischemia and could be a false-positive ECG response. Diagnosis of ischemia in this situation requires radionuclide or echocardiogram confirmation. See 4.00C12 and 4.00C13.

e. Listing 4.04A3 requires a decrease in systolic blood pressure below the baseline level (taken in the standing position immediately prior to exercise) or below any systolic pressure reading recorded during exercise. This is the same finding required in 4.02B3c. See 4.00D4d for full details.

f. In 4.04B, each of the three ischemic episodes must require revascularization or be not amenable to treatment. *Revascularization* means angioplasty (with or without stent placement) or bypass surgery. However, reocclusion that occurs after a revascularization procedure but during the same hospitalization and that requires a second procedure during the same hospitalization will not be counted as another ischemic episode. Not amenable means that the revascularization procedure could not be done because of another medical impairment or because the vessel was not suitable for revascularization.

g. We will use 4.04C only when you have symptoms due to myocardial ischemia as described in 4.00E3–4.00E7 while on a regimen of prescribed treatment, you are at risk for exercise testing (see 4.00C8), and we do not have a timely ETT or a timely normal drug-induced stress test for you. See 4.00C9 for what we mean by a timely test.

h. In 4.04C1 the term *nonbypassed* means that the blockage is in a vessel that is potentially bypassable; that is, large enough to be bypassed and considered to be a cause of your ischemia. These vessels are usually major arteries or one of a major artery's major branches. A vessel that has become obstructed again after angioplasty or stent placement and has remained obstructed or is not amenable to another revascularization is considered a nonbypassed vessel for purposes of this listing. When you have had revascularization, we will not use the preoperative findings to assess the current severity of your coronary artery disease under 4.04C, although we will consider the severity and duration of your impairment prior to your surgery in making our determination or decision.

F. *Evaluating Arrhythmias*

1. *What is an arrhythmia?* An *arrhythmia* is a change in the regular beat of the heart. Your heart may seem to skip a beat or beat irregularly, very quickly (tachycardia), or very slowly (bradycardia).

2. *What are the different types of arrhythmias?*

a. There are many types of arrhythmias. Arrhythmias are identified by where they occur in the heart (atria or ventricles) and by what happens to the heart's rhythm when they occur.

b. Arrhythmias arising in the cardiac atria (upper chambers of the heart) are called atrial or supraventricular arrhythmias. Ventricular arrhythmias begin in the ventricles (lower chambers). In general, ventricular arrhythmias caused by heart disease are the most serious.

3. *How do we evaluate arrhythmias using 4.05?*

a. We will use 4.05 when you have arrhythmias that are not fully controlled by medication, an implanted pacemaker, or an implanted cardiac defibrillator and you have uncontrolled recurrent episodes of syncope or near syncope. If your arrhythmias are controlled, we will evaluate your underlying heart disease using the appropriate listing. For other considerations when we evaluate arrhythmias in the presence of an implanted cardiac defibrillator, see 4.00F4.

b. We consider *near syncope* to be a period of altered consciousness, since syncope is a loss of consciousness or a faint. It is not merely a feeling of lightheadedness, momentary weakness, or dizziness.

c. For purposes of 4.05, there must be a documented association between the syncope or near syncope and the recurrent arrhythmia. The recurrent arrhythmia, not some other cardiac or non-cardiac disorder, must be established as the cause of the associated symptom. This documentation of the association between the symptoms and the arrhythmia may come from the usual diagnostic methods, including Holter monitoring (also called ambulatory electrocardiography) and tilt-table testing with a concurrent ECG. Although an arrhythmia may be a coincidental finding on an ETT, we will not purchase an ETT to document the presence of a cardiac arrhythmia.

4. *What will we consider when you have an implanted cardiac defibrillator and you do not have arrhythmias that meet the requirements of 4.05?*

a. Implanted cardiac defibrillators are used to prevent sudden cardiac death in individuals who have had, or are at high risk for, cardiac arrest from life-threatening ventricular arrhythmias. The largest group at risk for sudden cardiac death consists of individuals with cardiomyopathy (ischemic or non-ischemic) and reduced ventricular function. However, life-threatening ventricular arrhythmias can also occur in individuals with little or no ventricular dysfunction. The shock from the implanted cardiac defibrillator is a unique form of treatment; it rescues an individual from what may have been cardiac arrest. However, as a consequence of the shock(s), individuals may experience psychological distress, which we may evaluate under the mental disorders listings in 12.00ff.

b. Most implantable cardiac defibrillators have rhythm-correcting and pacemaker capabilities. In some individuals, these functions may result in the termination of ventricular arrhythmias without an otherwise painful shock. (The shock is like being kicked in the chest.) Implanted cardiac defibrillators may deliver inappropriate shocks, often repeatedly, in response to benign arrhythmias or electrical malfunction. Also, exposure to strong electrical or magnetic fields, such as from MRI (magnetic resonance imaging), can trigger or reprogram an implanted cardiac defibrillator, resulting in inappropriate shocks. We must consider the frequency of, and the reason(s) for, the shocks when evaluating the severity and duration of your impairment.

c. In general, the exercise limitations imposed on individuals with an implanted cardiac defibrillator are those dictated by the underlying heart impairment. However, the exercise limitations may be greater when the implanted cardiac defibrillator delivers an inappropriate shock in response to the increase in heart rate with exercise, or when there is exercise-induced ventricular arrhythmia.

G. *Evaluating Peripheral Vascular Disease*

1. *What is peripheral vascular disease (PVD)?* Generally, *PVD* is any impairment that affects either the arteries (peripheral arterial disease) or the veins (venous insufficiency) in the extremities, particularly the lower extremities. The usual effect is blockage of the flow of blood either from the heart (arterial) or back to the heart (venous). If you have peripheral arterial disease, you may have pain in your calf after walking a distance that goes away when you rest (intermittent claudication); at more advanced stages, you may have pain in your calf at rest or you may develop ulceration or gangrene. If you have venous insufficiency, you may have swelling, varicose veins, skin pigmentation changes, or skin ulceration.

2. *How do we assess limitations resulting from PVD?* We will assess your limitations based on your symptoms together with physical findings, Doppler studies, other appropriate non-invasive studies, or angiographic findings. However, if the PVD has resulted in amputation, we will evaluate any limitations related to the amputation under the musculoskeletal listings, 1.00ff.

3. *What is brawny edema? Brawny edema* (4.11A) is swelling that is usually dense and feels firm due to the presence of increased connective tissue; it is also associated with characteristic skin pigmentation changes. It is not the same thing as pitting edema. Brawny edema generally does not pit (indent on pressure), and the terms are not interchangeable. Pitting edema does not satisfy the requirements of 4.11A.

4. *What is lymphedema and how will we evaluate it?*

a. *Lymphedema* is edema of the extremities due to a disorder of the lymphatic circulation; at its worst, it is called elephantiasis. Primary lymphedema is caused by abnormal development of lymph vessels and may be present at birth (congenital lymphedema), but more often develops during the teens (lymphedema praecox). It may also appear later, usually after age 35 (lymphedema tarda). Secondary lymphedema is due to obstruction or destruction of normal lymphatic channels due to tumor, surgery, repeated infections, or parasitic infection such as filariasis. Lymphedema most commonly affects one extremity.

b. Lymphedema does not meet the requirements of 4.11, although it may medically equal the severity of that listing. We will evaluate lymphedema by considering whether the underlying cause meets or medically equals any listing or whether the lymphedema medically equals a cardiovascular listing, such as 4.11, or a musculoskeletal listing, such as 1.02A or 1.03. If no listing is met or medically equaled, we will evaluate any functional limitations imposed by your lymphedema when we assess your residual functional capacity.

5. *When will we purchase exercise Doppler studies for evaluating peripheral arterial disease (PAD)?* If we need additional evidence of your PAD, we will generally purchase exercise Doppler studies (see 4.00C16 and 4.00C17) when your resting ankle/brachial systolic blood pressure ratio is at least 0.50 but less than 0.80, and only rarely when it is 0.80 or above. We will not purchase exercise Doppler testing if you have a disease that results in abnormal arterial calcification or small vessel disease, but will use your resting toe systolic blood pressure or resting toe/brachial systolic blood pressure ratio. (See 4.00G7c and 4.00G8.) There are no current medical standards for evaluating exercise toe pressures. Because any exercise test stresses your entire cardiovascular system, we will purchase exercise Doppler studies only after an MC, preferably one with experience in the care of patients with cardiovascular disease, has determined that the test would not present a significant risk to you and that there is no other medical reason not to purchase the test (see 4.00C6, 4.00C7, and 4.00C8).

6. *Are there any other studies that are helpful in evaluating PAD?* Doppler studies done using a recording ultrasonic Doppler unit and strain-gauge plethysmography are other useful tools for evaluating PAD. A recording Doppler, which prints a tracing of the arterial pulse wave in the femoral, popliteal, dorsalis pedis, and posterior tibial arteries, is an excellent evaluation tool to compare wave forms in normal and compromised peripheral blood flow. Qualitative analysis of the pulse wave is very helpful in the overall assessment of the severity of the occlusive disease. Tracings are especially helpful in assessing severity if you have small vessel disease related to diabetes mellitus or other diseases with similar vascular changes, or diseases causing medial calcifications when ankle pressure is either normal or falsely high.

7. *How do we evaluate PAD under 4.12?*

a. The ankle blood pressure referred to in 4.12A and B is the higher of the pressures recorded from the posterior tibial and dorsalis pedis arteries in the affected leg. The higher pressure recorded from the two sites is the more significant measurement in assessing the extent of arterial insufficiency. Techniques for obtaining ankle systolic blood pressures include Doppler (See 4.00C16 and 4.00C17), plethysmographic studies, or other techniques. We will request any available tracings generated by these studies so that we can review them.

b. In 4.12A, the ankle/brachial systolic blood pressure ratio is the ratio of the systolic blood pressure at the ankle to the systolic blood pressure at the brachial artery; both taken at the same time while you are lying on your back. We do not require that the ankle and brachial pressures be taken on the same side of your body. This is because, as with the ankle pressure, we will use the higher brachial systolic pressure measured. Listing 4.12A is met when your resting ankle/brachial systolic blood pressure ratio is less than 0.50. If your resting ankle/brachial systolic blood pressure ratio is 0.50 or above, we will use 4.12B to evaluate the severity of your PAD, unless you also have a disease causing abnormal arterial calcification or small vessel disease, such as diabetes mellitus. See 4.00G7c and 4.00G8.

c. We will use resting toe systolic blood pressures or resting toe/brachial systolic blood pressure ratios (determined the same way as ankle/brachial ratios, see 4.00G7b) when you have intermittent claudication and a disease that results in abnormal arterial calcification (for example, Monckeberg's sclerosis or diabetes mellitus) or small vessel disease (for example, diabetes mellitus). These diseases may result in misleadingly high blood pressure readings at the ankle. However, high blood pressures due to vascular changes related to these diseases seldom occur at the toe level. While the criteria in 4.12Cand 4.12D are intended primarily for individuals who have a disease causing abnormal arterial calcification or small vessel disease, we may also use them for evaluating anyone with PAD.

8. *How are toe pressures measured?* Toe pressures are measured routinely in most vascular laboratories through one of three methods: most frequently, photoplethysmography; less frequently, plethysmography using strain gauge cuffs; and Doppler ultrasound. Toe pressure can also be measured by using any blood pressure cuff that fits snugly around the big toe and is neither too tight nor too loose. A neonatal cuff or a cuff designed for use on fingers or toes can be used in the measurement of toe pressure.

9. *How do we use listing 4.12 if you have had a peripheral graft?* Peripheral grafting serves the same purpose as coronary grafting; that is, to bypass a narrow or obstructed arterial segment. If intermittent claudication recurs or persists after peripheral grafting, we may purchase Doppler studies to assess the flow of blood through the bypassed vessel and to establish the current severity of the peripheral arterial impairment. However, if you have had peripheral grafting done for your PAD, we will not use the findings from before the surgery to assess the current severity of your impairment, although we will consider the severity and duration of your impairment prior to your surgery in making our determination or decision.

H. *Evaluating Other Cardiovascular Impairments*

1. *How will we evaluate hypertension?* Because *hypertension* (high blood pressure) generally causes disability through its effects on other body systems, we will evaluate it by reference to the specific body system(s) affected (heart, brain, kidneys, or eyes) when we consider its effects under the listings. We will also consider any limitations imposed by your hypertension when we assess your residual functional capacity.

2. *How will we evaluate symptomatic congenital heart disease? Congenital heart disease* is any abnormality of the heart or the major blood vessels that is present at birth. Because of improved treatment methods, more children with congenital heart disease are living to adulthood. Although some types of congenital heart disease may be corrected by surgery, many individuals with treated congenital heart disease continue to have problems throughout their lives (symptomatic congenital heart disease). If you have congenital heart disease that results in chronic heart failure with evidence of ventricular dysfunction or in recurrent arrhythmias, we will evaluate your impairment under 4.02 or 4.05. Otherwise, we will evaluate your impairment under 4.06.

3. *What is cardiomyopathy and how will we evaluate it? Cardiomyopathy* is a disease of the heart muscle. The heart loses its ability to pump blood (heart failure), and in some instances, heart rhythm is disturbed, leading to irregular heartbeats (arrhythmias). Usually, the exact cause of the muscle damage is never found (idiopathic cardiomyopathy). There are various types of cardiomyopathy, which fall into two major categories: *Ischemic* and *nonischemic* cardiomyopathy. Ischemic cardiomyopathy typically refers to heart muscle damage that results from coronary artery disease, including heart attacks. Nonischemic cardiomyopathy includes several types: Dilated, hypertrophic, and restrictive. We will evaluate cardiomyopathy under 4.02, 4.04, 4.05, or 11.04, depending on its effects on you.

4. *How will we evaluate valvular heart disease?* We will evaluate valvular heart disease under the listing appropriate for its effect on you. Thus, we may use 4.02, 4.04, 4.05, 4.06,or an appropriate neurological listing in 11.00ff.

5. *What do we consider when we evaluate heart transplant recipients?*

a. After your heart transplant, we will consider you disabled for 1 year following the surgery because there is a greater likelihood of rejection of the organ and infection during the first year.

b. However, heart transplant patients generally meet our definition of disability before they undergo transplantation. We will determine the onset of your disability based on the facts in your case.

c. We will not assume that you became disabled when your name was placed on a transplant waiting list. This is because you may be placed on a waiting list soon after diagnosis of the cardiac disorder that may eventually require a transplant. Physicians recognize that candidates for transplantation often have to wait months or even years before a suitable donor heart is found, so they place their patients on the list as soon as permitted.

d. When we do a continuing disability review to determine whether you are still disabled, we will evaluate your residual impairment(s), as shown by symptoms, signs, and laboratory findings, including any side effects of medication. We will consider any remaining symptoms, signs, and laboratory findings indicative of cardiac dysfunction in deciding whether medical improvement (as defined in §§ 404.1594 and 416.994) has occurred.

6. *When does an aneurysm have "dissection not controlled by prescribed treatment," as required under 4.10?* An aneurysm (or bulge in the aorta or one of its major branches) is *dissecting* when the inner lining of the artery begins to separate from the arterial wall. We consider the dissection not controlled when you have persistence of chest pain due to progression of the dissection, an increase in the size of the aneurysm, or compression of one or more branches of the aorta supplying the heart, kidneys, brain, or other organs. An aneurysm with dissection can cause heart failure, renal (kidney) failure, or neurological complications. If you have an aneurysm that does not meet the requirements of 4.10 and you have one or more of these associated conditions, we will evaluate the condition(s) using the appropriate listing.

7. *What is hyperlipidemia and how will we evaluate it? Hyperlipidemia*is the general term for an elevation of any or all of the lipids (fats or cholesterol) in the blood; for example, hypertriglyceridemia, hypercholesterolemia, and hyperlipoproteinemia. These disorders of lipoprotein metabolism and transport can cause defects throughout the body. The effects most likely to interfere with function are those produced by atherosclerosis (narrowing of the arteries) and coronary artery disease. We will evaluate your lipoprotein disorder by considering its effects on you.

8. *What is Marfan syndrome and how will we evaluate it?*

a. Marfan syndrome is a genetic connective tissue disorder that affects multiple body systems, including the skeleton, eyes, heart, blood vessels, nervous system, skin, and lungs. There is no specific laboratory test to diagnose Marfan syndrome. The diagnosis is generally made by medical history, including family history, physical examination, including an evaluation of the ratio of arm/leg size to trunk size, a slit lamp eye examination, and a heart test(s), such as an echocardiogram. In some cases, a genetic analysis may be useful, but such analyses may not provide any additional helpful information.

b. The effects of Marfan syndrome can range from mild to severe. In most cases, the disorder progresses as you age. Most individuals with Marfan syndrome have abnormalities associated with the heart and blood vessels. Your heart's mitral valve may leak, causing a heart murmur. Small leaks may not cause symptoms, but larger ones may cause shortness of breath, fatigue, and palpitations. Another effect is that the wall of the aorta may be weakened and abnormally stretch (aortic dilation). This aortic dilation may tear, dissect, or rupture, causing serious heart problems or sometimes sudden death. We will evaluate the manifestations of your Marfan syndrome under the appropriate body system criteria, such as 4.10, or if necessary, consider the functional limitations imposed by your impairment.

I. *Other Evaluation Issues*

1. *What effect does obesity have on the cardiovascular system and how will we evaluate it?* Obesity is a medically determinable impairment that is often associated with disorders of the cardiovascular system. Disturbance of this system can be a major cause of disability if you have obesity. Obesity may affect the cardiovascular system because of the increased workload the additional body mass places on the heart. Obesity may make it harder for the chest and lungs to expand. This can mean that the respiratory system must work harder to provide needed oxygen. This in turn would make the heart work harder to pump blood to carry oxygen to the body. Because the body would be working harder at rest, its ability to perform additional work would be less than would otherwise be expected. Thus, the combined effects of obesity with cardiovascular impairments can be greater than the effects of each of the impairments considered separately. We must consider any additional and cumulative effects of obesity when we determine whether you have a severe cardiovascular impairment or a listing-level cardiovascular impairment (or a combination of impairments that medically equals the severity of a listed impairment), and when we assess your residual functional capacity.

2. *How do we relate treatment to functional status?* In general, conclusions about the severity of a cardiovascular impairment cannot be made on the basis of type of treatment rendered or anticipated. The amount of function restored and the time required for improvement after treatment (medical, surgical, or a prescribed program of progressive physical activity) vary with the nature and extent of the disorder, the type of treatment, and other factors. Depending upon the timing of this treatment in relation to the alleged onset date of disability, we may need to defer evaluation of the impairment for a period of up to 3 months from the date treatment began to permit consideration of treatment effects, unless we can make a determination or decision using the evidence we have. See 4.00B4.

3. *How do we evaluate impairments that do not meet one of the cardiovascular listings?*

a. These listings are only examples of common cardiovascular impairments that we consider severe enough to prevent you from doing any gainful activity. If your severe impairment(s) does not meet the criteria of any of these listings, we must also consider whether you have an impairment(s) that satisfies the criteria of a listing in another body system.

b. If you have a severe medically determinable impairment(s) that does not meet a listing, we will determine whether your impairments(s) medically equals a listing. (See §§ 404.1526 and 416.926.) If you have a severe impairment(s) that does not meet or medically equal the criteria of a listing, you may or may not have the residual functional capacity to engage in substantial gainful activity. Therefore, we proceed to the fourth and, if necessary, the fifth steps of the sequential evaluation process in §§ 404.1520 and 416.920. If you are an adult, we use the rules in §§ 404.1594 or 416.994, as appropriate, when we decide whether you continue to be disabled.

4.01 Category of Impairments, Cardiovascular System

4.02 ***Chronic heart failure*** while on a regimen of prescribed treatment, with symptoms and signs described in 4.00D2. The required level of severity for this impairment is met when the requirements in *both A and B* are satisfied.

A. Medically documented presence of one of the following:

1. Systolic failure (see 4.00D1a(i)), with left ventricular end diastolic dimensions greater than 6.0 cm or ejection fraction of 30 percent or less during a period of stability (not during an episode of acute heart failure); or

2. Diastolic failure (see 4.00D1a(ii)), with left ventricular posterior wall plus septal thickness totaling 2.5 cm or greater on imaging, with an enlarged left atrium greater than or equal to 4.5 cm, with normal or elevated ejection fraction during a period of stability (not during an episode of acute heart failure);

AND

B. Resulting in one of the following:

1. Persistent symptoms of heart failure which very seriously limit the ability to independently initiate, sustain, or complete activities of daily living in an individual for whom an MC, preferably one experienced in the care of patients with cardiovascular disease, has concluded that the performance of an exercise test would present a significant risk to the individual; or

2. Three or more separate episodes of acute congestive heart failure within a consecutive 12-month period (see 4.00A3e), with evidence of fluid retention (see 4.00D2b(ii)) from clinical and imaging assessments at the time of the episodes, requiring acute extended physician intervention such as hospitalization or emergency room treatment for 12 hours or more, separated by periods of stabilization (see 4.00D4c); or

3. Inability to perform on an exercise tolerance test at a workload equivalent to 5 METs or less due to:

a. Dyspnea, fatigue, palpitations, or chest discomfort; or

b. Three or more consecutive premature ventricular contractions (ventricular tachycardia), or increasing frequency of ventricular ectopy with at least 6 premature ventricular contractions per minute; or

c. Decrease of 10 mm Hg or more in systolic pressure below the baseline systolic blood pressure or the preceding systolic pressure measured during exercise (see 4.00D4d) due to left ventricular dysfunction, despite an increase in workload; or

d. Signs attributable to inadequate cerebral perfusion, such as ataxic gait or mental confusion.

4.04 Ischemic heart disease, with symptoms due to myocardial ischemia, as described in 4.00E3–4.00E7, while on a regimen of prescribed treatment (see 4.00B3 if there is no regimen of prescribed treatment), with one of the following:

A. Sign-or symptom-limited exercise tolerance test demonstrating at least one of the following manifestations at a workload equivalent to 5 METs or less:

1. Horizontal or downsloping depression, in the absence of digitalis glycoside treatment or hypokalemia, of the ST segment of at least –0.10 millivolts (–1.0 mm) in at least 3 consecutive complexes that are on a level baseline in any lead other than a VR, and depression of at least –0.10 millivolts lasting for at least 1 minute of recovery; or

2. At least 0.1 millivolt (1 mm) ST elevation above resting baseline in non-infarct leads during both exercise and 1 or more minutes of recovery; or

3. Decrease of 10 mm Hg or more in systolic pressure below the baseline blood pressure or the preceding systolic pressure measured during exercise (see 4.00E9e) due to left ventricular dysfunction, despite an increase in workload; or

4. Documented ischemia at an exercise level equivalent to 5 METs or less on appropriate medically acceptable imaging, such as radionuclide perfusion scans or stress echocardiography.

OR

B. Three separate ischemic episodes, each requiring revascularization or not amenable to revascularization (see 4.00E9f), within a consecutive 12-month period (see 4.00A3e).

OR

C. Coronary artery disease, demonstrated by angiography (obtained independent of Social Security disability evaluation) or other appropriate medically acceptable imaging, and in the absence of a timely exercise tolerance test or a timely normal drug-induced stress test, an MC, preferably one experienced in the care of patients with cardiovascular disease, has concluded that performance of exercise tolerance testing would present a significant risk to the individual, with both 1 and 2:

1. Angiographic evidence showing:

a. 50 percent or more narrowing of a nonbypassed left main coronary artery; or

b. 70 percent or more narrowing of another nonbypassed coronary artery; or

c. 50 percent or more narrowing involving a long (greater than 1 cm) segment of a nonbypassed coronary artery; or

d. 50 percent or more narrowing of at least two nonbypassed coronary arteries; or

e. 70 percent or more narrowing of a bypass graft vessel; and

2. Resulting in very serious limitations in the ability to independently initiate, sustain, or complete activities of daily living.

4.05 Recurrent arrhythmias, not related to reversible causes, such as electrolyte abnormalities or digitalis glycoside or antiarrhythmic drug toxicity, resulting in uncontrolled (see 4.00A3f), recurrent (see 4.00A3c) episodes of cardiac syncope or near syncope (see 4.00F3b), despite prescribed treatment(see 4.00B3 if there is no prescribed treatment), and documented by resting or ambulatory (Holter) electrocardiography, or by other appropriate medically acceptable testing, coincident with the occurrence of syncope or near syncope (see 4.00F3c).

4.06 Symptomatic congenital heart disease (cyanotic or acyanotic), documented by appropriate medically acceptable imaging (see 4.00A3d) or cardiac catheterization, with one of the following:

A. Cyanosis at rest, and:

1. Hematocrit of 55 percent or greater; or

2. Arterial O_2 saturation of less than 90 percent in room air, or resting arterial PO_2 of 60 Torr or less.

OR

B. Intermittent right-to-left shunting resulting in cyanosis on exertion (e.g., Eisenmenger's physiology) and with arterial PO_2 of 60 Torr or less at a workload equivalent to 5 METs or less.

OR

C. Secondary pulmonary vascular obstructive disease with pulmonary arterial systolic pressure elevated to at least 70 percent of the systemic arterial systolic pressure.

4.09 Heart transplant. Consider under a disability for 1 year following surgery; thereafter, evaluate residual impairment under the appropriate listing.

4.10 Aneurysm of aorta or major branches, due to any cause (e.g., atherosclerosis, cystic medial necrosis, Marfan syndrome, trauma), demonstrated by appropriate medically acceptable imaging, with dissection not controlled by prescribed treatment (see 4.00H6).

4.11 Chronic venous insufficiency of a lower extremity with incompetency or obstruction of the deep venous system and one of the following:

A. Extensive brawny edema (see 4.00G3) involving at least two-thirds of the leg between the ankle and knee or the distal one-third of the lower extremity between the ankle and hip.

OR

B. Superficial varicosities, stasis dermatitis, and either recurrent ulceration or persistent ulceration that has not healed following at least 3 months of prescribed treatment.

4.12 Peripheral arterial disease, as determined by appropriate medically acceptable imaging (see 4.00A3d, 4.00G2, 4.00G5, and 4.00G6), causing intermittent claudication (see 4.00G1) and one of the following:

A. Resting ankle/brachial systolic blood pressure ratio of less than 0.50.

OR

B. Decrease in systolic blood pressure at the ankle on exercise (see 4.00G7a and 4.00C16–4.00C17) of 50 percent or more of pre-exercise level and requiring 10 minutes or more to return to pre-exercise level.

OR

C. Resting toe systolic pressure of less than 30 mm Hg (see 4.00G7c and 4.00G8).

OR

D. Resting toe/brachial systolic blood pressure ratio of less than 0.40 (see 4.00G7c).

5.00 Digestive System

A. *What kinds of disorders do we consider in the digestive system?* Disorders of the digestive system include gastrointestinal hemorrhage, hepatic (liver) dysfunction, inflammatory bowel disease, short bowel syndrome, and malnutrition. They may also lead to complications, such as obstruction, or be accompanied by manifestations in other body systems.

B. *What documentation do we need?* We need a record of your medical evidence, including clinical and laboratory findings. The documentation should include appropriate medically acceptable imaging studies and reports of endoscopy, operations, and pathology, as appropriate to each listing, to document the severity and duration of your digestive disorder. Medically acceptable imaging includes, but is not limited to, x-ray imaging, sonography, computerized axial tomography (CAT scan), magnetic resonance imaging (MRI), and radionuclide scans. *Appropriate* means that the technique used is the proper one to support the evaluation and diagnosis of the disorder. The findings required by these listings must occur within the period we are considering in connection with your application or continuing disability review.

C. *How do we consider the effects of treatment?*

1. Digestive disorders frequently respond to medical or surgical treatment; therefore, we generally consider the severity and duration of these disorders within the context of prescribed treatment.

2. We assess the effects of treatment, including medication, therapy, surgery, or any other form of treatment you receive, by determining if there are improvements in the symptoms, signs, and laboratory findings of your digestive disorder. We also assess any side effects of your treatment that may further limit your functioning.

3. To assess the effects of your treatment, we may need information about:

a. The treatment you have been prescribed (for example, the type of medication or therapy, or your use of parenteral (intravenous) nutrition or supplemental enteral nutrition via a gastrostomy);

b. The dosage, method, and frequency of administration;

c. Your response to the treatment;

d. Any adverse effects of such treatment; and

e. The expected duration of the treatment.

4. Because the effects of treatment may be temporary or long-term, in most cases we need information about the impact of your treatment, including its expected duration and side effects, over a sufficient period of time to help us assess its outcome. When adverse effects of treatment contribute to the severity of your impairment(s), we will consider the duration or expected duration of the treatment when we assess the duration of your impairment(s).

5. If you need parenteral (intravenous) nutrition or supplemental enteral nutrition via a gastrostomy to avoid debilitating complications of a digestive disorder, this treatment will not, in itself, indicate that you are unable to do any gainful activity, except under 5.07, short bowel syndrome (see 5.00F).

6. If you have not received ongoing treatment or have not had an ongoing relationship with the medical community despite the existence of a severe impairment(s), we will evaluate the severity and duration of your digestive impairment on the basis of the current medical and other evidence in your case record. If you have not received treatment, you may not be able to show an impairment that meets the criteria of one of the digestive system listings, but your digestive impairment may medically equal a listing or be disabling based on consideration of your residual functional capacity, age, education, and work experience.

D. *How do we evaluate chronic liver disease?*

1. *General. Chronic liver disease* is characterized by liver cell necrosis, inflammation, or scarring (fibrosis or cirrhosis), due to any cause, that persists for more than 6 months. Chronic liver disease may result in portal hypertension, cholestasis (suppression of bile flow), extrahepatic manifestations, or liver cancer. (We evaluate liver cancer under 13.19.) Significant loss of liver function may be manifested by hemorrhage from varices or portal hypertensive gastropathy,

ascites (accumulation of fluid in the abdominal cavity), hydrothorax (ascitic fluid in the chest cavity), or encephalopathy. There can also be progressive deterioration of laboratory findings that are indicative of liver dysfunction. Liver transplantation is the only definitive cure for end stage liver disease (ESLD).

2. *Examples of chronic liver disease* include, but are not limited to, chronic hepatitis, alcoholic liver disease, non-alcoholic steatohepatitis (NASH), primary biliary cirrhosis (PBC), primary sclerosing cholangitis (PSC), autoimmune hepatitis, hemochromatosis, drug-induced liver disease, Wilson's disease, and serum alpha-1 antitrypsin deficiency. Acute hepatic injury is frequently reversible, as in viral, drug-induced, toxin-induced, alcoholic, and ischemic hepatitis. In the absence of evidence of a chronic impairment, episodes of acute liver disease do not meet 5.05.

3. *Manifestations of chronic liver disease.*

a. *Symptoms* may include, but are not limited to, pruritis (itching), fatigue, nausea, loss of appetite, or sleep disturbances. Symptoms of chronic liver disease may have a poor correlation with the severity of liver disease and functional ability.

b. *Signs* may include, but are not limited to, jaundice, enlargement of the liver and spleen, ascites, peripheral edema, and altered mental status.

c. *Laboratory findings* may include, but are not limited to, increased liver enzymes, increased serum total bilirubin, increased ammonia levels, decreased serum albumin, and abnormal coagulation studies, such as increased International Normalized Ratio (INR) or decreased platelet counts. Abnormally low serum albumin or elevated INR levels indicate loss of synthetic liver function, with increased likelihood of cirrhosis and associated complications. However, other abnormal lab tests, such as liver enzymes, serum total bilirubin, or ammonia levels, may have a poor correlation with the severity of liver disease and functional ability. A liver biopsy may demonstrate the degree of liver cell necrosis, inflammation, fibrosis, and cirrhosis. If you have had a liver biopsy, we will make every reasonable effort to obtain the results; however, we will not purchase a liver biopsy. Imaging studies (CAT scan, ultrasound, MRI) may show the size and consistency (fatty liver, scarring) of the liver and document ascites (see 5.00D6).

4. *Chronic viral hepatitis infections.*

a. *General.*

(i) *Chronic viral hepatitis* infections are commonly caused by hepatitis C virus (HCV), and to a lesser extent, hepatitis B virus (HBV). Usually, these are slowly progressive disorders that persist over many years during which the symptoms and signs are typically nonspecific, intermittent, and mild (for example, fatigue, difficulty with concentration, or right upper quadrant pain). Laboratory findings (liver enzymes, imaging studies, liver biopsy pathology) and complications are generally similar in HCV and HBV. The spectrum of these chronic viral hepatitis infections ranges widely and includes an asymptomatic state; insidious disease with mild to moderate symptoms associated with fluctuating liver tests; extrahepatic manifestations; cirrhosis, both compensated and decompensated; ESLD with the need for liver transplantation; and liver cancer. Treatment for chronic viral hepatitis infections varies considerably based on medication tolerance, treatment response, adverse effects of treatment, and duration of the treatment. Comorbid disorders, such as HIV infection, may accelerate the clinical course of viral hepatitis infection(s) or may result in a poorer response to medical treatment.

(ii) We evaluate all types of chronic viral hepatitis infections under 5.05or any listing in an affected body system(s). If your impairment(s) does not meet or medically equal a listing, we will consider the effects of your hepatitis when we assess your residual functional capacity.

b. *Chronic hepatitis B virus (HBV) infection.*

(i) *Chronic HBV infection* can be diagnosed by the detection of hepatitis B surface antigen (HBsAg) or hepatitis B virus DNA (HBV DNA) in the blood for at least 6 months. In addition, detection of the hepatitis B e antigen (HBeAg) suggests an increased likelihood of progression to cirrhosis, ESLD, and hepatocellular carcinoma. (HBeAg may also be referred to as "hepatitis B early antigen" or "hepatitis B envelope antigen.")

(ii) The therapeutic goal of treatment is to suppress HBV replication and thereby prevent progression to cirrhosis, ESLD, and hepatocellular carcinoma. Treatment usually includes interferon injections, oral antiviral agents, or a combination of both. Common adverse effects of treatment are the same as noted in 5.00D4c(ii) for HCV, and generally end within a few days after treatment is discontinued.

c. *Chronic hepatitis C virus (HCV) infection.*

(i) *Chronic HCV infection* is diagnosed by the detection of hepatitis C viral RNA in the blood for at least 6 months. Documentation of the therapeutic response to treatment is also monitored by the quantitative assay of serum HCV RNA ("HCV viral load"). Treatment usually includes a combination of interferon injections and oral ribavirin; whether a therapeutic response has occurred is usually assessed after 12 weeks of treatment by checking the HCV viral load. If there has been a substantial reduction in HCV viral load (also known as early viral response, or EVR), this reduction is predictive of sustained viral response with completion of treatment. Combined therapy is commonly discontinued after 12 weeks when there is no early viral response, since in that circumstance there is little chance of obtaining a sustained viral response (SVR). Otherwise, treatment is usually continued for a total of 48 weeks.

(ii) Combined interferon and ribavirin treatment may have significant adverse effects that may require dosing reduction, planned interruption of treatment, or discontinuation of treatment. Adverse effects may include: Anemia (ribavirin-induced hemolysis), neutropenia, thrombocytopenia, fever, cough, fatigue, myalgia, arthralgia, nausea, loss of appetite, pruritis, and insomnia. Behavioral side effects may also occur. Influenza-like symptoms are generally worse in the first 4 to 6 hours after each interferon injection and during the first weeks of treatment. Adverse effects generally end within a few days after treatment is discontinued.

d. *Extrahepatic manifestations of HBV and HCV.* In addition to their hepatic manifestations, both HBV and HCV may have significant extrahepatic manifestations in a variety of body systems. These include, but are not limited to: Keratoconjunctivitis (sicca syndrome), glomerulonephritis, skin disorders (for example, lichen planus, porphyria cutanea tarda), neuropathy, and immune dysfunction (for example, cryoglobulinemia, Sjögren's syndrome, and vasculitis). The extrahepatic manifestations of HBV and HCV may not correlate with the severity of your hepatic impairment. If you impairment(s) does not meet or medically equal a listing in an affected body system(s), we will consider the effects of your extrahepatic manifestations when we assess your residual functional capacity.

5. *Gastrointestinal hemorrhage* (5.02 and 5.05A). Gastrointestinal hemorrhaging can result in hematemesis (vomiting of blood), melena (tarry stools), or hematochezia (bloody stools). Under 5.02, the required transfusions of at least 2 units of blood must be at least 30 days apart and occur at least three times during a consecutive 6-month period. Under 5.05A, *hemodynamic instability* is diagnosed with signs such as pallor (pale skin), diaphoresis (profuse perspiration), rapid pulse, low blood pressure, postural hypotension (pronounced fall in blood pressure when arising to an upright position from lying down) or syncope (fainting). Hemorrhaging that results in hemodynamic instability is potentially life-threatening and therefore requires hospitalization for transfusion and supportive care. Under 5.05A, we require only one hospitalization for transfusion of at least 2 units of blood.

6. *Ascites or hydrothorax* (5.05B) indicates significant loss of liver function due to chronic liver disease. We evaluate ascites or hydrothorax that is not attributable to other causes under 5.05B. The required findings must be present on at least two evaluations at least 60 days apart within a consecutive 6-month period and despite continuing treatment as prescribed.

7. *Spontaneous bacterial peritonitis* (5.05C) is an infectious complication of chronic liver disease. It is diagnosed by ascitic peritoneal fluid that is documented to contain an absolute neutrophil count of at least 250 cells/mm3. The required finding in 5.05C is satisfied with one evaluation documenting peritoneal fluid infection. We do not evaluate other causes of peritonitis that are unrelated to chronic liver disease, such as tuberculosis, malignancy, and perforated bowel,

under this listing. We evaluate these other causes of peritonitis under the appropriate body system listings.

8. *Hepatorenal syndrome* (5.05D) is defined as functional renal failure associated with chronic liver disease in the absence of underlying kidney pathology. Hepatorenal syndrome is documented by elevation of serum creatinine, marked sodium retention, and oliguria (reduced urine output). The requirements of 5.05D are satisfied with documentation of any one of the three laboratory findings on one evaluation. We do not evaluate known causes of renal dysfunction, such as glomerulonephritis, tubular necrosis, drug-induced renal disease, and renal infections, under this listing. We evaluate these other renal impairments under 6.00ff.

9. *Hepatopulmonary syndrome* (5.05E) is defined as arterial deoxygenation (hypoxemia) that is associated with chronic liver disease due to intrapulmonary arteriovenous shunting and vasodilatation in the absence of other causes of arterial deoxygenation. Clinical manifestations usually include dyspnea, orthodeoxia (increasing hypoxemia with erect position), platypnea (improvement of dyspnea with flat position), cyanosis, and clubbing. The requirements of 5.05E are satisfied with documentation of any one of the findings on one evaluation. In 5.05E1, we require documentation of the altitude of the testing facility because altitude affects the measurement of arterial oxygenation. We will not purchase the specialized studies described in 5.05E2; however, if you have had these studies at a time relevant to your claim, we will make every reasonable effort to obtain the reports for the purpose of establishing whether your impairment meets 5.05E2.

10. *Hepatic encephalopathy* (5.05F).

a. *General.* Hepatic encephalopathy usually indicates severe loss of hepatocellular function. We define hepatic encephalopathy under 5.05F as a recurrent or chronic neuropsychiatric disorder, characterized by abnormal behavior, cognitive dysfunction, altered state of consciousness, and ultimately coma and death. The diagnosis is established by changes in mental status associated with fleeting neurological signs, including "flapping tremor" (asterixis), characteristic electroencephalographic (EEG) abnormalities, or abnormal laboratory values that indicate loss of synthetic liver function. We will not purchase the EEG testing described in 5.05F3b; however, if you have had this test at a time relevant to your claim, we will make every reasonable effort to obtain the report for the purpose of establishing whether your impairment meets 5.05F.

b. *Acute encephalopathy.* We will not evaluate your acute encephalopathy under 5.05F if it results from conditions other than chronic liver disease, such as vascular events and neoplastic diseases. We will evaluate these other causes of acute encephalopathy under the appropriate body system listings.

11. *End stage liver disease (ESLD) documented by scores from the SSA Chronic Liver Disease (SSA CLD) calculation* (5.05G).

a. We will use the SSA CLD score to evaluate your ESLD under 5.05G. We explain how we calculate the SSA CLD score in b. through g. of this section.

b. To calculate the SSA CLD score, we use a formula that includes three laboratory values: Serum total bilirubin (mg/dL), serum creatinine (mg/dL), and International Normalized Ratio (INR). The formula for the SSA CLD score calculation is:

9.57 × [Loge(serum creatinine mg/dL)]

+ 3.78 × [Loge(serum total bilirubin mg/dL)]

+ 11.2 × [Loge(INR)]

+ 6.43

c. When we indicate "Loge" in the formula for the SSA CLD score calculation, we mean the "base *e* logarithm" or "natural logarithm" (ln) of a numerical laboratory value, not the "base 10 logarithm" or "common logarithm" (log) of the laboratory value, and not the actual laboratory value. For example, if an individual has laboratory values of serum creatinine 1.2 mg/dL, serum total bilirubin 2.2 mg/dL, and INR 1.0, we would compute the SSA CLD score as follows:

9.57 × [Loge(serum creatinine 1.2 mg/dL) = 0.182]

+ 3.78 × [Loge(serum total bilirubin 2.2 mg/dL) = 0.788]

+ 11.2 × [Loge(INR 1.0) = 0]

+ 6.43

= 1.74 + 2.98 + 0 + 6.43

= 11.15, which is then rounded to an SSA CLD score of 11.

d. For any SSA CLD score calculation, all of the required laboratory values must have been obtained within 30 days of each other. If there are multiple laboratory values within the 30-day interval for any given laboratory test (serum total bilirubin, serum creatinine, or INR), we will use the highest value for the SSA CLD score calculation. We will round all laboratory values less than 1.0 up to 1.0.

e. Listing 5.05G requires two SSA CLD scores. The laboratory values for the second SSA CLD score calculation must have been obtained at least 60 days after the latest laboratory value for the first SSA CLD score and within the required 6-month period. We will consider the date of each SSA CLD score to be the date of the first laboratory value used for its calculation.

f. If you are in renal failure or on dialysis within a week of any serum creatinine test in the period used for the SSA CLD calculation, we will use a serum creatinine of 4, which is the maximum serum creatinine level allowed in the calculation, to calculate your SSA CLD score.

g. If you have the two SSA CLD scores required by 5.05G, we will find that your impairment meets the criteria of the listing from at least the date of the first SSA CLD score.

12. *Liver transplantation* (5.09) may be performed for metabolic liver disease, progressive liver failure, life-threatening complications of liver disease, hepatic malignancy, and acute fulminant hepatitis (viral, drug-induced, or toxin-induced). We will consider you to be disabled for 1 year from the date of the transplantation. Thereafter, we will evaluate your residual impairment(s) by considering the adequacy of post-transplant liver function, the requirement for post-transplant antiviral therapy, the frequency and severity of rejection episodes, comorbid complications, and all adverse treatment effects.

E. *How do we evaluate inflammatory bowel disease (IBD)?*

1. *Inflammatory bowel disease* (5.06) includes, but is not limited to, Crohn's disease and ulcerative colitis. These disorders, while distinct entities, share many clinical, laboratory, and imaging findings, as well as similar treatment regimens. Remissions and exacerbations of variable duration are the hallmark of IBD. Crohn's disease may involve the entire alimentary tract from the mouth to the anus in a segmental, asymmetric fashion. Obstruction, stenosis, fistulization, perineal involvement, and extraintestinal manifestations are common. Crohn's disease is rarely curable and recurrence may be a lifelong problem, even after surgical resection. In contrast, ulcerative colitis only affects the colon. The inflammatory process may be limited to the rectum, extend proximally to include any contiguous segment, or involve the entire colon. Ulcerative colitis may be cured by total colectomy.

2. Symptoms and signs of IBD include diarrhea, fecal incontinence, rectal bleeding, abdominal pain, fatigue, fever, nausea, vomiting, arthralgia, abdominal tenderness, palpable abdominal mass (usually inflamed loops of bowel) and perineal disease. You may also have signs or laboratory findings indicating malnutrition, such as weight loss, edema, anemia, hypoalbuminemia, hypokalemia, hypocalcemia, or hypomagnesemia.

3. IBD may be associated with significant extraintestinal manifestations in a variety of body systems. These include, but are not limited to, involvement of the eye (for example, uveitis, episcleritis, iritis); hepatobiliary disease (for example, gallstones, primary sclerosing cholangitis); urologic disease (for example, kidney stones, obstructive hydronephrosis); skin involvement (for example, erythema nodosum, pyoderma gangrenosum); or non-destructive inflammatory arthritis. You may also have associated thromboembolic disorders or vascular disease. These manifestations may not correlate with the severity of your IBD. If your

impairment does not meet any of the criteria of 5.06, we will consider the effects of your extraintestinal manifestations in determining whether you have an impairment(s) that meets or medically equals another listing, and we will also consider the effects of your extraintestinal manifestations when we assess your residual functional capacity.

4. Surgical diversion of the intestinal tract, including ileostomy and colostomy, does not preclude gainful activity if you are able to maintain adequate nutrition and function of the stoma. However, if you are not able to maintain adequate nutrition, we will evaluate your impairment under 5.08.

F. *How do we evaluate short bowel syndrome (SBS)?*

1. *Short bowel syndrome* (5.07) is a disorder that occurs when ischemic vascular insults (for example, volvulus), trauma, or IBD complications require surgical resection of more than one-half of the small intestine, resulting in the loss of intestinal absorptive surface and a state of chronic malnutrition. The management of SBS requires long-term parenteral nutrition via an indwelling central venous catheter (central line); the process is often referred to as *hyperalimentation* or *total parenteral nutrition* (TPN). Individuals with SBS can also feed orally, with variable amounts of nutrients being absorbed through their remaining intestine. Over time, some of these individuals can develop additional intestinal absorptive surface, and may ultimately be able to be weaned off their parenteral nutrition.

2. Your impairment will continue to meet 5.07 as long as you remain dependent on daily parenteral nutrition via a central venous catheter for most of your nutritional requirements. Long-term complications of SBS and parenteral nutrition include central line infections (with or without septicemia), thrombosis, hepatotoxicity, gallstones, and loss of venous access sites. Intestinal transplantation is the only definitive treatment for individuals with SBS who remain chronically dependent on parenteral nutrition.

3. To document SBS, we need a copy of the operative report of intestinal resection, the summary of the hospitalization(s) including: Details of the surgical findings, medically appropriate postoperative imaging studies that reflect the amount of your residual small intestine, or if we cannot get one of these reports, other medical reports that include details of the surgical findings. We also need medical documentation that you are dependent on daily parenteral nutrition to provide most of your nutritional requirements.

G. *How do we evaluate weight loss due to any digestive disorder?*

1. In addition to the impairments specifically mentioned in these listings, other digestive disorders, such as esophageal stricture, pancreatic insufficiency, and malabsorption, may result in significant weight loss. We evaluate weight loss due to any digestive disorder under 5.08 by using the Body Mass Index (BMI). We also provide a criterion in 5.06B for lesser weight loss resulting from IBD.

2. BMI is the ratio of your weight to the square of your height. Calculation and interpretation of the BMI are independent of gender in adults.

a. We calculate BMI using inches and pounds, meters and kilograms, centimeters and kilograms. We must have measurements of your weight and height without shoes for these calculations.

b. We calculate BMI using one of the following formulas:

English Formula

BMI = Weight in Pounds / (Height in Inches × Height in Inches) × 703

Metric Formulas

BMI = Weight in Kilograms / (Height in Meters × Height in Meters)

BMI = Weight in Kilograms / (Height in Centimeters × Height in Centimeters) × 10,000

H. *What do we mean by the phrase "consider under a disability for 1 year"?* We use the phrase "consider under a disability for 1 year" following a specific event in 5.02, 5.05A, and 5.09 to explain how long your impairment can meet the requirements of those particular listings. This phrase does not refer to the date on which your disability began, only to the date on which we must reevaluate whether your impairment continues to meet a listing or is otherwise disabling. For example, if you have received a liver transplant, you may have become disabled before the transplant because of chronic liver disease. Therefore, we do not restrict our determination of the onset of disability to the date of the specified event. We will establish an onset date earlier than the date of the specified event if the evidence in your case record supports such a finding.

I. *How do we evaluate impairments that do not meet one of the digestive disorder listings?*

1. These listings are only examples of common digestive disorders that we consider severe enough to prevent you from doing any gainful activity. If your impairment(s) does not meet the criteria of any of these listings, we must also consider whether you have an impairment(s) that satisfies the criteria of a listing in another body system. For example, if you have hepatitis B or C and you are depressed, we will evaluate your impairment under 12.04.

2. If you have a severe medically determinable impairment(s) that does not meet a listing, we will determine whether your impairment(s) medically equals a listing. (See §§ 404.1526 and 416.926.) If your impairment(s) does not meet or medically equal a listing, you may or may not have the residual functional capacity to engage in substantial gainful activity. In this situation, we will proceed to the fourth, and if necessary, the fifth steps of the sequential evaluation process in §§ 404.1520 and 416.920. When we decide whether you continue to be disabled, we use the rules in §§ 404.1594, 416.994, and 416.994a as appropriate.

5.01 Category of Impairments, Digestive System

5.02 Gastrointestinal hemorrhaging from any cause, requiring blood transfusion (with or without hospitalization) of at least 2 units of blood per transfusion, and occurring at least three times during a consecutive 6-month-period. The transfusions must be at least 30 days apart within the 6-month period. Consider under a disability for 1 year following the last documented transfusion; thereafter, evaluate the residual impairment(s).

5.03 [Reserved]

5.04 [Reserved]

5.05 Chronic liver disease, with:

A. Hemorrhaging from esophageal, gastric, or ectopic varices or from portal hypertensive gastropathy, demonstrated by endoscopy, x-ray, or other appropriate medically acceptable imaging, resulting in hemodynamic instability as defined in 5.00D5, and requiring hospitalization for transfusion of at least 2 units of blood. Consider under disability for 1 year following the last documented transfusion; thereafter, evaluate the residual impairment(s).

OR

B. Ascites or hydrothorax not attributable to other causes, despite continuing treatment as prescribed, present on at least 2 evaluations at least 60 days apart within a consecutive 6-month period. Each evaluation must be documented by:

1. Paracentesis or thoracentesis; or

2. Appropriate medically acceptable imaging or physical examination and one of the following:

a. Serum albumin of 3.0 g/dL or less; or

b. International Normalized Ratio (INR) of at least 1.5.

OR

C. Spontaneous bacterial peritonitis with peritoneal fluid containing an absolute neutrophil count of at least 250 cells/mm^3.

OR

D. Hepatorenal syndrome as described in 5.00D8, with one of the following:

1. Serum creatinine elevation of at least 2 mg/dL; or

2. Oliguria with 24-hour urine output less than 500 mL; or

3. Sodium retention with urine sodium less than 10 mEq per liter.

OR

E. Hepatopulmonary syndrome as described in 5.00D9, with:

1. Arterial oxygenation (PaO2) on room air of:

a. 60 mm Hg or less, at test sites less than 3000 feet above sea level, or

b. 55 mm Hg or less, at test sites from 3000 to 6000 feet, or

c. 50 mm Hg or less, at test sites above 6000 feet; or

2. Documentation of intrapulmonary arteriovenous shunting by contrast-enhanced echocardiography or macroaggregated albumin lung perfusion scan.

OR

F. Hepatic encephalopathy as described in 5.00D10, with 1 and either 2 or 3:

1. Documentation of abnormal behavior, cognitive dysfunction, changes in mental status, or altered state of consciousness (for example, confusion, delirium, stupor, or coma), present on at least two evaluations at least 60 days apart within a consecutive 6-month period; and

2. History of transjugular intrahepatic portosystemic shunt (TIPS) or any surgical portosystemic shunt; or

3. One of the following occurring on at least two evaluations at least 60 days apart within the same consecutive 6-month period as in F1:

a. Asterixis or other fluctuating physical neurological abnormalities; or

b. Electroencephalogram (EEG) demonstrating triphasic slow wave activity; or

c. Serum albumin of 3.0 g/dL or less; or

d. International Normalized Ratio (INR) of 1.5 or greater.

OR

G. End stage liver disease with SSA CLD scores of 22 or greater calculated as described in 5.00D11. Consider under a disability from at least the date of the first score.

5.06 Inflammatory bowel disease (IBD) documented by endoscopy, biopsy, appropriate medically acceptable imaging, or operative findings with:

A. Obstruction of stenotic areas (not adhesions) in the small intestine or colon with proximal dilatation, confirmed by appropriate medically acceptable imaging or in surgery, requiring hospitalization for intestinal decompression or for surgery, and occurring on at least two occasions at least 60 days apart within a consecutive 6-month period.

OR

B. Two of the following despite continuing treatment as prescribed and occurring within the same consecutive 6-month period:

1. Anemia with hemoglobin of less than 10.0 g/dL, present on at least two evaluations at least 60 days apart; or

2. Serum albumin of 3.0 g/dL or less, present on at least two evaluations at least 60 days apart; or

3. Clinically documented tender abdominal mass palpable on physical examination with abdominal pain or cramping that is not completely controlled by prescribed narcotic medication, present on at least two evaluations at least 60 days apart; or

4. Perineal disease with a draining abscess or fistula, with pain that is not completely controlled by prescribed narcotic medication, present on at least two evaluations at least 60 days apart; or

5. Involuntary weight loss of at least 10 percent from baseline, as computed in pounds, kilograms, or BMI, present on at least two evaluations at least 60 days apart; or

6. Need for supplemental daily enteral nutrition via a gastrostomy or daily parenteral nutrition via a central venous catheter.

5.07 Short bowel syndrome (SBS), due to surgical resection of more than one-half of the small intestine, with dependence on daily parenteral nutrition via a central venous catheter (see 5.00F).

5.08 Weight loss due to any digestive disorder despite continuing treatment as prescribed, with BMI of less than 17.50 calculated on at least two evaluations at least 60 days apart within a consecutive 6-month period.

5.09 Liver transplantation. Consider under a disability for 1 year following the date of transplantation; thereafter, evaluate the residual impairment(s) (see 5.00D12 and 5.00H).

6.00 Genitourinary Disorders

A. *Which disorders do we evaluate under these listings?*

We evaluate genitourinary disorders resulting in chronic kidney disease (CKD). Examples of such disorders include chronic glomerulonephritis, hypertensive nephropathy, diabetic nephropathy, chronic obstructive uropathy, and hereditary nephropathies. We also evaluate nephrotic syndrome due to glomerular dysfunction under these listings.

B. *What evidence do we need?*

1. We need evidence that documents the signs, symptoms, and laboratory findings of your CKD. This evidence should include reports of clinical examinations, treatment records, and documentation of your response to treatment. Laboratory findings, such as serum creatinine or serum albumin

levels, may document your kidney function. We generally need evidence covering a period of at least 90 days unless we can make a fully favorable determination or decision without it.

2. *Estimated glomerular filtration rate (eGFR).* The eGFR is an estimate of the filtering capacity of the kidneys that takes into account serum creatinine concentration and other variables, such as your age, gender, and body size. If your medical evidence includes eGFR findings, we will consider them when we evaluate your CKD under 6.05

3. *Kidney or bone biopsy.* If you have had a kidney or bone biopsy, we need a copy of the pathology report. When we cannot get a copy of the pathology report, we will accept a statement from an acceptable medical source verifying that a biopsy was performed and describing the results.

C. What other factors do we consider when we evaluate your genitourinary disorder?

1. *Chronic hemodialysis or peritoneal dialysis.*
   a. Dialysis is a treatment for CKD that uses artificial means to remove toxic metabolic byproducts from the blood. Hemodialysis uses an artificial kidney machine to clean waste products from the blood; peritoneal dialysis uses a dialyzing solution that is introduced into and removed from the abdomen (peritoneal cavity) either continuously or intermittently. Under 6.03, your ongoing dialysis must have lasted or be expected to last for a continuous period of at least 12 months. To satisfy the requirements in 6.03, we will accept a report from an acceptable medical source that describes your CKD and your current dialysis, and indicates that your dialysis will be ongoing.
   b. If you are undergoing chronic hemodialysis or peritoneal dialysis, your CKD may meet our definition of disability before you started dialysis. We will determine the onset of your disability based on the facts in your case record.
2. *Kidney transplant.*
   a. If you receive a kidney transplant, we will consider you to be disabled under 6.04 for 1 year from the date of transplant. After that, we will evaluate your residual impairment(s) by considering your post-transplant function, any rejection episodes you have had, complications in other body systems, and any adverse effects related to ongoing treatment.
   b. If you received a kidney transplant, your CKD may meet our definition of disability before you received the transplant. We will determine the onset of your disability based on the facts in your case record.
3. *Renal osteodystrophy.* This condition is the bone degeneration resulting from chronic kidney disease-mineral and bone disorder (CKD-MBD). CKD-MBD occurs when the kidneys are unable to maintain the necessary levels of minerals, hormones, and vitamins required for bone structure and function.

Under 6.05B1, "severe bone pain" means frequent or intractable (resistant to treatment) bone pain that interferes with physical activity or mental functioning.

4. *Peripheral neuropathy.* This disorder results when the kidneys do not adequately filter toxic substances from the blood. These toxins can adversely affect nerve tissue. The resulting neuropathy may affect peripheral motor or sensory nerves, or both, causing pain, numbness, tingling, and muscle weakness in various parts of the body. Under 6.05B2, the peripheral neuropathy must be a severe impairment. (See §§ 404.1520(c), 404.1521, 416.920(c), and 416.921of this chapter.) It must also have lasted or be expected to last for a continuous period of at least 12 months.
5. *Fluidoverload syndrome.* This condition occurs when excess sodium and water retention in the body due to CKD results in vascular congestion. Under 6.05B3, we need a description of a physical examination that documents signs and symptoms of vascular congestion, such as congestive heart failure, pleural effusion (excess fluid in the chest), ascites (excess fluid in the abdomen), hypertension, fatigue, shortness of breath, or peripheral edema.
6. *Anasarca* (generalized massive edema or swelling). Under 6.05B3 and 6.06B, we need a description of the extent of edema, including pretibial (in front of the tibia), periorbital (around the eyes), or presacral (in front of the sacrum) edema. We also need a description of any ascites, pleural effusion, or pericardial effusion.
7. *Anorexia (diminished appetite) with weight loss.* Anorexia is a frequent sign of CKD and can result in weight loss. We will use body mass index (BMI) to determine the severity of your weight loss under 6.05B4. (BMI is the ratio of your measured weight to the square of your measured height.) The formula for calculating BMI is in section 5.00G.
8. *Complications of CKD.* The hospitalizations in 6.09 may be for different complications of CKD. Examples of complications from CKD that may result in hospitalization include stroke, congestive heart failure, hypertensive crisis, or acute kidney failure requiring a short course of hemodialysis. If the CKD complication occurs during a hospitalization that was initially for a co-occurring condition, we will evaluate it under our rules for determining medical equivalence. (See §§ 404.1526 and 416.926 of this chapter.) We will evaluate co-occurring conditions, including those that result in hospitalizations, under the listings for the affected body system or under our rules for medical equivalence.

D. *How do we evaluate disorders that do not meet one of the genitourinary listings?*

1. The listed disorders are only examples of common genitourinary disorders that we consider severe enough to prevent you from doing any gainful activity. If your impairment(s) does not meet the criteria of any of these listings, we must also consider whether you have an impairment(s) that satisfies the criteria of a listing in another body system.

2. If you have a severe medically determinable impairment(s) that does not meet a listing, we will determine whether your impairment(s) medically equals a listing. (See §§ 404.1526 and 416.926 of this chapter.) Genitourinary disorders may be associated with disorders in other body systems, and we consider the combined effects of multiple impairments when we determine whether they medically equal a listing. If your impairment(s) does not meet or medically equal the criteria of a listing, you may or may not have the residual functional capacity to engage in substantial gainful activity. We proceed to the fourth and, if necessary, the fifth steps of the sequential evaluation process in §§ 404.1520 and 416.920 of this chapter. We use the rules in §§ 404.1594 and 416.994 of this chapter, as appropriate, when we decide whether you continue to be disabled.

6.01 Category of Impairments, Genitourinary Disorders

6.03 ***Chronic kidney disease,*** with chronic hemodialysis or peritoneal dialysis (see 6.00C1).

6.04 ***Chronic kidney disease,*** with kidney transplant. Consider under a disability for 1 year following the transplant; thereafter, evaluate the residual impairment (see 6.00C2).

6.05 ***Chronic kidney disease,*** with impairment of kidney function, with A and B:

A. Reduced glomerular filtration evidenced by one of the following laboratory findings documented on at least two occasions at least 90 days apart during a consecutive 12-month period:

1. Serum creatinine of 4 mg/dL or greater; or
2. Creatinine clearance of 20 ml/min. or less; or
3. Estimated glomerular filtration rate (eGFR) of 20 ml/min/1.73m2 or less.

AND

B. One of the following:

1. Renal osteodystrophy (see 6.00C3) with severe bone pain and imaging studies documenting bone abnormalities, such as osteitis fibrosa, osteomalacia, or pathologic fractures; or
2. Peripheral neuropathy (see 6.00C4); or
3. Fluid overload syndrome (see 6.00C5) documented by one of the following:
    a. Diastolic hypertension greater than or equal to diastolic blood pressure of 110 mm Hg despite at least 90 consecutive days of prescribed therapy, documented by at least two measurements of diastolic blood pressure at least 90 days apart during a consecutive 12-month period; or

b. Signs of vascular congestion or anasarca (see 6.00C6) despite at least 90 consecutive days of prescribed therapy, documented on at least two occasions at least 90 days apart during a consecutive 12-month period; or

4. Anorexia with weight loss (see 6.00C7) determined by body mass index (BMI) of 18.0 or less, calculated on at least two occasions at least 90 days apart during a consecutive 12-month period.

6.06 *Nephrotic syndrome,* with A and B

A. Laboratory findings as described in 1 or 2, documented on at least two occasions at least 90 days apart during a consecutive 12-month period:

1. Proteinuria of 10.0 g or greater per 24 hours; or
2. Serum albumin of 3.0 g/dL or less, and
   a. Proteinuria of 3.5 g or greater per 24 hours; or
   b. Urine total-protein-to-creatinine ratio of 3.5 or greater.

AND

B. Anasarca (see 6.00C6) persisting for at least 90 days despite prescribed treatment.

6.09 *Complications of chronic kidney disease* (see 6.00C8) requiring at least three hospitalizations within a consecutive 12-month period and occurring at least 30 days apart. Each hospitalization must last at least 48 hours, including hours in a hospital emergency department immediately before the hospitalization.

7.00 Hematological Disorders

A. *What hematological disorders do we evaluate under these listings?*

1. We evaluate non-malignant (non-cancerous) hematological disorders, such as hemolytic anemias (7.05), disorders of thrombosis and hemostasis (7.08), and disorders of bone marrow failure (7.10). These disorders disrupt the normal development and function of white blood cells, red blood cells, platelets, and clotting-factor proteins (factors).
2. We evaluate malignant (cancerous) hematological disorders, such as lymphoma, leukemia, and multiple myeloma, under the appropriate listings in 13.00, except for two lymphomas associated with human immunodeficiency virus (HIV) infection. We evaluate primary central nervous system lymphoma associated with HIV infection under 14.11B, and primary effusion lymphoma associated with HIV infection under 14.11C.

B. *What evidence do we need to document that you have a hematological disorder?* We need the following evidence to document that you have a hematological disorder:

1. A laboratory report of a definitive test that establishes a hematological disorder, signed by a physician; or
2. A laboratory report of a definitive test that establishes a hematological disorder that is not signed by a physician and a report from a physician that states you have the disorder; or
3. When we do not have a laboratory report of a definitive test, a persuasive report from a physician that a diagnosis of your hematological disorder was confirmed by appropriate laboratory analysis or other diagnostic method(s). To be persuasive, this report must state that you had the appropriate definitive laboratory test or tests for diagnosing your disorder and provide the results, or explain how your diagnosis was established by other diagnostic method(s) consistent with the prevailing state of medical knowledge and clinical practice.
4. We will make every reasonable effort to obtain the results of appropriate laboratory testing you have had. We will not purchase complex, costly, or invasive tests, such as tests of clotting-factor proteins, and bone marrow aspirations.

C. *What are hemolytic anemias, and how do we evaluate them under 7.05?*

1. *Hemolytic anemias, both congenital and acquired*, are disorders that result in premature destruction of red blood cells (RBCs). Hemolytic disorders include abnormalities of hemoglobin structure (hemoglobinopathies), abnormal RBC enzyme content and function, and RBC membrane (envelope) defects that are congenital or acquired. The diagnosis of hemolytic anemia is based on hemoglobin electrophoresis or analysis of the contents of the RBC (enzymes) and membrane. Examples of congenital hemolytic anemias include sickle cell disease, thalassemia and their variants, and hereditary spherocytosis. Acquired hemolytic anemias may result from autoimmune disease (for example, systemic lupus erythematosus) or mechanical devices (for example, heart valves, intravascular patches).
2. The hospitalizations in 7.05B do not all have to be for the same complication of the hemolytic anemia. They may be for three different complications of the disorder. Examples of complications of hemolytic anemia that may result in hospitalization include osteomyelitis, painful (vaso-occlusive) crisis, pulmonary infections or infarctions, acute chest syndrome, pulmonary hypertension, chronic heart failure, gallbladder disease, hepatic (liver) failure, renal (kidney) failure, nephrotic syndrome, aplastic crisis, and stroke. We will count the hours you receive emergency treatment in a comprehensive sickle cell disease center immediately before the hospitalization if this treatment is comparable to the treatment provided in a hospital emergency department.
3. For 7.05C, we do not require hemoglobin to be measured during a period in which you are free of pain or other symptoms of your disorder. We will

accept hemoglobin measurements made while you are experiencing complications of your hemolytic anemia.

4. 7.05D refers to the most serious type of beta thalassemia major in which the bone marrow cannot produce sufficient numbers of normal RBCs to maintain life. The only available treatments for beta thalassemia major are lifelong RBC transfusions (sometimes called hypertransfusion) or bone marrow transplantation. For purposes of 7.05D, we do not consider prophylactic RBC transfusions to prevent strokes or other complications in sickle cell disease and its variants to be of equal significance to life-saving RBC transfusions for beta thalassemia major. However, we will consider the functional limitations associated with prophylactic RBC transfusions and any associated side effects (for example, iron overload) under 7.18 and any affected body system(s). We will also evaluate strokes and resulting complications under 11.00 and 12.00.

D. *What are disorders of thrombosis and hemostasis, and how do we evaluate them under 7.08?*

1. *Disorders of thrombosis and hemostasis* include both clotting and bleeding disorders, and may be congenital or acquired. These disorders are characterized by abnormalities in blood clotting that result in hypercoagulation (excessive blood clotting) or hypocoagulation (inadequate blood clotting). The diagnosis of a thrombosis or hemostasis disorder is based on evaluation of plasma clotting-factor proteins (factors) and platelets. Protein C or protein S deficiency and Factor V Leiden are examples of hypercoagulation disorders. Hemophilia, von Willebrand disease, and thrombocytopenia are examples of hypocoagulation disorders. Acquired excessive blood clotting may result from blood protein defects and acquired inadequate blood clotting (for example, acquired hemophilia A) may be associated with inhibitor autoantibodies.
2. The hospitalizations in 7.08 do not all have to be for the same complication of a disorder of thrombosis and hemostasis. They may be for three different complications of the disorder. Examples of complications that may result in hospitalization include anemias, thromboses, embolisms, and uncontrolled bleeding requiring multiple factor concentrate infusions or platelet transfusions. We will also consider any surgery that you have, even if it is not related to your hematological disorder, to be a complication of your disorder of thrombosis and hemostasis if you require treatment with clotting-factor proteins (for example, factor VIII or factor IX) or anticoagulant medication to control bleeding or coagulation in connection with your surgery. We will count the hours you receive emergency treatment in a comprehensive hemophilia treatment center immediately before the hospitalization if this treatment is comparable to the treatment provided in a hospital emergency department.

E. *What are disorders of bone marrow failure, and how do we evaluate them under 7.10?*

1. *Disorders of bone marrow failure* may be congenital or acquired, characterized by bone marrow that does not make enough healthy RBCs, platelets, or granulocytes (specialized types of white blood cells); there may also be a combined failure of these bone marrow-produced cells. The diagnosis is based on peripheral blood smears and bone marrow aspiration or bone marrow biopsy, but not peripheral blood smears alone. Examples of these disorders are myelodysplastic syndromes, aplastic anemia, granulocytopenia, and myelofibrosis. Acquired disorders of bone marrow failure may result from viral infections, chemical exposure, or immunologic disorders.
2. The hospitalizations in 7.10A do not all have to be for the same complication of bone marrow failure. They may be for three different complications of the disorder. Examples of complications that may result in hospitalization include uncontrolled bleeding, anemia, and systemic bacterial, viral, or fungal infections.
3. For 7.10B, the requirement of life-long RBC transfusions to maintain life in myelodysplastic syndromes or aplastic anemias has the same meaning as it does for beta thalassemia major (see 7.00C4).

F. *How do we evaluate bone marrow or stem cell transplantation under 7.17?* We will consider you to be disabled for 12 months from the date of bone marrow or stem cell transplantation, or we may consider you to be disabled for a longer period if you are experiencing any serious post-transplantation complications, such as graft-versus-host (GVH) disease, frequent infections after immunosuppressive therapy, or significant deterioration of organ systems. We do not restrict our determination of the onset of disability to the date of the transplantation in 7.17. We may establish an earlier onset date of disability due to your transplantation if evidence in your case record supports such a finding.

G. *How do we use the functional criteria in 7.18?*

1. When we use the functional criteria in 7.18, we consider all relevant information in your case record to determine the impact of your hematological disorder on your ability to function independently, appropriately, effectively, and on a sustained basis in a work setting. Factors we will consider when we evaluate your functioning under 7.18 include, but are not limited to: your symptoms, the frequency and duration of complications of your hematological disorder, periods of exacerbation and remission, and the functional impact of your treatment, including the side effects of your medication.
2. *Repeated complications* means that the complications occur on an average of three times a year, or once every 4 months, each lasting 2 weeks or more; or the complications do not last for 2 weeks but occur substantially more frequently than three times in a year or once every 4 months; or they occur less frequently than an average of three times a year or once every 4 months but

last substantially longer than 2 weeks. Your impairment will satisfy this criterion regardless of whether you have the same kind of complication repeatedly, all different complications, or any other combination of complications; for example, two of the same kind of complication and a different one. You must have the required number of complications with the frequency and duration required in this section. Additionally, the complications must occur within the period we are considering in connection with your application or continuing disability review.

3. To satisfy the functional criteria in 7.18, your hematological disorder must result in a "marked" level of limitation in one of three general areas of functioning: activities of daily living, social functioning, or difficulties in completing tasks due to deficiencies in concentration, persistence, or pace. Functional limitations may result from the impact of the disease process itself on your mental functioning, physical functioning, or both your mental and physical functioning. This limitation could result from persistent or intermittent symptoms, such as pain, severe fatigue, or malaise, resulting in a limitation of your ability to do a task, to concentrate, to persevere at a task, or to perform the task at an acceptable rate of speed. (*Severe fatigue* means a frequent sense of exhaustion that results in significant reduced physical activity or mental function. *Malaise* means frequent feelings of illness, bodily discomfort, or lack of well-being that result in significantly reduced physical activity or mental function.) You may also have limitations because of your treatment and its side effects.

4. *Marked* limitation means that the symptoms and signs of your hematological disorder interfere *seriously* with your ability to function. Although we do not require the use of such a scale, "marked" would be the fourth point on a five-point scale consisting of no limitation, mild limitation, moderate limitation, marked limitation, and extreme limitation. We do not define "marked" by a specific number of different activities of daily living or different behaviors in which your social functioning is impaired, or a specific number of tasks that you are able to complete, but by the nature and overall degree of interference with your functioning. You may have a marked limitation when several activities or functions are impaired, or even when only one is impaired. Additionally, you need not be totally precluded from performing an activity to have a marked limitation, as long as the degree of limitation interferes seriously with your ability to function independently, appropriately, and effectively. The term "marked" does not imply that you must be confined to bed, hospitalized, or in a nursing home.

5. *Activities of daily living* include, but are not limited to, such activities as doing household chores, grooming and hygiene, using a post office, taking public transportation, or paying bills. We will find that you have a "marked" limitation in activities of daily living if you have a serious limitation in your ability to maintain a household or take public transportation because of

symptoms such as pain, severe fatigue, anxiety, or difficulty concentrating, caused by your hematological disorder (including complications of the disorder) or its treatment, even if you are able to perform some self-care activities.

6. *Social functioning* includes the capacity to interact with others independently, appropriately, effectively, and on a sustained basis. It includes the ability to communicate effectively with others. We will find that you have a "marked" limitation in maintaining social functioning if you have a serious limitation in social interaction on a sustained basis because of symptoms such as pain, severe fatigue, anxiety, or difficulty concentrating, or a pattern of exacerbation and remission, caused by your hematological disorder (including complications of the disorder) or its treatment, even if you are able to communicate with close friends or relatives.
7. *Completing tasks in a timely manner* involves the ability to sustain concentration, persistence, or pace to permit timely completion of tasks commonly found in work settings. We will find that you have a "marked" limitation in completing tasks if you have a serious limitation in your ability to sustain concentration or pace adequate to complete work-related tasks because of symptoms, such as pain, severe fatigue, anxiety, or difficulty concentrating caused by your hematological disorder (including complications of the disorder) or its treatment, even if you are able to do some routine activities of daily living.

H. *How do we consider your symptoms, including your pain, severe fatigue, and malaise?* Your symptoms, including pain, severe fatigue, and malaise, may be important factors in our determination whether your hematological disorder(s) meets or medically equals a listing, or in our determination whether you are otherwise able to work. We cannot consider your symptoms unless you have medical signs or laboratory findings showing the existence of a medically determinable impairment(s) that could reasonably be expected to produce the symptoms. If you have such an impairment(s), we will evaluate the intensity, persistence, and functional effects of your symptoms using the rules throughout 7.00 and in our other regulations. (See sections 404.1521, 404.1529, 416.921, and 416.929 of this chapter) Additionally, when we assess the credibility of your complaints about your symptoms and their functional effects, we will not draw any inferences from the fact that you do not receive treatment or that you are not following treatment without considering all of the relevant evidence in your case record, including any explanations you provide that may explain why you are not receiving or following treatment.

I. *How do we evaluate episodic events in hematological disorders?* Some of the listings in this body system require a specific number of events within a consecutive 12-month period. (See 7.05, 7.08, and 7.10A.) When we use such criteria, a consecutive 12-month period means a period of 12 consecutive months, all or part of which must occur within the period we are considering in connection with your application or continuing disability review. These events must occur at least 30 days apart to ensure that we are evaluating separate events.

J. *How do we evaluate hematological disorders that do not meet one of these listings?*

1. These listings are only common examples of hematological disorders that we consider severe enough to prevent a person from doing any gainful activity. If your disorder does not meet the criteria of any of these listings, we must consider whether you have a disorder that satisfies the criteria of a listing in another body system. For example, we will evaluate hemophilic joint deformity or bone or joint pain from myelofibrosis under 1.00; polycythemia vera under 3.00, 4.00, or 11.00; chronic iron overload resulting from repeated RBC transfusion (transfusion hemosiderosis) under 3.00, 4.00, or 5.00; and the effects of intracranial bleeding or stroke under 11.00 or 12.00.
2. If you have a severe medically determinable impairment(s) that does not meet a listing, we will determine whether your impairment(s) medically equals a listing. (See sections 404.1526 and 416.926 of this chapter.) Hematological disorders may be associated with disorders in other body systems, and we consider the combined effects of multiple impairments when we determine whether they medically equal a listing. If your impairment(s) does not medically equal a listing, you may or may not have the residual functional capacity to engage in substantial gainful activity. We proceed to the fourth, and, if necessary, the fifth steps of the sequential evaluation process in sections 404.1520 and 416.920. We use the rules in sections 404.1594, 416.994, and 416.994a of this chapter, as appropriate, when we decide whether you continue to be disabled.

7.01 Category of Impairments, Hematological Disorders

7.05 *Hemolytic anemias,* including sickle cell disease, thalassemia, and their variants (see 7.00C), with:

A. Documented painful (vaso-occlusive) crises requiring parenteral (intravenous or intramuscular) narcotic medication, occurring at least six times within a 12-month period with at least 30 days between crises.

OR

B. Complications of hemolytic anemia requiring at least three hospitalizations within a 12-month period and occurring at least 30 days apart. Each hospitalization must last at least 48 hours, which can include hours in a hospital emergency department or comprehensive sickle cell disease center immediately before the hospitalization (see 7.00C2)

OR

C. Hemoglobin measurements of 7.0 grams per deciliter (g/dL) or less, occurring at least three times within a 12-month period with at least 30 days between measurements.

OR

D. Beta thalassemia major requiring life-long RBC transfusions at least once every 6 weeks to maintain life (see 7.00C4).

7.08 ***Disorders of thrombosis and hemostasis***, including hemophilia and thrombocytopenia (see 7.00D), with complications requiring at least three hospitalizations within a 12 month period and occurring at least 30 days apart prior to adjudication. Each hospitalization must last at least 48 hours, which can include hours in the hospital emergency department or comprehensive hemophilia treatment center immediately before the hospitalization (see 7.00D2).

7.10 ***Disorders of bone marrow failure,*** including myelodysplastic syndromes, aplastic anemia, granulocytopenia, and myelofibrosis (see 7.00E), with:

A. Complications of bone marrow failure requiring at least three hospitalizations within a 12-month period and occurring at least 30 days apart. Each hospitalization must last at least 48 hours, which can include hours in a hospital emergency department immediately before the hospitalization (see 7.00E2).

OR

B. Myelodysplastic syndromes or aplastic anemias requiring life-long RBC transfusions at least once every 6 weeks to maintain life (see 7.00E3).

7.17 ***Hematological disorders treated by bone marrow or stem cell transplantation (see 7.00F)***. Consider under a disability for at least 12 consecutive months from the date of transplantation. After that, evaluate any residual impairment(s) under the criteria for the affected body system.

7.18 ***Repeated complications of hematological disorders (see 7.00G2)*** including those complications listed in 7.05, 7.08, and 7.10 but without the requisite findings for those listings, or other complications (for example, anemia, osteonecrosis, retinopathy, skin ulcers, silent central nervous system infarction, cognitive or other mental limitation, or limitation of joint movement), resulting in significant, documented symptoms or signs (for example, pain, severe fatigue, malaise, fever, night sweats, headaches, joint or muscle swelling, or shortness of breath), and one of the following at the marked level (see 7.00G4)

A. Limitation of activities of daily living (see 7.00G5).

B. Limitation in maintaining social functioning (see 7.00G6).

C. Limitation in completing tasks in a timely manner due to deficiencies in concentration, persistence, or pace (see 7.00G7).

8.00 Skin Disorders

A. *What skin disorders do we evaluate with these listings?*

We use these listings to evaluate skin disorders that may result from hereditary, congenital, or acquired pathological processes. The kinds of impairments covered by these listings are: Ichthyosis, bullous diseases, chronic infections of the skin or mucous membranes, dermatitis, hidradenitis suppurativa, genetic photosensitivity disorders, and burns.

B. *What documentation do we need?*

When we evaluate the existence and severity of your skin disorder, we generally need information about the onset, duration, frequency of flare-ups, and prognosis of your skin disorder; the location, size, and appearance of lesions; and, when applicable, history of exposure to toxins, allergens, or irritants, familial incidence, seasonal variation, stress factors, and your ability to function outside of a highly protective environment. To confirm the diagnosis, we may need laboratory findings (for example, results of a biopsy obtained independently of Social Security disability evaluation or blood tests) or evidence from other medically acceptable methods consistent with the prevailing state of medical knowledge and clinical practice.

C. *How do we assess the severity of your skin disorder(s)?*

We generally base our assessment of severity on the extent of your skin lesions, the frequency of flare-ups of your skin lesions, how your symptoms (including pain) limit you, the extent of your treatment, and how your treatment affects you.

1. *Extensive skin lesions.*

Extensive skin lesions are those that involve multiple body sites or critical body areas, and result in a very serious limitation. Examples of extensive skin lesions that result in a very serious limitation include but are not limited to:

a. Skin lesions that interfere with the motion of your joints and that very seriously limit your use of more than one extremity; that is, two upper extremities, two lower extremities, or one upper and one lower extremity.

b. Skin lesions on the palms of both hands that very seriously limit your ability to do fine and gross motor movements.

c. Skin lesions on the soles of both feet, the perineum, or both inguinal areas that very seriously limit your ability to ambulate.

2. *Frequency of flare-ups.*

If you have skin lesions, but they do not meet the requirements of any of the listings in this body system, you may still have an impairment that prevents you from doing any gainful activity when we consider your condition over time, especially if your flare-ups result in extensive skin lesions, as defined in C1 of this section. Therefore, if you have frequent flare-ups, we may find that your impairment(s) is medically equal to one of these listings even though you have some periods during which your condition is in remission. We will consider how frequent and serious your flare-ups are, how quickly they resolve, and how you function between flare-ups to determine whether you have been unable to do any gainful activity for a continuous period of at least 12 months or can be expected to be unable to do any gainful activity for a continuous period of at least 12 months. We will also consider the frequency of your flare-ups when we determine whether you have a severe impairment and when we need to assess your residual functional capacity.

3. *Symptoms (including pain).*

Symptoms (including pain) may be important factors contributing to the severity of your skin disorder(s). We assess the impact of symptoms as explained in §§ 404.1521, 404.1529, 416.921, and 416.929 of this chapter.

4. *Treatment.*

We assess the effects of medication, therapy, surgery, and any other form of treatment you receive when we determine the severity and duration of your impairment(s). Skin disorders frequently respond to treatment; however, response to treatment can vary widely, with some impairments becoming resistant to treatment. Some treatments can have side effects that can in themselves result in limitations.

a. We assess the effects of continuing treatment as prescribed by determining if there is improvement in the symptoms, signs, and laboratory findings of your disorder, and if you experience side effects that result in functional limitations. To assess the effects of your treatment, we may need information about:

i. The treatment you have been prescribed (for example, the type, dosage, method, and frequency of administration of medication or therapy);
ii. Your response to the treatment;
iii. Any adverse effects of the treatment; and
iv. The expected duration of the treatment.

b. Because treatment itself or the effects of treatment may be temporary, in most cases sufficient time must elapse to allow us to evaluate the impact and expected duration of treatment and its side effects. Except under 8.07 and 8.08, you must follow continuing treatment as prescribed for at least 3 months before your impairment can be determined to meet the requirements of a skin disorder listing. (See 8.00H if you are not undergoing treatment or did not have treatment for 3 months.) We consider your specific response to treatment when we evaluate the overall severity of your impairment.

D. *How do we assess impairments that may affect the skin and other body systems?*

When your impairment affects your skin and has effects in other body systems, we first evaluate the predominant feature of your impairment under the appropriate body system. Examples include, but are not limited to the following.

1. *Tuberous sclerosis* primarily affects the brain. The predominant features are seizures, which we evaluate under the neurological listings in 11.00, and developmental delays or other mental disorders, which we evaluate under the mental disorders listings in 12.00.

2. *Malignant tumors of the skin* (for example, malignant melanomas) are cancers, or neoplastic diseases, which we evaluate under the listings in 13.00.

3. *Autoimmune disorders* and other immune system disorders (for example, systemic lupus erythematosus (SLE), scleroderma, human immunodeficiency virus (HIV) infection, and Sjögren's syndrome) often involve more than one body system. We first evaluate these disorders under the immune system disorders listings in 14.00. We evaluate SLE under 14.02, scleroderma under 14.04, Sjögren's syndrome under 14.10, and HIV infection under 14.11.

4. *Disfigurement or deformity* resulting from skin lesions may result in loss of sight, hearing, speech, and the ability to chew (mastication). We evaluate these impairments and their effects under the special senses and speech listings in 2.00 and the digestive system listings in 5.00. Facial disfigurement or other physical deformities may also have effects we evaluate under the mental disorders listings in 12.00, such as when they affect mood or social functioning.

E. *How do we evaluate genetic photosensitivity disorders?*

1. Xeroderma pigmentosum (XP). When you have XP, your impairment meets the requirements of 8.07A if you have clinical and laboratory findings showing that you have the disorder. (See 8.00E3.) People who have XP have a lifelong hypersensitivity to all forms of ultraviolet light and generally lead extremely restricted lives in highly protective environments in order to prevent skin cancers from developing. Some people with XP also experience problems with their eyes, neurological problems, mental disorders, and problems in other body systems.

2. *Other genetic photosensitivity disorders.*

Other genetic photosensitivity disorders may vary in their effects on different people, and may not result in an inability to engage in any gainful activity for a continuous period of at least 12 months. Therefore, if you have a genetic photosensitivity disorder other than XP (established by clinical and laboratory findings as described in 8.00E3), you must show that you have either extensive skin lesions or an inability to function outside of a highly protective environment to meet the requirements of 8.07B.

You must also show that your impairment meets the duration requirement. By inability to function outside of a highly protective environment we mean that you must avoid exposure to ultraviolet light (including sunlight passing through windows and light from unshielded fluorescent bulbs), wear protective clothing and eyeglasses, and use opaque broad spectrum sunscreens in order to avoid skin cancer or other serious effects. Some genetic photosensitivity disorders can have very serious effects in other body systems, especially special senses and speech (2.00), neurological (11.00), mental (12.00), and neoplastic (13.00). We will evaluate the predominant feature of your impairment under the appropriate body system, as explained in 8.00D.

3. *Clinical and laboratory findings.*

a. *General.* We need documentation from an acceptable medical source to establish that you have a medically determinable impairment. In general, we must have evidence of appropriate laboratory testing showing that you have XP or another genetic photosensitivity disorder. We will find that you have XP or another genetic photosensitivity disorder based on a report from an acceptable medical source indicating that you have the impairment, supported by definitive genetic laboratory studies documenting appropriate chromosomal changes, including abnormal DNA repair or another DNA or genetic abnormality specific to your type of photosensitivity disorder.

b. *What we will accept as medical evidence instead of the actual laboratory report.* When we do not have the actual laboratory report, we need evidence from an acceptable medical source that includes appropriate clinical findings for your impairment and that is persuasive that a positive diagnosis has been confirmed by appropriate laboratory testing at some time prior to our evaluation. To be persuasive, the report must state that the appropriate definitive genetic laboratory study was conducted and that the results confirmed the diagnosis. The report must be consistent with other evidence in your case record.

F. *How do we evaluate burns?*

Electrical, chemical, or thermal burns frequently affect other body systems; for example, musculoskeletal, special senses and speech, respiratory, cardiovascular, renal, neurological, or mental. Consequently, we evaluate burns the way we evaluate other disorders that can affect the skin and other body systems, using the listing for the predominant feature of your impairment. For example, if your soft tissue injuries are under continuing surgical management (as defined in 1.00M), we will evaluate your impairment under 1.08. However, if your burns do not meet the requirements of 1.08 and you have extensive skin lesions that result in a very serious limitation (as defined in 8.00C1) that has lasted or can be expected to last for a continuous period of at least 12 months, we will evaluate them under 8.08.

G. *How do we determine if your skin disorder(s) will continue at a disabling level of severity in order to meet the duration requirement?*

For all of these skin disorder listings except 8.07 and 8.08, we will find that your impairment meets the duration requirement if your skin disorder results in extensive skin lesions that persist for at least 3 months despite continuing treatment as prescribed. By persist, we mean that the longitudinal clinical record shows that, with few exceptions, your lesions have been at the level of severity specified in the listing. For 8.07A, we will presume that you meet the duration requirement. For 8.07B and 8.08, we will consider all of the relevant medical and other information in your case record to determine whether your skin disorder meets the duration requirement.

H. *How do we assess your skin disorder(s) if your impairment does not meet the requirements of one of these listings?*

1. These listings are only examples of common skin disorders that we consider severe enough to prevent you from engaging in any gainful activity. For most of these listings, if you do not have continuing treatment as prescribed, if your treatment has not lasted for at least 3 months, or if you do not have extensive skin lesions that have persisted for at least 3 months, your impairment cannot meet the requirements of these skin disorder listings. (This provision does not apply to 8.07 and 8.08.) However, we may still find that you are disabled because your impairment(s) meets the requirements of a listing in another body system or medically equals the severity of a listing. (See §§ 404.1526 and 416.926 of this chapter.) We may also find you disabled at the last step of the sequential evaluation process.

2. If you have not received ongoing treatment or do not have an ongoing relationship with the medical community despite the existence of a severe impairment(s), or if your skin lesions have not persisted for at least 3 months but you are undergoing continuing treatment as prescribed, you may still have an impairment(s) that meets a listing in another body system or that medically equals a listing. If you do not have an impairment(s) that meets or medically equals a listing, we will assess your residual functional capacity and proceed to the fourth and, if necessary, the fifth step of the sequential evaluation process in §§ 404.1520 and 416.920 of this chapter. When we decide whether you continue to be disabled, we use the rules in §§ 404.1594 and 416.994 of this chapter.

8.01 Category of Impairments, Skin Disorders

8.02 ***Ichthyosis,*** with extensive skin lesions that persist for at least 3 months despite continuing treatment as prescribed.

8.03 ***Bullous disease*** (for example, pemphigus, erythema multiforme bullosum, epidermolysis bullosa, bullous pemphigoid, dermatitis herpetiformis), with extensive skin lesions that persist for at least 3 months despite continuing treatment as prescribed.

8.04 ***Chronic infections of the skin or mucous membranes,*** with extensive fungating or extensive ulcerating skin lesions that persist for at least 3 months despite continuing treatment as prescribed.

8.05 ***Dermatitis*** (for example, psoriasis, dyshidrosis, atopic dermatitis, exfoliative dermatitis, allergic contact dermatitis), with extensive skin lesions that persist for at least 3 months despite continuing treatment as prescribed.

8.06 ***Hidradenitis suppurativa,*** with extensive skin lesions involving both axillae, both inguinal areas or the perineum that persist for at least 3 months despite continuing treatment as prescribed.

8.07 Genetic photosensitivity disorders, established as described in 8.00E.

A. Xeroderma pigmentosum. Consider the individual disabled from birth.

B. Other genetic photosensitivity disorders, with:

1. Extensive skin lesions that have lasted or can be expected to last for a continuous period of at least 12 months,

OR

2. Inability to function outside of a highly protective environment for a continuous period of at least 12 months (see 8.00E2).

8.08 Burns, with extensive skin lesions that have lasted or can be expected to last for a continuous period of at least 12 months (see 8.00F).

9.00 Endocrine Disorders

A. *What is an endocrine disorder?*

An endocrine disorder is a medical condition that causes a hormonal imbalance. When an endocrine gland functions abnormally, producing either too much of a specific hormone (hyperfunction) or too little (hypofunction), the hormonal imbalance can cause various complications in the body. The major glands of the endocrine system are the pituitary, thyroid, parathyroid, adrenal, and pancreas.

B. *How do we evaluate the effects of endocrine disorders?* We evaluate impairments that result from endocrine disorders under the listings for other body systems. For example:

1. *Pituitary gland disorders* can disrupt hormone production and normal functioning in other endocrine glands and in many body systems. The effects of pituitary gland disorders vary depending on which hormones are involved. For example, when pituitary hypofunction affects water and electrolyte balance in the kidney and leads to diabetes insipidus, we evaluate the effects of recurrent dehydration under 6.00.

2. *Thyroid gland disorders* affect the sympathetic nervous system and normal metabolism. We evaluate thyroid-related changes in blood pressure and heart rate that cause arrhythmias or other cardiac dysfunction under 4.00; thyroid-related weight loss under 5.00; hypertensive cerebrovascular accidents (strokes)

under 11.00; and cognitive limitations, mood disorders, and anxiety under 12.00.

3. *Parathyroid gland disorders* affect calcium levels in bone, blood, nerves, muscle, and other body tissues. We evaluate parathyroid-related osteoporosis and fractures under 1.00; abnormally elevated calcium levels in the blood (hypercalcemia) that lead to cataracts under 2.00; kidney failure under 6.00; and recurrent abnormally low blood calcium levels (hypocalcemia) that lead to increased excitability of nerves and muscles, such as tetany and muscle spasms, under 11.00.

4. *Adrenal gland disorders* affect bone calcium levels, blood pressure, metabolism, and mental status. We evaluate adrenal-related osteoporosis with fractures that compromises the ability to walk or to use the upper extremities under 1.00; adrenal-related hypertension that worsens heart failure or causes recurrent arrhythmias under 4.00; adrenal-related weight loss under 5.00; and mood disorders under 12.00.

5. *Diabetes mellitus and other pancreatic gland disorders* disrupt the production of several hormones, including insulin, that regulate metabolism and digestion. Insulin is essential to the absorption of glucose from the bloodstream into body cells for conversion into cellular energy. The most common pancreatic gland disorder is *diabetes mellitus* (DM). There are two major types of DM: type 1 and type 2. Both type 1 and type 2 DM are chronic disorders that can have serious disabling complications that meet the duration requirement. Type 1 DM—previously known as "juvenile diabetes" or "insulin-dependent diabetes mellitus" (IDDM) —is an absolute deficiency of insulin production that commonly begins in childhood and continues throughout adulthood. Treatment of type 1 DM always requires lifelong daily insulin. With type 2 DM—previously known as "adult-onset diabetes mellitus" or "non-insulin-dependent diabetes mellitus" (NIDDM)—the body's cells resist the effects of insulin, impairing glucose absorption and metabolism. Treatment of type 2 DM generally requires lifestyle changes, such as increased exercise and dietary modification, and sometimes insulin in addition to other medications. While both type 1 and type 2 DM are usually controlled, some persons do not achieve good control for a variety of reasons including, but not limited to, hypoglycemia unawareness, other disorders that can affect blood glucose levels, inability to manage DM due to a mental disorder, or inadequate treatment.

a. *Hyperglycemia*. Both types of DM cause hyperglycemia, which is an abnormally high level of blood glucose that may produce acute and long-term complications. Acute complications of hyperglycemia include diabetic ketoacidosis. Long-term complications of chronic hyperglycemia include many conditions affecting various body systems.

(i) *Diabetic ketoacidosis (DKA)*. DKA is an acute, potentially life-threatening complication of DM in which the chemical balance of the body becomes dangerously hyperglycemic and acidic. It results from a severe insulin deficiency, which can occur due to missed or inadequate daily insulin therapy or in association with an acute illness. It usually requires hospital treatment to correct the acute complications of dehydration, electrolyte imbalance, and insulin deficiency. You may have serious complications resulting from your treatment, which we evaluate under the affected body system. For example, we evaluate cardiac arrhythmias under 4.00, intestinal necrosis under 5.00, and cerebral edema and seizures under 11.00. Recurrent episodes of DKA may result from mood or eating disorders, which we evaluate under 12.00.

(ii) *Chronic hyperglycemia*. Chronic hyperglycemia, which is longstanding abnormally high levels of blood glucose, leads to long-term diabetic complications by disrupting nerve and blood vessel functioning. This disruption can have many different effects in other body systems. For example, we evaluate diabetic peripheral neurovascular disease that leads to gangrene and subsequent amputation of an extremity under 1.00; diabetic retinopathy under 2.00; coronary artery disease and peripheral vascular disease under 4.00; diabetic gastroparesis that results in abnormal gastrointestinal motility under 5.00; diabetic nephropathy under 6.00; poorly healing bacterial and fungal skin infections under 8.00; diabetic peripheral and sensory neuropathies under 11.00; and cognitive impairments, depression, and anxiety under 12.00.

b. *Hypoglycemia*. Persons with DM may experience episodes of hypoglycemia, which is an abnormally low level of blood glucose. Most adults recognize the symptoms of hypoglycemia and reverse them by consuming substances containing glucose; however, some do not take this step because of hypoglycemia unawareness. Severe hypoglycemia can lead to complications, including seizures or loss of consciousness, which we evaluate under 11.00, or altered mental status and cognitive deficits, which we evaluate under 12.00.

C. *How do we evaluate endocrine disorders that do not have effects that meet or medically equal the criteria of any listing in other body systems?* If your impairment(s) does not meet or medically equal a listing in another body system, you may or may not have the residual functional capacity to engage in substantial gainful activity. In this situation, we proceed to the fourth and, if necessary, the fifth steps of the sequential evaluation process in §§ 404.1520 and 416.920. When we decide whether you continue to be disabled, we use the rules in §§ 404.1594, 416.994, and 416.994a.

10.00 Congenital Disorders that Affect Multiple Body Systems

A. *Which disorder do we evaluate under this body system?* Although Down syndrome exists in non-mosaic and mosaic forms, we evaluate only non-mosaic Down syndrome under this body system.

B. *What is non-mosaic Down syndrome?* Non-mosaic Down syndrome is a genetic disorder. Most people with non-mosaic Down syndrome have three copies of chromosome 21 in all of their cells (chromosome 21 trisomy); some have an extra copy of chromosome 21 attached to a different chromosome in all of their cells (chromosome 21 translocation). Virtually all people with non-mosaic Down syndrome have characteristic facial or other physical features, delayed physical development, and intellectual disability. People with non-mosaic Down syndrome may also have congenital heart disease, impaired vision, hearing problems, and other disorders. We evaluate non-mosaic Down syndrome under 10.06. If you have non-mosaic Down syndrome documented as described in 10.00C, we consider you disabled from birth.

C. *What evidence do we need to document non-mosaic Down syndrome under 10.06?*

1. Under 10.06A, we will find you disabled based on laboratory findings.

a. To find that your disorder meets 10.06A, we need a copy of the laboratory report of karyotype analysis, which is the definitive test to establish non-mosaic Down syndrome. We will not purchase karyotype analysis. We will not accept a fluorescence in situ hybridization (FISH) test because it does not distinguish between the mosaic and non-mosaic forms of Down syndrome.

b. If a physician (see §§ 404.1513(a)(1) and 416.913(a)(1) of this chapter) has not signed the laboratory report of karyotype analysis, the evidence must also include a physician's statement that you have Down syndrome.

c. For purposes of 10.06A, we do not require additional evidence stating that you have the distinctive facial or other physical features of Down syndrome.

2. If we do not have a laboratory report of karyotype analysis showing that you have non-mosaic Down syndrome, we may find you disabled under 10.06B or 10.06C.

a. Under 10.06B, we need a physician's report stating: (i) your karyotype diagnosis or evidence that documents your type of Down syndrome is consistent with prior karyotype analysis (for example, reference to a diagnosis of "trisomy 21"), and (ii) that you have the distinctive facial or other physical features of Down syndrome. We do not require a detailed description of the facial or other physical features of the disorder. However, we will not find that your disorder meets 10.06B if we have evidence—such as evidence of functioning inconsistent with the diagnosis—that indicates that you do not have non-mosaic Down syndrome.

b. If we do not have evidence of prior karyotype analysis (you did not have testing, or you had testing but we do not have information from a physician about the test results), we will find that your disorder meets 10.06C if we have: (i) a physician's report stating that you have the distinctive facial or other physical features of Down syndrome, and (ii) evidence that your functioning is consistent with a diagnosis of non-mosaic Down syndrome. This evidence may include medical or nonmedical information about your physical and mental abilities, including information about your education, work history, or the results of psychological testing. However, we will not find that your disorder meets 10.06C if we have evidence—such as evidence of functioning inconsistent with the diagnosis—that indicates that you do not have non-mosaic Down syndrome.

D. *How do we evaluate mosaic Down syndrome and other congenital disorders that affect multiple body systems?*

1. *Mosaic Down syndrome.* Approximately 2 percent of people with Down syndrome have the mosaic form. In mosaic Down syndrome, there are some cells with an extra copy of chromosome 21 and other cells with the normal two copies of chromosome 21. Mosaic Down syndrome can be so slight as to be undetected clinically, but it can also be profound and disabling, affecting various body systems.

2. *Other congenital disorders that affect multiple body systems.* Other congenital disorders, such as congenital anomalies, chromosomal disorders, dysmorphic syndromes, inborn metabolic syndromes, and perinatal infectious diseases, can cause deviation from, or interruption of, the normal function of the body or can interfere with development. Examples of these disorders include both the juvenile and late-onset forms of Tay-Sachs disease, trisomy x syndrome (XXX syndrome), fragile x syndrome, phenylketonuria (PKU), caudal regression syndrome, and fetal alcohol syndrome. For these disorders and other disorders like them, the degree of deviation, interruption, or interference, as well as the resulting functional limitations and their progression, may vary widely from person to person and may affect different body systems.

3. *Evaluating the effects of mosaic Down syndrome or another congenital disorder under the listings.* When the effects of mosaic Down syndrome or another congenital disorder that affects multiple body systems are sufficiently severe we evaluate the disorder under the appropriate affected body system(s), such as musculoskeletal, special senses and speech, neurological, or mental disorders. Otherwise, we evaluate the specific functional limitations that result from the disorder under our other rules described in 10.00E.

E. *What if your disorder does not meet a listing?* If you have a severe medically determinable impairment(s) that does not meet a listing, we will consider whether your impairment(s) medically equals a listing. See §§ 404.1526 and 416.926 of this chapter. If your impairment(s) does not meet or medically equal a listing, you may or may not have the residual functional capacity to engage in substantial gainful activity. We proceed to the fourth, and if necessary, the fifth steps of the sequential evaluation process in §§ 404.1520 and 416.920 of this chapter. We use the rules in §§ 404.1594 and 416.994 of this chapter, as appropriate, when we decide whether you continue to be disabled.

10.01 Category of Impairments, Congenital Disorders That Affect Multiple Body Systems

10.06 ***Non-mosaic Down syndrome,*** (chromosome 21 trisomy or chromosome 21 translocation), documented by:

A. A laboratory report of karyotype analysis signed by a physician, or both a laboratory report of karyotype analysis not signed by a physician *and* a statement by a physician that you have Down syndrome (see 10.00C1).

OR

B. A physician's report stating that you have chromosome 21 trisomy or chromosome 21 translocation consistent with prior karyotype analysis with the distinctive facial or other physical features of Down syndrome (see 10.00C2a).

OR

C. A physician's report stating that you have Down syndrome with the distinctive facial or other physical features *and* evidence demonstrating that you function at a level consistent with non-mosaic Down syndrome (see 10.00C2b).

11.00 Neurological

A. *Which neurological disorders do we evaluate under these listings?*

We evaluate epilepsy, amyotrophic lateral sclerosis, coma or persistent vegetative state (PVS), and neurological disorders that cause disorganization of motor function, bulbar and neuromuscular dysfunction, communication impairment, or a combination of limitations in physical and mental functioning such as early-onset Alzheimer's disease. We evaluate neurological disorders that may manifest in a combination of limitations in physical and mental functioning. For example, if you have a neurological disorder that causes mental limitations, such as Huntington's disease, which may limit executive functioning (e.g., regulating attention, planning, inhibiting responses, decision-making), we evaluate your limitations using the functional criteria under these listings (see 11.00G). Under this body system, we evaluate the limitations resulting from the impact of the neurological disease process itself. If your neurological disorder results in only mental impairment or if you have a co-occurring mental condition that is not caused by your neurological disorder (for example, dementia), we will evaluate your mental impairment under the mental disorders body system, 12.00.

B. *What evidence do we need to document your neurological disorder?*

1. We need both medical and non-medical evidence (signs, symptoms, and laboratory findings) to assess the effects of your neurological disorder. Medical evidence should include your medical history, examination findings,

relevant laboratory tests, and the results of imaging. Imaging refers to medical imaging techniques, such as x-ray, computerized tomography (CT), magnetic resonance imaging (MRI), and electroencephalography (EEG). The imaging must be consistent with the prevailing state of medical knowledge and clinical practice as the proper technique to support the evaluation of the disorder. In addition, the medical evidence may include descriptions of any prescribed treatment and your response to it. We consider non-medical evidence such as statements you or others make about your impairments, your restrictions, your daily activities, or your efforts to work.

2. We will make every reasonable effort to obtain the results of your laboratory and imaging evidence. When the results of any of these tests are part of the existing evidence in your case record, we will evaluate the test results and all other relevant evidence. We will not purchase imaging, or other diagnostic tests, or laboratory tests that are complex, may involve significant risk, or that are invasive. We will not routinely purchase tests that are expensive or not readily available.

C. *How do we consider adherence to prescribed treatment in neurological disorders?*

In 11.02 (Epilepsy), 11.06 (Parkinsonian syndrome), and 11.12 (Myasthenia gravis), we require that limitations from these neurological disorders exist despite adherence to prescribed treatment. "Despite adherence to prescribed treatment" means that you have taken medication(s) or followed other treatment procedures for your neurological disorder(s) as prescribed by a physician for three consecutive months but your impairment continues to meet the other listing requirements despite this treatment. You may receive your treatment at a health care facility that you visit regularly, even if you do not see the same physician on each visit.

D. *What do we mean by disorganization of motor function?*

1. *Disorganization of motor function* means interference, due to your neurological disorder, with movement of two extremities; i.e., the lower extremities, or upper extremities (including fingers, wrists, hands, arms, and shoulders). By two extremities we mean both lower extremities, or both upper extremities, or one upper extremity and one lower extremity. All listings in this body system, except for 11.02 (Epilepsy), 11.10 (Amyotrophic lateral sclerosis), and 11.20 (Coma and persistent vegetative state), include criteria for disorganization of motor function that results in an extreme limitation in your ability to:
   - Stand up from a seated position; or
   - Balance while standing or walking; or
   - Use the upper extremities (including fingers, wrists, hands, arms, and shoulders).
2. *Extreme limitation* means the inability to stand up from a seated position, maintain balance in a standing position and while walking, or use your

upper extremities to independently initiate, sustain, and complete work-related activities. The assessment of motor function depends on the degree of interference with standing up; balancing while standing or walking; or using the upper extremities (including fingers, hands, arms, and shoulders).

a. Inability to stand up from a seated position means that once seated you are unable to stand and maintain an upright position without the assistance of another person or the use of an assistive device, such as a walker, two crutches, or two canes.
b. Inability to maintain balance in a standing position means that you are unable to maintain an upright position while standing or walking without the assistance of another person or an assistive device, such as a walker, two crutches, or two canes.
c. Inability to use your upper extremities means that you have a loss of function of both upper extremities (including fingers, wrists, hands, arms, and shoulders) that very seriously limits your ability to independently initiate, sustain, and complete work-related activities involving fine and gross motor movements. Inability to perform fine and gross motor movements could include not being able to pinch, manipulate, and use your fingers; or not being able to use your hands, arms, and shoulders to perform gross motor movements, such as handling, gripping, grasping, holding, turning, and reaching; or not being able to engage in exertional movements such a lifting, carrying, pushing, and pulling.

E. *How do we evaluate communication impairments under these listings?* We must have a description of a recent comprehensive evaluation including all areas of communication, performed by an acceptable medical source, to document a communication impairment associated with a neurological disorder. A communication impairment may occur when a medically determinable neurological impairment results in dysfunction in the parts of the brain responsible for speech and language. We evaluate communication impairments associated with neurological disorders under 11.04A, 11.07C, or 11.11B. We evaluate communication impairments due to non-neurological disorders under 2.09.

1. Under 11.04A, we need evidence documenting that your central nervous system vascular accident or insult (CVA) and sensory or motor aphasia have resulted in ineffective speech or communication. *Ineffective speech or communication* means there is an extreme limitation in your ability to understand or convey your message in simple spoken language resulting in your inability to demonstrate basic communication skills, such as following one-step commands or telling someone about your basic personal needs without assistance.
2. Under 11.07C, we need evidence documenting that your cerebral palsy has resulted in significant interference in your ability to speak, hear, or

see. We will find you have "significant interference" in your ability to speak, hear, or see if your signs, such as aphasia, strabismus, or sensorineural hearing loss, seriously limit your ability to communicate on a sustained basis.

3. Under 11.11B, we need evidence documenting that your post-polio syndrome has resulted in the inability to produce intelligible speech.

F. *What do we mean by bulbar and neuromuscular dysfunction?* The bulbar region of the brain is responsible for controlling the bulbar muscles in the throat, tongue, jaw, and face. Bulbar and neuromuscular dysfunction refers to weakness in these muscles, resulting in breathing, swallowing, and speaking impairments. Listings 11.11 (Post-polio syndrome), 11.12 (Myasthenia gravis), and 11.22 (Motor neuron disorders other than ALS) include criteria for evaluating bulbar and neuromuscular dysfunction. If your neurological disorder has resulted in a breathing disorder, we may evaluate that condition under the respiratory system, 3.00.

G. *How do we evaluate limitations in physical and mental functioning under these listings?*

1. Neurological disorders may manifest in a combination of limitations in physical and mental functioning. We consider all relevant information in your case record to determine the effects of your neurological disorder on your physical and mental functioning. To satisfy the requirement described under 11.00G, your neurological disorder must result in a marked limitation in physical functioning and a marked limitation in at least one of four areas of mental functioning: understanding, remembering, or applying information; interacting with others; concentrating, persisting, or maintaining pace; or adapting or managing oneself. If your neurological disorder results in an extreme limitation in at least one of the four areas of mental functioning, or results in marked limitation in at least two of the four areas of mental functioning, but you do not have at least a marked limitation in your physical functioning, we will consider whether your condition meets or medically equals one of the mental disorders body system listings, 12.00.
2. *Marked Limitation.* To satisfy the requirements of the functional criteria, your neurological disorder must result in a marked limitation in physical functioning and a marked limitation in one of the four areas of mental functioning (see 11.00G3). Although we do not require the use of such a scale, "marked" would be the fourth point on a five-point scale consisting of no limitation, mild limitation, moderate limitation, marked limitation, and extreme limitation. We consider the nature and overall degree of interference with your functioning. The term "marked" does not require that you must be confined to bed, hospitalized, or in a nursing home.
   a. *Marked limitation and physical functioning.* For this criterion, a marked limitation means that, due to the signs and symptoms of your

neurological disorder, you are seriously limited in the ability to independently initiate, sustain, and complete work-related physical activities (see 11.00G3). You may have a marked limitation in your physical functioning when your neurological disease process causes persistent or intermittent symptoms that affect your abilities to independently initiate, sustain, and complete work-related activities, such as standing, balancing, walking, using both upper extremities for fine and gross movements, or results in limitations in using one upper and one lower extremity. The persistent and intermittent symptoms must result in a serious limitation in your ability to do a task or activity on a sustained basis. We do not define "marked" by a specific number of different physical activities or tasks that demonstrate your ability, but by the overall effects of your neurological symptoms on your ability to perform such physical activities on a consistent and sustained basis. You need not be totally precluded from performing a function or activity to have a marked limitation, as long as the degree of limitation seriously limits your ability to independently initiate, sustain, and complete work-related physical activities.

b. *Marked limitation and mental functioning.* For this criterion, a marked limitation means that, due to the signs and symptoms of your neurological disorder, you are seriously limited in the ability to function independently, appropriately, effectively, and on a sustained basis in work settings (see 11.03G3). We do not define "marked" by a specific number of mental activities, such as: the number of activities that demonstrate your ability to understand, remember, and apply information; the number of tasks that demonstrate your ability to interact with others; a specific number of tasks that demonstrate you are able to concentrate, persist or maintain pace; or a specific number of tasks that demonstrate you are able to manage yourself. You may have a marked limitation in your mental functioning when several activities or functions are impaired, or even when only one is impaired. You need not be totally precluded from performing an activity to have a marked limitation, as long as the degree of limitation seriously limits your ability to function independently, appropriately, and effectively on a sustained basis, and complete work-related mental activities.

3. *Areas of physical and mental functioning.*

   a. *Physical functioning.* Examples of this criterion include specific motor abilities, such as independently initiating, sustaining, and completing the following activities: standing up from a seated position, balancing while standing or walking, or using both your upper extremities for fine and gross movements (see 11.00D). Physical functioning may also include functions of the body that support motor abilities, such as the abilities to see, breathe, and swallow (see 11.00E and 11.00F). Examples of when your limitation in seeing, breathing, or swallowing may, on its own, rise to a "marked" limitation include: prolonged and uncorrectable double vision causing difficulty with balance; prolonged difficulty breathing requiring the use of a prescribed assistive breathing device, such as a portable continuous positive airway pressure machine; or repeated instances, occurring at least weekly, of aspiration without causing aspiration pneumonia. Alternatively, you may have a combination of limitations due to your neurological disorder that together rise to a "marked" limitation in physical functioning. We may also find that you have a "marked" limitation in this area if, for example, your symptoms, such as pain or fatigue (see 11.00T), as documented in your medical record, and caused by your neurological disorder or its treatment, seriously limit your ability to independently initiate, sustain, and complete these work-related motor functions, or the other physical functions or physiological processes that support those motor functions. We may also find you seriously limited in an area if, while you retain some ability to perform the function, you are unable to do so consistently and on a sustained basis. The limitation in your physical functioning must last or be expected to last at least 12 months. These examples illustrate the nature of physical functioning. We do not require documentation of all of the examples.

b. *Mental functioning.*

   i. *Understanding, remembering, or applying information.* This area of mental functioning refers to the abilities to learn, recall, and use information to perform work activities. Examples include: understanding and learning terms, instructions, procedures; following one- or two-step oral instructions to carry out a task; describing work activity to someone else; asking and answering questions and providing explanations; recognizing a mistake and correcting it; identifying and solving problems; sequencing multi-step activities; and using reason and judgment to make work-related decisions. These examples illustrate the nature of this area of mental functioning. We do not require documentation of all of the examples.

   ii. *Interacting with others.* This area of mental functioning refers to the abilities to relate to and work with supervisors, co-workers, and the public. Examples include: cooperating with others; asking for help when needed; handling conflicts with others; stating your own point of view; initiating or sustaining conversation; understanding and responding to social cues (physical, verbal, emotional); responding to requests, suggestions, criticism, correction, and challenges; and keeping social interactions free of excessive irritability, sensitivity, argumentativeness, or suspiciousness. These examples illustrate the nature of this area of mental functioning. We do not require documentation of all of the examples.

iii. *Concentrating, persisting, or maintaining pace.* This area of mental functioning refers to the abilities to focus attention on work activities and to stay on-task at a sustained rate. Examples include: initiating and performing a task that you understand and know how to do; working at an appropriate and consistent pace; completing tasks in a timely manner; ignoring or avoiding distractions while working; changing activities or work settings without being disruptive; working close to or with others without interrupting or distracting them; sustaining an ordinary routine and regular attendance at work; and working a full day without needing more than the allotted number or length of rest periods during the day. These examples illustrate the nature of this area of mental functioning. We do not require documentation of all of the examples.

iv. *Adapting or managing oneself.* This area of mental functioning refers to the abilities to regulate emotions, control behavior, and maintain well-being in a work setting. Examples include: responding to demands; adapting to changes; managing your psychologically based symptoms; distinguishing between acceptable and unacceptable work performance; setting realistic goals; making plans for yourself independently of others; maintaining personal hygiene and attire appropriate to a work setting; and being aware of normal hazards and taking appropriate precautions. These examples illustrate the nature of this area of mental functioning. We do not require documentation of all of the examples.

4. *Signs and symptoms of your disorder and the effects of treatment.*

   a. We will consider your signs and symptoms and how they affect your ability to function in the work place. When we evaluate your functioning, we will consider whether your signs and symptoms are persistent or intermittent, how frequently they occur and how long they last, their intensity, and whether you have periods of exacerbation and remission.

   b. We will consider the effectiveness of treatment in improving the signs, symptoms, and laboratory findings related to your neurological disorder, as well as any aspects of treatment that may interfere with your ability to function. We will consider, for example: the effects of medications you take (including side effects); the time-limited efficacy of some medications; the intrusiveness, complexity, and duration of your treatment (for example, the dosing schedule or need for injections); the effects of treatment, including medications, therapy, and surgery, on your functioning; the variability of your response to treatment; and any drug interactions.

H. *What is epilepsy, and how do we evaluate it under 11.02?*

1. *Epilepsy* is a pattern of recurrent and unprovoked seizures that are manifestations of abnormal electrical activity in the brain. There are various types of

generalized and "focal" or partial seizures. However, psychogenic nonepileptic seizures and pseudoseizures are not epileptic seizures for the purpose of 11.02. We evaluate psychogenic seizures and pseudoseizures under the mental disorders body system, 12.00. In adults, the most common potentially disabling seizure types are *generalized tonic-clonic seizures* and *dyscognitive seizures* (formerly complex partial seizures).

a. *Generalized tonic-clonic seizures* are characterized by loss of consciousness accompanied by a tonic phase (sudden muscle tensing causing the person to lose postural control) followed by a clonic phase (rapid cycles of muscle contraction and relaxation, also called convulsions). Tongue biting and incontinence may occur during generalized tonic-clonic seizures, and injuries may result from falling.

b. *Dyscognitive seizures* are characterized by alteration of consciousness without convulsions or loss of muscle control. During the seizure, blank staring, change of facial expression, and automatisms (such as lip smacking, chewing or swallowing, or repetitive simple actions, such as gestures or verbal utterances) may occur. During its course, a dyscognitive seizure may progress into a generalized tonic-clonic seizure (see 11.00H1a).

2. *Description of seizure.* We require at least one detailed description of your seizures from someone, preferably a medical professional, who has observed at least one of your typical seizures. If you experience more than one type of seizure, we require a description of each type.

3. *Serum drug levels.* We do not require serum drug levels; therefore, we will not purchase them. However, if serum drug levels are available in your medical records, we will evaluate them in the context of the other evidence in your case record.

4. *Counting seizures.* The period specified in 11.02A, B, or C cannot begin earlier than one month after you began prescribed treatment. The required number of seizures must occur within the period we are considering in connection with your application or continuing disability review. When we evaluate the frequency of your seizures, we also consider your adherence to prescribed treatment (see 11.00C). When we determine the number of seizures you have had in the specified period, we will:

a. Count multiple seizures occurring in a 24-hour period as one seizure.

b. Count status epilepticus (a continuous series of seizures without return to consciousness between seizures) as one seizure.

c. Count a dyscognitive seizure that progresses into a generalized tonic-clonic seizure as one generalized tonic-clonic seizure.

d. We do not count seizures that occur during a period when you are not adhering to prescribed treatment without good reason. When we determine that you had good reason for not adhering to prescribed treatment, we will consider your physical, mental, educational, and communicative limitations (including any language barriers). We will consider you to have good reason for not following prescribed treatment if, for example, the treatment is very risky for you due to its consequences or unusual nature, or if you are unable to afford prescribed treatment that you are willing to accept, but for which no free community resources are available. We will follow guidelines found in our policy, such as §§ 404.1530(c) and 416.930(c) of this chapter, when we determine whether you have a good reason for not adhering to prescribed treatment.

e. We do not count psychogenic nonepileptic seizures or pseudoseizures under 11.02. We evaluate these seizures under the mental disorders body system, 12.00.

5. *Electroencephalography (EEG) testing.* We do not require EEG test results; therefore, we will not purchase them. However, if EEG test results are available in your medical records, we will evaluate them in the context of the other evidence in your case record.

I. *What is vascular insult to the brain, and how do we evaluate it under 11.04?*

1. *Vascular insult to the brain* (cerebrum, cerebellum, or brainstem), commonly referred to as stroke or cerebrovascular accident (CVA), is brain cell death caused by an interruption of blood flow within or leading to the brain, or by a hemorrhage from a ruptured blood vessel or aneurysm in the brain. If you have a vision impairment resulting from your vascular insult, we may evaluate that impairment under the special senses body system, 2.00.
2. We need evidence of sensory or motor aphasia that results in ineffective speech or communication under 11.04A (see 11.00E). We may evaluate your communication impairment under listing 11.04C if you have marked limitation in physical functioning and marked limitation in one of the four areas of mental functioning.
3. We generally need evidence from at least 3 months after the vascular insult to evaluate whether you have disorganization of motor functioning under 11.04B, or the impact that your disorder has on your physical and mental functioning under 11.04C. In some cases, evidence of your vascular insult is sufficient to allow your claim within 3 months post-vascular insult. If we are unable to allow your claim within 3 months after your vascular insult, we will defer adjudication of the claim until we obtain evidence of your neurological disorder at least 3 months post-vascular insult.

J. *What are benign brain tumors, and how do we evaluate them under 11.05?* Benign brain tumors are noncancerous (nonmalignant) abnormal growths of tissue in or on the brain that invade healthy brain tissue or apply pressure on the brain or cranial nerves. We evaluate their effects on your functioning as discussed in 11.00D and 11.00G. We evaluate malignant brain tumors under the cancer body system in 13.00. If you have a vision impairment resulting from your benign brain tumor, we may evaluate that impairment under the special senses body system, 2.00.

K. *What is Parkinsonian syndrome, and how do we evaluate it under 11.06?* Parkinsonian syndrome is a term that describes a group of chronic, progressive movement disorders resulting from loss or decline in the function of dopamine-producing brain cells. Dopamine is a neurotransmitter that regulates muscle movement throughout the body. When we evaluate your Parkinsonian syndrome, we will consider your adherence to prescribed treatment (see 11.00C).

L. *What is cerebral palsy, and how do we evaluate it under 11.07?*

1. *Cerebral palsy (CP)* is a term that describes a group of static, nonprogressive disorders caused by abnormalities within the brain that disrupt the brain's ability to control movement, muscle coordination, and posture. The resulting motor deficits manifest very early in a person's development, with delayed or abnormal progress in attaining developmental milestones. Deficits may become more obvious as the person grows and matures over time.
2. We evaluate your signs and symptoms, such as ataxia, spasticity, flaccidity, athetosis, chorea, and difficulty with precise movements when we determine your ability to stand up, balance, walk, or perform fine and gross motor movements. We will also evaluate your signs, such as dysarthria and apraxia of speech, and receptive and expressive language problems when we determine your ability to communicate.
3. We will consider your other impairments or signs and symptoms that develop secondary to the disorder, such as post-impairment syndrome (a combination of pain, fatigue, and weakness due to muscle abnormalities); overuse syndromes (repetitive motion injuries); arthritis; abnormalities of proprioception (perception of the movements and position of the body); abnormalities of stereognosis (perception and identification of objects by touch); learning problems; anxiety; and depression.

M. *What are spinal cord disorders, and how do we evaluate them under 11.08?*

1. *Spinal cord disorders* may be congenital or caused by injury to the spinal cord. Motor signs and symptoms of spinal cord disorders include paralysis, flaccidity, spasticity, and weakness.
2. *Spinal cord disorders with complete loss of function* (11.08A) addresses spinal cord disorders that result in a complete lack of motor, sensory, and autonomic function of the affected part(s) of the body.
3. *Spinal cord disorders with disorganization of motor function* (11.08B) addresses spinal cord disorders that result in less than a complete loss of function of

the affected part(s) of the body, reducing, but not eliminating, motor, sensory, and autonomic function.

4. When we evaluate your spinal cord disorder, we generally need evidence from at least 3 months after your symptoms began in order to evaluate your disorganization of motor function. In some cases, evidence of your spinal cord disorder may be sufficient to allow your claim within 3 months after the spinal cord disorder. If the medical evidence demonstrates total cord transection causing a loss of motor and sensory functions below the level of injury, we will not wait 3 months but will make the allowance decision immediately.

N. *What is multiple sclerosis, and how do we evaluate it under 11.09?*

1. *Multiple sclerosis (MS)* is a chronic, inflammatory, degenerative disorder that damages the myelin sheath surrounding the nerve fibers in the brain and spinal cord. The damage disrupts the normal transmission of nerve impulses within the brain and between the brain and other parts of the body, causing impairment in muscle coordination, strength, balance, sensation, and vision. There are several forms of MS, ranging from mildly to highly aggressive. Milder forms generally involve acute attacks (exacerbations) with partial or complete recovery from signs and symptoms (remissions). Aggressive forms generally exhibit a steady progression of signs and symptoms with few or no remissions. The effects of all forms vary from person to person.

2. We evaluate your signs and symptoms, such as flaccidity, spasticity, spasms, incoordination, imbalance, tremor, physical fatigue, muscle weakness, dizziness, tingling, and numbness when we determine your ability to stand up, balance, walk, or perform fine and gross motor movements. When determining whether you have limitations of physical and mental functioning, we will consider your other impairments or signs and symptoms that develop secondary to the disorder, such as fatigue; visual loss; trouble sleeping; impaired attention, concentration, memory, or judgment; mood swings; and depression. If you have a vision impairment resulting from your MS, we may evaluate that impairment under the special senses body system, 2.00.

O. *What is amyotrophic lateral sclerosis, and how do we evaluate it under 11.10? Amyotrophic lateral sclerosis (ALS)* is a type of motor neuron disorder that rapidly and progressively attacks the nerve cells responsible for controlling voluntary muscles. We establish ALS under 11.10 when you have a documented diagnosis of ALS. We require documentation based on generally accepted methods consistent with the prevailing state of medical knowledge and clinical practice. We require laboratory testing to establish the diagnosis when the clinical findings of upper and lower motor neuron disease are not present in three or more regions. Electrophysiological studies, such as nerve conduction velocity studies and electromyography (EMG), may support your diagnosis of ALS; however, we will not purchase these studies.

P. *What are neurodegenerative disorders of the central nervous system, such as Huntington's disease, Friedreich's ataxia, and spinocerebellar degeneration, and how do we evaluate them under 11.17?* Neurodegenerative disorders of the central nervous system are disorders characterized by progressive and irreversible degeneration of neurons or their supporting cells. Over time, these disorders impair many of the body's motor, cognitive, and other mental functions. We consider neurodegenerative disorders of the central nervous system under 11.17 that we do not evaluate elsewhere in section 11.00, such as Huntington's disease (HD), Friedreich's ataxia, spinocerebellar degeneration, Creutzfeldt-Jakob disease (CJD), progressive supranuclear palsy (PSP), early-onset Alzheimer's disease, and frontotemporal dementia (Pick's disease). When these disorders result in solely cognitive and other mental function effects, we will evaluate the disorder under the mental disorder listings.

Q. *What is traumatic brain injury, and how do we evaluate it under 11.18?*

1. *Traumatic brain injury (TBI)* is damage to the brain resulting from skull fracture, collision with an external force leading to a closed head injury, or penetration by an object that enters the skull and makes contact with brain tissue. We evaluate TBI that results in coma or persistent vegetative state (PVS) under 11.20.
2. We generally need evidence from at least 3 months after the TBI to evaluate whether you have disorganization of motor function under 11.18A or the impact that your disorder has on your physical and mental functioning under 11.18B. In some cases, evidence of your TBI is sufficient to determine disability within 3 months post-TBI. If we are unable to allow your claim within 3 months post-TBI, we will defer adjudication of the claim until we obtain evidence of your neurological disorder at least 3 months post-TBI. If a finding of disability still is not possible at that time, we will again defer adjudication of the claim until we obtain evidence at least 6 months after your TBI.

R. *What are coma and persistent vegetative state, and how do we evaluate them under 11.20?* Coma is a state of unconsciousness in which a person does not exhibit a sleep/wake cycle, and is unable to perceive or respond to external stimuli. People who do not fully emerge from coma may progress into a persistent vegetative state (PVS). PVS is a condition of partial arousal in which a person may have a low level of consciousness but is still unable to react to external stimuli. In contrast to coma, a person in a PVS retains sleep/wake cycles and may exhibit some key lower brain functions, such as spontaneous movement, opening and moving eyes, and grimacing. Coma or PVS may result from TBI, a nontraumatic insult to the brain (such as a vascular insult, infection, or brain tumor), or a neurodegenerative or metabolic disorder. Medically induced comas are not considered under 11.20 and should be considered under the section pertaining to the underlying reason the coma was medically induced and not under this section.

S. *What are motor neuron disorders, other than ALS, and how do we evaluate them under 11.22?* Motor neuron disorders such as progressive bulbar palsy, primary lateral sclerosis (PLS), and spinal muscular atrophy (SMA) are progressive neurological disorders that destroy the cells that control voluntary muscle activity, such as walking, breathing, swallowing, and speaking. We evaluate the effects of these disorders on motor functioning, bulbar and neuromuscular functioning, oral communication, or limitations in physical and mental functioning.

T. *How do we consider symptoms of fatigue in these listings?* Fatigue is one of the most common and limiting symptoms of some neurological disorders, such as multiple sclerosis, post-polio syndrome, and myasthenia gravis. These disorders may result in physical fatigue (lack of muscle strength) or mental fatigue (decreased awareness or attention). When we evaluate your fatigue, we will consider the intensity, persistence, and effects of fatigue on your functioning. This may include information such as the clinical and laboratory data and other objective evidence concerning your neurological deficit, a description of fatigue considered characteristic of your disorder, and information about your functioning. We consider the effects of physical fatigue on your ability to stand up, balance, walk, or perform fine and gross motor movements using the criteria described in 11.00D. We consider the effects of physical and mental fatigue when we evaluate your physical and mental functioning described in 11.00G.

U. *How do we evaluate your neurological disorder when it does not meet one of these listings?*

1. If your neurological disorder does not meet the criteria of any of these listings, we must also consider whether your impairment(s) meets the criteria of a listing in another body system. If you have a severe medically determinable impairment(s) that does not meet a listing, we will determine whether your impairment(s) medically equals a listing. See §§ 404.1526 and 416.926 of this chapter.
2. If your impairment(s) does not meet or medically equal the criteria of a listing, you may or may not have the residual functional capacity to perform your past relevant work or adjust to other work that exists in significant numbers in the national economy, which we determine at the fourth and, if necessary, the fifth steps of the sequential evaluation process in §§ 404.1520 and 416.920 of this chapter.
3. We use the rules in §§ 404.1594 and 416.994 of this chapter, as appropriate, when we decide whether you continue to be disabled.

11.01 Category of Impairments, Neurological Disorders

11.02 ***Epilepsy*****, documented by a detailed description of a typical seizure and characterized by A, B, C, or D:**

A. Generalized tonic-clonic seizures (see 11.00H1a), occurring at least once a month for at least 3 consecutive months (see 11.00H4) despite adherence to prescribed treatment (see 11.00C).

OR

B. Dyscognitive seizures (see 11.00H1b), occurring at least once a week for at least 3 consecutive months (see 11.00H4) despite adherence to prescribed treatment (see 11.00C).

OR

C. Generalized tonic-clonic seizures (see 11.00H1a), occurring at least once every 2 months for at least 4 consecutive months (see 11.00H4) despite adherence to prescribed treatment (see 11.00C); and a marked limitation in one of the following:

1. Physical functioning (see 11.00G3a); or
2. Understanding, remembering, or applying information (see 11.00G3b(i)); or
3. Interacting with others (see 11.00G3b(ii)); or
4. Concentrating, persisting, or maintaining pace (see 11.00G3b(iii)); or
5. Adapting or managing oneself (see 11.00G3b(iv)).

OR

D. Dyscognitive seizures (see 11.00H1b), occurring at least once every 2 weeks for at least 3 consecutive months (see 11.00H4) despite adherence to prescribed treatment (see 11.00C); and a marked limitation in one of the following:

1. Physical functioning (see 11.00G3a); or
2. Understanding, remembering, or applying information (see 11.00G3b(i)); or
3. Interacting with others (see 11.00G3b(ii)); or
4. Concentrating, persisting, or maintaining pace (see 11.00G3b(iii)); or
5. Adapting or managing oneself (see 11.00G3b(iv)).

11.03 [Reserved]

11.04 *Vascular insult to the brain*, characterized by A, B, or C:

A. Sensory or motor aphasia resulting in ineffective speech or communication (see 11.00E1) persisting for at least 3 consecutive months after the insult.

OR

B. Disorganization of motor function in two extremities (see 11.00D1), resulting in an extreme limitation (see 11.00D2) in the ability to stand up from a seated position, balance while standing or walking, or use the upper extremities, persisting for at least 3 consecutive months after the insult.

OR

C. Marked limitation (see 11.00G2) in physical functioning (see 11.00G3a) and in one of the following areas of mental functioning, both persisting for at least 3 consecutive months after the insult:

1. Understanding, remembering, or applying information (see 11.00G3b(i)); or
2. Interacting with others (see 11.00G3b(ii)); or
3. Concentrating, persisting, or maintaining pace (see 11.00G3b(iii)); or
4. Adapting or managing oneself (see 11.00G3b(iv)).

11.05 *Benign brain tumors*, characterized by A or B:

A. Disorganization of motor function in two extremities (see 11.00D1), resulting in an extreme limitation (see 11.00D2) in the ability to stand up from a seated position, balance while standing or walking, or use the upper extremities.

OR

B. Marked limitation (see 11.00G2) in physical functioning (see 11.00G3a), and in one of the following:

1. Understanding, remembering, or applying information (see 11.00G3b(i)); or
2. Interacting with others (see 11.00G3b(ii)); or
3. Concentrating, persisting, or maintaining pace (see 11.00G3b(iii)); or
4. Adapting or managing oneself (see 11.00G3b(iv)).

11.06 ***Parkinsonian syndrome***, characterized by A or B despite adherence to prescribed treatment for at least 3 consecutive months (see 11.00C):

A. Disorganization of motor function in two extremities (see 11.00D1), resulting in an extreme limitation (see 11.00D2) in the ability to stand up from a seated position, balance while standing or walking, or use the upper extremities.

OR

B. Marked limitation (see 11.00G2) in physical functioning (see 11.00G3a), and in one of the following:

1. Understanding, remembering, or applying information (see 11.00G3b(i)); or
2. Interacting with others (see 11.00G3b(ii)); or
3. Concentrating, persisting, or maintaining pace (see 11.00G3b(iii)); or
4. Adapting or managing oneself (see 11.00G3b(iv)).

11.07 ***Cerebral palsy***, characterized by A, B, or C:

A. Disorganization of motor function in two extremities (see 11.00D1), resulting in an extreme limitation (see 11.00D2) in the ability to stand up from a seated position, balance while standing or walking, or use the upper extremities.

OR

B. Marked limitation (see 11.00G2) in physical functioning (see 11.00G3a), and in one of the following:

1. Understanding, remembering, or applying information (see 11.00G3b(i)); or

2. Interacting with others (see 11.00G3b(ii)); or
3. Concentrating, persisting, or maintaining pace (see 11.00G3b(iii)); or
4. Adapting or managing oneself (see 11.00G3b(iv)).

OR

C. Significant interference in communication due to speech, hearing, or visual deficit (see 11.00E2).

11.08 ***Spinal cord disorders***, characterized by A, B, or C:

A. Complete loss of function, as described in 11.00M2, persisting for 3 consecutive months after the disorder (see 11.00M4).

OR

B. Disorganization of motor function in two extremities (see 11.00D1), resulting in an extreme limitation (see 11.00D2) in the ability to stand up from a seated position, balance while standing or walking, or use the upper extremities persisting for 3 consecutive months after the disorder (see 11.00M4).

OR

C. Marked limitation (see 11.00G2) in physical functioning (see 11.00G3a) and in one of the following areas of mental functioning, both persisting for 3 consecutive months after the disorder (see 11.00M4):

1. Understanding, remembering, or applying information (see 11.00G3b(i)); or
2. Interacting with others (see 11.00G3b(ii)); or
3. Concentrating, persisting, or maintaining pace (see 11.00G3b(iii)); or
4. Adapting or managing oneself (see 11.00G3b(iv)).

11.09 ***Multiple sclerosis***, characterized by A or B:

A. Disorganization of motor function in two extremities (see 11.00D1), resulting in an extreme limitation (see 11.00D2) in the ability to stand up from a seated position, balance while standing or walking, or use the upper extremities.

OR

B. Marked limitation (see 11.00G2) in physical functioning (see 11.00G3a), and in one of the following:

1. Understanding, remembering, or applying information (see 11.00G3b(i)); or
2. Interacting with others (see 11.00G3b(ii)); or
3. Concentrating, persisting, or maintaining pace (see 11.00G3b(iii)); or
4. Adapting or managing oneself (see 11.00G3b(iv)).

11.10 *Amyotrophic lateral sclerosis (ALS)* established by clinical and laboratory findings (see 11.00O).

11.11 *Post-polio syndrome*, characterized by A, B, C, or D:

A. Disorganization of motor function in two extremities (see 11.00D1), resulting in an extreme limitation (see 11.00D2) in the ability to stand up from a seated position, balance while standing or walking, or use the upper extremities.

OR

B. Unintelligible speech (see 11.00E3).

OR

C. Bulbar and neuromuscular dysfunction (see 11.00F), resulting in:

1. Acute respiratory failure requiring mechanical ventilation; or
2. Need for supplemental enteral nutrition via a gastrostomy or parenteral nutrition via a central venous catheter.

OR

D. Marked limitation (see 11.00G2) in physical functioning (see 11.00G3a), and in one of the following:

1. Understanding, remembering, or applying information (see 11.00G3b(i)); or
2. Interacting with others (see 11.00G3b(ii)); or
3. Concentrating, persisting, or maintaining pace (see 11.00G3b(iii)); or
4. Adapting or managing oneself (see 11.00G3b(iv)).

11.12 *Myasthenia gravis*, characterized by A, B, or C despite adherence to prescribed treatment for at least 3 months (see 11.00C):

A. Disorganization of motor function in two extremities (see 11.00D1), resulting in an extreme limitation (see 11.00D2) in the ability to stand up from a seated position, balance while standing or walking, or use the upper extremities.

OR

B. Bulbar and neuromuscular dysfunction (see 11.00F), resulting in:

1. One myasthenic crisis requiring mechanical ventilation; or
2. Need for supplemental enteral nutrition via a gastrostomy or parenteral nutrition via a central venous catheter.

OR

C. Marked limitation (see 11.00G2) in physical functioning (see 11.00G3a), and in one of the following:

1. Understanding, remembering, or applying information (see 11.00G3b(i)); or
2. Interacting with others (see 11.00G3b(ii)); or
3. Concentrating, persisting, or maintaining pace (see 11.00G3b(iii)); or
4. Adapting or managing oneself (see 11.00G3b(iv)).

11.13 ***Muscular dystrophy***, characterized by A or B:

A. Disorganization of motor function in two extremities (see 11.00D1), resulting in an extreme limitation (see 11.00D2) in the ability to stand up from a seated position, balance while standing or walking, or use the upper extremities.

OR

B. Marked limitation (see 11.00G2) in physical functioning (see 11.00G3a), and in one of the following:

1. Understanding, remembering, or applying information (see 11.00G3b(i)); or
2. Interacting with others (see 11.00G3b(ii)); or
3. Concentrating, persisting, or maintaining pace (see 11.00G3b(iii)); or
4. Adapting or managing oneself (see 11.00G3b(iv)).

11.14 ***Peripheral neuropathy***, characterized by A or B:

A. Disorganization of motor function in two extremities (see 11.00D1), resulting in an extreme limitation (see 11.00D2) in the ability to stand up from a seated position, balance while standing or walking, or use the upper extremities.

OR

B. Marked limitation (see 11.00G2) in physical functioning (see 11.00G3a), and in one of the following:

1. Understanding, remembering, or applying information (see 11.00G3b(i)); or
2. Interacting with others (see 11.00G3b(ii)); or
3. Concentrating, persisting, or maintaining pace (see 11.00G3b(iii)); or
4. Adapting or managing oneself (see 11.00G3b(iv)).

11.15 [Reserved]

11.16 [Reserved]

11.17 ***Neurodegenerative disorders of the central nervous system, such as Huntington's disease, Friedreich's ataxia, and spinocerebellar degeneration***, characterized by A or B:

A. Disorganization of motor function in two extremities (see 11.00D1), resulting in an extreme limitation (see 11.00D2) in the ability to stand up from a seated position, balance while standing or walking, or use the upper extremities.

OR

B. Marked limitation (see 11.00G2) in physical functioning (see 11.00G3a), and in one of the following:

1. Understanding, remembering, or applying information (see 11.00G3b(i)); or
2. Interacting with others (see 11.00G3b(ii)); or
3. Concentrating, persisting, or maintaining pace (see 11.00G3b(iii)); or
4. Adapting or managing oneself (see 11.00G3b(iv)).

11.18 ***Traumatic brain injury***, characterized by A or B:

A. Disorganization of motor function in two extremities (see 11.00D1), resulting in an extreme limitation (see 11.00D2) in the ability to stand up from a seated position, balance while standing or walking, or use the upper extremities, persisting for at least 3 consecutive months after the injury.

OR

B. Marked limitation (see 11.00G2) in physical functioning (see 11.00G3a), and in one of the following areas of mental functioning, persisting for at least 3 consecutive months after the injury:

1. Understanding, remembering, or applying information (see 11.00G3b(i)); or
2. Interacting with others (see 11.00G3b(ii)); or
3. Concentrating, persisting, or maintaining pace (see 11.00G3b(iii)); or
4. Adapting or managing oneself (see 11.00G3b(iv)).

11.19 [Reserved]

11.20 ***Coma or persistent vegetative state*, persisting for at least 1 month**.

11.21 [Reserved]

11.22 ***Motor neuron disorders other than ALS***, characterized by A, B, or C:

A. Disorganization of motor function in two extremities (see 11.00D1), resulting in an extreme limitation (see 11.00D2) in the ability to stand up from a seated position, balance while standing or walking, or use the upper extremities.

OR

B. Bulbar and neuromuscular dysfunction (see 11.00F), resulting in:

1. Acute respiratory failure requiring invasive mechanical ventilation; or
2. Need for supplemental enteral nutrition via a gastrostomy or parenteral nutrition via a central venous catheter.

C. Marked limitation (see 11.00G2) in physical functioning (see 11.00G3a), and in one of the following:

1. Understanding, remembering, or applying information (see 11.00G3b(i)); or
2. Interacting with others (see 11.00G3b(ii)); or
3. Concentrating, persisting, or maintaining pace (see 11.00G3b(iii)); or
4. Adapting or managing oneself (see 11.00G3b(iv)).

12.00 Mental Disorders

A. How are the listings for mental disorders arranged, and what do they require?

1. The listings for mental disorders are arranged in 11 categories: neurocognitive disorders (12.02); schizophrenia spectrum and other psychotic disorders (12.03); depressive, bipolar and related disorders (12.04); intellectual disorder (12.05); anxiety and obsessive-compulsive disorders (12.06); somatic symptom and related disorders (12.07); personality and impulse-control disorders (12.08); autism spectrum disorder (12.10); neurodevelopmental disorders (12.11); eating disorders (12.13); and trauma- and stressor-related disorders (12.15).
2. Listings 12.07, 12.08, 12.10, 12.11, and 12.13 have two paragraphs, designated A and B; your mental disorder must satisfy the requirements of both paragraphs A and B. Listings 12.02, 12.03, 12.04, 12.06, and 12.15 have three paragraphs, designated A, B, and C; your mental disorder must satisfy the requirements of both paragraphs A and B, or the requirements of both paragraphs A and C. Listing 12.05 has two paragraphs that are unique to that listing (see 12.00A3); your mental disorder must satisfy the requirements of either paragraph A or paragraph B.
   a. Paragraph A of each listing (except 12.05) includes the medical criteria that must be present in your medical evidence.
   b. Paragraph B of each listing (except 12.05) provides the functional criteria we assess, in conjunction with a rating scale (see 12.00E and 12.00F), to evaluate how your mental disorder limits your functioning. These criteria represent the areas of mental functioning a person uses in a work setting. They are: understand, remember, or apply information; interact with others; concentrate, persist, or maintain pace; and adapt or manage oneself. We will determine the degree to which your medically determinable mental impairment affects the four areas of mental functioning and your ability to function independently, appropriately, effectively, and on a sustained basis (see 404.1520a(c)(2) and 416.920a(c)(2) of this chapter). To satisfy the paragraph B criteria, your mental disorder must result in "extreme" limitation of one, or "marked" limitation of two, of the four areas of mental functioning. (When we refer to "paragraph B criteria" or "area[s] of mental functioning" in the introductory text of this body system, we mean the criteria in paragraph B of every listing except 12.05.)

c. Paragraph C of listings 12.02, 12.03, 12.04, 12.06, and 12.15provides the criteria we use to evaluate "serious and persistent mental disorders." To satisfy the paragraph C criteria, your mental disorder must be "serious and persistent"; that is, there must be a medically documented history of the existence of the disorder over a period of at least 2 years, and evidence that satisfies the criteria in both C1 and C2 (see 12.00G). (When we refer to "paragraph C" or "the paragraph C criteria" in the introductory text of this body system, we mean the criteria in paragraph C of listings 12.02, 12.03, 12.04, 12.06, and 12.15.)

3. Listing 12.05 has two paragraphs, designated A and B, that apply to only intellectual disorder. Each paragraph requires that you have significantly subaverage general intellectual functioning; significant deficits in current adaptive functioning; and evidence that demonstrates or supports (is consistent with) the conclusion that your disorder began prior to age 22.

B. Which mental disorders do we evaluate under each listing category?

1. *Neurocognitive disorders (12.02).*
   a. These disorders are characterized by a clinically significant decline in cognitive functioning. Symptoms and signs may include, but are not limited to, disturbances in memory, executive functioning (that is, higher-level cognitive processes; for example, regulating attention, planning, inhibiting responses, decision-making), visual-spatial functioning, language and speech, perception, insight, judgment, and insensitivity to social standards.
   b. Examples of disorders that we evaluate in this category include major neurocognitive disorder; dementia of the Alzheimer type; vascular dementia; dementia due to a medical condition such as a metabolic disease (for example, late-onset Tay-Sachs disease), human immunodeficiency virus infection, vascular malformation, progressive brain tumor, neurological disease (for example, multiple sclerosis, Parkinsonian syndrome, Huntington disease), or traumatic brain injury; or substance-induced cognitive disorder associated with drugs of abuse, medications, or toxins. (We evaluate neurological disorders under that body system (see 11.00). We evaluate cognitive impairments that result from neurological disorders under 12.02 if they do not satisfy the requirements in 11.00 (see 11.00G).)
   c. This category does not include the mental disorders that we evaluate under intellectual disorder (12.05), autism spectrum disorder (12.10), and neurodevelopmental disorders (12.11).
2. *Schizophrenia spectrum and other psychotic disorders (12.03).*
   a. These disorders are characterized by delusions, hallucinations, disorganized speech, or grossly disorganized or catatonic behavior, causing a clinically significant decline in functioning. Symptoms and signs may

include, but are not limited to, inability to initiate and persist in goal-directed activities, social withdrawal, flat or inappropriate affect, poverty of thought and speech, loss of interest or pleasure, disturbances of mood, odd beliefs and mannerisms, and paranoia.

   b. Examples of disorders that we evaluate in this category include schizophrenia, schizoaffective disorder, delusional disorder, and psychotic disorder due to another medical condition.

3. *Depressive, bipolar and related disorders (12.04).*

   a. These disorders are characterized by an irritable, depressed, elevated, or expansive mood, or by a loss of interest or pleasure in all or almost all activities, causing a clinically significant decline in functioning. Symptoms and signs may include, but are not limited to, feelings of hopelessness or guilt, suicidal ideation, a clinically significant change in body weight or appetite, sleep disturbances, an increase or decrease in energy, psychomotor abnormalities, disturbed concentration, pressured speech, grandiosity, reduced impulse control, sadness, euphoria, and social withdrawal.

   b. Examples of disorders that we evaluate in this category include bipolar disorders (I or II), cyclothymic disorder, major depressive disorder, persistent depressive disorder (dysthymia), and bipolar or depressive disorder due to another medical condition.

4. *Intellectual disorder (12.05).*

   a. This disorder is characterized by significantly subaverage general intellectual functioning, significant deficits in current adaptive functioning, and manifestation of the disorder before age 22. Signs may include, but are not limited to, poor conceptual, social, or practical skills evident in your adaptive functioning.

   b. The disorder that we evaluate in this category may be described in the evidence as intellectual disability, intellectual developmental disorder, or historically used terms such as "mental retardation."

   c. This category does not include the mental disorders that we evaluate under neurocognitive disorders (12.02), autism spectrum disorder (12.10), or neurodevelopmental disorders (12.11).

5. *Anxiety and obsessive-compulsive disorders (12.06).*

   a. These disorders are characterized by excessive anxiety, worry, apprehension, and fear, or by avoidance of feelings, thoughts, activities, objects, places, or people. Symptoms and signs may include, but are not limited to, restlessness, difficulty concentrating, hyper-vigilance, muscle tension, sleep disturbance, fatigue, panic attacks, obsessions and compulsions, constant thoughts and fears about safety, and frequent physical complaints.

b. Examples of disorders that we evaluate in this category include social anxiety disorder, panic disorder, generalized anxiety disorder, agoraphobia, and obsessive-compulsive disorder.

c. This category does not include the mental disorders that we evaluate under trauma- and stressor-related disorders (12.15).

6. *Somatic symptom and related disorders (12.07).*

a. These disorders are characterized by physical symptoms or deficits that are not intentionally produced or feigned, and that, following clinical investigation, cannot be fully explained by a general medical condition, another mental disorder, the direct effects of a substance, or a culturally sanctioned behavior or experience. These disorders may also be characterized by a preoccupation with having or acquiring a serious medical condition that has not been identified or diagnosed. Symptoms and signs may include, but are not limited to, pain and other abnormalities of sensation, gastrointestinal symptoms, fatigue, a high level of anxiety about personal health status, abnormal motor movement, pseudoseizures, and pseudoneurological symptoms, such as blindness or deafness.

b. Examples of disorders that we evaluate in this category include somatic symptom disorder, illness anxiety disorder, and conversion disorder.

7. *Personality and impulse-control disorders (12.08).*

a. These disorders are characterized by enduring, inflexible, maladaptive, and pervasive patterns of behavior. Onset typically occurs in adolescence or young adulthood. Symptoms and signs may include, but are not limited to, patterns of distrust, suspiciousness, and odd beliefs; social detachment, discomfort, or avoidance; hypersensitivity to negative evaluation; an excessive need to be taken care of; difficulty making independent decisions; a preoccupation with orderliness, perfectionism, and control; and inappropriate, intense, impulsive anger and behavioral expression grossly out of proportion to any external provocation or psychosocial stressors.

b. Examples of disorders that we evaluate in this category include paranoid, schizoid, schizotypal, borderline, avoidant, dependent, obsessive-compulsive personality disorders, and intermittent explosive disorder.

8. *Autism spectrum disorder (12.10).*

a. These disorders are characterized by qualitative deficits in the development of reciprocal social interaction, verbal and nonverbal communication skills, and symbolic or imaginative activity; restricted repetitive and stereotyped patterns of behavior, interests, and activities; and stagnation of development or loss of acquired skills early in life. Symptoms and signs may include, but are not limited to, abnormalities and unevenness in the development of cognitive skills; unusual responses to sensory stimuli; and behavioral difficulties, including hyperactivity, short attention span, impulsivity, aggressiveness, or self-injurious actions.

b. Examples of disorders that we evaluate in this category include autism spectrum disorder with or without accompanying intellectual impairment, and autism spectrum disorder with or without accompanying language impairment.

c. This category does not include the mental disorders that we evaluate under neurocognitive disorders (12.02), intellectual disorder (12.05), and neurodevelopmental disorders (12.11).

9. *Neurodevelopmental disorders (12.11).*

a. These disorders are characterized by onset during the developmental period, that is, during childhood or adolescence, although sometimes they are not diagnosed until adulthood. Symptoms and signs may include, but are not limited to, underlying abnormalities in cognitive processing (for example, deficits in learning and applying verbal or non-verbal information, visual perception, memory, or a combination of these); deficits in attention or impulse control; low frustration tolerance; excessive or poorly planned motor activity; difficulty with organizing (time, space, materials, or tasks); repeated accidental injury; and deficits in social skills. Symptoms and signs specific to tic disorders include sudden, rapid, recurrent, non-rhythmic, motor movement or vocalization.

b. Examples of disorders that we evaluate in this category include specific learning disorder, borderline intellectual functioning, and tic disorders (such as Tourette syndrome).

c. This category does not include the mental disorders that we evaluate under neurocognitive disorders (12.02), autism spectrum disorder (12.10), or personality and impulse-control disorders (12.08).

10. *Eating disorders (12.13).*

a. These disorders are characterized by disturbances in eating behavior and preoccupation with, and excessive self-evaluation of, body weight and shape. Symptoms and signs may include, but are not limited to, restriction of energy consumption when compared with individual requirements; recurrent episodes of binge eating or behavior intended to prevent weight gain, such as self-induced vomiting, excessive exercise, or misuse of laxatives; mood disturbances, social withdrawal, or irritability; amenorrhea; dental problems; abnormal laboratory findings; and cardiac abnormalities.

b. Examples of disorders that we evaluate in this category include anorexia nervosa, bulimia nervosa, binge-eating disorder, and avoidant/restrictive food disorder.

11. *Trauma- and stressor-related disorders (12.15).*
    a. These disorders are characterized by experiencing or witnessing a traumatic or stressful event, or learning of a traumatic event occurring to a close family member or close friend, and the psychological aftermath of clinically significant effects on functioning. Symptoms and signs may include, but are not limited to, distressing memories, dreams, and flashbacks related to the trauma or stressor; avoidant behavior; diminished interest or participation in significant activities; persistent negative emotional states (for example, fear, anger) or persistent inability to experience positive emotions (for example, satisfaction, affection); anxiety; irritability; aggression; exaggerated startle response; difficulty concentrating; and sleep disturbance.
    b. Examples of disorders that we evaluate in this category include posttraumatic stress disorder and other specified trauma- and stressor-related disorders (such as adjustment-like disorders with prolonged duration without prolonged duration of stressor).
    c. This category does not include the mental disorders that we evaluate under anxiety and obsessive-compulsive disorders (12.06), and cognitive impairments that result from neurological disorders, such as a traumatic brain injury, which we evaluate under neurocognitive disorders (12.02).

C. What evidence do we need to evaluate your mental disorder?

1. *General.* We need objective medical evidence from an acceptable medical source to establish that you have a medically determinable mental disorder. We also need evidence to assess the severity of your mental disorder and its effects on your ability to function in a work setting. We will determine the extent and kinds of evidence we need from medical and nonmedical sources based on the individual facts about your disorder. For additional evidence requirements for intellectual disorder (12.05), see 12.00H. For our basic rules on evidence, see 404.1512, 404.1513, 404.1520b,416.912, 416.913, and 416.920b of this chapter. For our rules on evaluating medical opinions, see 404.1520c, 404.1527, 416.920c, and 416.927 of this chapter. For our rules on evidence about your symptoms, see 404.1529 and 416.929 of this chapter.
2. *Evidence from medical sources.* We will consider all relevant medical evidence about your disorder from your physician, psychologist, and other medical sources, which include health care providers such as physician assistants, psychiatric nurse practitioners, licensed clinical social workers, and clinical mental health counselors. Evidence from your medical sources may include:
    a. Your reported symptoms.
    b. Your medical, psychiatric, and psychological history.
    c. The results of physical or mental status examinations, structured clinical interviews, psychiatric or psychological rating scales, measures of adaptive functioning, or other clinical findings.

d. Psychological testing, imaging results, or other laboratory findings.
e. Your diagnosis.
f. The type, dosage, and beneficial effects of medications you take.
g. The type, frequency, duration, and beneficial effects of therapy you receive.
h. Side effects of medication or other treatment that limit your ability to function.
i. Your clinical course, including changes in your medication, therapy, or other treatment, and the time required for therapeutic effectiveness.
j. Observations and descriptions of how you function during examinations or therapy.
k. Information about sensory, motor, or speech abnormalities, or about your cultural background (for example, language or customs) that may affect an evaluation of your mental disorder.
l. The expected duration of your symptoms and signs and their effects on your functioning, both currently and in the future.

3. *Evidence from you and people who know you.* We will consider all relevant evidence about your mental disorder and your daily functioning that we receive from you and from people who know you. We will ask about your symptoms, your daily functioning, and your medical treatment. We will ask for information from third parties who can tell us about your mental disorder, but you must give us permission to do so. This evidence may include information from your family, caregivers, friends, neighbors, clergy, case managers, social workers, shelter staff, or other community support and outreach workers. We will consider whether your statements and the statements from third parties are consistent with the medical and other evidence we have.
4. *Evidence from school, vocational training, work, and work-related programs.*
   a. *School.* You may have recently attended or may still be attending school, and you may have received or may still be receiving special education services. If so, we will try to obtain information from your school sources when we need it to assess how your mental disorder affects your ability to function. Examples of this information include your Individualized Education Programs (IEPs), your Section 504 plans, comprehensive evaluation reports, school-related therapy progress notes, information from your teachers about how you function in a classroom setting, and information about any special services or accommodations you receive at school.
   b. *Vocational training, work, and work-related programs.* You may have recently participated in or may still be participating in vocational training, work-related programs, or work activity. If so, we will try to obtain information from your training program or your employer when we

need it to assess how your mental disorder affects your ability to function. Examples of this information include training or work evaluations, modifications to your work duties or work schedule, and any special supports or accommodations you have required or now require in order to work. If you have worked or are working through a community mental health program, sheltered or supported work program, rehabilitation program, or transitional employment program, we will consider the type and degree of support you have received or are receiving in order to work (see 12.00D).

5. *Need for longitudinal evidence.*
   a. *General.* Longitudinal medical evidence can help us learn how you function over time, and help us evaluate any variations in the level of your functioning. We will request longitudinal evidence of your mental disorder when your medical providers have records concerning you and your mental disorder over a period of months or perhaps years (see 404.1512(d) and 416.912(d) of this chapter).
   b. *Non-medical sources of longitudinal evidence.* Certain situations, such as chronic homelessness, may make it difficult for you to provide longitudinal medical evidence. If you have a severe mental disorder, you will probably have evidence of its effects on your functioning over time, even if you have not had an ongoing relationship with the medical community or are not currently receiving treatment. For example, family members, friends, neighbors, former employers, social workers, case managers, community support staff, outreach workers, or government agencies may be familiar with your mental health history. We will ask for information from third parties who can tell us about your mental disorder, but you must give us permission to do so.
   c. *Absence of longitudinal evidence.* In the absence of longitudinal evidence, we will use current objective medical evidence and all other relevant evidence available to us in your case record to evaluate your mental disorder. If we purchase a consultative examination to document your disorder, the record will include the results of that examination (see 404.1514 and 416.914 of this chapter). We will take into consideration your medical history, symptoms, clinical and laboratory findings, and medical source opinions. If you do not have longitudinal evidence, the current evidence alone may not be sufficient or appropriate to show that you have a disorder that meets the criteria of one of the mental disorders listings. In that case, we will follow the rules in 12.00J.
6. *Evidence of functioning in unfamiliar situations or supportive situations.*
   a. *Unfamiliar situations.* We recognize that evidence about your functioning in unfamiliar situations does not necessarily show how you would function on a sustained basis in a work setting. In one-time, time-

limited, or other unfamiliar situations, you may function differently than you do in familiar situations. In unfamiliar situations, you may appear more, or less, limited than you do on a daily basis and over time.

b. *Supportive situations.* Your ability to complete tasks in settings that are highly structured, or that are less demanding or more supportive than typical work settings does not necessarily demonstrate your ability to complete tasks in the context of regular employment during a normal workday or work week.

c. *Our assessment.* We must assess your ability to complete tasks by evaluating all the evidence, such as reports about your functioning from you and third parties who are familiar with you, with an emphasis on how independently, appropriately, and effectively you are able to complete tasks on a sustained basis.

D. How do we consider psychosocial supports, structured settings, living arrangements, and treatment?

1. *General.* Psychosocial supports, structured settings, and living arrangements, including assistance from your family or others, may help you by reducing the demands made on you. In addition, treatment you receive may reduce your symptoms and signs and possibly improve your functioning, or may have side effects that limit your functioning. Therefore, when we evaluate the effects of your mental disorder and rate the limitation of your areas of mental functioning, we will consider the kind and extent of supports you receive, the characteristics of any structured setting in which you spend your time, and the effects of any treatment. This evidence may come from reports about your functioning from you or third parties who are familiar with you, and other third-party statements or information. Following are some examples of the supports you may receive:

   a. You receive help from family members or other people who monitor your daily activities and help you to function. For example, family members administer your medications, remind you to eat, shop for you and pay your bills, or change their work hours so you are never home alone.

   b. You participate in a special education or vocational training program, or a psychosocial rehabilitation day treatment or community support program, where you receive training in daily living and entry-level work skills.

   c. You participate in a sheltered, supported, or transitional work program, or in a competitive employment setting with the help of a job coach or supervisor.

   d. You receive comprehensive "24/7 wrap-around" mental health services while living in a group home or transitional housing, while participating in a semi-independent living program, or while living in individual housing (for example, your own home or apartment).

e. You live in a hospital or other institution with 24-hour care.

f. You receive assistance from a crisis response team, social workers, or community mental health workers who help you meet your physical needs, and who may also represent you in dealings with government or community social services.

g. You live alone and do not receive any psychosocial support(s); however, you have created a highly structured environment by eliminating all but minimally necessary contact with the world outside your living space.

2. *How we consider different levels of support and structure in psychosocial rehabilitation programs.*

   a. Psychosocial rehabilitation programs are based on your specific needs. Therefore, we cannot make any assumptions about your mental disorder based solely on the fact that you are associated with such a program. We must know the details of the program(s) in which you are involved and the pattern(s) of your involvement over time.

   b. The kinds and levels of supports and structures in psychosocial rehabilitation programs typically occur on a scale of "most restrictive" to "least restrictive." Participation in a psychosocial rehabilitation program at the most restrictive level would suggest greater limitation of your areas of mental functioning than would participation at a less restrictive level. The length of time you spend at different levels in a program also provides information about your functioning. For example, you could begin participation at the most restrictive crisis intervention level but gradually improve to the point of readiness for a lesser level of support and structure and possibly some form of employment.

3. *How we consider the help or support you receive.*

   a. We will consider the complete picture of your daily functioning, including the kinds, extent, and frequency of help and support you receive, when we evaluate your mental disorder and determine whether you are able to use the four areas of mental functioning in a work setting. The fact that you have done, or currently do, some routine activities without help or support does not necessarily mean that you do not have a mental disorder or that you are not disabled. For example, you may be able to take care of your personal needs, cook, shop, pay your bills, live by yourself, and drive a car. You may demonstrate both strengths and deficits in your daily functioning.

   b. You may receive various kinds of help and support from others that enable you to do many things that, because of your mental disorder, you might not be able to do independently. Your daily functioning may depend on the special contexts in which you function. For example, you may spend your time among only familiar people or surroundings, in a simple and steady routine or an unchanging environment, or in a highly structured setting. However, this does not necessarily show how you would function in a work setting on a sustained basis, throughout a normal workday and workweek. (See 12.00H for further discussion of these issues regarding significant deficits in adaptive functioning for the purpose of 12.05.)

4. *How we consider treatment.* We will consider the effect of any treatment on your functioning when we evaluate your mental disorder. Treatment may include medication(s), psychotherapy, or other forms of intervention, which you receive in a doctor's office, during a hospitalization, or in a day program at a hospital or outpatient treatment program. With treatment, you may not only have your symptoms and signs reduced, but may also be able to function in a work setting. However, treatment may not resolve all of the limitations that result from your mental disorder, and the medications you take or other treatment you receive for your disorder may cause side effects that limit your mental or physical functioning. For example, you may experience drowsiness, blunted affect, memory loss, or abnormal involuntary movements.

E. What are the paragraph B criteria?

1. *Understand, remember, or apply information (paragraph B1).* This area of mental functioning refers to the abilities to learn, recall, and use information to perform work activities. Examples include: understanding and learning terms, instructions, procedures; following one- or two-step oral instructions to carry out a task; describing work activity to someone else; asking and answering questions and providing explanations; recognizing a mistake and correcting it; identifying and solving problems; sequencing multi-step activities; and using reason and judgment to make work-related decisions. These examples illustrate the nature of this area of mental functioning. We do not require documentation of all of the examples.
2. *Interact with others (paragraph B2).* This area of mental functioning refers to the abilities to relate to and work with supervisors, co-workers, and the public. Examples include: cooperating with others; asking for help when needed; handling conflicts with others; stating own point of view; initiating or sustaining conversation; understanding and responding to social cues (physical, verbal, emotional); responding to requests, suggestions, criticism, correction, and challenges; and keeping social interactions free of excessive irritability, sensitivity, argumentativeness, or suspiciousness. These examples illustrate the nature of this area of mental functioning. We do not require documentation of all of the examples.
3. *Concentrate, persist, or maintain pace (paragraph B3).* This area of mental functioning refers to the abilities to focus attention on work activities and stay on task at a sustained rate. Examples include: initiating and performing a task that you understand and know how to do; working at an appropriate and

consistent pace; completing tasks in a timely manner; ignoring or avoiding distractions while working; changing activities or work settings without being disruptive; working close to or with others without interrupting or distracting them; sustaining an ordinary routine and regular attendance at work; and working a full day without needing more than the allotted number or length of rest periods during the day. These examples illustrate the nature of this area of mental functioning. We do not require documentation of all of the examples.

4. *Adapt or manage oneself (paragraph B4).* This area of mental functioning refers to the abilities to regulate emotions, control behavior, and maintain well-being in a work setting. Examples include: responding to demands; adapting to changes; managing your psychologically based symptoms; distinguishing between acceptable and unacceptable work performance; setting realistic goals; making plans for yourself independently of others; maintaining personal hygiene and attire appropriate to a work setting; and being aware of normal hazards and taking appropriate precautions. These examples illustrate the nature of this area of mental functioning. We do not require documentation of all of the examples.

F. How do we use the paragraph B criteria to evaluate your mental disorder?

1. *General.* We use the paragraph B criteria, in conjunction with a rating scale (see 12.00F2), to rate the degree of your limitations. We consider only the limitations that result from your mental disorder(s). We will determine whether you are able to use each of the paragraph B areas of mental functioning in a work setting. We will consider, for example, the kind, degree, and frequency of difficulty you would have; whether you could function without extra help, structure, or supervision; and whether you would require special conditions with regard to activities or other people (see 12.00D).
2. *The five-point rating scale.* We evaluate the effects of your mental disorder on each of the four areas of mental functioning based on a five-point rating scale consisting of none, mild, moderate, marked, and extreme limitation. To satisfy the paragraph B criteria, your mental disorder must result in extreme limitation of one, or marked limitation of two, paragraph B areas of mental functioning. Under these listings, the five rating points are defined as follows:
   a. *No limitation (or none).* You are able to function in this area independently, appropriately, effectively, and on a sustained basis.
   b. *Mild limitation.* Your functioning in this area independently, appropriately, effectively, and on a sustained basis is slightly limited.
   c. *Moderate limitation.* Your functioning in this area independently, appropriately, effectively, and on a sustained basis is fair.

d. *Marked limitation.* Your functioning in this area independently, appropriately, effectively, and on a sustained basis is seriously limited.

e. *Extreme limitation.* You are not able to function in this area independently, appropriately, effectively, and on a sustained basis.

3. *Rating the limitations of your areas of mental functioning.*

a. *General.* We use all of the relevant medical and non-medical evidence in your case record to evaluate your mental disorder: the symptoms and signs of your disorder, the reported limitations in your activities, and any help and support you receive that is necessary for you to function. The medical evidence may include descriptors regarding the diagnostic stage or level of your disorder, such as "mild" or "moderate." Clinicians may use these terms to characterize your medical condition. However, these terms will not always be the same as the degree of your limitation in a paragraph B area of mental functioning.

b. *Areas of mental functioning in daily activities.* You use the same four areas of mental functioning in daily activities at home and in the community that you would use to function at work. With respect to a particular task or activity, you may have trouble using one or more of the areas. For example, you may have difficulty understanding and remembering what to do; or concentrating and staying on task long enough to do it; or engaging in the task or activity with other people; or trying to do the task without becoming frustrated and losing self-control. Information about your daily functioning can help us understand whether your mental disorder limits one or more of these areas; and, if so, whether it also affects your ability to function in a work setting.

c. *Areas of mental functioning in work settings.* If you have difficulty using an area of mental functioning from day-to-day at home or in your community, you may also have difficulty using that area to function in a work setting. On the other hand, if you are able to use an area of mental functioning at home or in your community, we will not necessarily assume that you would also be able to use that area to function in a work setting where the demands and stressors differ from those at home. We will consider all evidence about your mental disorder and daily functioning before we reach a conclusion about your ability to work.

d. *Overall effect of limitations.* Limitation of an area of mental functioning reflects the overall degree to which your mental disorder interferes with that area. The degree of limitation is how we document our assessment of your limitation when using the area of mental functioning independently, appropriately, effectively, and on a sustained basis. It does not necessarily reflect a specific type or number of activities, including activities of daily living, that you have difficulty doing. In addition, no single piece of information (including test results) can establish the degree of limitation of an area of mental functioning.

e. *Effects of support, supervision, structure on functioning.* The degree of limitation of an area of mental functioning also reflects the kind and extent of supports or supervision you receive and the characteristics of any structured setting where you spend your time, which enable you to function. The more extensive the support you need from others or the more structured the setting you need in order to function, the more limited we will find you to be (see 12.00D).

f. *Specific instructions for paragraphs B1, B3, and B4.* For paragraphs B1, B3, and B4, the greatest degree of limitation of any part of the area of mental functioning directs the rating of limitation of that whole area of mental functioning.

   i. To do a work-related task, you must be able to understand *and* remember *and* apply information required by the task. Similarly, you must be able to concentrate *and* persist *and* maintain pace in order to complete the task, and adapt *and* manage yourself in the workplace. Limitation in any one of these parts (understand *or* remember *or* apply; concentrate *or* persist *or* maintain pace; adapt *or* manage oneself) may prevent you from completing a work-related task.

   ii. We will document the rating of limitation of the whole area of mental functioning, not each individual part. We will not add ratings of the parts together. For example, with respect to paragraph B3, if you have marked limitation in maintaining pace, and mild or moderate limitations in concentrating and persisting, we will find that you have marked limitation in the whole paragraph B3 area of mental functioning.

   iii. Marked limitation in more than one part of the same paragraph B area of mental functioning does not satisfy the requirement to have marked limitation in two paragraph B areas of mental functioning.

4. *How we evaluate mental disorders involving exacerbations and remissions.*

   a. When we evaluate the effects of your mental disorder, we will consider how often you have exacerbations and remissions, how long they last, what causes your mental disorder to worsen or improve, and any other relevant information. We will assess any limitation of the affected paragraph B area(s) of mental functioning using the rating scale for the paragraph B criteria. We will consider whether you can use the area of mental functioning on a regular and continuing basis (8 hours a day, 5 days a week, or an equivalent work schedule). We will not find that you are able to work solely because you have a period(s) of improvement (remission), or that you are disabled solely because you have a period of worsening (exacerbation), of your mental disorder.

   b. If you have a mental disorder involving exacerbations and remissions, you may be able to use the four areas of mental functioning to work for a few weeks or months. Recurrence or worsening of symptoms and signs, however, can interfere enough to render you unable to sustain the work.

G. What are the paragraph C criteria, and how do we use them to evaluate your mental disorder?

1. *General.* The paragraph C criteria are an alternative to the paragraph B criteria under listings 12.02, 12.03, 12.04, 12.06, and 12.15. We use the paragraph C criteria to evaluate mental disorders that are "serious and persistent." In the paragraph C criteria, we recognize that mental health interventions may control the more obvious symptoms and signs of your mental disorder.
2. *Paragraph C criteria.*
   a. We find a mental disorder to be "serious and persistent" when there is a medically documented history of the existence of the mental disorder in the listing category over a period of at least 2 years, and evidence shows that your disorder satisfies both C1 and C2.
   b. The criterion in C1 is satisfied when the evidence shows that you rely, on an ongoing basis, upon medical treatment, mental health therapy, psychosocial support(s), or a highly structured setting(s), to diminish the symptoms and signs of your mental disorder (see 12.00D). We consider that you receive ongoing medical treatment when the medical evidence establishes that you obtain medical treatment with a frequency consistent with accepted medical practice for the type of treatment or evaluation required for your medical condition. We will consider periods of inconsistent treatment or lack of compliance with treatment that may result from your mental disorder. If the evidence indicates that the inconsistent treatment or lack of compliance is a feature of your mental disorder, and it has led to an exacerbation of your symptoms and signs, we will not use it as evidence to support a finding that you have not received ongoing medical treatment as required by this paragraph.
   c. The criterion in C2 is satisfied when the evidence shows that, despite your diminished symptoms and signs, you have achieved only marginal adjustment. "Marginal adjustment" means that your adaptation to the requirements of daily life is fragile; that is, you have minimal capacity to adapt to changes in your environment or to demands that are not already part of your daily life. We will consider that you have achieved only marginal adjustment when the evidence shows that changes or increased demands have led to exacerbation of your symptoms and signs and to deterioration in your functioning; for example, you have become unable to function outside of your home or a more restrictive setting, without substantial psychosocial supports (see 12.00D). Such deterioration may have necessitated a significant change

in medication or other treatment. Similarly, because of the nature of your mental disorder, evidence may document episodes of deterioration that have required you to be hospitalized or absent from work, making it difficult for you to sustain work activity over time.

H. How do we document and evaluate intellectual disorder under 12.05?

1. *General.* Listing 12.05 is based on the three elements that characterize intellectual disorder: significantly subaverage general intellectual functioning; significant deficits in current adaptive functioning; and the disorder manifested before age 22.
2. *Establishing significantly subaverage general intellectual functioning.*
   a. *Definition.* Intellectual functioning refers to the general mental capacity to learn, reason, plan, solve problems, and perform other cognitive functions. Under 12.05A, we identify significantly subaverage general intellectual functioning by the cognitive inability to function at a level required to participate in standardized intelligence testing. Our findings under 12.05A are based on evidence from an acceptable medical source. Under 12.05B, we identify significantly subaverage general intellectual functioning by an IQ score(s) on an individually administered standardized test of general intelligence that meets program requirements and has a mean of 100 and a standard deviation of 15. A qualified specialist (see 12.00H2c) must administer the standardized intelligence testing.

   b. *Psychometric standards.* We will find standardized intelligence test results usable for the purposes of 12.05B1 when the measure employed meets contemporary psychometric standards for validity, reliability, normative data, and scope of measurement; and a qualified specialist has individually administered the test according to all pre-requisite testing conditions.

   c. *Qualified specialist.* A "qualified specialist" is currently licensed or certified at the independent level of practice in the State where the test was performed, and has the training and experience to administer, score, and interpret intelligence tests. If a psychological assistant or paraprofessional administered the test, a supervisory qualified specialist must interpret the test findings and co-sign the examination report.

   d. *Responsibility for conclusions based on testing.* We generally presume that your obtained IQ score(s) is an accurate reflection of your general intellectual functioning, unless evidence in the record suggests otherwise. Examples of this evidence include: a statement from the test administrator indicating that your obtained score is not an accurate reflection of your general intellectual functioning, prior or internally inconsistent IQ scores, or information about your daily functioning. Only qualified specialists, Federal and State agency medical and psychological consultants, and other contracted medical and psychological experts may conclude that your obtained IQ score(s) is not an accurate reflection of your general intellectual functioning. This conclusion must be well supported by appropriate clinical and laboratory diagnostic techniques and must be based on relevant evidence in the case record, such as:

i. The data obtained in testing;

ii. Your developmental history, including when your signs and symptoms began;

iii. Information about how you function on a daily basis in a variety of settings; and

iv. Clinical observations made during the testing period, such as your ability to sustain attention, concentration, and effort; to relate appropriately to the examiner; and to perform tasks independently without prompts or reminders.

3. Establishing significant deficits in adaptive functioning.

a. Definition. Adaptive functioning refers to how you learn and use conceptual, social, and practical skills in dealing with common life demands. It is your typical functioning at home and in the community, alone or among others. Under 12.05A, we identify significant deficits in adaptive functioning based on your dependence on others to care for your personal needs, such as eating and bathing. We will base our conclusions about your adaptive functioning on evidence from a variety of sources (see 12.00H3b) and not on your statements alone. Under 12.05B2, we identify significant deficits in adaptive functioning based on whether there is extreme limitation of one, or marked limitation of two, of the paragraph B criteria (see 12.00E; 12.00F).

b. Evidence. Evidence about your adaptive functioning may come from:

i. Medical sources, including their clinical observations;

ii. Standardized tests of adaptive functioning (see 12.00H3c);

iii. Third party information, such as a report of your functioning from a family member or friend;

iv. School records, if you were in school recently;

v. Reports from employers or supervisors; and

vi. Your own statements about how you handle all of your daily activities.

c. Standardized tests of adaptive functioning. We do not require the results of an individually administered standardized test of adaptive functioning. If your case record includes these test results, we will consider the results along with all other relevant evidence; however, we will use the guidelines in 12.00E and F to evaluate and determine the degree of your deficits in adaptive functioning, as required under 12.05B2.

d. *How we consider common everyday activities.*

   i. The fact that you engage in common everyday activities, such as caring for your personal needs, preparing simple meals, or driving a car, will not always mean that you do not have deficits in adaptive functioning as required by 12.05B2. You may demonstrate both strengths and deficits in your adaptive functioning. However, a lack of deficits in one area does not negate the presence of deficits in another area. When we assess your adaptive functioning, we will consider all of your activities and your performance of them.

   ii. Our conclusions about your adaptive functioning rest on whether you do your daily activities independently, appropriately, effectively, and on a sustained basis. If you receive help in performing your activities, we need to know the kind, extent, and frequency of help you receive in order to perform them. We will not assume that your ability to do some common everyday activities, or to do some things without help or support, demonstrates that your mental disorder does not meet the requirements of 12.05B2. (See 12.00D regarding the factors we consider when we evaluate your functioning, including how we consider any help or support you receive.)

e. How we consider work activity. The fact that you have engaged in work activity, or that you work intermittently or steadily in a job commensurate with your abilities, will not always mean that you do not have deficits in adaptive functioning as required by 12.05B2. When you have engaged in work activity, we need complete information about the work, and about your functioning in the work activity and work setting, before we reach any conclusions about your adaptive functioning. We will consider all factors involved in your work history before concluding whether your impairment satisfies the criteria for intellectual disorder under 12.05B. We will consider your prior and current work history, if any, and various other factors influencing how you function. For example, we consider whether the work was in a supported setting, whether you required more supervision than other employees, how your job duties compared to others in the same job, how much time it took you to learn the job duties, and the reason the work ended, if applicable.

4. Establishing that the disorder began before age 22. We require evidence that demonstrates or supports (is consistent with) the conclusion that your mental disorder began prior to age 22. We do not require evidence that your impairment met all of the requirements of 12.05A or 12.05B prior to age 22. Also, we do not require you to have met our statutory definition of disability prior to age 22. When we do not have evidence that was recorded before you attained age 22, we need evidence about your current intellectual and adaptive functioning and the history of your disorder that supports the

conclusion that the disorder began before you attained age 22. Examples of evidence that can demonstrate or support this conclusion include:

a. Tests of intelligence or adaptive functioning;
b. School records indicating a history of special education services based on your intellectual functioning;
c. An Individualized Education Program (IEP), including your transition plan;
d. Reports of your academic performance and functioning at school;
e. Medical treatment records;
f. Interviews or reports from employers;
g. Statements from a supervisor in a group home or a sheltered workshop; and
h. Statements from people who have known you and can tell us about your functioning in the past and currently.

I. How do we evaluate substance use disorders? If we find that you are disabled and there is medical evidence in your case record establishing that you have a substance use disorder, we will determine whether your substance use disorder is a contributing factor material to the determination of disability (see §§ 404.1535 and 416.935 of this chapter).

J. How do we evaluate mental disorders that do not meet one of the mental disorders listings?

1. These listings include only examples of mental disorders that we consider serious enough to prevent you from doing any gainful activity. If your severe mental disorder does not meet the criteria of any of these listings, we will consider whether you have an impairment(s) that meets the criteria of a listing in another body system. You may have another impairment(s) that is secondary to your mental disorder. For example, if you have an eating disorder and develop a cardiovascular impairment because of it, we will evaluate your cardiovascular impairment under the listings for the cardiovascular body system.
2. If you have a severe medically determinable impairment(s) that does not meet a listing, we will determine whether your impairment(s) medically equals a listing (see 404.1526 and 416.926of this chapter).
3. If your impairment(s) does not meet or medically equal a listing, we will assess your residual functional capacity for engaging in substantial gainful activity (see 404.1545 and 416.945 of this chapter). When we assess your residual functional capacity, we consider all of your impairment-related mental and physical limitations. For example, the side effects of some medications may reduce your general alertness, concentration, or physical stamina, affecting your residual functional capacity for non-exertional or exertional work activities. Once we have determined your residual functional capacity, we proceed to the fourth, and if necessary, the fifth steps of

the sequential evaluation process in 404.1520 and 416.920 of this chapter. We use the rules in 404.1594 and 416.994of this chapter, as appropriate, when we decide whether you continue to be disabled.

12.01 Category of Impairments, Mental Disorders

12.02 Neurocognitive disorders (see 12.00B1), satisfied by A and B, or A and C:

A. Medical documentation of a significant cognitive decline from a prior level of functioning in *one* or more of the cognitive areas:

1. Complex attention;
2. Executive function;
3. Learning and memory;
4. Language;
5. Perceptual-motor; or
6. Social cognition.

AND

B. Extreme limitation of one, or marked limitation of two, of the following areas of mental functioning (see 12.00F):

1. Understand, remember, or apply information (see 12.00E1).
2. Interact with others (see 12.00E2).
3. Concentrate, persist, or maintain pace (see 12.00E3).
4. Adapt or manage oneself (see 12.00E4).

OR

C. Your mental disorder in this listing category is "serious and persistent;" that is, you have a medically documented history of the existence of the disorder over a period of at least 2 years, and there is evidence of both:

1. Medical treatment, mental health therapy, psychosocial support(s), or a highly structured setting(s) that is ongoing and that diminishes the symptoms and signs of your mental disorder (see 12.00G2b); *and*
2. Marginal adjustment, that is, you have minimal capacity to adapt to changes in your environment or to demands that are not already part of your daily life (see 12.00G2c).

12.03 Schizophrenia spectrum and other psychotic disorders (see 12.00B2), satisfied by A and B, or A and C:

A. Medical documentation of *one* or more of the following:

1. Delusions or hallucinations;

2. Disorganized thinking (speech); or
3. Grossly disorganized behavior or catatonia.

AND

B. Extreme limitation of one, or marked limitation of two, of the following areas of mental functioning (see 12.00F):

1. Understand, remember, or apply information (see 12.00E1).
2. Interact with others (see 12.00E2).
3. Concentrate, persist, or maintain pace (see 12.00E3).
4. Adapt or manage oneself (see 12.00E4).

OR

C. Your mental disorder in this listing category is "serious and persistent;" that is, you have a medically documented history of the existence of the disorder over a period of at least 2 years, and there is evidence of both:

1. Medical treatment, mental health therapy, psychosocial support(s), or a highly structured setting(s) that is ongoing and that diminishes the symptoms and signs of your mental disorder (see 12.00G2b); *and*
2. Marginal adjustment, that is, you have minimal capacity to adapt to changes in your environment or to demands that are not already part of your daily life (see 12.00G2c).

12.04 Depressive, bipolar and related disorders (see 12.00B3), satisfied by A and B, or A and C:

A. Medical documentation of the requirements of paragraph 1 or 2:

1. Depressive disorder, characterized by *five* or more of the following:
   a. Depressed mood;
   b. Diminished interest in almost all activities;
   c. Appetite disturbance with change in weight;
   d. Sleep disturbance;
   e. Observable psychomotor agitation or retardation;
   f. Decreased energy;
   g. Feelings of guilt or worthlessness;
   h. Difficulty concentrating or thinking; or
   i. Thoughts of death or suicide.
2. Bipolar disorder, characterized by *three* or more of the following:
   a. Pressured speech;
   b. Flight of ideas;

c. Inflated self-esteem;
d. Decreased need for sleep;
e. Distractibility;
f. Involvement in activities that have a high probability of painful consequences that are not recognized; or
g. Increase in goal-directed activity or psychomotor agitation.

AND

B. Extreme limitation of one, or marked limitation of two, of the following areas of mental functioning (see 12.00F):

1. Understand, remember, or apply information (see 12.00E1).
2. Interact with others (see 12.00E2).
3. Concentrate, persist, or maintain pace (see 12.00E3).
4. Adapt or manage oneself (see 12.00E4).

OR

C. Your mental disorder in this listing category is "serious and persistent;" that is, you have a medically documented history of the existence of the disorder over a period of at least 2 years, and there is evidence of both:

1. Medical treatment, mental health therapy, psychosocial support(s), or a highly structured setting(s) that is ongoing and that diminishes the symptoms and signs of your mental disorder (see 12.00G2b); *and*
2. Marginal adjustment, that is, you have minimal capacity to adapt to changes in your environment or to demands that are not already part of your daily life (see 12.00G2c).

12.05 Intellectual disorder (see 12.00B4), satisfied by A or B:

A. Satisfied by 1, 2, and 3 (see 12.00H):

1. Significantly subaverage general intellectual functioning evident in your cognitive inability to function at a level required to participate in standardized testing of intellectual functioning; and
2. Significant deficits in adaptive functioning currently manifested by your dependence upon others for personal needs (for example, toileting, eating, dressing, or bathing); and
3. The evidence about your current intellectual and adaptive functioning and about the history of your disorder demonstrates or supports the conclusion that the disorder began prior to your attainment of age 22.

OR

B. Satisfied by 1, 2, and 3 (see 12.00H):

1. Significantly subaverage general intellectual functioning evidenced by a or b:
   a. A full scale (or comparable) IQ score of 70 or below on an individually administered standardized test of general intelligence; or
   b. A full scale (or comparable) IQ score of 71-75 accompanied by a verbal or performance IQ score (or comparable part score) of 70 or below on an individually administered standardized test of general intelligence; and
2. Significant deficits in adaptive functioning currently manifested by extreme limitation of one, or marked limitation of two, of the following areas of mental functioning:
   a. Understand, remember, or apply information (see 12.00E1); or
   b. Interact with others (see 12.00E2); or
   c. Concentrate, persist, or maintain pace (see 12.00E3); or
   d. Adapt or manage oneself (see 12.00E4); and
3. The evidence about your current intellectual and adaptive functioning and about the history of your disorder demonstrates or supports the conclusion that the disorder began prior to your attainment of age 22.

12.06 Anxiety and obsessive-compulsive disorders (see 12.00B5), satisfied by A and B, or A and C:

A. Medical documentation of the requirements of paragraph 1, 2, or 3:

1. Anxiety disorder, characterized by *three* or more of the following;
   a. Restlessness;
   b. Easily fatigued;
   c. Difficulty concentrating;
   d. Irritability;
   e. Muscle tension; or
   f. Sleep disturbance.
2. Panic disorder or agoraphobia, characterized by *one* or both:
   a. Panic attacks followed by a persistent concern or worry about additional panic attacks or their consequences; or
   b. Disproportionate fear or anxiety about at least two different situations (for example, using public transportation, being in a crowd, being in a line, being outside of your home, being in open spaces).
3. Obsessive-compulsive disorder, characterized by *one* or both:
   a. Involuntary, time-consuming preoccupation with intrusive, unwanted thoughts; or
   b. Repetitive behaviors aimed at reducing anxiety.

AND

B. Extreme limitation of one, or marked limitation of two, of the following areas of mental functioning (see 12.00F):

1. Understand, remember, or apply information (see 12.00E1).
2. Interact with others (see 12.00E2).
3. Concentrate, persist, or maintain pace (see 12.00E3).
4. Adapt or manage oneself (see 12.00E4).

OR

C. Your mental disorder in this listing category is "serious and persistent;" that is, you have a medically documented history of the existence of the disorder over a period of at least 2 years, and there is evidence of both:

1. Medical treatment, mental health therapy, psychosocial support(s), or a highly structured setting(s) that is ongoing and that diminishes the symptoms and signs of your mental disorder (see 12.00G2b); *and*
2. Marginal adjustment, that is, you have minimal capacity to adapt to changes in your environment or to demands that are not already part of your daily life (see 12.00G2c).

12.07 Somatic symptom and related disorders (see 12.00B6), satisfied by A and B:

A. Medica documentation of *one* or more of the following:

1. Symptoms of altered voluntary motor or sensory function that are not better explained by another medical or mental disorder;
2. One or more somatic symptoms that are distressing, with excessive thoughts, feelings, or behaviors related to the symptoms; or
3. Preoccupation with having or acquiring a serious illness without significant symptoms present.

AND

B. Extreme limitation of one, or marked limitation of two, of the following areas of mental functioning (see 12.00F):

1. Understand, remember, or apply information (see 12.00E1).
2. Interact with others (see 12.00E2).
3. Concentrate, persist, or maintain pace (see 12.00E3).
4. Adapt or manage oneself (see 12.00E4).

12.08 Personality and impulse-control disorders (see 12.00B7), satisfied by A and B:

A. Medical documentation of a pervasive pattern of *one* or more of the following:

1. Distrust and suspiciousness of others;
2. Detachment from social relationships;
3. Disregard for and violation of the rights of others;
4. Instability of interpersonal relationships;
5. Excessive emotionality and attention seeking;
6. Feelings of inadequacy;
7. Excessive need to be taken care of;
8. Preoccupation with perfectionism and orderliness; or
9. Recurrent, impulsive, aggressive behavioral outbursts.

AND

B. Extreme limitation of one, or marked limitation of two, of the following areas of mental functioning (see 12.00F):

1. Understand, remember, or apply information (see 12.00E1).
2. Interact with others (see 12.00E2).
3. Concentrate, persist, or maintain pace (see 12.00E3).
4. Adapt or manage oneself (see 12.00E4).

12.09 [Reserved]

12.10 Autism spectrum disorder (see 12.00B8), satisfied by A and B:

A. Medical documentation of *both* of the following:

1. Qualitative deficits in verbal communication, nonverbal communication, and social interaction; and
2. Significantly restricted, repetitive patterns of behavior, interests, or activities.

AND

B. Extreme limitation of one, or marked limitation of two, of the following areas of mental functioning (see 12.00F):

1. Understand, remember, or apply information (see 12.00E1).
2. Interact with others (see 12.00E2).
3. Concentrate, persist, or maintain pace (see 12.00E3).
4. Adapt or manage oneself (see 12.00E4).

12.11 Neurodevelopmental disorders (see 12.00B9), satisfied by A and B:

A. Medical documentation of the requirements of paragraph 1, 2, or 3:

1. *One* or both of the following:
   a. Frequent distractibility, difficulty sustaining attention, and difficulty organizing tasks; or
   b. Hyperactive and impulsive behavior (for example, difficulty remaining seated, talking excessively, difficulty waiting, appearing restless, or behaving as if being "driven by a motor").
2. Significant difficulties learning and using academic skills; or
3. Recurrent motor movement or vocalization.

AND

B. Extreme limitation of one, or marked limitation of two, of the following areas of mental functioning (see 12.00F):

1. Understand, remember, or apply information (see 12.00E1).
2. Interact with others (see 12.00E2).
3. Concentrate, persist, or maintain pace (see 12.00E3).
4. Adapt or manage oneself (see 12.00E4).

12.12 [Reserved]

12.13 Eating disorders (see 12.00B10), satisfied by A and B:

A. Medical documentation of a persistent alteration in eating or eating-related behavior that results in a change in consumption or absorption of food and that significantly impairs physical or psychological health.

AND

B. Extreme limitation of one, or marked limitation of two, of the following areas of mental functioning (see 12.00F):

1. Understand, remember, or apply information (see 12.00E1).
2. Interact with others (see 12.00E2).
3. Concentrate, persist, or maintain pace (see 12.00E3).
4. Adapt or manage oneself (see 12.00E4).

12.15 Trauma- and stressor-related disorders (see 12.00B11), satisfied by A and B, or A and C:

A. Medical documentation of *all* of the following:

1. Exposure to actual or threatened death, serious injury, or violence;

2. Subsequent involuntary re-experiencing of the traumatic event (for example, intrusive memories, dreams, or flashbacks);
3. Avoidance of external reminders of the event;
4. Disturbance in mood and behavior; and
5. Increases in arousal and reactivity (for example, exaggerated startle response, sleep disturbance).

AND

B. Extreme limitation of one, or marked limitation of two, of the following areas of mental functioning (see 12.00F):

1. Understand, remember, or apply information (see 12.00E1).
2. Interact with others (see 12.00E2).
3. Concentrate, persist, or maintain pace (see 12.00E3).
4. Adapt or manage oneself (see 12.00E4).

OR

C. Your mental disorder in this listing category is "serious and persistent;" that is, you have a medically documented history of the existence of the disorder over a period of at least 2 years, and there is evidence of both:

1. Medical treatment, mental health therapy, psychosocial support(s), or a highly structured setting(s) that is ongoing and that diminishes the symptoms and signs of your mental disorder (see 12.00G2b); *and*
2. Marginal adjustment, that is, you have minimal capacity to adapt to changes in your environment or to demands that are not already part of your daily life (see 12.00G2c).

13.00 Cancer

A. ***What impairments do these listings cover?*** We use these listings to evaluate all

cancers (malignant neoplastic diseases) except certain cancers associated with human immunodeficiency virus (HIV) infection. We use the criteria in 14.11B to evaluate primary central nervous system lymphoma, 14.11C to evaluate primary effusion lymphoma, and 14.11E to evaluate pulmonary Kaposi sarcoma if you also have HIV infection. We evaluate all other cancers associated with HIV infection, for example, Hodgkin lymphoma or non-pulmonary Kaposi sarcoma, under this body system or under 14.11F–I in the immune system disorders body system.

B. ***What do we consider when we evaluate cancer under these listings?*** We consider factors including:

1. Origin of the cancer.

2. Extent of involvement.

3. Duration, frequency, and response to anticancer therapy.

4. Effects of any post-therapeutic residuals.

C. ***How do we apply these listings?*** We apply the criteria in a specific listing to a cancer originating from that specific site.

D. ***What evidence do we need?***

1. We need medical evidence that specifies the type, extent, and site of the primary, recurrent, or metastatic lesion. When the primary site cannot be identified, we will use evidence documenting the site(s) of metastasis to evaluate the impairment under 13.27.

2. For operative procedures, including a biopsy or a needle aspiration, we generally need a copy of both the:

a. Operative note, and

b. Pathology report.

3. When we cannot get these documents, we will accept the summary of hospitalization(s) or other medical reports. This evidence should include details of the findings at surgery and, whenever appropriate, the pathological findings.

4. In some situations we may also need evidence about recurrence, persistence, or progression of the cancer, the response to therapy, and any significant residuals. (See 13.00G.)

E. ***When do we need longitudinal evidence?***

1. ***Cancer with distant metastases.*** We generally do not need longitudinal evidence for cancer that has metastasized beyond the regional lymph nodes because this cancer usually meets the requirements of a listing. Exceptions are for cancer with distant metastases that we expect to respond to anticancer therapy. For these exceptions, we usually need a longitudinal record of 3 months after therapy starts to determine whether the therapy achieved its intended effect, and whether this effect is likely to persist.

2. ***Other cancers.*** When there are no distant metastases, many of the listings require that we consider your response to initial anticancer therapy; that is, the initial planned treatment regimen. This therapy may consist of a single modality or a combination of modalities; that is, multimodal therapy (see 13.00I4).

3. ***Types of Treatment.***

a. Whenever the initial planned therapy is a single modality, enough time must pass to allow a determination about whether the therapy will achieve its intended effect. If the treatment fails, the failure often happens within 6 months after the treatment starts, and there will often be a change in the treatment regimen.

b. Whenever the initial planned therapy is multimodal, we usually cannot make a determination about the effectiveness of the therapy until we can determine the effects of all the planned modalities. In some cases, we may need to defer adjudication until we can assess the effectiveness of therapy. However, we do not need to defer adjudication to determine whether the therapy will achieve its intended effect if we can make a fully favorable determination or decision based on the length and effects of therapy, or the residuals of the cancer or therapy (see 13.00G).

c. We need evidence under 13.02E, 13.11D, and 13.14C to establish that your treating source initiated multimodal anticancer therapy. We do not need to make a determination about the length or effectiveness of your therapy. Multimodal therapy has been initiated, and satisfies the requirements in 13.02E, 13.11D, and 13.14C, when your treating source starts the first modality. We may defer adjudication if your treating source plans multimodal therapy and has not initiated it.

F. ***How do we evaluate impairments that do not meet one of the cancer listings?***

1. These listings are only examples of cancer that we consider severe enough to prevent you from doing any gainful activity. If your severe impairment(s) does not meet the criteria of any of these listings, we must also consider whether you have an impairment(s) that meets the criteria of a listing in another body system.

2. If you have a severe medically determinable impairment(s) that does not meet a listing, we will determine whether your impairment(s) medically equals a listing. (See §§ 404.1526 and 416.926 of this chapter.) If your impairment(s) does not meet or medically equal a listing, you may or may not have the residual functional capacity to engage in substantial gainful activity. In that situation, we proceed to the fourth, and, if necessary, the fifth steps of the sequential evaluation process in §§ 404.1520 and 416.920 of this chapter. We use the rules in §§ 404.1594 and 416.994 of this chapter, as appropriate, when we decide whether you continue to be disabled.

G. ***How do we consider the effects of anticancer therapy?***

1. ***How we consider the effects of anticancer therapy under the listings.*** In many cases, cancers meet listing criteria only if the therapy is not effective and the cancer persists, progresses, or recurs. However, as explained in the following paragraphs, we will not delay adjudication if we can make a fully favorable determination or decision based on the evidence in the case record.

2. ***Effects can vary widely.***

a. We consider each case on an individual basis because the therapy and its toxicity may vary widely. We will request a specific description of the therapy, including these items:

i. Drugs given.

ii. Dosage.

iii. Frequency of drug administration.

iv. Plans for continued drug administration.

v. Extent of surgery.

vi. Schedule and fields of radiation therapy.

b. We will also request a description of the complications or adverse effects of therapy, such as the following:

i. Continuing gastrointestinal symptoms.

ii. Persistent weakness.

iii. Neurological complications.

iv. Cardiovascular complications.

v. Reactive mental disorders.

3. ***Effects of therapy may change.*** The severity of the adverse effects of anticancer therapy may change during treatment; therefore, enough time must pass to allow us to evaluate the therapy's effect. The residual effects of treatment are temporary in most instances; however on occasion, the effects may be disabling for a consecutive period of at least 12 months. In some situations, very serious adverse effects may interrupt and prolong multimodal anticancer therapy for a continuous period of almost 12 months. In these situations, we may determine there is an expectation that your impairment will preclude you from engaging in any gainful activity for at least 12 months.

4. ***When the initial anticancer therapy is effective.*** We evaluate any post-therapeutic residual impairment(s) not included in these listings under the criteria for the affected body system. We must consider any complications of therapy. When the residual impairment(s) does not meet or medically equal a listing, we must consider its effect on your ability to do substantial gainful activity.

H. ***How long do we consider your impairment to be disabling?***

1. In some listings, we specify that we will consider your impairment to be disabling until a particular point in time (for example, until at least 12 months from the date of transplantation). We may consider your impairment to be disabling beyond this point when the medical and other evidence justifies it.

2. When a listing does not contain such a specification, we will consider an impairment(s) that meets or medically equals a listing in this body system to be disabling until at least 3 years after onset of complete remission. When the impairment(s) has been in complete remission for at least 3 years, that is, the original tumor or a recurrence (or relapse) and any metastases have not been evident for at least 3 years, the impairment(s) will no longer meet or medically equal the criteria of a listing in this body system.

3. Following the appropriate period, we will consider any residuals, including residuals of the cancer or therapy (see 13.00G), in determining whether you are disabled. If you have a recurrence or relapse of your cancer, your impairment may meet or medically equal one of the listings in this body system again.

I. ***What do we mean by the following terms?***

1. ***Anticancer therapy*** means surgery, radiation, chemotherapy, hormones, immunotherapy, or bone marrow or stem cell transplantation. When we refer to surgery as an anticancer treatment, we mean surgical excisions for treatment, not for diagnostic purposes.

2. ***Inoperable*** means surgery is thought to be of no therapeutic value or the surgery cannot be performed; for example, when you cannot tolerate anesthesia or surgery because of another impairment(s), or you have a cancer that is too large or that has invaded crucial structures. This term does not include situations in which your cancer could have been surgically removed but another method of treatment was chosen; for example, an attempt at organ preservation. Your physician may determine whether the cancer is inoperable before or after you receive neoadjuvant therapy. *Neoadjuvant therapy* is anticancer therapy, such as chemotherapy or radiation, given before surgery in order to reduce the size of the cancer.

3. ***Metastases*** means the spread of cancer cells by blood, lymph, or other body fluid. This term does not include the spread of cancer cells by direct extension of the cancer to other tissues or organs.

4. ***Multimodal therapy*** means anticancer therapy that is a combination of at least two types of treatment given in close proximity as a unified whole and usually planned before any treatment has begun. There are three types of treatment modalities: surgery, radiation, and systemic drug therapy (chemotherapy, hormone therapy, and immunotherapy or biological modifier therapy. Examples of multimodal therapy include:

a. Surgery followed by chemotherapy or radiation.

b. Chemotherapy followed by surgery.

c. Chemotherapy and concurrent radiation.

5. ***Persistent*** means the planned initial anticancer therapy failed to achieve a complete remission of your cancer; that is, your cancer is evident, even if smaller, after the therapy has ended.

6. ***Progressive*** Progressive means the cancer becomes more extensive after treatment; that is, there is evidence that your cancer is growing after you have completed at least half of your planned initial anticancer therapy.

7. ***Recurrent, relapse*** means the cancer that was in complete remission or entirely removed by surgery has returned.

8. ***Unresectable*** means surgery or surgeries did not completely remove the cancer. This term includes situations in which your cancer is incompletely resected or the surgical margins are positive. It does not include situations in which there is a finding of a positive margin(s) if additional surgery obtains a margin(s) that is clear. It does not include situations in which the cancer is completely resected but you are receiving adjuvant therapy. Adjuvant therapy is anticancer therapy, such as chemotherapy or radiation, given after surgery in order to eliminate any remaining cancer cells and lessen the chance of recurrence.

J. ***Can we establish the existence of a disabling impairment prior to the date of the evidence that shows the cancer satisfies the criteria of a listing?*** Yes. We will consider factors such as:

1. The type of cancer and its location.

2. The extent of involvement when the cancer was first demonstrated.

3. Your symptoms.

K. *How do we evaluate specific cancers?*

1. ***Lymphoma.***

a. Many indolent (non-aggressive) lymphomas are controlled by well-tolerated treatment modalities, although the lymphomas may produce intermittent symptoms and signs. We may defer adjudicating these cases for an appropriate period after therapy is initiated to determine whether the therapy will achieve its intended effect, which is usually to stabilize the disease process. (See 13.00E3.) Once your disease stabilizes, we will assess severity based on the extent of involvement of other organ systems and residuals from therapy.

b. A change in therapy for indolent lymphomas is usually an indicator that the therapy is not achieving its intended effect. However, your impairment will not meet the requirements of 13.05A2 if your therapy is changed solely because you or your physician chooses to change it, and not because of a failure to achieve stability.

c. We consider Hodgkin lymphoma that recurs more than 12 months after completing initial anticancer therapy to be a new disease rather than a recurrence.

2. ***Leukemia.***

a. ***Acute leukemia.*** The initial diagnosis of acute leukemia, including the accelerated or blast phase of chronic myelogenous (granulocytic) leukemia, is based upon definitive bone marrow examination. Additional diagnostic information is based on chromosomal analysis, cytochemical and surface marker studies on the abnormal cells, or other methods consistent with the prevailing state of medical knowledge and clinical practice. Recurrent disease must be documented by peripheral blood, bone marrow, or cerebrospinal fluid examination, or by testicular biopsy. The initial and follow-up pathology reports should be included.

b. ***Chronic myelogenous leukemia (CML).*** We need a diagnosis of CML based upon documented granulocytosis, including immature forms such as differentiated or undifferentiated myelocytes and myeloblasts, and a chromosomal analysis that demonstrates the Philadelphia chromosome. In the absence of a chromosomal analysis, or if the Philadelphia chromosome is not present, the diagnosis may be made by other methods consistent with the prevailing state of medical knowledge and clinical practice. The requirement of CML in the accelerated or blast phase is met in 13.06B if laboratory findings show the proportion of blast (immature) cells in the peripheral blood or bone marrow is 10 percent or greater.

c. ***Chronic lymphocytic leukemia.***

i. We require the diagnosis of chronic lymphocytic leukemia (CLL) to be documented by evidence of a chronic lymphocytosis of at least 10,000/mm3 for 3 months or longer, or other acceptable diagnostic techniques consistent with the prevailing state of medical knowledge and clinical practice.

ii. We evaluate the complications and residual impairment(s) from CLL under the appropriate listings, such as 13.05A2, or the hematological listings (7.00).

d. ***Elevated white cell count.*** In cases of chronic leukemia (either myelogenous or lymphocytic), an elevated white cell count, in itself, is not a factor in determining the severity of the impairment.

3. ***Macroglobulinemia or heavy chain disease.*** We require the diagnosis of these diseases to be confirmed by protein electrophoresis or immunoelectrophoresis. We evaluate the resulting impairment(s) under the appropriate listings, such as 13.05A2 or the hematological listings (7.00).

4. ***Primary breast cancer.***

a. We evaluate bilateral primary breast cancer (synchronous or metachronous) under 13.10A, which covers local primary disease, and not as a primary disease that has metastasized.

b. We evaluate secondary lymphedema that results from anticancer therapy for breast cancer under 13.10E if the lymphedema is treated by surgery to salvage or restore the functioning of an upper extremity. Secondary lymphedema is edema that results from obstruction or destruction of normal lymphatic channels. We may not restrict our determination of the onset of disability to the date of the surgery; we may establish an earlier onset date of disability if the evidence in your case record supports such a finding.

5. ***Carcinoma-in-situ***. Carcinoma-in-situ, or preinvasive carcinoma, usually responds to treatment. When we use the term "carcinoma" in these listings, it does not include carcinoma-in-situ.

6. ***Primary central nervous system (CNS) cancers.*** We use the criteria in 13.13 to evaluate cancers that originate within the CNS (that is, brain and spinal cord cancers).

a. The CNS cancers listed in 13.13A1 are highly malignant and respond poorly to treatment, and therefore we do not require additional criteria to evaluate them. We do not list pituitary gland cancer (for example, pituitary gland carcinoma) in 13.13A1, although this CNS cancer is highly malignant and responds poorly to treatment. We evaluate pituitary gland cancer under 13.13A1 and do not require additional criteria to evaluate it.

b. We consider a CNS tumor to be malignant if it is classified as Grade II, Grade III, or Grade IV under the World Health Organization (WHO) classification of tumors of the CNS (*WHO Classification of Tumours of the Central Nervous System, 2007*).

c. We evaluate benign (for example, WHO Grade I) CNS tumors under 11.05. We evaluate metastasized CNS cancers from non-CNS sites under the primary cancers (see 13.00C). We evaluate any complications of CNS cancers, such as resultant neurological or psychological impairments, under the criteria for the affected body system.

7. ***Primary peritoneal carcinoma.*** We use the criteria in 13.23E to evaluate primary peritoneal carcinoma in women because this cancer is often indistinguishable from ovarian cancer and is generally treated the same way as ovarian cancer. We use the criteria in 13.15A to evaluate primary peritoneal carcinoma in men because many of these cases are similar to malignant mesothelioma.

8. ***Prostate cancer.*** We exclude "biochemical recurrence" in 13.24A, which is defined as an increase in the serum prostate-specific antigen (PSA) level following the completion of the hormonal intervention therapy. We need corroborating evidence to document recurrence, such as radiological studies or findings on physical examination.

9. ***Melanoma.*** We evaluate malignant melanoma that affects the skin (cutaneous melanoma), eye (ocular melanoma), or mucosal membranes (mucosal melanoma) under 13.29. We evaluate melanoma that is not malignant that affects the skin (benign melanocytic tumor) under the listings in 8.00 or other affected body systems.

L. ***How do we evaluate cancer treated by bone marrow or stem cell transplantation, including transplantation using stem cells from umbilical cord blood?*** Bone marrow or stem cell transplantation is performed for a variety of cancers. We require the transplantation to occur before we evaluate it under these listings. We do not need to restrict our determination of the onset of disability to the date of the transplantation (13.05, 13.06, or 13.07) or the date of first treatment under the treatment plan that includes transplantation (13.28). We may be able to establish an earlier onset date of disability due to your transplantation if the evidence in your case record supports such a finding.

1. ***Acute leukemia (including T-cell lymphoblastic lymphoma) or accelerated or blast phase of CML.*** If you undergo bone marrow or stem cell transplantation for any of these disorders, we will consider you to be disabled until at least 24 months from the date of diagnosis or relapse, or at least 12 months from the date of transplantation, whichever is later.

2. ***Lymphoma, multiple myeloma, or chronic phase of CML.*** If you undergo bone marrow or stem cell transplantation for any of these disorders, we will consider you to be disabled until at least 12 months from the date of transplantation.

3. ***Other cancers.*** We will evaluate any other cancer treated with bone marrow or stem cell transplantation under 13.28, regardless of whether there is another listing that addresses that impairment. The length of time we will consider you to be disabled depends on whether you undergo allogeneic or autologous transplantation.

a. ***Allogeneic bone marrow or stem cell transplantation.*** If you undergo allogeneic transplantation (transplantation from an unrelated donor or a related donor other than an identical twin), we will consider you to be disabled until at least 12 months from the date of transplantation.

b. ***Autologous bone marrow or stem cell transplantation***. If you undergo autologous transplantation (transplantation of your own cells or cells from your identical twin (syngeneic transplantation)), we will consider you to be disabled until at least 12 months from the date of the first treatment under the treatment plan that includes transplantation. The first treatment usually refers to the initial therapy given to prepare you for transplantation.

4. ***Evaluating disability after the appropriate time period has elapsed.*** We consider any residual impairment(s), such as complications arising from:

a. Graft-versus-host (GVH) disease.

b. Immunosuppressant therapy, such as frequent infections.

c. Significant deterioration of other organ systems.

13.01 Category of Impairments, Cancer *(malignant neoplastic diseases)*

13.02 Soft tissue cancer of the head and neck (except salivary glands—13.08—and thyroid gland—13.09).

A. Inoperable or unresectable.

OR

B. Persistent or recurrent disease following initial anticancer therapy, except persistence or recurrence in the true vocal cord.

OR

C. With metastases beyond the regional lymph nodes.

OR

D. Small cell (oat cell) carcinoma.

OR

E. Soft tissue cancers originating in the head and neck treated with multimodal anticancer therapy (see 13.00E3c). Consider under a disability until at least 18 months from the date of diagnosis. Thereafter, evaluate any residual impairment(s) under the criteria for the affected body system.

13.03 Skin.

A. Sarcoma or carcinoma with metastases to or beyond the regional lymph nodes.

OR

B. Carcinoma invading deep extradermal structures (for example, skeletal muscle, cartilage, or bone).

13.04 Soft tissue sarcoma.

A. With regional or distant metastases.

OR

B. Persistent or recurrent following initial anticancer therapy.

13.05 Lymphoma (including mycosis fungoides, but excluding T-cell lymphoblastic lymphoma-13.06). (See 13.00K1 and 13.00K2c.)

A. Non-Hodgkin lymphoma, as described in 1 or 2:

1. Aggressive lymphoma (including diffuse large B-cell lymphoma) persistent or recurrent following initial anticancer therapy.

2: Indolent lymphoma (including mycosis fungoides and follicular small cleaved cell) requiring initiation of more than one (single mode or multimodal) anticancer treatment regimen within a period of 12 consecutive months. Consider under a disability from at least the date of initiation of the treatment regimen that failed within 12 months.

OR

B. Hodgkin lymphoma with failure to achieve clinically complete remission, or recurrent lymphoma within 12 months of completing initial anticancer therapy.

OR

C. With bone marrow or stem cell transplantation. Consider under a disability until at least 12 months from the date of transplantation. Thereafter, evaluate any residual impairment(s) under the criteria for the affected body system.

OR

D. Mantle cell lymphoma.

13.06 Leukemia. (See 13.00K2.)

A. Acute leukemia (including T-cell lymphoblastic lymphoma). Consider under a disability until at least 24 months from the date of diagnosis or relapse, or at least 12 months from the date of bone marrow or stem cell transplantation, whichever is later. Thereafter, evaluate any residual impairment(s) under the criteria for the affected body system.

OR

B. Chronic myelogenous leukemia, as described in 1 or 2:

1. Accelerated or blast phase (see 13.00K2b). Consider under a disability until at least 24 months from the date of diagnosis or relapse, or at least 12 months from the date of bone marrow or stem cell transplantation, whichever is later. Thereafter, evaluate any residual impairment(s) under the criteria for the affected body system.

2. Chronic phase, as described in a or b:

a. Consider under a disability until at least 12 months from the date of bone marrow or stem cell transplantation. Thereafter, evaluate any residual impairment(s) under the criteria for the affected body system.

b. Progressive disease following initial anticancer therapy.

13.07 Multiple myeloma (confirmed by appropriate serum or urine protein electrophoresis and bone marrow findings).

A. Failure to respond or progressive disease following initial anticancer therapy.

OR

B. With bone marrow or stem cell transplantation. Consider under a disability until at least 12 months from the date of transplantation. Thereafter, evaluate any residual impairment(s) under the criteria for the affected body system.

13.08 Salivary glands—carcinoma or sarcoma with metastases beyond the regional lymph nodes.

13.09 Thyroid gland.

A. Anaplastic (undifferentiated) carcinoma.

OR

B. Carcinoma with metastases beyond the regional lymph nodes progressive despite radioactive iodine therapy.

OR

C. Medullary carcinoma with metastases beyond the regional lymph nodes.

13.10 Breast (except sarcoma—13.04) *(See 13.00K4.)*

A. Locally advanced cancer (inflammatory carcinoma, cancer of any size with direct extension to the chest wall or skin, or cancer of any size with metastases to the ipsilateral internal mammary nodes).

OR

B. Carcinoma with metastases to the supraclavicular or infraclavicular nodes, to 10 or more axillary nodes, or with distant metastases.

OR

C. Recurrent carcinoma, except local recurrence that remits with anticancer therapy.

OR

D. Small-cell (oat cell) carcinoma.

OR

E. With secondary lymphedema that is caused by anticancer therapy and treated by surgery to salvage or restore the functioning of an upper extremity. (See 13.00K4b.) Consider under a disability until at least 12 months from the date of the surgery that treated the secondary lymphedema. Thereafter, evaluate any residual impairment(s) under the criteria for the affected body system.

13.11 Skeletal system—sarcoma.

A. Inoperable or unresectable.

OR

B. Recurrent cancer (except local recurrence) after initial anticancer therapy.

OR

C. With distant metastases.

OR

D. All other cancer originating in bone with multimodal anticancer therapy (see 13.00E3c). Consider under a disability for 12 months from the date of diagnosis.

Thereafter, evaluate any residual impairment(s) under the criteria for the affected body system.

13.12 Maxilla, orbit, or temporal fossa.

A. Sarcoma or carcinoma of any type with regional or distant metastases.

OR

B. Carcinoma of the antrum with extension into the orbit or ethmoid or sphenoid sinus.

OR

C. Cancer with extension to the orbit, meninges, sinuses, or base of the skull.

13.13 Nervous system. (See 13.00K6.)

A. Primary central nervous system (CNS; that is brain and spinal cord) cancers, as described in 1,2 or 3:

1. Glioblastoma multiforme, ependymoblastoma, and diffuse intrinsic brain stem gliomas (see 13.00K6a).

2. Any Grade III or Grade IV CNS cancer (see 13.00K6b), including astrocytomas, sarcomas, and medulloblastoma and other primitive neuroectodermal tumors (PNETs).

3. Any primary CNS cancer, as described in a or b:

a. Metastatic.

b. Progressive or recurrent following initial anticancer therapy.

OR

B. Primary peripheral nerve or spinal root cancers, as described in 1 or 2:

1. Metastatic.

2. Progressive or recurrent following initial anticancer therapy.

13.14 Lungs.

A. Non-small-cell carcinoma—inoperable, unresectable, recurrent, or metastatic disease to or beyond the hilar nodes.

OR

B. Small-cell (oat cell) carcinoma.

OR

C. Carcinoma of the superior sulcus (including Pancoast tumors) with multimodal anticancer therapy (see 13.00E3c). Consider under a disability until at least 18 months from the date of diagnosis. Thereafter, evaluate any residual impairment(s) under the criteria for the affected body system.

13.15 Pleura or mediastinum.

A. Malignant mesothelioma of pleura.

OR

B. Tumors of the mediastinum, as described in 1 or 2:

1. With metastases to or beyond the regional lymph nodes.

2. Persistent or recurrent following initial anticancer therapy.

OR

C. Small-cell (oat cell) carcinoma.

13.16 Esophagus or stomach.

A. Carcinoma or sarcoma of the esophagus.

OR

B. Carcinoma or sarcoma of the stomach, as described in 1 or 2:

1. Inoperable, unresectable, extending to surrounding structures, or recurrent.

2. With metastases to or beyond the regional lymph nodes.

OR

C. Small-cell (oat cell) carcinoma.

13.17 Small intestine—carcinoma, sarcoma, or carcinoid.

A. Inoperable, unresectable, or recurrent.

OR

B. With metastases beyond the regional lymph nodes.

OR

C. Small-cell (oat cell) carcinoma.

13.18 Large intestine (from ileocecal valve to and including anal canal).

A. Adenocarcinoma that is inoperable, unresectable, or recurrent.

OR

B. Squamous cell carcinoma of the anus, recurrent after surgery.

OR

C. With metastases beyond the regional lymph nodes.

OR

D. Small-cell (oat cell) carcinoma.

13.19 Liver or gallbladder—cancer of the liver, gallbladder, or bile ducts.

13.20 Pancreas.

A. Carcinoma (except islet cell carcinoma).

OR

B. Islet cell carcinoma that is physiologically active and is either inoperable or unresectable.

13.21 Kidneys, adrenal glands, or ureters—carcinoma.

A. Inoperable, unresectable, or recurrent.

OR

B. With metastases to or beyond the regional lymph nodes.

13.22 Urinary bladder—carcinoma.

A. With infiltration beyond the bladder wall.

OR

B. Recurrent after total cystectomy.

OR

C. Inoperable or unresectable.

OR

D. With metastases to or beyond the regional lymph nodes.

OR

E. Small-cell (oat cell) carcinoma.

13.23 Cancers of the female genital tract—carcinoma or sarcoma (including primary peritoneal carcinoma).

A. Uterus (corpus), as described in 1, 2, or 3:

1. Invading adjoining organs.

2. With metastases to or beyond the regional lymph nodes.

3. Persistent or recurrent following initial anticancer therapy.

OR

B. Uterine cervix, as described in 1, 2 or 3:

1. Extending to the pelvic wall, lower portion of the vagina, or adjacent or distant organs.

2. Persistent or recurrent following initial anticancer therapy.

3. With metastases to distant (for example, para-aortic or supraclavicular) lymph nodes.

OR

C. Vulva or vagina, as described in 1, 2, or 3:

1. Invading adjoining organs.

2. With metastases to or beyond the regional lymph nodes.

3. Persistent or recurrent following initial anticancer therapy.

OR

D. Fallopian tubes, as described in 1 or 2:

1. Extending to the serosa or beyond.

2. Persistent or recurrent following initial anticancer therapy.

OR

E. Ovaries, as described in 1 or 2:

1. All cancers except germ-cell cancers, with at least one of the following:

a. Extension beyond the pelvis; for example, implants on, or direct extension to, peritoneal, omental, or bowel surfaces.

b. Metastases to or beyond the regional lymph nodes.

c. Recurrent following initial anticancer therapy.

2. Germ-cell cancer—progressive or recurrent following initial anticancer therapy.

OR

F. Small-cell (oat cell) carcinoma.

13.24 Prostate gland—carcinoma.

A. Progressive or recurrent (not including biochemical recurrence) despite initial hormonal intervention. (See 13.00K8.)

OR

B. With visceral metastases (metastases to internal organs).

OR

C. Small-cell (oat cell) carcinoma.

13.25 Testicles—cancer with metastatic disease progressive or recurrent following initial chemotherapy.

13.26 Penis—carcinoma with metastases to or beyond the regional lymph nodes.

13.27 Primary site unknown after appropriate search for primary—metastatic carcinoma or sarcoma, except for squamous cell carcinoma confined to the neck nodes.

13.28 Cancer treated by bone marrow or stem cell transplantation. (See 13.00L.)

A. Allogeneic transplantation. Consider under a disability until at least 12 months from the date of transplantation. Thereafter, evaluate any residual impairment(s) under the criteria for the affected body system.

OR

B. Autologous transplantation. Consider under a disability until at least 12 months from the date of the first treatment under the treatment plan that includes transplantation. Thereafter, evaluate any residual impairment(s) under the criteria for the affected body system.

13.29 Malignant melanoma (including skin, ocular, or mucosal melanomas), as described in either A, B, or C:

A. Recurrent (except an additional primary melanoma at a different site, which is not considered to be recurrent disease) following either 1 or 2:

1. Wide excision (skin melanoma).

2. Enucleation of the eye (ocular melanoma).

OR

B. With metastases as described in 1, 2, or 3:

1. Metastases to one or more clinically apparent nodes; that is, nodes that are detected by imaging studies (excluding lymphoscintigraphy) or by clinical evaluation (palpable).

2. If the nodes are not clinically apparent, with metastases to four or more nodes.

3. Metastases to adjacent skin (satellite lesions) or distant sites (for example, liver, lung, or brain).

OR

C. Mucosal melanoma.

14.00 Immune System Disorders

A. *What disorders do we evaluate under the immune system disorders listings?*

1. *We evaluate immune system disorders that cause dysfunction in one or more components of your immune system.*

a. The dysfunction may be due to problems in antibody production, impaired cell-mediated immunity, a combined type of antibody/cellular deficiency, impaired phagocytosis, or complement deficiency.

b. Immune system disorders may result in recurrent and unusual infections, or inflammation and dysfunction of the body's own tissues. Immune system disorders can cause a deficit in a single organ or body system that results in extreme (that is, very serious) loss of function. They can also cause lesser degrees of limitations in two or more organs or body systems, and when associated with symptoms or signs, such as severe fatigue, fever, malaise, diffuse musculoskeletal pain, or involuntary weight loss, can also result in extreme limitation.

c. We organize the discussions of immune system disorders in three categories: Autoimmune disorders; Immune deficiency disorders, excluding human immunodeficiency virus (HIV) infection; and HIV infection.

2. *Autoimmune disorders (14.00D).* Autoimmune disorders are caused by dysfunctional immune responses directed against the body's own tissues, resulting in chronic, multisystem impairments that differ in clinical manifestations, course, and outcome. They are sometimes referred to as rheumatic diseases, connective tissue disorders, or collagen vascular disorders. Some of the features of autoimmune disorders in adults differ from the features of the same disorders in children.

3. *Immune deficiency disorders, excluding HIV infection (14.00E).* Immune deficiency disorders are characterized by recurrent or unusual infections that respond poorly to treatment, and are often associated with complications affecting other parts of the body. Immune deficiency disorders are classified as either *primary* (congenital) or *acquired*. Individuals with immune deficiency disorders also have an increased risk of malignancies and of having autoimmune disorders.

4. *Human immunodeficiency virus (HIV) infection (14.00F).* HIV infection may be characterized by increased susceptibility to common infections as well as opportunistic infections, cancers, or other conditions listed in 14.11.

B. *What information do we need to show that you have an immune system disorder?* Generally, we need your medical history, a report(s) of a physical examination, a report(s) of laboratory findings, and in some instances, appropriate medically acceptable imaging or tissue biopsy reports to show that you have an immune system disorder. Therefore, we will make every reasonable effort to obtain your medical history, medical findings, and results of laboratory tests. We explain the information we need in more detail in the sections below.

C. *Definitions*

1. *Appropriate medically acceptable imaging* includes, but is not limited to, angiography, x-ray imaging, computerized axial tomography (CAT scan) or magnetic resonance imaging (MRI), with or without contrast material, myelography, and radionuclear bone scans. "Appropriate" means that the technique used is the proper one to support the evaluation and diagnosis of the impairment.

2. *Constitutional symptoms or signs*, as used in these listings, means severe fatigue, fever, malaise, or involuntary weight loss. *Severe fatigue* means a frequent sense

of exhaustion that results in significantly reduced physical activity or mental function. *Malaise* means frequent feelings of illness, bodily discomfort, or lack of well-being that result in significantly reduced physical activity or mental function.

3. *Disseminated* means that a condition is spread over a considerable area. The type and extent of the spread will depend on your specific disease.

4. *Dysfunction* means that one or more of the body regulatory mechanisms are impaired, causing either an excess or deficiency of immunocompetent cells or their products.

5. *Extra-articular* means "other than the joints"; for example, an organ(s) such as the heart, lungs, kidneys, or skin.

6. *Inability to ambulate effectively* has the same meaning as in 1.00B2b.

7. *Inability to perform fine and gross movements effectively* has the same meaning as in 1.00B2c.

8. *Major peripheral joints* has the same meaning as in 1.00F.

9. *Persistent* means that a sign(s) or symptom(s) has continued over time. The precise meaning will depend on the specific immune system disorder, the usual course of the disorder, and the other circumstances of your clinical course.

10. *Recurrent* means that a condition that previously responded adequately to an appropriate course of treatment returns after a period of remission or regression. The precise meaning, such as the extent of response or remission and the time periods involved, will depend on the specific disease or condition you have, the body system affected, the usual course of the disorder and its treatment, and the other facts of your particular case.

11. *Resistant to treatment* means that a condition did not respond adequately to an appropriate course of treatment. Whether a response is adequate or a course of treatment is appropriate will depend on the specific disease or condition you have, the body system affected, the usual course of the disorder and its treatment, and the other facts of your particular case.

12. *Severe* means medical severity as used by the medical community. The term does not have the same meaning as it does when we use it in connection with a finding at the second step of the sequential evaluation processes in §§ 404.1520, 416.920, and 416.924.

D. *How do we document and evaluate the listed autoimmune disorders?*

1. *Systemic lupus erythematosus (14.02).*

a. *General.* Systemic lupus erythematosus (SLE) is a chronic inflammatory disease that can affect any organ or body system. It is frequently, but not always, accompanied by constitutional symptoms or signs (severe fatigue, fever, malaise, involuntary weight loss). Major organ or body system involvement can include: Respiratory (pleuritis, pneumonitis), cardiovascular (endocarditis, myocarditis, pericarditis, vasculitis), renal (glomerulonephritis), hematologic (anemia, leukopenia, thrombocytopenia), skin (photosensitivity), neurologic (seizures), mental (anxiety, fluctuating cognition ("lupus fog"), mood disorders, organic brain syndrome, psychosis), or immune system disorders (inflammatory arthritis). Immunologically, there is an array of circulating serum auto-antibodies and pro- and anti-coagulant proteins that may occur in a highly variable pattern.

b. *Documentation of SLE.* Generally, but not always, the medical evidence will show that your SLE satisfies the criteria in the current "Criteria for the Classification of Systemic Lupus Erythematosus" by the American College of Rheumatology found in the most recent edition of the *Primer on the Rheumatic Diseases* published by the Arthritis Foundation.

2. *Systemic vasculitis (14.03).*

a. *General.*

(i) Vasculitis is an inflammation of blood vessels. It may occur acutely in association with adverse drug reactions, certain chronic infections, and occasionally, malignancies. More often, it is chronic and the cause is unknown. Symptoms vary depending on which blood vessels are involved. Systemic vasculitis may also be associated with other autoimmune disorders; for example, SLE or dermatomyositis.

(ii) There are several clinical patterns, including but not limited to polyarteritis nodosa, Takayasu's arteritis (aortic arch arteritis), giant cell arteritis (temporal arteritis), and Wegener's granulomatosis.

b. *Documentation of systemic vasculitis.* Angiography or tissue biopsy confirms a diagnosis of systemic vasculitis when the disease is suspected clinically. When you have had angiography or tissue biopsy for systemic vasculitis, we will make every reasonable effort to obtain reports of the results of that procedure. However, we will not purchase angiography or tissue biopsy.

3. *Systemic sclerosis (scleroderma) (14.04).*

a. *General.* Systemic sclerosis (scleroderma) constitutes a spectrum of disease in which thickening of the skin is the clinical hallmark. Raynaud's phenomenon, often medically severe and progressive, is present frequently and may be the peripheral manifestation of a vasospastic abnormality in the heart, lungs, and kidneys. The CREST syndrome (calcinosis, Raynaud's phenomenon, esophageal dysmotility, sclerodactyly, and telangiectasia) is a variant that may slowly progress over years to the generalized process, systemic sclerosis.

b. *Diffuse cutaneous systemic sclerosis.* In diffuse cutaneous systemic sclerosis (also known as diffuse scleroderma), major organ or systemic involvement can include the gastrointestinal tract, lungs, heart, kidneys, and muscle in addition to skin or blood vessels. Although arthritis can occur, joint dysfunction results primarily from soft tissue/cutaneous thickening, fibrosis, and contractures.

c. *Localized scleroderma (linear scleroderma and morphea).*

(i) Localized scleroderma (linear scleroderma and morphea) is more common in children than in adults. However, this type of scleroderma can persist into adulthood. To assess the severity of the impairment, we need a description of the extent of involvement of linear scleroderma and the location of the lesions. For example, linear scleroderma involving the arm but not crossing any joints is not as functionally limiting as sclerodactyly (scleroderma localized to the fingers). Linear scleroderma of a lower extremity involving skin thickening and atrophy of underlying muscle or bone can result in contractures and leg length discrepancy. In such cases, we may evaluate your impairment under the musculoskeletal listings (1.00).

(ii) When there is isolated morphea of the face causing facial disfigurement from unilateral hypoplasia of the mandible, maxilla, zygoma, or orbit, adjudication may be more appropriate under the criteria in the affected body system, such as special senses and speech (2.00) or mental disorders (12.00).

(iii) Chronic variants of these syndromes include disseminated morphea, Shulman's disease (diffuse fasciitis with eosinophilia), and eosinophilia-myalgia syndrome (often associated with toxins such as toxic oil or contaminated tryptophan), all of which can impose medically severe musculoskeletal dysfunction and may also lead to restrictive pulmonary disease. We evaluate these variants of the disease under the criteria in the musculoskeletal listings (1.00) or respiratory system listings (3.00).

d. *Documentation of systemic sclerosis (scleroderma).* Documentation involves differentiating the clinical features of systemic sclerosis (scleroderma) from other autoimmune disorders. However, there may be an overlap.

4. *Polymyositis and dermatomyositis (14.05).*

a. *General.* Polymyositis and dermatomyositis are related disorders that are characterized by an inflammatory process in striated muscle, occurring alone or in association with other autoimmune disorders or malignancy. The most common manifestations are symmetric weakness, and less frequently, pain and tenderness of the proximal limb-girdle (shoulder or pelvic) musculature. There may also be involvement of the cervical, cricopharyngeal, esophageal, intercostal, and diaphragmatic muscles.

b. *Documentation of polymyositis and dermatomyositis.* Generally, but not always, polymyositis is associated with elevated serum muscle enzymes (creatine phosphokinase (CPK), aminotransferases, and aldolase), and characteristic abnormalities on electromyography and muscle biopsy. In dermatomyositis there are characteristic skin findings in addition to the findings of polymyositis. When you have had electromyography or muscle biopsy for polymyositis or dermatomyositis, we will make every reasonable effort to obtain reports of the results of that procedure. However, we will not purchase electromyography or muscle biopsy.

c. *Additional information about how we evaluate polymyositis and dermatomyositis under the listings.*

(i) Weakness of your pelvic girdle muscles that results in your inability to rise independently from a squatting or sitting position or to climb stairs may be an indication that you are unable to ambulate effectively. Weakness of your shoulder girdle muscles may result in your inability to perform lifting, carrying, and reaching overhead, and also may seriously affect your ability to perform activities requiring fine movements. We evaluate these limitations under 14.05A.

(ii) We use the malignant neoplastic diseases listings (13.00) to evaluate malignancies associated with polymyositis or dermatomyositis. We evaluate the involvement of other organs/body systems under the criteria for the listings in the affected body system.

5. *Undifferentiated and mixed connective tissue disease (14.06).*

a. *General.* This listing includes syndromes with clinical and immunologic features of several autoimmune disorders, but which do not satisfy the criteria for any of the specific disorders described. For example, you may have clinical features of SLE and systemic vasculitis, and the serologic (blood test) findings of rheumatoid arthritis.

b. *Documentation of undifferentiated and mixed connective tissue disease.* Undifferentiated connective tissue disease is diagnosed when clinical features and serologic (blood test) findings, such as rheumatoid factor or antinuclear antibody (consistent with an autoimmune disorder) are present but do not satisfy the criteria for a specific disease. Mixed connective tissue disease (MCTD) is diagnosed when clinical features and serologic findings of two or more autoimmune diseases overlap.

6. *Inflammatory arthritis (14.09).*

a. *General.* The spectrum of inflammatory arthritis includes a vast array of disorders that differ in cause, course, and outcome. Clinically, inflammation of major peripheral joints may be the dominant manifestation causing difficulties with ambulation or fine and gross movements; there may be joint pain, swelling, and tenderness. The arthritis may affect other joints, or cause less limitation in ambulation or the performance of fine and gross movements. However, in combination with extra-articular features, including constitutional symptoms or signs (severe fatigue, fever, malaise, involuntary weight loss), inflammatory arthritis may result in an extreme limitation.

b. *Inflammatory arthritis involving the axial spine (spondyloarthropathy).* In adults, inflammatory arthritis involving the axial spine may be associated with disorders such as:

(i) Reiter's syndrome;

(ii) Ankylosing spondylitis;

(iii) Psoriatic arthritis;

(iv) Whipple's disease;

(v) Behçet's disease; and

(vi) Inflammatory bowel disease.

c. *Inflammatory arthritis involving the peripheral joints.* In adults, inflammatory arthritis involving peripheral joints may be associated with disorders such as:

(i) Rheumatoid arthritis;

(ii) Sjögren's syndrome;

(iii) Psoriatic arthritis;

(iv) Crystal deposition disorders (gout and pseudogout);

(v) Lyme disease; and

(vi) Inflammatory bowel disease.

d. *Documentation of inflammatory arthritis.* Generally, but not always, the diagnosis of inflammatory arthritis is based on the clinical features and serologic findings described in the most recent edition of the Primer on the Rheumatic Diseases published by the Arthritis Foundation.

e. *How we evaluate inflammatory arthritis under the listings.*

(i) Listing-level severity in 14.09A and 14.09C1 is shown by an impairment that results in an "extreme" (very serious) limitation. In 14.09A, the criterion is satisfied with persistent inflammation or deformity in one major peripheral weight-bearing joint resulting in the inability to ambulate effectively (as defined in 14.00C6) or one major peripheral joint in each upper extremity resulting in the inability to perform fine and gross movements effectively (as defined in 14.00C7). In 14.09C1, if you have the required ankylosis (fixation) of your cervical or dorsolumbar spine, we will find that you have an extreme limitation in your ability to see in front of you, above you, and to the side. Therefore, inability to ambulate effectively is implicit in 14.09C1, even though you might not require bilateral upper limb assistance.

(ii) Listing-level severity is shown in 14.09B, 14.09C2, and 14.09D by inflammatory arthritis that involves various combinations of complications of one or more major peripheral joints or other joints, such as inflammation or deformity, extra-articular features, repeated manifestations, and constitutional symptoms or signs. Extra-articular impairments may also meet listings in other body systems.

(iii) Extra-articular features of inflammatory arthritis may involve any body system; for example: Musculoskeletal (heel enthesopathy), ophthalmologic (iridocyclitis, keratoconjunctivitis sicca, uveitis), pulmonary (pleuritis, pulmonary fibrosis or nodules, restrictive lung disease), cardiovascular (aortic valve insufficiency, arrhythmias, coronary arteritis, myocarditis, pericarditis, Raynaud's phenomenon, systemic vasculitis), renal (amyloidosis of the kidney), hematologic (chronic anemia, thrombocytopenia), neurologic (peripheral neuropathy, radiculopathy, spinal cord or cauda equina compression with sensory and motor loss), mental (cognitive dysfunction, poor memory), and immune system (Felty's syndrome (hypersplenism with compromised immune competence)).

(iv) If both inflammation and chronic deformities are present, we evaluate your impairment under the criteria of any appropriate listing.

7. *Sjögren's syndrome (14.10).*

a. *General.*

(i) Sjögren's syndrome is an immune-mediated disorder of the exocrine glands. Involvement of the lacrimal and salivary glands is the hallmark feature, resulting in symptoms of dry eyes and dry mouth, and possible complications, such as corneal damage, blepharitis (eyelid inflammation), dysphagia (difficulty in swallowing), dental caries, and the inability to speak for extended periods of time. Involvement of the exocrine glands of the upper airways may result in persistent dry cough.

(ii) Many other organ systems may be involved, including musculoskeletal (arthritis, myositis), respiratory (interstitial fibrosis), gastrointestinal (dysmotility, dysphagia, involuntary weight loss), genitourinary (interstitial cystitis, renal tubular acidosis), skin (purpura, vasculitis), neurologic (central nervous system disorders, cranial and peripheral neuropathies), mental (cognitive dysfunction, poor memory), and neoplastic (lymphoma). Severe fatigue and malaise are frequently reported. Sjögren's syndrome may be associated with other autoimmune disorders (for example, rheumatoid arthritis or SLE); usually the clinical features of the associated disorder predominate.

b. *Documentation of Sjögren's syndrome.* If you have Sjögren's syndrome, the medical evidence will generally, but not always, show that your disease satisfies the criteria in the current "Criteria for the Classification of Sjögren's Syndrome" by the American College of Rheumatology found in the most recent edition of the *Primer on the Rheumatic Diseases* published by the Arthritis Foundation.

E. How do we document and evaluate immune deficiency disorders, excluding HIV infection?

1. *General.*

a. Immune deficiency disorders can be classified as:

(i) *Primary* (congenital); for example, X-linked agammaglobulinemia, thymic hypoplasia (DiGeorge syndrome), severe combined immunodeficiency (SCID), chronic granulomatous disease (CGD), C1 esterase inhibitor deficiency.

(ii) *Acquired;* for example, medication-related.

b. Primary immune deficiency disorders are seen mainly in children. However, recent advances in the treatment of these disorders have allowed many affected children to survive well into adulthood. Occasionally, these disorders are first diagnosed in adolescence or adulthood.

2. *Documentation of immune deficiency disorders.* The medical evidence must include documentation of the specific type of immune deficiency. Documentation may be by laboratory evidence or by other generally acceptable methods consistent with the prevailing state of medical knowledge and clinical practice.

3. *Immune deficiency disorders treated by stem cell transplantation.*

a. *Evaluation in the first 12 months.* If you undergo stem cell transplantation for your immune deficiency disorder, we will consider you disabled until at least 12 months from the date of the transplant.

b. *Evaluation after the 12-month period has elapsed.* After the 12-month period has elapsed, we will consider any residuals of your immune deficiency disorder as well as any residual impairment(s) resulting from the treatment, such as complications arising from:

(i) Graft-versus-host (GVH) disease.

(ii) Immunosuppressant therapy, such as frequent infections.

(iii) Significant deterioration of other organ systems.

4. *Medication-induced immune suppression.* Medication effects can result in varying degrees of immune suppression, but most resolve when the medication is ceased. However, if you are prescribed medication for long-term immune suppression, such as after an organ transplant, we will evaluate:

a. The frequency and severity of infections.

b. Residuals from the organ transplant itself, after the 12-month period has elapsed.

c. Significant deterioration of other organ systems.

F. How do we document and evaluate HIV infection?

Any individual with HIV infection, including one with a diagnosis of acquired immune deficiency syndrome (AIDS), may be found disabled under 14.11 if his or her impairment meets the criteria in that listing or is medically equivalent to the criteria in that listing.

1. *Documentation of HIV infection.*

a. *Definitive documentation of HIV infection.* We may document a diagnosis of HIV infection by positive findings on one or more of the following definitive laboratory tests:

(i) HIV antibody screening test (for example, enzyme immunoassay, or EIA), confirmed by a supplemental HIV antibody test such as the Western blot (immunoblot), an immunofluorescence assay, or an HIV-1/HIV-2 antibody differentiation immunoassay.

(ii) HIV nucleic acid (DNA or RNA) detection test (for example, polymerase chain reaction, or PCR).

(iii) HIV p24 antigen (p24Ag) test.

(iv) Isolation of HIV in viral culture.

(v) Other tests that are highly specific for detection of HIV and that are consistent with the prevailing state of medical knowledge.

b. We will make every reasonable effort to obtain the results of your laboratory testing. Pursuant to §§ 404.1519f and 416.919f, we will purchase examinations or tests necessary to make a determination in your claim if no other acceptable documentation exists.

c. *Other acceptable documentation of HIV infection.* We may also document HIV infection without definitive laboratory evidence.

(i) We will accept a persuasive report from a physician that a positive diagnosis of your HIV infection was confirmed by an appropriate laboratory test(s), such as those described in 14.00F1a. To be persuasive, this report must state that you had the appropriate definitive laboratory test(s) for diagnosing your HIV infection and provide the results. The report must also be consistent with the remaining evidence of record.

(ii) We may also document HIV infection by the medical history, clinical and laboratory findings, and diagnosis(es) indicated in the medical evidence, provided that such documentation is consistent with the prevailing state of medical knowledge and clinical practice and is consistent with the other evidence in your case record. For example, we will accept a diagnosis of HIV infection without definitive laboratory evidence of the HIV infection if you have an opportunistic disease that is predictive of a defect in cell-mediated immunity (for example, toxoplasmosis of the brain or Pneumocystis pneumonia (PCP)), and there is no other known cause of diminished resistance to that disease (for example, long-term steroid treatment or lymphoma). In such cases, we will make every reasonable effort to obtain full details of the history, medical findings, and results of testing.

2. *Documentation of the manifestations of HIV infection.*

a. *Definitive documentation of manifestations of HIV infection.* We may document manifestations of HIV infection by positive findings on definitive laboratory tests, such as culture, microscopic examination of biopsied tissue or other material (for example, bronchial washings), serologic tests, or on other generally acceptable definitive tests consistent with the prevailing state of medical knowledge and clinical practice.

b. We will make every reasonable effort to obtain the results of your laboratory testing. Pursuant to §§ 404.1519f and 416.919f, we will purchase examinations or tests necessary to make a determination of your claim if no other acceptable documentation exists.

c. *Other acceptable documentation of manifestations of HIV infection.* We may also document manifestations of HIV infection without definitive laboratory evidence.

(i) We will accept a persuasive report from a physician that a positive diagnosis of your manifestation of HIV infection was confirmed by an appropriate laboratory test(s). To be persuasive, this report must state that you had the appropriate definitive laboratory test(s) for diagnosing your manifestation of HIV infection and provide the results. The report must also be consistent with the remaining evidence of record.

(ii) We may also document manifestations of HIV infection without the definitive laboratory evidence described in 14.00F2a, provided that such documentation is consistent with the prevailing state of medical knowledge and clinical practice and is consistent with the other evidence in your case record. For example, many conditions are now commonly diagnosed based on some or all of the following: Medical history, clinical manifestations, laboratory findings (including appropriate medically acceptable imaging), and treatment responses. In such cases, we will make every reasonable effort to obtain full details of the history, medical findings, and results of testing.

3. *Disorders associated with HIV infection (14.11A–E).*

a. *Multicentric Castleman disease* (MCD, 14.11A) affects multiple groups of lymph nodes and organs containing lymphoid tissue. This widespread involvement distinguishes MCD from *localized* (or unicentric) Castleman disease, which affects only a single set of lymph nodes. While not a cancer, MCD is known as a lymphoproliferative disorder. Its clinical presentation and progression is similar to that of lymphoma, and its treatment may include radiation or chemotherapy. We require characteristic findings on microscopic examination of the biopsied lymph nodes or other generally acceptable methods consistent with the prevailing state of medical knowledge and clinical practice to establish the diagnosis. Localized (or unicentric) Castleman disease does not meet or medically equal the criterion in 14.11A, but we may evaluate it under the criteria in 14.11H or 14.11I.

b. *Primary central nervous system lymphoma* (PCNSL, 14.11B) originates in the brain, spinal cord, meninges, or eye. Imaging tests (for example, MRI) of the brain, while not diagnostic, may show a single lesion or multiple lesions in the white matter of the brain. We require characteristic findings on microscopic examination of the cerebral spinal fluid or of the biopsied brain tissue, or other generally acceptable methods consistent with the prevailing state of medical knowledge and clinical practice to establish the diagnosis.

c. *Primary effusion lymphoma* (PEL, 14.11C) is also known as body cavity lymphoma. We require characteristic findings on microscopic examination of the effusion fluid or of the biopsied tissue from the affected internal organ, or other generally acceptable methods consistent with the prevailing state of medical knowledge and clinical practice to establish the diagnosis.

d. *Progressive multifocal leukoencephalopathy* (PML, 14.11D) is a progressive neurological degenerative syndrome caused by the John Cunningham (JC) virus in immunosuppressed individuals. Clinical findings of PML include clumsiness, progressive weakness, and visual and speech changes. Personality and cognitive changes may also occur. We require appropriate clinical findings, characteristic white matter lesions on MRI, and a positive PCR test for the JC virus in the cerebrospinal fluid to establish the diagnosis. We also accept a positive brain biopsy for JC virus or other generally acceptable methods consistent with the prevailing state of medical knowledge and clinical practice to establish the diagnosis.

e. *Pulmonary Kaposi sarcoma* (Kaposi sarcoma in the lung, 14.11E) is the most serious form of Kaposi sarcoma (KS). Other internal KS tumors (for example, tumors of the gastrointestinal tract) have a more variable prognosis. We require characteristic findings on microscopic examination of the induced sputum, bronchoalveolar lavage washings, or of the biopsied transbronchial tissue, or by other generally acceptable methods consistent with the prevailing state of medical knowledge and clinical practice to establish the diagnosis.

4. *CD4 measurement (14.11F).* To evaluate your HIV infection under 14.11F, we require one measurement of your absolute CD4 count (also known as CD4 count or CD4+ T-helper lymphocyte count). This measurement must occur within the period we are considering in connection with your application or continuing disability review. If you have more than one measurement of your absolute CD4 count within this period, we will use your lowest absolute CD4 count.

5. *Measurement of CD4 and either body mass index or hemoglobin*(14.11G). To evaluate your HIV infection under 14.11G, we require one measurement of your absolute CD4 count or your CD4 percentage, and either a measurement of your body mass index (BMI) or your hemoglobin. These measurements must occur within the period we are considering in connection with your application or continuing disability review. If you have more than one measurement of your CD4 (absolute count or percentage), BMI, or hemoglobin within this period, we will use the lowest of your CD4 (absolute count or percentage), BMI, or hemoglobin. The date of your lowest CD4 (absolute count or percentage) measurement may be different from the date of your lowest BMI or hemoglobin measurement. We calculate your BMI using the formulas in 5.00G2.

6. *Complications of HIV infection requiring hospitalization (14.11H).*

a. Complications of HIV infection may include infections (common or opportunistic), cancers, and other conditions. Examples of complications that may result in hospitalization include: Depression; diarrhea; immune reconstitution inflammatory syndrome; malnutrition; and PCP and other severe infections.

b. Under 14.11H, we require three hospitalizations within a 12-month period that are at least 30 days apart and that result from a complication(s) of HIV infection. The hospitalizations may be for the same complication or different complications of HIV infection and are not limited to the examples of complications that may result in hospitalization listed in 14.00F6a. All three hospitalizations must occur within the period we are considering in connection with your application or continuing disability review. Each hospitalization must last at least 48 hours, including hours in a hospital emergency department immediately before the hospitalization.

c. We will use the rules on medical equivalence in §§ 404.1526 and 416.926 to evaluate your HIV infection if you have fewer, but longer, hospitalizations, or more frequent, but shorter, hospitalizations, or if you receive nursing, rehabilitation, or other care in alternative settings.

7. *HIV infection manifestations specific to women.*

a. General. Most women with severe immunosuppression secondary to HIV infection exhibit the typical opportunistic infections and other conditions, such as PCP, *Candida* esophagitis, wasting syndrome, cryptococcosis, and toxoplasmosis. However, HIV infection may have different manifestations in women than in men. Adjudicators must carefully scrutinize the medical evidence and be alert to the variety of medical conditions specific to, or common in, women with HIV infection that may affect their ability to function in the workplace.

b. Additional considerations for evaluating HIV infection in women. Many of these manifestations (for example, vulvovaginal candidiasis or pelvic inflammatory disease) occur in women with or without HIV infection, but can be more severe or resistant to treatment, or occur more frequently in a woman whose immune system is suppressed. Therefore, when evaluating the claim of a woman with HIV infection, it is important to consider gynecologic and other problems specific to women, including any associated symptoms (for example, pelvic pain), in assessing the severity of the impairment and resulting functional limitations. We may evaluate manifestations of HIV infection in women under 14.11H-I, or under the criteria for the appropriate body system (for example, cervical cancer under 13.23).

8. *HIV-associated dementia* (HAD). HAD is an advanced neurocognitive disorder, characterized by a significant decline in cognitive functioning. We evaluate HAD under 14.11I. Other names associated with neurocognitive disorders due to HIV infection include: AIDS dementia complex, HIV dementia, HIV encephalopathy, and major neurocognitive disorder due to HIV infection.

G. How do we consider the effects of treatment in evaluating your autoimmune disorder, immune deficiency disorder, or HIV infection?

1. *General.* If your impairment does not otherwise meet the requirements of a listing, we will consider your medical treatment in terms of its effectiveness in improving the signs, symptoms, and laboratory abnormalities of your specific immune system disorder or its manifestations, and in terms of any side effects that limit your functioning. We will make every reasonable effort to obtain a specific description of the treatment you receive (including surgery) for your immune system disorder. We consider:

a. The effects of medications you take.

b. Adverse side effects (acute and chronic).

c. The intrusiveness and complexity of your treatment (for example, the dosing schedule, need for injections).

d. The effect of treatment on your mental functioning (for example, cognitive changes, mood disturbance).

e. Variability of your response to treatment (see 14.00G2).

f. The interactive and cumulative effects of your treatments. For example, many individuals with immune system disorders receive treatment both for their immune system disorders and for the manifestations of the disorders or co-occurring impairments, such as treatment for HIV infection and hepatitis C. The interactive and cumulative effects of these treatments may be greater than the effects of each treatment considered separately.

g. The duration of your treatment.

h. Any other aspects of treatment that may interfere with your ability to function.

2. *Variability of your response to treatment.* Your response to treatment and the adverse or beneficial consequences of your treatment may vary widely. The effects of your treatment may be temporary or long term. For example, some individuals may show an initial positive response to a drug or combination of drugs followed by a decrease in effectiveness. When we evaluate your response to treatment and how your treatment may affect you, we consider such factors as disease activity before treatment, requirements for changes in therapeutic regimens, the time required for therapeutic effectiveness of a particular drug or drugs, the limited number of drug combinations that may be available for your impairment(s), and the time-limited efficacy of some drugs. For example, an individual with HIV infection or another immune deficiency disorder who develops pneumonia or tuberculosis may not respond to the same antibiotic regimen used in treating individuals without HIV infection or another immune deficiency disorder, or may not respond to an antibiotic that he or she responded to before. Therefore, we must consider the effects of your treatment on an individual basis, including the effects of your treatment on your ability to function.

3. *How we evaluate the effects of treatment for autoimmune disorders on your ability to function.* Some medications may have acute or long-term side effects. When we consider the effects of corticosteroids or other treatments for autoimmune disorders on your ability to function, we consider the factors in 14.00G1 and 14.00G2. Long-term corticosteroid treatment can cause ischemic necrosis of bone, posterior subcapsular cataract, weight gain, glucose intolerance, increased susceptibility to infection, and osteoporosis that may result in a loss of function. In addition, medications used in the treatment of autoimmune disorders may also have effects on mental functioning, including cognition (for example, memory), concentration, and mood.

4. *How we evaluate the effects of treatment for immune deficiency disorders, excluding HIV infection, on your ability to function.* When we consider the effects of your treatment for your immune deficiency disorder on your ability to function, we consider the factors in 14.00G1and 14.00G2. A frequent need for treatment such as intravenous immunoglobulin and gamma interferon therapy can be intrusive and interfere with your ability to work. We will also consider whether you have chronic side effects from these or other medications, including severe fatigue, fever, headaches, high blood pressure, joint swelling, muscle aches, nausea, shortness of breath, or limitations in mental function including cognition (for example, memory), concentration, and mood.

5. *How we evaluate the effects of treatment for HIV infection on your ability to function.*

a. *General.* When we consider the effects of antiretroviral drugs (including the effects of highly active antiretroviral therapy (HAART)) and the effects of treatments for the manifestations of HIV infection on your ability to function, we consider the factors in 14.00G1 and 14.00G2. Side effects of antiretroviral drugs include, but are not limited to: Bone marrow suppression, pancreatitis, gastrointestinal intolerance (nausea, vomiting, diarrhea), neuropathy, rash, hepatotoxicity, lipodystrophy (fat redistribution, such as "buffalo hump"), glucose intolerance, and lactic acidosis. In addition, medications used in the treatment of HIV infection may also have effects on mental functioning, including cognition (for example, memory), concentration, and mood, and may result in malaise, severe fatigue, joint and muscle pain, and insomnia. The symptoms of HIV infection and the side effects of medication may be indistinguishable from each other. We will consider all of your functional limitations, whether they result from your symptoms or signs of HIV infection or the side effects of your treatment.

b. *Structured treatment interruptions.* A structured treatment interruption (STI, also called a "drug holiday") is a treatment practice during which your treating source advises you to stop taking your medications temporarily. An STI in itself does not imply that your medical condition has improved; nor does it imply that you are noncompliant with your treatment because you are following your treating source's advice. Therefore, if you have stopped taking medication because your treating source prescribed or recommended an STI, we will not find that you are failing to follow treatment or draw inferences about the severity of your impairment on this fact alone. We will consider why your treating source has prescribed or recommended an STI and all the other information in your case record when we determine the severity of your impairment.

6. *When there is no record of ongoing treatment.* If you have not received ongoing treatment or have not had an ongoing relationship with the medical community despite the existence of a severe impairment(s), we will evaluate the medical severity and duration of your immune system disorder on the basis of the current objective medical evidence and other evidence in your case record, taking into consideration your medical history, symptoms, clinical and laboratory findings, and medical source opinions. If you have just begun treatment and we cannot determine whether you are disabled based on the evidence we have, we may need to wait to determine the effect of the treatment on your ability to function. The amount of time we need to wait will depend on the facts of your case. If you have not received treatment, you may not be able to show an impairment that meets the criteria of one of the immune system disorders listings, but your immune system disorder may medically equal a listing or be disabling based on a consideration of your residual functional capacity, age, education, and work experience.

H. *How do we consider your symptoms, including your pain, severe fatigue, and malaise?*

Your symptoms, including pain, severe fatigue, and malaise, may be important factors in our determination whether your immune system disorder(s) meets or medically equals a listing or in our determination whether you are otherwise able to work. In order for us to consider your symptoms, you must have medical signs or laboratory findings showing the existence of a medically determinable impairment(s) that could reasonably be expected to produce the symptoms. If you have such an impairment(s), we will evaluate the intensity, persistence, and functional effects of your symptoms using the rules throughout 14.00and in our other regulations. See §§ 404.1521, 404.1529, 416.921, and 416.929. Additionally, when we assess the credibility of your complaints about your symptoms and their functional effects, we will not draw any inferences from the fact that you do not receive treatment or that you are not following treatment without considering all of the relevant evidence in your case record, including any explanations you provide that may explain why you are not receiving or following treatment.

I. *How do we use the functional criteria in these listings?*

1. The following listings in this body system include standards for evaluating the functional limitations resulting from immune system disorders: 14.02B, for systemic lupus erythematosus; 14.03B, for systemic vasculitis; 14.04D, for systemic sclerosis (scleroderma); 14.05E, for polymyositis and dermatomyositis; 14.06B,

for undifferentiated and mixed connective tissue disease; 14.07C, for immune deficiency disorders, excluding HIV infection; 14.09D, for inflammatory arthritis;14.10B, for Sjögren's syndrome; and 14.11I, for HIV infection.

2. When we use one of the listings cited in 14.00I1, we will consider all relevant information in your case record to determine the full impact of your immune system disorder on your ability to function on a sustained basis. Important factors we will consider when we evaluate your functioning under these listings include, but are not limited to: Your symptoms, the frequency and duration of manifestations of your immune system disorder, periods of exacerbation and remission, and the functional impact of your treatment, including the side effects of your medication.

3. As used in these listings, "repeated" means that the manifestations occur on an average of three times a year, or once every 4 months, each lasting 2 weeks or more; or the manifestations do not last for 2 weeks but occur substantially more frequently than three times in a year or once every 4 months; or they occur less frequently than an average of three times a year or once every 4 months but last substantially longer than 2 weeks. Your impairment will satisfy this criterion regardless of whether you have the same kind of manifestation repeatedly, all different manifestations, or any other combination of manifestations; for example, two of the same kind of manifestation and a different one. You must have the required number of manifestations with the frequency and duration required in this section. Also, the manifestations must occur within the period covered by your claim.

4. To satisfy the functional criterion in a listing, your immune system disorder must result in a "marked" level of limitation in one of three general areas of functioning: Activities of daily living, social functioning, or difficulties in completing tasks due to deficiencies in concentration, persistence, or pace. Functional limitation may result from the impact of the disease process itself on your mental functioning, physical functioning, or both your mental and physical functioning. This could result from persistent or intermittent symptoms, such as depression, severe fatigue, or pain, resulting in a limitation of your ability to do a task, to concentrate, to persevere at a task, or to perform the task at an acceptable rate of speed. You may also have limitations because of your treatment and its side effects (see 14.00G).

5. *Marked* limitation means that the signs and symptoms of your immune system disorder interfere seriously with your ability to function. Although we do not require the use of such a scale, "marked" would be the fourth point on a five-point scale consisting of no limitation, mild limitation, moderate limitation, marked limitation, and extreme limitation.

You may have a marked limitation when several activities or functions are impaired, or even when only one is impaired. Also, you need not be totally precluded from performing an activity to have a marked limitation, as long as the degree of limitation seriously interferes with your ability to function independently, appropriately, and effectively. The term "marked" does not imply that you must be confined to bed, hospitalized, or in a nursing home.

6. *Activities of daily living* include, but are not limited to, such activities as doing household chores, grooming and hygiene, using a post office, taking public transportation, or paying bills. We will find that you have a "marked" limitation of activities of daily living if you have a serious limitation in your ability to maintain a household or take public transportation because of symptoms, such as pain, severe fatigue, anxiety, or difficulty concentrating, caused by your immune system disorder (including manifestations of the disorder) or its treatment, even if you are able to perform some self-care activities.

7. *Social functioning* includes the capacity to interact independently, appropriately, effectively, and on a sustained basis with others. It includes the ability to communicate effectively with others. We will find that you have a "marked" limitation in maintaining social functioning if you have a serious limitation in social interaction on a sustained basis because of symptoms, such as pain, severe fatigue, anxiety, or difficulty concentrating, or a pattern of exacerbation and remission, caused by your immune system disorder (including manifestations of the disorder) or its treatment, even if you are able to communicate with close friends or relatives.

8. *Completing tasks in a timely manner* involves the ability to sustain concentration, persistence, or pace to permit timely completion of tasks commonly found in work settings. We will find that you have a "marked" limitation in completing tasks if you have a serious limitation in your ability to sustain concentration or pace adequate to complete work-related tasks because of symptoms, such as pain, severe fatigue, anxiety, or difficulty concentrating, caused by your immune system disorder (including manifestations of the disorder) or its treatment, even if you are able to do some routine activities of daily living.

J. *How do we evaluate your immune system disorder when it does not meet one of the listings?*

1. These listings are only examples of immune system disorders that we consider severe enough to prevent you from doing any gainful activity. If your impairment(s) does not meet the criteria of any of these listings, we must also consider whether you have an impairment(s) that satisfies the criteria of a listing in another body system.

2. Individuals with immune system disorders, including HIV infection, may manifest signs or symptoms of a mental impairment or of another physical impairment. For example, HIV infection may accelerate the onset of conditions such as diabetes or affect the course of or treatment options for diseases such as cardiovascular disease or hepatitis. We may evaluate these impairments under the affected body system.

3. If you have a severe medically determinable impairment(s) that does not meet a listing, we will determine whether your impairment(s) medically equals a listing. (See §§ 404.1526 and 416.926.) If it does not, you may or may not have the residual functional capacity to engage in substantial gainful activity. Therefore, we proceed to the fourth, and if necessary, the fifth steps of the sequential evaluation process in §§ 404.1520 and 416.920. We use the rules in §§ 404.1594, 416.994, and 416.994a as appropriate, when we decide whether you continue to be disabled.

14.01 Category of Impairments, Immune System Disorders

14.02 Systemic lupus erythematosus. As described in 14.00D1. With:

A. Involvement of two or more organs/body systems, with:

1. One of the organs/body systems involved to at least a moderate level of severity; and

2. At least two of the constitutional symptoms or signs (severe fatigue, fever, malaise, or involuntary weight loss).

OR

B. Repeated manifestations of SLE, with at least two of the constitutional symptoms or signs (severe fatigue, fever, malaise, or involuntary weight loss) and one of the following at the marked level:

1. Limitation of activities of daily living.

2. Limitation in maintaining social functioning.

3. Limitation in completing tasks in a timely manner due to deficiencies in concentration, persistence, or pace.

14.03 Systemic vasculitis. As described in 14.00D2. With:

A. Involvement of two or more organs/body systems, with:

1. One of the organs/body systems involved to at least a moderate level of severity; and

2. At least two of the constitutional symptoms or signs (severe fatigue, fever, malaise, or involuntary weight loss).

OR

B. Repeated manifestations of systemic vasculitis, with at least two of the constitutional symptoms or signs (severe fatigue, fever, malaise, or involuntary weight loss) and one of the following at the marked level:

1. Limitation of activities of daily living.

2. Limitation in maintaining social functioning.

3. Limitation in completing tasks in a timely manner due to deficiencies in concentration, persistence, or pace.

14.04 Systemic sclerosis (scleroderma) As described in 14.00D3. With:

A. Involvement of two or more organs/body systems, with:

1. One of the organs/body systems involved to at least a moderate level of severity; and

2. At least two of the constitutional symptoms or signs (severe fatigue, fever, malaise, or involuntary weight loss).

OR

B. With one of the following:

1. Toe contractures or fixed deformity of one or both feet, resulting in the inability to ambulate effectively as defined in 14.00C6; or

2. Finger contractures or fixed deformity in both hands, resulting in the inability to perform fine and gross movements effectively as defined in 14.00C7; or

3. Atrophy with irreversible damage in one or both lower extremities, resulting in the inability to ambulate effectively as defined in 14.00C6; or

4. Atrophy with irreversible damage in both upper extremities, resulting in the inability to perform fine and gross movements effectively as defined in 14.00C7.

OR

C. Raynaud's phenomenon, characterized by:

1. Gangrene involving at least two extremities; or

2. Ischemia with ulcerations of toes or fingers, resulting in the inability to ambulate effectively or to perform fine and gross movements effectively as defined in 14.00C6 and 14.00C7;

OR

D. Repeated manifestations of systemic sclerosis (scleroderma), with at least two of the constitutional symptoms or signs (severe fatigue, fever, malaise, or involuntary weight loss) and one of the following at the marked level:

1. Limitation of activities of daily living.

2. Limitation in maintaining social functioning.

3. Limitation in completing tasks in a timely manner due to deficiencies in concentration, persistence, or pace.

14.05 Polymyositis and dermatomyositis. As described in 14.00D4. With:

A. Proximal limb-girdle (pelvic or shoulder) muscle weakness, resulting in inability to ambulate effectively or inability to perform fine and gross movements effectively as defined in 14.00C6 and 14.00C7.

OR

B. Impaired swallowing (dysphagia) with aspiration due to muscle weakness.

OR

C. Impaired respiration due to intercostal and diaphragmatic muscle weakness.

OR

D. Diffuse calcinosis with limitation of joint mobility or intestinal motility.

OR

E. Repeated manifestations of polymyositis or dermatomyositis, with at least two of the constitutional symptoms or signs (severe fatigue, fever, malaise, or involuntary weight loss) and one of the following at the marked level:

1. Limitation of activities of daily living.

2. Limitation in maintaining social functioning.

3. Limitation in completing tasks in a timely manner due to deficiencies in concentration, persistence, or pace.

14.06 Undifferentiated and mixed connective tissue disease. As described in 14.00D5. With:

A. Involvement of two or more organs/body systems, with:

1. One of the organs/body systems involved to at least a moderate level of severity; and

2. At least two of the constitutional symptoms or signs (severe fatigue, fever, malaise, or involuntary weight loss).

OR

B. Repeated manifestations of undifferentiated or mixed connective tissue disease, with at least two of the constitutional symptoms or signs (severe fatigue, fever, malaise, or involuntary weight loss) and one of the following at the marked level:

1. Limitation of activities of daily living.

2. Limitation in maintaining social functioning.

3. Limitation in completing tasks in a timely manner due to deficiencies in concentration, persistence, or pace.

14.07 Immune deficiency disorders, excluding HIV infection. As described in 14.00E. With:

A. One or more of the following infections. The infection(s) must either be resistant to treatment or require hospitalization or intravenous treatment three or more times in a 12-month period.

1. Sepsis; or

2. Meningitis; or

3. Pneumonia; or

4. Septic arthritis; or

5. Endocarditis; or

6. Sinusitis documented by appropriate medically acceptable imaging.

OR

B. Stem cell transplantation as described under 14.00E3. Consider under a disability until at least 12 months from the date of transplantation. Thereafter, evaluate any residual impairment(s) under the criteria for the affected body system.

OR

C. Repeated manifestations of an immune deficiency disorder, with at least two of the constitutional symptoms or signs (severe fatigue, fever, malaise, or involuntary weight loss) and one of the following at the marked level:

1. Limitation of activities of daily living.

2. Limitation in maintaining social function.

3. Limitation in completing tasks in a timely manner due to deficiencies in concentration, persistence, or pace.

14.08 [Reserved]

14.09 Inflammatory arthritis. As described in 14.00D6. With:

A. Persistent inflammation or persistent deformity of:

1. One or more major peripheral weight-bearing joints resulting in the inability to ambulate effectively (as defined in 14.00C6); or

2. One or more major peripheral joints in each upper extremity resulting in the inability to perform fine and gross movements effectively (as defined in 14.00C7).

OR

B. Inflammation or deformity in one or more major peripheral joints with:

1. Involvement of two or more organs/body systems with one of the organs/body systems involved to at least a moderate level of severity; and

2. At least two of the constitutional symptoms or signs (severe fatigue, fever, malaise, or involuntary weight loss).

OR

C. Ankylosing spondylitis or other spondyloarthropathies, with:

1. Ankylosis (fixation) of the dorsolumbar or cervical spine as shown by appropriate medically acceptable imaging and measured on physical examination at 45° or more of flexion from the vertical position (zero degrees); or

2. Ankylosis (fixation) of the dorsolumbar or cervical spine as shown by appropriate medically acceptable imaging and measured on physical examination at 30° or more of flexion (but less than 45°) measured from the vertical position (zero degrees), and involvement of two or more organs/body systems with one of the organs/body systems involved to at least a moderate level of severity.

OR

D. Repeated manifestations of inflammatory arthritis, with at least two of the constitutional symptoms or signs (severe fatigue, fever, malaise, or involuntary weight loss) and one of the following at the marked level:

1. Limitation of activities of daily living.

2. Limitation in maintaining social functioning.

3. Limitation in completing tasks in a timely manner due to deficiencies in concentration, persistence, or pace.

14.10 Sjögren's syndrome. As described in 14.00D7. With:

A. Involvement of two or more organs/body systems, with:

1. One of the organs/body systems involved to at least a moderate level of severity; and

2. At least two of the constitutional symptoms or signs (severe fatigue, fever, malaise, or involuntary weight loss).

OR

B. Repeated manifestations of Sjögren's syndrome, with at least two of the constitutional symptoms or signs (severe fatigue, fever, malaise, or involuntary weight loss) and one of the following at the marked level:

1. Limitation of activities of daily living.

2. Limitation in maintaining social functioning.

3. Limitation in completing tasks in a timely manner due to deficiencies in concentration, persistence, or pace.

14.11 ***Human immunodeficiency virus (HIV) infection.*** With documentation as described in 14.00F1 and one of the following:

A. Multicentric (not localized or unicentric) Castleman disease affecting multiple groups of lymph nodes or organs containing lymphoid tissue (see 14.00F3a).

OR

B. Primary central nervous system lymphoma (see 14.00F3b).

OR

C. Primary effusion lymphoma (see 14.00F3c).

OR

D. Progressive multifocal leukoencephalopathy (see 14.00F3d).

OR

E. Pulmonary Kaposi sarcoma (see 14.00F3e).

OR

F. Absolute CD4 count of 50 cells/mm3 or less (see 14.00F4).

OR

G. Absolute CD4 count of less than 200 cells/mm3 or CD4 percentage of less than 14 percent, *and* one of the following (values do not have to be measured on the same date) (see 14.00F5):

1. BMI measurement of less than 18.5; or

2. Hemoglobin measurement of less than 8.0 grams per deciliter (g/dL).

OR

H. Complication(s) of HIV infection requiring at least three hospitalizations within a 12-month period and at least 30 days apart (see 14.00F6). Each hospitalization must last at least 48 hours, including hours in a hospital emergency department immediately before the hospitalization.

OR

I. Repeated (as defined in 14.00I3) manifestations of HIV infection, including those listed in 14.11A-H, but without the requisite findings for those listings (for example, Kaposi sarcoma not meeting the criteria in 14.11E), or other manifestations (including, but not limited to, cardiovascular disease (including myocarditis, pericardial effusion, pericarditis, endocarditis, or pulmonary arteritis), diarrhea, distal sensory polyneuropathy, glucose intolerance, gynecologic conditions (including cervical cancer or pelvic inflammatory disease, see 14.00F7), hepatitis, HIV-associated dementia, immune reconstitution inflammatory syndrome (IRIS), infections (bacterial, fungal, parasitic, or viral), lipodystrophy (lipoatrophy or lipohypertrophy), malnutrition, muscle weakness, myositis, neurocognitive or other mental limitations not meeting the criteria in 12.00, oral hairy leukoplakia, osteoporosis, pancreatitis, peripheral neuropathy) resulting in significant, documented symptoms or signs (for example, but not limited to, fever, headaches, insomnia, involuntary weight loss, malaise, nausea, night sweats, pain, severe fatigue, or vomiting) and one of the following at the marked level:

1. Limitation of activities of daily living.

2. Limitation in maintaining social functioning.

3. Limitation in completing tasks in a timely manner due to deficiencies in concentration, persistence, or pace.

APPENDIX B

Listing of Impairments (Child)

Disability Evaluation under Social Security

Listing of Impairments—Childhood Listings (Part B)

The following sections contain medical criteria that apply only to the evaluation of impairments in children under age 18.

100.00 Low Birth Weight and Failure to Thrive

A. What conditions do we evaluate under these listings? We evaluate low birth weight (LBW) in infants from birth to attainment of age 1 and failure to thrive (FTT) in infants and toddlers from birth to attainment of age 3.

B. How do we evaluate disability based on LBW under 100.04? In 100.04A and 100.04B, we use an infant's birth weight as documented by an original or certified copy of the infant's birth certificate or by a medical record signed by a physician. *Birth weight* means the first weight recorded after birth. In 100.04B, *gestational age* is the infant's age based on the date of conception as recorded in the medical record. If the infant's impairment meets the requirements for listing 100.04A or 100.04B, we will follow the rules in § 416.990(b)(11) of this chapter.

Source: Code of Federal Regulations, Title 20, Chapter III, Part 404, Subpart P, Appendix 1. Available online at https://www.govinfo.gov/app/details/CFR-2012-title20-vol2/CFR-2012-title20-vol2-part404-subpartP-app1.

C. How do we evaluate disability under 100.05?

1. *General.* We establish FTT with or without a known cause when we have documentation of an infant's or toddler's growth failure and developmental delay from an acceptable medical source(s) as defined in § 416.913(a) of this chapter. We require documentation of growth measurements in 100.05A and developmental delay in 100.05B or 100.05C within the same consecutive 12-month period. The dates of developmental testing and reports may be different from the dates of the growth measurements. After the attainment of age 3, we evaluate growth failure under the affected body system(s).

2. *Growth failure.* Under 100.05A, we use the appropriate table(s) under 105.08B in the digestive system to determine whether a child's growth is less than the third percentile. The child does not need to have a digestive disorder for the purposes of 100.05.

a. For children from birth to attainment of age 2, we use the weight-for-length table corresponding to the child's gender (Table I or Table II).

b. For children age 2 to the attainment of age 3, we use the body mass index (BMI)-for-age table corresponding to the child's gender (Table III or Table IV).

c. BMI is the ratio of a child's weight to the square of his or her height. We calculate BMI using the formulas in 105.00G2c.

d. *Growth measurements.* The weight-for-length measurements for children from birth to attainment of age 2 and BMI-for-age measurements in children age 2 to attainment of age 3 that are required for this listing must be obtained within a 12-month period and at least 60 days apart. If a child attains 2 during the evaluation period, additional measurements are not needed. Any measurements taken before the child attains age 2 can be used to evaluate the impairment under the appropriate listing for the child's age. If the child attains age 3 during the evaluation period, the measurements can be used to evaluate the impairment in the affected body system.

3. *Developmental Delay.*

a. Under 100.05B and C, we use reports from acceptable medical sources to establish delay in a child's development.

b. Under 100.05B, we document the severity of developmental delay with results from a standardized developmental assessment, which compares a child's level of development to the level typically expected for his or her chronological age. If the child was born prematurely, we may use the corrected chronological age (CCA) for comparison. (See § 416.924b(b) of this chapter.) CCA is the chronological age adjusted by a period of gestational prematurity. CCA = (chronological age)—(number of weeks premature). Acceptable medical sources or early intervention specialists, physical or occupational therapists, and other sources may conduct standardized developmental assessments and developmental screenings. The results of these tests and screening must be accompanied by a statement or records from an acceptable medical source who established the child has a developmental delay.

c. Under 100.05C, when there are no results from a standardized developmental assessment in the case record, we need narrative developmental reports from the child's medical sources in sufficient detail to assess the severity of his or her developmental delay. A narrative developmental report is based on clinical observations, progress notes, and well-baby check-ups. To meet the requirements for 100.05C, the report must include: the child's developmental history; examination findings (with abnormal findings noted on repeated examinations); and an overall assessment of the child's development (that is, more than one or two isolated skills) by the medical source. Some narrative developmental reports may include results from developmental screening tests, which can identify a child who is not developing or achieving skills within expected timeframes. Although medical sources may refer to screening test results as supporting evidence in the narrative developmental report, screening test results alone cannot establish a diagnosis or the severity of developmental delay.

D. How do we evaluate disorders that do not meet one of our listings?

1. We may find infants disabled due to other disorders when their birth weights are greater than 1200 grams but less than 2000 grams and their weight and gestational age do not meet listing 100.04. The most common disorders of prematurity and LBW include retinopathy of prematurity (ROP), chronic lung disease of infancy (CLD, previously known as bronchopulmonary dysplasia, or BPD), intraventricular hemorrhage (IVH), necrotizing enterocolitis (NEC), and periventricular leukomalacia (PVL). Other disorders include poor nutrition and growth failure, hearing disorders, seizure disorders, cerebral palsy, and developmental disorders. We evaluate these disorders under the affected body systems.

2. We may evaluate infants and toddlers with growth failure that is associated with a known medical disorder under the body system of that medical disorder, for example, the respiratory or digestive body systems.

3. If an infant or toddler has a severe medical determinable impairment(s) that does not meet the criteria of any listing, we must also consider whether the child has an impairment(s) that medically equals a listing (see § 416.926 of this chapter). If the child's impairment(s) does not meet or medically equal a listing, we will determine whether the child's impairment(s) functionally equals the listings (see § 416.926a of this chapter) considering the factors in § 416.924a of this chapter. We use the rules in § 416.994a of this chapter when we decide whether a child continues to be disabled.

100.01 Category of Impairments, Low Birth Weight and Failure to Thrive

100.04 Low birth weight in infants from birth to attainment of age 1.

A. Birth weight (see 100.00B) of less than 1200 grams.

OR

B. The following gestational age and birth weight:

Gestational Age (in weeks)	Birth Weight
37–40	2000 grams or less
36	1875 grams or less
35	1700 grams or less
34	1500 grams or less
33	1325 grams or less
32	1250 grams or less

100.05 Failure to thrive in children from birth to attainment of age 3 (see 100.00C), documented by A and B, or A and C.

A. Growth failure as required in 1 or 2:

1. *For children from birth to attainment of age 2,* three weight-for-length measurements that are:

a. Within a consecutive 12-month period; and

b. At least 60 days apart; and

c. Less than the third percentile on the appropriate weight-for-length table under 105.08B1; or

2. *For children age 2 to attainment of age 3,* three BMI-for-age measurements that are:

a. Within a consecutive 12-month period; and

b. At least 60 days apart; and

c. Less than the third percentile on the appropriate BMI-for-age table under 105.08B2.

AND

B. Developmental delay (see 100.00C1 and C3), established by an acceptable medical source and documented by findings from one current report of a standardized developmental assessment (see 100.00C3b) that:

1. Shows development not more than two-thirds of the level typically expected for the child's age; or

2. Results in a valid score that is at least two standard deviations below the mean.

OR

C. Developmental delay (see 100.00C3), established by an acceptable medical source and documented by findings from two narrative developmental reports (see 100.00C3c) that:

1. Are dated at least 120 days apart (see 100.00C1); and

2. Indicate current development not more than two-thirds of the level typically expected for the child's age.

101.00 Musculoskeletal System

A. Disorders of the musculoskeletal system may result from hereditary, congenital, or acquired pathologic processes. Impairments may result from infectious, inflammatory, or degenerative processes, traumatic or developmental events, or neoplastic, vascular, or toxic/metabolic diseases.

B. Loss of function.

1. General. We evaluate impairments with neurological causes under 111.00, as appropriate.

2. How we define loss of function in these listings.

a. General. Regardless of the cause(s) of a musculoskeletal impairment, functional loss for purposes of these listings is defined as the inability to ambulate effectively on a sustained basis for any reason, including pain associated with the underlying musculoskeletal impairment, or the inability to perform fine and gross movements effectively on a sustained basis for any reason, including pain associated with the underlying musculoskeletal impairment.

The inability to ambulate effectively or the inability to perform fine and gross movements effectively must have lasted, or be expected to last, for at least 12 months. For the purposes of these criteria, consideration of the ability to perform these activities must be from a physical standpoint alone. When there is an inability to perform these activities due to a mental impairment, the criteria in 112.00ff are to be used. We will determine whether a child can ambulate effectively or can perform fine and gross movements effectively based on the medical and other evidence in the case record, generally without developing additional evidence about the child's ability to perform the specific activities listed as examples in 101.00B2b(2) and (3) and 101.00B2c(2) and (3).

b. What we mean by inability to ambulate effectively.

(1) Definition. Inability to ambulate effectively means an extreme limitation of the ability to walk; i.e., an impairment that interferes very seriously with the

child's ability to independently initiate, sustain, or complete activities. Ineffective ambulation is defined generally as having insufficient lower extremity functioning (see 101.00J) to permit independent ambulation without the use of a hand-held assistive device(s) that limits the functioning of both upper extremities. (Listing 101.05C is an exception to this general definition because the child has the use of only one upper extremity due to amputation of a hand.)

(2) How we assess inability to ambulate effectively for children too young to be expected to walk independently. For children who are too young to be expected to walk independently, consideration of function must be based on assessment of limitations in the ability to perform comparable age-appropriate activities with the lower extremities, given normal developmental expectations. For such children, an extreme level of limitation means skills or performance at no greater than one-half of age-appropriate expectations based on an overall developmental assessment rather than on one or two isolated skills.

(3) How we assess inability to ambulate effectively for older children. Older children, who would be expected to be able to walk when compared to other children the same age who do not have impairments, must be capable of sustaining a reasonable walking pace over a sufficient distance to be able to carry out age-appropriate activities. They must have the ability to travel age-appropriately without extraordinary assistance to and from school or a place of employment.

Therefore, examples of ineffective ambulation for older children include, but are not limited to, the inability to walk without the use of a walker, two crutches or two canes, the inability to walk a block at a reasonable pace on rough or uneven surfaces, the inability to use standard public transportation, the inability to carry out age-appropriate school activities independently, and the inability to climb a few steps at a reasonable pace with the use of a single hand rail. The ability to walk independently about the child's home or a short distance at school without the use of assistive devices does not, in and of itself, constitute effective ambulation.

c. What we mean by inability to perform fine and gross movements effectively.

(1) *Definition*. Inability to perform fine and gross movements effectively means an extreme loss of function of both upper extremities; i.e., an impairment that interferes very seriously with the child's ability to independently initiate, sustain, or complete activities. To use their upper extremities effectively, a child must be capable of sustaining such functions as reaching, pushing, pulling, grasping, and fingering in an age-appropriate manner to be able to carry out age-appropriate activities.

(2) How we assess inability to perform fine and gross movements in very young children. For very young children, we consider limitations in the ability to perform comparable age-appropriate activities involving the upper extremities

compared to the ability of children the same age who do not have impairments. For such children, an extreme level of limitation means skills or performance at no greater than one-half of age-appropriate expectations based on an overall developmental assessment.

(3) How we assess inability to perform fine and gross movements in older children. For older children, examples of inability to perform fine and gross movements effectively include, but are not limited to, the inability to prepare a simple meal and feed oneself, the inability to take care of personal hygiene, or the inability to sort and handle papers or files, depending upon which activities are age-appropriate.

d. Pain or other symptoms. Pain or other symptoms may be an important factor contributing to functional loss. In order for pain or other symptoms to be found to affect a child's ability to function in an age-appropriate manner or to perform basic work activities, medical signs or laboratory findings must show the existence of a medically determinable impairment(s) that could reasonably be expected to produce the pain or other symptoms.

The musculoskeletal listings that include pain or other symptoms among their criteria also include criteria for limitations in functioning as a result of the listed impairment, including limitations caused by pain. It is, therefore, important to evaluate the intensity and persistence of such pain or other symptoms carefully in order to determine their impact on the child's functioning under these listings. See also §§ 404.1525(f) and 404.1529 of this part, and §§ 416.925(f) and 416.929 of part 416 of this chapter.

C. Diagnosis and evaluation.

1. General. Diagnosis and evaluation of musculoskeletal impairments should be supported, as applicable, by detailed descriptions of the joints, including ranges of motion, condition of the musculature (e.g., weakness, atrophy), sensory or reflex changes, circulatory deficits, and laboratory findings, including findings on x-ray or other appropriate medically acceptable imaging. Medically acceptable imaging includes, but is not limited to, x-ray imaging, computerized axial tomography (CAT scan) or magnetic resonance imaging (MRI), with or without contrast material, myelography, and radionuclear bone scans. "Appropriate" means that the technique used is the proper one to support the evaluation and diagnosis of the impairment.

2. Purchase of certain medically acceptable imaging. While any appropriate medically acceptable imaging is useful in establishing the diagnosis of musculoskeletal impairments, some tests, such as CAT scans and MRIs, are quite expensive, and we will not routinely purchase them. Some, such as myelograms, are invasive and may involve significant risk. We will not order such tests. However, when the results of any of these tests are part of the existing evidence in the case record we will consider them together with the other relevant evidence.

3. Consideration of electrodiagnostic procedures. Electrodiagnostic procedures may be useful in establishing the clinical diagnosis, but do not constitute alternative criteria to the requirements of 101.04.

D. The physical examination must include a detailed description of the rheumatological, orthopedic, neurological, and other findings appropriate to the specific impairment being evaluated. These physical findings must be determined on the basis of objective observation during the examination and not simply a report of the child's allegation; e.g., "He says his leg is weak, numb."

Alternative testing methods should be used to verify the abnormal findings; e.g., a seated straight-leg raising test in addition to a supine straight-leg raising test. Because abnormal physical findings may be intermittent, their presence over a period of time must be established by a record of ongoing management and evaluation. Care must be taken to ascertain that the reported examination findings are consistent with the child's age and activities.

E. Examination of the spine.

1. General. Examination of the spine should include a detailed description of gait, range of motion of the spine given quantitatively in degrees from the vertical position (zero degrees) or, for straight-leg raising from the sitting and supine position (zero degrees), any other appropriate tension signs, motor and sensory abnormalities, muscle spasm, when present, and deep tendon reflexes. Observations of the child during the examination should be reported; e.g., how he or she gets on and off the examination table.

Inability to walk on the heels or toes, to squat, or to arise from a squatting position, when appropriate, may be considered evidence of significant motor loss. However, a report of atrophy is not acceptable as evidence of significant motor loss without circumferential measurements of both thighs and lower legs, or both upper and lower arms, as appropriate, at a stated point above and below the knee or elbow given in inches or centimeters. Additionally, a report of atrophy should be accompanied by measurement of the strength of the muscle(s) in question generally based on a grading system of 0 to 5, with 0 being complete loss of strength and 5 being maximum strength. A specific description of atrophy of hand muscles is acceptable without measurements of atrophy but should include measurements of grip and pinch strength. However, because of the unreliability of such measurement in younger children, these data are not applicable to children under 5 years of age.

2. When neurological abnormalities persist. Neurological abnormalities may not completely subside after treatment or with the passage of time. Therefore, residual neurological abnormalities that persist after it has been determined clinically or by direct surgical or other observation that the ongoing or progressive condition is no longer present will not satisfy the required findings in 101.04. More serious neurological deficits (paraparesis, paraplegia) are to be evaluated under the criteria in 111.00ff.

F. Major joints refers to the major peripheral joints, which are the hip, knee, shoulder, elbow, wrist-hand, and ankle-foot, as opposed to other peripheral joints (e.g., the joints of the hand or forefoot) or axial joints (i.e., the joints of the spine.) The wrist and hand are considered together as one major joint, as are the ankle and foot. Since only the ankle joint, which consists of the juncture of the bones of the lower leg (tibia and fibula) with the hindfoot (tarsal bones), but not the forefoot, is crucial to weight bearing, the ankle and foot are considered separately in evaluating weight bearing.

G. Measurements of joint motion are based on the techniques described in the chapter on the extremities, spine, and pelvis in the current edition of the "Guides to the Evaluation of Permanent Impairment" published by the American Medical Association.

H. Documentation.

1. General. Musculoskeletal impairments frequently improve with time or respond to treatment. Therefore, a longitudinal clinical record is generally important for the assessment of severity and expected duration of an impairment unless the child is a newborn or the claim can be decided favorably on the basis of the current evidence.

2. Documentation of medically prescribed treatment and response. Many children, especially those who have listing-level impairments, will have received the benefit of medically prescribed treatment. Whenever evidence of such treatment is available it must be considered.

3. When there is no record of ongoing treatment. Some children will not have received ongoing treatment or have an ongoing relationship with the medical community despite the existence of a severe impairment(s). In such cases, evaluation will be made on the basis of the current objective medical evidence and other available evidence, taking into consideration the child's medical history, symptoms, and medical source opinions. Even though a child who does not receive treatment may not be able to show an impairment that meets the criteria of one of the musculoskeletal listings, the child may have an impairment(s) that is either medically or, in the case of a claim for benefits under part 416 of this chapter, functionally equivalent in severity to one of the listed impairments.

4. Evaluation when the criteria of a musculoskeletal listing are not met. These listings are only examples of common musculoskeletal disorders that are severe enough to find a child disabled. Therefore, in any case in which a child has a medically determinable impairment that is not listed, an impairment that does not meet the requirements of a listing, or a combination of impairments no one of which meets the requirements of a listing, we will consider whether the child's impairment(s) is medically or, in the case of a claim for benefits under part 416 of this chapter, functionally equivalent in severity to the criteria of a listing. (See §§ 404.1526, 416.926, and 416.926a.)

Individuals with claims for benefits under part 404, who have an impairment(s) with a level of severity that does not meet or equal the criteria of the musculoskeletal listings may or may not have the RFC that would enable them to engage in substantial gainful activity. Evaluation of the impairment(s) of these individuals should proceed through the final steps of the sequential evaluation process in §§ 404.1520 (or, as appropriate, the steps in the medical improvement review standard in §§ 404.1594).

I. Effects of treatment.

1. General. Treatments for musculoskeletal disorders may have beneficial effects or adverse side effects. Therefore, medical treatment (including surgical treatment) must be considered in terms of its effectiveness in ameliorating the signs, symptoms, and laboratory abnormalities of the disorder, and in terms of any side effects that may further limit the child.

2. Response to treatment. Response to treatment and adverse consequences of treatment may vary widely. For example, a pain medication may relieve a child's pain completely, partially, or not at all. It may also result in adverse effects, e.g., drowsiness, dizziness, or disorientation, that compromise the child's ability to function. Therefore, each case must be considered on an individual basis, and include consideration of the effects of treatment on the child's ability to function.

3. Documentation. A specific description of the drugs or treatment given (including surgery), dosage, frequency of administration, and a description of the complications or response to treatment should be obtained. The effects of treatment may be temporary or long-term. As such, the finding regarding the impact of treatment must be based on a sufficient period of treatment to permit proper consideration or judgment about future functioning.

J. Orthotic, prosthetic, or assistive devices.

1. General. Consistent with clinical practice, children with musculoskeletal impairments may be examined with and without the use of any orthotic, prosthetic, or assistive devices as explained in this section.

2. Orthotic devices. Examination should be with the orthotic device in place and should include an evaluation of the child's maximum ability to function effectively with the orthosis. It is unnecessary to routinely evaluate the child's ability to function without the orthosis in place. If the child has difficulty with, or is unable to use, the orthotic device, the medical basis for the difficulty should be documented. In such cases, if the impairment involves a lower extremity or extremities, the examination should include information on the child's ability to ambulate effectively without the device in place unless contraindicated by the medical judgment of a physician who has treated or examined the child.

3. Prosthetic devices. Examination should be with the prosthetic device in place. In amputations involving a lower extremity or extremities, it is unnecessary to

evaluate the child's ability to walk without the prosthesis in place. However, the child's medical ability to use a prosthesis to ambulate effectively, as defined in 101.00B2b, should be evaluated. The condition of the stump should be evaluated without the prosthesis in place.

4. Hand-held assistive devices. When a child with an impairment involving a lower extremity or extremities uses a hand-held assistive device, such as a cane, crutch or walker, examination should be with and without the use of the assistive device unless contraindicated by the medical judgment of a physician who has treated or examined the child. The child's ability to ambulate with and without the device provides information as to whether, or the extent to which, the child is able to ambulate without assistance. The medical basis for the use of any assistive device (e.g., instability, weakness) should be documented. The requirement to use a hand-held assistive device may also impact on the child's functional capacity by virtue of the fact that one or both upper extremities are not available for such activities as lifting, carrying, pushing, and pulling.

K. Disorders of the spine, listed in 101.04, result in limitations because of distortion of the bony and ligamentous architecture of the spine and associated impingement on nerve roots (including the cauda equina) or spinal cord. Such impingement on nerve tissue may result from a herniated nucleus pulposus, spinal stenosis, arachnoditis, or other miscellaneous conditions.

1. Herniated nucleus pulposus is a disorder frequently associated with the impingement of a nerve root, but occurs infrequently in children. Nerve root compression results in a specific neuro-anatomic distribution of symptoms and signs depending upon the nerve root(s) compromised.

2. Other miscellaneous conditions that may cause weakness of the lower extremities, sensory changes, areflexia, trophic ulceration, bladder or bowel incontinence, and that should be evaluated under 101.04 include, but are not limited to, lysosomal disorders, metabolic disorders, vertebral osteomyelitis, vertebral fractures and achondroplasia. Disorders such as spinal dysrhaphism, (e.g., spina bifida) diastematomyelia, and tethered cord syndrome may also cause such abnormalities. In these cases, there may be gait difficulty and deformity of the lower extremities based on neurological abnormalities, and the neurological effects are to be evaluated under the criteria in 111.00ff.

L. Abnormal curvatures of the spine. Abnormal curvatures of the spine (specifically, scoliosis, kyphosis and kyphoscoliosis) can result in impaired ambulation, but may also adversely affect functioning in body systems other than the musculoskeletal system. For example, an individual's ability to breathe may be affected; there may be cardiac difficulties (e.g., impaired myocardial function); or there may be disfigurement resulting in withdrawal or isolation. When there is impaired ambulation, evaluation of equivalence may be made by reference to 114.09A. When the abnormal curvature of the spine results in symptoms related to fixation of the dorsolumbar or cervical spine, evaluation of equivalence may be made by reference to 114.09C. When there is respiratory or cardiac involvement or an associated mental disorder, evaluation may be made under 103.00ff,104.00ff, or 112.00ff, as appropriate. Other consequences should be evaluated according to the listing for the affected body system.

M. Under continuing surgical management, as used in 101.07 and 101.08, refers to surgical procedures and any other associated treatments related to the efforts directed toward the salvage or restoration of functional use of the affected part. It may include such factors as post-surgical procedures, surgical complications, infections, or other medical complications, related illnesses, or related treatments that delay the child's attainment of maximum benefit from therapy. When burns are not under continuing surgical management, see 108.00F.

N. After maximum benefit from therapy has been achieved in situations involving fractures of an upper extremity (101.07), or soft tissue injuries (101.08), i.e., there have been no significant changes in physical findings or on appropriate medically acceptable imaging for any 6-month period after the last definitive surgical procedure or other medical intervention, evaluation must be made on the basis of the demonstrable residuals, if any. A finding that 101.07 or 101.08 is met must be based on a consideration of the symptoms, signs, and laboratory findings associated with recent or anticipated surgical procedures and the resulting recuperative periods, including any related medical complications, such as infections, illnesses, and therapies which impede or delay the efforts toward restoration of function.

Generally, when there has been no surgical or medical intervention for 6 months after the last definitive surgical procedure, it can be concluded that maximum therapeutic benefit has been reached. Evaluation at this point must be made on the basis of the demonstrable residual limitations, if any, considering the child's impairment-related symptoms, signs, and laboratory findings, any residual symptoms, signs, and laboratory findings associated with such surgeries, complications, and recuperative periods, and other relevant evidence.

O. Major function of the face and head, for purposes of listing 101.08, relates to impact on any or all of the activities involving vision, hearing, speech, mastication, and the initiation of the digestive process.

P. When surgical procedures have been performed, documentation should include a copy of the operative notes and available pathology reports.

101.01 Category of Impairments, Musculoskeletal

101.02 ***Major dysfunction of a joint(s) (due to any cause):*** Characterized by gross anatomical deformity (e.g., subluxation, contracture, bony or fibrous ankylosis, instability) and chronic joint pain and stiffness with signs of limitation of motion or other abnormal motion of the affected joint(s), and findings on appropriate medically acceptable imaging of joint space narrowing, bony destruction, or ankylosis of the affected joint(s). With:

A. Involvement of one major peripheral weight-bearing joint (i.e., hip, knee, or ankle), resulting in inability to ambulate effectively, as defined in 101.00B2b;

or

B. Involvement of one major peripheral joint in each upper extremity (i.e., shoulder, elbow, or wrist-hand), resulting in inability to perform fine and gross movements effectively, as defined in 101.00B2c.

101.03 ***Reconstructive surgery or surgical arthrodesis of a major weight-bearing joint***, with inability to ambulate effectively, as defined in 101.00B2b, and return to effective ambulation did not occur, or is not expected to occur, within 12 months of onset.

101.04 ***Disorders of the spine*** (e.g., lysosomal disorders, metabolic disorders, vertebral osteomyelitis, vertebral fracture, achondroplasia) resulting in compromise of a nerve root (including the cauda equina) or the spinal cord, with evidence of nerve root compression characterized by neuro-anatomic distribution of pain, limitation of motion of the spine, motor loss (atrophy with associated muscle weakness or muscle weakness) accompanied by sensory or reflex loss and, if there is involvement of the lower back, positive straight-leg raising test (sitting and supine).

101.05 ***Amputation (due to any cause)***.

A. Both hands;

or

B. One or both lower extremities at or above the tarsal region, with stump complications resulting in medical inability to use a prosthetic device to ambulate effectively, as defined in 101.00B2b, which have lasted or are expected to last for at least 12 months;

or

C. One hand and one lower extremity at or above the tarsal region, with inability to ambulate effectively, as defined in 101.00B2b;

or

D. Hemipelvectomy or hip disarticulation.

101.06 ***Fracture of the femur, tibia, pelvis, or one or more of the tarsal bones***. With:

A. Solid union not evident on appropriate medically acceptable imaging, and not clinically solid;

and

B. Inability to ambulate effectively, as defined in 101.00B2b, and return to effective ambulation did not occur or is not expected to occur within 12 months of onset.

101.07 ***Fracture of an upper extremity*** with nonunion of a fracture of the shaft of the humerus, radius, or ulna, under continuing surgical management, as defined in 101.00M, directed toward restoration of functional use of the extremity, and such function was not restored or expected to be restored within 12 months of onset.

101.08 ***Soft tissue injury (e.g., burns)*** of an upper or lower extremity, trunk, or face and head, under continuing surgical management, as defined in 101.00M, directed toward the salvage or restoration of major function, and such major function was not restored or expected to be restored within 12 months of onset. Major function of the face and head is described in 101.00O.

102.00 Special Senses and Speech

A. *How do we evaluate visual disorders?*

1. ***What are visual disorders?*** Visual disorders are abnormalities of the eye, the optic nerve, the optic tracts, or the brain that may cause a loss of visual acuity or visual fields. A loss of visual acuity limits your ability to distinguish detail, read, do fine work, or perform other age-appropriate activities. A loss of visual fields limits your ability to perceive visual stimuli in the peripheral extent of vision.

2. ***How do we define statutory blindness?*** Statutory blindness is blindness as defined in sections 216(i)(1) and 1614(a)(2) of the Social Security Act (Act).

a. The Act defines blindness as central visual acuity of 20/200 or less in the better eye with the use of a correcting lens. We use your best-corrected central visual acuity for distance in the better eye when we determine if this definition is met. (For visual acuity testing requirements, see 102.00A5.)

b. The Act also provides that an eye that has a visual field limitation such that the widest diameter of the visual field subtends an angle no greater than 20 degrees is considered as having a central visual acuity of 20/200 or less. (For visual field testing requirements, see 102.00A6.)

c. You have statutory blindness only if your visual disorder meets the criteria of 102.02A, 102.02B, or 102.03A. You do not have statutory blindness if your visual disorder medically equals the criteria of 102.02A, 102.02B, or 102.03A or meets or medically equals the criteria of 102.03B, 102.03C, 102.04A, or 102.04B because your disability is based on criteria other than those in the statutory definition of blindness.

3. ***What evidence do we need to establish statutory blindness under title XVI?*** To establish that you have statutory blindness under title XVI, we need evidence showing only that your central visual acuity in your better eye or your visual

field in your better eye meets the criteria in 102.00A2, provided that those measurements are consistent with the other evidence in your case record. We do not need documentation of the cause of your blindness. Also, there is no duration requirement for statutory blindness under title XVI (see §§416.981 and 416.983 of this chapter).

4. ***What evidence do we need to evaluate visual disorders, including those that result in statutory blindness under title II?*** To evaluate your visual disorder, we usually need a report of an eye examination that includes measurements of your best-corrected central visual acuity (see 102.00A5) or the extent of your visual fields (see 102.00A6), as appropriate. If you have visual acuity or visual field loss, we need documentation of the cause of the loss. A standard eye examination will usually indicate the cause of any visual acuity loss. A standard eye examination can also indicate the cause of some types of visual field deficits. Some disorders, such as cortical visual disorders, may result in abnormalities that do not appear on a standard eye examination. If the standard eye examination does not indicate the cause of your vision loss, we will request the information used to establish the presence of your visual disorder. If your visual disorder does not satisfy the criteria in 102.02, 102.03, or 102.04, we will request a description of how your visual disorder affects your ability to function.

5. ***How do we measure best-corrected visual acuity?***

a. *Visual acuity testing.* When we need to measure your best-corrected central visual acuity, which is your optimal visual acuity attainable with the use of a corrective lens, we use visual acuity testing for distance that was carried out using Snellen methodology or any other testing methodology that is comparable to Snellen methodology.

(i) Your best-corrected central visual acuity for distance is usually measured by determining what you can see from 20 feet. If your visual acuity is measured for a distance other than 20 feet, we will convert it to a 20-foot measurement. For example, if your visual acuity is measured at 10 feet and is reported as 10/40, we will convert this measurement to 20/80.

(ii) A visual acuity recorded as CF (counts fingers), HM (hand motion only), LP or LPO (light perception or light perception only), or NLP (no light perception) indicates that no optical correction will improve your visual acuity. If your central visual acuity in an eye is recorded as CF, HM, LP or LPO, or NLP, we will determine that your best-corrected central visual acuity is 20/200 or less in that eye.

(iii) We will not use the results of pinhole testing or automated refraction acuity to determine your best-corrected central visual acuity. These tests provide an estimate of potential visual acuity but not an actual measurement of your best-corrected central visual acuity.

(iv) Very young children, such as infants and toddlers, cannot participate in testing using Snellen methodology or other comparable testing. If you are unable to participate in testing using Snellen methodology or other comparable testing due to your young age, we will consider clinical findings of your fixation and visual-following behavior. If both these behaviors are absent, we will consider the anatomical findings or the results of neuroimaging, electroretinogram, or visual evoked response (VER) testing when this testing has been performed.

b. *Other test charts.*

(i) Children between the ages of 3 and 5 often cannot identify the letters on a Snellen or other letter test chart. Specialists with expertise in assessment of childhood vision use alternate methods for measuring visual acuity in young children. We consider alternate methods, for example, the Landolt C test or the tumbling-E test, which are used to evaluate young children who are unable to participate in testing using Snellen methodology, to be comparable to testing using Snellen methodology.

(ii) Most test charts that use Snellen methodology do not have lines that measure visual acuity between 20/100 and 20/200. Some test charts, such as the Bailey-Lovie or the Early Treatment Diabetic Retinopathy Study (ETDRS), used mostly in research settings, have such lines. If your visual acuity is measured with one of these charts, and you cannot read any of the letters on the 20/100 line, we will determine that you have statutory blindness based on a visual acuity of 20/200 or less. For example, if your best-corrected central visual acuity for distance in the better eye is 20/160 using an ETDRS chart, we will find that you have statutory blindness. Regardless of the type of test chart used, you do not have statutory blindness if you can read at least one letter on the 20/100 line. For example, if your best-corrected central visual acuity for distance in the better eye is 20/125+1 using an ETDRS chart, we will find that you do not have statutory blindness because you are able to read one letter on the 20/100 line.

c. *Testing using a specialized lens.* In some instances, you may perform visual acuity testing using a specialized lens, such as a contact lens. We will use the visual acuity measurements obtained with a specialized lens only if you have demonstrated the ability to use the specialized lens on a sustained basis. We will not use visual acuity measurements obtained with telescopic lenses.

d. *Cycloplegic refraction* is an examination of the eye performed after administering cycloplegic eye drops capable of relaxing the ability of the pupil to become smaller and temporarily paralyzing the focusing muscles. If your case record contains the results of cycloplegic refraction, we may use the results to determine your best-corrected central visual acuity. We will not purchase cycloplegic refraction.

e. *VER testing* measures your response to visual events and can often detect dysfunction that is undetectable through other types of examinations. If you have an absent response to VER testing in your better eye, we will determine that your best-corrected central visual acuity is 20/200 or less in that eye and that your visual acuity loss satisfies the criterion in 102.02A or 102.02B4, as appropriate, when these test results are consistent with the other evidence in your case record. If you have a positive response to VER testing in an eye, we will not use that result to determine your best-corrected central visual acuity in that eye.

6. ***How do we measure visual fields?***

a. *General.* We generally need visual field testing when you have a visual disorder that could result in visual field loss, such as glaucoma, retinitis pigmentosa, or optic neuropathy, or when you display behaviors that suggest a visual field loss. When we need to measure the extent of your visual field loss, we use visual field testing (also referred to as perimetry) carried out using automated static threshold perimetry performed on an acceptable perimeter. (For perimeter requirements, see 102.00A9.)

b. *Automated static threshold perimetry requirements.*

(i) The test must use a white size III Goldmann stimulus and a 31.5 apostilb (asb) white background (or a 10 candela per square meter (cd/m^2) white background). The stimuli test locations must be no more than 6 degrees apart horizontally or vertically. Measurements must be reported on standard charts and include a description of the size and intensity of the test stimulus.

(ii) We measure the extent of your visual field loss by determining the portion of the visual field in which you can see a white III4e stimulus. The "III" refers to the standard Goldmann test stimulus size III (4 mm^2), and the "4e" refers to the standard Goldmann intensity filter (0 decibel (dB) attenuation, which allows presentation of the maximum luminance) used to determine the intensity of the stimulus.

(iii) In automated static threshold perimetry, the intensity of the stimulus varies. The intensity of the stimulus is expressed in decibels (dB). A perimeter's maximum stimulus luminance is usually assigned the value 0 dB. We need to determine the dB level that corresponds to a 4e intensity for the particular perimeter being used. We will then use the dB printout to determine which points you see at a 4e intensity level (a "seeing point"). For example:

A. When the maximum stimulus luminance (0 dB stimulus) on an acceptable perimeter is 10,000 asb, a 10 dB stimulus is equivalent to a 4e stimulus. Any point you see at 10 dB or greater is a seeing point.

B. When the maximum stimulus luminance (0 dB stimulus) on an acceptable perimeter is 4,000 asb, a 6 dB stimulus is equivalent to a 4e stimulus. Any point you see at 6 dB or greater is a seeing point.

C. When the maximum stimulus luminance (0 dB stimulus) on an acceptable perimeter is 1,000 asb, a 0 dB stimulus is equivalent to a 4e stimulus. Any point you see at 0 dB or greater is a seeing point.

c. *Evaluation under* 102.03A. To determine statutory blindness based on visual field loss in your better eye (102.03A), we need the results of a visual field test that measures the central 24 to 30 degrees of your visual field; that is, the area measuring 24 to 30 degrees from the point of fixation. Acceptable tests include the Humphrey Field Analyzer (HFA) 30–2, HFA 24–2, and Octopus 32.

d. *Evaluation under* 102.03B. To determine whether your visual field loss meets listing 102.03B, we use the mean deviation or defect (MD) from acceptable automated static threshold perimetry that measures the central 30 degrees of the visual field. MD is the average sensitivity deviation from normal values for all measured visual field locations. When using results from HFA tests, which report the MD as a negative number, we use the absolute value of the MD to determine whether your visual field loss meets listing 102.03B. We cannot use tests that do not measure the central 30 degrees of the visual field, such as the HFA 24–2, to determine if your impairment meets or medically equals 102.03B.

e. *Other types of perimetry.* If your case record contains visual field measurements obtained using manual or automated kinetic perimetry, such as Goldmann perimetry or the HFA "SSA Test Kinetic," we can generally use these results if the kinetic test was performed using a white III4e stimulus projected on a white 31.5 asb (10 cd/m^2) background. Automated kinetic perimetry, such as the HFA "SSA Test Kinetic," does not detect limitations in the central visual field because testing along a meridian stops when you see the stimulus. If your visual disorder has progressed to the point at which it is likely to result in a significant limitation in the central visual field, such as a scotoma (see 102.00A6h), we will not use *automated* kinetic perimetry to determine the extent of your visual field loss. Instead, we will determine the extent of your visual field loss using automated static threshold perimetry or manual kinetic perimetry.

f. *Screening tests.* We will not use the results of visual field screening tests, such as confrontation tests, tangent screen tests, or automated static screening tests, to determine that your impairment meets or medically equals a listing, or functionally equals the listings. We can consider normal results from visual field screening tests to determine whether your visual disorder is severe when these test results are consistent with the other evidence in your case record. (See §416.924(c) of this chapter.) We will not consider normal test results to be consistent with the other evidence if the clinical findings indicate that your visual disorder has progressed to the point that it is likely to cause visual field loss, or you have a history of an operative procedure for retinal detachment.

g. *Use of corrective lenses.* You must not wear eyeglasses during visual field testing because they limit your field of vision. You may wear contact lenses to correct your visual acuity during the visual field test to obtain the most accurate visual field measurements. For this single purpose, you do not need to demonstrate that you have the ability to use the contact lenses on a sustained basis.

h. *Scotoma.* A scotoma is a field defect or non-seeing area (also referred to as a "blind spot") in the visual field surrounded by a normal field or seeing area. When we measure your visual field, we subtract the length of any scotoma, other than the normal blind spot, from the overall length of any diameter on which it falls.

7. ***How do we determine your visual acuity efficiency, visual field efficiency, and visual efficiency?***

a. *General. Visual efficiency*, a calculated value of your remaining visual function, is the combination of your *visual acuity efficiency* and your *visual field efficiency* expressed as a percentage.

b. *Visual acuity efficiency.* Visual acuity efficiency is a percentage that corresponds to the best-corrected central visual acuity for distance in your better eye. See Table 1.

c. *Visual field efficiency.* Visual field efficiency is a percentage that corresponds to the visual field in your better eye. Under 102.03C, we require kinetic perimetry to determine your visual field efficiency percentage. We calculate the visual field efficiency percentage by adding the number of degrees you see along the eight principal meridians found on a visual field chart (0, 45, 90, 135, 180, 225, 270, and 315) in your better eye and dividing by 5. For example, in Figure 1:

A. The diagram of the left eye illustrates a visual field, as measured with a III4e stimulus, contracted to 30 degrees in two meridians (180 and 225) and to 20 degrees in the remaining six meridians. The visual efficiency percentage of this field is: ((2 x 30) + (6 x 20)) / 5 = 36 percent.

Table 1—Visual Acuity Efficiency

Snellen best-corrected central visual acuity for distance		**Visual acuity efficiency (%) (102.04A)**
English	**Metric**	
20/16	6/5	100
20/20	6/6	100
20/25	6/7.5	95
20/30	6/9	90
20/40	6/12	85
20/50	6/15	75
20/60	6/18	70
20/70	6/21	65
20/80	6/24	60
20/100	6/30	50

B. The diagram of the right eye illustrates the extent of a normal visual field as measured with a III4e stimulus. The sum of the eight principal meridians of this field is 500 degrees. The visual efficiency percentage of this field is 500 / 5 = 100 percent.

d. *Visual efficiency.* Under 102.04A, we calculate the visual efficiency percentage by multiplying your visual acuity efficiency percentage (see 102.00A7b) by your visual field efficiency percentage (see 102.00A7c) and dividing by 100. For example, if your visual acuity efficiency percentage is 75 and your visual field efficiency percentage is 36, your visual efficiency percentage is: (75 x 36) / 100 = 27 percent.

8. *How do we determine your visual acuity impairment value, visual field impairment value, and visual impairment value?*

a. *General. Visual impairment value*, a calculated value of your loss of visual function, is the combination of your *visual acuity impairment value* and your *visual field impairment value.*

b. *Visual acuity impairment value.* Your visual acuity impairment value corresponds to the best-corrected central visual acuity for distance in your better eye. See Table 2.

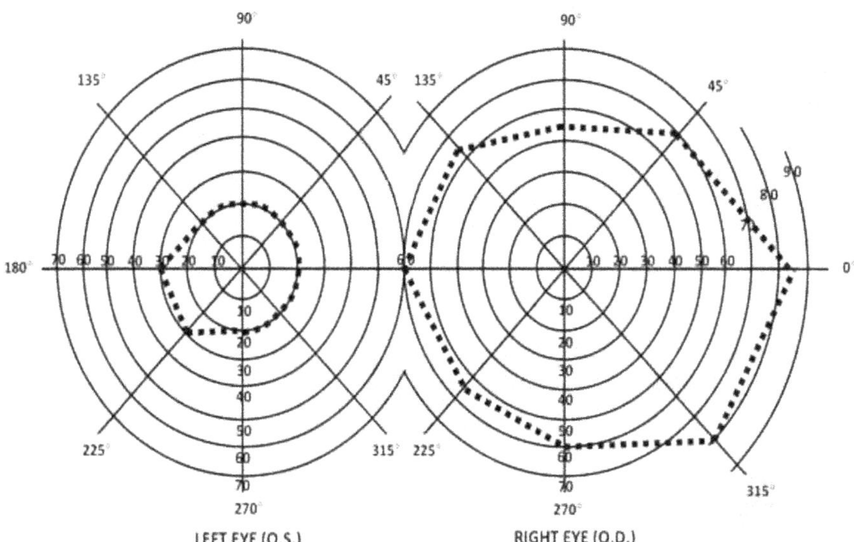

Figure 1

Table 2—Visual Acuity Impairment Value

Snellen best-corrected central visual acuity for distance		Visual acuity impairment value (102.04B)
English	**Metric**	
20/16	6/5	0.00
20/20	6/6	0.00
20/25	6/7.5	0.10
20/30	6/9	0.18
20/40	6/12	0.30
20/50	6/15	0.40
20/60	6/18	0.48
20/70	6/21	0.54
20/80	6/24	0.60
20/100	6/30	0.70

c. *Visual field impairment value.* Your visual field impairment value corresponds to the visual field in your better eye. Using the MD from acceptable automated static threshold perimetry, we calculate the visual field impairment value by dividing the absolute value of the MD by 22. For example, if your MD on an HFA 30–2 is –16, your visual field impairment value is: |–16| / 22 = 0.73.

d. *Visual impairment value.* Under 102.04B, we calculate the visual impairment value by adding your visual acuity impairment value (see 102.00A8b) and your visual field impairment value (see 102.00A8c). For example, if your visual acuity impairment value is 0.48 and your visual field impairment value is 0.73, your visual impairment value is: 0.48 + 0.73 = 1.21.

9. ***What are our requirements for an acceptable perimeter?*** We will use results from automated static threshold perimetry performed on a perimeter that:

a. Uses optical projection to generate the test stimuli.

b. Has an internal normative database for automatically comparing your performance with that of the general population.

c. Has a statistical analysis package that is able to calculate visual field indices, particularly mean deviation or mean defect.

d. Demonstrates the ability to correctly detect visual field loss and correctly identify normal visual fields.

e. Demonstrates good test-retest reliability.

f. Has undergone clinical validation studies by three or more independent laboratories with results published in peer-reviewed ophthalmic journals.

B. How do we evaluate hearing loss?

1. What evidence do we need?

a. We need evidence showing that you have a medically determinable impairment that causes your hearing loss and audiometric measurements of the severity of your hearing loss. We generally require both an otologic examination and audiometric testing to establish that you have a medically determinable impairment that causes your hearing loss. You should have this audiometric testing within 2 months of the otologic examination. Once we have evidence that you have a medically determinable impairment, we can use the results of later audiometric testing to assess the severity of your hearing loss without another otologic examination. We will consider your test scores together with any other relevant information we have about your hearing, including information from outside of the test setting.

b. The otologic examination must be performed by a licensed physician (medical or osteopathic doctor) or audiologist. It must include your medical history, your description of how your hearing loss affects you, and the physician's or audiologist's description of the appearance of the external ears (pinnae and external ear canals), evaluation of the tympanic membranes, and assessment of any middle ear abnormalities.

c. Audiometric testing must be performed by, or under the direct supervision of, a licensed audiologist or an otolaryngologist.

2. What audiometric testing do we need when you do not have a cochlear implant?

a. **General.** We need either physiologic or behavioral testing (other than screening testing, see 102.00B2g) that is appropriate for your age at the time of testing. See 102.00B2c–102.00B2f. We will make every reasonable effort to obtain the results of physiologic testing that has been done; however, we will not purchase such testing.

b. **Testing requirements.** The testing must be conducted in accordance with the most recently published standards of the American National Standards Institute (ANSI). You must not wear hearing aids during the testing. Additionally, a person described in 102.00B1c must perform an otoscopic examination immediately before the audiometric testing. (An **otoscopic examination** provides a description of the appearance of your external ear canals and an evaluation of the tympanic membranes. In these rules, we use the term to include otoscopic examinations performed by physicians and otoscopic inspections performed by audiologists and others.) The otoscopic examination must show that there are no conditions that would prevent valid audiometric testing, such as fluid in the ear, ear infection, or obstruction in an ear canal. The person performing the test should also report on any other factors, such as your ability to maintain attention, that can affect the interpretation of the test results.

c. Children from birth to the attainment of age 6 months.

(i) We need physiologic testing, such as auditory brainstem response (ABR) testing.

(ii) To determine whether your hearing loss meets 102.10A, we will average your hearing thresholds at 500, 1000, 2000, and 4000 Hertz (Hz). If you do not have a response at a particular frequency, we will use a threshold of 5 decibels (dB) over the limit of the audiometer.

d. Children from age 6 months to the attainment of age 2.

(i) We need air conduction thresholds determined by a behavioral assessment, usually visual reinforcement audiometry (VRA). We can use ABR testing if the behavioral assessment cannot be completed or if the results are inconclusive or unreliable.

(ii) To determine whether your hearing loss meets 102.10A, we will average your hearing thresholds at 500, 1000, 2000, and 4000 Hz. If you do not have a response at a particular frequency, we will use a threshold of 5 dB over the limit of the audiometer.

(iii) For this age group, behavioral assessments are often performed in a sound field, and each ear is not tested separately. If each ear is not tested separately, we will consider the test results to represent the hearing in the better ear.

e. Children from age 2 to the attainment of age 5.

(i) We need air conduction thresholds determined by a behavioral assessment, such as conditioned play audiometry (CPA), tangible or visually reinforced operant conditioning audiometry (TROCA, VROCA), or VRA. If you have had ABR testing, we can use the results of that testing if the behavioral assessment cannot be completed or the results are inconclusive or unreliable.

(ii) To determine whether your hearing loss meets 102.10A, we will average your hearing thresholds at 500, 1000, 2000, and 4000 Hz. If you do not have a response at a particular frequency, we will use a threshold of 5 dB over the limit of the audiometer.

(iii) For this age group, behavioral assessments are often performed in a sound field and each ear is not tested separately. If each ear is not tested separately, we will consider the test results to represent the hearing in the better ear.

f. Children from age 5 to the attainment of age 18.

(i) We generally need pure tone air conduction and bone conduction testing, speech reception threshold (SRT) testing (also referred to as "spondee threshold" or "ST" testing), and word recognition testing (also referred to as "word discrimination" or "speech discrimination" testing). This testing must be conducted in a sound-treated booth or room and must be in accordance with the most recently published ANSI standards. Each ear must be tested separately.

(ii) To determine whether your hearing loss meets the air and bone conduction criterion in 102.10B1 or 102.10B3, we will average your hearing thresholds at 500, 1000, 2000, and 4000 Hz. If you do not have a response at a particular frequency, we will use a threshold of 5 dB over the limit of the audiometer.

(iii) The SRT is the minimum dB level required for you to recognize 50 percent of the words on a standard list of spondee words. (Spondee words are two-syllable words that have equal stress on each syllable.) The SRT is usually within 10 dB of the average pure tone air conduction hearing thresholds at 500, 1000, and 2000 Hz. If the SRT is not within 10 dB of the average pure tone air conduction threshold, the reason for the discrepancy must be documented. If we cannot determine that there is a medical basis for the discrepancy, we will not use the results of the testing to determine whether your hearing loss meets a listing.

(iv) Word recognition testing determines your ability to recognize an age-appropriate, standardized list of phonetically balanced monosyllabic words in the absence of any visual cues. This testing must be performed in quiet. The list may be recorded or presented live, but in either case, the words should be presented at a level of amplification that will measure your maximum ability to discriminate words, usually 35 to 40 dB above your SRT. However, the amplification level used in the testing must be medically appropriate, and you must be able to tolerate it. If you cannot be tested at 35 to 40 dB above your SRT, the person who performs the test should report your word recognition testing score at your highest comfortable level of amplification.

g. **Screening testing.** Physiologic testing, such as ABR and otoacoustic emissions (OAE), and pure tone testing can be used as hearing screening tests. We will not use these tests to determine that your hearing loss meets or medically equals a listing, or to assess functional limitations due to your hearing loss, when they are used only as screening tests. We can consider normal results from hearing screening tests to determine that your hearing loss is not "severe" when these test results are consistent with the other evidence in your case record. See Sec. 416.924(c).

3. *What audiometric testing do we need when you have a cochlear implant?*

a. If you have a cochlear implant, we will consider you to be disabled until age 5, or for 1 year after initial implantation, whichever is later.

b. After that period, we need word recognition testing performed with any age-appropriate version of the Hearing in Noise Test (HINT) or the Hearing in Noise Test for Children (HINT-C) to determine whether your impairment meets 102.11B. This testing must be conducted in quiet in a sound field. Your implant must be functioning properly and adjusted to your normal settings. The sentences should be presented at 60 dB HL (Hearing Level) and without any visual cues.

4. How do we evaluate your word recognition ability if you are not fluent in English?

If you are not fluent in English, you should have word recognition testing using an appropriate word list for the language in which you are most fluent. The person conducting the test should be fluent in the language used for the test. If there is no appropriate word list or no person who is fluent in the language and qualified to perform the test, it may not be possible to measure your word recognition ability. If your word recognition ability cannot be measured, your hearing loss cannot meet 102.10B2 or 102.11B. Instead, we will consider the facts of your case to determine whether you have difficulty understanding words in the language in which you are most fluent, and if so, whether that degree of difficulty medically equals 102.10B2 or 102.11B. For example, we will consider how you interact with family members, interpreters, and other persons who speak the language in which you are most fluent.

5. What do we mean by a marked limitation in speech or language as used in 102.10B3?

a. We will consider you to have a marked limitation in speech if:

(i) Entire phrases or sentences in your conversation are intelligible to unfamiliar listeners at least 50 percent (half) of the time but no more than 67 percent (two-thirds) of the time on your first attempt; and

(ii) Your sound production or phonological patterns (the ways in which you combine speech sounds) are atypical for your age.

b. We will consider you to have a marked limitation in language when your current and valid test score on an appropriate comprehensive, standardized test of overall language functioning is at least two standard deviations below the mean. In addition, the evidence of your daily communication functioning must be consistent with your test score. If you are not fluent in English, it may not be possible to test your language performance. If we cannot test your language performance, your hearing loss cannot meet 102.10B3. Instead, we will consider the facts of your case to determine whether your hearing loss medically equals 102.10B3.

C. How do we evaluate impairments that do not meet one of the special senses and speech listings?

1. These listings are only examples of common special senses and speech disorders that we consider severe enough to result in marked and severe functional limitations. If your impairment(s) does not meet the criteria of any of these listings, we must also consider whether you have an impairment(s) that satisfies the criteria of a listing in another body system.

2. If you have a medically determinable impairment(s) that does not meet a listing, we will determine whether the impairment(s) medically equals a listing or

functionally equals the listings. (See §§ 416.926 and 416.926a.) We use the rules in § 416.994a when we decide whether you continue to be disabled.

102.01 Category of Impairments, Special Senses and Speech

102.02 Loss of central visual acuity.

A. Remaining vision in the better eye after best correction is 20/200 or less.

OR

B. An inability to participate in visual acuity testing using Snellen methodology or other comparable testing, clinical findings that fixation and visual-following behavior are absent in the better eye, and one of the following:

1. Abnormal anatomical findings indicating a visual acuity of 20/200 or less in the better eye (such as the presence of Stage III or worse retinopathy of prematurity despite surgery, hypoplasia of the optic nerve, albinism with macular aplasia, or bilateral optic atrophy); or

2. Abnormal neuroimaging documenting damage to the cerebral cortex which would be expected to prevent the development of a visual acuity better than 20/200 in the better eye (such as neuroimaging showing bilateral encephalomyelitis or bilateral encephalomalacia); or

3. Abnormal electroretinogram documenting the presence of Leber's congenital amaurosis or achromatopsia in the better eye; or

4. An absent response to VER testing in the better eye.

102.03 Contraction of the visual field in the better eye, with:

A. The widest diameter subtending an angle around the point of fixation no greater than 20 degrees.

OR

B. An MD of 22 decibels or greater, determined by automated static threshold perimetry that measures the central 30 degrees of the visual field (see 102.00A6d).

OR

C. A visual field efficiency of 20 percent or less, determined by kinetic perimetry (see 102.00A7c).

102.04 Loss of visual efficiency, or visual impairment, in the better eye:

A. A visual efficiency percentage of 20 or less after best correction (see 102.00A7d).

OR

B. A visual impairment value of 1.00 or greater after best correction (see 102.00A8d).

102.10 Hearing loss not treated with cochlear implantation.

A. For children from birth to the attainment of age 5, an average air conduction hearing threshold of 50 decibels or greater in the better ear (see 102.00B2).

OR

B. For children from age 5 to the attainment of age 18:

1. An average air conduction hearing threshold of 70 decibels or greater in the better ear and an average bone conduction hearing threshold of 40 decibels or greater in the better ear (see 102.00B2f); or

2. A word recognition score of 40 percent or less in the better ear determined using a standardized list of phonetically balanced monosyllabic words (see 102.00B2f); or

3. An average air conduction hearing threshold of 50 decibels or greater in the better ear and a marked limitation in speech or language (see 102.00B2f and 102.00B5).

102.11 Hearing loss treated with cochlear implantation.

A. Consider under a disability until the attainment of age 5 or for 1 year after initial implantation, whichever is later.

OR

B. Upon the attainment of age 5 or 1 year after initial implantation, whichever is later, a word recognition score of 60 percent or less determined using the HINT or the HINT-C (see 102.00B3b).

103.00 Respiratory Disorders

A. Which disorders do we evaluate in this body system?

1. We evaluate respiratory disorders that result in obstruction (difficulty moving air out of the lungs) or restriction (difficulty moving air into the lungs), or that interfere with diffusion (gas exchange) across cell membranes in the lungs. Examples of such disorders and the listings we use to evaluate them include chronic obstructive pulmonary disease (103.02), chronic lung disease of infancy (also known as bronchopulmonary dysplasia, 103.02C or 103.02E), pulmonary fibrosis (103.02), asthma (103.02 or 103.03), and cystic fibrosis (103.04). We also use listings in this body system to evaluate

respiratory failure resulting from an underlying chronic respiratory disorder (103.04E or 103.14) and lung transplantation (103.11).

2. We evaluate cancers affecting the respiratory system under the listings in 113.00. We evaluate the pulmonary effects of neuromuscular and autoimmune disorders under these listings or under the listings in 111.00 or 114.00, respectively.

B. *What are the symptoms and signs of respiratory disorders?*

Symptoms and signs of respiratory disorders include dyspnea (shortness of breath), chest pain, coughing, wheezing, sputum production, hemoptysis (coughing up blood from the respiratory tract), use of accessory muscles of respiration, and tachypnea (rapid rate of breathing).

C. *What abbreviations do we use in this body system?*

1. *BiPAP* means bi-level positive airway pressure ventilation.
2. *BTPS* means body temperature and ambient pressure, saturated with water vapor.
3. *CF* means cystic fibrosis.
4. *CFRD* means CF-related diabetes.
5. *CFTR* means CF transmembrane conductance regulator.
6. *CLD* means chronic lung disease of infancy.
7. FEV_1 means forced expiratory volume in the first second of a forced expiratory maneuver.
8. *FVC* means forced vital capacity.
9. *L* means liter.

D. *What documentation do we need to evaluate your respiratory disorder?*

1. We need *medical evidence* to document and assess the severity of your respiratory disorder. Medical evidence should include your medical history, physical examination findings, the results of imaging (see 103.00D3), spirometry (see 103.00E), other relevant laboratory tests, and descriptions of any prescribed treatment and your response to it. We may not need all of this evidence depending on your particular respiratory disorder and its effects on you.
2. If you use *supplemental oxygen*, we still need medical evidence to establish the severity of your respiratory disorder.
3. *Imaging* refers to medical imaging techniques, such as x-ray and computerized tomography. The imaging must be consistent with the prevailing state of medical knowledge and clinical practice as the proper technique to support the evaluation of the disorder.

E. What is spirometry and what are our requirements for an acceptable test and report?

1. Spirometry, which measures how well you move air into and out of your lungs, involves at least three forced expiratory maneuvers during the same test session. A forced expiratory maneuver is a maximum inhalation followed by a forced maximum exhalation, and measures exhaled volumes of air over time. The volume of air you exhale in the first second of the forced expiratory maneuver is the FEV_1. The total volume of air that you exhale during the entire forced expiratory maneuver is the FVC. We use your highest FEV_1 value to evaluate your respiratory disorder under 103.02A and 103.04A, and your highest FVC value to evaluate your respiratory disorder under 103.02B, regardless of whether the values are from the same forced expiratory maneuver or different forced expiratory maneuvers. We will not purchase spirometry for children who have not attained age 6.
2. We have the following requirements for spirometry under these listings:
   a. You must be medically stable at the time of the test. Examples of when we would not consider you to be medically stable include when you are:
      i. Within 2 weeks of a change in your prescribed respiratory medication.
      ii. Experiencing, or within 30 days of completion of treatment for, a lower respiratory tract infection.
      iii. Experiencing, or within 30 days of completion of treatment for, an acute exacerbation (temporary worsening) of a chronic respiratory disorder. Wheezing by itself does not indicate that you are not medically stable.

   b. During testing, if your FEV_1 is less than 70 percent of your predicted normal value, we require repeat spirometry after inhalation of a bronchodilator to evaluate your respiratory disorder under these listings, unless it is medically contraindicated. If you used a bronchodilator before the test and your FEV_1 is less than 70 percent of your predicted normal value, we still require repeat spirometry after inhalation of a bronchodilator unless the supervising physician determines that it is not safe for you to take a bronchodilator again (in which case we may need to reschedule the test). If you do not have post-bronchodilator spirometry, the test report must explain why. We can use the results of spirometry administered without bronchodilators when the use of bronchodilators is medically contraindicated.

   c. Your forced expiratory maneuvers must be satisfactory. We consider a forced expiratory maneuver to be satisfactory when you exhale with maximum effort following a full inspiration, and when the test tracing has a sharp takeoff and rapid rise to peak flow, has a smooth contour, and either lasts for at least 6 seconds (for children age 10 and older) or for at least 3 seconds (for children who have not attained age 10), or maintains a plateau for at least 1 second.

3. The spirometry report must include the following information:
   a. The date of the test and your name, age or date of birth, gender, and height without shoes. (We will assume that your recorded height on the date of the test is without shoes, unless we have evidence to the contrary.) If your spine is abnormally curved (for example, you have kyphoscoliosis), we will substitute the longest distance between your outstretched fingertips with your arms abducted 90 degrees in place of your height when this measurement is greater than your standing height without shoes.
   b. Any factors, if applicable, that can affect the interpretation of the test results (for example, your cooperation or effort in doing the test).
   c. Legible tracings of your forced expiratory maneuvers in a volume-time format showing your name and the date of the test for each maneuver.
4. If you have attained age 6, we may need to purchase spirometry to determine whether your disorder meets a listing, unless we can make a fully favorable determination or decision on another basis.
5. Before we purchase spirometry for a child age 6 or older, a medical consultant (see § 416.1016 of this chapter), preferably one with experience in the care of children with respiratory disorders, must review your case record to determine if we need the test. If we purchase spirometry, the medical source we designate to administer the test is solely responsible for deciding whether it is safe for you to do the test and for how to administer it.

F. *What is CLD and how do we evaluate it?*

1. *CLD*, also known as bronchopulmonary dysplasia, or BPD, is scarring of the immature lung. CLD may develop as a complication of mechanical ventilation and oxygen therapy for infants with significant neonatal respiratory problems. Within the first 6 months of life, most infants with CLD are successfully weaned from mechanical ventilation, and then weaned from oxygen supplementation. We evaluate CLD under 103.02C, 103.02E, or if you are age 2 or older, under 103.03 or another appropriate listing.
2. If you have CLD, are not yet 6 months old, and need 24-hour-per-day oxygen supplementation, we will not evaluate your CLD under 103.02C until you are 6 months old. Depending on the evidence in your case record, we may make a fully favorable determination or decision under other rules before you are 6 months old.
3. We evaluate your CLD under 103.02C if you are at least 6 months old and you need 24-hour-per-day oxygen supplementation. (If you were born

prematurely, we use your corrected chronological age. See § 416.924b(b) of this chapter.) We also evaluate your CLD under 103.02C if you were weaned off oxygen supplementation but needed it again by the time you were 6 months old or older.

4. We evaluate your CLD under 103.02E if you are any age from birth to the attainment of age 2 and have CLD exacerbations or complications (for example, wheezing, lower respiratory tract infections, or acute respiratory distress) that require hospitalization. For the purpose of 103.02E, we count your initial birth hospitalization as one hospitalization. The phrase "consider under a disability for 1 year from the discharge date of the last hospitalization *or* until the attainment of age 2, whichever is later" in 103.02E does not refer to the date on which your disability began, only to the date on which we must reevaluate whether your impairment(s) continues to meet a listing or is otherwise disabling.

G. *What is asthma and how do we evaluate it?*

1. *Asthma* is a chronic inflammatory disorder of the lung airways that we evaluate under 103.02 or 103.03. If you have respiratory failure resulting from chronic asthma (see 103.00J), we will evaluate it under 103.14.
2. For the purposes of 103.03:
   a. The phrase "consider under a disability for 1 year" explains how long your asthma can meet the requirements of the listing. It does not refer to the date on which your disability began, only to the date on which we must reevaluate whether your asthma continues to meet a listing or is otherwise disabling.
   b. We determine the onset of your disability based on the facts of your case, but it will be no later than the admission date of your first of three hospitalizations that satisfy the criteria of 103.03.

H. *What is CF and how do we evaluate it?*

1. *General.* We evaluate *CF*, a genetic disorder that results in abnormal salt and water transport across cell membranes in the lungs, pancreas, and other body organs, under 103.04. We need the evidence described in 103.00H2 to establish that you have CF.
2. *Documentation of CF.* We need a report signed by a physician (see § 416.913(a) of this chapter) showing both a *and* b:
   a. One of the following:
      i. A positive newborn screen for CF; or
      ii. A history of CF in a sibling; or
      iii. Documentation of at least one specific CF phenotype or clinical criterion (for example, chronic sino-pulmonary disease with

persistent colonization or infections with typical CF pathogens, pancreatic insufficiency, or salt-loss syndromes); *and*

b. One of the following definitive laboratory tests:

   i. An elevated sweat chloride concentration equal to or greater than 60 millimoles per L; or

   ii. The identification of two CF gene mutations affecting the CFTR; or

   iii. Characteristic abnormalities in ion transport across the nasal epithelium.

c. When we have the report showing a and b, but it is not signed by a physician, we also need a report from a physician stating that you have CF.

d. When we do not have the report showing a and b, we need a report from a physician that is persuasive that a positive diagnosis of CF was confirmed by an appropriate definitive laboratory test. To be persuasive, this report must include a statement by the physician that you had the appropriate definitive laboratory test for diagnosing CF. The report must provide the test results or explain how your diagnosis was established that is consistent with the prevailing state of medical knowledge and clinical practice.

3. *CF pulmonary exacerbations.* Examples of CF pulmonary exacerbations include increased cough and sputum production, hemoptysis, increased shortness of breath, increased fatigue, and reduction in pulmonary function. Treatment usually includes intravenous antibiotics and intensified airway clearance therapy (for example, increased frequencies of chest percussion or increased use of inhaled nebulized therapies, such as bronchodilators or mucolytics).

4. For 103.04G, we require any two exacerbations or complications from the list in 103.04G1 through 103.04G4 within a 12-month period. You may have two of the same exacerbation or complication or two different ones.

   a. If you have two of the acute exacerbations or complications we describe in 103.04G1 and 103.04G2, there must be at least 30 days between the two.

   b. If you have one of the acute exacerbations or complications we describe in 103.04G1 and 103.04G2 and one of the chronic complications we describe in 103.04G3 and 103.04G4, the two can occur during the same time. For example, your CF meets 103.04G if you have the pulmonary hemorrhage we describe in 103.04G2 and the weight loss we describe in 103.04G3 even if the pulmonary hemorrhage occurs during the 90-day period in 103.04G3.

   c. Your CF also meets 103.04G if you have both of the chronic complications in 103.04G3 and 103.04G4.

5. CF may also affect other body systems such as digestive or endocrine. If your CF, including pulmonary exacerbations and nonpulmonary complications,

does not meet or medically equal a respiratory disorders listing, we may evaluate your CF-related impairments under the listings in the affected body system.

I. *How do we evaluate lung transplantation?* If you receive a lung transplant (or a lung transplant simultaneously with other organs, such as the heart), we will consider you to be disabled under 103.11 for 3 years from the date of the transplant. After that, we evaluate your residual impairment(s) by considering the adequacy of your post-transplant function, the frequency and severity of any rejection episodes you have, complications in other body systems, and adverse treatment effects. Children who receive organ transplants generally have impairments that meet our definition of disability before they undergo transplantation. The phrase "consider under a disability for 3 years" in 103.11 does not refer to the date on which your disability began, only to the date on which we must reevaluate whether your impairment(s) continues to meet a listing or is otherwise disabling. We determine the onset of your disability based on the facts of your case.

J. *What is respiratory failure and how do we evaluate it?* Respiratory failure is the inability of the lungs to perform their basic function of gas exchange. We evaluate respiratory failure under 103.04E if you have CF-related respiratory failure, or under 103.14 if you have respiratory failure due to any other *chronic* respiratory disorder. Continuous positive airway pressure does not satisfy the criterion in 103.04E or 103.14, and cannot be substituted as an equivalent finding, for invasive mechanical ventilation or noninvasive ventilation with BiPAP.

K. *How do we evaluate growth failure due to any chronic respiratory disorder?*

1. To evaluate growth failure due to any chronic respiratory disorder, we require documentation of the oxygen supplementation described in 103.06A and the growth measurements in 103.06B within the same consecutive 12-month period. The dates of oxygen supplementation may be different from the dates of growth measurements.
2. Under 103.06B, we use the appropriate table(s) under 105.08B in the digestive system to determine whether a child's growth is less than the third percentile.
   a. For children from birth to attainment of age 2, we use the weight-for-length table corresponding to the child's gender (Table I or Table II).
   b. For children age 2 to attainment of age 18, we use the body mass index (BMI)-for-age table corresponding to the child's gender (Table III or Table IV).
   c. BMI is the ratio of a child's weight to the square of his or her height. We calculate BMI using the formulas in 105.00G2c.

L. *How do we evaluate respiratory disorders that do not meet one of these listings?*

1. These listings are only examples of common respiratory disorders that we consider severe enough to result in marked and severe functional limitations. If your impairment(s) does not meet the criteria of any of these listings, we must also consider whether you have an impairment(s) that meets the criteria of a listing in another body system. For example, if your CF has resulted in chronic pancreatic or hepatobiliary disease, we evaluate your impairment under the listings in 105.00.
2. If you have a severe medically determinable impairment(s) that does not meet a listing, we will determine whether your impairment(s) medically equals a listing. See § 416.926 of this chapter. Respiratory disorders may be associated with disorders in other body systems, and we consider the combined effects of multiple impairments when we determine whether they medically equal a listing. If your impairment(s) does not meet or medically equal a listing, we will also consider whether it functionally equals the listings. See § 416.926a of this chapter. We use the rules in § 416.994a of this chapter when we decide whether you continue to be disabled.

103.01 Category of Impairments, Respiratory Disorders

103.02 ***Chronic respiratory disorders*** due to any cause except CF (for CF, see 103.04), with A, B, C, D, or E:

A. FEV_1 (see 103.00E) less than or equal to the value in Table I-A or I-B for your age, gender, and height without shoes (see 103.00E3a).

Table I: FEV_1 Criteria for 103.02A

Table I-A

	Age 6 to attainment of age 13 (For both females and males)	
Height without shoes *(centimeters)* < means *less than*	**Height without shoes *(inches)* < means *less than***	**FEV_1 less than or equal to (L, BTPS)**
<123.0	<48.50	0.80
123.0 to <129.0	48.50 to <50.75	0.90
129.0 to <134.0	50.75 to <52.75	1.00
134.0 to <139.0	52.75 to <54.75	1.10
139.0 to <144.0	54.75 to <56.75	1.20
144.0 to <149.0	56.75 to <58.75	1.30
149.0 or more	58.75 or more	1.40

Table I-B

Age 13 to attainment of age 18			
Height without shoes *(centimeters)* < means *less than*	**Height without shoes *(inches)* < means *less than***	***Females*** **FEV_1 less than or equal to (L, BTPS)**	***Males*** **FEV_1 less than or equal to (L, BTPS)**
<153.0	<60.25	1.35	1.40
153.0 to <159.0	60.25 to <62.50	1.45	1.50
159.0 to <164.0	62.50 to <64.50	1.55	1.60
164.0 to <169.0	64.50 to <66.50	1.65	1.70
169.0 to <174.0	66.50 to <68.50	1.75	1.85
174.0 to <180.0	68.50 to <70.75	1.85	2.00
180.0 or more	70.75 or more	1.95	2.10

OR

B. FVC (see 103.00E) less than or equal to the value in Table II-A or II-B for your age, gender, and height without shoes (see 103.00E3a).

Table II: FVC Criteria for 103.02B

Table II-A

Age 6 to attainment of age 13 (For both females and males)		
Height without shoes *(centimeters)* < means *less than*	**Height without shoes *(inches)* < means *less than***	**FVC less than or equal to (L, BTPS)**
<123.0	<48.50	0.85
123.0 to <129.0	48.50 to <50.75	1.00
129.0 to <134.0	50.75 to <52.75	1.10
134.0 to <139.0	52.75 to <54.75	1.30
139.0 to <144.0	54.75 to <56.75	1.40
144.0 to <149.0	56.75 to <58.75	1.55
149.0 or more	58.75 or more	1.70

Table II-B

Age 13 to attainment of age 18			
Height without shoes *(centimeters)* < means *less than*	**Height without shoes *(inches)* < means *less than***	***Females* FVC less than or equal to (L, BTPS)**	***Males* FVC less than or equal to (L, BTPS)**
<153.0	<60.25	1.65	1.65
153.0 to <159.0	60.25 to <62.50	1.70	1.80
159.0 to <164.0	62.50 to <64.50	1.80	1.95
164.0 to <169.0	64.50 to <66.50	1.95	2.10
169.0 to <174.0	66.50 to <68.50	2.05	2.25
174.0 to <180.0	68.50 to <70.75	2.20	2.45
180.0 or more	70.75 or more	2.30	2.55

OR

C. Hypoxemia with the need for at least 1.0 L per minute of continuous (24 hours per day) oxygen supplementation for at least 90 consecutive days.

OR

D. The presence of a tracheostomy.

1. Consider under a disability until the attainment of age 3; or
2. Upon the attainment of age 3, documented need for mechanical ventilation via a tracheostomy for at least 4 hours per day and for at least 90 consecutive days.

OR

E. For children who have not attained age 2, CLD (see 103.00F) with exacerbations or complications requiring three hospitalizations within a 12-month period and at least 30 days apart (the 12-month period must occur within the period we are considering in connection with your application or continuing disability review). Each hospitalization must last at least 48 hours, including hours in a hospital emergency department immediately before the hospitalization. (A child's initial birth hospitalization when CLD is first diagnosed counts as one hospitalization.) Consider under a disability for 1 year from the discharge date of the last hospitalization *or* until the attainment of age 2, whichever is later. After that, evaluate the impairment(s) under 103.03 or another appropriate listing.

103.03 ***Asthma***. (see 103.00G) with exacerbations or complications requiring three hospitalizations within a 12-month period and at least 30 days apart (the

12-month period must occur within the period we are considering in connection with your application or continuing disability review). Each hospitalization must last at least 48 hours, including hours in a hospital emergency department immediately before the hospitalization. Consider under a disability for 1 year from the discharge date of the last hospitalization; after that, evaluate the residual impairment(s) under 103.03 or another appropriate listing.

103.04 ***Cystic fibrosis***. (documented as described in 103.00H), with A, B, C, D, E, F, or G:

A. FEV_1 (see 103.00E) less than or equal to the value in Table III-A or Table III-B for your age, gender, and height without shoes (see 103.00E3a).

OR

B. For children who have not attained age 6, findings on imaging (see 103.00D3) of thickening of the proximal bronchial airways, nodular-cystic lesions, segmental or lobular atelectasis, or consolidation, *and* documentation of one of the following:

1. Shortness of breath with activity; or
2. Accumulation of secretions as manifested by repetitive coughing; or
3. Bilateral rales or rhonchi, or reduction of breath sounds.

OR

C. Exacerbations or complications (see 103.00H3) requiring three hospitalizations of any length within a 12-month period and at least 30 days apart (the 12-month period must occur within the period we are considering in connection with your application or continuing disability review).

OR

D. Spontaneous pneumothorax, secondary to CF, requiring chest tube placement.

OR

E. Respiratory failure (see 103.00J) requiring invasive mechanical ventilation, noninvasive ventilation with BiPAP, or a combination of both treatments, for a continuous period of at least 48 hours, or for a continuous period of at least 72 hours if postoperatively.

OR

F. Pulmonary hemorrhage requiring vascular embolization to control bleeding.

OR

G. Two of the following exacerbations or complications (either two of the same or two different, see 103.00H3 and 103.00H4) within a 12-month period (the

Table III: FEV_1 Criteria for 103.04A

Table III-A

Age 6 to attainment of age 13 (For both females and males)		
Height without shoes *(centimeters)* **< means** *less than*	**Height without shoes** *(inches)* **< means** *less than*	**FEV_1 less than or equal to (L, BTPS)**
<123.0	<48.50	1.00
123.0 to <129.0	48.50 to <50.75	1.15
129.0 to <134.0	50.75 to <52.75	1.25
134.0 to <139.0	52.75 to <54.75	1.40
139.0 to <144.0	54.75 to <56.75	1.50
144.0 to <149.0	56.75 to <58.75	1.70
149.0 or more	58.75 or more	1.80

Table III-B

Age 13 to attainment of age 18			
Height without shoes *(centimeters)* **< means** *less than*	**Height without shoes** *(inches)* **< means** *less than*	*Females* **FEV_1 less than or equal to (L, BTPS)**	*Males* **FEV_1 less than or equal to (L, BTPS)**
<153.0	<60.25	1.75	1.85
153.0 to <159.0	60.25 to <62.50	1.85	2.05
159.0 to <164.0	62.50 to <64.50	1.95	2.15
164.0 to <169.0	64.50 to <66.50	2.10	2.30
169.0 to <174.0	66.50 to <68.50	2.25	2.45
174.0 to <180.0	68.50 to <70.75	2.35	2.60
180.0 or more	70.75 or more	2.50	2.70

12-month period must occur within the period we are considering in connection with your application or continuing disability review):

1. Pulmonary exacerbation requiring 10 consecutive days of intravenous antibiotic treatment.
2. Pulmonary hemorrhage (hemoptysis with more than blood-streaked sputum but not requiring vascular embolization) requiring hospitalization of any length.

3. Weight loss requiring daily supplemental enteral nutrition via a gastrostomy for at least 90 consecutive days *or* parenteral nutrition via a central venous catheter for at least 90 consecutive days.
4. CFRD requiring daily insulin therapy for at least 90 consecutive days.

103.05 [Reserved]

103.06 Growth failure due to any chronic respiratory disorder (see 103.00K), documented by:

A. Hypoxemia with the need for at least 1.0 L per min of oxygen supplementation for at least 4 hours per day and for at least 90 consecutive days.

AND

B. Growth failure as required in 1 or 2:

1. *For children from birth to attainment of age 2*, three weight-for-length measurements that are:
   a. Within a consecutive 12-month period; and
   b. At least 60 days apart; and
   c. Less than the third percentile on the appropriate weight-for-length table under 105.08B1; or
2. *For children age 2 to attainment of age 18*, three BMI-for-age measurements that are:
   a. Within a consecutive 12-month period; and
   b. At least 60 days apart; and
   c. Less than the third percentile on the appropriate BMI-for-age table under 105.08B2.

103.07 [Reserved]

103.08 [Reserved]

103.09 [Reserved]

103.10 [Reserved]

103.11 Lung transplantation (see 103.00I). Consider under a disability for 3 years from the date of the transplant; after that, evaluate the residual impairment(s).

103.12 [Reserved]

103.13 [Reserved]

103.14 Respiratory failure (see 103.00J) resulting from any underlying chronic respiratory disorder except CF (for CF, see 103.04E), requiring invasive mechanical ventilation, noninvasive ventilation with BiPAP, or a combination of both treatments, for a continuous period of at least 48 hours, or for a continuous period of at least 72 hours if postoperatively, *twice* within a 12-month period and at least 30 days apart (the 12-month period must occur within the period we are considering in connection with your application or continuing disability review).

104.00 Cardiovascular System

A. *General*

1. *What do we mean by a cardiovascular impairment?*

a. We mean any disorder that affects the proper functioning of the heart or the circulatory system (that is, arteries, veins, capillaries, and the lymphatic drainage). The disorder can be congenital or acquired.

b. Cardiovascular impairment results from one or more of four consequences of heart disease:

(i) Chronic heart failure or ventricular dysfunction.

(ii) Discomfort or pain due to myocardial ischemia, with or without necrosis of heart muscle.

(iii) Syncope, or near syncope, due to inadequate cerebral perfusion from any cardiac cause, such as obstruction of flow or disturbance in rhythm or conduction resulting in inadequate cardiac output.

(iv) Central cyanosis due to right-to-left shunt, reduced oxygen concentration in the arterial blood, or pulmonary vascular disease.

c. Disorders of the veins or arteries (for example, obstruction, rupture, or aneurysm) may cause impairments of the lower extremities (peripheral vascular disease), the central nervous system, the eyes, the kidneys, and other organs. We will evaluate peripheral vascular disease under 4.11 or 4.12 in part A, and impairments of another body system(s) under the listings for that body system(s).

2. *What do we consider in evaluating cardiovascular impairments?* The listings in this section describe cardiovascular impairments based on symptoms, signs, laboratory findings, response to a regimen of prescribed treatment, and functional limitations.

3. *What do the following terms or phrases mean in these listings?*

a. *Medical consultant* is an individual defined in §§404.1616(a) and 416.1016(a). This term does not include medical sources who provide consultative examinations for us. We use the abbreviation "MC" throughout this section to designate a medical consultant.

b. *Persistent* means that the longitudinal clinical record shows that, with few exceptions, the required finding(s) has been present, or is expected to be present, for a continuous period of at least 12 months, such that a pattern of continuing severity is established.

c. *Recurrent* means that the longitudinal clinical record shows that, within a consecutive 12-month period, the finding(s) occurs at least three times, with intervening periods of improvement of sufficient duration that it is clear that separate events are involved.

d. *Appropriate medically acceptable imaging* means that the technique used is the proper one to evaluate and diagnose the impairment and is commonly recognized as accurate for assessing the cited finding.

e. *A consecutive 12-month period* means a period of 12 consecutive months, all or part of which must occur within the period we are considering in connection with an application or continuing disability review.

f. *Currently present* means that the finding is present at the time of adjudication.

g. *Uncontrolled* means the impairment does not respond adequately to standard prescribed medical treatment.

B. *Documenting Cardiovascular Impairment*

1. *What basic documentation do we need?* We need sufficiently detailed reports of history, physical examinations, laboratory studies, and any prescribed treatment and response to allow us to assess the severity and duration of your cardiovascular impairment. A longitudinal clinical record covering a period of not less than 3 months of observations and treatment is usually necessary, unless we can make a determination or decision based on the current evidence.

2. *Why is a longitudinal clinical record important?* We will usually need a longitudinal clinical record to assess the severity and expected duration of your impairment(s). If you have a listing-level impairment, you probably will have received medically prescribed treatment. Whenever there is evidence of such treatment, your longitudinal clinical record should include a description of the ongoing management and evaluation provided by your treating or other medical source. It should also include your response to this medical management, as well as information about the nature and severity of your impairment. The record will provide us with information on your functional status over an extended period of time and show whether your ability to function is improving, worsening, or unchanging.

3. *What if you have not received ongoing medical treatment?*

a. You may not have received ongoing treatment or have an ongoing relationship with the medical community despite the existence of a severe impairment(s). In this situation, we will base our evaluation on the current objective medical evidence and the other evidence we have. If you do not receive treatment, you cannot show an impairment that meets the criteria of these listings. However, we may find you disabled because you have another impairment(s) that in combination with your cardiovascular impairment medically equals the severity of a listed impairment or that functionally equals the listings.

b. Unless we can decide your claim favorably on the basis of the current evidence, a longitudinal record is still important. In rare instances where there is no or insufficient longitudinal evidence, we may purchase a consultative examination(s) to help us establish the severity and duration of your impairment.

4. *When will we wait before we ask for more evidence?*

a. We will wait when we have information showing that your impairment is not yet stable and the expected change in your impairment might affect our determination or decision. In these situations, we need to wait to properly evaluate the severity and duration of your impairment during a stable period. Examples of when we might wait are:

(i) If you have had a recent acute event; for example, acute rheumatic fever.

(ii) If you have recently had a corrective cardiac procedure; for example, open-heart surgery.

(iii) If you have started new drug therapy and your response to this treatment has not yet been established; for example, beta-blocker therapy for dilated congestive cardiomyopathy.

b. In these situations, we will obtain more evidence 3 months following the event before we evaluate your impairment. However, we will not wait if we have enough information to make a determination or decision based on all of the relevant evidence in your case.

5. *Will we purchase any studies?* In appropriate situations, we will purchase studies necessary to substantiate the diagnosis or to document the severity of your impairment, generally after we have evaluated the medical and other evidence we already have. We will not purchase studies involving exercise testing if there is significant risk involved or if there is another medical reason not to perform the test. We will follow sections 4.00C6, 4.00C7, 4.00C8, and 104.00B7 when we decide whether to purchase exercise testing. We will make a reasonable effort to obtain any additional studies from a qualified medical source in an office or center experienced in pediatric cardiac assessment. (See §416.919g.)

6. *What studies will we not purchase?* We will not purchase any studies involving cardiac catheterization, such as coronary angiography, arteriograms, or electrophysiological studies. However, if the results of catheterization are part of the existing evidence we have, we will consider them together with the other relevant evidence. See 4.00C15a in part A.

7. *Will we use exercise tolerance tests (ETTs) for evaluating children with cardiovascular impairment?*

a. ETTs, though increasingly used, are still less frequently indicated in children than in adults, and can rarely be performed successfully by children under 6 years of age. An ETT may be of value in the assessment of some arrhythmias, in the assessment of the severity of chronic heart failure, and in the assessment of recovery of function following cardiac surgery or other treatment.

b. We will purchase an ETT in a childhood claim only if we cannot make a determination or decision based on the evidence we have and an MC, preferably one with experience in the care of children with cardiovascular impairments, has determined that an ETT is needed to evaluate your impairment. We will not purchase an ETT if you are less than 6 years of age. If we do purchase an ETT for a child age 12 or younger, it must be performed by a qualified medical source in a specialty center for pediatric cardiology or other facility qualified to perform exercise tests of children.

c. For full details on ETT requirements and usage, see 4.00C in part A.

C. *Evaluating Chronic Heart Failure*

1. *What is chronic heart failure (CHF)?*

a. *CHF* is the inability of the heart to pump enough oxygenated blood to body tissues. This syndrome is characterized by symptoms and signs of pulmonary or systemic congestion (fluid retention) or limited cardiac output. Certain laboratory findings of cardiac functional and structural abnormality support the diagnosis of CHF.

b. CHF is considered in these listings as a single category whether due to atherosclerosis (narrowing of the arteries), cardiomyopathy, hypertension, or rheumatic, congenital, or other heart disease. However, if the CHF is the result of primary pulmonary hypertension secondary to disease of the lung (cor pulmonale), we will evaluate your impairment using 3.09 in the respiratory system listings in part A.

2. *What evidence of CHF do we need?*

a. Cardiomegaly or ventricular dysfunction must be present and demonstrated by appropriate medically acceptable imaging, such as chest x-ray, echocardiography (M-Mode, 2-dimensional, and Doppler), radionuclide studies, or cardiac catheterization.

(i) Cardiomegaly is present when:

(A) Left ventricular diastolic dimension or systolic dimension is greater than 2 standard deviations above the mean for the child's body surface area;

(B) Left ventricular mass is greater than 2 standard deviations above the mean for the child's body surface area; or

(C) Chest x-ray (6 foot PA film) is indicative of cardiomegaly if the cardiothoracic ratio is over 60 percent at 1 year of age or less, or 55 percent or greater at more than 1 year of age.

(ii) Ventricular dysfunction is present when indices of left ventricular function, such as fractional shortening or ejection fraction (the percentage of the blood in the ventricle actually pumped out with each contraction), are greater than 2 standard deviations below the mean for the child's age. (Fractional shortening, also called shortening fraction, reflects the left ventricular systolic function in the absence of segmental wall motion abnormalities and has a linear correlation with ejection fraction. In children, fractional shortening is more commonly used than ejection fraction.)

(iii) However, these measurements alone do not reflect your functional capacity, which we evaluate by considering all of the relevant evidence.

(iv) Other findings on appropriate medically acceptable imaging may include increased pulmonary vascular markings, pleural effusion, and pulmonary edema. These findings need not be present on each report, since CHF may be controlled by prescribed treatment.

b. To establish that you have *chronic* heart failure, we require that your medical history and physical examination describe characteristic symptoms and signs of pulmonary or systemic congestion or of limited cardiac output associated with the abnormal findings on appropriate medically acceptable imaging. When a remediable factor, such as an arrhythmia, triggers an acute episode of heart failure, you may experience restored cardiac function and a chronic impairment may not be present.

(i) Symptoms of congestion or of limited cardiac output include easy fatigue, weakness, shortness of breath (dyspnea), cough, or chest discomfort at rest or with activity. Children with CHF may also experience shortness of breath on lying flat (orthopnea) or episodes of shortness of breath that wake them from sleep (paroxysmal nocturnal dyspnea). They may also experience cardiac arrhythmias resulting in palpitations, lightheadedness, or fainting. Fatigue or exercise intolerance in an infant may be manifested by prolonged feeding time, often associated with excessive respiratory effort and sweating.

(ii) During infancy, other manifestations of chronic heart failure may include repeated lower respiratory tract infections.

(iii) Signs of congestion may include hepatomegaly, ascites, increased jugular venous distention or pressure, rales, peripheral edema, rapid shallow breathing (tachypnea), or rapid weight gain. However, these signs need not be found on all examinations because fluid retention may be controlled by prescribed treatment.

3. How do we evaluate growth failure due to CHF?

a. To evaluate growth failure due to CHF, we require documentation of the clinical findings of CHF described in 104.00C2 and the growth measurements in 104.02C within the same consecutive 12-month period. The dates of clinical findings may be different from the dates of growth measurements.

b. Under 104.02C, we use the appropriate table(s) under 105.08B in the digestive system to determine whether a child's growth is less than the third percentile.

(i) For Children from birth to attainment of age 2, we use the weight-for-length table corresponding to the child's gender (Table I or Table II).

(ii) For children age 2 to attainment of of age 18, we use the body mass index (BMI)-for-age table corresponding to the child's gender (Table III or Table IV).

(iii) BMI is the ratio of a child's weight to the square of his or her height. We calculate BMI using the formulas in 105.00G2c.

D. *Evaluating Congenital Heart Disease*

1. *What is congenital heart disease?* Congenital heart disease is any abnormality of the heart or the major blood vessels that is present at birth. Examples include:

a. *Abnormalities of cardiac septation,* including ventricular septal defect or atrioventricular canal;

b. *Abnormalities resulting in cyanotic heart disease,* including tetralogy of Fallot or transposition of the great arteries;

c. *Valvular defects or obstructions to ventricular outflow,* including pulmonary or aortic stenosis or coarctation of the aorta; and

d. *Major abnormalities of ventricular development,* including hypoplastic left heart syndrome or pulmonary tricuspid atresia with hypoplastic right ventricle.

2. *How will we evaluate symptomatic congenital heart disease?*

a. Because of improved treatment methods, more children with congenital heart disease are living longer. Although some types of congenital heart disease may be corrected by surgery, many children with treated congenital heart disease continue to have problems throughout their lives (symptomatic congenital heart disease). If you have congenital heart disease that results in chronic heart failure with evidence of ventricular dysfunction or in recurrent arrhythmias, we will evaluate your impairment under 104.02 or 104.05. Otherwise, we will evaluate your impairment under 104.06.

b. For 104.06A2, we will accept pulse oximetry measurements instead of arterial O2, but the arterial O2 values are preferred, if available.

c. For 104.06D, examples of impairments that in most instances will require life-saving surgery or a combination of surgery and other major interventional procedures (for example, multiple "balloon" catheter procedures) before age 1 include, but are not limited to, the following:

(i) Hypoplastic left heart syndrome,

(ii) Critical aortic stenosis with neonatal heart failure,

(iii) Critical coarctation of the aorta, with or without associated anomalies,

(iv) Complete atrioventricular canal defects,

(v) Transposition of the great arteries,

(vi) Tetralogy of Fallot,

(vii) Pulmonary atresia with intact ventricular septum,

(viii) Single ventricle,

(ix) Tricuspid atresia, and

(x) Multiple ventricular septal defects.

E. *Evaluating Arrhythmias*

1. *What is an arrhythmia?* An *arrhythmia* is a change in the regular beat of the heart. Your heart may seem to skip a beat or beat irregularly, very quickly (tachycardia), or very slowly (bradycardia).

2. *What are the different types of arrhythmias?*

a. There are many types of arrhythmias. Arrhythmias are identified by where they occur in the heart (atria or ventricles) and by what happens to the heart's rhythm when they occur.

b. Arrhythmias arising in the cardiac atria (upper chambers of the heart) are called atrial or supraventricular arrhythmias. Ventricular arrhythmias begin in the ventricles (lower chambers). In general, ventricular arrhythmias caused by heart disease are the most serious.

3. *How do we evaluate arrhythmias using 104.05?*

a. We will use 104.05 when you have arrhythmias that are not fully controlled by medication, an implanted pacemaker, or an implanted cardiac defibrillator and you have uncontrolled recurrent episodes of syncope or near syncope. If your arrhythmias are controlled, we will evaluate your underlying heart disease using the appropriate listing. For other considerations when we evaluate arrhythmias in the presence of an implanted cardiac defibrillator, see 104.00E4.

b. We consider *near syncope* to be a period of altered consciousness, since syncope is a loss of consciousness or a faint. It is not merely a feeling of light-headedness, momentary weakness, or dizziness.

c. For purposes of 104.05, there must be a documented association between the syncope or near syncope and the recurrent arrhythmia. The recurrent arrhythmia, not some other cardiac or non-cardiac disorder, must be established as the cause of the associated symptom. This documentation of the association between the symptoms and the arrhythmia may come from the usual diagnostic methods, including Holter monitoring (also called ambulatory electrocardiography) and tilt-table testing with a concurrent ECG. Although an arrhythmia may be a coincidental finding on an ETT, we will not purchase an ETT to document the presence of a cardiac arrhythmia.

4. *What will we consider when you have an implanted cardiac defibrillator and you do not have arrhythmias that meet the requirements of 104.05?*

a. Implanted cardiac defibrillators are used to prevent sudden cardiac death in children who have had, or are at high risk for, cardiac arrest from life-threatening ventricular arrhythmias. The largest group of children at risk for sudden cardiac death consists of children with cardiomyopathy (ischemic or non-ischemic) and reduced ventricular function. However, life-threatening ventricular arrhythmias can also occur in children with little or no ventricular dysfunction. The shock from the implanted cardiac defibrillator is a unique form of treatment; it rescues a child from what may have been cardiac arrest. However, as a consequence of the shock(s), children may experience psychological distress, which we may evaluate under the mental disorders listings in 112.00ff.

b. Most implantable cardiac defibrillators have rhythm-correcting and pacemaker capabilities. In some children, these functions may result in the termination of ventricular arrhythmias without an otherwise painful shock. (The shock is like being kicked in the chest.) Implanted cardiac defibrillators may deliver inappropriate shocks, often repeatedly, in response to benign arrhythmias or electrical malfunction. Also, exposure to strong electrical or magnetic fields, such as from MRI (magnetic resonance imaging), can trigger or reprogram an implanted cardiac defibrillator, resulting in inappropriate shocks. We must consider the frequency of, and the reason(s) for, the shocks when evaluating the severity and duration of your impairment.

c. In general, the exercise limitations imposed on children with an implanted cardiac defibrillator are those dictated by the underlying heart impairment. However, the exercise limitations may be greater when the implanted cardiac defibrillator delivers an inappropriate shock in response to the increase in heart rate with exercise, or when there is exercise-induced ventricular arrhythmia.

F. *Evaluating Other Cardiovascular Impairments*

1. *What is ischemic heart disease (IHD) and how will we evaluate it in children?* IHD results when one or more of your coronary arteries is narrowed or obstructed or,

in rare situations, constricted due to vasospasm, interfering with the normal flow of blood to your heart muscle (ischemia). The obstruction may be the result of an embolus, a thrombus, or plaque. When heart muscle tissue dies as a result of the reduced blood supply, it is called a myocardial infarction (heart attack). Ischemia is rare in children, but when it occurs, its effects on children are the same as on adults. If you have IHD, we will evaluate it under 4.00E and 4.04 in part A.

2. *How will we evaluate hypertension?* Because *hypertension* (high blood pressure) generally causes disability through its effects on other body systems, we will evaluate it by reference to the specific body system(s) affected (heart, brain, kidneys, or eyes) when we consider its effects under the listings. We will also consider any limitations imposed by your hypertension when we consider whether you have an impairment that functionally equals the listings.

3. *What is cardiomyopathy and how will we evaluate it? Cardiomyopathy* is a disease of the heart muscle. The heart loses its ability to pump blood (heart failure), and in some instances, heart rhythm is disturbed, leading to irregular heartbeats (arrhythmias). Usually, the exact cause of the muscle damage is never found (idiopathic cardiomyopathy). There are various types of cardiomyopathy, which fall into two major categories: *Ischemic* and *nonischemic* cardiomyopathy. Ischemic cardiomyopathy typically refers to heart muscle damage that results from coronary artery disease, including heart attacks. Nonischemic cardiomyopathy includes several types: Dilated, hypertrophic, and restrictive. We will evaluate cardiomyopathy under 4.04 in part A, 104.02, 104.05, or 111.06, depending on its effects on you.

4. *How will we evaluate valvular heart disease?* We will evaluate valvular heart disease under the listing appropriate for its effect on you. Thus, we may use 4.04 in part A, 104.02, 104.05, 104.06, or an appropriate neurological listing in 111.00ff.

5. *What do we consider when we evaluate heart transplant recipients?*

a. After your heart transplant, we will consider you disabled for 1 year following the surgery because there is a greater likelihood of rejection of the organ and infection during the first year.

b. However, heart transplant patients generally meet our definition of disability before they undergo transplantation. We will determine the onset of your disability based on the facts in your case.

c. We will not assume that you became disabled when your name was placed on a transplant waiting list. This is because you may be placed on a waiting list soon after diagnosis of the cardiac disorder that may eventually require a transplant. Physicians recognize that candidates for transplantation often have to wait months or even years before a suitable donor heart is found, so they place their patients on the list as soon as permitted.

d. When we do a continuing disability review to determine whether you are still disabled, we will evaluate your residual impairment(s), as shown by symptoms, signs, and laboratory findings, including any side effects of medication. We will consider any remaining symptoms, signs, and laboratory findings indicative of cardiac dysfunction in deciding whether medical improvement (as defined in §416.994a) has occurred.

6. *How will we evaluate chronic rheumatic fever or rheumatic heart disease?* The diagnosis should be made in accordance with the current revised Jones criteria for guidance in the diagnosis of rheumatic fever. We will evaluate persistence of rheumatic fever activity under 104.13. If you have evidence of chronic heart failure or recurrent arrhythmias associated with rheumatic heart disease, we will use 104.02 or 104.05.

7. *What is hyperlipidemia and how will we evaluate it? Hyperlipidemia*is the general term for an elevation of any or all of the lipids (fats or cholesterol) in the blood; for example, hypertriglyceridemia, hypercholesterolemia, and hyperlipoproteinemia. These disorders of lipoprotein metabolism and transport can cause defects throughout the body. The effects most likely to interfere with function are those produced by atherosclerosis (narrowing of the arteries) and coronary artery disease. We will evaluate your lipoprotein disorder by considering its effects on you.

8. *How will we evaluate Kawasaki disease?* We will evaluate Kawasaki disease under the listing appropriate to its effects on you, which may include major coronary artery aneurysm or heart failure. A major coronary artery aneurysm may cause ischemia or arrhythmia, which we will evaluate under 4.04 in part A or 104.05. We will evaluate chronic heart failure under 104.02.

9. *What is lymphedema and how will we evaluate it?*

a. *Lymphedema* is edema of the extremities due to a disorder of the lymphatic circulation; at its worst, it is called elephantiasis. Primary lymphedema is caused by abnormal development of lymph vessels and may be present at birth (congenital lymphedema), but more often develops during the teens (lymphedema praecox). Secondary lymphedema is due to obstruction or destruction of normal lymphatic channels due to tumor, surgery, repeated infections, or parasitic infection such as filariasis. Lymphedema most commonly affects one extremity.

b. Lymphedema does not meet the requirements of 4.11 in part A, although it may medically equal the severity of that listing. We will evaluate lymphedema by considering whether the underlying cause meets or medically equals any listing or whether the lymphedema medically equals a cardiovascular listing, such as 4.11, or a musculoskeletal listing, such as 101.02A or 101.03. If no listing is met or medically equaled, we will evaluate any functional limitations imposed by your lymphedema when we consider whether you have an impairment that functionally equals the listings.

10. *What is Marfan syndrome and how will we evaluate it?*

a. Marfan syndrome is a genetic connective tissue disorder that affects multiple body systems, including the skeleton, eyes, heart, blood vessels, nervous system, skin, and lungs. There is no specific laboratory test to diagnose Marfan syndrome. The diagnosis is generally made by medical history, including family history, physical examination, including an evaluation of the ratio of arm/leg size to trunk size, a slit lamp eye examination, and a heart test(s), such as an echocardiogram. In some cases, a genetic analysis may be useful, but such analyses may not provide any additional helpful information.

b. The effects of Marfan syndrome can range from mild to severe. In most cases, the disorder progresses as you age. Most individuals with Marfan syndrome have abnormalities associated with the heart and blood vessels. Your heart's mitral valve may leak, causing a heart murmur. Small leaks may not cause symptoms, but larger ones may cause shortness of breath, fatigue, and palpitations. Another effect is that the wall of the aorta may be weakened and stretch (aortic dilation). This aortic dilation may tear, dissect, or rupture, causing serious heart problems or sometimes sudden death. We will evaluate the manifestations of your Marfan syndrome under the appropriate body system criteria, such as 4.10 in part A, or if necessary consider the functional limitations imposed by your impairment.

G. *Other Evaluation Issues*

1. *What effect does obesity have on the cardiovascular system and how will we evaluate it?* Obesity is a medically determinable impairment that is often associated with disorders of the cardiovascular system. Disturbance of this system can be a major cause of disability in children with obesity. Obesity may affect the cardiovascular system because of the increased workload the additional body mass places on the heart. Obesity may make it harder for the chest and lungs to expand. This can mean that the respiratory system must work harder to provide needed oxygen. This in turn would make the heart work harder to pump blood to carry oxygen to the body. Because the body would be working harder at rest, its ability to perform additional work would be less than would otherwise be expected. Thus, the combined effects of obesity with cardiovascular impairments can be greater than the effects of each of the impairments considered separately. We must consider any additional and cumulative effects of obesity when we determine whether you have a severe cardiovascular impairment or a listing-level cardiovascular impairment (or a combination of impairments that medically equals a listing), and when we determine whether your impairment(s) functionally equals the listings.

2. *How do we relate treatment to functional status?* In general, conclusions about the severity of a cardiovascular impairment cannot be made on the basis of type of treatment rendered or anticipated. The amount of function restored and the time required for improvement after treatment (medical, surgical, or a

prescribed program of progressive physical activity) vary with the nature and extent of the disorder, the type of treatment, and other factors. Depending upon the timing of this treatment in relation to the alleged onset date of disability, we may need to defer evaluation of the impairment for a period of up to 3 months from the date treatment began to permit consideration of treatment effects, unless we can make a determination or decision using the evidence we have. See 104.00B4.

3. *How do we evaluate impairments that do not meet one of the cardiovascular listings?*

a. These listings are only examples of common cardiovascular disorders that we consider severe enough to result in marked and severe functional limitations. If your severe impairment(s) does not meet the criteria of any of these listings, we must also consider whether you have an impairment(s) that satisfies the criteria of a listing in another body system.

b. If you have a severe medically determinable impairment(s) that does not meet a listing, we will determine whether your impairment(s) medically equals a listing. (See §416.926.) If you have a severe impairment(s) that does not meet or medically equal the criteria of a listing, we will consider whether it functionally equals the listings. (See §416.926a.) When we decide whether you continue to be disabled, we use the rules in §416.994a.

104.01 Category of Impairments, Cardiovascular System

104.02 Chronic heart failure while on a regimen of prescribed treatment with symptoms and signs described in 104.00C2 and with one of the following:

A. Persistent tachycardia at rest (see Table I);

OR

B. Persistent tachypnea at rest (see Table II) or markedly decreased exercise tolerance (see 104.00C2b);

OR

C. Growth failure as required in 1 or 2:

1. *For children from birth to attainment of age* 2, three weight-for-length measurements that are:

a. Within a consecutive 12-month period; and

b. At least 60 days apart; and

c. Less than the third percentile on the appropriate weight-for-length Table I or II under 105.08B1; or

Table I—Tachycardia at Rest

Age	Apical heart rate (beats per minute)
Under 1 year	150
1 through 3 years	130
4 through 9 years	120
10 through 15 years	110
Over 15 years	100

Table II—Tachypnea at Rest

Age	Respiratory rate over (per minute)
Under 1 year	40
1 through 5 years	35
6 through 9 years	30
Over 9 years	25

2. *For children age 2 to attainment of age 18,* three BMI-for-age measurements that are:

a. Within a consecutive 12-month period; and

b. At least 60 days apart; and

c. Less than the third percentile on the appropriate BMI-for-age Table III or IV under 105.08B2.

104.05 Recurrent arrhythmias, not related to reversible causes such as electrolyte abnormalities or digitalis glycoside or antiarrhythmic drug toxicity, resulting in uncontrolled (see 104.00A3g), recurrent (see 104.00A3c) episodes of cardiac syncope or near syncope (see 104.00E3b), despite prescribed treatment (see 104.00B3 if there is no prescribed treatment), and documented by resting or ambulatory (Holter) electrocardiography, or by other appropriate medically acceptable testing, coincident with the occurrence of syncope or near syncope (see 104.00E3c).

104.06 Congenital heart disease, documented by appropriate medically acceptable imaging (see 104.00A3d) or cardiac catheterization, with one of the following:

A. Cyanotic heart disease, with persistent, chronic hypoxemia as manifested by:

1. Hematocrit of 55 percent or greater on two evaluations 3 months or more apart within a consecutive 12-month period (see 104.00A3e); or

2. Arterial O2 saturation of less than 90 percent in room air, or resting arterial PO2 of 60 Torr or less; or

3. Hypercyanotic spells, syncope, characteristic squatting, or other incapacitating symptoms directly related to documented cyanotic heart disease; or

4. Exercise intolerance with increased hypoxemia on exertion.

OR

B. Secondary pulmonary vascular obstructive disease with pulmonary arterial systolic pressure elevated to at least 70 percent of the systemic arterial systolic pressure.

OR

C. Symptomatic acyanotic heart disease, with ventricular dysfunction interfering very seriously with the ability to independently initiate, sustain, or complete activities.

OR

D. For infants under 12 months of age at the time of filing, with life-threatening congenital heart impairment that will require or already has required surgical treatment in the first year of life, and the impairment is expected to be disabling (because of residual impairment following surgery, or the recovery time required, or both) until the attainment of at least 1 year of age, consider the infant to be under disability until the attainment of at least age 1; thereafter, evaluate impairment severity with reference to the appropriate listing.

104.09 Heart transplant. Consider under a disability for 1 year following surgery; thereafter, evaluate residual impairment under the appropriate listing.

104.13 Rheumatic heart disease, with persistence of rheumatic fever activity manifested by significant murmurs(s), cardiac enlargement or ventricular dysfunction (see 104.00C2a), and other associated abnormal laboratory findings; for example, an elevated sedimentation rate or ECG findings, for 6 months or more in a consecutive 12-month period (see 104.00A3e). Consider under a disability for 18 months from the established onset of impairment, then evaluate any residual impairment(s).

105.00 Digestive System

A. *What kinds of disorders do we consider in the digestive system?* Disorders of the digestive system include gastrointestinal hemorrhage, hepatic (liver) dysfunction, inflammatory bowel disease, short bowel syndrome, and malnutrition. They may also lead to complications, such as obstruction, or be accompanied by manifestations in other body systems. Congenital abnormalities involving the organs of the gastrointestinal system may interfere with the ability to maintain adequate nutrition, growth, and development.

B. *What documentation do we need?* We need a record of your medical evidence, including clinical and laboratory findings. The documentation should include appropriate medically acceptable imaging studies and reports of endoscopy, operations, and pathology, as appropriate to each listing, to document the severity and duration of your digestive disorder. We may also need assessments of your growth and development. Medically acceptable imaging includes, but is not limited to, x-ray imaging, computerized axial tomography (CAT scan), magnetic resonance imaging (MRI), and radionuclide scans. *Appropriate* means that the technique used is the proper one to support the evaluation and diagnosis of the disorder. The findings required by these listings must occur within the period we are considering in connection with your application or continuing disability review.

C. *How do we consider the effects of treatment?*

1. Digestive disorders frequently respond to medical or surgical treatment; therefore, we generally consider the severity and duration of these disorders within the context of prescribed treatment.

2. We assess the effects of treatment, including medication, therapy, surgery, or any other form of treatment you receive, by determining if there are improvements in the symptoms, signs, and laboratory findings of your digestive disorder. We also assess any side effects of your treatment that may further limit your functioning.

3. To assess the effects of your treatment, we may need information about:

a. The treatment you have been prescribed (for example, the type of medication or therapy, or your use of parenteral (intravenous) nutrition or supplemental enteral nutrition via a gastrostomy);

b. The dosage, method, and frequency of administration;

c. Your response to the treatment;

d. Any adverse effects of such treatment; and

e. The expected duration of the treatment.

4. Because the effects of treatment may be temporary or long-term, in most cases we need information about the impact of your treatment, including its expected duration and side effects, over a sufficient period of time to help us assess its outcome. When adverse effects of treatment contribute to the severity of your impairment(s), we will consider the duration or expected duration of the treatment when we assess the duration of your impairment(s).

5. If you need parenteral (intravenous) nutrition or supplemental enteral nutrition via a gastrostomy to avoid debilitating complications of a digestive disorder, this

treatment will not, in itself, indicate that you have marked and severe functional limitations. The exceptions are 105.07, short bowel syndrome, and 105.10, for children who have not attained age 3 and who require supplemental daily enteral feedings via a gastrostomy (see 105.00F and 105.00H).

6. If you have not received ongoing treatment or have not had an ongoing relationship with the medical community despite the existence of a severe impairment(s), we will evaluate the severity and duration of your digestive impairment on the basis of the current medical and other evidence in your case record. If you have not received treatment, you may not be able to show an impairment that meets the criteria of one of the digestive system listings, but your digestive impairment may medically equal a listing or functionally equal the listings.

D. *How do we evaluate chronic liver disease?*

1. *General. Chronic liver disease* is characterized by liver cell necrosis, inflammation, or scarring (fibrosis or cirrhosis), due to any cause, that persists for more than 6 months. Chronic liver disease may result in portal hypertension, cholestasis (suppression of bile flow), extrahepatic manifestations, or liver cancer. (We evaluate liver cancer under 113.03.) Significant loss of liver function may be manifested by hemorrhage from varices or portal hypertensive gastropathy, ascites (accumulation of fluid in the abdominal cavity), hydrothorax (ascitic fluid in the chest cavity), or encephalopathy. There can also be progressive deterioration of laboratory findings that are indicative of liver dysfunction. Liver transplantation is the only definitive cure for end stage liver disease (ESLD).

2. *Examples of chronic liver disease* include, but are not limited to, biliary atresia, chronic hepatitis, non-alcoholic steatohepatitis (NASH), primary biliary cirrhosis (PBC), primary sclerosing cholangitis (PSC), autoimmune hepatitis, hemochromatosis, drug-induced liver disease, Wilson's disease, and serum alpha-1 antitrypsin deficiency. Children can also have congenital abnormalities of abdominal organs or inborn metabolic disorders that result in chronic liver disease. Acute hepatic injury is frequently reversible, as in viral, drug-induced, toxin-induced, and ischemic hepatitis. In the absence of evidence of a chronic impairment, episodes of acute liver disease do not meet 105.05.

3. *Manifestations of chronic liver disease.*

a. *Symptoms* may include, but are not limited to, pruritis (itching), fatigue, nausea, loss of appetite, or sleep disturbances. Children can also have associated developmental delays or poor school performance. Symptoms of chronic liver disease may have a poor correlation with the severity of liver disease and functional ability.

b. *Signs* may include, but are not limited to, jaundice, enlargement of the liver and spleen, ascites, peripheral edema, and altered mental status.

c. *Laboratory findings* may include, but are not limited to, increased liver enzymes, increased serum total bilirubin, increased ammonia levels, decreased serum albumin, and abnormal coagulation studies, such as increased International Normalized Ratio (INR) or decreased platelet counts. Abnormally low serum albumin or elevated INR levels indicate loss of synthetic liver function, with increased likelihood of cirrhosis and associated complications. However, other abnormal lab tests, such as liver enzymes, serum total bilirubin, or ammonia levels, may have a poor correlation with the severity of liver disease and functional ability. A liver biopsy may demonstrate the degree of liver cell necrosis, inflammation, fibrosis, and cirrhosis. If you have had a liver biopsy, we will make every reasonable effort to obtain the results; however, we will not purchase a liver biopsy. Imaging studies (CAT scan, ultrasound, MRI) may show the size and consistency (fatty liver, scarring) of the liver and document ascites (see 105.00D6).

4. *Chronic viral hepatitis infections.*

a. *General.*

(i) *Chronic viral hepatitis* infections are commonly caused by hepatitis C virus (HCV), and to a lesser extent, hepatitis B virus (HBV). Usually, these are slowly progressive disorders that persist over many years during which the symptoms and signs are typically nonspecific, intermittent, and mild (for example, fatigue, difficulty with concentration, or right upper quadrant pain). Laboratory findings (liver enzymes, imaging studies, liver biopsy pathology) and complications are generally similar in HCV and HBV. The spectrum of these chronic viral hepatitis infections ranges widely and includes an asymptomatic state; insidious disease with mild to moderate symptoms associated with fluctuating liver tests; extrahepatic manifestations; cirrhosis, both compensated and decompensated; ESLD with the need for liver transplantation; and liver cancer. Treatment for chronic viral hepatitis infections varies considerably based on age, medication tolerance, treatment response, adverse effects of treatment, and duration of the treatment. Comorbid disorders, such as HIV infection, may accelerate the clinical course of viral hepatitis infection(s) or may result in a poorer response to medical treatment.

(ii) We evaluate all types of chronic viral hepatitis infections under 105.05 or any listing in an affected body system(s). If your impairment(s) does not meet or medically equal a listing, we will consider the effects of your hepatitis when we assess whether your impairment(s) functionally equals the listings.

b. *Chronic hepatitis B virus (HBV) infection.*

(i) *Chronic HBV infection* can be diagnosed by the detection of hepatitis B surface antigen (HBsAg) or hepatitis B virus DNA (HBV DNA) in the blood for at least 6 months. In addition, detection of the hepatitis B e antigen (HBeAg) suggests an increased likelihood of progression to cirrhosis, ESLD, and hepatocellular carcinoma. (HBeAg may also be referred to as "hepatitis B early antigen" or "hepatitis B envelope antigen.")

(ii) The therapeutic goal of treatment is to suppress HBV replication and thereby prevent progression to cirrhosis, ESLD, and hepatocellular carcinoma. Treatment usually includes interferon injections, oral antiviral agents, or a combination of both. Common adverse effects of treatment are the same as noted in 105.00D4c(ii) for HCV, and generally end within a few days after treatment is discontinued.

c. *Chronic hepatitis C virus (HCV) infection.*

(i) *Chronic HCV infection* is diagnosed by the detection of hepatitis C viral RNA in the blood for at least 6 months. Documentation of the therapeutic response to treatment is also monitored by the quantitative assay of serum HCV RNA ("HCV viral load"). Treatment usually includes a combination of interferon injections and oral ribavirin; whether a therapeutic response has occurred is usually assessed after 12 weeks of treatment by checking the HCV viral load. If there has been a substantial reduction in HCV viral load (also known as early viral response, or EVR), this reduction is predictive of sustained viral response with completion of treatment. Combined therapy is commonly discontinued after 12 weeks when there is no early viral response, since in that circumstance there is little chance of obtaining a sustained viral response (SVR). Otherwise, treatment is usually continued for a total of 48 weeks.

(ii) Combined interferon and ribavirin treatment may have significant adverse effects that may require dosing reduction, planned interruption of treatment, or discontinuation of treatment. Adverse effects may include: Anemia (ribavirin-induced hemolysis), neutropenia, thrombocytopenia, fever, cough, fatigue, myalgia, arthralgia, nausea, loss of appetite, pruritis, and insomnia. Behavioral side effects may also occur. Influenza-like symptoms are generally worse in the first 4 to 6 hours after each interferon injection and during the first weeks of treatment. Adverse effects generally end within a few days after treatment is discontinued.

d. *Extrahepatic manifestations of HBV and HCV.* In addition to their hepatic manifestations, both HBV and HCV may have significant extrahepatic manifestations in a variety of body systems. These include, but are not limited to: Keratoconjunctivitis (sicca syndrome), glomerulonephritis, skin disorders (for example, lichen planus, porphyria cutanea tarda), neuropathy, and immune dysfunction (for example, cryoglobulinemia, Sjögren's syndrome, and vasculitis). The extrahepatic manifestations of HBV and HCV may not correlate with the severity of your hepatic impairment. If you impairment(s) does not meet or medically equal a listing in an affected body system(s), we will consider the effects of your extrahepatic manifestations when we determine whether your impairment(s) functionally equals the listings.

5. *Gastrointestinal hemorrhage* (105.02 and 105.05A). Gastrointestinal hemorrhaging can result in hematemesis (vomiting of blood), melena (tarry stools), or

hematochezia (bloody stools). Under 105.02, the required transfusions of at least 10 cc of blood/kg of body weight must be at least 30 days apart and occur at least three times during a consecutive 6-month period. Under 105.05A, *hemodynamic instability* is diagnosed with signs such as pallor (pale skin), diaphoresis (profuse perspiration), rapid pulse, low blood pressure, postural hypotension (pronounced fall in blood pressure when arising to an upright position from lying down) or syncope (fainting). Hemorrhaging that results in hemodynamic instability is potentially life-threatening and therefore requires hospitalization for transfusion and supportive care. Under 105.05A, we require only one hospitalization for transfusion of at least 10 cc of blood/kg of body weight.

6. *Ascites or hydrothorax* (105.05B) indicates significant loss of liver function due to chronic liver disease. We evaluate ascites or hydrothorax that is not attributable to other causes under 105.05B. The required findings must be present on at least two evaluations at least 60 days apart within a consecutive 6-month period and despite continuing treatment as prescribed.

7. *Spontaneous bacterial peritonitis* (105.05C) is an infectious complication of chronic liver disease. It is diagnosed by ascitic peritoneal fluid that is documented to contain an absolute neutrophil count of at least 250 cells/mm3. The required finding in 105.05C is satisfied with one evaluation documenting peritoneal fluid infection. We do not evaluate other causes of peritonitis that are unrelated to chronic liver disease, such as tuberculosis, malignancy, and perforated bowel, under this listing. We evaluate these other causes of peritonitis under the appropriate body system listings.

8. *Hepatorenal syndrome* (105.05D) is defined as functional renal failure associated with chronic liver disease in the absence of underlying kidney pathology. Hepatorenal syndrome is documented by elevation of serum creatinine, marked sodium retention, and oliguria (reduced urine output). The requirements of 105.05D are satisfied with documentation of any one of the three laboratory findings on one evaluation. We do not evaluate known causes of renal dysfunction, such as glomerulonephritis, tubular necrosis, drug-induced renal disease, and renal infections, under this listing. We evaluate these other renal impairments under 106.00ff.

9. *Hepatopulmonary syndrome* (105.05E) is defined as arterial deoxygenation (hypoxemia) that is associated with chronic liver disease due to intrapulmonary arteriovenous shunting and vasodilatation in the absence of other causes of arterial deoxygenation. Clinical manifestations usually include dyspnea, orthodeoxia (increasing hypoxemia with erect position), platypnea (improvement of dyspnea with flat position), cyanosis, and clubbing. The requirements of 105.05E are satisfied with documentation of any one of the findings on one evaluation. In 105.05E1, we require documentation of the altitude of the testing facility because altitude affects the measurement of arterial oxygenation. We will not purchase

the specialized studies described in 105.05E2; however, if you have had these studies at a time relevant to your claim, we will make every reasonable effort to obtain the reports for the purpose of establishing whether your impairment meets 105.05E2.

10. *Hepatic encephalopathy* (105.05F).

a. *General.* Hepatic encephalopathy usually indicates severe loss of hepatocellular function. We define hepatic encephalopathy under 105.05F as a recurrent or chronic neuropsychiatric disorder, characterized by abnormal behavior, cognitive dysfunction, altered state of consciousness, and ultimately coma and death. The diagnosis is established by changes in mental status associated with fleeting neurological signs, including "flapping tremor" (asterixis), characteristic electroencephalographic (EEG) abnormalities, or abnormal laboratory values that indicate loss of synthetic liver function. We will not purchase the EEG testing described in 105.05F3b; however, if you have had this test at a time relevant to your claim, we will make every reasonable effort to obtain the report for the purpose of establishing whether your impairment meets 105.05F.

b. *Acute encephalopathy.* We will not evaluate your acute encephalopathy under 105.05F if it results from conditions other than chronic liver disease, such as vascular events and neoplastic diseases. We will evaluate these other causes of acute encephalopathy under the appropriate body system listings.

11. *End stage liver disease (ESLD) documented by scores from the SSA Chronic Liver Disease (SSA CLD) calculation* (*105.05G1*) *and SSA Chronic Liver Disease-Pediatric (SSA CLD-P) calculation* (*105.05G2*).

a. *SSA CLD score.*

(i) If you are age 12 or older, we will use the SSA CLD score to evaluate your ESLD under 105.05G1. We explain how we calculate the SSA CLD score in a(ii) through a(vii) of this section.

(ii) To calculate the SSA CLD score, we use a formula that includes three laboratory values: Serum total bilirubin (mg/dL), serum creatinine (mg/dL), and International Normalized Ratio (INR). The formula for the SSA CLD score calculation is:

9.57 × [Loge(serum creatinine mg/dL)]
+ 3.78 × [Loge(serum total bilirubin mg/dL)]
+ 11.2 × [Loge(INR)]
+ 6.43

(iii) When we indicate "Loge" in the formula for the SSA CLD score calculation, we mean the "base *e* logarithm" or "natural logarithm" (ln) of a numerical laboratory value, not the "base 10 logarithm" or "common logarithm" (log) of the laboratory value, and not the actual laboratory value. For an example of SSA CLD calculation, see 5.00D11c.

(iv) For any SSA CLD score calculation, all of the required laboratory values must have been obtained within 30 days of each other. If there are multiple laboratory values within the 30-day interval for any given laboratory test (serum total bilirubin, serum creatinine, or INR), we will use the highest value for the SSA CLD score calculation. We will round all laboratory values less than 1.0 up to 1.0.

(v) Listing 105.05G requires two SSA CLD scores. The laboratory values for the second SSA CLD score calculation must have been obtained at least 60 days after the latest laboratory value for the first SSA CLD score and within the required 6-month period. We will consider the date of each SSA CLD score to be the date of the first laboratory value used for its calculation.

(vi) If you are in renal failure or on dialysis within a week of any serum creatinine test in the period used for the SSA CLD calculation, we will use a serum creatinine of 4, which is the maximum serum creatinine level allowed in the calculation, to calculate your SSA CLD score.

(vii) If you have the two SSA CLD scores required by 105.05G1, we will find that your impairment meets the criteria of the listing from at least the date of the first SSA CLD score.

b. *SSA CLD-P score.*

(i) If you have not attained age 12, we will use the SSA CLD-P score to evaluate your ESLD under 105.05G2. We explain how we calculate the SSA CLD-P score in b(ii) through b(vii) of this section.

(ii) To calculate the SSA CLD-P score, we use a formula that includes four parameters: Serum total bilirubin (mg/dL), International Normalized Ratio (INR), serum albumin (g/dL), and whether growth failure is occurring. The formula for the SSA CLD-P score calculation is:

4.80 × [Loge(serum total bilirubin mg/dL)]

+ 18.57 × [Loge(INR)]

– 6.87 × [Loge(serum albumin g/dL)]

+ 6.67 if the child has growth failure (<–2 standard deviations for weight or height)

(iii) When we indicate "Loge" in the formula for the SSA CLD-P score calculation, we mean the "base *e* logarithm" or "natural logarithm" (ln) of a numerical laboratory value, not the "base 10 logarithm" or "common logarithm" (log) of the laboratory value, and not the actual laboratory value. For example, if a female child is 4.0 years old, has a current weight of 13.5 kg (10th percentile for age) and height of 92 cm (less than the third percentile for age), and has laboratory values of serum total bilirubin 2.2 mg/dL, INR 1.0, and serum albumin 3.5 g/dL, we will compute the SSA CLD-P score as follows:

4.80 × [Loge(serum total bilirubin 2.2 mg/dL) = 0.788]
+ 18.57 × [Loge(INR 1.0) = 0]
- 6.87 × [Loge(serum albumin 3.5 g/dL) = 1.253]
+ 6.67 if the child has growth failure (<–2 standard deviations for weight or *height)*
= 3.78 + 0 - 8.61 + 6.67
= 1.84, which is then rounded to an SSA CLD-P score of 2

(iv) For any SSA CLD-P score calculation, all of the required laboratory values (serum total bilirubin, INR, or serum albumin) must have been obtained within 30 days of each other. We will not purchase INR values for children who have not attained age 12. If there is no INR value for a child under 12 within the applicable time period, we will use an INR value of 1.1 to calculate the SSA CLD-P score. If there are multiple laboratory values within the 30-day interval for any given laboratory test, we will use the highest serum total bilirubin and INR values and the lowest serum albumin value for the SSA CLD-P score calculation. We will round all laboratory values less than 1.0 up to 1.0.

(v) The weight and length/height measurements used for the calculation must be obtained from one evaluation within the same 30-day period as in D11b(iv).

(vi) Listing 105.05G2 requires two SSA CLD-P scores. The laboratory values for the second SSA CLD-P score calculation must have been obtained at least 60 days after the latest laboratory value for the first SSA CLD-P score and within the required 6-month period. We will consider the date of each SSA CLD-P score to be the date of the first laboratory value used for its calculation.

(vii) If you have the two SSA CLD-P scores required by listing 105.05G2, we will find that your impairment meets the criteria of the listing from at least the date of the first SSA CLD-P score.

12. *Extrahepatic biliary atresia (EBA)* (105.05H) usually presents itself in the first 2 months of life with persistent jaundice. The impairment meets 105.05H if the diagnosis of EBA is confirmed by liver biopsy or intraoperative cholangiogram that shows obliteration of the extrahepatic biliary tree. EBA is usually surgically treated by portoenterostomy (for example, Kasai procedure). If this surgery is not performed in the first months of life or is not completely successful, liver transplantation is indicated. If you have had a liver transplant, we will evaluate your impairment under 105.09.

13. *Liver transplantation* (105.09) may be performed for metabolic liver disease, progressive liver failure, life-threatening complications of liver disease, hepatic

malignancy, and acute fulminant hepatitis (viral, drug-induced, or toxin-induced). We will consider you to be disabled for 1 year from the date of the transplantation. Thereafter, we will evaluate your residual impairment(s) by considering the adequacy of post-transplant liver function, the requirement for post-transplant antiviral therapy, the frequency and severity of rejection episodes, comorbid complications, and all adverse treatment effects.

E. *How do we evaluate inflammatory bowel disease (IBD)?*

1. *Inflammatory bowel disease* (105.06) includes, but is not limited to, Crohn's disease and ulcerative colitis. These disorders, while distinct entities, share many clinical, laboratory, and imaging findings, as well as similar treatment regimens. Remissions and exacerbations of variable duration are the hallmark of IBD. Crohn's disease may involve the entire alimentary tract from the mouth to the anus in a segmental, asymmetric fashion. Obstruction, stenosis, fistulization, perineal involvement, and extraintestinal manifestations are common. Crohn's disease is rarely curable and recurrence may be a lifelong problem, even after surgical resection. In contrast, ulcerative colitis only affects the colon. The inflammatory process may be limited to the rectum, extend proximally to include any contiguous segment, or involve the entire colon. Ulcerative colitis may be cured by total colectomy.

2. Symptoms and signs of IBD include diarrhea, fecal incontinence, rectal bleeding, abdominal pain, fatigue, fever, nausea, vomiting, arthralgia, abdominal tenderness, palpable abdominal mass (usually inflamed loops of bowel) and perineal disease. You may also have signs or laboratory findings indicating malnutrition, such as weight loss, edema, anemia, hypoalbuminemia, hypokalemia, hypocalcemia, or hypomagnesemia.

3. IBD may be associated with significant extraintestinal manifestations in a variety of body systems. These include, but are not limited to, involvement of the eye (for example, uveitis, episcleritis, iritis); hepatobiliary disease (for example, gallstones, primary sclerosing cholangitis); urologic disease (for example, kidney stones, obstructive hydronephrosis); skin involvement (for example, erythema nodosum, pyoderma gangrenosum); or non-destructive inflammatory arthritis. You may also have associated thromboembolic disorders or vascular disease. These manifestations may not correlate with the severity of your IBD. If your impairment does not meet any of the criteria of 105.06, we will consider the effects of your extraintestinal manifestations in determining whether you have an impairment(s) that meets or medically equals another listing, and we will also consider the effects of your extraintestinal manifestations when we determine whether your impairment(s) functionally equal the listings.

4. Surgical diversion of the intestinal tract, including ileostomy and colostomy, does not very seriously interfere with age-appropriate functioning if you are able to maintain adequate nutrition and function of the stoma. However, if you are not

able to maintain adequate nutrition, we will evaluate your impairment under 105.08.

F. *How do we evaluate short bowel syndrome (SBS)?*

1. *Short bowel syndrome* (105.07) is a disorder that occurs when congenital intestinal abnormalities, ischemic vascular insults (for example, necrotizing enterocolitis, volvulus), trauma, or IBD complications require surgical resection of more than one-half of the small intestine, resulting in the loss of intestinal absorptive surface and a state of chronic malnutrition. The management of SBS requires long-term parenteral nutrition via an indwelling central venous catheter (central line); the process is often referred to as *hyperalimentation* or *total parenteral nutrition* (TPN). Children with SBS can also feed orally, with variable amounts of nutrients being absorbed through their remaining intestine. Over time, some of these children can develop additional intestinal absorptive surface, and may ultimately be able to be weaned off their parenteral nutrition.

2. Your impairment will continue to meet 105.07 as long as you remain dependent on daily parenteral nutrition via a central venous catheter for most of your nutritional requirements. Long-term complications of SBS and parenteral nutrition include abnormal growth rates, central line infections (with or without septicemia), thrombosis, hepatotoxicity, gallstones, and loss of venous access sites. Intestinal transplantation is the only definitive treatment for children with SBS who remain chronically dependent on parenteral nutrition.

3. To document SBS, we need a copy of the operative report of intestinal resection, the summary of the hospitalization(s) including: Details of the surgical findings, medically appropriate postoperative imaging studies that reflect the amount of your residual small intestine, or if we cannot get one of these reports, other medical reports that include details of the surgical findings. We also need medical documentation that you are dependent on daily parenteral nutrition to provide most of your nutritional requirements.

G. *How do we evaluate growth failure due to any digestive disorder?*

1. To evaluate growth failure due to any digestive disorder, we require documentation of the laboratory findings of chronic nutritional deficiency described in 105.08A and the growth measurements in 105.08B within the same consecutive 12-month period. The dates of laboratory findings may be different from the dates of growth measurements.

2. Under 105.08B, we evaluate a child's growth failure by using the appropriate table for age and gender.

a. For children from birth to attainment of age 2, we use the weight-for-length table (see Table I or Table II).

b. For children age 2 to attainment of age 18, we use the body mass index (BMI)-for-age table (see Table III or Table IV).

c. BMI is the ratio of a child's weight to the square of the child's height. We calculate BMI using one of the following formulas:

English Formula

BMI = [Weight in Pounds / (Height in Inches x Height in Inches)] x 703

Metric Formulas

BMI = Weight in Kilograms / (Height in Meters x Height in Meters)

BMI = [Weight in Kilograms / (Height in Centimeters x Height in Centimeters)] x 10,000

H. *How do we evaluate the need for supplemental daily enteral feeding via a gastrostomy?*

1. *General.* Infants and young children may have anatomical, neurological, or developmental disorders that interfere with their ability to feed by mouth, resulting in inadequate caloric intake to meet their growth needs. These disorders frequently result in the medical necessity to supplement caloric intake and to bypass the anatomical feeding route of mouth-throat-esophagus into the stomach.

2. Children who have not attained age 3 and who require supplemental daily enteral nutrition via a feeding gastrostomy meet 105.10 regardless of the medical reason for the gastrostomy. Thereafter, we evaluate growth impairment under 100.02, malnutrition under 105.08, or other medical or developmental disorder(s) (including the disorder(s) that necessitated gastrostomy placement) under the appropriate listing(s).

I. *How do we evaluate esophageal stricture or stenosis?* Esophageal stricture or stenosis (narrowing) from congenital atresia (absence or abnormal closure of a tubular body organ) or destructive esophagitis may result in malnutrition or the need for gastrostomy placement, which we evaluate under 105.08 or 105.10. Esophageal stricture or stenosis may also result in complications such as pneumonias due to frequent aspiration, or difficulty in maintaining nutritional status short of listing-level severity. While none of these complications may be of such severity that they would meet the criteria of another listing, the combination of impairments may medically equal the severity of a listing or functionally equal the listings.

J. *What do we mean by the phrase "consider under a disability for 1 year"?* We use the phrase "consider under a disability for 1 year" following a specific event in 105.02, 105.05A, and 105.09 to explain how long your impairment can meet the requirements of those particular listings. This phrase does not refer to the date on which your disability began, only to the date on which we must reevaluate whether your impairment continues to meet a listing or is otherwise disabling. For example, if you have received a liver transplant, you may have become disabled before the transplant because of chronic liver disease. Therefore, we do not restrict our determination of the onset of disability to the date of the specified event. We will establish an onset date earlier than the date of the specified event if the evidence in your case record supports such a finding.

K. *How do we evaluate impairments that do not meet one of the digestive disorder listings?*

1. These listings are only examples of common digestive disorders that we consider severe enough to result in marked and severe functional limitations. If your impairment(s) does not meet the criteria of any of these listings, we must also consider whether you have an impairment(s) that satisfies the criteria of a listing in another body system. For example:

a. If you have hepatitis B or C and you are depressed, we will evaluate your impairment under 112.04.

b. If you have multiple congenital abnormalities, we will evaluate your impairment(s) under the criteria in the listings for impairments that affect multiple body systems (110.00) or the criteria of listings in other affected body systems.

c. If you have digestive disorders that interfere with intake, digestion, or absorption of nutrition, and result in a reduction in your rate of growth, and your impairment does not satisfy the criteria in the malnutrition listing (105.08), we will evaluate your impairment under the growth impairment listings (100.00).

2. If you have a severe medically determinable impairment(s) that does not meet a listing, we will determine whether your impairment(s) medically equals a listing. (See §416.926.) If your impairment(s) does not meet or medically equal a listing, you may or may not have an impairment(s) that functionally equals the listings. (See §416.926a.) When we decide whether you continue to be disabled, we use the rules in §416.994a.

105.01 Category of Impairments, Digestive System

105.02 Gastrointestinal hemorrhaging from any cause, requiring blood transfusion (with or without hospitalization) of at least 10 cc of blood/kg of body weight, and occurring at least three times during a consecutive 6-month period. The transfusions must be at least 30 days apart within the 6-month period. Consider under a disability for 1 year following the last documented transfusion; thereafter, evaluate the residual impairment(s).

105.03 [Reserved]

105.04 [Reserved]

105.05 Chronic liver disease, with:

A. Hemorrhaging from esophageal, gastric, or ectopic varices or from portal hypertensive gastropathy, demonstrated by endoscopy, x-ray, or other appropriate medically acceptable imaging, resulting in hemodynamic instability as defined in 105.00D5, and requiring hospitalization for transfusion of at least 10 cc of blood/kg of body weight. Consider under a disability for 1 year following the last documented transfusion; thereafter, evaluate the residual impairment(s).

OR

B. Ascites or hydrothorax not attributable to other causes, despite continuing treatment as prescribed, present on at least two evaluations at least 60 days apart within a consecutive 6-month period. Each evaluation must be documented by:

1. Paracentesis or thoracentesis; or

2. Appropriate medically acceptable imaging or physical examination and one of the following:

a. Serum albumin of 3.0g/dL or less; or

b. International Normalized Ratio (INR) of at least 1.5.

OR

C. Spontaneous bacterial peritonitis with peritoneal fluid containing an absolute neutrophil count of at least 250 cells/mm3.

OR

D. Hepatorenal syndrome as described in 105.00D8, with one of the following:

1. Serum creatinine elevation of at least 2 mg/dL; or

2. Oliguria with 24-hour urine output less than 1 mL/kg/hr; or

3. Sodium retention with urine sodium less than 10 mEq per liter.

OR

E. Hepatopulmonary syndrome as described in 105.00D9, with:

1. Arterial oxygenation (PaO2) on room air of:

a. 60 mm Hg or less, at test sites less than 3000 feet above sea level, or

b. 55 mm Hg or less, at test sites from 3000 to 6000 feet, or

c. 50 mm Hg or less, at test sites above 6000 feet; or

2. Documentation of intrapulmonary arteriovenous shunting by contrast-enhanced echocardiography or macroaggregated albumin lung perfusion scan.

OR

F. Hepatic encephalopathy as described in 105.00D10, with 1 and either 2 or 3:

1. Documentation of abnormal behavior, cognitive dysfunction, changes in mental status, or altered state of consciousness (for example, confusion, delirium, stupor, or coma), present on at least two evaluations at least 60 days apart within a consecutive 6-month period; and

2. History of transjugular intrahepatic portosystemic shunt (TIPS) or any surgical portosystemic shunt; or

3. One of the following occurring on at least two evaluations at least 60 days apart within the same consecutive 6-month period as in F1:

a. Asterixis or other fluctuating physical neurological abnormalities; or

b. Electroencephalogram (EEG) demonstrating triphasic slow wave activity; or

c. Serum albumin of 3.0 g/dL or less; or

d. International Normalized Ratio (INR) of 1.5 or greater.

OR

G. End Stage Liver Disease, with:

1. For children 12 years of age or older, SSA CLD scores of 22 or greater calculated as described in 105.00D11a. Consider under a disability from at least the date of the first score.

2. For children who have not attained age 12, SSA CLD-P scores of 11 or greater calculated as described in 105.00D11b. Consider under a disability from at least the date of the first score.

OR

H. Extrahepatic biliary atresia as diagnosed on liver biopsy or intraoperative cholangiogram. Consider under a disability for 1 year following diagnosis; thereafter, evaluate the residual liver function.

105.06 Inflammatory bowel disease (IBD) documented by endoscopy, biopsy, appropriate medically acceptable imaging, or operative findings with:

A. Obstruction of stenotic areas (not adhesions) in the small intestine or colon with proximal dilatation, confirmed by appropriate medically acceptable imaging or in surgery, requiring hospitalization for intestinal decompression or for surgery, and occurring on at least two occasions at least 60 days apart within a consecutive 6-month period;

OR

B. Two of the following despite continuing treatment as prescribed and occurring within the same consecutive 6-month period:

1. Anemia with hemoglobin less than 10.0 g/dL, present on at least two evaluations at least 60 days apart; or

2. Serum albumin of 3.0 g/dL or less, present on at least two evaluations at least 60 days apart; or

3. Clinically documented tender abdominal mass palpable on physical examination with abdominal pain or cramping that is not completely controlled by prescribed narcotic mediation, present on at least two evaluations at least 60 days apart; or

4. Perineal disease with a draining abscess or fistula, with pain that is not completely controlled by prescribed narcotic medication, present on at least two evaluations at least 60 days apart; or

5. Need for supplemental daily enteral nutrition via a gastrostomy or daily parenteral nutrition via a central venous catheter. (See 105.10 for children who have not attained age 3.)

105.07 Short bowel syndrome (SBS), *due to surgical resection of more than one-half of the small intestine, with dependence on daily parenteral nutrition via a central venous catheter (see 105.00F).*

105.08 Growth Failure due to any digestive disorder *(see 105.00G), documented by A and B:*

A. Chronic nutritional deficiency present on at least two evaluations at least 60 days apart within a consecutive 12-month period documented by one of the following:

1. Anemia with hemoglobin less than 10.0 g/dL; or

2. Serum albumin of 3.0 g/dL or less

AND

B. Growth failure as required in 1 or 2:

1. *For children from birth to attainment of age 2,* three weight-for-length measurements that are:

a. Within a 12-month period; and

b. At least 60 days apart; and

c. Less than the third percentile on Table I or Table II; or

Third Percentile Values for Weight-for Length

Length (Centimeters)	Weight (kilograms) Table I—Males Birth to Attainment of Age 2	Table II—Females Birth to Attainment of Age 2
45.0	1.597	1.613
45.5	1.703	1.724
46.5	1.919	1.946
47.5	2.139	2.171
48.5	2.364	2.397
49.5	2.592	2.624
50.5	2.824	2.852
51.5	3.058	3.081
52.5	3.294	3.310
53.5	3.532	3.538
54.5	3.771	3.767
55.5	4.010	3.994
56.5	4.250	4.220
57.5	4.489	4.445
58.5	4.728	4.669
59.5	4.966	4.892
60.5	5.203	5.113
61.5	5.438	5.333
62.5	5.671	5.552
63.5	5.903	5.769
64.5	6.132	5.985
65.5	6.359	6.200
66.5	6.584	6.413
67.5	6.807	6.625
68.5	7.027	6.836
69.5	7.245	7.046
70.5	7.461	7.254
71.5	7.674	7.461
72.5	7.885	7.667
73.5	8.094	7.871
74.5	8.301	8.075
75.5	8.507	8.277
76.5	8.710	8.479

(continued)

Third Percentile Values for Weight-for Length (*continued*)

Length (Centimeters)	Weight (kilograms)	
	Table I—Males Birth to Attainment of Age 2	Table II—Females Birth to Attainment of Age 2
77.5	8.913	8.679
78.5	9.113	8.879
79.5	9.313	9.078
80.5	9.512	9.277
81.5	9.710	9.476
82.5	9.907	9.674
83.5	10.104	9.872
84.5	10.301	10.071
85.5	10.499	10.270
86.5	10.696	10.469
87.5	10.895	10.670
88.5	11.095	10.871
89.5	11.296	11.074
90.5	11.498	11.278
91.5	11.703	11.484
92.5	11.910	11.691
93.5	12.119	11.901
94.5	12.331	12.112
95.5	12.546	12.326
96.5	12.764	12.541
97.5	12.987	12.760
98.5	13.213	12.981
99.5	13.443	13.205
100.5	13.678	13.431
101.5	13.918	13.661
102.5	14.163	13.895
103.5	14.413	14.132

2. *For children age 2 to attainment of age 18*, three (BMI)-for-age measurements that are:

a. Within a consecutive 12-month period; and

b. At least 60 days apart; and

c. Less than the third percentile on Table III or Table IV

Third Percentile Values for BMI-for-Age

Table III—Males Age 2 to Attainment of Age 18		Table IV—Females Age 2 to Attainment of Age 18	
Age (yrs. and mos.)	**BMI**	**Age (yrs. and mos.)**	**BMI**
2.0 to 2.1	14.5	2.0 to 2.2	14.1
2.2 to 2.4	14.4	2.3 to 2.6	14.0
2.5 to 2.7	14.3	2.7 to 2.10	13.9
2.8 to 2.11	14.2	2.11 to 3.2	13.8
3.0 to 3.2	14.1	3.3 to 3.6	13.7
3.3 to 3.6	14.0	3.7 to 3.11	13.6
3.7 to 3.11	13.9	4.0 to 4.4	13.5
4.0 to 4.5	13.8	4.5 to 4.11	13.4
4.6 to 5.0	13.7	5.0 to 5.9	13.3
5.1 to 6.0	13.6	5.10 to 7.6	13.2
6.1 to 7.6	13.5	7.7 to 8.4	13.3
7.7 to 8.6	13.6	8.05 to 8.10	13.4
8.7 to 9.1	13.7	8.11 to 9.3	13.5
9.2 to 9.6	13.8	9.4 to 9.8	13.6
9.7 to 9.11	13.9	9.9 to 10.0	13.7
10.0 to 10.3	14.0	10.1 to 10.4	13.8
10.4 to 10.7	14.1	10.5 to 10.7	13.9
10.8 to 10.10	14.2	10.8 to 10.10	14.0
10.11 to 11.2	14.3	10.11 to 11.2	14.1
11.3 to 11.5	14.4	11.3 to 11.5	14.2
11.6 to 11.8	14.5	11.6 to 11.7	14.3
11.9 to 11.11	14.6	11.8 to 11.10	14.4
12.0 to 12.1	14.7	11.11 to 12.1	14.5
12.2 to 12.4	14.8	12.2 to 12.4	14.6
12.5 to 12.7	14.9	12.5 to 12.6	14.7
12.8 to 12.9	15.0	12.7 to 12.9	14.8
12.10 to 13.0	15.1	12.10 to 12.11	14.9
13.1 to 13.2	15.2	13.0 to 13.2	15.0
13.3 to 13.4	15.3	13.3 to 13.4	15.1
13.5 to 13.7	15.4	13.5 to 13.7	15.2

(continued)

Third Percentile Values for BMI-for-Age (*continued*)

Table III—Males Age 2 to Attainment of Age 18		Table IV—Females Age 2 to Attainment of Age 18	
Age (yrs. and mos.)	**BMI**	**Age (yrs. and mos.)**	**BMI**
13.8 to 13.9	15.5	13.8 to 13.9	15.3
13.10 to 13.11	15.6	13.10 to 14.0	15.4
14.0 to 14.1	15.7	14.1 to 14.2	15.5
14.2 to 14.4	15.8	14.3 to 14.5	15.6
14.5 to 14.6	15.9	14.6 to 14.7	15.7
14.7 to 14.8	16.0	14.8 to 14.9	15.8
14.9 to 14.10	16.1	14.10 to 15.0	15.9
14.11 to 15.0	16.2	15.1 to 15.2	16.0
15.1 to 15.3	16.3	15.3 to 15.5	16.1
15.4 to 15.5	16.4	15.6 to 15.7	16.2
15.6 to 15.7	16.5	15.8 to 15.10	16.3
15.8 to 15.9	16.6	15.11 to 16.0	16.4
15.10 to 15.11	16.7	16.1 to 16.3	16.5
16.0 to 16.1	16.8	16.4 to 16.6	16.6
16.2 to 16.3	16.9	16.7 to 16.9	16.7
16.4 to 16.5	17.0	16.10 to 17.0	16.8
16.6 to 16.8	17.1	17.1 to 17.3	16.9
16.9 to 16.10	17.2	17.4 to 17.7	17.0
16.11 to 17.0	17.3	17.8 to 17.11	17.1
17.1 to 17.2	17.4		
17.3 to 17.5	17.5		
17.6 to 17.7	17.6		
17.8 to 17.9	17.7		
17.10 to 17.11	17.8		

105.09 Liver transplantation. Consider under a disability for 1 year following the date of transplantation; thereafter, evaluate the residual impairment(s) (see 105.00D13 and 105.00J).

105.10 Need for supplemental daily enteral feeding via a gastrostomy due to any cause, for children who have not attained age 3; thereafter, evaluate the residual impairment(s) (see 105.00H).

106.00 Genitourinary Disorders

A. *Which disorders do we evaluate under these listings?*

We evaluate genitourinary disorders resulting in chronic kidney disease (CKD). Examples of such disorders include chronic glomerulonephritis, hypertensive nephropathy, diabetic nephropathy, chronic obstructive uropathy, and hereditary nephropathies. We also evaluate nephrotic syndrome due to glomerular dysfunction, and congenital genitourinary disorders, such as ectopic ureter, exstrophic urinary bladder, urethral valves, and Eagle-Barrett syndrome (prune belly syndrome), under these listings.

B. *What evidence do we need?*

1. We need evidence that documents the signs, symptoms, and laboratory findings of your CKD. This evidence should include reports of clinical examinations, treatment records, and documentation of your response to treatment. Laboratory findings, such as serum creatinine or serum albumin levels, may document your kidney function. We generally need evidence covering a period of at least 90 days unless we can make a fully favorable determination or decision without it.
2. *Estimated glomerular filtration rate (eGFR).* The eGFR is an estimate of the filtering capacity of the kidneys that takes into account serum creatinine concentration and other variables, such as your age, gender, and body size. If your medical evidence includes eGFR findings, we will consider them when we evaluate your CKD under 106.05.
3. *Kidney or bone biopsy.* If you have had a kidney or bone biopsy, we need a copy of the pathology report. When we cannot get a copy of the pathology report, we will accept a statement from an acceptable medical source verifying that a biopsy was performed and describing the results.

C. *What other factors do we consider when we evaluate your genitourinary disorder?*

1. *Chronic hemodialysis or peritoneal dialysis.*
   a. Dialysis is a treatment for CKD that uses artificial means to remove toxic metabolic byproducts from the blood. Hemodialysis uses an artificial kidney machine to clean waste products from the blood; peritoneal dialysis uses a dialyzing solution that is introduced into and removed from the abdomen (peritoneal cavity) either continuously or intermittently. Under 106.03, your ongoing dialysis must have lasted or be expected to last for a continuous period of at least 12 months. To satisfy the requirement in 106.03, we will accept a report from an acceptable medical source that describes your CKD and your current dialysis, and indicates that your dialysis will be ongoing.
   b. If you are undergoing chronic hemodialysis or peritoneal dialysis, your CKD may meet our definition of disability before you started dialysis.

We will determine the onset of your disability based on the facts in your case record.

2. *Kidney transplant.*
   a. If you receive a kidney transplant, we will consider you to be disabled under 106.04 for 1 year from the date of transplant. After that, we will evaluate your residual impairment(s) by considering your post-transplant function, any rejection episodes you have had, complications in other body systems, and any adverse effects related to ongoing treatment.
   b. If you received a kidney transplant, your CKD may meet our definition of disability before you received the transplant. We will determine the onset of your disability based on the facts in your case record.
3. *Anasarca* (generalized massive edema or swelling). Under 106.06B, we need a description of the extent of edema, including pretibial (in front of the tibia), periorbital (around the eyes), or presacral (in front of the sacrum) edema. We also need a description of any ascites, pleural effusion, or pericardial effusion.
4. *Congenital genitourinary disorder.* Procedures such as diagnostic cystoscopy or circumcision do not satisfy the requirement for urologic surgical procedures in 106.07.
5. *Growth failure due to any chronic renal disease.*
   a. To evaluate growth failure due to any chronic renal disease, we require documentation of the laboratory findings described in 106.08A and the growth measurements in 106.08B within the same consecutive 12-month period. The dates of laboratory findings may be different from the dates of growth measurements.
   b. Under 106.08B, we use the appropriate table(s) under 105.08B in the digestive system to determine whether a child's growth is less than the third percentile.
      (i) For children from birth to attainment of age 2, we use the weight-for-length table corresponding to the child's gender (Table I or Table II).
      (ii) For children age 2 to attainment of age 18, we use the body mass index (BMI)-for-age table corresponding to the child's gender (Table III or Table IV).
      (iii) BMI is the ratio of a child's weight to the square of his or her height. We calculate BMI using the formulas in 105.00G2c.
6. *Complications of CKD.*

   The hospitalizations in 106.09 may be for different complications of CKD. Examples of complications from CKD that may result in hospitalization include stroke, congestive heart failure, hypertensive crisis, or acute kidney failure requiring a short course of hemodialysis. If the CKD complication occurs during a hospitalization that was initially for a co-occurring condition, we will evaluate it under our rules for determining medical equivalence. (See § 416.926 of this chapter.) We will evaluate co-occurring conditions, including those that result in hospitalizations, under the listings for the affected body system or under our rules for medical equivalence.

D. *How do we evaluate disorders that do not meet one of the genitourinary listings?*

1. The listed disorders are only examples of common genitourinary disorders that we consider severe enough to result in marked and severe functional limitations. If your impairment(s) does not meet the criteria of any of these listings, we must also consider whether you have an impairment(s) that satisfies the criteria of a listing in another body system.
2. If you have a severe medically determinable impairment(s) that does not meet a listing, we will determine whether your impairment(s) medically equals a listing. (See §416.926 of this chapter.) Genitourinary disorders may be associated with disorders in other body systems, and we consider the combined effects of multiple impairments when we determine whether they medically equal a listing. If your impairment(s) does not medically equal a listing, we will also consider whether it functionally equals the listings. (See §416.926a of this chapter.) We use the rules in §416.994a of this chapter when we decide whether you continue to be disabled.

106.01 Category of Impairments, Genitourinary Disorders

106.03 ***Chronic kidney disease,*** with chronic hemodialysis or peritoneal dialysis (see 106.00C1).

106.04 ***Chronic kidney disease,*** with kidney transplant. Consider under a disability for 1 year following the transplant; thereafter, evaluate the residual impairment (see 106.00C2).

106.05 ***Chronic kidney disease,*** with impairment of kidney function, with one of the following documented on at least two occasions at least 90 days apart during a consecutive 12-month period:

A. Serum creatinine of 3 mg/dL or greater;

OR

B. Creatinine clearance of 30 ml/min/1.73m2 or less;

OR

C. Estimated glomerular filtration rate (eGFR) of 30 ml/min/1.73m2 or less.

106.06 Nephrotic syndrome, with A and B:

A. Laboratory findings as described in 1 or 2, documented on at least two occasions at least 90 days apart during a consecutive 12-month period:

1. Serum albumin of 3.0 g/dL or less, or
2. Proteinuria of 40 mg/m2/hr or greater;

AND

B. Anasarca (see 106.00C3) persisting for at least 90 days despite prescribed treatment.

106.07 Congenital genitourinary disorder (see 106.00C4) requiring urologic surgical procedures at least three times in a consecutive 12-month period, with at least 30 days between procedures. Consider under a disability for 1 year following the date of the last surgery; thereafter, evaluate the residual impairment.

106.08 Growth failure due to any chronic renal disease (see 106.00C5), with:

A. Serum creatinine of 2 mg/dL or greater, documented at least two times within a consecutive 12-month period with at least 60 days between measurements.

AND

B. Growth failure as required in 1 or 2:

1. *For children from birth to attainment of age 2*, three weight-for length measurements that are:

a. Within a consecutive 12-month period; and

b. At least 60 days apart; and

c. Less than the third percentile on the appropriate weight-for-length table under 105.08B1; or

2. For children age 2 to attainment of age 18, three BMI-for-age measurements that are:

a. Within a consecutive 12-month period; and

b. At least 60 days apart; and

c. Less than the third percentile on the appropriate weight-for-length table under 105.08B2.

106.09 Complications of chronic kidney disease (see 106.00C5) requiring at least three hospitalizations within a consecutive 12-month period and occurring at least 30 days apart. Each hospitalization must last at least 48 hours, including hours in a hospital emergency department immediately before the hospitalization.

107.00 Hematological Disorders

A. *What hematological disorders do we evaluate under these listings?*

1. We evaluate non-malignant (non-cancerous) hematological disorders, such as hemolytic anemias (107.05), disorders of thrombosis and hemostasis (107.08), and disorders of bone marrow failure (107.10). These disorders disrupt the normal development and function of white blood cells, red blood cells, platelets, and clotting-factor proteins (factors).
2. We evaluate malignant (cancerous) hematological disorders, such as lymphoma, leukemia, and multiple myeloma, under the appropriate listings in 13.00, except for two lymphomas associated with human immunodeficiency virus (HIV) infection. We evaluate primary central nervous system lymphoma associated with HIV infection under 114.11B, and primary effusion lymphoma associated with HIV infection under 114.11C.

B. *What evidence do we need to document that you have a hematological disorder?* We need the following evidence to document that you have a hematological disorder:

1. A laboratory report of a definitive test that establishes a hematological disorder, signed by a physician; or
2. A laboratory report of a definitive test that establishes a hematological disorder that is not signed by a physician and a report from a physician that states you have the disorder; or
3. When we do not have a laboratory report of a definitive test, a persuasive report from a physician that a diagnosis of your hematological disorder was confirmed by appropriate laboratory analysis or other diagnostic method(s). To be persuasive, this report must state that you had the appropriate definitive laboratory test or tests for diagnosing your disorder and provide the results, or explain how your diagnosis was established by other diagnostic method(s) consistent with the prevailing state of medical knowledge and clinical practice.
4. We will make every reasonable effort to obtain the results of appropriate laboratory testing you have had. We will not purchase complex, costly, or invasive tests, such as tests of clotting-factor proteins, and bone marrow aspirations.

C. *What are hemolytic anemias, and how do we evaluate them under 107.05?*

1. *Hemolytic anemias, both congenital and acquired*, are disorders that result in premature destruction of red blood cells (RBCs). Hemolytic anemias include abnormalities of hemoglobin structure (hemoglobinopathies), abnormal RBC enzyme content and function, and RBC membrane (envelope) defects that are congenital or acquired. The diagnosis of hemolytic anemia is based on hemoglobin electrophoresis or analysis of the contents of the RBC

(enzymes) and membrane. Examples of congenital hemolytic anemias include sickle cell disease, thalassemia, and their variants, and hereditary spherocytosis. Acquired hemolytic anemias may result from autoimmune disease (for example, systemic lupus erythematosus) or mechanical devices (for example, heart valves, intravascular patches).

2. The hospitalizations in 107.05B do not all have to be for the same complication of the hemolytic anemia. They may be for three different complications of the disorder. Examples of complications of hemolytic anemia that may result in hospitalization include dactylitis, osteomyelitis, painful (vaso-occlusive) crisis, pulmonary infections or infarctions, acute chest syndrome, pulmonary hypertension, chronic heart failure, gallbladder disease, hepatic (liver) failure, renal (kidney) failure, nephrotic syndrome, aplastic crisis, and strokes. We will count the hours you receive emergency treatment in a comprehensive sickle cell disease center immediately before the hospitalization if this treatment is comparable to the treatment provided in a hospital emergency department.
3. For 107.05C, we do not require hemoglobin to be measured during a period in which you are free of pain or other symptoms of your disorder. We will accept hemoglobin measurements made while you are experiencing complications of your hemolytic anemia.
4. 107.05D refers to the most serious type of beta thalassemia major in which the bone marrow cannot produce sufficient numbers of normal RBCs to maintain life. The only available treatments for beta thalassemia major are life-long RBC transfusions (sometimes called hypertransfusion) or bone marrow transplantation. For purposes of 107.05D, we do not consider prophylactic RBC transfusions to prevent strokes or other complications in sickle cell disease and its variants to be of equal significance to life-saving RBC transfusions for beta thalassemia major. However, we will consider the functional limitations associated with prophylactic RBC transfusions and any associated side effects (for example, iron overload) under functional equivalence and any affected body system(s). We will also evaluate strokes and resulting complications under 111.00 and 112.00.

D. *What are disorders of thrombosis and hemostasis, and how do we evaluate them under 107.08?*

1. *Disorders of thrombosis and hemostasis* include both clotting and bleeding disorders, and may be congenital or acquired. These disorders are characterized by abnormalities in blood clotting that result in hypercoagulation (excessive blood clotting) or hypocoagulation (inadequate blood clotting). The diagnosis of a thrombosis or hemostasis disorder is based on evaluation of plasma clotting-factor proteins (factors) and platelets. Protein C or protein S deficiency and Factor V Leiden are examples of hypercoagulation disorders. Hemophilia, von Willebrand disease, and thrombocytopenia are

examples of hypocoagulation disorders. Acquired excessive blood clotting may result from blood protein defects and acquired inadequate blood clotting (for example, acquired hemophilia A) may be associated with inhibitor autoantibodies.

2. The hospitalizations in 107.08 do not all have to be for the same complication of a disorder of thrombosis and hemostasis. They may be for three different complications of the disorder. Examples of complications that may result in hospitalization include anemias, thromboses, embolisms, and uncontrolled bleeding requiring multiple factor concentrate infusions or platelet transfusions. We will also consider any surgery that you have, even if it is not related to your hematological disorder, to be a complication of your disorder of thrombosis and hemostasis if you require treatment with clotting-factor proteins (for example, factor VIII or IX) or anticoagulant medication to control bleeding or coagulation in connection with your surgery. We will count the hours you receive emergency treatment in a comprehensive hemophilia treatment center immediately before the hospitalization if this treatment is comparable to the treatment provided in a hospital emergency department.

E. *What are disorders of bone marrow failure, and how do we evaluate them under 107.10?*

1. *Disorders of bone marrow failure* may be congenital or acquired, characterized by bone marrow that does not make enough healthy RBCs, platelets, or granulocytes (specialized types of white blood cells); there may also be a combined failure of these bone marrow-producing cells. The diagnosis is based on peripheral blood smears and bone marrow aspiration or bone marrow biopsy, but not peripheral blood smears alone. Examples of these disorders are myelodysplastic syndromes, aplastic anemia, granulocytopenia, and myelofibrosis. Acquired disorders of bone marrow failure may result from viral infections, chemical exposure, or immunologic disorders.
2. The hospitalizations in 107.10A do not all have to be for the same complication of bone marrow failure. They may be for three different complications of the disorder. Examples of complications that may result in hospitalization include uncontrolled bleeding, anemia, and systemic bacterial, viral, or fungal infections.
3. For 107.10B, the requirement of life-long RBC transfusions to maintain life in myelodysplastic syndromes or aplastic anemias has the same meaning as it does for beta thalassemia major. (See 107.00C4.)

F. *How do we evaluate bone marrow or stem cell transplantation under 107.17?* We will consider you to be disabled for 12 months from the date of bone marrow or stem cell transplantation, or we may consider you to be disabled for a longer period if you are experiencing any serious post-transplantation complications, such as graft-versus-host (GVH) disease, frequent infections after immunosuppressive therapy, or significant deterioration of organ systems. We do not restrict our determination of the onset of disability to the date of the transplantation in 107.17. We may establish an earlier onset of disability due to your transplantation if evidence in your case record supports such a finding.

G. *How do we consider your symptoms, including your pain, severe fatigue, and malaise?* Your symptoms, including pain, severe fatigue, and malaise, may be important factors in our determination whether your hematological disorder meets or medically equals a listing, or in our determination whether you otherwise have marked and severe functional limitations. We cannot consider your symptoms unless you have medical signs or laboratory findings showing the existence of a medically determinable impairment(s) that could reasonably be expected to produce the symptoms. If you have such an impairment(s), we will evaluate the intensity, persistence, and functional effects of your symptoms using the rules throughout 107.00 and in our other regulations. (See sections 416.921 and 416.929 of this chapter.) Additionally, when we assess the credibility of your complaints about your symptoms and their functional effects, we will not draw any inferences from the fact that you do not receive treatment or that you are not following treatment without considering all of the relevant evidence in your case record, including any explanations you provide on why you are not receiving or following treatment.

H. *How do we evaluate episodic events in hematological disorders?* Some of the listings in this body system require a specific number of events within a consecutive 12-month period. (See 107.05, 107.08, and 107.10A.) When we use such criteria, a consecutive 12-month period means a period of 12 consecutive months, all or part of which must occur within the period we are considering in connection with your application or continuing disability review. These events must occur at least 30 days apart to ensure that we are evaluating separate events.

I. *How do we evaluate hematological disorders that do not meet one of these listings?*

1. These listings are only common examples of hematological disorders that we consider severe enough to result in marked and severe functional limitations. If your disorder does not meet the criteria of any of these listings, we must consider whether you have a disorder that satisfies the criteria of a listing in another body system. For example, we will evaluate hemophilic joint deformity under 101.00; polycythemia vera under 103.00, 104.00, or 111.00; chronic iron overload resulting from repeated RBC transfusion (transfusion hemosiderosis) under 103.00, 104.00, or 105.00; and the effects of intracranial bleeding or stroke under 111.00 or 112.00.
2. If you have a severe medically determinable impairment(s) that does not meet a listing, we will determine whether your impairment(s) medically equals a listing. (See section 416.926 of this chapter.) Hematological disorders may be associated with disorders in other body systems, and we consider the combined effects of multiple impairments when we determine

whether they medically equal a listing. If your impairment(s) does not medically equal a listing, we will also consider whether it functionally equals the listings. (See section 416.926a of this chapter.) We use the rules in section 416.994a of this chapter when we decide whether you continue to be disabled.

107.01 Category of Impairments, Hematological Disorders

107.05 ***Hemolytic anemias,*** *including sickle cell disease, thalassemia, and their variants (see 107.00C),* with:

A. Documented painful (vaso-occlusive) crises requiring parenteral (intravenous or intramuscular) narcotic medication, occurring at least six times within a 12-month period with at least 30 days between crises.

OR

B. Complications of hemolytic anemia requiring at least three hospitalizations within a 12-month period and occurring at least 30 days apart. Each hospitalization must last at least 48 hours, which can include hours in a hospital emergency department or comprehensive sickle cell disease center immediately before the hospitalization (see 107.00C2).

OR

C. Hemoglobin measurements of 7.0 grams per deciliter (g/dL) or less, occurring at least three times within a 12-month period with at least 30 days between measurements.

OR

D. Beta thalassemia major requiring life-long RBC transfusions at least once every 6 weeks to maintain life (see 107.00C4).

107.08 ***Disorders of thrombosis and hemostasis,*** including hemophilia and thrombocytopenia (see 107.00D), with complications requiring at least three hospitalizations within a 12-month period and occurring at least 30 days apart. Each hospitalization must last at least 48 hours, which can include hours in a hospital emergency department or comprehensive hemophilia treatment center immediately before the hospitalization (see 107.00D2).

107.10 ***Disorders of bone marrow failure,*** including myelodysplastic syndromes, aplastic anemia, granulocytopenia, and myelofibrosis (see 107.00E), with:

A. Complications of bone marrow failure requiring at least three hospitalizations within a 12-month period and occurring at least 30 days apart. Each hospitalization must last at least 48 hours, which can include hours in a hospital emergency department immediately before the hospitalization (see 107.00E2).

OR

B. Myelodysplastic syndromes or aplastic anemias requiring life-long RBC transfusions at least once every 6 weeks to maintain life (see 107.00E3).

107.17 *Hematological disorders treated by bone marrow or stem cell transplantation* (see 107.00F). Consider under a disability for at least 12 consecutive months from the date of transplantation. After that, evaluate any residual impairment(s) under the criteria for the affected body system.

108.00 Skin Disorders

A. *What skin disorders do we evaluate with these listings?*

We use these listings to evaluate skin disorders that may result from hereditary, congenital, or acquired pathological processes. The kinds of impairments covered by these listings are: Ichthyosis, bullous diseases, chronic infections of the skin or mucous membranes, dermatitis, hidradenitis suppurativa, genetic photosensitivity disorders, and burns.

B. *What documentation do we need?*

When we evaluate the existence and severity of your skin disorder, we generally need information about the onset, duration, frequency of flare-ups, and prognosis of your skin disorder; the location, size, and appearance of lesions; and, when applicable, history of exposure to toxins, allergens, or irritants, familial incidence, seasonal variation, stress factors, and your ability to function outside of a highly protective environment. To confirm the diagnosis, we may need laboratory findings (for example, results of a biopsy obtained independently of Social Security disability evaluation or blood tests) or evidence from other medically acceptable methods consistent with the prevailing state of medical knowledge and clinical practice.

C. *How do we assess the severity of your skin disorders(s)?*

We generally base our assessment of severity on the extent of your skin lesions, the frequency of flare-ups of your skin lesions, how your symptoms (including pain) limit you, the extent of your treatment, and how your treatment affects you.

1. *Extensive skin lesions.* Extensive skin lesions are those that involve multiple body sites or critical body areas, and result in a very serious limitation. Examples of extensive skin lesions that result in a very serious limitation include but are not limited to:

a. Skin lesions that interfere with the motion of your joints and that very seriously limit your use of more than one extremity; that is, two upper extremities, two lower extremities, or one upper and one lower extremity.

b. Skin lesions on the palms of both hands that very seriously limit your ability to do fine and gross motor movements.

c. Skin lesions on the soles of both feet, the perineum, and both inguinal areas that very seriously limit your ability to ambulate.

2. *Frequency of flare-ups.* If you have skin lesions, but they do not meet the requirements of any of the listings in this body system, you may still have an impairment that results in marked and severe functional limitations when we consider your condition over time, especially if your flare-ups result in extensive skin lesions, as defined in C1 of this section. Therefore, if you have frequent flare-ups, we may find that your impairment(s) is medically equal to one of these listings even though you have some periods during which your condition is in remission. We will consider how frequent and serious your flare-ups are, how quickly they resolve, and how you function between flare-ups to determine whether you have marked and severe functional limitations that have lasted for a continuous period of at least 12 months or that can be expected to last for a continuous period of at least 12 months. We will also consider the frequency of your flare-ups when we determine whether you have a severe impairment and when we need to assess functional equivalence.

3. *Symptoms (including pain).* Symptoms (including pain) may be important factors contributing to the severity of your skin disorder(s). We assess the impact of symptoms as explained in §§ 416.921 and 416.929 of this chapter.

4. *Treatment.* We assess the effects of medication, therapy, surgery, and any other form of treatment you receive when we determine the severity and duration of your impairment(s). Skin disorders frequently respond to treatment; however, response to treatment can vary widely, with some impairments becoming resistant to treatment. Some treatments can have side effects that can in themselves result in limitations.

a. We assess the effects of continuing treatment as prescribed by determining if there is improvement in the symptoms, signs, and laboratory findings of your disorder, and if you experience side effects that result in functional limitations. To assess the effects of your treatment, we may need information about:

i. The treatment you have been prescribed (for example, the type, dosage, method and frequency of administration of medication or therapy);

ii. Your response to the treatment;

iii. Any adverse effects of the treatment; and

iv. The expected duration of the treatment.

b. Because treatment itself or the effects of treatment may be temporary, in most cases sufficient time must elapse to allow us to evaluate the impact and expected duration of treatment and its side effects. Except under 108.07 and 108.08, you must follow continuing treatment as prescribed for at least 3 months before your impairment can be determined to meet the requirements of a skin disorder listing. (See 108.00H if you are not undergoing treatment or did not have treatment for 3 months.) We consider your specific response to treatment when we evaluate the overall severity of your impairment.

D. *How do we assess impairments that may affect the skin and other body systems?*

When your impairment affects your skin and has effects in other body systems, we first evaluate the predominant feature of your impairment under the appropriate body system. Examples include, but are not limited to the following.

1. *Tuberous sclerosis* primarily affects the brain. The predominant features are seizures, which we evaluate under the neurological listings in 111.00, and developmental delays or other mental disorders, which we evaluate under the mental disorders listings in 112.00.

2. *Malignant tumors of the skin* (for example, malignant melanoma) are cancers, or neoplastic diseases, which we evaluate under the listings in 113.00.

3. *Autoimmune disorders* and other immune system disorders (for example, systemic lupus erythematosus (SLE), scleroderma, human immunodeficiency virus (HIV) infection, and Sjögren's syndrome) often involve more than one body system. We evaluate SLE under 114.02, scleroderma under 114.04, Sjögren's syndrome under 114.10, and HIV infection under 114.11.

4. *Disfigurement or deformity* resulting from skin lesions may result in loss of sight, hearing, speech, and the ability to chew (mastication). We evaluate these impairments and their effects under the special senses and speech listings in 102.00 and the digestive system listings in 105.00. Facial disfigurement or other physical deformities may also have effects we evaluate under the mental disorders listings in 112.00, such as when they affect mood or social functioning.

5. We evaluate *erythropoietic porphyries* under the hemic and lymphatic listings in 107.00.

6. We evaluate *hemangiomas associated with thrombocytopenia and hemorrhage* (for example, Kasabach-Merritt syndrome) involving coagulation defects, under the hemic and lymphatic listings in 107.00. But, when hemangiomas impinge on vital structures or interfere with function, we evaluate their primary effects under the appropriate body system.

E. *How do we evaluate genetic photosensitivity disorders?*

1. *Xeroderma pigmentosum* (XP). When you have XP, your impairment meets the requirements of 108.07A if you have clinical and laboratory findings showing that you have the disorder. (See 108.00E3.) People who have XP have a lifelong hypersensitivity to all forms of ultraviolet light and generally lead extremely restricted lives in highly protective environments in order to prevent skin cancers from developing. Some people with XP also experience problems with their eyes, neurological problems, mental disorders, and problems in other body systems.

2. *Other genetic photosensitivity disorders.* Other genetic photosensitivity disorders may vary in their effects on different people, and may not result in marked and severe functional limitations for a continuous period of at least 12 months. Therefore, if you have a genetic photosensitivity disorder other than XP (established by clinical and laboratory findings as described in 108.00E3), you must show that you have either extensive skin lesions or an inability to function outside of a highly protective environment to meet the requirements of 108.07B. You must also show that your impairment meets the duration requirement. By *inability to function outside of a highly protective environment* we mean that you must avoid exposure to ultraviolet light (including sunlight passing through windows and light from unshielded fluorescent bulbs), wear protective clothing and eyeglasses, and use opaque broad-spectrum sunscreens in order to avoid skin cancer or other serious effects. Some genetic photosensitivity disorders can have very serious effects in other body systems, especially special senses and speech (102.00), neurological (111.00), mental (112.00), and neoplastic (113.00). We will evaluate the predominant feature of your impairment under the appropriate body system, as explained in 108.00D.

3. *Clinical and laboratory findings.*

a. *General.* We need documentation from an acceptable medical source to establish that you have a medically determinable impairment. In general, we must have evidence of appropriate laboratory testing showing that you have XP or another genetic photosensitivity disorder. We will find that you have XP or another genetic photosensitivity disorder based on a report from an acceptable medical source indicating that you have the impairment, supported by definitive genetic laboratory studies documenting appropriate chromosomal changes, including abnormal DNA repair or another DNA or genetic abnormality specific to your type of photosensitivity disorder.

b. *What we will accept as medical evidence instead of the actual laboratory report.* When we do not have the actual laboratory report, we need evidence from an acceptable medical source that includes appropriate clinical findings for your impairment and that is persuasive that a positive diagnosis has been confirmed by appropriate laboratory testing at some time prior to our evaluation. To be persuasive, the report must state that the appropriate definitive genetic laboratory study was conducted and that the results confirmed the diagnosis. The report must be consistent with other evidence in your case record.

F. *How do we evaluate burns?*

Electrical, chemical, or thermal burns frequently affect other body systems; for example, musculoskeletal, special senses and speech, respiratory, cardiovascular, renal, neurological, or mental. Consequently, we evaluate burns the way we evaluate other disorders that can affect the skin and other body systems, using the listing for the predominant feature of your impairment. For example, if your soft tissue injuries are under continuing surgical management (as defined in 101.00M), we will evaluate your impairment under 101.08. However, if your burns do not meet the requirements of 101.08 and you have extensive skin lesions that result in a very serious limitation (as defined in 108.00C1) that has lasted or can be expected to last for a continuous period of at least 12 months, we will evaluate them under 108.08.

G. *How do we determine if your skin disorder(s) will continue at a disabling level of severity in order to meet the duration requirement?*

For all of these skin disorder listings except 108.07 and 108.08, we will find that your impairment meets the duration requirement if your skin disorder results in extensive skin lesions that persist for at least 3 months despite continuing treatment as prescribed. By persist, we mean that the longitudinal clinical record shows that, with few exceptions, your lesions have been at the level of severity specified in the listing. For 108.07A, we will presume that you meet the duration requirement. For 108.07B and 108.08, we will consider all of the relevant medical and other information in your case record to determine whether your skin disorder meets the duration requirement.

H. *How do we assess your skin disorder(s) if your impairment does not meet the requirements of one of these listings?*

1. These listings are only examples of common skin disorders that we consider severe enough to result in marked and severe functional limitations. For most of these listings, if you do not have continuing treatment as prescribed, if your treatment has not lasted for at least 3 months, or if you do not have extensive skin lesions that have persisted for at least 3 months, your impairment cannot meet the requirements of these skin disorder listings. (This provision does not apply to 108.07 and 108.08.) However, we may still find that you are disabled because your impairment(s) meets the requirements of a listing in another body system, medically equals (see §§ 404.1526 and 416.926 of this chapter) the severity of a listing, or functionally equals the severity of the listings.

2. If you have not received ongoing treatment or do not have an ongoing relationship with the medical community despite the existence of a severe impairment(s), or if your skin lesions have not persisted for at least 3 months but you are undergoing continuing treatment as prescribed, you may still have an impairment(s) that meets a listing in another body system or that medically equals a listing. If you do not have an impairment(s) that meets or medically equals a listing, we will consider whether your impairment(s) functionally equals the listings. (See § 416.924 of this chapter.) When we decide whether you continue to be disabled, we use the rules in § 416.994a of this chapter.

108.01 Category of Impairments, Skin Disorders

108.02 Ichthyosis, with extensive skin lesions that persist for at least 3 months despite continuing treatment as prescribed.

108.03 Bullous disease (for example, pemphigus, erythema multiforme bullosum, epidermolysis bullosa, bullous pemphigoid, dermatitis herpetiformis), with extensive skin lesions that persist for at least 3 months despite continuing treatment as prescribed.

108.04 Chronic infections of the skin or mucous membranes, with extensive fungating or extensive ulcerating skin lesions that persist for at least 3 months despite continuing treatment as prescribed.

108.05 Dermatitis (for example, psoriasis, dyshidrosis, atopic dermatitis, exfoliative dermatitis, allergic contact dermatitis), with extensive skin lesions that persist for at least 3 months despite continuing treatment as prescribed.

108.06 Hidradenitis suppurativa, with extensive skin lesions involving both axillae, both inguinal areas, or the perineum that persist for at least 3 months despite continuing treatment as prescribed.

108.07 Genetic photosensitivity disorders, established as described in 108.00E.

A. Xeroderma pigmentosum. Consider the individual disabled from birth.

B. Other genetic photosensitivity disorders, with:

1. Extensive skin lesions that have lasted or can be expected to last for a continuous period of at least 12 months,

OR

2. Inability to function outside of a highly protective environment for a continuous period of at least 12 months (see 108.00E2).

108.08 Burns, with extensive skin lesions that have lasted or can be expected to last for a continuous period of at least 12 months. (See 108.00F).

109.00 Endocrine Disorders

A. *What is an endocrine disorder?*

An endocrine disorder is a medical condition that causes a hormonal imbalance. When an endocrine gland functions abnormally, producing either too much of a specific hormone (hyperfunction) or too little (hypofunction), the hormonal imbalance can cause various complications in the body. The major glands of the endocrine system are the pituitary, thyroid, parathyroid, adrenal, and pancreas.

B. *How do we evaluate the effects of endocrine disorders?* The only listing in this body system addresses children from birth to the attainment of age 6 who have diabetes mellitus (DM) and require daily insulin. We evaluate other impairments that result from endocrine disorders under the listings for other body systems. For example:

1. *Pituitary gland disorders* can disrupt hormone production and normal functioning in other endocrine glands and in many body systems. The effects of pituitary gland disorders vary depending on which hormones are involved. For example, when pituitary growth hormone deficiency in growing children limits bone maturation and results in pathological short stature, we evaluate this linear growth impairment under 100.00. When pituitary hypofunction affects water and electrolyte balance in the kidney and leads to diabetes insipidus, we evaluate the effects of recurrent dehydration under 106.00.

2. *Thyroid gland disorders* affect the sympathetic nervous system and normal metabolism. We evaluate thyroid-related changes in linear growth under 100.00; thyroid-related changes in blood pressure and heart rate that cause cardiac arrhythmias or other cardiac dysfunction under 104.00; thyroid-related weight loss under 105.00; and cognitive limitations, mood disorders, and anxiety under 112.00.

3. *Parathyroid gland disorders* affect calcium levels in bone, blood, nerves, muscle, and other body tissues. We evaluate parathyroid-related osteoporosis and fractures under 101.00; abnormally elevated calcium levels in the blood (hypercalcemia) that lead to cataracts under 102.00; kidney failure under 106.00; and recurrent abnormally low blood calcium levels (hypocalcemia) that lead to increased excitability of nerves and muscles, such as tetany and muscle spasms, under 111.00.

4. *Adrenal gland disorders* affect bone calcium levels, blood pressure, metabolism, and mental status. We evaluate adrenal-related linear growth impairments under 100.00; adrenal-related osteoporosis with fractures that compromises the ability to walk or to use the upper extremities under 101.00; adrenal-related hypertension that worsens heart failure or causes recurrent arrhythmias under 104.00; adrenal-related weight loss under 105.00; and mood disorders under 112.00.

5. *Diabetes mellitus and other pancreatic gland disorders* disrupt the production of several hormones, including insulin, that regulate metabolism and digestion. Insulin is essential to the absorption of glucose from the bloodstream into body cells for conversion into cellular energy. The most common pancreatic gland disorder is diabetes mellitus (DM). There are two major types of DM: type 1 and type 2. Both type 1 and type 2 DM are chronic disorders that can have serious,

disabling complications that meet the duration requirement. Type 1 DM—previously known as "juvenile diabetes" or "insulin-dependent diabetes mellitus" (IDDM) —is an absolute deficiency of insulin secretion that commonly begins in childhood and continues throughout adulthood. Treatment of type 1 DM always requires lifelong daily insulin. With type 2 DM—previously known as "adult-onset diabetes mellitus" or "non-insulin-dependent diabetes mellitus" (NIDDM) —the body's cells resist the effects of insulin, impairing glucose absorption and metabolism. Type 2 is less common than type 1 DM in children, but physicians are increasingly diagnosing type 2 DM before age 18. Treatment of type 2 DM generally requires lifestyle changes, such as increased exercise and dietary modification, and sometimes insulin in addition to other medications. While both type 1 and type 2 DM are usually controlled, some children do not achieve good control for a variety of reasons including, but not limited to, hypoglycemia unawareness, other disorders that can affect blood glucose levels, inability to manage DM due to a mental disorder, or inadequate treatment.

a. *Hyperglycemia*. Both types of DM cause hyperglycemia, which is an abnormally high level of blood glucose that may produce acute and long-term complications. Acute complications of hyperglycemia include diabetic ketoacidosis. Long-term complications of chronic hyperglycemia include many conditions affecting various body systems but are rare in children.

b. *Diabetic ketoacidosis (DKA)*. DKA is an acute, potentially life-threatening complication of DM in which the chemical balance of the body becomes dangerously hyperglycemic and acidic. It results from a severe insulin deficiency, which can occur due to missed or inadequate daily insulin therapy or in association with an acute illness. It usually requires hospital treatment to correct the acute complications of dehydration, electrolyte imbalance, and insulin deficiency. You may have serious complications resulting from your treatment, which we evaluate under the affected body system. For example, we evaluate cardiac arrhythmias under 104.00, intestinal necrosis under 105.00, and cerebral edema and seizures under 111.00. Recurrent episodes of DKA in adolescents may result from mood or eating disorders, which we evaluate under 112.00.

c. *Hypoglycemia*. Children with DM may experience episodes of hypoglycemia, which is an abnormally low level of blood glucose. Most children age 6 and older recognize the symptoms of hypoglycemia and reverse them by consuming substances containing glucose; however, some do not take this step because of hypoglycemia unawareness. Severe hypoglycemia can lead to complications, including seizures or loss of consciousness, which we evaluate under 111.00, or altered mental status, cognitive deficits, and permanent brain damage, which we evaluate under 112.00.

C. *How do we evaluate DM in children?*

Listing 109.08 is only for children with DM who have not attained age 6 and who require daily insulin. For all other children (that is, children with DM who are age 6 or older and require daily insulin, and children of any age with DM who do not require daily insulin), we follow our rules for determining whether the DM is severe, alone or in combination with another impairment, whether it meets or medically equals the criteria of a listing in another body system, or functionally equals the listings under the criteria in §416.926a, considering the factors in §416.924a. The management of DM in children can be complex and variable from day to day, and all children with DM require some level of adult supervision. For example, if a child age 6 or older has a medical need for 24-hour-a-day adult supervision of insulin treatment, food intake, and physical activity to ensure survival, we will find that the child's impairment functionally equals the listings based on the example in §416.926a(m)(5).

D. *How do we evaluate other endocrine disorders that do not have effects that meet or medically equal the criteria of any listing in other body systems?* If your impairment(s) does not meet or medically equal a listing in another body system, we will consider whether your impairment(s) functionally equals the listings under the criteria in §416.926a, considering the factors in §416.924a. When we decide whether you continue to be disabled, we use the rules in §416.994a.

110.00 Congenital Disorders that Affect Multiple Body Systems

A. *Which disorders do we evaluate under this body system?* We evaluate non-mosaic Down syndrome and catastrophic congenital disorders under this body system.

B. *What is non-mosaic Down syndrome?* Non-mosaic Down syndrome is a genetic disorder. Most children with non-mosaic Down syndrome have three copies of chromosome 21 in all of their cells (chromosome 21 trisomy); some have an extra copy of chromosome 21 attached to a different chromosome in all of their cells (chromosome 21 translocation). Virtually all children with non-mosaic Down syndrome have characteristic facial or other physical features, delayed physical development, and intellectual disability. Children with non-mosaic Down syndrome may also have congenital heart disease, impaired vision, hearing problems, and other disorders. We evaluate non-mosaic Down syndrome under 110.06. If you have non-mosaic Down syndrome documented as described in 110.00C, we consider you disabled from birth.

C. *What evidence do we need to document non-mosaic Down syndrome under 110.06?*

1. Under 110.06A, we will find you disabled based on laboratory findings.

a. To find that your disorder meets 110.06A, we need a copy of the laboratory report of karyotype analysis, which is the definitive test to establish non-mosaic Down syndrome. We will not purchase karyotype analysis. We will not accept a fluorescence in situ hybridization (FISH) test because it does not distinguish between the mosaic and non-mosaic forms of Down syndrome.

b. If a physician (see §§404.1513(a)(1) and 416.913(a)(1) of this chapter) has not signed the laboratory report of karyotype analysis, the evidence must also include a physician's statement that you have Down syndrome.

c. For purposes of 110.06A, we do not require evidence stating that you have the distinctive facial or other physical features of Down syndrome.

2. If we do not have a laboratory report of karyotype analysis documenting that you have non-mosaic Down syndrome, we may find you disabled under 110.06B or 110.06C.

a. Under 110.06B, we need a physician's report stating: (i) your karyotype diagnosis or evidence that documents your type of Down syndrome that is consistent with prior karyotype analysis (for example, reference to a diagnosis of "trisomy 21") and (ii) that you have the distinctive facial or other physical features of Down syndrome. We do not require a detailed description of the facial or other physical features of the disorder. However, we will not find that your disorder meets 110.06B if we have evidence—such as evidence of functioning inconsistent with the diagnosis—that indicates that you do not have non-mosaic Down syndrome.

b. If we do not have evidence of prior karyotype analysis (you did not have testing, or you had testing but we do not have information from a physician about the test results), we will find that your disorder meets 110.06C if we have: (i) a physician's report stating that you have the distinctive facial or other physical features of Down syndrome and (ii) evidence that your functioning is consistent with a diagnosis of non-mosaic Down syndrome. This evidence may include medical or nonmedical information about your physical and mental abilities, including information about your development, education, work history, or the results of psychological testing. However, we will not find that your disorder meets 110.06C if we have evidence—such as evidence of functioning inconsistent with the diagnosis—that indicates that you do not have non-mosaic Down syndrome.

D. *What are catastrophic congenital disorders?* Some catastrophic congenital disorders, such as anencephaly, cyclopia, chromosome 13 trisomy (Patau syndrome or trisomy D), and chromosome 18 trisomy (Edwards' syndrome or trisomy E), are usually expected to result in early death. Others such as cri du chat syndrome (chromosome 5p deletion syndrome) and the infantile onset form of Tay-Sachs disease interfere very seriously with development. We evaluate catastrophic congenital disorders under 110.08. The term "very seriously" in 110.08 has the same meaning as in the term "extreme" in §416.926a(e)(3) of this chapter.

E. *What evidence do we need under 110.08?*

We need one of the following to determine if your disorder meets 110.08A or B:

1. A laboratory report of the definitive test that documents your disorder (for example, genetic analysis or evidence of biochemical abnormalities) signed by a physician.

2. A laboratory report of the definitive test that documents your disorder that is not signed by a physician *and* a report from a physician stating that you have the disorder.

3. A report from a physician stating that you have the disorder with the typical clinical features of the disorder and that you had definitive testing that documented your disorder. In this case, we will find that your disorder meets 110.08A or B unless we have evidence that indicates that you do not have the disorder.

4. If we do not have the definitive laboratory evidence we need under E1, E2, or E3, we will find that your disorder meets 110.08A or B if we have: (i) a report from a physician stating that you have the disorder and that you have the typical clinical features of the disorder, *and* (ii) other evidence that supports the diagnosis. This evidence may include medical or nonmedical information about your development and functioning.

5. For obvious catastrophic congenital anomalies that are expected to result in early death, such as anencephaly and cyclopia, we need evidence from a physician that demonstrates that the infant has the characteristic physical features of the disorder. In these rare cases, we do not need laboratory testing or any other evidence that confirms the disorder.

F. *How do we evaluate mosaic Down syndrome and other congenital disorders that affect multiple body systems?*

1. *Mosaic Down syndrome.* Approximately 2 percent of children with Down syndrome have the mosaic form. In mosaic Down syndrome, there are some cells with an extra copy of chromosome 21 and other cells with the normal two copies of chromosome 21. Mosaic Down syndrome can be so slight as to be undetected clinically, but it can also be profound and disabling, affecting various body systems.

2. *Other congenital disorders that affect multiple body systems.* Other congenital disorders, such as congenital anomalies, chromosomal disorders, dysmorphic syndromes, inborn metabolic syndromes, and perinatal infectious diseases, can cause deviation from, or interruption of, the normal function of the body or can interfere with development. Examples of these disorders include both the juvenile and late-onset forms of Tay-Sachs disease, trisomy X syndrome (XXX syndrome), fragile X syndrome, phenylketonuria (PKU), caudal regression syndrome, and fetal alcohol syndrome. For these disorders and other disorders like them, the degree of deviation, interruption, or interference, as well as the resulting functional limitations and their progression, may vary widely from child to child and may affect different body systems.

3. *Evaluating the effects of mosaic Down syndrome or another congenital disorder under the listings.* When the effects of mosaic Down syndrome or another congenital disorder that affects multiple body systems are sufficiently severe we evaluate the disorder under the appropriate affected body system(s), such as musculoskeletal, special senses and speech, neurological, or mental disorders.

Otherwise, we evaluate the specific functional limitations that result from the disorder under our other rules described in 110.00G.

G. *What if your disorder does not meet a listing?* If you have a severe medically determinable impairment(s) that does not meet a listing, we will consider whether your impairment(s) medically equals a listing. See §416.926 of this chapter. If your impairment(s) does not meet or medically equal a listing, we will consider whether it functionally equals the listings. See §§416.924a and 416.926a of this chapter. We use the rules in §416.994a of this chapter when we decide whether you continue to be disabled.

110.01 Category of Impairments, Congenital Disorders That Affect Multiple Body Systems

110.06 Non-mosaic Down syndrome (chromosome 21 trisomy or chromosome 21 translocation), documented by:

A. A laboratory report of karyotype analysis signed by a physician, or both a laboratory report of karyotype analysis not signed by a physician *and* a statement by a physician that the child has Down syndrome (see 110.00C1).

OR

B. A physician's report stating that the child has chromosome 21 trisomy or chromosome 21 translocation consistent with karyotype analysis with the distinctive facial or other physical features of Down syndrome (see 110.00C2a).

OR

C. A physician's report stating that the child has Down syndrome with the distinctive facial or other physical features *and* evidence demonstrating that the child is functioning at the level of a child with non-mosaic Down syndrome (see 110.00C2b).

110.08 A catastrophic congenital disorder (see 110.00D and 110.00E) with:

A. Death usually expected within the first months of life.

OR

B. Very serious interference with development or functioning.

111.00 Neurological

A. *Which neurological disorders do we evaluate under these listings?*

We evaluate epilepsy, coma or persistent vegetative state (PVS), and neurological disorders that cause disorganization of motor function, bulbar and neuromuscular dysfunction, or communication impairment. Under this body system, we evaluate the limitations resulting from the impact of the neurological disease process itself. If you have a neurological disorder(s) that affects your physical and mental functioning, we will evaluate your impairments under the rules we use to determine functional equivalence. If your neurological disorder results in only mental impairment or if you have a co-occurring mental condition that is not caused by your neurological disorder (for example, Autism spectrum disorder), we will evaluate your mental impairment under the mental disorders body system, 112.00.

B. *What evidence do we need to document your neurological disorder?*

1. We need both medical and non-medical evidence (signs, symptoms, and laboratory findings) to assess the effects of your neurological disorder. Medical evidence should include your medical history, examination findings, relevant laboratory tests, and the results of imaging. Imaging refers to medical imaging techniques, such as x-ray, computerized tomography (CT), magnetic resonance imaging (MRI), and electroencephalography (EEG). The imaging must be consistent with the prevailing state of medical knowledge and clinical practice as the proper technique to support the evaluation of the disorder. In addition, the medical evidence may include descriptions of any prescribed treatment and your response to it. We consider non-medical evidence such as statements you or others make about your impairments, your restrictions, your daily activities, or, if you are an adolescent, your efforts to work.
2. We will make every reasonable effort to obtain the results of your laboratory and imaging evidence. When the results of any of these tests are part of the existing evidence in your case record, we will evaluate the test results and all other relevant evidence. We will not purchase imaging, or other diagnostic tests or laboratory tests that are complex, may involve significant risk, or that are invasive. We will not routinely purchase tests that are expensive or not readily available.

C. *How do we consider adherence to prescribed treatment in neurological disorders?* In 111.02 (Epilepsy) and 111.12 (Myasthenia gravis), we require that limitations from these neurological disorders exist despite adherence to prescribed treatment. "Despite adherence to prescribed treatment" means that you have taken medication(s) or followed other treatment procedures for your neurological disorder(s) as prescribed by a physician for three consecutive months but your impairment continues to meet the other listing requirements despite this treatment. You may receive your treatment at a health care facility that you visit regularly, even if you do not see the same physician on each visit.

D. *What do we mean by disorganization of motor function?*

1. Disorganization of motor function means interference, due to your neurological disorder, with movement of two extremities; i.e., the lower extremities, or upper extremities (including fingers, wrists, hands, arms, and shoulders). By

two extremities we mean both lower extremities, or both upper extremities, or one upper extremity and one lower extremity. All listings in this body system, except for 111.02 (Epilepsy) and 111.20 (Coma and persistent vegetative state), include criteria for disorganization of motor function that results in an extreme limitation in your ability to:

- o Stand up from a seated position; or
- o Balance while standing or walking; or
- o Use the upper extremities (e.g., fingers, wrists, hands, arms, and shoulders).

2. Extreme limitation means the inability to stand up from a seated position, maintain balance in a standing position and while walking, or use your upper extremities to independently initiate, sustain, and complete age-appropriate activities. The assessment of motor function depends on the degree of interference with standing up; balancing while standing or walking; or using the upper extremities (including fingers, hands, arms, and shoulders).
   a. Inability to stand up from a seated position means that once seated you are unable to stand and maintain an upright position without the assistance of another person or the use of an assistive device, such as a walker, two crutches, or two canes.
   b. Inability to maintain balance in a standing position means that you are unable to maintain an upright position while standing or walking without the assistance of another person or an assistive device, such as a walker, two crutches, or two canes.
   c. Inability to use your upper extremities means that you have a loss of function of both upper extremities (e.g., fingers, wrists, hands, arms, and shoulders) that very seriously limits your ability to independently initiate, sustain, and complete age- appropriate activities involving fine and gross motor movements. Inability to perform fine and gross motor movements could include not being able to pinch, manipulate, and use your fingers; or not being able to use your hands, arms, and shoulders to perform gross motor movements, such as handling, gripping, grasping, holding, turning, and reaching; or not being able to engage in exertional movements such a lifting, carrying, pushing, and pulling.

3. For children who are not yet able to balance, stand up, or walk independently, we consider their function based on assessments of limitations in the ability to perform comparable age-appropriate activities with the lower and upper extremities, given normal developmental milestones. For such children, an extreme level of limitation means developmental milestones at less than one-half of the child's chronological age.

E. *What do we mean by bulbar and neuromuscular dysfunction?* The bulbar region of the brain is responsible for controlling the bulbar muscles in the throat, tongue, jaw, and face. Bulbar and neuromuscular dysfunction refers to weakness in these muscles, resulting in breathing, swallowing, and speaking impairments. Listings 111.12 (Myasthenia gravis) and 111.22 (Motor neuron disorders) include criteria for evaluating bulbar and neuromuscular dysfunction. If your neurological disorder has resulted in a breathing disorder, we may evaluate that condition under the respiratory system, 103.00.

F. *What is epilepsy, and how do we evaluate it under 111.02?*

1. Epilepsy is a pattern of recurrent and unprovoked seizures that are manifestations of abnormal electrical activity in the brain. There are various types of generalized and "focal" or partial seizures. In children, the most common potentially disabling seizure types are generalized tonic-clonic seizures, dyscognitive seizures (formerly complex partial seizures), and absence seizures. However, psychogenic nonepileptic seizures and pseudoseizures are not epileptic seizures for the purpose of 111.02. We evaluate psychogenic seizures and pseudoseizures under the mental disorders body system, 112.00.
    a. Generalized tonic-clonic seizures are characterized by loss of consciousness accompanied by a tonic phase (sudden muscle tensing causing the child to lose postural control) followed by a clonic phase (rapid cycles of muscle contraction and relaxation, also called convulsions). Tongue biting and incontinence may occur during generalized tonic-clonic seizures, and injuries may result from falling.
    b. Dyscognitive seizures are characterized by alteration of consciousness without convulsions or loss of muscle control. During the seizure, blank staring, change of facial expression, and automatisms (such as lip smacking, chewing or swallowing, or repetitive simple actions, such as gestures or verbal utterances) may occur. During its course, a dyscognitive seizure may progress into a generalized tonic-clonic seizure (see 111.00F1a).
    c. Absence seizures (petit mal) are also characterized by an alteration in consciousness, but are shorter than other generalized seizures (e.g., tonic-clonic and dyscognitive) seizures, generally lasting for only a few seconds rather than minutes. They may present with blank staring, change of facial expression, lack of awareness and responsiveness, and a sense of lost time after the seizure. An aura never precedes absence seizures. Although absence seizures are brief, frequent occurrence may limit functioning. This type of seizure usually does not occur after adolescence.
    d. Febrile seizures may occur in young children in association with febrile illnesses. We will consider seizures occurring during febrile illnesses.

To meet 111.02, we require documentation of seizures during nonfebrile periods and epilepsy must be established.

2. Description of seizure. We require at least one detailed description of your seizures from someone, preferably a medical professional, who has observed at least one of your typical seizures. If you experience more than one type of seizure, we require a description of each type.
3. Serum drug levels. We do not require serum drug levels; therefore, we will not purchase them. However, if serum drug levels are available in your medical records, we will evaluate them in the context of the other evidence in your case record.
4. Counting seizures. The period specified in 111.02A or B cannot begin earlier than one month after you began prescribed treatment. The required number of seizures must occur within the period we are considering in connection with your application or continuing disability review. When we evaluate the frequency of your seizures, we also consider your adherence to prescribed treatment (see 111.00C). When we determine the number of seizures you have had in the specified period, we will:
    a. Count multiple seizures occurring in a 24-hour period as one seizure.
    b. Count status epilepticus (a continuous series of seizures without return to consciousness between seizures) as one seizure.
    c. Count a dyscognitive seizure that progresses into a generalized tonic-clonic seizure as one generalized tonic-clonic seizure.
    d. We do not count seizures that occur during a period when you are not adhering to prescribed treatment without good reason. When we determine that you had a good reason for not adhering to prescribed treatment, we will consider your physical, mental, educational, and communicative limitations (including any language barriers). We will consider you to have good reason for not following prescribed treatment if, for example, the treatment is very risky for you due to its consequences or unusual nature, or if you are unable to afford prescribed treatment that you are willing to accept, but for which no free community resources are available. We will follow guidelines found in our policy, such as § 416.930(c) of this chapter, when we determine whether you have a good reason for not adhering to prescribed treatment.
    e. We do not count psychogenic nonepileptic seizures or pseudoseizures under 111.02. We evaluate these seizures under the mental disorders body system, 112.00.
5. Electroencephalography (EEG) testing. We do not require EEG test results; therefore, we will not purchase them. However, if EEG test results are available in your medical records, we will evaluate them in the context of the other evidence in your case record.

G. *What is vascular insult to the brain, and how do we evaluate it under 111.04?*

1. Vascular insult to the brain (cerebrum, cerebellum, or brainstem), commonly referred to as stroke or cerebrovascular accident (CVA), is brain cell death caused by an interruption of blood flow within or leading to the brain, or by a hemorrhage from a ruptured blood vessel or aneurysm in the brain. If you have a vision impairment resulting from your vascular insult, we may evaluate that impairment under the special senses body system, 102.00.
2. We generally need evidence from at least 3 months after the vascular insult to determine whether you have disorganization of motor function under 111.04. In some cases, evidence of your vascular insult is sufficient to allow your claim within 3 months post-vascular insult. If we are unable to allow your claim within 3 months after your vascular insult, we will defer adjudication of the claim until we obtain evidence of your neurological disorder at least 3 months post-vascular insult.

H. *What are benign brain tumors, and how do we evaluate them under 111.05?* Benign brain tumors are noncancerous (nonmalignant) abnormal growths of tissue in or on the brain that invade healthy brain tissue or apply pressure on the brain or cranial nerves. We evaluate their effects on your functioning as discussed in 111.00D. We evaluate malignant brain tumors under the cancer body system in 113.00. If you have a vision impairment resulting from your benign brain tumor, we may evaluate that impairment under the special senses body system, 102.00.

I. *What is cerebral palsy, and how do we evaluate it under 111.07?*

1. Cerebral palsy (CP) is a term that describes a group of static, nonprogressive disorders caused by abnormalities within the brain that disrupt the brain's ability to control movement, muscle coordination, and posture. The resulting motor deficits manifest very early in a child's development, with delayed or abnormal progress in attaining developmental milestones; deficits may become more obvious as the child grows and matures over time.
2. We evaluate your signs and symptoms, such as ataxia, spasticity, flaccidity, athetosis, chorea, and difficulty with precise movements when we determine your ability to stand up, balance, walk, or perform fine and gross motor movements. We will also evaluate your signs, such as dysarthria and apraxia of speech, and receptive and expressive language problems when we determine your ability to communicate.
3. We will consider your other impairments or signs and symptoms that develop secondary to the disorder, such as post-impairment syndrome (a combination of pain, fatigue, and weakness due to muscle abnormalities); overuse syndromes (repetitive motion injuries); arthritis; abnormalities of proprioception (perception of the movements and position of the body); abnormalities of stereognosis (perception and identification of objects by touch); learning problems; anxiety; and depression.

J. *What are spinal cord disorders, and how do we evaluate them under 111.08?*

1. Spinal cord disorders may be congenital or caused by injury to the spinal cord. Motor signs and symptoms of spinal cord disorders include paralysis, flaccidity, spasticity, and weakness.
2. Spinal cord disorders with complete loss of function (111.08A) addresses spinal cord disorders that result in complete lack of motor, sensory, and autonomic function of the affected part(s) of the body.
3. Spinal cord disorders with disorganization of motor function (111.08B) addresses spinal cord disorders that result in less than complete loss of function of the affected part(s) of the body, reducing, but not eliminating, motor, sensory, and autonomic function.
4. When we evaluate your spinal cord disorder, we generally need evidence from at least 3 months after your symptoms began in order to evaluate your disorganization of motor function. In some cases, evidence of your spinal cord disorder may be sufficient to allow your claim within 3 months after the spinal cord disorder. If the medical evidence demonstrates total cord transection causing a loss of motor and sensory functions below the level of injury, we will not wait 3 months but will make the allowance decision immediately.

K. *What are communication impairments associated with neurological disorders, and how do we evaluate them under 111.09?*

1. Communication impairments result from medically determinable neurological disorders that cause dysfunction in the parts of the brain responsible for speech and language. Under 111.09, we must have recent comprehensive evaluation including all areas of affective and effective communication, performed by a qualified professional, to document a communication impairment associated with a neurological disorder.
2. Under 111.09A, we need documentation from a qualified professional that your neurological disorder has resulted in a speech deficit that significantly affects your ability to communicate. Significantly affects means that you demonstrate a serious limitation in communicating, and a person who is unfamiliar with you cannot easily understand or interpret your speech.
3. Under 111.09B, we need documentation from a qualified professional that shows that your neurological disorder has resulted in a comprehension deficit that results in ineffective verbal communication for your age. For the purposes of 111.09B, comprehension deficit means a deficit in receptive language. Ineffective verbal communication means that you demonstrate serious limitation in your ability to communicate orally on the same level as other children of the same age and level of development.

4. Under 111.09C, we need documentation of a neurological disorder that has resulted in hearing loss. Your hearing loss will be evaluated under listing 102.10 or 102.11.
5. We evaluate speech deficits due to non-neurological disorders under 2.09.

L. *What are neurodegenerative disorders of the central nervous system, such as Juvenile-onset Huntington's disease and Friedreich's ataxia, and how do we evaluate them under 111.17?* Neurodegenerative disorders of the central nervous system are disorders characterized by progressive and irreversible degeneration of neurons or their supporting cells. Over time, these disorders impair many of the body's motor or cognitive and other mental functions. We consider neurodegenerative disorders of the central nervous system under 111.17 that we do not evaluate elsewhere in section 111.00, such as juvenile-onset Huntington's disease (HD) and Friedreich's ataxia. When these disorders result in solely cognitive and other mental functional limitations, we will evaluate the disorder under the mental disorder listings, 112.00.

M. *What is traumatic brain injury, and how do we evaluate it under 111.18?*

1. Traumatic brain injury (TBI) is damage to the brain resulting from skull fracture, collision with an external force leading to a closed head injury, or penetration by an object that enters the skull and makes contact with brain tissue. We evaluate a TBI that results in coma or persistent vegetative state (PVS) under 111.20.
2. We generally need evidence from at least 3 months after the TBI to evaluate whether you have disorganization of motor function under 111.18. In some cases, evidence of your TBI is sufficient to determine disability. If we are unable to allow your claim within 3 months post-TBI, we will defer adjudication of the claim until we obtain evidence of your neurological disorder at least 3 months post-TBI. If a finding of disability still is not possible at that time, we will again defer adjudication of the claim until we obtain evidence at least 6 months after your TBI.

N. *What are coma and persistent vegetative state, and how do we evaluate them under 111.20?* Coma is a state of unconsciousness in which a child does not exhibit a sleep/wake cycle, and is unable to perceive or respond to external stimuli. Children who do not fully emerge from coma may progress into persistent vegetative state (PVS). PVS is a condition of partial arousal in which a child may have a low level of consciousness but is still unable to react to external stimuli. In contrast to coma, a child in a PVS retains sleep/wake cycles and may exhibit some key lower brain functions, such as spontaneous movement, opening and moving eyes, and grimacing. Coma or PVS may result from a TBI, a nontraumatic insult to the brain (such as a vascular insult, infection, or brain tumor), or a neurodegenerative or metabolic disorder. Medically induced comas should be considered under the section pertaining to the underlying reason the coma was medically induced and not under this section.

O. *What is multiple sclerosis, and how do we evaluate it under 111.21?*

1. Multiple sclerosis (MS) is a chronic, inflammatory, degenerative disorder that damages the myelin sheath surrounding the nerve fibers in the brain and spinal cord. The damage disrupts the normal transmission of nerve impulses within the brain and between the brain and other parts of the body causing impairment in muscle coordination, strength, balance, sensation, and vision. There are several forms of MS, ranging from slightly to highly aggressive. Milder forms generally involve acute attacks (exacerbations) with partial or complete recovery from signs and symptoms (remissions). Aggressive forms generally exhibit a steady progression of signs and symptoms with few or no remissions. The effects of all forms vary from child to child.
2. We evaluate your signs and symptoms, such as flaccidity, spasticity, spasms, incoordination, imbalance, tremor, physical fatigue, muscle weakness, dizziness, tingling, and numbness when we determine your ability to stand up, balance, walk, or perform fine and gross motor movements, such as using your arms, hands, and fingers. If you have a vision impairment resulting from your MS, we may evaluate that impairment under the special senses body system, 102.00.

P. *What are motor neuron disorders, and how do we evaluate them under 111.22?* Motor neuron disorders are progressive neurological disorders that destroy the cells that control voluntary muscle activity, such as walking, breathing, swallowing, and speaking. The most common motor neuron disorders in children are progressive bulbar palsy and spinal muscular dystrophy syndromes. We evaluate the effects of these disorders on motor functioning or bulbar and neuromuscular functioning.

Q. *How do we consider symptoms of fatigue in these listings?* Fatigue is one of the most common and limiting symptoms of some neurological disorders, such as multiple sclerosis and myasthenia gravis. These disorders may result in physical fatigue (lack of muscle strength) or mental fatigue (decreased awareness or attention). When we evaluate your fatigue, we will consider the intensity, persistence, and effects of fatigue on your functioning. This may include information such as the clinical and laboratory data and other objective evidence concerning your neurological deficit, a description of fatigue considered characteristic of your disorder, and information about your functioning. We consider the effects of physical fatigue on your ability to stand up, balance, walk, or perform fine and gross motor movements using the criteria described in 111.00D.

R. *How do we evaluate your neurological disorder when it does not meet one of these listings?*

1. If your neurological disorder does not meet the criteria of any of these listings, we must also consider whether your impairment(s) meets the criteria of

a listing in another body system. If you have a severe medically determinable impairment(s) that does not meet a listing, we will determine whether your impairment(s) medically equals a listing. See § 416.926 of this chapter.

2. If your impairment(s) does not meet or medically equal a listing, we will consider whether your impairment(s) functionally equals the listings. See § 416.926a of this chapter.
3. We use the rules in § 416.994a of this chapter when we decide whether you continue to be disabled.

111.01 Category of Impairments, Neurological Disorders

111.02 Epilepsy, documented by a detailed description of a typical seizure and characterized by A or B:

A. Generalized tonic-clonic seizures (see 111.00F1a), occurring at least once a month for at least 3 consecutive months (see 111.00F4) despite adherence to prescribed treatment (see 111.00C).

OR

B. Dyscognitive seizures (see 111.00F1b) or absence seizures (see 111.00F1c), occurring at least once a week for at least 3 consecutive months (see 111.00F4) despite adherence to prescribed treatment (see 111.00C).

111.03 [Reserved]

111.04 Vascular insult to the brain, characterized by disorganization of motor function in two extremities (see 111.00D1), resulting in an extreme limitation (see 111.00D2) in the ability to stand up from a seated position, balance while standing or walking, or use the upper extremities, persisting for at least 3 consecutive months after the insult.

111.05 Benign brain tumors, characterized by disorganization of motor function in two extremities (see 111.00D1), resulting in an extreme limitation (see 111.00D2) in the ability to stand up from a seated position, balance while standing or walking, or use the upper extremities.

111.06 [Reserved]

111.07 Cerebral palsy, characterized by disorganization of motor function in two extremities (see 111.00D1), resulting in an extreme limitation (see 111.00D2) in the ability to stand up from a seated position, balance while standing or walking, or use the upper extremities.

111.08 Spinal cord disorders, characterized by A or B:

A. Complete loss of function, as described in 111.00J2, persisting for 3 consecutive months after the disorder (see 111.00J4).

OR

B. Disorganization of motor function in two extremities (see 111.00D1), resulting in an extreme limitation (see 111.00D2) in the ability to stand up from a seated position, balance while standing or walking, or use the upper extremities persisting for 3 consecutive months after the disorder (see 111.00J4).

111.09 Communication impairment, associated with documented neurological disorder and one of the following:

A. Documented speech deficit that significantly affects (see 111.00K1) the clarity and content of the speech.

OR

B. Documented comprehension deficit resulting in ineffective verbal communication (see 111.00K2) for age.

OR

C. Impairment of hearing as described under the criteria in 102.10 or 102.11.

111.10 [Reserved]

111.11 [Reserved]

111.12 Myasthenia gravis, characterized by A or B despite adherence to prescribed treatment for at least 3 months (see 111.00C):

A. Disorganization of motor function in two extremities (see 111.00D1), resulting in an extreme limitation (see 111.00D2) in the ability to stand up from a seated position, balance while standing or walking, or use the upper extremities.

OR

B. Bulbar and neuromuscular dysfunction (see 111.00E), resulting in:

1. One myasthenic crisis requiring mechanical ventilation; or
2. Need for supplemental enteral nutrition via a gastrostomy or parenteral nutrition via a central venous catheter.

111.13 Muscular dystrophy, characterized by disorganization of motor function in two extremities (see 111.00D1), resulting in an extreme limitation (see 111.00D2) in the ability to stand up from a seated position, balance while standing or walking, or use the upper extremities.

111.14 Peripheral neuropathy, characterized by disorganization of motor function in two extremities (see 111.00D1), resulting in an extreme limitation (see 111.00D2) in the ability to stand up from a seated position, balance while standing or walking, or use the upper extremities.

111.15 [Reserved]

111.16 [Reserved]

111.17 Neurodegenerative disorders of the central nervous system, such as Juvenile-onset Huntington's disease and Friedreich's ataxia, characterized by disorganization of motor function in two extremities (see 111.00D1), resulting in an extreme limitation (see 111.00D2) in the ability to stand up from a seated position, balance while standing or walking, or use the upper extremities.

111.18 Traumatic brain injury, characterized by disorganization of motor function in two extremities (see 111.00D1), resulting in an extreme limitation (see 111.00D2) in the ability to stand up from a seated position, balance while standing or walking, or use the upper extremities, persisting for at least 3 consecutive months after the injury.

111.19 [Reserved]

111.20 Coma or persistent vegetative state, persisting for at least 1 month.

111.21 Multiple sclerosis, characterized by disorganization of motor function in two extremities (see 111.00D1), resulting in an extreme limitation (see 111.00D2) in the ability to stand up from a seated position, balance while standing or walking, or use the upper extremities.

111.22 Motor neuron disorders, characterized by A or B:

A. Disorganization of motor function in two extremities (see 111.00D1), resulting in an extreme limitation (see 111.00D2) in the ability to stand up from a seated position, balance while standing or walking, or use the upper extremities.

OR

B. Bulbar and neuromuscular dysfunction (see 111.00E), resulting in:

1. Acute respiratory failure requiring invasive mechanical ventilation; or
2. Need for supplemental enteral nutrition via a gastrostomy or parenteral nutrition via a central venous catheter.

112.00 Mental Disorders

A. How are the listings for mental disorders for children arranged, and what do they require?

1. The listings for mental disorders for children are arranged in 12 categories: neurocognitive disorders (112.02); schizophrenia spectrum and other psychotic disorders (112.03); depressive, bipolar and related disorders (112.04);

intellectual disorder (112.05); anxiety and obsessive-compulsive disorders (112.06); somatic symptom and related disorders (112.07); personality and impulse-control disorders (112.08); autism spectrum disorder (112.10); neurodevelopmental disorders (112.11); eating disorders (112.13); developmental disorders in infants and toddlers (112.14); and trauma- and stressor-related disorders (112.15). All of these listings, with the exception of 112.14, apply to children from age three to attainment of age 18. Listing 112.14 is for children from birth to attainment of age 3.

2. Listings 112.07, 112.08, 112.10, 112.11, 112.13, and 112.14 have two paragraphs, designated A and B; your mental disorder must satisfy the requirements of both paragraphs A and B. Listings 112.02, 112.03, 112.04, 112.06, and 112.15 have three paragraphs, designated A, B, and C; your mental disorder must satisfy the requirements of both paragraphs A and B, or the requirements of both paragraphs A and C. Listing 112.05 has two paragraphs that are unique to that listing (see 112.00A3); your mental disorder must satisfy the requirements of either paragraph A or paragraph B.

   a. Paragraph A of each listing (except 112.05) includes the medical criteria that must be present in your medical evidence.

   b. Paragraph B of each listing (except 112.05) provides the functional criteria we assess to evaluate how your mental disorder limits your functioning. For children ages 3 to 18, these criteria represent the areas of mental functioning a child uses to perform age-appropriate activities. They are: understand, remember, or apply information; interact with others; concentrate, persist, or maintain pace; and adapt or manage oneself. (See 112.00I for a discussion of the criteria for children from birth to attainment of age 3 under 112.14.) We will determine the degree to which your medically determinable mental impairment affects the four areas of mental functioning and your ability to function age-appropriately in a manner comparable to that of other children your age who do not have impairments. (Hereinafter, the words "age-appropriately" incorporate the qualifying statement, "in a manner comparable to that of other children your age who do not have impairments.") To satisfy the paragraph B criteria, your mental disorder must result in "extreme" limitation of one, or "marked" limitation of two, of the four areas of mental functioning. (When we refer to "paragraph B criteria" or "area[s] of mental functioning" in the introductory text of this body system, we mean the criteria in paragraph B of every listing except 112.05and 112.14.)

   c. Paragraph C of listings 112.02, 112.03, 112.04, 112.06, and 112.15 provides the criteria we use to evaluate "serious and persistent mental disorders." To satisfy the paragraph C criteria, your mental disorder must be "serious and persistent"; that is, there must be a medically documented history of the existence of the disorder over a period of at least 2 years, and evidence that satisfies the criteria in both C1 and C2 (see 112.00G). (When we refer to "paragraph C" or "the paragraph C criteria" in the introductory text of this body system, we mean the criteria in paragraph C of listings 112.02, 112.03, 112.04, 112.06, and 112.15.)

3. Listing 112.05 has two paragraphs, designated A and B, that apply to only intellectual disorder. Each paragraph requires that you have significantly subaverage general intellectual functioning and significant deficits in current adaptive functioning.

B. Which mental disorders do we evaluate under each listing category for children?

1. *Neurocognitive disorders (112.02).*
   a. These disorders are characterized in children by a clinically significant deviation in normal cognitive development or by a decline in cognitive functioning. Symptoms and signs may include, but are not limited to, disturbances in memory, executive functioning (that is, higher-level cognitive processes; for example, regulating attention, planning, inhibiting responses, decision-making), visual-spatial functioning, language and speech, perception, insight, and judgment.
   b. Examples of disorders that we evaluate in this category include major neurocognitive disorder; mental impairments resulting from medical conditions such as a metabolic disease (for example, juvenile Tay-Sachs disease), human immunodeficiency virus infection, vascular malformation, progressive brain tumor, or traumatic brain injury; or substance-induced cognitive disorder associated with drugs of abuse, medications, or toxins. (We evaluate neurological disorders under that body system (see 111.00). We evaluate cognitive impairments that result from neurological disorders under 112.02 if they do not satisfy the requirements in 111.00. We evaluate catastrophic genetic disorders under listings in 110.00, 111.00, or 112.00, as appropriate. We evaluate genetic disorders that are not catastrophic under the affected body system(s).)
   c. This category does not include the mental disorders that we evaluate under intellectual disorder (112.05), autism spectrum disorder (112.10), and neurodevelopmental disorders (112.11).
2. *Schizophrenia spectrum and other psychotic disorders (112.03).*
   a. These disorders are characterized by delusions, hallucinations, disorganized speech, or grossly disorganized or catatonic behavior, causing a clinically significant decline in functioning. Symptoms and signs may include, but are not limited to, inability to initiate and persist in goal-directed activities, social withdrawal, flat or inappropriate affect,

poverty of thought and speech, loss of interest or pleasure, disturbances of mood, odd beliefs and mannerisms, and paranoia.

b. Examples of disorders that we evaluate in this category include schizophrenia, schizoaffective disorder, delusional disorder, and psychotic disorder due to another medical condition.

3. *Depressive, bipolar and related disorders (112.04).*

   a. These disorders are characterized by an irritable, depressed, elevated, or expansive mood, or by a loss of interest or pleasure in all or almost all activities, causing a clinically significant decline in functioning. Symptoms and signs may include, but are not limited to, feelings of hopelessness or guilt, suicidal ideation, a clinically significant change in body weight or appetite, sleep disturbances, an increase or decrease in energy, psychomotor abnormalities, disturbed concentration, pressured speech, grandiosity, reduced impulse control, sadness, euphoria, and social withdrawal. Depending on a child's age and developmental stage, certain features, such as somatic complaints, irritability, anger, aggression, and social withdrawal may be more commonly present than other features.

   b. Examples of disorders that we evaluate in this category include bipolar disorders (I or II), cyclothymic disorder, disruptive mood dysregulation disorder, major depressive disorder, persistent depressive disorder (dysthymia), and bipolar or depressive disorder due to another medical condition.

4. *Intellectual disorder (112.05).*

   a. This disorder is characterized by significantly subaverage general intellectual functioning and significant deficits in current adaptive functioning. Signs may include, but are not limited to, poor conceptual, social, or practical skills evident in your adaptive functioning.

   b. The disorder that we evaluate in this category may be described in the evidence as intellectual disability, intellectual developmental disorder, or historically used terms such as "mental retardation."

   c. This category does not include the mental disorders that we evaluate under neurocognitive disorders (112.02), autism spectrum disorder (112.10), or neurodevelopmental disorders (112.11).

5. *Anxiety and obsessive-compulsive disorders (112.06).*

   a. These disorders are characterized by excessive anxiety, worry, apprehension, and fear, or by avoidance of feelings, thoughts, activities, objects, places, or people. Symptoms and signs may include, but are not limited to, restlessness, difficulty concentrating, hyper-vigilance, muscle tension, sleep disturbance, fatigue, panic attacks, obsessions and compulsions, constant thoughts and fears about safety, and frequent physical complaints. Depending on a child's age and developmental stage, other features may also include refusal to go to school, academic failure, frequent stomachaches and other physical complaints, extreme worries about sleeping away from home, being overly clinging, and exhibiting tantrums at times of separation from caregivers.

b. Examples of disorders that we evaluate in this category include separation anxiety disorder, social anxiety disorder, panic disorder, generalized anxiety disorder, agoraphobia, and obsessive-compulsive disorder.

c. This category does not include the mental disorders that we evaluate under trauma- and stressor-related disorders (112.15).

6. *Somatic symptom and related disorders (112.07).*

   a. These disorders are characterized by physical symptoms or deficits that are not intentionally produced or feigned, and that, following clinical investigation, cannot be fully explained by a general medical condition, another mental disorder, the direct effects of a substance, or a culturally sanctioned behavior or experience. Symptoms and signs may include, but are not limited to, pain and other abnormalities of sensation, gastrointestinal symptoms, fatigue, abnormal motor movement, pseudoseizures, and pseudoneurological symptoms, such as blindness or deafness.

   b. Examples of disorders that we evaluate in this category include somatic symptom disorder and conversion disorder.

7. *Personality and impulse-control disorders (112.08).*

   a. These disorders are characterized by enduring, inflexible, maladaptive, and pervasive patterns of behavior. Onset may occur in childhood but more typically occurs in adolescence or young adulthood. Symptoms and signs may include, but are not limited to, patterns of distrust, suspiciousness, and odd beliefs; social detachment, discomfort, or avoidance; hypersensitivity to negative evaluation; an excessive need to be taken care of; difficulty making independent decisions; a preoccupation with orderliness, perfectionism, and control; and inappropriate, intense, impulsive anger and behavioral expression grossly out of proportion to any external provocation or psychosocial stressors.

   b. Examples of disorders that we evaluate in this category include paranoid, schizoid, schizotypal, borderline, avoidant, dependent, obsessive-compulsive personality disorders, and intermittent explosive disorder.

8. *Autism spectrum disorder (112.10).*

   a. These disorders are characterized by qualitative deficits in the development of reciprocal social interaction, verbal and nonverbal communication skills, and symbolic or imaginative play; restricted repetitive and stereotyped patterns of behavior, interests, and activities; and stagnation of development or loss of acquired skills. Symptoms and signs may include, but are not limited to, abnormalities and unevenness in the development of cognitive skills; unusual responses to sensory stimuli; and behavioral difficulties, including hyperactivity, short attention span, impulsivity, aggressiveness, or self-injurious actions.

b. Examples of disorders that we evaluate in this category include autism spectrum disorder with or without accompanying intellectual impairment, and autism spectrum disorder with or without accompanying language impairment.

c. This category does not include the mental disorders that we evaluate under neurocognitive disorders (112.02), intellectual disorder (112.05), and neurodevelopmental disorders (112.11).

9. *Neurodevelopmental disorders (112.11).*

   a. These disorders are characterized by onset during the developmental period, that is, during childhood or adolescence, although sometimes they are not diagnosed until adulthood. Symptoms and signs may include, but are not limited to, underlying abnormalities in cognitive processing (for example, deficits in learning and applying verbal or nonverbal information, visual perception, memory, or a combination of these); deficits in attention or impulse control; low frustration tolerance; excessive or poorly planned motor activity; difficulty with organizing (time, space, materials, or tasks); repeated accidental injury; and deficits in social skills. Symptoms and signs specific to tic disorders include sudden, rapid, recurrent, non-rhythmic, motor movement or vocalization.

   b. Examples of disorders that we evaluate in this category include specific learning disorder, borderline intellectual functioning, and tic disorders (such as Tourette syndrome).

   c. This category does not include the mental disorders that we evaluate under neurocognitive disorders (112.02), autism spectrum disorder (112.10), or personality and impulse-control disorders (112.08).

10. *Eating disorders (112.13).*

   a. These disorders are characterized in young children by persistent eating of nonnutritive substances or repeated episodes of regurgitation and rechewing of food, or by persistent failure to consume adequate nutrition by mouth. In adolescence, these disorders are characterized by disturbances in eating behavior and preoccupation with, and excessive self-evaluation of, body weight and shape. Symptoms and signs may include, but are not limited to, failure to make expected weight gains; restriction of energy consumption when compared with individual requirements; recurrent episodes of binge eating or behavior intended to prevent weight gain, such as self-induced vomiting, excessive exercise, or misuse of laxatives; mood disturbances, social withdrawal, or irritability; amenorrhea; dental problems; abnormal laboratory findings; and cardiac abnormalities.

b. Examples of disorders that we evaluate in this category include anorexia nervosa, bulimia nervosa, binge-eating disorder, and avoidant/restrictive food disorder.

11. *Developmental disorders in infants and toddlers (112.14).*

a. Developmental disorders are characterized by a delay or deficit in the development of age-appropriate skills, or a loss of previously acquired skills, involving motor planning and control, learning, relating and communicating, and self-regulating.

b. Examples of disorders that we evaluate in this category include developmental coordination disorder, separation anxiety disorder, autism spectrum disorder, and regulation disorders of sensory processing (difficulties in regulating emotions, behaviors, and motor abilities in response to sensory stimulation). Some infants and toddlers may have only a general diagnosis of "developmental delay."

c. This category does not include eating disorders related to low birth weight and failure to thrive, which we evaluate under that body system (100.00).

12. *Trauma- and stressor-related disorders (112.15).*

a. These disorders are characterized by experiencing or witnessing a traumatic or stressful event, or learning of a traumatic event occurring to a close family member or close friend, and the psychological aftermath of clinically significant effects on functioning. Symptoms and signs may include, but are not limited to, distressing memories, dreams, and flashbacks related to the trauma or stressor; avoidant or withdrawn behavior; constriction of play and significant activities; increased frequency of negative emotional states (for example, fear, sadness) or reduced expression of positive emotions (for example, satisfaction, affection); anxiety; irritability; aggression; exaggerated startle response; difficulty concentrating; sleep disturbance; and a loss of previously acquired developmental skills.

b. Examples of disorders that we evaluate in this category include posttraumatic stress disorder, reactive attachment disorder, and other specified trauma- and stressor-related disorders (such as adjustment-like disorders with prolonged duration without prolonged duration of stressor).

c. This category does not include the mental disorders that we evaluate under anxiety and obsessive-compulsive disorders (112.06), and cognitive impairments that result from neurological disorders, such as a traumatic brain injury, which we evaluate under neurocognitive disorders (112.02).

C. What evidence do we need to evaluate your mental disorder?

1. *General.* We need objective medical evidence from an acceptable medical source to establish that you have a medically determinable mental disorder. We also need evidence to assess the severity of your mental disorder and its effects on your ability to function age-appropriately. We will determine the extent and kinds of evidence we need from medical and nonmedical sources based on the individual facts about your disorder. For additional evidence requirements for intellectual disorder (112.05), see 112.00H. For our basic rules on evidence, see §§ 416.912, 416.913, and 416.920b of this chapter. For our rules on evaluating medical opinions, see §§ 416.1520c and 416.927 of this chapter. For our rules on evidence about your symptoms, see § 416.929 of this chapter.
2. *Evidence from medical sources.* We will consider all relevant medical evidence about your disorder from your physician, psychologist, and other medical sources, which include health care providers such as physician assistants, psychiatric nurse practitioners, licensed clinical social workers, and clinical mental health counselors. Evidence from your medical sources may include:
    a. Your reported symptoms.
    b. Your developmental, medical, psychiatric, and psychological history.
    c. The results of physical or mental status examinations, structured clinical interviews, psychiatric or psychological rating scales, measures of adaptive functioning, or other clinical findings.
    d. Developmental assessments, psychological testing, imaging results, or other laboratory findings.
    e. Your diagnosis.
    f. The type, dosage, and beneficial effects of medications you take.
    g. The type, frequency, duration, and beneficial effects of therapy you receive.
    h. Side effects of medication or other treatment that limit your ability to function.
    i. Your clinical course, including changes in your medication, therapy, or other treatment, and the time required for therapeutic effectiveness.
    j. Observations and descriptions of how you function during examinations or therapy.
    k. Information about sensory, motor, or speech abnormalities, or about your cultural background (for example, language or customs) that may affect an evaluation of your mental disorder.
    l. The expected duration of your symptoms and signs and their effects on your ability to function age-appropriately, both currently and in the future.

3. *Evidence from you and people who know you.* We will consider all relevant evidence about your mental disorder and your daily functioning that we receive from you and from people who know you. If you are too young or unable to describe your symptoms and your functioning, we will ask for a description from the person who is most familiar with you. We will ask about your symptoms, your daily functioning, and your medical treatment. We will ask for information from third parties who can tell us about your mental disorder, but we must have permission to do so. This evidence may include information from your family, caregivers, teachers, other educators, neighbors, clergy, case managers, social workers, shelter staff, or other community support and outreach workers. We will consider whether your statements and the statements from third parties are consistent with the medical and other evidence we have.
4. *Evidence from early intervention programs, school, vocational training, work, and work-related programs.*
   a. *Early intervention programs.* You may receive services in an Early Intervention Program (EIP) to help you with your developmental needs. If so, we will consider information from your Individualized Family Service Plan (IFSP) and the early intervention specialists who help you.
   b. *School.* You may receive special education or related services at your preschool or school. If so, we will try to obtain information from your school sources when we need it to assess how your mental disorder affects your ability to function. Examples of this information include your Individualized Education Programs (IEPs), your Section 504 plans, comprehensive evaluation reports, school-related therapy progress notes, information from your teachers about how you function in a classroom setting, and information from special educators, nurses, school psychologists, and occupational, physical, and speech/language therapists about any special education services or accommodations you receive at school.
   c. *Vocational training, work, and work-related programs.* You may have recently participated in or may still be participating in vocational training, work-related programs, or work activity. If so, we will try to obtain information from your training program or your employer when we need it to assess how your mental disorder affects your ability to function. Examples of this information include training or work evaluations, modifications to your work duties or work schedule, and any special supports or accommodations you have required or now require in order to work. If you have worked or are working through a community mental health program, sheltered or supported work program, rehabilitation program, or transitional employment program, we will consider the type and degree of support you have received or are receiving in order to work (see 112.00D).

5. *Need for longitudinal evidence.*

   a. *General.* Longitudinal medical evidence can help us learn how you function over time, and help us evaluate any variations in the level of your functioning. We will request longitudinal evidence of your mental disorder when your medical providers have records concerning you and your mental disorder over a period of months or perhaps years (see § 416.912(d) of this chapter).

   b. *Non-medical sources of longitudinal evidence.* Certain situations, such as chronic homelessness, may make it difficult for you to provide longitudinal medical evidence. If you have a severe mental disorder, you will probably have evidence of its effects on your functioning over time, even if you have not had an ongoing relationship with the medical community or are not currently receiving treatment. For example, family members, caregivers, teachers, neighbors, former employers, social workers, case managers, community support staff, outreach workers, or government agencies may be familiar with your mental health history. We will ask for information from third parties who can tell us about your mental disorder, but you must give us permission to do so.

   c. *Absence of longitudinal evidence.* In the absence of longitudinal evidence, we will use current objective medical evidence and all other relevant evidence available to us in your case record to evaluate your mental disorder. If we purchase a consultative examination to document your disorder, the record will include the results of that examination (see § 416.914 of this chapter). We will take into consideration your medical history, symptoms, clinical and laboratory findings, and medical source opinions. If you do not have longitudinal evidence, the current evidence alone may not be sufficient or appropriate to show that you have a disorder that meets the criteria of one of the mental disorders listings. In that case, we will follow the rules in 112.00K.

6. *Evidence of functioning in unfamiliar situations or supportive situations.*

   a. *Unfamiliar situations.* We recognize that evidence about your functioning in unfamiliar situations does not necessarily show how you would function on a sustained basis in a school or other age-appropriate setting. In one-time, time-limited, or other unfamiliar situations, you may function differently than you do in familiar situations. In unfamiliar situations, you may appear more, or less, limited than you do on a daily basis and over time.

   b. *Supportive situations.* Your ability to function in settings that are highly structured, or that are less demanding or more supportive than settings in which children your age without impairments typically function, does not necessarily demonstrate your ability to function age-appropriately.

c. *Our assessment.* We must assess your ability to function age-appropriately by evaluating all the evidence, such as reports about your functioning from third parties who are familiar with you, with an emphasis on how well you can initiate, sustain, and complete age-appropriate activities despite your impairment(s), compared to other children your age who do not have impairments.

D. How do we consider psychosocial supports, structured settings, living arrangements, and treatment when we evaluate the functioning of children?

1. *General.* Psychosocial supports, structured settings, and living arrangements, including assistance from your family or others, may help you by reducing the demands made on you. In addition, treatment you receive may reduce your symptoms and signs and possibly improve your functioning, or may have side effects that limit your functioning. Therefore, when we evaluate the effects of your mental disorder and rate the limitation of your areas of mental functioning, we will consider the kind and extent of supports you receive, the characteristics of any structured setting in which you spend your time (compared to children your age without impairments), and the effects of any treatment. This evidence may come from reports about your functioning from third parties who are familiar with you, and other third-party statements or information. Following are some examples of the supports you may receive:

   a. You receive help from family members or other people in ways that children your age without impairments typically do not need in order to function age-appropriately. For example, an aide may accompany you on the school bus to help you control your actions or to monitor you to ensure you do not injure yourself or others.

   b. You receive one-on-one assistance in your classes every day; or you have a full-time personal aide who helps you to function in your classroom; or you are a student in a self-contained classroom; or you attend a separate or alternative school where you receive special education services.

   c. You participate in a special education or vocational training program, or a psychosocial rehabilitation day treatment or community support program, where you receive training in daily living and entry-level work skills.

   d. You participate in a sheltered, supported, or transitional work program, or in a competitive employment setting with the help of a job coach or supervisor.

   e. You receive comprehensive "24/7 wrap-around" mental health services while living in a group home or transitional housing, while participating in a semi-independent living program, or while living at home.

f. You live in a residential school, hospital, or other institution with 24-hour care.

g. You receive assistance from a crisis response team, social workers, or community mental health workers who help you meet your physical needs, and who may also represent you in dealings with government or community social services.

2. *How we consider different levels of support and structure in psychosocial rehabilitation programs.*

   a. Psychosocial rehabilitation programs are based on your specific needs. Therefore, we cannot make any assumptions about your mental disorder based solely on the fact that you are associated with such a program. We must know the details of the program(s) in which you are involved and the pattern(s) of your involvement over time.

   b. The kinds and levels of supports and structures in psychosocial rehabilitation programs typically occur on a scale of "most restrictive" to "least restrictive." Participation in a psychosocial rehabilitation program at the most restrictive level would suggest greater limitation of your areas of mental functioning than would participation at a less restrictive level. The length of time you spend at different levels in a program also provides information about your functioning. For example, you could begin participation at the most restrictive crisis intervention level but gradually improve to the point of readiness for a lesser level of support and structure and, if you are an older adolescent, possibly some form of employment.

3. *How we consider the help or support you receive.*

   a. We will consider the complete picture of your daily functioning, including the kinds, extent, and frequency of help and support you receive, when we evaluate your mental disorder and determine whether you are able to use the four areas of mental functioning age-appropriately. The fact that you have done, or currently do, some routine activities without help or support does not necessarily mean that you do not have a mental disorder or that you are not disabled. For example, you may be able to take age-appropriate care of your personal needs, or you may be old enough and able to cook, shop, and take public transportation. You may demonstrate both strengths and deficits in your daily functioning.

   b. You may receive various kinds of help and support from others that enable you to do many things that, because of your mental disorder, you might not be able to do independently. Your daily functioning may depend on the special contexts in which you function. For example, you may spend your time among only familiar people or surroundings, in a simple and steady routine or an unchanging environment, or in a highly structured classroom or alternative school. However, this does not necessarily show whether you would function age-appropriately without those supports or contexts. (See 112.00H for further discussion of these issues regarding significant deficits in adaptive functioning for the purpose of 112.05.)

4. *How we consider treatment.* We will consider the effect of any treatment on your functioning when we evaluate your mental disorder. Treatment may include medication(s), psychotherapy, or other forms of intervention, which you receive in a doctor's office, during a hospitalization, or in a day program at a hospital or outpatient treatment program. With treatment, you may not only have your symptoms and signs reduced, but may also be able to function age-appropriately. However, treatment may not resolve all of the limitations that result from your mental disorder, and the medications you take or other treatment you receive for your disorder may cause side effects that limit your mental or physical functioning. For example, you may experience drowsiness, blunted affect, memory loss, or abnormal involuntary movements.

E. What are the paragraph B criteria for children age 3 to the attainment of age 18?

1. *Understand, remember, or apply information (paragraph B1).* This area of mental functioning refers to the abilities to learn, recall, and use information to perform age-appropriate activities. Examples include: understanding and learning terms, instructions, procedures; following one- or two-step oral instructions to carry out a task; describing an activity to someone else; asking and answering questions and providing explanations; recognizing a mistake and correcting it; identifying and solving problems; sequencing multi-step activities; and using reason and judgment to make decisions. These examples illustrate the nature of the area of mental functioning. We do not require documentation of all of the examples. How you manifest this area of mental functioning and your limitations in using it depends, in part, on your age.
2. *Interact with others (paragraph B2).* This area of mental functioning refers to the abilities to relate to others age-appropriately at home, at school, and in the community. Examples include: engaging in interactive play; cooperating with others; asking for help when needed; initiating and maintaining friendships; handling conflicts with others; stating own point of view; initiating or sustaining conversation; understanding and responding to social cues (physical, verbal, emotional); responding to requests, suggestions, criticism, correction, and challenges; and keeping social interactions free of excessive irritability, sensitivity, argumentativeness, or suspiciousness. These examples illustrate the nature of this area of mental functioning. We do not require documentation of all of the examples. How you manifest this area of mental functioning and your limitations in using it depends, in part, on your age.

3. *Concentrate, persist, or maintain pace (paragraph B3).* This area of mental functioning refers to the abilities to focus attention on activities and stay on task age-appropriately. Examples include: initiating and performing an activity that you understand and know how to do; engaging in an activity at home or in school at an appropriate and consistent pace; completing tasks in a timely manner; ignoring or avoiding distractions while engaged in an activity or task; changing activities without being disruptive; engaging in an activity or task close to or with others without interrupting or distracting them; sustaining an ordinary routine and regular attendance at school; and engaging in activities at home, school, or in the community without needing an unusual amount of rest. These examples illustrate the nature of this area of mental functioning. We do not require documentation of all of the examples. How you manifest this area of mental functioning and your limitations in using it depends, in part, on your age.
4. *Adapt or manage oneself (paragraph B4).* This area of mental functioning refers to the abilities to regulate emotions, control behavior, and maintain well-being in age-appropriate activities and settings. Examples include: responding to demands; adapting to changes; managing your psychologically based symptoms; distinguishing between acceptable and unacceptable performance in community- or school-related activities; setting goals; making plans independently of others; maintaining personal hygiene; and protecting yourself from harm and exploitation by others. These examples illustrate the nature of this area of mental functioning. We do not require documentation of all of the examples. How you manifest this area of mental functioning and your limitations in using it depends, in part, on your age.

F. How do we use the paragraph B criteria to evaluate mental disorders in children?

1. *General.* We use the paragraph B criteria to rate the degree of your limitations. We consider only the limitations that result from your mental disorder(s). We will determine whether you are able to use each of the paragraph B areas of mental functioning in age-appropriate activities in a manner comparable to that of other children your age who do not have impairments. We will consider, for example, the range of your activities and whether they are age-appropriate; how well you can initiate, sustain, and complete your activities; the kinds and frequency of help or supervision you receive; and the kinds of structured or supportive settings you need in order to function age-appropriately (see 112.00D).
2. *Degrees of limitation.* We evaluate the effects of your mental disorder on each of the four areas of mental functioning. To satisfy the paragraph B criteria, your mental disorder must result in extreme limitation of one, or marked limitation of two, paragraph B areas of mental functioning. See §§ 416.925(b)(2)(ii) and 416.926a(e) of this chapter for the definitions of the terms marked and extreme as they apply to children.

3. *Rating the limitations of your areas of mental functioning.*
   a. *General.* We use all of the relevant medical and non-medical evidence in your case record to evaluate your mental disorder: the symptoms and signs of your disorder, the reported limitations in your activities, and any help and support you receive that is necessary for you to function. The medical evidence may include descriptors regarding the diagnostic stage or level of your disorder, such as "mild" or "moderate." Clinicians may use these terms to characterize your medical condition. However, these terms will not always be the same as the degree of your limitation in a paragraph B area of mental functioning.
   b. *Areas of mental functioning in daily activities.* You use the same four areas of mental functioning in daily activities at home, at school, and in the community. With respect to a particular task or activity, you may have trouble using one or more of the areas. For example, you may have difficulty understanding and remembering what to do; or concentrating and staying on task long enough to do it; or engaging in the task or activity with other people; or trying to do the task without becoming frustrated and losing self-control. Information about your daily functioning in your activities at home, at school, or in your community can help us understand whether your mental disorder limits one or more of these areas; and, if so, whether it also affects your ability to function age-appropriately.
   c. *Overall effect of limitations.* Limitation of an area of mental functioning reflects the overall degree to which your mental disorder interferes with that area. The degree of limitation does not necessarily reflect a specific type or number of activities, including activities of daily living, that you have difficulty doing. In addition, no single piece of information (including test results) can establish whether you have extreme or marked limitation of an area of mental functioning.
   d. *Effects of support, supervision, structure on functioning.* The degree of limitation of an area of mental functioning also reflects the kind and extent of supports or supervision you receive (beyond what other children your age without impairments typically receive) and the characteristics of any structured setting where you spend your time, which enable you to function. The more extensive the support you need from others (beyond what is age-appropriate) or the more structured the setting you need in order to function, the more limited we will find you to be (see 112.00D).
   e. *Specific instructions for paragraphs B1, B3, and B4.* For paragraphs B1, B3, and B4, the greatest degree of limitation of any part of the area of mental functioning directs the rating of limitation of that whole area of mental functioning.
      i. To do an age-appropriate activity, you must be able to understand *and* remember *and* apply information required by the activity.

Similarly, you must be able to concentrate *and* persist *and* maintain pace in order to complete the activity, and adapt *and* manage yourself age-appropriately. Limitation in any one of these parts (understand *or* remember *or* apply; concentrate *or* persist *or* maintain pace; adapt *or* manage oneself) may prevent you from completing age-appropriate activities.

ii. We will document the rating of limitation of the whole area of mental functioning, not each individual part. We will not add ratings of the parts together. For example, with respect to paragraph B3, if you have marked limitation in concentrating, but your limitations in persisting and maintaining pace do not rise to a marked level, we will find that you have marked limitation in the whole paragraph B3 area of mental functioning.

iii. Marked limitation in more than one part of the same paragraph B area of mental functioning does not satisfy the requirement to have marked limitation in two paragraph B areas of mental functioning.

4. *How we evaluate mental disorders involving exacerbations and remissions.*

   a. When we evaluate the effects of your mental disorder, we will consider how often you have exacerbations and remissions, how long they last, what causes your mental disorder to worsen or improve, and any other relevant information. We will assess whether your mental impairment(s) causes marked or extreme limitation of the affected paragraph B area(s) of mental functioning (see 112.00F2). We will consider whether you can use the area of mental functioning age-appropriately on a sustained basis. We will not find that you function age-appropriately solely because you have a period(s) of improvement (remission), or that you are disabled solely because you have a period of worsening (exacerbation), of your mental disorder.

   b. If you have a mental disorder involving exacerbations and remissions, you may be able to use the four areas of mental functioning at home, at school, or in the community for a few weeks or months. Recurrence or worsening of symptoms and signs, however, can interfere enough to render you unable to function age-appropriately.

G. What are the paragraph C criteria, and how do we use them to evaluate mental disorders in children age 3 to the attainment of age 18?

1. *General.* The paragraph C criteria are an alternative to the paragraph B criteria under listings 112.02, 112.03, 112.04, 112.06, and 112.15. We use the paragraph C criteria to evaluate mental disorders that are "serious and persistent." In the paragraph C criteria, we recognize that mental health interventions may control the more obvious symptoms and signs of your mental disorder.

2. *Paragraph C criteria.*
   a. We find a mental disorder to be "serious and persistent" when there is a medically documented history of the existence of the mental disorder in the listing category over a period of at least 2 years, and evidence shows that your disorder satisfies both C1 and C2.
   b. The criterion in C1 is satisfied when the evidence shows that you rely, on an ongoing basis, upon medical treatment, mental health therapy, psychosocial support(s), or a highly structured setting(s), to diminish the symptoms and signs of your mental disorder (see 112.00D). We consider that you receive ongoing medical treatment when the medical evidence establishes that you obtain medical treatment with a frequency consistent with accepted medical practice for the type of treatment or evaluation required for your medical condition. We will consider periods of inconsistent treatment or lack of compliance with treatment that may result from your mental disorder. If the evidence indicates that the inconsistent treatment or lack of compliance is a feature of your mental disorder, and it has led to an exacerbation of your symptoms and signs, we will not use it as evidence to support a finding that you have not received ongoing medical treatment as required by this paragraph.
   c. The criterion in C2 is satisfied when the evidence shows that, despite your diminished symptoms and signs, you have achieved only marginal adjustment. "Marginal adjustment" means that your adaptation to the requirements of daily life is fragile; that is, you have minimal capacity to adapt to changes in your environment or to demands that are not already part of your daily life. We will consider that you have achieved only marginal adjustment when the evidence shows that changes or increased demands have led to exacerbation of your symptoms and signs and to deterioration in your functioning; for example, you have become unable to function outside of your home or a more restrictive setting, without substantial psychosocial supports (see 112.00D). Such deterioration may have necessitated a significant change in medication or other treatment. Similarly, because of the nature of your mental disorder, evidence may document episodes of deterioration that have required you to be hospitalized or absent from school, making it difficult for you to sustain age-appropriate activity over time.

H. How do we document and evaluate intellectual disorder under 112.05?

1. *General.* Listing 112.05 is based on the two elements that characterize intellectual disorder for children up to age 18: significantly subaverage general intellectual functioning and significant deficits in current adaptive functioning.
2. *Establishing significantly subaverage general intellectual functioning.*
   a. *Definition.* Intellectual functioning refers to the general mental capacity to learn, reason, plan, solve problems, and perform other cognitive

functions. Under 112.05A, we identify significantly subaverage general intellectual functioning by the cognitive inability to function at a level required to participate in standardized intelligence testing. Our findings under 112.05A are based on evidence from an acceptable medical source. Under 112.05B, we identify significantly subaverage general intellectual functioning by an IQ score(s) on an individually administered standardized test of general intelligence that meets program requirements and has a mean of 100 and a standard deviation of 15. A qualified specialist (see 112.00H2c) must administer the standardized intelligence testing.

b. *Psychometric standards.* We will find standardized intelligence test results usable for the purposes of 112.05B1 when the measure employed meets contemporary psychometric standards for validity, reliability, normative data, and scope of measurement; and a qualified specialist has individually administered the test according to all pre-requisite testing conditions.

c. *Qualified specialist.* A "qualified specialist" is currently licensed or certified at the independent level of practice in the State where the test was performed, and has the training and experience to administer, score, and interpret intelligence tests. If a psychological assistant or paraprofessional administered the test, a supervisory qualified specialist must interpret the test findings and co-sign the examination report.

d. *Responsibility for conclusions based on testing.* We generally presume that your obtained IQ score(s) is an accurate reflection of your general intellectual functioning, unless evidence in the record suggests otherwise. Examples of this evidence include: a statement from the test administrator indicating that your obtained score is not an accurate reflection of your general intellectual functioning, prior or internally inconsistent IQ scores, or information about your daily functioning. Only qualified specialists, Federal and State agency medical and psychological consultants, and other contracted medical and psychological experts may conclude that your obtained IQ score(s) is not an accurate reflection of your general intellectual functioning. This conclusion must be well supported by appropriate clinical and laboratory diagnostic techniques and must be based on relevant evidence in the case record, such as:

    i. The data obtained in testing;

    ii. Your developmental history, including when your signs and symptoms began;

    iii. Information about how you function on a daily basis in a variety of settings; and

    iv. Clinical observations made during the testing period, such as your ability to sustain attention, concentration, and effort; to relate appropriately to the examiner; and to perform tasks independently without prompts or reminders.

3. Establishing significant deficits in adaptive functioning.
    a. Definition. Adaptive functioning refers to how you learn and use conceptual, social, and practical skills in dealing with common life demands. It is your typical functioning at home, at school, and in the community, alone or among others. Under 112.05A, we identify significant deficits in adaptive functioning based on your dependence on others to care for your personal needs, such as eating and bathing (grossly in excess of age-appropriate dependence). We will base our conclusions about your adaptive functioning on evidence from a variety of sources (see 112.00H3b) and not on your statements alone. Under 112.05B2, we identify significant deficits in adaptive functioning based on whether there is extreme limitation of one, or marked limitation of two, of the paragraph B criteria (see 112.00E; 112.00F).
    b. Evidence. Evidence about your adaptive functioning may come from:
        i. Medical sources, including their clinical observations;
        ii. Standardized tests of adaptive functioning (see 112.00H3c);
        iii. Third party information, such as a report of your functioning from a family member or your caregiver;
        iv. School records;
        v. A teacher questionnaire;
        vi. Reports from employers or supervisors; and
        vii. Your own statements about how you handle all of your daily activities.
    c. Standardized tests of adaptive functioning. We do not require the results of an individually administered standardized test of adaptive functioning. If your case record includes these test results, we will consider the results along with all other relevant evidence; however, we will use the guidelines in 112.00E and F to evaluate and determine the degree of your deficits in adaptive functioning, as required under 112.05B2.
    d. Standardized developmental assessments. We do not require the results of standardized developmental assessments, which compare your level of development to the level typically expected for your chronological age. If your case record includes test results, we will consider the results along with all other relevant evidence. However, we will use the guidelines in 112.00E and F to evaluate and determine the degree of your deficits in adaptive functioning, as required under 112.05B2.
    e. How we consider common everyday activities.
        i. The fact that you engage in common everyday activities, such as caring for your personal needs, preparing simple meals, or driving a car, will not always mean that you do not have deficits in adaptive

functioning as required by 112.05B2. You may demonstrate both strengths and deficits in your adaptive functioning. However, a lack of deficits in one area does not negate the presence of deficits in another area. When we assess your adaptive functioning, we will consider all of your activities and your performance of them.

ii. Our conclusions about your adaptive functioning rest on the quality of your daily activities and whether you do them age-appropriately. If you receive help in performing your activities, we need to know the kind, extent, and frequency of help you receive in order to perform them. We will not assume that your ability to do some common everyday activities, or to do some things without help or support, demonstrates that your mental disorder does not meet the requirements of 112.05B2. (See 112.00D regarding the factors we consider when we evaluate your functioning, including how we consider any help or support you receive.)

f. *How we consider work activity.* The fact that you have engaged in work activity, or that you work intermittently or steadily in a job commensurate with your abilities, will not always mean that you do not have deficits in adaptive functioning as required by 112.05B2. When you have engaged in work activity, we need complete information about the work, and about your functioning in the work activity and work setting, before we reach any conclusions about your adaptive functioning. We will consider all factors involved in your work history before concluding whether your impairment satisfies the criteria for intellectual disorder under 112.05B. We will consider your prior and current work history, if any, and various other factors influencing how you function. For example, we consider whether the work was in a supported setting, whether you required more supervision than other employees, how your job duties compared to others in the same job, how much time it took you to learn the job duties, and the reason the work ended, if applicable.

I. What additional considerations do we use to evaluate developmental disorders of infants and toddlers?

1. *General.* We evaluate developmental disorders from birth to attainment of age 3 under 112.14. We evaluate your ability to acquire and maintain the motor, cognitive, social/communicative, and emotional skills that you need to function age-appropriately. When we rate your impairment-related limitations for this listing (see §§ 416.925(b)(2)(ii) and 416.926a(e) of this chapter), we consider only limitations you have because of your developmental disorder. If you have a chronic illness or physical abnormality(ies), we will evaluate it under the affected body system, for example, the cardiovascular or musculoskeletal system.

2. *Age and typical development in early childhood.*
   a. *Prematurity and age.* If you were born prematurely, we will use your corrected chronological age (CCA) for comparison. CCA is your chronological age adjusted by a period of gestational prematurity. CCA = (chronological age) – (number of weeks premature). If you have not attained age 1, we will correct your chronological age, using the same formula. If you are over age 1, we will decide whether to correct your chronological age, based on our judgment and all the facts of your case (see § 416.924b(b) of this chapter).
   b. *Developmental assessment.* We will use the results from a standardized developmental assessment to compare your level of development with that typically expected for your chronological age. When there are no results from a comprehensive standardized developmental assessment in the case record, we need narrative developmental reports from your medical sources in sufficient detail to assess the limitations resulting from your developmental disorder.
   c. *Variation.* When we evaluate your developmental disorder, we will consider the wide variation in the range of normal or typical development in early childhood. At the end of a recognized milestone period, new skills typically begin to emerge. If your new skills begin to emerge later than is typically expected, the timing of their emergence may or may not indicate that you have a developmental delay or deficit that can be expected to last for 1 year.
3. *Evidence.*
   a. *Standardized developmental assessments.* We use standardized test reports from acceptable medical sources or from early intervention specialists, physical or occupational therapists, and other qualified professionals. Only the qualified professional who administers the test, Federal and State agency medical and psychological consultants, and other contracted medical and psychological experts may conclude that the assessment results are not an accurate reflection of your development. This conclusion must be well supported by appropriate clinical and laboratory diagnostic techniques and must be based on relevant evidence in the case record. If the assessment results are not an accurate reflection of your development, we may purchase a new developmental assessment If the developmental assessment is inconsistent with other information in your case record, we will follow the guidelines in § 416.920b of this chapter.
   b. *Narrative developmental reports.* A narrative developmental report is based on clinical observations, progress notes, and well-baby check-ups, and includes your developmental history, examination findings (with abnormal findings noted on repeated examinations), and an

overall assessment of your development (that is, more than one or two isolated skills) by the medical source. Although medical sources may refer to screening test results as supporting evidence in the narrative developmental report, screening test results alone cannot establish a diagnosis or the severity of developmental disorder.

4. *What are the paragraph B criteria for 112.14?*

   a. *General.* The paragraph B criteria for 112.14 are slightly different from the paragraph B criteria for the other listings. They are the developmental abilities that infants and toddlers use to acquire and maintain the skills needed to function age-appropriately. An infant or toddler is expected to use his or her developmental abilities to achieve a recognized pattern of milestones, over a typical range of time, in order to acquire and maintain the skills needed to function age-appropriately. We will find that your developmental disorder satisfies the requirements of 112.14 if it results in extreme limitation of one, or marked limitation of two, of the 112.14 paragraph B criteria. (See §§ 416.925(b)(2)(ii) and 416.926a(e) of this chapter for the definitions of the terms marked and extreme as they apply to children.)

   b. *Definitions of the 112.14 paragraph B developmental abilities.*

      i. *Ability to plan and control motor movement.* This criterion refers to the developmental ability to plan, remember, and execute controlled motor movements by integrating and coordinating perceptual and sensory input with motor output. Using this ability develops gross and fine motor skills, and makes it possible for you to engage in age-appropriate symmetrical or alternating motor activities. You use this ability when, for example, you grasp and hold objects with one or both hands, pull yourself up to stand, walk without holding on, and go up and down stairs with alternating feet. These examples illustrate the nature of the developmental ability. We do not require documentation of all of the examples. How you manifest this developmental ability and your limitations in using it depends, in part, on your age.

      ii. *Ability to learn and remember.* This criterion refers to the developmental ability to learn by exploring the environment, engaging in trial-and-error experimentation, putting things in groups, understanding that words represent things, and participating in pretend play. Using this ability develops the skills that help you understand what things mean, how things work, and how you can make things happen. You use this ability when, for example, you show interest in objects that are new to you, imitate simple actions, name body parts, understand simple cause-and-effect relationships, remember simple directions, or figure out how to take something apart. These examples illustrate the nature of the developmental ability. We do not require documentation of all of the examples. How you manifest this developmental ability and your limitations in using it depends, in part, on your age.

iii. *Ability to interact with others.* This criterion refers to the developmental ability to participate in reciprocal social interactions and relationships by communicating your feelings and intents through vocal and visual signals and exchanges; physical gestures and contact; shared attention and affection; verbal turn taking; and understanding and sending increasingly complex messages. Using this ability develops the social skills that make it possible for you to influence others (for example, by gesturing for a toy or saying "no" to stop an action); invite someone to interact with you (for example, by smiling or reaching); and draw someone's attention to what interests you (for example, by pointing or taking your caregiver's hand and leading that person). You use this ability when, for example, you use vocalizations to initiate and sustain a "conversation" with your caregiver; respond to limits set by an adult with words, gestures, or facial expressions; play alongside another child; or participate in simple group activities with adult help. These examples illustrate the nature of the developmental ability. We do not require documentation of all of the examples. How you manifest this developmental ability and your limitations in using it depends, in part, on your age.

iv. *Ability to regulate physiological functions, attention, emotion, and behavior.* This criterion refers to the developmental ability to stabilize biological rhythms (for example, by developing an age-appropriate sleep/wake cycle); control physiological functions (for example, by achieving regular patterns of feeding); and attend, react, and adapt to environmental stimuli, persons, objects, and events (for example, by becoming alert to things happening around you and in relation to you, and responding without overreacting or underreacting). Using this ability develops the skills you need to regulate yourself and makes it possible for you to achieve and maintain a calm, alert, and organized physical and emotional state. You use this ability when, for example, you recognize your body's needs for food or sleep, focus quickly and pay attention to things that interest you, cry when you are hurt but become quiet when your caregiver holds you, comfort yourself with your favorite toy when you are upset, ask for help when something frustrates you, or refuse help from your caregiver when trying to do something for yourself. These examples illustrate the nature of the developmental ability. We do not require documentation of all of the examples. How you manifest this developmental ability and your limitations in using it depends, in part, on your age.

5. *Deferral of determination.*
   a. *Full-term infants.* In the first few months of life, full-term infants typically display some irregularities in observable behaviors (for example, sleep cycles, feeding, responding to stimuli, attending to faces, self-calming), making it difficult to assess the presence, extent, and duration of a developmental disorder. When the evidence indicates that you may have a significant developmental delay, but there is insufficient evidence to make a determination, we will defer making a disability determination under 112.14 until you are at least 6 months old. This deferral will allow us to obtain a longitudinal medical history so that we can more accurately evaluate your developmental patterns and functioning over time. In most cases, when you are at least 6 months old, any developmental delay you may have can be better assessed, and you can undergo standardized developmental testing, if indicated.
   b. *Premature infants.* When the evidence indicates that you may have a significant developmental delay, but there is insufficient evidence to make a determination, we will defer your case until you attain a CCA (see 112.00I2a) of at least 6 months in order to better evaluate your developmental delay.
   c. *When we will not defer a determination.* We will not defer our determination if we have sufficient evidence to determine that you are disabled under 112.14 or any other listing, or that you have an impairment or combination of impairments that functionally equals the listings. In addition, we will not defer our determination if the evidence demonstrates that you are not disabled.

J. How do we evaluate substance use disorders? If we find that you are disabled and there is medical evidence in your case record establishing that you have a substance use disorder, we will determine whether your substance use disorder is a contributing factor material to the determination of disability (see § 416.935 of this chapter).

K. How do we evaluate mental disorders that do not meet one of the mental disorders listings?

1. These listings include only examples of mental disorders that we consider serious enough to result in marked and severe functional limitations. If your severe mental disorder does not meet the criteria of any of these listings, we will consider whether you have an impairment(s) that meets the criteria of a listing in another body system. You may have another impairment(s) that is secondary to your mental disorder. For example, if you have an eating disorder and develop a cardiovascular impairment because of it, we will evaluate your cardiovascular impairment under the listings for the cardiovascular body system.
2. If you have a severe medically determinable impairment(s) that does not meet a listing, we will determine whether your impairment(s) medically equals a listing (see § 416.926 of this chapter).

3. If your impairment(s) does not meet or medically equal a listing, we will consider whether you have an impairment(s) that functionally equals the listings (see § 416.926a of this chapter).
4. Although we present these alternatives in a specific sequence above, each represents listing-level severity, and we can evaluate your claim in any order. For example, if the factors of your case indicate that the combination of your impairments may functionally equal the listings, we may start with that analysis. We use the rules in § 416.994a of this chapter, as appropriate, when we decide whether you continue to be disabled.

112.01 Category of Impairments, Mental Disorders

112.02 Neurocognitive disorders (see 112.00B1), for children age 3 to attainment of age 18, satisfied by A and B, or A and C:

A. Medical documentation of a clinically significant deviation in normal cognitive development or by significant cognitive decline from a prior level of functioning in *one* or more of the cognitive areas:

1. Complex attention;
2. Executive function;
3. Learning and memory;
4. Language;
5. Perceptual-motor; or
6. Social cognition.

AND

B. Extreme limitation of one, or marked limitation of two, of the following areas of mental functioning (see 112.00F):

1. Understand, remember, or apply information (see 112.00E1).
2. Interact with others (see 112.00E2).
3. Concentrate, persist, or maintain pace (see 112.00E3).
4. Adapt or manage oneself (see 112.00E4).

OR

C. Your mental disorder in this listing category is "serious and persistent;" that is, you have a medically documented history of the existence of the disorder over a period of at least 2 years, and there is evidence of both:

1. Medical treatment, mental health therapy, psychosocial support(s), or a highly structured setting(s) that is ongoing and that diminishes the symptoms and signs of your mental disorder (see 112.00G2b); *and*
2. Marginal adjustment, that is, you have minimal capacity to adapt to changes in your environment or to demands that are not already part of your daily life (see 112.00G2c).

112.03 Schizophrenia spectrum and other psychotic disorders (see 112.00B2), for children age 3 to attainment of age 18, satisfied by A and B, or A and C:

A. Medical documentation of *one* or more of the following:

1. Delusions or hallucinations;
2. Disorganized thinking (speech); or
3. Grossly disorganized behavior or catatonia.

AND

B. Extreme limitation of one, or marked limitation of two, of the following areas of mental functioning (see 112.00F):

1. Understand, remember, or apply information (see 112.00E1).
2. Interact with others (see 112.00E2).
3. Concentrate, persist, or maintain pace (see 112.00E3).
4. Adapt or manage oneself (see 112.00E4).

OR

C. Your mental disorder in this listing category is "serious and persistent"; that is, you have a medically documented history of the existence of the disorder over a period of at least 2 years, and there is evidence of both:

1. Medical treatment, mental health therapy, psychosocial support(s), or a highly structured setting(s) that is ongoing and that diminishes the symptoms and signs of your mental disorder (see 112.00G2b); *and*
2. Marginal adjustment, that is, you have minimal capacity to adapt to changes in your environment or to demands that are not already part of your daily life (see 112.00G2c).

112.04 Depressive, bipolar and related disorders (see 112.00B3), for children age 3 to attainment of age 18, satisfied by A and B, or A and C:

A. Medical documentation of the requirements of paragraph 1, 2, or 3:

1. Depressive disorder, characterized by *five* or more of the following:
    a. Depressed or irritable mood;
    b. Diminished interest in almost all activities;
    c. Appetite disturbance with change in weight (or a failure to achieve an expected weight gain);
    d. Sleep disturbance;
    e. Observable psychomotor agitation or retardation;
    f. Decreased energy;

  g. Feelings of guilt or worthlessness;
  h. Difficulty concentrating or thinking; or
  i. Thoughts of death or suicide.
2. Bipolar disorder, characterized by *three* or more of the following:
  a. Pressured speech;
  b. Flight of ideas;
  c. Inflated self-esteem;
  d. Decreased need for sleep;
  e. Distractibility;
  f. Involvement in activities that have a high probability of painful consequences that are not recognized; or
  g. Increase in goal-directed activity or psychomotor agitation.
3. Disruptive mood dysregulation disorder, beginning prior to age 10, and *all* of the following:
  a. Persistent, significant irritability or anger;
  b. Frequent, developmentally inconsistent temper outbursts; and
  c. Frequent aggressive or destructive behavior.

AND

B. Extreme limitation of one, or marked limitation of two, of the following areas of mental functioning (see 112.00F):

1. Understand, remember, or apply information (see 112.00E1).
2. Interact with others (see 112.00E2).
3. Concentrate, persist, or maintain pace (see 112.00E3).
4. Adapt or manage oneself (see 112.00E4).

OR

C. Your mental disorder in this listing category is "serious and persistent"; that is, you have a medically documented history of the existence of the disorder over a period of at least 2 years, and there is evidence of both:

1. Medical treatment, mental health therapy, psychosocial support(s), or a highly structured setting(s) that is ongoing and that diminishes the symptoms and signs of your mental disorder (see 112.00G2b); *and*
2. Marginal adjustment, that is, you have minimal capacity to adapt to changes in your environment or to demands that are not already part of your daily life (see 112.00G2c).

112.05 Intellectual disorder (see 112.00B4), for children age 3 to attainment of age 18, satisfied by A or B:

A. Satisfied by 1 and 2 (see 112.00H):

1. Significantly subaverage general intellectual functioning evident in your cognitive inability to function at a level required to participate in standardized testing of intellectual functioning; and
2. Significant deficits in adaptive functioning currently manifested by your dependence upon others for personal needs (for example, toileting, eating, dressing, or bathing) in excess of age-appropriate dependence.

OR

B. Satisfied by 1 and 2 (see 112.00H):

1. Significantly subaverage general intellectual functioning evidenced by a or b:
    a. A full scale (or comparable) IQ score of 70 or below on an individually administered standardized test of general intelligence; or
    b. A full scale (or comparable) IQ score of 71-75 accompanied by a verbal or performance IQ score (or comparable part score) of 70 or below on an individually administered standardized test of general intelligence; and
2. Significant deficits in adaptive functioning currently manifested by extreme limitation of one, or marked limitation of two, of the following areas of mental functioning:
    a. Understand, remember, or apply information (see 112.00E1); or
    b. Interact with others (see 112.00E2); or
    c. Concentrate, persist, or maintain pace (see 112.00E3); or
    d. Adapt or manage oneself (see 112.00E4).

112.06 Anxiety and obsessive-compulsive disorders (see 112.00B5), for children age 3 to attainment of age 18, satisfied by A and B, or A and C:

A. Medical documentation of the requirements of paragraph 1, 2, 3, or 4:

1. Anxiety disorder, characterized by *one* or more of the following:
    a. Restlessness;
    b. Easily fatigued;
    c. Difficulty concentrating;
    d. Irritability;
    e. Muscle tension; or
    f. Sleep disturbance.

2. Panic disorder or agoraphobia, characterized by *one* or both:
    a. Panic attacks followed by a persistent concern or worry about additional panic attacks or their consequences; or
    b. Disproportionate fear or anxiety about at least two different situations (for example, using public transportation, being in a crowd, being in a line, being outside of your home, being in open spaces).
3. Obsessive-compulsive disorder, characterized by *one* or both:
    a. Involuntary, time-consuming preoccupation with intrusive, unwanted thoughts; or;
    b. Repetitive behaviors that appear aimed at reducing anxiety.
4. Excessive fear or anxiety concerning separation from those to whom you are attached.

AND

B. Extreme limitation of one, or marked limitation of two, of the following areas of mental functioning (see 112.00F):

1. Understand, remember, or apply information (see 112.00E1).
2. Interact with others (see 112.00E2).
3. Concentrate, persist, or maintain pace (see 112.00E3).
4. Adapt or manage oneself (see 112.00E4).

OR

C. Your mental disorder in this listing category is "serious and persistent"; that is, you have a medically documented history of the existence of the disorder over a period of at least 2 years, and there is evidence of both:

1. Medical treatment, mental health therapy, psychosocial support(s), or a highly structured setting(s) that is ongoing and that diminishes the symptoms and signs of your mental disorder (see 112.00G2b); *and*
2. Marginal adjustment, that is, you have minimal capacity to adapt to changes in your environment or to demands that are not already part of your daily life (see 112.00G2c).

112.07 Somatic symptom and related disorders (see 112.00B6), for children age 3 to attainment of age 18, satisfied by A and B:

A. Medical documentation of *one* or both of the following:

1. Symptoms of altered voluntary motor or sensory function that are not better explained by another medical or mental disorder; or
2. One or more somatic symptoms that are distressing, with excessive thoughts, feelings, or behaviors related to the symptoms.

AND

B. Extreme limitation of one, or marked limitation of two, of the following areas of mental functioning (see 112.00F):

1. Understand, remember, or apply information (see 112.00E1).
2. Interact with others (see 112.00E2).
3. Concentrate, persist, or maintain pace (see 112.00E3).
4. Adapt or manage oneself (see 112.00E4).

112.08 Personality and impulse-control disorders (see 112.00B7), for children age 3 to attainment of age 18, satisfied by A and B:

A. Medical documentation of a pervasive pattern of *one* or more of the following:

1. Distrust and suspiciousness of others;
2. Detachment from social relationships;
3. Disregard for and violation of the rights of others;
4. Instability of interpersonal relationships;
5. Excessive emotionality and attention seeking;
6. Feelings of inadequacy;
7. Excessive need to be taken care of;
8. Preoccupation with perfectionism and orderliness; or
9. Recurrent, impulsive, aggressive behavioral outbursts.

AND

B. Extreme limitation of one, or marked limitation of two, of the following areas of mental functioning (see 112.00F):

1. Understand, remember, or apply information (see 112.00E1).
2. Interact with others (see 112.00E2).
3. Concentrate, persist, or maintain pace (see 112.00E3).
4. Adapt or manage oneself (see 112.00E4).

112.09 [Reserved]

112.10 Autism spectrum disorder (see 112.00B8), for children age 3 to attainment of age 18), satisfied by A and B:

A. Medical documentation of *both* of the following:

1. Qualitative deficits in verbal communication, nonverbal communication, and social interaction; and
2. Significantly restricted, repetitive patterns of behavior, interests, or activities.

AND

B. Extreme limitation of one, or marked limitation of two, of the following areas of mental functioning (see 112.00F):

1. Understand, remember, or apply information (see 112.00E1).
2. Interact with others (see 112.00E2).
3. Concentrate, persist, or maintain pace (see 112.00E3).
4. Adapt or manage oneself (see 112.00E4).

112.11 Neurodevelopmental disorders (see 112.00B9), for children age 3 to attainment of age 18, satisfied by A and B:

A. Medical documentation of the requirements of paragraph 1, 2, or 3:

1. *One* or both of the following:
    a. Frequent distractibility, difficulty sustaining attention, and difficulty organizing tasks; or
    b. Hyperactive and impulsive behavior (for example, difficulty remaining seated, talking excessively, difficulty waiting, appearing restless, or behaving as if being "driven by a motor").
2. Significant difficulties learning and using academic skills; or
3. Recurrent motor movement or vocalization.

AND

B. Extreme limitation of one, or marked limitation of two, of the following areas of mental functioning (see 112.00F):

1. Understand, remember, or apply information (see 112.00E1).
2. Interact with others (see 112.00E2).
3. Concentrate, persist, or maintain pace (see 112.00E3).
4. Adapt or manage oneself (see 112.00E4).

112.12 [Reserved]

112.13 Eating disorders (see 112.00B10), for children age 3 to attainment of age 18, satisfied by A and B:

A. Medical documentation of a persistent alteration in eating or eating-related behavior that results in a change in consumption or absorption of food and that significantly impairs physical or psychological health.

AND

B. Extreme limitation of one, or marked limitation of two, of the following areas of mental functioning (see 112.00F):

1. Understand, remember, or apply information (see 112.00E1).

2. Interact with others (see 112.00E2).
3. Concentrate, persist, or maintain pace (see 112.00E3).
4. Adapt or manage oneself (see 112.00E4).

112.14 Developmental disorders in infants and toddlers (see 112.00B11, 112.00I), satisfied by A and B:

A. Medical documentation of *one* or both of the following:

1. A delay or deficit in the development of age-appropriate skills; or
2. A loss of previously acquired skills.

AND

B. Extreme limitation of one, or marked limitation of two, of the following developmental abilities (see 112.00F):

1. Plan and control motor movement (see 112.00I4b(i)).
2. Learn and remember (see 112.00I4b(ii)).
3. Interact with others (see 112.00I4b(iii)).
4. Regulate physiological functions, attention, emotion, and behavior (see 112.00I4b(iv)).

112.15 Trauma- and stressor-related disorders (see 112.00B11), for children age 3 to attainment of age 18, satisfied by A and B, or A and C:

A. Medical documentation of the requirements of paragraph 1 or 2:

1. Posttraumatic stress disorder, characterized by *all* of the following:
    a. Exposure to actual or threatened death, serious injury, or violence;
    b. Subsequent involuntary re-experiencing of the traumatic event (for example, intrusive memories, dreams, or flashbacks);
    c. Avoidance of external reminders of the event;
    d. Disturbance in mood and behavior (for example, developmental regression, socially withdrawn behavior); and
    e. Increases in arousal and reactivity (for example, exaggerated startle response, sleep disturbance).
2. Reactive attachment disorder, characterized by *two* or all of the following:
    a. Rarely seeks comfort when distressed;
    b. Rarely responds to comfort when distressed; or
    c. Episodes of unexplained emotional distress.

AND

B. Extreme limitation of one, or marked limitation of two, of the following areas of mental functioning (see 112.00F):

1. Understand, remember, or apply information (see 112.00E1).
2. Interact with others (see 112.00E2).
3. Concentrate, persist, or maintain pace (see 112.00E3).
4. Adapt or manage oneself (see 112.00E4).

OR

C. Your mental disorder in this listing category is "serious and persistent;" that is, you have a medically documented history of the existence of the disorder over a period of at least 2 years, and there is evidence of both:

1. Medical treatment, mental health therapy, psychosocial support(s), or a highly structured setting(s) that is ongoing and that diminishes the symptoms and signs of your mental disorder (see 112.00G2b); *and*
2. Marginal adjustment, that is, you have minimal capacity to adapt to changes in your environment or to demands that are not already part of your daily life (see 112.00G2c).

113.00 Cancer

A. *What impairments do these listings cover?* We use these listings to evaluate all cancers (malignant neoplastic diseases) except certain cancers associated with human immunodeficiency virus (HIV) infection. We use the criteria in 114.11B to evaluate primary central nervous system lymphoma, 114.11C to evaluate primary effusion lymphoma, and 114.11E to evaluate pulmonary Kaposi sarcoma if you also have HIV infection. We evaluate all other cancers associated with HIV infection, for example, Hodgkin lymphoma or non-pulmonary Kaposi sarcoma, under this body system or under 114.11F–I in the immune system disorders body system.

B. *What do we consider when we evaluate cancer under these listings?* We consider factors including:

1. Origin of the cancer.

2. Extent of involvement.

3. Duration, frequency, and response to therapy.

4. Effects of any post-therapeutic residuals.

C. *How do we apply these listings?* We apply the criteria in a specific listing to a cancer originating from that specific site.

D. *What evidence do we need?*

1. We need medical evidence that specifies the type, extent, and site of the primary, recurrent, or metastatic lesion. In the rare situation in which the primary site cannot be identified, we will use evidence documenting the site(s) of metastasis to evaluate the impairment under 13.27 in part A.

2. For operative procedures, including a biopsy or a needle aspiration, we generally need a copy of both the:

a. Operative note, and

b. Pathology report.

3. When we cannot get these documents, we will accept the summary of hospitalization(s) or other medical reports. This evidence should include details of the findings at surgery and, whenever appropriate, the pathological findings.

4. In some situations we may also need evidence about recurrence, persistence, or progression of the cancer, the response to therapy, and any significant residuals. (See 113.00G.)

E. *When do we need longitudinal evidence?*

1. *Cancer with distant metastases.* Most cancer of childhood consist of a local lesion with metastases to regional lymph nodes and, less often, distant metastases. We generally do not need longitudinal evidence for cancer that has metastasized beyond the regional lymph nodes because this cancer usually meets the requirements of a listing. Exceptions are for cancer with distant metastases that we expect to respond to anticancer therapy. For these exceptions, we usually need a longitudinal record of 3 months after therapy starts to determine whether the therapy achieved its intended effect, and whether this effect is likely to persist.

2. *Other cancers.* When there are no distant metastases, many of the listings require that we consider your response to initial anticancer therapy; that is, the initial planned treatment regimen. This therapy may consist of a single modality or a combination of modalities; that is, multimodal therapy (see 113.00I3).

3. *Types of treatment.*

   a. Whenever the initial planned therapy is a single modality, enough time must pass to allow a determination about whether the therapy will achieve its intended effect. If the treatment fails, the failure will often happen within 6 months after treatment starts, and there will often be a change in the treatment regimen.

   b. Whenever the initial planned therapy is multimodal, we usually cannot make a determination about the effectiveness of the therapy until we can determine the effects of all the planned modalities. In some cases, we may need to defer adjudication until we can assess the effectiveness of therapy. However, we do not need to defer adjudication to determine whether the therapy will achieve its intended effect if we can make a fully favorable determination or decision based on the length and effects of therapy, or the residuals of the cancer or therapy (see 113.00G).

F. *How do we evaluate impairments that do not meet one of the cancer listings?*

1. These listings are only examples of cancer that we consider severe enough to result in marked and severe functional limitations. If your impairment(s) does not meet the criteria of any of these listings, we must also consider whether you have an impairment(s) that meets the criteria of a listing in another body system.

2. If you have a severe medically determinable impairment(s) that does not meet a listing, we will determine whether your impairment(s) medically equals a listing. (See §§404.1526 and 416.926 of this chapter.) If your impairment(s) does not meet or medically equal a listing, we will also consider whether you have an impairment(s) that functionally equals the listings. (See §416.926a of this chapter.) We use the rules in §§416.994a of this chapter when we decide whether you continue to be disabled.

G. *How do we consider the effects of anticancer therapy?*

1. *How we consider the effects of therapy under the listings.* In many cases, cancers meet listing criteria only if the therapy is not effective and the cancer persists, progresses, or recurs. However, as explained in the following paragraphs, we will not delay adjudication if we can make a fully favorable determination or decision based on the evidence in the case record.

2. *Effects can vary widely.*

a. We consider each case on an individual basis because the therapy and its toxicity may vary widely. We will request a specific description of the therapy, including these items:

i. Drugs given.

ii. Dosage.

iii. Frequency of drug administration.

iv. Plans for continued drug administration.

v. Extent of surgery.

vi. Schedule and fields of radiation therapy.

b. We will also request a description of the complications or adverse effects of therapy, such as the following:

i. Continuing gastrointestinal symptoms.

ii. Persistent weakness.

iii. Neurological complications.

iv. Cardiovascular complications.

v. Reactive mental disorders.

3. *Effects of therapy may change.* The severity of the adverse effects of anticancer therapy may change during treatment; therefore, enough time must pass to allow us to evaluate the therapy's effect. The residual effects of treatment are temporary in most instances; however, on occasion, the effects may be disabling for a consecutive period of at least 12 months. In some situations, very serious adverse effects may interrupt and prolong multimodal anticancer therapy for a continuous period of almost 12 months. In these situations, we may determine there is an expectation that your impairment will preclude you from engaging in any age-appropriate activities for at least 12 months.

4. *When the initial anticancer therapy is effective.* We evaluate any post-therapeutic residual impairment(s) not included in these listings under the criteria for the affected body system. We must consider any complications of therapy. When the residual impairment(s) does not meet a listing, we must consider whether it medically equals a listing, or, as appropriate, functionally equals the listings.

H. *How long do we consider your impairment to be disabling?*

1. In some listings, we specify that we will consider your impairment to be disabling until a particular point in time (for example, until at least 12 months from the date of transplantation). We may consider your impairment to be disabling beyond this point when the medical and other evidence justifies it.

2. When a listing does not contain such a specification, we will consider an impairment(s) that meets or medically equals a listing in this body system to be disabling until at least 3 years after onset of complete remission. When the impairment(s) has been in complete remission for at least 3 years, that is, the original tumor or a recurrence (or relapse) and any metastases have not been evident for at least 3 years, the impairment(s) will no longer meet or medically equal the criteria of a listing in this body system.

3. Following the appropriate period, we will consider any residuals, including residuals of the cancer or therapy (see 113.00G), in determining whether you are disabled. If you have a recurrence or relapse of your cancer, your impairment may meet or medically equal one of the listings in this body system again.

I. *What do we mean by the following terms?*

1. *Anticancer therapy* means surgery, radiation, chemotherapy, hormones, immunotherapy, or bone marrow or stem cell transplantation. When we refer to surgery as an anticancer treatment, we mean surgical excision for treatment, not for diagnostic purposes.

2. *Metastases* means the spread of cancer cells by blood, lymph, or other body fluid. This term does not include the spread of cancer cells by direct extension of the cancer to other tissues or organs.

3. *Multimodal therapy* means anticancer therapy that is a combination of at least two types of treatment given in close proximity as a unified whole and usually planned before any treatment has begun. There are three types of treatment modalities: surgery, radiation, and systemic drug therapy (chemotherapy, hormone therapy, and immunotherapy or biological modifier therapy). Examples of multimodal therapy include:

a. Surgery followed by chemotherapy or radiation.

b. Chemotherapy followed by surgery.

c. Chemotherapy and concurrent radiation.

4. *Persistent* means the planned initial anticancer therapy failed to achieve a complete remission of your cancer; that is, your cancer is evident, even if smaller, after the therapy has ended.

5. *Progressive* means the cancer becomes more extensive after treatment; that is, there is evidence that your cancer is growing after you have completed at least half of your planned initial anticancer therapy.

6. *Recurrent, relapse* means the cancer that was in complete remission or entirely removed by surgery has returned.

J. *Can we establish the existence of a disabling impairment prior to the date of the evidence that shows the cancer satisfies the criteria of a listing?* Yes. We will consider factors such as:

1. The type of cancer and its location.

2. The extent of involvement when the cancer was first demonstrated.

3. Your symptoms.

K. *How do we evaluate specific cancers?*

1. *Lymphoma.*

a. We provide criteria for evaluating aggressive lymphomas that are disseminated or have not responded to anticancer therapy in 113.05.

b. Lymphoblastic lymphoma is treated with leukemia-based protocols, so we will evaluate this type of cancer under 113.06.

2. *Leukemia.*

a. *Acute leukemia.* The initial diagnosis of acute leukemia, including the accelerated or blast phase of chronic myelogenous (granulocytic) leukemia, is based upon definitive bone marrow examination. Additional diagnostic information is based on chromosomal analysis, cytochemical and surface marker studies on the abnormal cells, or other methods consistent with the prevailing state of medical knowledge and clinical practice. Recurrent disease must be documented by peripheral blood, bone marrow, or cerebrospinal fluid examination, or by testicular biopsy. The initial and follow-up pathology reports should be included.

b. *Chronic myelogenous leukemia (CML).* We need a diagnosis of CML based upon documented granulocytosis, including immature forms such as differentiated or undifferentiated myelocytes and myeloblasts, and a chromosomal analysis that demonstrates the Philadelphia chromosome. In the absence of a chromosomal analysis, or if the Philadelphia chromosome is not present, the diagnosis may be made by other methods consistent with the prevailing state of medical knowledge and clinical practice. The requirement of CML in the accelerated or blast phase is met in 113.06B if laboratory findings show the proportion of blast (immature) cells in the peripheral blood or bone marrow is 10 percent or greater.

c. *Juvenile chronic myelogenous leukemia (JCML).* JCML is a rare, Philadelphia-chromosome-negative childhood leukemia that is aggressive and clinically similar to acute myelogenous leukemia. We evaluate JCML under 113.06A.

d. *Elevated white cell count.* In cases of chronic leukemia (either myelogenous or lymphocytic), an elevated white cell count, in itself, is not a factor in determining the severity of the impairment.

3. *Malignant solid tumors.* The tumors we consider under 113.03 include the histiocytosis syndromes except for solitary eosinophilic granuloma. We do not evaluate thyroid cancer (see 113.09), retinoblastomas (see 113.12), primary central nervous system (CNS) cancers (see 113.13), neuroblastomas (see 113.21), or malignant melanoma (see 113.29) under this listing.

4. *Primary central nervous system (CNS) cancers.* We use the criteria in 113.13 to evaluate cancers that originate within the CNS (that is, brain and spinal cord cancers).

a. The CNS cancers listed in 113.13A1 are highly malignant and respond poorly to treatment, and therefore we do not require additional criteria to evaluate them. We do not list pituitary gland cancer (for example, pituitary gland carcinoma) in 113.13A1, although this CNS cancer is highly malignant and responds poorly to treatment. We evaluate pituitary gland cancer under 113.13A1 and do not require additional criteria to evaluate it.

b. We consider a CNS tumor to be malignant if it is classified as Grade II, Grade III, or Grade IV under the World Health Organization (WHO) classification of tumors of the CNS (*WHO Classification of Tumours of the Central Nervous System, 2007*).

c. We evaluate benign (for example, WHO Grade I) CNS tumors under 111.05. We evaluate metastasized CNS cancers from non-CNS sites under the primary cancers (see 113.00C). We evaluate any complications of CNS cancers, such as resultant neurological or psychological impairments, under the criteria for the affected body system.

5. *Retinoblastoma*. The treatment for bilateral retinoblastoma usually results in a visual impairment. We will evaluate any resulting visual impairment under 102.02.

6. *Melanoma* We evaluate malignant melanoma that affects the skin (cutaneous melanoma), eye (ocular melanoma), or mucosal membranes (mucosal melanoma) under 113.29. We evaluate melanoma that is not malignant that affects the skin (benign melanocytic tumor) under the listings in 108.00 or other affected body systems.

L. *How do we evaluate cancer treated by bone marrow or stem cell transplantation, including transplantation using stem cells from umbilical cord blood?* Bone marrow or stem cell transplantation is performed for a variety of cancers. We require the transplantation to occur before we evaluate it under these listings. We do not need to restrict our determination of the onset of disability to the date of the transplantation (113.05 or 113.06). We may be able to establish an earlier onset date of disability due to your transplantation if the evidence in your case record supports such a finding.

1. *Acute leukemia (including all types of lymphoblastic lymphoma and JCML) or accelerated or blast phase of CML*. If you undergo bone marrow or stem cell transplantation for any of these disorders, we will consider you to be disabled until at least 24 months from the date of diagnosis or relapse, or at least 12 months from the date of transplantation, whichever is later.

2. *Lymphoma or chronic phase of CML*. If you undergo bone marrow or stem cell transplantation for any of these disorders, we will consider you to be disabled until at least 12 months from the date of transplantation.

3. *Evaluating disability after the appropriate time period has elapsed*. We consider any residual impairment(s), such as complications arising from:

a. Graft-versus-host (GVH) disease.

b. Immunosuppressant therapy, such as frequent infections.

c. Significant deterioration of other organ systems.

113.01 ***Category of Impairments, Cancer (Malignant Neoplastic Diseases)***

113.03 ***Malignant solid tumors*** Consider under a disability:

A. For 24 months from the date of initial diagnosis. Thereafter, evaluate any residual impairment(s) under the criteria for the affected body system.

OR

B. For 24 months from the date of recurrence of active disease. Thereafter, evaluate any residual impairment(s) under the criteria for the affected body system..

113.05 ***Lymphoma (excluding all types of lymphoblastic lymphoma— 113.06)*** (See 113.00K1)

A. Non-Hodgkin lymphoma (including Burkitt's and anaplastic large cell), with either 1 or 2:

1. Bone marrow, brain, spinal cord, liver, or lung involvement at initial diagnosis. Consider under a disability for 24 months from the date of diagnosis. Thereafter, evaluate under 113.05A2, or any residual impairment(s) under the criteria for the affected body system.

2. Persistent or recurrent following initial anticancer therapy.

OR

B. Hodgkin lymphoma, with either 1 or 2:

1. Bone marrow, brain, spinal cord, liver, or lung involvement at initial diagnosis. Consider under a disability for 24 months from the date of diagnosis. Thereafter, evaluate under 113.05B2, or any residual impairment(s) under the criteria for the affected body system.

2. Persistent or recurrent following initial anticancer therapy.

OR

C. With bone marrow or stem cell transplantation. Consider under a disability until at least 12 months from the date of transplantation. Thereafter, evaluate any residual impairment(s) under the criteria of the affected body system.

OR

D. Mantle cell lymphoma.

113.06 ***Leukemia*** (See 113.00K2)

A. Acute leukemia (including all types of lymphoblastic lymphoma and juvenile chronic myelogenous leukemia (JCML). Consider under a disability until at least 24 months from the date of diagnosis or relapse, or at least 12 months from the date of bone marrow or stem cell transplantation, whichever is later. Thereafter, evaluate any residual impairment(s) under the criteria for the affected body system.

OR

B. Chronic myelogenous leukemia (except JCML), as described in 1 or 2:

1. Accelerated or blast phase (see 113.00K2b). Consider under a disability until at least 24 months from the date of diagnosis or relapse, or at least 12 months from the date of bone marrow or stem cell transplantation, whichever is later. Thereafter, evaluate any residual impairment(s) under the criteria for the affected body system.

2. Chronic phase, as described in a or b:

a. Consider under a disability until at least 12 months from the date of bone marrow or stem cell transplantation. Thereafter, evaluate any residual impairment(s) under the criteria for the affected body system.

b. Progressive disease following initial anticancer therapy.

113.09 ***Thyroid gland***

A. Anaplastic (undifferentiated) carcinoma.

OR

B. Carcinoma with metastases beyond the regional lymph nodes progressive despite radioactive iodine therapy.

OR

C. Medullary carcinoma with metastases beyond the regional lymph nodes.

113.12 ***Retinoblastoma***

A. With extension beyond the orbit.

OR

B. Persistent or recurrent following initial anticancer therapy.

OR

C. With regional or distant metastases.

113.13 ***Nervous system*** (See 113.00K4.) Primary central nervous system (CNS; that is, brain and spinal cord) cancers, as described in A, B, or C:

A. Glioblastoma multiforme, ependymoblastoma, and diffuse intrinsic brain stem gliomas (see 113.00K4a).

B. Any Grade III or Grade IV CNS cancer (see 113.00K4b), including astrocytomas, sarcomas, and medulloblastoma and other primitive neuroectodermal tumors (PNETs).

C. Any primary CNS cancer, as described in 1 or 2:

1. Metastatic.

2. Progressive or recurrent following initial anticancer therapy.

113.21 ***Neuroblastoma***

A. With extension across the midline.

OR

B. With distant metastases.

OR

C. Recurrent.

OR

D. With onset at age 1 year or older.

113.29 ***Malignant melanoma*** (including skin, ocular, or mucosal melanomas), as described in either A, B, or C:

A. Recurrent (except an additional primary melanoma at a different site, which is not considered to be recurrent disease) following either 1 or 2:

1. Wide excision (skin melanoma).

2. Enucleation of the eye (ocular melanoma).

OR

B. With metastases as described in 1, 2, or 3:

1. Metastases to one or more clinically apparent nodes; that is, nodes that are detected by imaging studies (excluding lymphoscintigraphy) or by clinical evaluation (palpable).

2. If the nodes are not clinically apparent, with metastases to four or more nodes.

3. Metastases to adjacent skin (satellite lesions) or distant sites (for example, liver, lung, or brain).

OR

C. Mucosal melanoma.

114.00 Immune System Disorders

A. *What disorders do we evaluate under the immune system disorders listings?*

1. *We evaluate immune system disorders that cause dysfunction in one or more components of your immune system.*

a. The dysfunction may be due to problems in antibody production, impaired cell-mediated immunity, a combined type of antibody/cellular deficiency, impaired phagocytosis, or complement deficiency.

b. Immune system disorders may result in recurrent and unusual infections, or inflammation and dysfunction of the body's own tissues. Immune system disorders can cause a deficit in a single organ or body system that results in extreme (that is, very serious) loss of function. They can also cause lesser degrees of limitations in two or more organs or body systems, and when associated with symptoms or signs, such as severe fatigue, fever, malaise, diffuse musculoskeletal pain, or involuntary weight loss, can also result in extreme limitation. In children, immune system disorders or their treatment may also affect growth, development, and the performance of age-appropriate activities.

c. We organize the discussions of immune system disorders in three categories: Autoimmune disorders; Immune deficiency disorders, excluding human immunodeficiency virus (HIV) infection; and HIV infection.

2. *Autoimmune disorders (114.00D).* Autoimmune disorders are caused by dysfunctional immune responses directed against the body's own tissues, resulting in chronic, multisystem impairments that differ in clinical manifestations, course, and outcome. They are sometimes referred to as rheumatic diseases, connective tissue disorders, or collagen vascular disorders. Some of the features of autoimmune disorders in children differ from the features of the same disorders in adults. The impact of the disorders or their treatment on physical, psychological, and developmental growth of pre-pubertal children may be considerable, and often differs from that of post-pubertal adolescents or adults.

3. *Immune deficiency disorders, excluding HIV infection (114.00E).* Immune deficiency disorders are characterized by recurrent or unusual infections that respond poorly to treatment, and are often associated with complications affecting other parts of the body. Immune deficiency disorders are classified as either *primary* (congenital) or *acquired.* Children with immune deficiency disorders also have an increased risk of malignancies and of having autoimmune disorders.

4. *Human immunodeficiency virus (HIV) infection (114.00F).* HIV infection may be characterized by increased susceptibility to common infections as well as opportunistic infections, cancers, or other conditions listed in 114.11.

B. *What information do we need to show that you have an immune system disorder?* Generally, we need your medical history, a report(s) of a physical examination, a report(s) of laboratory findings, and in some instances, appropriate medically acceptable imaging or tissue biopsy reports to show that you have an immune system disorder. Therefore, we will make every reasonable effort to obtain your medical history, medical findings, and results of laboratory tests. We explain the information we need in more detail in the sections below.

C. *Definitions*

1. *Appropriate medically acceptable imaging* includes, but is not limited to, angiography, x-ray imaging, computerized axial tomography (CAT scan) or magnetic resonance imaging (MRI), with or without contrast material, myelography, and radionuclear bone scans. "Appropriate" means that the technique used is the proper one to support the evaluation and diagnosis of the impairment.

2. *Constitutional symptoms or signs*, as used in these listings, means severe fatigue, fever, malaise, or involuntary weight loss. *Severe fatigue* means a frequent sense of exhaustion that results in significantly reduced physical activity or mental function. *Malaise* means frequent feelings of illness, bodily discomfort, or lack of well-being that result in significantly reduced physical activity or mental function.

3. *Disseminated* means that a condition is spread over a considerable area. The type and extent of the spread will depend on your specific disease.

4. *Dysfunction* means that one or more of the body regulatory mechanisms are impaired, causing either an excess or deficiency of immunocompetent cells or their products.

5. *Extra-articular* means "other than the joints"; for example, an organ(s) such as the heart, lungs, kidneys, or skin.

6. *Inability to ambulate effectively* has the same meaning as in 101.00B2b.

7. *Inability to perform fine and gross movements effectively* has the same meaning as in 101.00B2c.

8. *Major peripheral joints* has the same meaning as in 101.00F.

9. *Persistent* means that a sign(s) or symptom(s) has continued over time. The precise meaning will depend on the specific immune system disorder, the usual course of the disorder, and the other circumstances of your clinical course.

10. *Recurrent* means that a condition that previously responded adequately to an appropriate course of treatment returns after a period of remission or regression. The precise meaning, such as the extent of response or remission and the time periods involved, will depend on the specific disease or condition you have, the body system affected, the usual course of the disorder and its treatment, and the other facts of your particular case.

11. *Resistant to treatment* means that a condition did not respond adequately to an appropriate course of treatment. Whether a response is adequate or a course of treatment is appropriate will depend on the specific disease or condition you have, the body system affected, the usual course of the disorder and its treatment, and the other facts of your particular case.

12. *Severe* means medical severity as used by the medical community. The term does not have the same meaning as it does when we use it in connection with a finding at the second step of the sequential evaluation process in § 416.924.

D. *How do we document and evaluate the listed autoimmune disorders?*

1. *Systemic lupus erythematosus (114.02).*

a. *General.* Systemic lupus erythematosus (SLE) is a chronic inflammatory disease that can affect any organ or body system. It is frequently, but not always, accompanied by constitutional symptoms or signs (severe fatigue, fever, malaise, involuntary weight loss). Major organ or body system involvement can include: Respiratory (pleuritis, pneumonitis), cardiovascular (endocarditis, myocarditis, pericarditis, vasculitis), renal (glomerulonephritis), hematologic (anemia, leukopenia, thrombocytopenia), skin (photosensitivity), neurologic (seizures), mental (anxiety, fluctuating cognition ("lupus fog"), mood disorders, organic brain syndrome, psychosis), or immune system disorders (inflammatory arthritis). Immunologically, there is an array of circulating serum auto-antibodies and pro- and anti-coagulant proteins that may occur in a highly variable pattern.

b. *Documentation of SLE.* Generally, but not always, the medical evidence will show that your SLE satisfies the criteria in the current "Criteria for the Classification of Systemic Lupus Erythematosus" by the American College of Rheumatology found in the most recent edition of the *Primer on the Rheumatic Diseases* published by the Arthritis Foundation.

2. *Systemic vasculitis (114.03).*

a. *General.*

(i) Vasculitis is an inflammation of blood vessels. It may occur acutely in association with adverse drug reactions, certain chronic infections, and occasionally, malignancies. More often, it is chronic and the cause is unknown. Symptoms vary depending on which blood vessels are involved. Systemic vasculitis may also be associated with other autoimmune disorders; for example, SLE or dermatomyositis.

(ii) Children can develop the vasculitis of Kawasaki disease, of which the most serious manifestation is formation of coronary artery aneurysms and related complications. We evaluate heart problems related to Kawasaki disease under the criteria in the cardiovascular listings (104.00). Children can also develop the vasculitis of anaphylactoid purpura (Henoch-Schoenlein purpura), which may cause intestinal and renal disorders. We evaluate intestinal and renal disorders related to vasculitis of anaphylactoid purpura under the criteria in the digestive (105.00) or genitourinary (106.00) listings. Other clinical patterns include, but are not limited to, polyarteritis nodosa, Takayasu's arteritis (aortic arch arteritis), and Wegener's granulomatosis.

b. *Documentation of systemic vasculitis.* Angiography or tissue biopsy confirms a diagnosis of systemic vasculitis when the disease is suspected clinically. When you have had angiography or tissue biopsy for systemic vasculitis, we will make every reasonable effort to obtain reports of the results of that procedure. However, we will not purchase angiography or tissue biopsy.

3. *Systemic sclerosis (scleroderma) (114.04).*

a. *General.* Systemic sclerosis (scleroderma) constitutes a spectrum of disease in which thickening of the skin is the clinical hallmark. Raynaud's phenomenon, often medically severe and progressive, is present frequently and may be the peripheral manifestation of a vasospastic abnormality in the heart, lungs, and kidneys. The CREST syndrome (calcinosis, Raynaud's phenomenon, esophageal dysmotility, sclerodactyly, and telangiectasia) is a variant that may slowly progress over years to the generalized process, systemic sclerosis.

b. *Diffuse cutaneous systemic sclerosis.* In diffuse cutaneous systemic sclerosis (also known as diffuse scleroderma), major organ or systemic involvement can include the gastrointestinal tract, lungs, heart, kidneys, and muscle in addition to skin or blood vessels. Although arthritis can occur, joint dysfunction results primarily from soft tissue/cutaneous thickening, fibrosis, and contractures.

c. *Localized scleroderma (linear scleroderma and morphea).*

(i) Localized scleroderma (linear scleroderma and morphea) is more common in children than systemic scleroderma. To assess the severity of the impairment, we need a description of the extent of involvement of linear scleroderma and the location of the lesions. For example, linear scleroderma involving the arm but not crossing any joints is not as functionally limiting as sclerodactyly (scleroderma localized to the fingers). Linear scleroderma of a lower extremity involving skin thickening and atrophy of underlying muscle or bone can result in contractures and leg length discrepancy. In such cases, we may evaluate your impairment under the musculoskeletal listings (101.00).

(ii) When there is isolated morphea of the face causing facial disfigurement from unilateral hypoplasia of the mandible, maxilla, zygoma, or orbit, adjudication may be more appropriate under the criteria in the affected body system, such as special senses and speech (102.00) or mental disorders (112.00).

(iii) Chronic variants of these syndromes include disseminated morphea, Shulman's disease (diffuse fasciitis with eosinophilia), and eosinophilia-myalgia syndrome (often associated with toxins such as toxic oil or contaminated tryptophan), all of which can impose medically severe musculoskeletal dysfunction and may also lead to restrictive pulmonary disease. We evaluate these variants of the disease under the criteria in the musculoskeletal listings (101.00) or respiratory system listings (103.00).

d. *Documentation of systemic sclerosis (scleroderma).* Documentation involves differentiating the clinical features of systemic sclerosis (scleroderma) from other autoimmune disorders. However, there may be an overlap.

4. *Polymyositis and dermatomyositis (114.05).*

a. *General.*

(i) Polymyositis and dermatomyositis are related disorders that are characterized by an inflammatory process in striated muscle, occurring alone or in association with other autoimmune disorders. The most common manifestations are symmetric weakness, and less frequently, pain and tenderness of the proximal limb-girdle (shoulder or pelvic) musculature. There may also be involvement of the cervical, cricopharyngeal, esophageal, intercostal, and diaphragmatic muscles.

(ii) Polymyositis occurs rarely in children; the more common presentation in children is dermatomyositis with symmetric proximal muscle weakness and characteristic skin findings. The clinical course of dermatomyositis can be more severe when it is accompanied by systemic vasculitis rather than just localized to striated muscle. Late in the disease, some children with dermatomyositis develop calcinosis of the skin and subcutaneous tissues, muscles, and joints. We evaluate the involvement of other organs/body systems under the criteria for the listings in the affected body system.

b. *Documentation of polymyositis and dermatomyositis.* Generally, but not always, polymyositis is associated with elevated serum muscle enzymes (creatine phosphokinase (CPK), aminotransferases, and aldolase), and characteristic abnormalities on electromyography and muscle biopsy. In children, the diagnosis of dermatomyositis is supported largely by medical history, findings on physical examination that include the characteristic skin findings, and elevated serum muscle enzymes. Muscle inflammation or vasculitis depicted on MRI is additional evidence supporting the diagnosis of childhood dermatomyositis. When you have had electromyography, muscle biopsy, or MRI for polymyositis or dermatomyositis, we will make every reasonable effort to obtain reports of the results of that procedure. However, we will not purchase electromyography, muscle biopsy, or MRI.

c. *Additional information about how we evaluate polymyositis and dermatomyositis under the listings.*

(i) In newborn and younger infants (birth to attainment of age 1), we consider muscle weakness that affects motor skills, such as head control, reaching, grasping, taking solids, or self-feeding, under 114.05A. In older infants and toddlers (age 1 to attainment of age 3), we also consider muscle weakness affecting your ability to roll over, sit, crawl, or walk under 114.05A.

(ii) If you are of preschool age through adolescence (age 3 to attainment of age 18), weakness of your pelvic girdle muscles that results in your inability to rise independently from a squatting or sitting position or to climb stairs may be an indication that you are unable to ambulate effectively. Weakness of your shoulder girdle muscles may result in your inability to perform lifting, carrying, and reaching overhead, and also may seriously affect your ability to perform activities requiring fine movements. We evaluate these limitations under 114.05A.

5. *Undifferentiated and mixed connective tissue disease (114.06).*

a. *General.* This listing includes syndromes with clinical and immunologic features of several autoimmune disorders, but which do not satisfy the criteria for any of the specific disorders described. For example, you may have clinical features of SLE and systemic vasculitis, and the serologic (blood test) findings of rheumatoid arthritis. The most common pattern of undifferentiated autoimmune disorders in children is mixed connective tissue disease (MCTD).

b. *Documentation of undifferentiated and mixed connective tissue disease.* Undifferentiated connective tissue disease is diagnosed when clinical features and serologic (blood test) findings, such as rheumatoid factor or antinuclear antibody (consistent with an autoimmune disorder) are present but do not satisfy the criteria for a specific disease. Children with MCTD have laboratory findings of extremely high antibody titers to extractable nuclear antigen (ENA) or ribonucleoprotein (RNP) without high titers of anti-dsDNA or anti-SM antibodies. There are often clinical findings suggestive of SLE or childhood dermatomyositis. Many children later develop features of scleroderma.

6. *Inflammatory arthritis (114.09).*

a. *General.* The spectrum of inflammatory arthritis includes a vast array of disorders that differ in cause, course, and outcome. Clinically, inflammation of major peripheral joints may be the dominant manifestation causing difficulties with ambulation or fine and gross movements; there may be joint pain, swelling, and tenderness. The arthritis may affect other joints, or cause less limitation in ambulation or the performance of fine and gross movements. However, in combination with extra-articular features, including constitutional symptoms or signs (severe fatigue, fever, malaise, involuntary weight loss), inflammatory arthritis may result in an extreme limitation. You may also have impaired growth as a result of the inflammatory arthritis because of its effects on the immature skeleton, open epiphyses, and young cartilage and bone. We evaluate any associated growth impairment under the criteria in 100.00.

b. *Inflammatory arthritis involving the axial spine (spondyloarthropathy).* In children, inflammatory arthritis involving the axial spine may be associated with disorders such as:

(i) Reactive arthropathies;

(ii) Juvenile ankylosing spondylitis;

(iii) Psoriatic arthritis;

(iv) SEA syndrome (seronegative enthesopathy arthropathy syndrome);

(v) Behçet's disease; and

(vi) Inflammatory bowel disease.

c. *Inflammatory arthritis involving the peripheral joints.* In children, inflammatory arthritis involving peripheral joints may be associated with disorders such as:

(i) Juvenile rheumatoid arthritis;

(ii) Sjögren's syndrome;

(iii) Psoriatic arthritis;

(iv) Crystal deposition disorders (gout and pseudogout);

(v) Lyme disease; and

(vi) Inflammatory bowel disease.

d. *Documentation of inflammatory arthritis.* Generally, but not always, the diagnosis of inflammatory arthritis is based on the clinical features and serologic findings described in the most recent edition of the *Primer on the Rheumatic Diseases* published by the Arthritis Foundation.

e. *How we evaluate inflammatory arthritis under the listings.*

(i) Listing-level severity in 114.09A and 114.09C1 is shown by an impairment that results in an "extreme" (very serious) limitation. In 114.09A, the criterion is satisfied with persistent inflammation or deformity in one major peripheral weight-bearing joint resulting in the inability to ambulate effectively (as defined in 114.00C6) or one major peripheral joint in each upper extremity resulting in the inability to perform fine and gross movements effectively (as defined in 114.00C7). In 114.09C1, if you have the required ankylosis (fixation) of your cervical or dorsolumbar spine, we will find that you have an extreme limitation in your ability to see in front of you, above you, and to the side. Therefore, inability to ambulate effectively is implicit in 114.09C1, even though you might not require bilateral upper limb assistance.

(ii) Listing-level severity is shown in 114.09B, 114.09C2, and 114.09D by inflammatory arthritis that involves various combinations of complications of one or more major peripheral joints or involves other joints, such as inflammation or deformity, extra-articular features, repeated manifestations, and constitutional symptoms and signs. Extra-articular impairments may also meet listings in other body systems.

(iii) Extra-articular features of inflammatory arthritis may involve any body system; for example: Musculoskeletal (heel enthesopathy), ophthalmologic (iridocyclitis, keratoconjunctivitis sicca, uveitis), pulmonary (pleuritis, pulmonary fibrosis or nodules, restrictive lung disease), cardiovascular (aortic valve insufficiency, arrhythmias, coronary arteritis, myocarditis, pericarditis, Raynaud's phenomenon, systemic vasculitis), renal (amyloidosis of the kidney), hematologic (chronic anemia, thrombocytopenia), neurologic (peripheral neuropathy, radiculopathy, spinal cord or cauda equina compression with sensory and motor loss), mental (cognitive dysfunction, poor memory), and immune system (Felty's syndrome (hypersplenism with compromised immune competence)).

(iv) If both inflammation and chronic deformities are present, we evaluate your impairment under the criteria of any appropriate listing.

7. *Sjögren's syndrome (114.10).*

a. *General.*

(i) Sjögren's syndrome is an immune-mediated disorder of the exocrine glands. Involvement of the lacrimal and salivary glands is the hallmark feature, resulting in symptoms of dry eyes and dry mouth, and possible complications, such as corneal damage, blepharitis (eyelid inflammation), dysphagia (difficulty in swallowing), dental caries, and the inability to speak for extended periods of time. Involvement of the exocrine glands of the upper airways may result in persistent dry cough.

(ii) Many other organ systems may be involved, including musculoskeletal (arthritis, myositis), respiratory (interstitial fibrosis), gastrointestinal (dysmotility, dysphagia, involuntary weight loss), genitourinary (interstitial cystitis, renal tubular acidosis), skin (purpura, vasculitis,), neurologic (central nervous system disorders, cranial and peripheral neuropathies), mental (cognitive dysfunction, poor memory), and neoplastic (lymphoma). Severe fatigue and malaise are frequently reported. Sjögren's syndrome may be associated with other autoimmune disorders (for example, rheumatoid arthritis or SLE); usually the clinical features of the associated disorder predominate.

b. *Documentation of Sjögren's syndrome.* If you have Sjögren's syndrome, the medical evidence will generally, but not always, show that your disease satisfies the criteria in the current "Criteria for the Classification of Sjögren's Syndrome" by the American College of Rheumatology found in the most recent edition of the *Primer on the Rheumatic Diseases* published by the Arthritis Foundation.

E. *How do we document and evaluate immune deficiency disorders, excluding HIV infection?*

1. *General.*

a. Immune deficiency disorders can be classified as:

(i) *Primary* (congenital); for example, X-linked agammaglobulinemia, thymic hypoplasia (DiGeorge syndrome), severe combined immunodeficiency (SCID), chronic granulomatous disease (CGD), C1 esterase inhibitor deficiency.

(ii) *Acquired;* for example, medication-related.

b. Primary immune deficiency disorders are seen mainly in children. However, recent advances in the treatment of these disorders have allowed many affected children to survive well into adulthood. Occasionally, these disorders are first diagnosed in adolescence or adulthood.

2. *Documentation of immune deficiency disorders.* The medical evidence must include documentation of the specific type of immune deficiency. Documentation may be by laboratory evidence or by other generally acceptable methods consistent with the prevailing state of medical knowledge and clinical practice.

3. *Immune deficiency disorders treated by stem cell transplantation.*

a. *Evaluation in the first 12 months.* If you undergo stem cell transplantation for your immune deficiency disorder, we will consider you disabled until at least 12 months from the date of the transplant.

b. *Evaluation after the 12-month period has elapsed.* After the 12-month period has elapsed, we will consider any residuals of your immune deficiency disorder as well as any residual impairment(s) resulting from the treatment, such as complications arising from:

(i) Graft-versus-host (GVH) disease.

(ii) Immunosuppressant therapy, such as frequent infections.

(iii) Significant deterioration of other organ systems.

4. *Medication-induced immune suppression.* Medication effects can result in varying degrees of immune suppression, but most resolve when the medication is ceased. However, if you are prescribed medication for long-term immune suppression, such as after an organ transplant, we will evaluate:

a. The frequency and severity of infections.

b. Residuals from the organ transplant itself, after the 12-month period has elapsed.

c. Significant deterioration of other organ systems.

F. *How do we document and evaluate HIV infection?* Any child with HIV infection, including one with a diagnosis of acquired immune deficiency syndrome (AIDS), may be found disabled under 114.11 if his or her impairment meets the criteria in that listing or is medically equivalent to the criteria in that listing.

1. *Documentation of HIV infection.*

a. *Definitive documentation of HIV infection.* We may document a diagnosis of HIV infection by positive findings on one or more of the following definitive laboratory tests:

(i) HIV antibody screening test (for example, enzyme immunoassay, or EIA), confirmed by a supplemental HIV antibody test such as the Western blot (immunoblot) or immunofluorescence assay, for any child age 18 months or older.

(ii) HIV nucleic acid (DNA or RNA) detection test (for example, polymerase chain reaction, or PCR).

(iii) HIV p24 antigen (p24Ag) test, for any child age 1 month or older.

(iv) Isolation of HIV in viral culture.

(v) Other tests that are highly specific for detection of HIV and that are consistent with the prevailing state of medical knowledge.

b. We will make every reasonable effort to obtain the results of your laboratory testing. Pursuant to § 416.919f, we will purchase examinations or tests necessary to make a determination in your claim if no other acceptable documentation exists.

c. *Other acceptable documentation of HIV infection.* We may also document HIV infection without definitive laboratory evidence.

(i) We will accept a persuasive report from a physician that a positive diagnosis of your HIV infection was confirmed by an appropriate laboratory test(s), such as those described in 114.00F1a. To be persuasive, this report must state that you had the appropriate definitive laboratory test(s) for diagnosing your HIV infection and provide the results. The report must also be consistent with the remaining evidence of record.

(ii) We may also document HIV infection by the medical history, clinical and laboratory findings, and diagnosis(es) indicated in the medical evidence, provided that such documentation is consistent with the prevailing state of medical knowledge and clinical practice and is consistent with the other evidence in your case record. For example, we will accept a diagnosis of HIV infection without definitive laboratory evidence of the HIV infection if you have an opportunistic disease that is predictive of a defect in cell-mediated immunity (for example, toxoplasmosis of the brain or Pneumocystis pneumonia (PCP)), and there is no other known cause of diminished resistance to that disease (for example, long-term steroid treatment or lymphoma). In such cases, we will make every reasonable effort to obtain full details of the history, medical findings, and results of testing.

2. *Documentation of the manifestations of HIV infection.*

a. *Definitive documentation of manifestations of HIV infection.* We may document manifestations of HIV infection by positive findings on definitive laboratory tests, such as culture, microscopic examination of biopsied tissue or other material (for example, bronchial washings), serologic tests, or on other generally acceptable definitive tests consistent with the prevailing state of medical knowledge and clinical practice.

b. We will make every reasonable effort to obtain the results of your laboratory testing. Pursuant to § 416.919f, we will purchase examinations or tests necessary to make a determination of your claim if no other acceptable documentation exists.

c. *Other acceptable documentation of manifestations of HIV infection.* We may also document manifestations of HIV infection without definitive laboratory evidence.

(i) We will accept a persuasive report from a physician that a positive diagnosis of your manifestation of HIV infection was confirmed by an appropriate laboratory test(s). To be persuasive, this report must state that you had the appropriate definitive laboratory test(s) for diagnosing your manifestation of HIV infection and provide the results. The report must also be consistent with the remaining evidence of record.

(ii) We may also document manifestations of HIV infection without the definitive laboratory evidence described in 114.00F2a, provided that such documentation is consistent with the prevailing state of medical knowledge and clinical practice and is consistent with the other evidence in your case record. For example, many conditions are now commonly diagnosed based on some or all of the following: Medical history, clinical manifestations, laboratory findings (including appropriate medically acceptable imaging), and treatment responses. In such cases, we will make every reasonable effort to obtain full details of the history, medical findings, and results of testing.

3. *Disorders associated with HIV infection (114.11A-E).*

a. *Multicentric Castleman disease* (MCD, 114.11A) affects multiple groups of lymph nodes and organs containing lymphoid tissue. This widespread involvement distinguishes MCD from *localized* (or unicentric) Castleman disease, which affects only a single set of lymph nodes. While not a cancer, MCD is known as a lymphoproliferative disorder. Its clinical presentation and progression is similar to that of lymphoma, and its treatment may include radiation or chemotherapy. We require characteristic findings on microscopic examination of the biopsied lymph nodes or other generally acceptable methods consistent with the prevailing state of medical knowledge and clinical practice to establish the diagnosis. Localized (or unicentric) Castleman disease does not meet or medically equal the criterion in 114.11A, but we may evaluate it under the criteria in 114.11G or 14.11I in part A.

b. *Primary central nervous system lymphoma* (PCNSL, 114.11B) originates in the brain, spinal cord, meninges, or eye. Imaging tests (for example, MRI) of the brain, while not diagnostic, may show a single lesion or multiple lesions in the white matter of the brain. We require characteristic findings on microscopic examination of the cerebral spinal fluid or of the biopsied brain tissue, or other generally acceptable methods consistent with the prevailing state of medical knowledge and clinical practice to establish the diagnosis.

c. *Primary effusion lymphoma* (PEL, 114.11C) is also known as body cavity lymphoma. We require characteristic findings on microscopic examination of the effusion fluid or of the biopsied tissue from the affected internal organ, or other generally acceptable methods consistent with the prevailing state of medical knowledge and clinical practice to establish the diagnosis.

d. *Progressive multifocal leukoencephalopathy* (PML, 114.11D) is a progressive neurological degenerative syndrome caused by the John Cunningham (JC) virus in immunosuppressed children. Clinical findings of PML include clumsiness, progressive weakness, and visual and speech changes. Personality and cognitive changes may also occur. We require appropriate clinical findings, characteristic white matter lesions on MRI, and a positive PCR test for the JC virus in the cerebrospinal fluid to establish the diagnosis. We also accept a positive brain biopsy for JC virus or other generally acceptable methods consistent with the prevailing state of medical knowledge and clinical practice to establish the diagnosis.

e. *Pulmonary Kaposi sarcoma* (Kaposi sarcoma in the lung, 114.11E) is the most serious form of Kaposi sarcoma (KS). Other internal KS tumors (for example, tumors of the gastrointestinal tract) have a more variable prognosis. We require characteristic findings on microscopic examination of the induced sputum, bronchoalveolar lavage washings, or of the biopsied transbronchial tissue, or other generally acceptable methods consistent with the prevailing state of medical knowledge and clinical practice to establish the diagnosis.

4. *CD4 measurement (114.11F).* To evaluate your HIV infection under 114.11F, we require one measurement of your absolute CD4 count (also known as CD4 count or CD4+ T-helper lymphocyte count) or CD4 percentage for children from birth to attainment of age 5, or one measurement of your absolute CD4 count for children from age 5 to attainment of age 18. These measurements (absolute CD4 count or CD4 percentage) must occur within the period we are considering in connection with your application or continuing disability review. If you have more than one CD4 measurement within this period, we will use your lowest absolute CD4 count or your lowest CD4 percentage.

5. *Complications of HIV infection requiring hospitalization (114.11G).*

a. Complications of HIV infection may include infections (common or opportunistic), cancers, and other conditions. Examples of complications that may result in hospitalization include: Depression; diarrhea; immune reconstitution inflammatory syndrome; malnutrition; and PCP and other severe infections.

b. Under 114.11G, we require three hospitalizations within a 12-month period that are at least 30 days apart and that result from a complication(s) of HIV infection. The hospitalizations may be for the same complication or different complications of HIV infection and are not limited to the examples of complications that may result in hospitalization listed in 114.00F5a. All three hospitalizations must occur within the period we are considering in connection with your application or continuing disability review. Each hospitalization must last at least 48 hours, including hours in a hospital emergency department immediately before the hospitalization.

c. We will use the rules on medical equivalence in § 416.926 to evaluate your HIV infection if you have fewer, but longer, hospitalizations, or more frequent, but shorter, hospitalizations, or if you receive nursing, rehabilitation, or other care in alternative settings.

6. *Neurological manifestations specific to children (114.11H).* The methods of identifying and evaluating neurological manifestations may vary depending on a

child's age. For example, in an infant, impaired brain growth can be documented by a decrease in the growth rate of the head. In an older child, impaired brain growth may be documented by brain atrophy on a CT scan or MRI. Neurological manifestations may present in the loss of acquired developmental milestones (developmental regression) in infants and young children or, in the loss of acquired intellectual abilities in school-age children and adolescents. A child may demonstrate loss of intellectual abilities by a decrease in IQ scores, by forgetting information previously learned, by inability to learn new information, or by a sudden onset of a new learning disability. When infants and young children present with serious developmental delays (without regression), we evaluate the child's impairment(s) under 112.00.

7. *Growth failure due to HIV immune suppression (114.11I).*

a. To evaluate growth failure due to HIV immune suppression, we require documentation of the laboratory values described in 114.11I1and the growth measurements in 114.11I2 or 114.11I3 within the same consecutive 12-month period. The dates of laboratory findings may be different from the dates of growth measurements.

b. Under 114.11I2 and 114.11I3, we use the appropriate table under 105.08B in the digestive system to determine whether a child's growth is less than the third percentile.

(i) For children from birth to attainment of age 2, we use the weight-for-length table corresponding to the child's gender (Table I or Table II).

(ii) For children from age 2 to attainment of age 18, we use the body mass index (BMI)-for-age corresponding to the child's gender (Table III or Table IV).

(iii) BMI is the ratio of a child's weight to the square of his or her height. We calculate BMI using the formulas in 105.00G2c.

G. *How do we consider the effects of treatment in evaluating your autoimmune disorder, immune deficiency disorder, or HIV infection?*

1. *General.* If your impairment does not otherwise meet the requirements of a listing, we will consider your medical treatment in terms of its effectiveness in improving the signs, symptoms, and laboratory abnormalities of your specific immune system disorder or its manifestations, and in terms of any side effects that limit your functioning. We will make every reasonable effort to obtain a specific description of the treatment you receive (including surgery) for your immune system disorder. We consider:

a. The effects of medications you take.

b. Adverse side effects (acute and chronic).

c. The intrusiveness and complexity of your treatment (for example, the dosing schedule, need for injections).

d. The effect of treatment on your mental functioning (for example, cognitive changes, mood disturbance).

e. Variability of your response to treatment (see 114.00G2).

f. The interactive and cumulative effects of your treatments. For example, many children with immune system disorders receive treatment both for their immune system disorders and for the manifestations of the disorders or co-occurring impairments, such as treatment for HIV infection and hepatitis C. The interactive and cumulative effects of these treatments may be greater than the effects of each treatment considered separately.

g. The duration of your treatment.

h. Any other aspects of treatment that may interfere with your ability to function.

2. *Variability of your response to treatment.* Your response to treatment and the adverse or beneficial consequences of your treatment may vary widely. The effects of your treatment may be temporary or long term. For example, some children may show an initial positive response to a drug or combination of drugs followed by a decrease in effectiveness. When we evaluate your response to treatment and how your treatment may affect you, we consider such factors as disease activity before treatment, requirements for changes in therapeutic regimens, the time required for therapeutic effectiveness of a particular drug or drugs, the limited number of drug combinations that may be available for your impairment(s), and the time-limited efficacy of some drugs. For example, a child with HIV infection or another immune deficiency disorder who develops otitis media may not respond to the same antibiotic regimen used in treating children without HIV infection or another immune deficiency disorder, or may not respond to an antibiotic that he or she responded to before. Therefore, we must consider the effects of your treatment on an individual basis, including the effects of your treatment on your ability to function.

3. *How we evaluate the effects of treatment for autoimmune disorders on your ability to function.* Some medications may have acute or long-term side effects. When we consider the effects of corticosteroids or other treatments for autoimmune disorders on your ability to function, we consider the factors in 114.00G1 and 114.00G2. Long-term corticosteroid treatment can cause ischemic necrosis of bone, posterior subcapsular cataract, impaired growth, weight gain, glucose intolerance, increased susceptibility to infection, and osteopenia that may result in a loss of function. In addition, medications used in the treatment of autoimmune disorders may also have effects on mental functioning, including cognition (for example, memory), concentration, and mood.

4. *How we evaluate the effects of treatment for immune deficiency disorders, excluding HIV infection, on your ability to function.* When we consider the effects of your treatment for your immune deficiency disorder on your ability to function, we

consider the factors in 114.00G1 and 114.00G2. A frequent need for treatment such as intravenous immunoglobulin and gamma interferon therapy can be intrusive and interfere with your ability to function. We will also consider whether you have chronic side effects from these or other medications, including severe fatigue, fever, headaches, high blood pressure, joint swelling, muscle aches, nausea, shortness of breath, or limitations in mental function including cognition (for example, memory) concentration, and mood.

5. *How we evaluate the effects of treatment for HIV infection on your ability to function.*

a. *General.* When we consider the effects of antiretroviral drugs (including the effects of highly active antiretroviral therapy (HAART)) and the effects of treatments for the manifestations of HIV infection on your ability to function, we consider the factors in 114.00G1 and 114.00G2. Side effects of antiretroviral drugs include, but are not limited to: Bone marrow suppression, pancreatitis, gastrointestinal intolerance (nausea, vomiting, diarrhea), neuropathy, rash, hepatotoxicity, lipodystrophy (fat redistribution, such as "buffalo hump"), glucose intolerance, and lactic acidosis. In addition, medications used in the treatment of HIV infection may also have effects on mental functioning, including cognition (for example, memory), concentration, and mood, and may result in malaise, severe fatigue, joint and muscle pain, and insomnia. The symptoms of HIV infection and the side effects of medication may be indistinguishable from each other. We will consider all of your functional limitations, whether they result from your symptoms or signs of HIV infection or the side effects of your treatment.

b. *Structured treatment interruptions.* A structured treatment interruption (STI, also called a "drug holiday") is a treatment practice during which your treating source advises you to stop taking your medications temporarily. An STI in itself does not imply that your medical condition has improved; nor does it imply that you are noncompliant with your treatment because you are following your treating source's advice. Therefore, if you have stopped taking medication because your treating source prescribed or recommended an STI, we will not find that you are failing to follow treatment or draw inferences about the severity of your impairment on this fact alone. We will consider why your treating source has prescribed or recommended an STI and all the other information in your case record when we determine the severity of your impairment.

6. *When there is no record of ongoing treatment.* If you have not received ongoing treatment or have not had an ongoing relationship with the medical community despite the existence of a severe impairment(s), we will evaluate the medical severity and duration of your immune system disorder on the basis of the current objective medical evidence and other evidence in your case record, taking into consideration your medical history, symptoms, clinical and laboratory findings, and medical source opinions. If you have just begun treatment and we cannot determine whether you are disabled based on the evidence we have, we may

need to wait to determine the effect of the treatment on your ability to develop and function in an age-appropriate manner. The amount of time we need to wait will depend on the facts of your case. If you have not received treatment, you may not be able to show an impairment that meets the criteria of one of the immune system disorders listings, but your immune system disorder may medically equal a listing or functionally equal the listings.

H. *How do we consider your symptoms, including your pain, severe fatigue, and malaise?* Your symptoms, including pain, severe fatigue, and malaise, may be important factors in our determination whether your immune system disorder(s) meets or medically equals a listing or in our determination whether you otherwise have marked and severe functional limitations. In order for us to consider your symptoms, you must have medical signs or laboratory findings showing the existence of a medically determinable impairment(s) that could reasonably be expected to produce the symptoms. If you have such an impairment(s), we will evaluate the intensity, persistence, and functional effects of your symptoms using the rules throughout 114.00 and in our other regulations. See §§ 416.921 and 416.929. Additionally, when we assess the credibility of your complaints about your symptoms and their functional effects, we will not draw any inferences from the fact that you do not receive treatment or that you are not following treatment without considering all of the relevant evidence in your case record, including any explanations you provide that may explain why you are not receiving or following treatment.

I. *How do we consider the impact of your immune system disorder on your functioning?*

1. We will consider all relevant information in your case record to determine the full impact of your immune system disorder, including HIV infection, on your ability to function. Functional limitation may result from the impact of the disease process itself on your mental functioning, physical functioning, or both your mental and physical functioning. This could result from persistent or intermittent symptoms, such as depression, diarrhea, severe fatigue, or pain, resulting in a limitation of your ability to acquire information, to concentrate, to persevere at a task, to interact with others, to move about, or to cope with stress. You may also have limitations because of your treatment and its side effects (see 114.00G).

2. Important factors we will consider when we evaluate your functioning include, but are not limited to: Your symptoms (see 114.00H), the frequency and duration of manifestations of your immune system disorder, periods of exacerbation and remission, and the functional impact of your treatment, including the side effects of your medication (see 114.00G). See §§ 416.924a and 416.926a for additional guidance on the factors we consider when we evaluate your functioning.

3. We will use the rules in §§ 416.924a and 416.926a to evaluate your functional limitations and determine whether your impairment functionally equals the listings.

J. *How do we evaluate your immune system disorder when it does not meet one of the listings?*

1. These listings are only examples of immune system disorders that we consider severe enough to result in marked and severe functional limitations. If your impairment(s) does not meet the criteria of any of these listings, we must also consider whether you have an impairment(s) that satisfies the criteria of a listing in another body system.

2. Individuals with immune system disorders, including HIV infection, may manifest signs or symptoms of a mental impairment or of another physical impairment. For example, HIV infection may accelerate the onset of conditions such as diabetes or affect the course of or treatment options for diseases such as cardiovascular disease or hepatitis. We may evaluate these impairments under the affected body system. For example, we will evaluate:

a. Growth impairment under 100.00.

b. Musculoskeletal involvement, such as surgical reconstruction of a joint, under 101.00.

c. Ocular involvement, such as dry eye, under 102.00.

d. Respiratory impairments, such as pleuritis, under 103.00.

e. Cardiovascular impairments, such as cardiomyopathy, under 104.00.

f. Digestive impairments, such as hepatitis (including hepatitis C) or weight loss as a result of HIV infection that affects the digestive system, under 105.00.

g. Genitourinary impairments, such as nephropathy, under 106.00.

h. Hematologic abnormalities, such as anemia, granulocytopenia, and thrombocytopenia, under 107.00.

i. Skin impairments, such as persistent fungal and other infectious skin eruptions, and photosensitivity, under 108.00.

j. Neurologic impairments, such as neuropathy or seizures, under 111.00.

k. Mental disorders, such as depression, anxiety, or cognitive deficits, under 112.00.

l. Allergic disorders, such as asthma or atopic dermatitis, under 103.00or 108.00 or under the criteria in another affected body system.

m. Syphilis or neurosyphilis under the criteria for the affected body system, for example, 102.00 Special senses and speech, 104.00Cardiovascular system, or 111.00 Neurological.

3. If you have a severe medically determinable impairment(s) that does not meet a listing, we will determine whether your impairment(s) medically equals a listing. (See § 416.926.) If it does not, we will also consider whether you have an

impairment(s) that functionally equals the listings. (See § 416.926a.) We use the rules in § 416.994a when we decide whether you continue to be disabled.

114.01 ***Category of Impairments, Immune System Disorders***

114.02 Systemic lupus erythematosus, as described in 114.00D1. With involvement of two or more organs/body systems, and with:

A. One of the organs/body systems involved to at least a moderate level of severity;

AND

B. At least two of the constitutional symptoms and signs (severe fatigue, fever, malaise, or involuntary weight loss).

114.03 Systemic vasculitis, as described in 114.00D2. With involvement of two or more organs/body systems, and with:

A. One of the organs/body systems involved to at least a moderate level of severity;

AND

B. At least two of the constitutional symptoms and signs (severe fatigue, fever, malaise, or involuntary weight loss).

114.04 Systemic sclerosis (scleroderma). As described in 114.00D3. With:

A. Involvement of two or more organs/body systems, with:

1. One of the organs/body systems involved to at least a moderate level of severity; and

2. At least two of the constitutional symptoms and signs (severe fatigue, fever, malaise, or involuntary weight loss).

OR

B. With one of the following:

1. Toe contractures or fixed deformity of one or both feet, resulting in the inability to ambulate effectively as defined in 114.00C6; or

2. Finger contractures or fixed deformity in both hands, resulting in the inability to perform fine and gross movements effectively as defined in 114.00C7; or

3. Atrophy with irreversible damage in one or both lower extremities, resulting in the inability to ambulate effectively as defined in 114.00C6; or

4. Atrophy with irreversible damage in both upper extremities, resulting in the inability to perform fine and gross movements effectively as defined in 114.00C7.

OR

C. Raynaud's phenomenon, characterized by:

1. Gangrene involving at least two extremities; or

2. Ischemia with ulcerations of toes or fingers, resulting in the inability to ambulate effectively or to perform fine and gross movements effectively as defined in 114.00C6 and 114.00C7.

114.05 Polymyositis and dermatomyositis. As described in 114.00D4. With:

A. Proximal limb-girdle (pelvic or shoulder) muscle weakness, resulting in inability to ambulate effectively or inability to perform fine and gross movements effectively as defined in 114.00C6 and 114.00C7.

OR

B. Impaired swallowing (dysphagia) with aspiration due to muscle weakness.

OR

C. Impaired respiration due to intercostal and diaphragmatic muscle weakness.

OR

D. Diffuse calcinosis with limitation of joint mobility or intestinal motility.

114.06 Undifferentiated and mixed connective tissue disease, as described in 114.00D5. With involvement of two or more organs/body systems, and with:

A. One of the organs/body systems involved to at least a moderate level of severity;

AND

B. At least two of the constitutional symptoms and signs (severe fatigue, fever, malaise, or involuntary weight loss).

114.07 Immune deficiency disorders, excluding HIV infection. As described in 114.00E. With:

A. One or more of the following infections. The infection(s) must either be resistant to treatment or require hospitalization or intravenous treatment three or more times in a 12-month period.

1. Sepsis; or

2. Meningitis; or

3. Pneumonia; or

4. Septic arthritis; or

5. Endocarditis; or

6. Sinusitis documented by appropriate medically acceptable imaging.

OR

B. Stem cell transplantation as described under 114.00E3. Consider under a disability until at least 12 months from the date of transplantation. Thereafter, evaluate any residual impairment(s) under the criteria for the affected body system.

114.08 [Reserved]

114.09 Inflammatory arthritis. As described in 114.00D6. With:

A. Persistent inflammation or persistent deformity of:

1. One or more major peripheral weight-bearing joints resulting in the inability to ambulate effectively (as defined in 114.00C6); or

2. One or more major peripheral joints in each upper extremity resulting in the inability to perform fine or gross movements effectively (as defined in 114.00C7).

OR

B. Inflammation or deformity in one or more major peripheral joints with:

1. Involvement of two or more organs/body systems with one of the organs/body systems involved to at least a moderate level of severity; and

2. At least two of the constitutional symptoms or signs (severe fatigue, fever, malaise, or involuntary weight loss).

OR

C. Ankylosing spondylitis or other spondyloarthropathies, with:

1. Ankylosis (fixation) of the dorsolumbar or cervical spine as shown by appropriate medically acceptable imaging and measured on physical examination at 45° or more of flexion from the vertical position (zero degrees); or

2. Ankylosis (fixation) of the dorsolumbar or cervical spine as shown by appropriate medically acceptable imaging and measured on physical examination at 30° or more of flexion (but less than 45°) measured from the vertical position (zero degrees), and involvement of two or more organs/body systems with one of the organs/body systems involved to at least a moderate level of severity.

114.10 Sjögren's syndrome, as described in 114.00D7. With involvement of two or more organs/body systems, and with:

A. One of the organs/body systems involved to at least a moderate level of severity;

AND

B. At least two of the constitutional symptoms and signs (severe fatigue, fever, malaise, or involuntary weight loss).

114.11 ***Human immunodeficiency virus (HIV) infection.*** With documentation as described in 114.00F1 and one of the following:

A. Multicentric (not localized or unicentric) Castleman disease affecting multiple groups of lymph nodes or organs containing lymphoid tissue (see 114.00F3a).

OR

B. Primary central nervous system lymphoma (see 114.00F3b).

OR

C. Primary effusion lymphoma (see 114.00F3c).

OR

D. Progressive multifocal leukoencephalopathy (see 114.00F3d).

OR

E. Pulmonary Kaposi sarcoma (see 114.00F3e).

OR

F. Absolute CD4 count or CD4 percentage (see 114.00F4):

1. For children from birth to attainment of age 1, absolute CD4 count of 500 cells/mm3 or less, or CD4 percentage of less than 15 percent; or

2. For children from age 1 to attainment of age 5, absolute CD4 count of 200 cells/mm3 or less, or CD4 percentage of less than 15 percent; or

3. For children from age 5 to attainment of age 18, absolute CD4 count of 50 cells/mm3 or less.

OR

G. Complication(s) of HIV infection requiring at least three hospitalizations within a 12-month period and at least 30 days apart (see 114.00F5). Each hospitalization must last at least 48 hours, including hours in a hospital emergency department immediately before the hospitalization.

OR

H. A neurological manifestation of HIV infection (for example, HIV encephalopathy or peripheral neuropathy) (see 114.00F6) resulting in one of the following:

1. Loss of previously acquired developmental milestones or intellectual ability (including the sudden onset of a new learning disability), documented on two examinations at least 60 days apart; or

2. Progressive motor dysfunction affecting gait and station or fine and gross motor skills, documented on two examinations at least 60 days apart; or

3. Microcephaly with head circumference that is less than the third percentile for age, documented on two examinations at least 60 days apart; or

4. Brain atrophy, documented by appropriate medically acceptable imaging.

OR

I. Immune suppression and growth failure (see 114.00F7) documented by 1 and 2, or by 1 and 3:

1. CD4 measurement:

a. For children from birth to attainment of age 5, CD4 percentage of less than 20 percent; or

b. For children from age 5 to attainment of age 18, absolute CD4 count of less than 200 cells/mm3 or CD4 percentage of less than 14 percent; and

2. For children from birth to attainment of age 2, three weight-for-length measurements that are:

a. Within a consecutive 12-month period; and

b. At least 60 days apart; and

c. Less than the third percentile on the appropriate weight-for-length table under 105.08B1; or

3. For children from age 2 to attainment of age 18, three BMI-for-age measurements that are:

a. Within a consecutive 12-month period; and

b. At least 60 days apart; and

c. Less than the third percentile on the appropriate BMI-for-age table under 105.08B2.

APPENDIX C

Functional Limitations Due to Physical Impairment Questionnaire (Adult)

Functional Limitations Due to Physical Impairment Questionnaire

Your patient has applied for disability benefits through Social Security. The Social Security Administration values the opinion of the treating clinician in the disability determination process. Please complete this questionnaire to assist the Administration's understanding of your patient's medical condition, symptoms, and their effect on functioning. Please provide opinions consistent with your patient's presentation, history, clinical findings, your professional experience, and treatment records. Thank you for your assistance and consideration.

Please print your responses clearly.

Re: (Name of Patient) ____________________ (Date of Birth)____/____/______

Name of Clinician: ____

Specialty: ____

Please answer the following questions concerning your patient's impairments and resultant limitations.

1. a. Date of first treatment. ____________________
   b. Date of most recent exam. ____________________
   c. Frequency of treatment. ____________________
2. What is your patient's diagnosis? ____________________
3. Prognosis: ____________________

4. Identify the positive clinical findings that demonstrate and/or support your diagnosis and indicate location where applicable.

____

____

5. Please list your patient's primary symptoms, including pain, loss of sensation, fatigue, malaise, etc.

____

____

6. Are your patient's symptoms and functional limitations reasonably consistent with the patient's physical and/or emotional impairments described in this evaluation?

   Yes _______ No _______

   If no, please explain _______________

7. If your patient has pain, please estimate the level of pain using an analog scale of 0 to 10, with 0 representing little or no pain and 10 representing the worst imaginable pain.

____

8. If your patient experiences fatigue, using the same analog scale, please estimate the fatigue experienced by your patient.

____

9. Does your patient's experience of pain, fatigue, and/or other symptoms interfere with activities of daily living? _______
10. Does your patient's experience of pain, fatigue, and/or other symptoms interfere with social functioning? _______
11. Does your patient's experience of pain, fatigue, and/or other symptoms limit his/her ability to complete tasks in a timely manner due to deficiencies in concentration, persistence, or pace? _______
12. As a result of my patient's physical impairments, he/she can perform the following activities rarely or never, occasionally (up to 1/3 of an eight-hour workday), frequently (up to 2/3 of an eight-hour workday), or constantly (2/3 or more of an eight-hour workday.

   a. Sit _______________
   b. Walk _______________
   c. Climb stairs/ramps _______________
   d. Push _______________
   e. Pull _______________
   f. Reach (not overhead) _______________
   g. Reach (overhead) _______________
   h. Lift up to 10 pounds _______________
   i. Lift up to 25 pounds _______________
   j. Lift up to 50 pounds _______________

k. Lift up to 100 pounds ____________

l. Lift more than 100 pounds ____________

m. Carry up to 10 pounds ____________

n. Carry up to 25 pounds ____________

o. Carry up to 50 pounds ____________

p. Carry up to 100 pounds ____________

q. Carry more than 100 pounds ____________

r. Grip or grasp with the right hand ____________

s. Grip or grasp with the left hand ____________

t. Handle with the right hand ____________

u. Handle with the left hand ____________

v. Finger with the right hand ____________

w. Finger with the left hand ____________

13. Please list medication(s) prescribed and dosage on the left column and any adverse side effects your patient has reported or you have observed on the right.

____________________ ____________

____________________ ____________

____________________ ____________

____________________ ____________

____________________ ____________

____________________ ____________

____________________ ____________

14. Have you substituted medications in an attempt to produce less symptomatology or relieve side effects? ____________________

15. List other treatment (e.g., hospitalizations, surgery, physical therapy) and complications, if any:____________________

____

____

16. Would your patient's symptoms likely increase if he/she were placed in a competitive work environment? __________

17. How often is your patient's experience of pain, fatigue, or other symptoms severe enough to interfere with attention and concentration? (rarely or never, occasionally (up to one-third of an eight-hour workday, frequently (up to two-thirds of an eight-hour workday) or constantly (more than two-thirds of an eight-hour workday) ____________________

18. Are your patient's impairments ongoing, creating an expectation on your part that they have lasted and/or will last at least 12 months?

    ____

19. Do emotional factors contribute to the severity of your patient's symptoms and functional limitations?

20. Is there any sign of malingering in your patient?

    ____

21. Is drug or alcohol use material to your patient's medical condition?

    ____

22. Do psychological or emotional factors play a role in your patient's medical condition? ______________________________

23. To what degree can your patient tolerate typical work stress?

    ____ Incapable of even "low stress"

    ____ Capable of low stress

    ____ Capable of moderate stress

    ____ Capable of high stress

24. If your patient were able to return to work, would your patient sometimes need to take unscheduled breaks to rest at unpredictable intervals during an eight-hour working day? (In California, full-time workers are entitled to two 10-minute rest breaks and one 30-minute meal break per eight-hour shift).

    ____

    If yes: a. How often do you think this will happen? __________

    b. How long (on average) will your patient need to rest before returning to work? ______________________________

25. Are your patient's impairments likely to produce "good days" and "bad days"?

    ____

26. Does your patient need to lie down and rest during an eight-hour period and if yes, how frequently and for what duration? __________

27. Does your patient require ready access to a restroom? ____ Yes ____ No. If yes, how frequently will your patient likely need to take restroom breaks (in addition to regularly scheduled breaks)? _____ Yes _____ No

28. Should your patient raise his/her leg(s) while sitting? If yes, to what height should the patient's legs be raised (eight inches to one foot above the floor, to hip level, or to chest level), and should they be raised occasionally (up to one-third of the eight-hour workday), frequently (up to two-thirds of the eight-hour workday) or constantly (more than two-thirds of the eight-hour workday)?

    ____

29. Please estimate, on the average, how often your patient is likely to be absent from work as a result of the impairments or treatment.

    ___ More than three times a month

    ___ About two to three times a month

    ___ About once a month

    ___ Less than once a month

30. Are there any other limitations that would affect your patient's ability to work at a regular job on a sustained basis (please check all that are applicable)?

    ___ psychological limitations

    ___ limited vision

    ___ limited hearing

    ___ need to avoid wetness

    ___ need to avoid temperature extremes

    ___ limited speech

    ___ need to avoid noise

    ___ need to avoid humidity

    ___ disbalance

    ___ need to avoid fumes

    ___ need to avoid dust

    ___ no bending

    ___ need to avoid gases

    ___ need to avoid heights

    ___ no stooping

    ___ learning differences

    ___ limited/no English fluency

    ___ illiteracy

    ___ other

Due to pain, fatigue, malaise, gastrointestinal symptoms, psychological symptoms, etc., will your patient likely be off task up to 10% of an eight-hour workday, off task up to 20% of an eight-hour workday, or off task more than 20% of an eight-hour workday on a consistent basis (two–three days per week)?

____

The Social Security Administration defines disability as a physical or mental impairment that is so severe that it prevents an individual from working at any full-time job (eight hours a day, 40 hours a week) in a competitive work environment without special modifications or accommodations. "Accommodations" refers to special consideration for the patient such as schedule flexibility, reduced hours, more frequent breaks, breaks of longer duration, reduced quotas, limited or no interaction with coworkers or the public, etc. In your professional opinion, does your patient meet these criteria? ____________________

Comments:____________________________________

____

____

____

____

____

____________________ Today's date

____________________ Signature of clinician

____________________ DEA or License #

____________________ Printed name of clinician

____________________ Supervisor (if required)

____________________ Supervisor's signature

Address of practice: ______________________________

____

____

Phone: ____________________ Fax: ________________

Email: ____________________

Please be sure to submit all treatment records, from date first seen to date last seen, to your patient's representative. Many thanks for your kind consideration in this matter.

APPENDIX D

Functional Limitations Due to Psychological Impairment Questionnaire (Adult)

Functional Limitations Due to Psychological Impairment (Adult)

Your patient has applied for disability benefits through Social Security. The Social Security Administration values the opinions of the treating clinician in the disability determination process. Please complete this questionnaire to assist the Administration's understanding of your patient's psychological condition, symptoms, and their effect on functioning. Please provide opinions that are consistent with your patient's presentation, history, clinical findings, your professional experience and your patient's treatment records. Your cooperation is essential to the positive outcome of your patient's claim. Thank you for your assistance and consideration.

Clinician's Name: ______________________ Specialty: ____________________

Patient: ______________________________ DOB: ______________________

Date you first saw patient professionally: ___________ Date of most recent visit: ________________

Diagnoses (per *DSM-5*): ____

____

____

____

GAF (or *DSM*-5 equivalent, WHODAS) at first session and currently ________

Prognosis: ____

____

If your patient experiences any concurrent medical condition(s) that result in pain, fatigue, or physical limitation(s) or affect cognitive, behavioral, psychological functioning, please explain: ____

____

____

____

____

Social Security defines disability as a physical or mental impairment that is so severe that it prevents an individual from performing any job on a full-time basis (eight hours a day, five days a week, with two 10-minute rest breaks and one 30-minute meal break per shift) in a competitive work setting without special modifications or accommodations. "Accommodations" refers to special consideration for the worker not available to every other worker at that workplace, such as schedule flexibility, reduced hours, additional rest breaks, breaks of longer duration, reduced quotas, limited or no interactions with coworkers or the public, continuous supervision, etc. In your professional opinion, does your patient meet these criteria? ____

Has your patient been hospitalized (including partial hospitalization) voluntarily or involuntarily for treatment of a psychological condition? ____________
If yes, when, where, and for how long?

____

____

____

Does your patient have a history of drug and/or alcohol abuse or dependence?

____

Is drug or alcohol abuse or dependence material to your patient's impairment(s)?

____

Is your patient a malingerer? ____

Can your patient tolerate typical stressors associated with work, such as meeting deadlines and quotas, accepting instruction and criticism from coworkers, interacting with coworkers and the public? ____

If my patient attempted to return to full-time competitive work, his/her symptoms would likely

___improve ___remain the same ___worsen

If my patient attempted to return to the full-time competitive workforce, his/her symptoms and their treatment would likely cause him/her to be absent

___one day per month ___two days per month ___three or more days per month

History and Symptom Checklist

___ Anhedonia
___ Depressed mood
___ Flight of ideas
___ Pressured speech
___ Distractibility
___ Disturbed or non-restorative sleep
___ Insomnia
___ Observable psychomotor agitation
___ Observable psychomotor retardation
___ Feelings of guilt
___ Feelings of worthlessness
___ Feelings of hopelessness
___ Poor memory for significant events or periods of time
___ Difficulty thinking
___ Difficulty concentrating
___ Problems with judgment
___ Problems with decision-making
___ Problems relating cause to effect
___ Social awkwardness
___ Easily fatigued
___ History of self-harm (self-injury, head-banging, scratching, cutting, food restriction, taking deliberate risks, etc.)
___ Generalized anxiety
___ Social anxiety
___ Panic attacks
___ History of suicide attempt
___ Suicidal ideation
___ Social isolation
___ History of failed or harmful interpersonal relationships
___ Chronic physical illness
___ Auditory, visual or perceptual hallucinations or distortions
___ Low energy
___ Intermittent disorientation to person, place and/or time
___ Distrust or suspiciousness of others
___ Change in appetite with weight loss
___ Change in appetite with weight gain
___ Irritability
___ Feelings of inadequacy
___ Obsessive and/or compulsive behaviors or thoughts
___ Psychosis or psychotic episodes
___ Obsessions or compulsions
___ History of recurrent, impulsive, aggressive behavioral outbursts

___ History of unstable interpersonal relationships

___ Phobias (claustrophobia, agoraphobia, etc.)

___ Paranoid ideas

___ Restlessness

___ Muscle tension

___ Blackouts or periods of time that cannot be accounted for

Prescribed Medications

Please list your patient's prescribed medications, dose and frequency, and any adverse effects (for example, unintended weight gain or weight loss, gastrointestinal distress, drowsiness, fatigue, etc.).

Medication	Dose	Frequency	Side effects, if any

Please provide your opinion on the effect of your patient's diagnoses, symptoms and treatment on the following. For purposes of this section, moderately impaired = off task 10% of the workday, severely impaired = off task 20% of the workday, extremely impaired = off task more than 20% of the workday.

	Moderately Impaired	Severely Impaired	Extremely Impaired
• Understand, remember, or apply information	______	______	______
• Interact with others	______	______	______
• Concentrate, persist, or maintain pace	______	______	______
• Adapt or manage oneself*	______	______	______

**This refers to the ability to regulate emotions, control behavior, and maintain well-being in a work setting.*

Work Limitations Related to Psychological Condition

Please check the boxes that correspond to your professional observations and experience, and your patient's history and treatment.

	Not Significantly Impaired (occasionally off task less than 10% of the workday)	Moderately Impaired (consistently off task 10% of the workday)	Markedly Impaired (consistently off task 20% of the workday)	Extremely Impaired (consistently off task more than 20% of the workday)
The ability to remember locations and work-like procedures				
The ability to understand and remember short and simple instructions				
The ability to understand and remember detailed instructions				
The ability to carry out very short and simple instructions				
The ability to carry out detailed instructions				
The ability to maintain attention and concentration for extended periods				
The ability to perform activities within a schedule, maintain regular attendance, and be punctual within customary tolerances				
The ability to sustain an ordinary routine without special supervision				

	Not Significantly Impaired (occasionally off task less than 10% of the workday)	Moderately Impaired (consistently off task 10% of the workday)	Markedly Impaired (consistently off task 20% of the workday)	Extremely Impaired (consistently off task more than 20% of the workday)
The ability to work in coordination with and proximity to others without being distracted by them				
The ability to make simple work-related decisions				
The ability to interact appropriately with the general public				
The ability to ask simple questions or request assistance				
The ability to accept instructions and respond appropriately to criticism from supervisors				
The ability to maintain socially appropriate behavior and to adhere to basic standards of neatness and cleanliness				
The ability to respond appropriately to changes in the work setting				
The ability to be aware of normal hazards and take appropriate precautions				
The ability to travel to unfamiliar places or use public transportation				

	Not Significantly Impaired (occasionally off task less than 10% of the workday)	Moderately Impaired (consistently off task 10% of the workday)	Markedly Impaired (consistently off task 20% of the workday)	Extremely Impaired (consistently off task more than 20% of the workday)
The ability to set realistic goals or make plans independently of others				

Comments: ______________________________

____

____

____

____

____

______________________ ______________________

Today's date Signature of clinician

______________________ ______________________

DEA or License # Printed name of clinician

____

Supervisor (if required)

____

Supervisor's signature

Address of practice: ______________________

____

____

Phone: ______________________ Fax: ______________________

Email: ______________________

Please be sure to submit all treatment records from date first seen to last seen to your patient's representative. Many thanks for your kind consideration in this matter.

APPENDIX E

Functional Limitations Due to Physical Impairment Questionnaire (Child)

Functional Limitations Due to Physical Impairment Questionnaire (Child)

Your patient has applied for disability benefits through Social Security. The Social Security Administration values the opinion of the treating clinician in the disability determination process. Please complete this questionnaire to assist the Administration's understanding of your patient's medical condition, symptoms, and their effect on functioning. Please provide opinions consistent with your patient's presentation, history, clinical findings, your professional experience, and treatment records. Thank you for your consideration.

Please print your responses clearly

From: ________________ (Name of Clinician) ______________ (Specialty)

Re: ________________ (Name of Patient) ______________ (Patient's DOB)

Parent/Guardian:

____

a. Date of first treatment. ______________________________

b. Date of most recent exam.______________________________

c. Frequency of treatment.______________________________

What are your patient's diagnoses? ____

____

____

____

When was your patient first diagnosed with each condition?

____

____

____

Prognoses:

____

____

____

Identify the positive **clinical findings** that demonstrate and/or support your diagnosis and indicate location where applicable.

____

____

____

Identify the **laboratory and diagnostic test results** that demonstrate and/or support your diagnosis.

____

____

____

Please list your patient's primary **symptoms**, including pain, loss of sensation, fatigue, gastrointestinal issues, etc.

____

____

____

Are your patient's symptoms and functional limitations **reasonably consistent** with the patient's physical and/or emotional impairments described in this evaluation?

________ Yes ________ No

If no, please explain.

____

____

____

Has your patient met all developmental milestones on schedule? __________

Has your patient learned age appropriate skills within the typical timeframe (toileting, shoe tying, self-dressing, etc.)? ____________________

Does your patient exhibit age-appropriate hand-eye coordination?

____

Is your patient attending school? ________ Grade? ________ Special education?

____

Does your patient perform at grade level? ____________________

Does your patient require assistive devices to ambulate? ____________________

Does your patient have significant limitations in performing repetitive reaching, handling, fingering or lifting? _____ Yes _____ No

Does your patient exhibit sensory deficits (hearing, seeing, speaking, tactile response)? ____________________

If yes, please explain.

____

Please describe the degree of limitation that your patient experiences using the upper extremities for gripping, grasping, handling, fingering, pushing, pulling and reaching.

____

____

On a scale of 0–10, with 10 being the most severe, what is your patient's estimated level of pain? ____________________

On a scale of 0–10, with 10 being most severe, what is your patient's estimated level of fatigue? ____________________

Does your patient have dietary restrictions? ____________________

Does your patient have environmental restrictions? ____________________

Please list medication(s) prescribed and dosage on the left column and any **adverse side effects** your patient has reported, or you have observed on the right.

____________________	____________________
____________________	____________________
____________________	____________________
____________________	____________________
____________________	____________________
____________________	____________________
____________________	____________________
____________________	____________________
____________________	____________________
____________________	____________________
____________________	____________________
____________________	____________________
____________________	____________________

Have you substituted medications in an attempt to produce less symptomatology or relieve side effects? _____ Yes _____ No

List other treatment (e.g., hospitalization [dates], surgery [dates], physical therapy) and complications, if any.

____

____

____

____

____

How often is your patient's experience of pain, fatigue or other symptoms severe enough to interfere with attention and concentration? (Please circle your response)

Never Seldom Periodically Frequently Constantly

Are your patient's impairments ongoing, creating an expectation on your part that they will last at least 12 months? _____ Yes _____ No

Do emotional factors contribute to the severity of your patient's symptoms and functional limitations? _____ Yes _____ No. If so, indicate what emotional factors affect your patient: ______________________________

____

____

To what degree can your patient tolerate stress associated with school or other scheduled and supervised activities?

___ Incapable of even "low stress" ___ Capable of moderate stress

___ Capable of low stress ___ Capable of high stress

What is the basis for your conclusions? ______________________________

Will your patient sometimes need to take unscheduled breaks to rest at unpredictable intervals during the day? _____ Yes _____ No.

If yes:

How **often** do you think this will happen? ______________________________

How **long** (on average) will your patient need to rest before returning to task

____

Are your patient's impairments likely to produce "good days" and "bad days"? _____ Yes _____ No

Does your patient require ready access to a restroom? _____ Yes _____ No.

If yes, how frequently will your patient likely need to take a restroom break?

____

Does your patient require assistance or supervision in the bathroom? _____ Yes _____ No

Please estimate, on the average, how often your patient is likely to be absent from school or other developmentally appropriate activity as a result of his/her impairments or treatment.

_______ More than three times a month _____ About two to three times a month

_______ About once a month _____ Less than once a month

Please estimate, on the average, how often your patient is likely to have to curtail his/her school or other developmentally appropriate activity by one hour or more by coming late or leaving early due to his/her condition or its treatment.

_____ More than three times a month _____ About two to three times a month

_____ About once a month _____ Less than once a month

Are there any other limitations that would affect your patient's ability to attend school or interact with others on a sustained basis (please check all that are applicable):

__ psychological limitations
__ limited vision
__ no pushing
__ need to avoid wetness
__ limited hearing
__ no pulling
__ need to avoid noise
__ need to avoid humidity
__ no kneeling
__ need to avoid fumes
__ need to avoid dust
__ no bending
__ need to avoid gases
__ need to avoid heights
__ no stooping
__ need to avoid repetitive handling
__ need to avoid temperature extremes
__ need to avoid repetitive fingering
__ other

____
____
____
____

The Social Security Administration considers a child between the ages of 0 and 18 disabled if he or she has a medically determinable physical or mental impairment (or combination of impairments); and the impairment(s) results in marked and severe functional limitations; and the impairment(s) has lasted (or is expected to last) for at least 12 months or is expected to result in death.

Does your patient's impairment conform to this definition? ________________

From what date has your patient been disabled according to the above definition? ____

Additional comments

____
____
____
____
____

______________ ________________________ ________________________

Date Signature Specialty

Print/Type Name

License #: _______ State: ______ DEA #: ______ Address and Phone Number:

____

____

____

Supervisor as necessary:

____________________	____________________	____________________
Date	Printed name	Signature

APPENDIX F

Functional Limitations Due to Psychological Impairment Questionnaire (Child)

Functional Limitations Due to Psychological Impairment (Child)

Your patient has applied for disability benefits through Social Security. The Social Security Administration values the opinions of the treating clinician in the disability determination process. Please complete this questionnaire to assist the Administration's understanding of your patient's psychological condition, symptoms, and their effect on functioning. Please provide opinions that are consistent with your patient's presentation, history, clinical findings, your professional experience, and your patient's treatment records. Your cooperation is essential to the positive outcome of your patient's claim. Thank you for your assistance and consideration.

Clinician's Name: ______________________ Specialty: ____________________

Patient: _______________________________ DOB: _______________________

Date you first saw patient professionally: _____ Date of most recent visit: _____

Diagnoses (per *DSM*-5): ____

____

____

____

GAF (or *DSM*-5 equivalent, WHODAS) at first session and currently

____

Prognosis: ____

____

If your patient experiences any concurrent medical condition(s) that result in pain, fatigue, or physical limitation(s) or affect cognitive, behavioral, psychological functioning, please explain: ____

____

____

____

____

Social Security defines disability as a physical or mental impairment that is so severe that it prevents an individual from any job on a full-time basis (eight hours a day, five days a week, with two 10-minute rest breaks and one 30-minute meal break per shift) in a competitive work setting without special modifications or accommodations. "Accommodations" refers to special consideration for the worker not available to every other worker at that workplace, such as schedule flexibility, reduced hours, additional rest breaks, breaks of longer duration, reduced quotas, limited or no interactions with coworkers or the public, continuous supervision, etc. In your professional opinion, does your patient meet these criteria? ____

Has your patient been hospitalized (including partial hospitalization) voluntarily or involuntarily for treatment of a psychological condition? __________ If yes, when, where, and for how long?

____

____

____

____

History and Symptom Checklist

___ Anhedonia

___ Depressed mood

___ Flight of ideas

___ Pressured speech

___ Distractibility

___ Disturbed or nonrestorative sleep

___ Insomnia

___ Observable psychomotor agitation

___ Observable psychomotor retardation

___ Feelings of guilt

___ Feelings of worthlessness
___ Feelings of hopelessness
___ Poor memory for significant events or periods of time
___ Difficulty thinking
___ Difficulty concentrating
___ Problems with judgment
___ Problems with decision-making
___ Problems relating cause to effect
___ Social awkwardness
___ Easily fatigued
___ Change in appetite with weight loss
___ Change in appetite with weight gain
___ Irritability
___ Feelings of inadequacy
___ Obsessive and/or compulsive behaviors or thoughts
___ Auditory, visual, or perceptual hallucinations or distortions
___ Low energy
___ Intermittent disorientation to person, place, and/or time
___ Distrust or suspiciousness of others
___ History of recurrent, impulsive, aggressive behavioral outbursts
___ History of unstable interpersonal relationships
___ Paranoid ideas
___ Restlessness
___ Muscle tension
___ Phobias (claustrophobia, agoraphobia, etc.)
___ Psychosis or psychotic episodes
___ Obsessions or compulsions
___ Blackouts or periods of time that cannot be accounted for
___ History of self-harm (self-injury, head-banging, scratching, cutting, food restriction, taking deliberate risks, etc.)
___ Generalized anxiety
___ Social anxiety
___ Panic attacks
___ History of suicide attempt
___ Suicidal ideation
___ Social isolation
___ History of failed or harmful interpersonal relationships
___ Chronic physical illness

Does your patient have a history of drug and/or alcohol abuse or dependence?
____

Is drug or alcohol abuse or dependence material to your patient's impairment(s)?
____

Is your patient a malingerer? ______________________________

Can your patient tolerate typical stressors associated with school such as meeting deadlines, accepting instruction and criticism from teachers, interacting with fellow students and peers?

____

My patient's symptoms and their treatment cause him/her to be absent ___ one day per month ___ two days per month ___ three or more days per month

Limitations Related to Psychological Condition

Please check the boxes that correspond to your professional observations and experience, and your patient's history and treatment.

	Not Significantly Impaired (occasionally off task less than 10% of the school day)	Moderately Impaired (consistently off task 10% of the school day)	Markedly Impaired (consistently off task 20% of the school day)	Extremely Impaired (consistently off task more than 20% of the school day)
The ability to remember locations and work-like procedures				
The ability to understand and remember short and simple instructions				
The ability to understand and remember detailed instructions				
The ability to carry out very short and simple instructions				
The ability to carry out detailed instructions				
The ability to maintain attention and concentration for extended periods				
The ability to perform activities within a schedule, maintain regular attendance, and be punctual within customary tolerances				

	Not Significantly Impaired (occasionally off task less than 10% of the school day)	Moderately Impaired (consistently off task 10% of the school day)	Markedly Impaired (consistently off task 20% of the school day)	Extremely Impaired (consistently off task more than 20% of the school day)
The ability to sustain an ordinary routine without special supervision				
The ability to work in coordination with and proximity to others without being distracted by them				
The ability to make simple task-related decisions				
The ability to interact appropriately with others				
The ability to ask simple questions or request assistance				
The ability to accept instructions and respond appropriately to criticism from teachers, parents, and authority figures				
The ability to maintain socially appropriate behavior and to adhere to basic standards of neatness and cleanliness				

	Not Significantly Impaired (occasionally off task less than 10% of the school day)	Moderately Impaired (consistently off task 10% of the school day)	Markedly Impaired (consistently off task 20% of the school day)	Extremely Impaired (consistently off task more than 20% of the school day)
The ability to respond appropriately to changes in the environment				
The ability to be aware of normal hazards and take appropriate precautions				
The ability to travel to unfamiliar places or use public transportation				
The ability to set realistic goals or make plans independently of others				

If your patient has a trauma-based disorder, does your patient meet **ALL** of the following criteria? ___ Yes ___ No

- Exposure to actual or threatened death, serious injury, or violence?
- Subsequent involuntary reexperiencing of the traumatic event (for example, intrusive memories, dreams, or flashbacks)?
- Avoidance of external reminders of the event?
- Disturbance in mood and behavior?
- Increases in arousal and reactivity (for example, exaggerated startle response, sleep disturbance)?

Please provide your opinion on the effect of your patient's diagnoses, symptoms and treatment on the following. For purposes of this section, moderately impaired = off task 10% of the workday, severely impaired = off task 20% of the school day, extremely impaired = off task more than 20% of the workday.

	Moderately Impaired	Severely Impaired	Extremely Impaired
• Understand, remember, or apply information	______	______	______
• Interact with others	______	______	______
• Concentrate, persist, or maintain pace	______	______	______
• Adapt or manage oneself*	______	______	______

**This area of mental functioning refers to the abilities to regulate emotions, control behavior, and maintain well-being in age-appropriate activities and settings.*

Prescribed Medications

Please list your patient's prescribed medications, dose and frequency, and any adverse effects (for example, unintended weight gain or weight loss, gastrointestinal distress, drowsiness, fatigue, etc.).

Medication **Dose** **Frequency** **Side effects, if any**

____

____

____

____

____

____

____

____

Comments: ____

____

____

____

____

____________________ Today's date	______________________________ Signature of clinician
____________________ DEA or License #	______________________________ Printed name of clinician
	______________________________ Supervisor (if required)
	______________________________ Supervisor's signature

Address of practice: ______________________________
____
____

Phone: ____________________ Fax: ______________

Email: ____________________

Please be sure to submit all treatment records, from date first seen to date last seen, to your patient's representative. Many thanks for your kind consideration in this matter.

APPENDIX G

Example of Social Security–Compatible Documentation of Psychological Services

Documentation of Psychological Services

Patient Name: ______________________ DOB: ___/___/___ DOS: ___/___/___

Scheduled time of session: _______ Arrival for session: ________ Length of Session: _______ Client Show/No Show _______ Client's appearance: ___________

Diagnosis: ____

____

Prognosis: ____

____

____

Symptoms observed or discussed this session:

____ Altered mental status
____ Anhedonia
____ Antisocial attitude/behaviors
____ Anxiety
____ Cognitive impairment
____ Decreased energy
____ Delusional thinking
____ Depressed mood
____ Difficulty concentrating/thinking
____ Fatigue
____ Feelings of guilt/worthlessness

____ Feelings of helplessness/hopelessness
____ Hallucinations (auditory/visual/tactile)
____ Manic episodes
____ Motor tension
____ Nightmares/night terrors
____ Obsessions/compulsions
____ Panic attack(s)
____ Paranoid thinking
____ Psychomotor agitation/retardation
____ Self-harm/self-mutilation
____ Social anxiety
____ Social withdrawal/isolation
____ Suicidal ideation
____ Suicide attempt(s)
____ Uncontrollable anger/rage

Behavioral observations this session:

____ Altered mental status
____ Anxiety
____ Autistic thinking
____ Compulsive behaviors
____ Depressed mood
____ Diaphoresis
____ Dissociation
____ Distractibility
____ Distracting behaviors
____ Flight of ideas
____ Hyperactivity
____ Hypervigilance
____ Impaired concentration
____ Impaired memory
____ Inappropriate affect
____ Mood swings
____ Poor attention
____ Poor eye contact
____ Pressured speech
____ Somnolence
____ Stutter
____ Tremor

Psychosocial and environmental problems addressed:

____ Adverse medication reaction
____ Child abuse victim
____ Crime victim
____ Disability
____ Domestic violence
____ Elder abuse victim
____ Homelessness
____ Interpersonal relationship
____ Legal problems
____ Limited access to health care
____ Pain
____ Physical limitations
____ Poor social support
____ Poverty
____ Transportation problems
____ Unemployment
____ Unstable finances
____ Unstable living condition

Risk issues addressed:

____	Suicide risk	____	Date of sobriety
____	Suicide plan	____	Legal problems
____	Domestic violence	____	Criminal activity
____	Financial hardship	____	Social services involvement
____	Dire need	____	Hospitalization recommended
____	ETOH/Drug use	____	Involuntary hospitalization

Current medications/dose/frequency/effectiveness/adverse effects:

____

____

____

____

____

Treatment goals: ____

____

Treatment plan: ____

____

____

____

____

Treatment compliance: ____

Evidence of malingering: ____

____

Medical necessity for past/current/future treatment: ______________________

____

____

____

____

Homework assignment for next session scheduled ___/___/___

____

____

Obstacles to sustained employment:

Maintaining a schedule ___________________________

Working independently ___________________________

Working at a pace consistent with workplace norms ___________________________

Concentrating for extended periods (two hours at a time)

____

Distracted by others ___________________________

Distracted by internal conflict ___________________________

Problems learning new tasks, ideas, concepts ___________________________

Problems with authority ___________________________

Periodically disoriented to person, place, time ___________________________

Interacting with others ___________________________

Disorganized thinking ___________________________

Adaptation to workplace changes ___________________________

Response to typical workplace stressors ___________________________

Additional Notes:

____

____

____

____

Signed (clinician): ___________________________ Dated: ___/___/___

Printed name: ___________________________ License#: ___________________________

Supervisor's name (if appropriate): ___________ Supervisor's License# ___________

Supervisor's signature: ___________________________ Dated: ___/___/___

Signed (patient): ___________________________ Dated: ___/___/___

APPENDIX H

Compassionate Allowance List (as of August 20, 2018)

Compassionate Allowance List (as of August 20, 2018)

1. Acute Leukemia
2. Adrenal Cancer—with distant metastases or inoperable, unresectable or recurrent
3. Adult Non-Hodgkin Lymphoma
4. Adult Onset Huntington Disease
5. Aicardi-Goutieres Syndrome
6. Alexander Disease (ALX)—Neonatal and Infantile
7. Allan-Herndon-Dudley Syndrome
8. Alobar Holoprosencephaly
9. Alpers Disease
10. Alpha Mannosidosis—Type II and III
11. ALS/Parkinsonism Dementia Complex
12. Alstrom Syndrome
13. Alveolar Soft Part Sarcoma
14. Amegakaryocytic Thrombocytopenia
15. Amyotrophic Lateral Sclerosis (ALS)
16. Anaplastic Adrenal Cancer—Adult with distant metastases or inoperable, unresectable or recurrent
17. Angelman Syndrome

18. Angiosarcoma
19. Aortic Atresia
20. Aplastic Anemia
21. Astrocytoma—Grade III and IV
22. Ataxia Telangiectasia
23. Atypical Teratoid/Rhabdoid Tumor
24. Batten Disease
25. Beta Thalassemia Major
26. Bilateral Optic Atrophy—Infantile
27. Bilateral Retinoblastoma
28. Bladder Cancer—with distant metastases or inoperable or unresectable
29. Breast Cancer—with distant metastases or inoperable or unresectable
30. Canavan Disease (CD)
31. CACH—Vanishing White Matter Disease-Infantile and Childhood Onset Forms
32. Carcinoma of Unknown Primary Site
33. Cardiac Amyloidosis—AL Type
34. Caudal Regression Syndrome—Types III and IV
35. Cerebro Oculo Facio Skeletal (COFS) Syndrome
36. Cerebrotendinous Xanthomatosis
37. Child Lymphoblastic Lymphoma
38. Child Lymphoma
39. Child Neuroblastoma—with distant metastases or recurrent
40. Chondrosarcoma—with multimodal therapy
41. Chronic Idiopathic Intestinal Pseudo Obstruction
42. Chronic Myelogenous Leukemia (CML)—Blast Phase
43. Coffin-Lowry Syndrome
44. Congenital Lymphedema
45. Congenital Myotonic Dystrophy
46. Cornelia de Lange Syndrome—Classic Form
47. Corticobasal Degeneration
48. Creutzfeldt-Jakob Disease (CJD)—Adult
49. Cri du Chat Syndrome
50. Degos Disease—Systemic
51. DeSanctis Cacchione Syndrome

52. Dravet Syndrome
53. Early-Onset Alzheimer's Disease
54. Edwards Syndrome (Trisomy 18)
55. Eisenmenger Syndrome
56. Endometrial Stromal Sarcoma
57. Endomyocardial Fibrosis
58. Ependymoblastoma (Child Brain Cancer)
59. Erdheim Chester Disease
60. Esophageal Cancer
61. Esthesioneuroblastoma
62. Ewing Sarcoma
63. Farber Disease (FD)—Infantile
64. Fatal Familial Insomnia
65. Fibrodysplasia Ossificans Progressiva
66. Fibrolamellar Cancer (Effective 8/20/2018)
67. Follicular Dendritic Cell Sarcoma—metastatic or recurrent
68. Friedreichs Ataxia (FRDA)
69. Frontotemporal Dementia (FTD), Picks Disease—Type A—Adult
70. Fryns Syndrome
71. Fucosidosis—Type 1
72. Fukuyama Congenital Muscular Dystrophy
73. Fulminant Giant Cell Myocarditis
74. Galactosialidosis—Early and Late Infantile Types
75. Gallbladder Cancer
76. Gaucher Disease (GD)—Type 2
77. Giant Axonal Neuropathy
78. Glioblastoma Multiforme (Brain Cancer)
79. Glioma Grade III and IV
80. Glutaric Acidemia—Type II
81. Head and Neck Cancers—with distant metastasis or inoperable or unresectable
82. Heart Transplant Graft Failure
83. Heart Transplant Wait List—1A/1B
84. Hemophagocytic Lymphohistiocytosis (HLH)—Familial Type
85. Hepatoblastoma

86. Hepatopulmonary Syndrome
87. Hepatorenal Syndrome
88. Histiocytosis Syndromes
89. Hoyeaal-Hreidarsson Syndrome
90. Hutchinson-Gilford Progeria Syndrome
91. Hydranencephaly
92. Hypocomplementemic Urticarial Vasculitis Syndrome
93. Hypophosphatasia Perinatal (Lethal) and Infantile Onset Types
94. Hypoplastic Left Heart Syndrome
95. I Cell Disease
96. Idiopathic Pulmonary Fibrosis
97. Infantile Free Sialic Acid Storage Disease
98. Infantile Neuroaxonal Dystrophy (INAD)
99. Infantile Neuronal Ceroid Lipofuscinoses
100. Inflammatory Breast Cancer (IBC)
101. Intracranial Hemangiopericytoma
102. Jervell and Lange-Nielsen Syndrome
103. Joubert Syndrome
104. Junctional Epidermolysis Bullosa—Lethal Type
105. Juvenile Onset Huntington Disease
106. Kidney Cancer—inoperable or unresectable
107. Kleefstra Syndrome
108. Krabbe Disease (KD)—Infantile
109. Kufs Disease—Type A and B
110. Large Intestine Cancer—with distant metastasis or inoperable, unresectable or recurrent
111. Late Infantile Neuronal Ceroid Lipofuscinoses
112. Leigh's Disease
113. Leiomyosarcoma
114. Leptomeningeal Carcinomatosis
115. Lesch-Nyhan Syndrome (LNS)
116. Lewy Body Dementia
117. Liposarcoma—metastatic or recurrent
118. Lissencephaly
119. Liver Cancer

120. Lowe Syndrome
121. Lymphomatoid Granulomatosis—Grade III
122. Malignant Brain Stem Gliomas—Childhood
123. Malignant Ectomesenchymoma
124. Malignant Gastrointestinal Stromal Tumor
125. Malignant Germ Cell Tumor
126. Malignant Multiple Sclerosis
127. Malignant Renal Rhabdoid Tumor
128. Mantle Cell Lymphoma (MCL)
129. Maple Syrup Urine Disease
130. Marshall-Smith Syndrome
131. Mastocytosis—Type IV
132. MECP2 Duplication Syndrome
133. Medulloblastoma—with metastases
134. Megacystis Microcolon Intestinal Hypoperistalsis Syndrome (Effective 8/20/2018)
135. Megalencephaly Capillary Malformation Syndrome (Effective 8/20/2018)
136. Menkes Disease—Classic or Infantile Onset Form
137. Merkel Cell Carcinoma—with metastases
138. Merosin Deficient Congenital Muscular Dystrophy
139. Metachromatic Leukodystrophy (MLD)—Late Infantile
140. Mitral Valve Atresia
141. Mixed Dementias
142. MPS I, formerly known as Hurler Syndrome
143. MPS II, formerly known as Hunter Syndrome
144. MPS III, formerly known as Sanfilippo Syndrome
145. Mucosal Malignant Melanoma
146. Multicentric Castleman Disease
147. Multiple System Atrophy
148. Myoclonic Epilepsy with Ragged Red Fibers Syndrome
149. Neonatal Adrenoleukodystrophy
150. Nephrogenic Systemic Fibrosis
151. Neurodegeneration with Brain Iron Accumulation—Types 1 and 2
152. NFU-1 Mitochondrial Disease
153. Niemann-Pick Disease (NPD)—Type A

154. Niemann-Pick Disease—Type C
155. Nonketotic Hyperglycinemia
156. Non-Small Cell Lung Cancer
157. Obliterative Bronchiolitis
158. Ohtahara Syndrome
159. Oligodendroglioma Brain Cancer—Grade III
160. Ornithine Transcarbamylase (OTC) Deficiency
161. Orthochromatic Leukodystrophy with Pigmented Glia
162. Osteogenesis Imperfecta (OI)—Type II
163. Osteosarcoma, formerly known as Bone Cancer—with distant metastases or inoperable or unresectable
164. Ovarian Cancer—with distant metastases or inoperable or unresectable
165. Pallister-Killian Syndrome
166. Pancreatic Cancer
167. Paraneoplastic Pemphigus
168. Patau Syndrome (Trisomy 13)
169. Pearson Syndrome
170. Pelizaeus-Merzbacher Disease—Classic Form
171. Pelizaeus-Merzbacher Disease—Connatal Form
172. Peripheral Nerve Cancer—metastatic or recurrent
173. Peritoneal Mesothelioma
174. Peritoneal Mucinous Carcinomatosis
175. Perry Syndrome
176. Phelan-McDermid Syndrome
177. Pleural Mesothelioma
178. Pompe Disease—Infantile
179. Primary Central Nervous System Lymphoma
180. Primary Effusion Lymphoma
181. Primary Progressive Aphasia
182. Progressive Bulbar Palsy
183. Progressive Multifocal Leukoencephalopathy
184. Progressive Supranuclear Palsy
185. Prostate Cancer—Hormone Refractory Disease—or with visceral metastases
186. Pulmonary Atresia
187. Pulmonary Kaposi Sarcoma

188. Retinopathy of Prematurity—Stage V
189. Rett (RTT) Syndrome
190. Revesz Syndrome
191. Rhabdomyosarcoma
192. Rhizomelic Chondrodysplasia Punctata
193. Roberts Syndrome
194. Salivary Cancers
195. Sandhoff Disease
196. Schindler Disease—Type 1
197. Seckel Syndrome
198. Severe Combined Immunodeficiency—Childhood
199. Single Ventricle
200. Sinonasal Cancer
201. Sjögren-Larsson Syndrome
202. Skin Malignant Melanoma with Metastases
203. Small Cell Cancer (Large Intestine, Prostate or Thymus)
204. Small Cell Cancer of the Female Genital Tract
205. Small Cell Lung Cancer
206. Small Intestine Cancer—with distant metastases or inoperable, unresectable or recurrent
207. Smith Lemli Opitz Syndrome
208. Soft Tissue Sarcoma—with distant metastases or recurrent
209. Spinal Muscular Atrophy (SMA)—Types 0 and 1
210. Spinal Nerve Root Cancer—metastatic or recurrent
211. Spinocerebellar Ataxia
212. Stiff Person Syndrome
213. Stomach Cancer—with distant metastases or inoperable, unresectable or recurrent
214. Subacute Sclerosing Panencephalitis
215. Superficial Siderosis of the Central Nervous System (Effective 8/20/2018)
216. Tabes Dorsalis
217. Tay Sachs Disease—Infantile Type
218. Tetrasomy 18p (Effective 8/20/2018)
219. Thanatophoric Dysplasia—Type 1
220. Thyroid Cancer

221. Transplant Coronary Artery Vasculopathy
222. Tricuspid Atresia
223. Ullrich Congenital Muscular Dystrophy
224. Ureter Cancer—with distant metastases or inoperable, unresectable or recurrent
225. Usher Syndrome—Type I
226. Ventricular Assist Device Recipient—Left, Right, or Biventricular
227. Walker Warburg Syndrome
228. Wolf-Hirschhorn Syndrome
229. Wolman Disease
230. X-Linked Lymphoproliferative Disease
231. X-Linked Myotubular Myopathy
232. Xeroderma Pigmentosum
233. Zellweger Syndrome

References

Alliance for Disability in Health Care Education. (2018). *Core competencies on disability for health care education*. Peapack, NJ: Author. Retrieved from http://www.adhce.org/2019/05/06/updated-core-competencies-for-health-care-education/

Amdur, M. A. (2018). Disability determination under Social Security: Increasing rates of approval. *Community Mental Health Journal, 55*(1), 38–41. doi:10.1007/s10597-018-0334-9

American Psychiatric Association (APA). (2000). *Diagnostic and statistical manual of mental disorders* (*DSM*-IV-TR). Arlington, VA: Author.

American Psychiatric Association (APA). (2013). *Diagnostic and statistical manual of mental disorders* (*DSM*-5). Arlington, VA: Author.

American Psychological Association (APA). (2002). Ethical principles of psychologists and code of conduct. *American Psychologist, 57*(12), 1060–1073. doi:10.1037/0003-066X.57.12.1060

Americans with Disabilities Act of 1990, as Amended, 42 U.S.C. 12101 *et seq.* (2008). Retrieved from https://www.ada.gov/pubs/adastatute08.htm

Conover, K. J. (2015). *Ableist microaggressions scale: Development, validation, and relationship with social support* (Unpublished doctoral dissertation). University of California, Santa Barbara, CA.

Corrigan, P. W., Kosyluk, K. A., & Rüsch, N. (2013). Reducing self-stigma by coming out proud. *American Journal of Public Health, 103*(5), 794–800. doi:10.2105/AJPH.2012.301037

Corrigan, P. W., & Watson, A. C. (2002). Understanding the impact of stigma on people with mental illness. *World Psychiatry, 1*(1), 16–20. Retrieved from https://www.ncbi.nlm.nih.gov/pmc/articles/PMC1489832/pdf/wpa010016.pdf

Dirth, T. P., & Branscombe, N. R. (2018). The social identity approach to disability: Bridging disability studies and psychological science. *Psychological Bulletin, 144*(12), 1300–1324. doi:10.1037/bul0000156

Disability Statistics and Demographics Rehabilitation and Research Training Center. (2014). Annual disability statistics compendium. Durham, NH: University of New Hampshire, Institute on Disability. Retrieved from http://www.disabilitycompendium.org/docs/default-source/2014-compendium/2014_compendium.pdf

Dorfman, D. (2017). Re-claiming disability: Identity, procedural justice, and the disability determination process. *Law & Social Inquiry, 42*(1), 195–231. doi:10.1111/lsi.12176

Dunn, D. S. (2019). Outsider privileges can lead to insider disadvantages: Some psychosocial aspects of ableism. *Journal of Social Issues*. Advance online publication. doi:10.1111/josi.12331

Employees' Benefits, 20 C.F.R. (revised as of April 1, 2018). Retrieved from http://www.ssa.gov/OP_Home/cfr20/cfrdoc.htm

Erickson Cornish, J. A., Gorgens, K. A., Monson, S. P., Olkin, R., Palombi, B. J., & Abels, A. V. (2008). Perspectives on ethical practice with people who have disabilities. *Professional Psychology: Research and Practice, 39*, 488–497.

Evans, H. D. (2019). "Trial by fire": Forms of impairment disclosure and implications for disability identity. *Disability & Society, 34*(5), 726–746. doi:10.1080/09687599.2019.1580187

Goldman, H. H., Frey, W. D., & Riley, J. K. (2018). Social Security and disability due to mental impairment in adults. *Annual Review of Clinical Psychology, 14*, 453–469. doi:10.1146/annurev-clinpsy-050817-084754

Graham, C. (2019, May 6). Updated core competencies for health care education. Retrieved from http://www.adhce.org/2019/05/06/updated-core-competencies-for-health-care-education/

Greenberg, M. H., & Baumohl, J. (1996). Income maintenance: Little help now, less on the way. In J. Baumohl (Ed.), *Homelessness in America* (pp. 63–78). Phoenix, AZ: Oryx Press.

Inaugural address by President Barack Obama. (2013, January 21). Retrieved from https://obamawhitehouse.archives.gov/the-press-office/2013/01/21/inaugural-address-president-barack-obama

Institute of Medicine. (2015). *Psychological testing in the service of disability determination*. Washington, DC: The National Academies Press.

Johnson, R. L. (2017, September). Navigating inherent bias in social security law [Web log post]. Retrieved from https://nwsidebar.wsba.org/2017/09/08/navigating-inherent-bias-in-social-security-law/

Kahle, D. B., & White, R. M. (1991). Attitudes toward alcoholism among psychologists and marriage, family and child counselors. *Journal of Studies on Alcohol, 52*(4), 321–324.

Kauff, J. F., Clary, E., Lupfer, K. S., & Fischer, P. J. (2016). An evaluation of SOAR: Implementation and outcomes of an effort to improve access to SSI and SSDI. *Psychiatric Services, 67*(10), 1098–1102. doi:10.1176/appi.ps.201500247

Khantzian, E. J., & Albanese, M. J. (2008). *Understanding addiction as self-medication: Finding hope behind the pain.* New York: Rowman & Littlefield.

Lowder, E. M., Desmarais, S. L., Neupert, S. D., & Truelove, M. A. (2017). SSI/SSDI Outreach, Access, and Recovery (SOAR): Disability application outcomes among homeless adults. *Psychiatric Services, 68*(11), 1189–1192. doi:10.1176/appi.ps.201600568

Lui, P. P., & Quezada, L. (2019). Associations between microaggression and adjustment outcomes: A meta-analytic and narrative review. *Psychological Bulletin, 145*(1), 45–78. doi:10.1037/bul0000172

Marfeo, E. E., Haley, S. M., Jette, A. M., Eisen, S. V., Pengsheng, B. C., Bogusz, K., . . . Rasch, E. K. (2013). Conceptual foundation for measures of physical function and behavioral health function for Social Security work disability evaluation. *Archives of Physical Medicine and Rehabilitation, 94*(9), 1645–1652.e2. doi:10.1016/j.apmr.2013.03.015

Merckelbach, H., Dandachi-FitzGerald, B., van Helvoort, D., Jelicic, M., & Otgaar, H. (2019). When patients overreport symptoms: More than just malingering. *Current Directions in Psychological Science, 28*(3), 321–326. doi:10.1177/0963721419837681

Nario-Redmond, M. R., Kemerling, A. A., & Silverman, A. (2019). Hostile, benevolent, and ambivalent ableism: Contemporary manifestations. *Journal of Social Issues.* Advance online publication. doi:10.1111/josi.12337

Noblitt, R., & Noblitt, P. (2010). Psychologists and the economics of Social Security disability programs. *Professional Psychology: Research and Practice, 4*(3), 274–279. doi:10.1037/a0019315

Noblitt, R., & Noblitt, P. (2012). Social Security disability criteria and substance abuse. *Professional Psychology: Research and Practice, 43*(2), 94–99. doi: 10.1037/a0027454

Noblitt, R., & Noblitt, P. (2017). The role of clinicians in Social Security disability determination. In A. Clark (Ed.), *Social Security: Programs, perspectives, and future directions* (pp. 35–20). Hauppauge, NY: Nova Science Publishers.

Norstedt, M. (2019). Work and invisible disabilities: Practices, experiences and understandings of (non)disclosure. *Scandinavian Journal of Disability Research, 21*(1), 14–24. doi:10.16993/sjdr.550

Religious Action Center of Reform Judaism. (n.d.). Jewish views on economic justice. Retrieved from https://reformjudaism.org/node/2457

Rosenbaum, S. (2018). Now welfare reform, of course. *The Milbank Quarterly, 96*(1), 13–16. doi:10.1111/1468-0009.12306

SAMHSA. (2019, March 29). SSI/SSDI Outreach, Access, and Recovery (SOAR). Retrieved from https://www.samhsa.gov/homelessness-programs-resources/grant-programs-services/soar

Simon, C. C. (2013, November 1). Disability studies: A new normal. *The New York Times.* Retrieved from https://www.nytimes.com/2013/11/03/education/edlife/disability-studies-a-new-normal.html

Stretton, M. S. (2017). Understanding the three types of evidence used by the Social Security Administration in resolving disability claims. In A. Clark (Ed.), *Social Security: Programs, perspectives, and future directions* (pp. 1–20). Hauppauge, NY: Nova Science Publishers.

UN General Assembly. (2007, January 24). *Convention on the rights of persons with disabilities*. Retrieved from https://www.refworld.org/docid/45f973632.html

Vendel, J. D. (2005). General bias and administrative law judges: Is there a remedy for Social Security Disability claimants? *Cornell Law Review, 90*, 769–810. Retrieved from http://scholarship.law.cornell.edu/clr/vol90/iss3/4

Whittle, H. J., Palar, K., Ranadive, N. A., Turan, J. M., Kushel, M., & Weiser, S. D. (2017). The land of the sick and the land of the healthy: Disability, bureaucracy, and stigma among people living with poverty and chronic illness in the United States. *Social Sciences & Medicine, 190*, 181–189. doi:10.1016/j.socscimed.2017.08.031

WHO. (2011). *World report on disability*. Retrieved from http://www.who.int/disabilities/world_report/2011/report.pdf

Glossary of Terms

Acceptable medical sources (AMSs)
Treating sources whose records and professional opinions are accepted as evidence for SSDI and SSI claims; they include licensed physicians (MDs and DOs) and licensed or certified psychologists at the independent practice level. AMSs may also be licensed or certified school psychologists or similarly qualified mental-health-care professionals in school settings (for impairments of intellectual ability, learning disabilities, or borderline intellectual functioning only); licensed optometrists (for visual disorders, visual acuity, and visual fields depending on state licensing limitations); licensed podiatrists (for foot and ankle impairments only); or licensed speech and language pathologists (for speech impairment only). For claims filed on or after March 27, 2017, additional AMSs include licensed physician assistants, licensed audiologists, and advanced practice nurses (APNs), including certified nurse midwives (CNWs), nurse practitioners (NPs), certified registered nurse anesthetists (CRNAs), and clinical nurse specialists (CNSs).

Accommodation
Any adjustment to the work environment, schedule, quotas, modifications, or procedures afforded an incapacitated worker but not to all other workers at the employment site, to facilitate the incapacitated worker's continued employment.

Administrative law judge (ALJ)
The trier of fact for disability determinations at the hearing level for SSDI and SSI benefits. The administrative law judge acts as representative for the commissioner of Social Security.

Alleged onset date (AOD)
The date from which the claimant for disability benefits became too impaired to perform past work or any other work. This date is used to determine eligibility for Medicare.

Americans with Disabilities Act (ADA, 1990) and Amended Act (ADAAA, 2008)
Provide federal protections to disabled individuals and apply penalties to noncompliant businesses and public premises to preserve the rights of disabled people to move about in public, use public transportation, and have safe access and egress to public buildings, public restrooms, hotels, restaurants, shops, and other businesses. Also protects the rights of the disabled to work and attend school by ensuring the availability of appropriate accommodations to make work and school participation possible.

Appeals Council (AC)
Reviews cases that originate in hearing offices throughout the United States, evaluates decisions based on the regulations, and may grant, deny, or dismiss a request for review. Cases that are granted a review may be decided by the Appeals Council or remanded (returned) to the administrative law judge for a new decision.

Application date
The date the application for benefits is filed. For SSI, the application date is considered the same as the onset date. For SSDI, the application date is used to calculate when back due benefits commence.

Average indexed monthly earnings (AIME)
The mechanism used to calculate a recipient's monthly OASDI primary insurance amount (PIA).

Closed period of disability
Claimants who apply for benefits but who recover sufficiently to return to the workforce may be eligible for a closed period of disability. Eligibility is based on demonstrating the presence of one or more medically determinable impairments where at least one is so severe that there were at least 12 months during which the claimant was unable to perform SGA in a competitive work setting.

Competitive work setting
Refers to a workplace with an eight-hour workday; a strictly enforced schedule that includes time-limited rest and meal breaks, quotas, or productivity goals; the ability to work in proximity to and cooperation with coworkers, supervisors, and the public; the ability to work independently and without constant supervision; the ability to concentrate for extended periods and to remember and perform at least simple, two-step instructions; the ability to sit, stand, walk, lift, carry, stoop, and engage in the postural requirements of an assigned job; and the ability to be present and available to work 40 hours a week without more than occasional absences.

Consultative examiner (CE)
This physician (MD or DO) or psychologist (PhD or PsyD) is contracted by the DDS to perform a one-time evaluation on an applicant for SSDI or SSI, review

available treatment records, and submit a written report that includes findings and offers opinions about the claimant's residual functional capacity (RFC).

Date last insured (DLI)
The period of insurability based on the claimant's work history and earnings record. A claimant must be insured to be eligible to receive SSDI benefits.

***Dictionary of Occupational Titles* (DOT)**
Volume produced by the Department of Labor describing occupations and their exertional, educational, and training requirements. Last revised in 1991 and used by Social Security to identify past relevant work, transferable skills, and other work that may be performed by the claimant.

Disability Determination Services (DDS)
A federally funded state agency tasked with evaluating medical records to determine disability eligibility for SSDI, SSI, and Medicaid in each state. Each state has at least one DDS office through which applications for SSDI, SSI, and Medicaid initial applications and reconsideration appeals are filtered. If medical evidence is unavailable, inconclusive, or does not provide an RFC, the DDS can refer the applicant to one or more CEs to provide greater clarity.

Exertional limitations (see also Nonexertional limitations)
Refers to the maximum physical effort the claimant can sustain in a competitive work setting.

Federal Insurance Contributions Act (FICA)
The mechanism through which payroll taxes are collected from employers and employees to fund Social Security programs.

Five-month waiting period
The waiting period, beginning with the alleged onset date (AOD), before cash benefits can be received. The 5-month waiting period is also applied in addition to the 24-month waiting period for Medicare eligibility. The five-month waiting period does not apply to SSI.

Five-step sequential evaluation process
Refers to the five basic criteria for establishing disability eligibility for Social Security programs.

HALLEX
Hearings, Appeals and Litigation Law Manual is a publication of the SSA that explains and details SSDI/SSI policies and procedures.

Health Insurance Portability and Accountability Act (HIPAA)
A major goal of HIPAA's Privacy Rule is to ensure that individuals' health information is properly protected while allowing the flow of health information needed to provide and promote high-quality health care and to protect the public's health and well-being. For more information, see https://www.hhs.gov/hipaa/for-professionals/privacy/laws-regulations/index.html.

Listing of Impairments
Medically determinable physical and mental conditions that, if supported by appropriate evidence, are considered disabling according to Social Security criteria.

Medicaid
Health insurance jointly funded by the federal government and individual states and administered by the state for low-income adults, children, pregnant women, elderly adults, and disabled people.

Medical expert (ME)
A physician or psychologist with expertise in the area the claimant's disabling medical or mental impairment, who reviews the claimant's medical records and offers testimony at the hearing.

Medical-Vocational Guidelines (grid rules)
Used at step 5 of the sequential evaluation process to analyze the claimant's capacity to perform past work or other work by assessing the combination of age, education, and work experience along with age and the claimant's maximum residual functional capacity.

Medically determinable impairment
Medical or mental condition that could be reasonably expected to produce symptoms that interfere with the ability to perform basic work activities.

Medicare
A federal health insurance program for adults aged 65 and older, younger individuals who receive SSDI benefits, and people with end-stage renal disease.

Nonexertional limitations (see also Exertional limitations)
Refers to cognitive, intellectual, behavioral, and emotional limitations that impede the claimant's ability to participate in the full-time competitive workforce.

Offices of Hearings Operations (OHO)
Is responsible for scheduling and holding hearings, issuing decisions, and reviewing post-hearing appeals for claims filed under Titles II and XVI of the Social Security Act.

Old-Age, Survivors, and Disability Insurance (OASDI)
A program designed to provide retirement benefits and disability insurance to workers who contribute to the policy through payroll contributions.

Past relevant work (PRW)
All paid work performed by the claimant for the 15 years prior to the alleged onset date.

Primary insurance amount (PIA)
The benefit (before rounding down to the nearest whole dollar) received by the retiring worker at the early-retirement age of 62 as the foundation for calculating SSDI monthly benefit.

Program Operations Manual System (POMS)
The operational reference utilized by SSA staff to conduct daily SSA business.

Protective filing date
The date that the claimant begins the application process for SSDI or SSI although the claimant may not complete the process until a later date. The SSA uses the protective filing date from which to calculate money benefits and back due benefits.

Representative payee
A third party designated to have control over money benefits for minor children and individuals who may be deemed incompetent to manage their own benefits.

Residual functional capacity (RFC)
A subjective assessment of the claimant's ability to perform typical work activities despite physical or mental limitations due to illness or injury.

Sheltered work setting
A protected environment for impaired workers providing flexible duties and schedules, reduced quotas or productivity requirements, close supervision, and other accommodations as needed. Often a family-held business that employs a family member with exertional or nonexertional limitations.

Social Security Disability Insurance (SSDI)
Under Title II of the Social Security Act, benefits including monthly funds and health insurance through Medicare made available to eligible disabled workers.

Supplemental Security Income (SSI)
Under Title XVI of the Social Security Act, benefits including monthly payments and health insurance through Medicaid are available to disabled individuals who meet eligibility requirements that include financial need.

Transferable skills
Skills acquired through education, training, and experience that can be applied to other jobs. Skills cannot be transferred from a semi-skilled job to a skilled job.

Trial work period
An opportunity for SSDI recipients to return to the workforce without losing benefits for a cumulative 9-month period during a rolling 60-month period of disability.

Unsuccessful work attempt
A work attempt not exceeding six months that fails due to the effects of the disabling condition.

Vocational expert (VE)
A vocational professional who provides impartial, expert-opinion evidence about a claimant's vocational abilities for an ALJ to consider when making a decision about disability.

Index

About the Authors

James Randall (Randy) Noblitt is a licensed psychologist in the state of Texas and a professor of clinical psychology and a member of the core faculty at the California School of Professional Psychology, Alliant International University, Los Angeles since 2006. He received his PhD in clinical psychology from University of North Texas in 1978. After serving as a psychologist in the USAF from 1973 to 1983, he established a private practice in Dallas, Texas (1983–2006).

Pamela Perskin Noblitt is a non-attorney (EDPNA) who has represented more than 1,000 claimants for Social Security disability benefits. Prior to her formally obtaining certification she assisted several of her husband's patients in getting their SSDI and SSI benefits, thus acquainting herself with the mysteries of Social Security.

www.ingramcontent.com/pod-product-compliance
Lightning Source LLC
Chambersburg PA
CBHW071821270326
41929CB00013B/1877
* 9 7 9 8 7 6 5 1 3 6 6 4 5 *